Contemporary Marxist Theory

Contemporary Marxist Theory

A Reader

ANDREW PENDAKIS,
JEFF DIAMANTI,
NICHOLAS BROWN,
JOSH ROBINSON,
AND
IMRE SZEMAN

Bloomsbury Academic
An imprint of Bloomsbury Publishing Inc

B L O O M S B U R Y
NEW YORK • LONDON • NEW DELHI • SYDNEY

Bloomsbury Academic

An imprint of Bloomsbury Publishing Inc

1385 Broadway	50 Bedford Square
New York	London
NY 10018	WC1B 3DP
USA	UK

www.bloomsbury.com

**BLOOMSBURY and the Diana logo are trademarks of
Bloomsbury Publishing Plc**

First published 2014

ISBN: HB: 978-1-4411-0342-0
PB: 978-1-4411-0628-5

Library of Congress Cataloging-in-Publication Data
Contemporary Marxist theory : a reader / edited by Andrew Pendakis,
Jeff Diamanti, Nicholas Brown, Josh Robinson, and Imre Szeman.
pages cm
Includes bibliographical references and index.
ISBN 978-1-4411-0342-0 (hardback : alk. paper) –
ISBN 978-1-4411-0628-5 (pbk. : alk. paper)
1. Socialism. 2. Communism. 3. Marx, Karl, 1818–1883. I. Pendakis, Andrew.
HX73.C657 2014
335.4–dc23
2014005606

Typeset by Newgen Knowledge Works (P) Ltd., Chennai, India

CONTENTS

Acknowledgments   viii

Introduction: Marxisms Lost and Found   1

PART ONE   Notes on the Conjuncture   19

1   Capitalistic Systems, Structures, and Processes
    Félix Guattari and Eric Alliez   25

2   Rethinking Marx's Critical Theory   *Moishe Postone*   41

3   The Impasses of Liberal Productivism   *Alan Lipietz*   55

4   Recapturing   *Paulin Hountondji*   67

5   Immaterial Labor   *Maurizio Lazzarato*   77

6   Women, Land Struggles, and Globalization:
    An International Perspective   *Silvia Federici*   93

7   The Idea of a "Chinese Model"   *Arif Dirlik*   109

PART TWO   Shapes of the Social   123

8   Is there a Neo-Racism?   *Étienne Balibar*   129

9   Marx after Marxism: A Subaltern Historian's
    Perspective   *Dipesh Chakrabarty*   141

10   The Logic of Gender: On the Separation of Spheres
     and the Process of Abjection   *Maya Gonzalez and
     Jeanne Neton*   149

11   Postmodernism or Class? Yes, Please   *Slavoj Žižek*   175

12 Communization in the Present Tense
   Théorie Communiste 203
13 Patriarchy and Commodity Society: Gender without
   the Body *Roswitha Scholz* 217

PART THREE Vicissitudes of Truth 233

14 Scattered Speculations on the Question of Value
   Gayatri Spivak 239
15 Philosophy as Operation *Pierre Macherey* 261
16 What is Transcritique? *Kojin Karatani* 275
17 The Idea of Communism *Alain Badiou* 295
18 The Kingdom of Philosophy: The Administration of
   Metanoia *Boris Groys* 309
19 Twenty-Five Theses on Philosophy in the Age of
   Finance Capital *Imre Szeman and Nicholas Brown* 321

PART FOUR Theories of Culture 337

20 Misplaced Ideas: Literature and Society in
   Late-Nineteenth-Century Brazil *Roberto Schwarz* 343
21 Traditionalism and the Quest for an African
   Literary Aesthetic *Chidi Amuta* 357
22 Marxist Literary Theory, Then and Now
   Imre Szeman 379
23 The Antinomies of Postmodernity *Fredric Jameson* 389
24 Reading Dialectically *Carolyn Lesjak* 407
25 Creative Labor *Sarah Brouillette* 441
26 The Work of Art in the Age of its Real Subsumption
   Under Capital *Nicholas Brown* 449

PART FIVE Machinations of the Political   469

27   State Crisis and Popular Power *Álvaro García Linera*   475

28   Constituent Power: The Concept of a Crisis
Antonio Negri   487

29   Radical Politics Today *Chantal Mouffe*   501

30   On Political Will *Peter Hallward*   515

31   Communicative Capitalism: Circulation and
the Foreclosure of Politics *Jodi Dean*   533

32   Ten Theses on Politics *Jacques Rancière*   555

33   A Contradiction between Matter and Form
Claus Peter Ortlieb   573

34   Misery and Debt: On the Logic and History of
Surplus Populations and Surplus Capital
Aaron Benanav and John Clegg   585

Sources   609

Index   613

ACKNOWLEDGMENTS

Free and unacknowledged labor is one of the worst consequences of a project this large. In the now three years since it began, countless hours from people all over the world have made it possible for this book to transform from concept into reality. Marie-Claire Antoine—the original editor of this project—and our current editorial leaders at Bloomsbury, Matthew Kopel and Kaitlin Fontana, have offered the best kind of support for which academics of our lot could hope. The Canada Research Chair program, through assistance with the cost of permissions and by providing funding for research assistants (RAs), has likewise made it possible to bring this book to life.

The work of a number of RAs have been indispensable to the creation of this anthology, including Alice Haisman at the University of Illinois-Chicago and Sarah Blacker and Justin Sully at the University of Alberta. Bringing the project to a close with countless hours of copyediting and grueling transcription were Zoran Vučkovac and Cynthia Spring. And without Sean O'Brien at the University of Alberta, the whole thing would have been impossibly clumsy and endlessly illegal.

Nicholas Brown mainly wants to thank everyone involved for putting up with his constant tardiness.

Jeff Diamanti: I owe a bunch to Imre Szeman, and everything else to Marija Cetinić. Mathias Nilges taught me Marxism. And Jason Potts showed me how to "make it cleaner." Some kind of beautiful force burst onto the scene in Edmonton, and I'll never think the same having been part of it. They're cut from that high-grade communist cloth we've all heard about. Brent Bellamy and David Janzen, who lent me eyes for this project, are good for the long haul. Alberto Toscano offered much needed commentary in OT. Marcel, finally, has shown me a thing or two about labor *for itself.*

Andrew Pendakis would like to thank his mom, Mary Pendakis, whose agapic Christian idealism found its way (inverted!) into the heart of his politics, and his dad, Paul Pendakis, who died after 30 years driving trucks and buses a few months into his retirement.

Josh Robinson: I should like to thank the President and Fellows of Queens' College, Cambridge and the School of English, Communication and Philosophy, Cardiff University. For support, encouragement, friendship, discussion, and disagreement of many kinds I'm grateful to friends and comrades including Andrea Trumann, Ben Trott, Bernadette Grubner, Christoph Plutte, David Graumann, Dirk Rudolph, Dorothea Hensel, Emma Dowling, Felix Kurz, Gabriele Lohß, Jeanne Neton, Karen Robertson, Katrin Scharnweber, Lis Paquette, Meade McCloughan, Nils Turnbull, Norbert Trenkle, Robert Ogman, Tadzio Müller, and Ziggy Melamed. Above all, thanks to Eef.

Imre Szeman: I feel fortunate to have been able to work with such generous and insightful co-editors. My colleagues and close friends have helped to make some difficult years into ones worth celebrating. Thanks to Brent Bellamy, Lauren Berlant, Sarah Blacker, Dominic Boyer, Sarah Brouillette, Anna Brown, Adam Carlson, Todd Dufresne, Jon Flatley, Matthew Flisfeder, Susan Hamilton, Dan Harvey, Andrew Johnson, Tim Kaposy, Marty Kreiswith, Leigh Claire La Berge, Graeme MacDonald, Mary O'Connor, Julie Rak, Valerie Savard, Will Straw, Joseph Szeman, Jennifer Wenzel, and Heather Zwicker—and others whom I've forgotten to list (you know who you are).

And to Pulpo: I know that our dream of becoming Chilangos and sharing coffee at the Vaca Oxidado is bound to become a reality.

Introduction: Marxisms Lost and Found

Andrew Pendakis and Imre Szeman

I

The confluence of the collapse of the Soviet Union with what was quickly framed as a new and inexhaustible paradigm of American-style growth worldwide, generated a tremendously persuasive historical narrative, one in which Marx became the signifier *par excellence* of theoretical hubris, redundancy, and error. In a flash, the Marxist cosmos, complete with whatever remained of its claim upon the future, disappeared. In its place emerged an order we once referred to euphemistically (and perhaps even a touch hopefully) as "globalization," but which we have since come to realize was little more than an ever fiercer and more menacing capitalism in disguise. Although continuously emphasizing its historical novelty, this was an order simultaneously convinced of its own eternity and naturalness, a system of living and believing that claimed to have left behind for good the petty limits and aporias of ideological thinking. Not only did neoliberal hegemony rewrite history, it elided our capacity to speculate (retrospectively) alternative narrative arcs and possibilities, negating the ontological right of the past to its own contingency and open-endedness. Although virtually no Sovietologist in the 1980s would have predicted the imminent fall of the Soviet Union, from the angle of the 1990s Marxism was not merely defeated, but born dead, *impossible from the very beginning.*

It is essential to remember that in 1979 there was no reason to believe that the election of Margaret Thatcher was anything but an anomaly on a planet that was still, if not really *moving* Left, at least idling there. Capitalism was in crisis, gripped by unemployment, inflation, recession, and industrial unrest. Marxism, though certainly beleaguered everywhere after 1980, was nevertheless a corporeal institutional universe. Included in this universe were not only those regimes explicitly governed by principles (ostensibly) derived from Marx's work—states governing almost one-third of the planet's population—but the whole ramifying complex of Marx-inflected political movements (in El Salvador, Afghanistan, Nicaragua, etc.), institutes, publications, union, and university connections that existed all over the world. From the vestigial Marxist-Leninist groupuscles and parties that still toiled from Paris to La Paz, to Western Marxist students and professors on university campuses around the world, to the material infrastructure and prestige of social democracy (surely an echo of Marx if ever there was one), Marxism then possessed a quiddity, *an empire of things* (MIGs, offices, rubles) such that it could in no way be placed *unequivocally* on the list of history's future extinct. It was a hundred years of ambivalent knowledge and practice, inseparable success, and failure, a vast, ambiguous configuration of inertia and possibility—and yet it was swept into oblivion at light speed.

This can be partially explained by the fact that the United States in the 1990s appeared to have definitively detached itself from a broad range of nagging twentieth-century materialities and limits. A novel species of growth—intensive rather than extensive, continuous rather than intermittent—seemed to be in the process of establishing itself, as business cycles and manufacturing-based trade surpluses dissolved into the debt-financed effervescence of the "new economy." Growth without inflation (and without explicit unemployment), the apparent stabilization of wages, housing, and stock prices that appeared to rise without a hint of ceiling: all of these had the effect of producing the fantasy of an economy capable of resolving every possible social contradiction and tension. Although growth has had associations with utopic, depoliticized abundance in the United States since at least World War II, the dependence of the 1990s on highly fetishized technological innovation, especially in communications and medicine, imbued it with an aura of qualitative difference, a new order charged with connotations of social connectivity, ontological variety, and novel forms of political liberty. Even if the Soviet Union hadn't collapsed, the disconnect between its extensive growth—"stupid" flows of steel and wheat—and the American magic of computers would have been enough to secure a narrative of socialist backwardness and failure. Compact discs and social networks on one side of the Berlin Wall, steam-belching Fordist factories encrusted with dirt and rust on the other: the Soviet Union wasn't just politically illegitimate, but an aesthetic failure.

For 20 years Marx was deprived the right to have even been the name for a process of thinking: he was no longer—whatever his limits and mistakes—a canonically un-ignorable philosopher, but a stick-figure killer, a blunderer, a brain on repeat. When not ignored entirely Marxism came to exist in most spaces of academic, journalistic, and governmental knowledge production as the easiest of foils, a laughable (though grimly brutal) form of secularized religion. Even if it were to be confined to a mere emendation in the history of ideas, we are happy to affirm that this period of caricature and ignorance vis-à-vis the work of Marx is now ending. Within the domain of what we still routinely call "theory" the status of Marx has changed so dramatically that any genuine reckoning with the scale of the shift requires a dreamy flashback sequence through the period furniture, gestures, and dress of twentieth-century *fin-de-siècle* critique. For those of us who floated in and out of universities, especially English and Comp. Lit. departments around this time, the 1990s strike us as now fully sutured to their own specificity, a process that is only now discernible as a completed historico-spiritual unit. These years have a discernible scent, a particular modulation of light, a tell-tale tone of the voice. Describing something as "problematic"—that was the 1990s. Garrulous paeans to the ineffable; denunciations of the violence inherent in universals and the impossibility of the general proposition; endless questing after innumerable limit-experiences, border zones, and outsides: whatever the continuing value of the theories informing these gestures, we can no longer deny that something has transpired within the intensity or coherence of their persuasiveness. Hegel's great innovation, one adapted brilliantly by Marx himself, was his method of determinate inquiry into all that is dead and alive in an age. We see as incontrovertible the necessity of curating this difficult eye to the historical metabolism of discourses. It is from this methodological starting-point that we want to suggest that the *spirit* of the 1990s is fled, even if its *letters*—the texts and theories on which it was based—must continue to be learned from, and remain, in some very real way, irreplaceable.

From the angle afforded today by retrospection, the factor most characteristic of 1990s criticism was the almost complete absence of political economy. This was a tendency inherited via the French post-Nietzscheanism upon which so much 1990s thinking relied for its style, objects, and method. Marxist economic analysis of the kind practiced by (say) Joan Robinson, Harry Magdoff, or Ernst Mandel operated within disciplinary and conceptual coordinates so foreign to those of post-1968 French thought that the former could only be perceived by thinkers influenced by the latter as archaic, determinist, and plagued by untheorized metaphysical remainders. The language of political economy, rarely stylized or self-reflexive, emptied of the ritual skepticism and play endemic to the writing of the period, to say nothing of the (mistakenly) intuited proximity of this language to the stale rhetoric of institutionalized communism allowed for its consignment to the invisibility of the already said. Political economy was to post-1968 thought what the Fordist factory was to the design aesthetic of Apple stores: heavy and left behind by time instead of light, futural, and effervescent. The shift away from an earlier Structuralist investment in the objectivity of the social sciences and toward a post-Heideggerian paradigm grounded in the epistemological fecundity of literature and artistic practice further marginalized economics as a particularly misguided echo from the ruined modern dream of a truth expressible in math.

This trend was only compounded by the sense that the century's communist revolutions, entranced by the deus ex machina of heavy infrastructure, had failed to de-link from the political space of nineteenth-century liberalism, conserving against (or within) their best intentions its disciplinary, statist, familialist, and productivist norms. Whether in the form of the self-transparent, rational *homo economicus* or a socialized new man, an isomorphism appeared from the perspective of the period between liberal and communist iterations of the economic. Both seemed to rely on rationalist, humanist subjects that were to varying extents grounded in nature (from Adam Smith's bartering essence to Marx's naturalized species being) just as both seemed intent on domesticating human experience in the normative disciplinary circuits of production/consumption. Economics became the very paradigm of disciplinarity, of a thought which, far from liberating bodies, worked instead to insidiously train and domesticate them.

Also at work behind the scenes was a certain discomfort with the entire conceptual terrain occupied by the motif of causality. Time and time again, Marx distinguishes historical materialist science from the vague—in fact idealist—moralisms of the "true socialists;" what they lack, according to Marx, is precisely an expository or analytic power, an understanding of just how it is that capitalism actually works. Although Marx's dialectical method protects him from allegations of positivism, he always conceived of his work as *within* the nineteenth-century tradition of scientific naturalism, and clearly believed that historical materialism unlocked provisionally not only the causal structure of the past, but that of the near future, insofar as it was tendentially contained within a dynamic, politically ambivalent present.

All of these ideas will fare badly in the context of the post-Nietzschean turn in French theory. Linked on the side of the object with Newtonian mechanism and on the side of the subject with crude associationism, causation would henceforth be largely seen as belonging to the same wrong-headed epistemological space as representation itself. In all of the great genealogical texts of Michel Foucault, and despite his avowed commitment to movement and flux, there is a clear—classically Structuralist—predilection for the synchronic: one gets complex snapshots of historical systems at different moments in time, but very little in the way of a concrete *narration* of the causal nexus which intermediates their difference. In the work of Gilles Deleuze and Félix Guattari, causal knowledge is to some extent forgone for a philosophy organized around the creation of percepts, affects, and concepts; knowledge, to paraphrase Foucault, is not made for understanding, but to cut, produce, or intervene.[1] In Jacques Derrida's corpus, the task is to dust away the layers of the palimpsest, rather than to articulate mediations within a broader, determinative causal context. Generally speaking, 1990s criticism—drawing on the sources mentioned above, and with the notable exception of the work of Fredric Jameson—eschewed a knowledge grounded in the uncovering of causes (often etiolated unfairly as "origins") for one anchored in the production and dispersion of effects. It was via this broad rejection of the category of causation that Marxism—always interested in the myriad ways in which culture, politics, and life are multiply determined (and determine) economic reality—could be reframed as determinist and necessitarian, the error of an enlightenment will to truth matched only by the proper name of (Pierre-Simon) Laplace.

Another factor in the theoretical eclipse of Marx was a key transformation in the way we understand power. With the post-1968 turn in French philosophy, exploitation notoriously drains out of its classical moorings in the primary capital/labor binary and saturates the whole field of social relations. This fission of exploitation into a fragmented cosmos of micro-oppressions characterized along axes of race, gender, and sexual orientation—a process which echoed urgent, contemporary social struggles—nevertheless scrambled the signal of Marx's universal subject of history, and with it the grandeur and mythos of the revolutionary project itself. These "others" were not uninvited guests whose arrival spoiled the party: the latter was in many ways already moribund and should in fact have been re-rejuvenated by these new energies of dissidence and rebellion. At the time, however, for reasons that are complex and retrospectively intelligible, this division between the multiple subjectivities excluded by history and the universal subject named by Marx could only be registered as crisis.

Although power and domination now flooded into the tiniest gestures—ranging from the operations of language to the movement of a gaze, from relations between a doctor and their patient to the ostensible violence of metaphysics itself—it paradoxically emptied out of precisely those domains previously understood under the category of the economic. The experience of exploitation undergone in an increasingly globalized, deregulated process of production; the low-wage, precarious, and benefit-less realities of life in the fast exploding service sector; the increasing financialization of existence, ranging from new practices of mass investment to unprecedented levels of personal and public indebtedness; the complete colonization of the time and space of experience by advertising and commodity exchange: all of this went largely unnoticed in the 1990s and has only been widely registered by critical and theoretical commentators in the last decade, often under the codewords of "globalization" or "neoliberalism." The critical practice known as "cultural studies," unmoored from its New Left origins and more and more widely practiced, *did* take note of some of these developments as they were occurring. But even in cultural studies, causation and political economy tended to be pushed aside in favor of a thematics of identity, meaning, and culture.

This was not conspiracy or malice, but that overcompensation and hiding that always takes place in the transition between the closing of one paradigm and the opening of another. From the angle of 1990s criticism talk of economic domination—and by this we do not merely point to the drama of labor, production, and distribution, but the power capital has over time, over the future, and over space, bodies, and practices—was largely bypassed as vestigial, a question subtended by a pre-Foucauldian conception of power that could no longer be taken seriously. With the ideas of the Marquis de Sade always there in the background of many of the period's most influential thinkers—Foucault, Pierre Klossowski, and Jean-François Lyotard come to mind—oppression itself lost its own transparency and social suffering became suddenly reinscribable as unconscious or transgressive pleasure. In the context of what was essentially a generalized nominalism, particularities, fragments, and identities flourished, and with them a conception of politics as privatized resistance or transgression. Revolution, not just as the description of a style of politics, but as the mere prospect of an outside to the general tenor of the present, now functioned as the very model of the violence always already present in the project of the universal. Although this again may be slavishly Hegelian on our part, we can't help but retrospectively name all of this as both *necessary* and *true*. Not only did the poststructural eclipse of Marx echo real conjunctural contradictions, it was in many ways the necessary precondition for the hybridization of a Marx much better equipped to grapple with and think the present. The flexibility and rigor of the Marxisms present in this anthology could not have come to be without the "excesses" and missed encounters of the interregnum of 1990s criticism, a moment that now seems as dated as the Soviet factories it once imagined itself to be leaping over into the future.

II

Just as Marxist analysis was eclipsed in line with the erasure of the economy as a viable category for thought, so too have its theoretical fortunes been revived alongside a renewed interest in economic forms. This is not merely some reflex epiphenomenon of 2008, the turn toward "alternatives" that even *The Economist* flirts with at the downside of every business cycle or protracted crisis. Certainly, the financial crisis and the Occupy movement it continues to gestate have dramatically placed back onto the radar of popular consciousness whole swaths of economic reality largely ignored for almost a quarter of a century. Inequality, unemployment, class, the role that finance plays in a deregulated neoliberal economy: these have all found their way into journalistic everydayness in a way unthinkable in the 1990s. What we might then call the "economic turn" is not just a whimsical shift in academic taste, that belatedness vis-à-vis "current events," which is always generating new, embarrassingly precise field names (9/11 studies being perhaps the most symptomatic). This turn goes far beyond a question of academic "interest" or "relevance;" it involves an intense, violent, and labyrinthine irruption of the economic itself. Like an iceberg striking the hull of a ship, it is a question of a shift in the ontology of the present, a situation as likely to produce new knowledge and practice as it is wide-eyed bewilderment and collapse.

One key factor in the recalibration of the cultural visibility of the economic was the string of wars initiated by the United States at the turn of the century. Although war is often misconstrued as the outside or limit of an economy's smooth reproduction, an extra-mundane exception to "business as usual," it became quickly apparent to the millions mobilized by the antiwar movement just how brazenly intertwined these phenomena were in an era dominated by fantasies of a "new American century." Of course, this relation has crucially sustained industrial demand in the United States since the 1940s and become an ever more critical element of its economic order since Ronald Reagan, but in this new conjuncture (national, capitalist) *Realpolitik*, industrial/corporate welfare and elite political cronyism merged so spectacularly that the relevance of that most Leninist of categories—imperialism itself—gained new theoretical purchase and texture (as captured so persuasively in David Harvey's *The New Imperialism* [2005]). The wars in Iraq and Afghanistan were like parodic object lessons in "vulgar" Marxism, events so clearly articulated at a distance from their explicit, liberal intentions—human, women's and minority rights—that not only the classic Marxist hypothesis of an analytically and causally primary infrastructural domain, but also that of a state-structure grounded in the false universality of a specific class interest, again became plausible—even indispensable—explanatory devices. War uncovered the economic, not in the mode of a machine silently subtending the future, but as a raw tissue of manipulations, interests, and brute force.

This image of the economy to some extent echoes the kind of inflated materialism one finds in Marx's writing between 1844 and 1846 at precisely the moment he is trying to emphatically distinguish his position from both idealism and the "contemplative" materialisms circumambient to the period. This is not the late Marx construed by Louis Althusser as having quietly embedded within the body of *Capital* an (inchoate) dialectical materialist epistemology, but that Marx, much closer to Lenin, of "real premises from which abstraction can only be made in the imagination."[2] In this sense, oil and blood, interest and falsehood stand to the avowed humanitarianism of United States' twenty-first-century wars with precisely the same ontological pretensions as Marx's "real individuals" do to the spiritual phantoms of the Young Hegelians: in each instant something palpable, gritty, and epistemologically unmediated is counterposed to the inexistence of the merely Ideal. This was, then, an ambivalent turn. On the one hand, the wars aggressively invalidated the digital economy's claim to an equilibrium without friction, one happily separated from the anachronistic *heaviness* of resources, scarcity, nation-states, and class. They belied dramatically its claims to ontological difference and newness. On the other hand, the casual Marxism resurrected by the wars had the drawback of injecting into our understanding of how an economy works a certain *atmosphere of conspiracy*—a conception of politics grounded in the intentional malevolence of a ruling class or cabal (themselves untouched by ideology). If it was tempting at the time to rephrase the ontological specificity of the economic in the language of a sinister holism—"the System" invoked darkly as an entity without parts or limits—the wars, and the economic strings to which they were attached, could just as easily be dismissed by liberal centrists as atomized exceptions to the good rule of sensible capital (the kind of position taken, for example, by Nobel Prize winning economist and *New York Times* columnist Paul Krugman).

Equally critical in the remattering of the economic as a usable epistemological category has been the explosion into consciousness, both "theoretical" and "popular," of what we sometimes call "the ecological crisis." However stalled and ineffective existing political responses to the crisis have been, and however far we are from even remotely beginning to assess its full import, the *presence to mind* of the crisis is now undeniable. Even if it is too often expressed in the same tone reserved for mundane changes in the weather—that tone set aside for banal, inevitable phenomena—we are nevertheless now keenly aware of our location on the edge of an ecological abyss. This has had an important number of effects on the discursive positioning of Marxist thought. First, the crisis has clearly displaced an earlier (poststructuralist) fascination with the workings of representation and language, and redirected attention to what we might call *an emergency of the object*. Although good dialecticians tirelessly remind us that neither crisis nor nature, nor even an imminent *nature in crisis* remotely compromise the rule of mediation, and though any notion of a return to a zero point of the object beyond language or discourse is pure fantasy, it is nevertheless the case that we are witnessing a broad return, whether via Graham Harman's object-oriented philosophy or a certain (often de-Marxified) Deleuze, to the object in all its complexity, immanence, and material thickness. If the gesture *par excellence* in the Derridean era was that of stammering—a lingering on the edge of the utterance, a certain pleasure taken in the surface of language—our own seems to be that of an excitement taken in the intricacy and complexity of that which is mediated by and produced through language, *the plenitude (and exigency) of the framed itself.* The sophistic, skeptical tendencies of the 1990s have been replaced, for example, by the kind of Deleuzian (actually Spinozist) realism found in the works of Antonio Negri, a realism that conceives of language not as a mere instrument of representation, nor as a Lacanian thorn in the flesh, but as a communal power that passionately links us to the world and to each other. In the wake of the exhaustion of epistemology and its impasses there is a new hunger for determinate material knowledge, a knowledge or research that is at the same instant indistinguishable from an engaged form of political practice.

With this new theoretical openness to an engagement with a properly planetary object—escaping the motif, popular in the 1990s, of a plurality of incommensurable worlds—a transformation has taken place in the valence of two concepts long seen as indispensible to the Marxist project. First, the planetary emergency has put a definitive end to the habits of mind that styled as statist, inherently violent, or Eurocentric the very idea of a determining economic totality. This is not just because the ecological itself requires an idea of interconnected structure, nor simply that globalization has dissolved any possibility of an enclave beyond the law of exchange, but also because the economic origins of the crisis are so patently obvious. Marxists are making use of complex totalities and a reconfigured notion of system completely de-linked from their early associations with spiritual holism or final causality, just as they have done away, once and for all, with any trace of an implied "scale of being" that locates particularities in a low and ontologically impoverished distance from the high, substantial, causal abstractions of capital and labor. At the same time, the crisis has seemed to generate the conditions for a new receptivity to the notion of political universality, one mirrored within the domain of capitalist production by the now global experience of precarity. Such a confluence, despite all of the theoretical and practical obstacles, creates obvious openings for the reintensification of the political scale indexed by the concept of revolution. To insist on the fact that everything must change no longer requires a subscription to moral or political perfectionism or a naïve, progressivist faith in the good-heartedness of history; it is not a question of human nature perfected or a society holistically "improved" (in the Baconian sense), but a series of globally localized technical problems linked to the urgent incompatibility of capitalism and life. Although such change might portend a thousand shifts in the distribution of dailiness—from the structure and feel of a workday to the ready availability of day care, from the shape of cities to the visual content of our cinemas—ecological crisis has made systemic change the necessary precondition for that most English (and "realist") of Hobbesian impulses—survival itself. Revolution, already fully domesticated by its expropriation by advertising, no longer draped in class terror or violence, is simply innovation, good, practical commonsensical thinking.

Also at work in the redistribution of interest in Marx is the waning of what we might call *the frission of the margin*, the orientation, long endemic to the poststructural, toward phenomena that take place at the borders, outskirts, and interstices of systems. With the shift away from an earlier Structuralist investment in the self-regulating and autonomous functioning of systems, and toward those qualities, phenomena, or events that consistently elude or violate them, came what was essentially a new regime of intellectual taste. Very schematically, we might say that this was a shift from the domain of Law to that of Crime. Madness, violence, error, the body, sex, forgetfulness, and death constituted a stable constellation of objects internally linked precisely via their shared distance from the old idealist norms and protocols—an idealism that was paradoxically expanded to include Marxist materialism as well! This was certainly a critical project and one that was in many ways invaluable: in an instant a whole terrain of phenomena long ignored as beneath or beyond the dignity of thought emerged into view and with it a completely reimagined sense for what could be done with thinking.

From today's vantage point, however, it sometimes appears as if this trend might itself have suffered from a one-sidedness popularly imputed (though mistakenly) to Marx himself: a certain incapacitating hatred of the bourgeoisie! This hatred of (really French) bourgeois culture—what Foucault once described in code as the whole realm of "mid-range pleasures" and which Deleuze and Guattari never tired of parodying—when translated into the recursive (and often very derivative) patterns of 1990s criticism became an obliviousness or indifference to all of the spaces and practices trafficked by commerce, property, and money.[3] Thought today no longer labors on the edges of normativity, but immerses itself in its concrete texture and details: the turn toward Marx and economics constitutes a different turn to the phenomena ignored by thought—a turn toward the banal and the barely noticed, toward objects so grey they're interesting. What can we learn about the literature of the World Bank? What would an ethnography of Wall Street tell us? What is the precise style of governance adopted by a neoliberal state? How does a factory in Guangzhou subjectivize its workers? What can be learned about the social ontology of the new communications technologies? What are the linkages between serial femicide in places like Ciudad Juarez and the social and phenomenological coordinates of the maquiladora? How does capital alter the logic of urban spaces? This generation appears more open to reading texts their subcultures have trained them to instinctively dislike; however much they might prefer to be reading de Sade, Nietzsche, or Georges Bataille, they have their noses in Adam Smith, John Locke, and Friedrich Hayek, and can even be found flipping (half-bored, half-fascinated) through the pages of the *Wall Street Journal*.

III

If there is anything, however, which has directly revivified interest in Marxist theory it is the sudden appearance on the scene, impossible to anticipate from the perspective of 1990s thinking, of a new generation of people for whom the word communism no longer merely signals stupidity, death, and failure, but a new horizon of political possibility and meaning. The specificity of the word matters here: the transfused energies of the word "communist" never cease to recall all that stands to be lost, botched, or destroyed by any genuine (transformative) political process. Unlike today's liberal democrats, whose political affiliation effortlessly channels associations with liberty and progress (wholly screening out its historical complicity with slavery, racism, pauperization, war, and other injustices), the communist elects to take on a political sign culturally saturated by the synecdoche of the gulag. In this sense, stupidity, death, and failure are the internalized (but not sufficient) first principles of every neocommunism, a nontransferable subjective debt that can in fact be dialectically (even ethically) fruitful, a testing spur to better thought and politics. For some, communism's abjection, its arrival from a space that is necessarily compromised and incomplete, is the very secret of its power: it is from this angle, one filtered through Jacques Lacan's suspicion of wholeness as intrinsically alienating, that Slavoj Žižek can produce his injunction to "fail better."[4] For most, however, an awareness of communist crime and the atmosphere of shame it produces is only a negative first moment in a much more capacious process of affirmation, one replete with positive new pleasures, concepts, forms of togetherness, and imagination. Neo-communism today marks out a terrain populated less by austere figures of organized militancy or dogma, than by a montage sequence of reading groups, free schools, art sites, graffiti, protest, and occupation. They come from everywhere, these new communists—these *communizers*—from anarchism and from Lenin, from Christianity and Yoga, from *Operaismo*, unemployment, and art. What they share is a common sense of revulsion in the face of consumerist banality and a conviction that there is more to life than work, debt, and insecurity. For those of us who haven't spent time on university campuses or with the urban youth and unemployed of Europe's sinking cities, or among a new generation of students in places like São Paulo, Cairo, or Shanghai, this is a phenomenon without an image or concept: such talk will be registered as little more than wishful thinking or fantasy. However fragile its numbers, however inchoate its organizational strategy and strength, it nevertheless remains that communism as a scattered concatenation of bodies, a desirous conception of the good life and as a style of passionate analysis and politics is again drifting around on the horizon. The full force of this shift has been echoed *in* a recent flood of texts ranging from Jodi Dean's *The Communist*

Horizon to Bruno Bosteels's *The Actuality of Communism*. The genealogy of this turn, conceived of in terms of dated publications, would appear to have begun in North America with 2001's *Empire* (through which the entire corpus of Antonio Negri was then rediscovered), with other textual landmarks along the way, including Retort's *Afflicted Powers* (2005), The Invisible Committee's *The Coming Insurrection* (2007), and, most recently, Alain Badiou's *The Communist Hypothesis* (2010). Conceived of in terms of political sequences, the new communism seems to have emerged in the West between Seattle and Occupy, a decade-long cycle of intermittent engagements that continues to draw on the political energies and organizational intelligence of movements (mostly South American) ranging from the Movimento Sem Terra in Brazil to Zapatismo in Oaxaca, from Venezuelan Bolivarianismo to Los Indignados in Argentina.

Often obscured by Marxism's traditional contempt for the disciplinary privacy and quietism of ethics are the contours of its own special ethico-affective dimension. We are not thinking here of a system of moral maxims or imperatives thought to undergird his politics, the unwritten ethical substrate of a society in which "the free development of each is the condition for the free development of all."[5] Nor do we have in mind the Hegelian residues of an early Marxist conception of communism that longed to mingle essence and nature, being and truth, in a political structure grounded in universal recognition. By ethics we don't mean the kind of individualist moral calculus often associated with the word, but an affective register at once personal and collective that is rarely associated with Marxism, but always present therewith. Marx's complex proximity to the discursive codes of nineteenth-century science as well as his suspicion (inherited in part from Hegel) toward bleeding-heart reformers and utopians, has covered over and concealed what we would simply like to note as *the pleasures of Marxism*.

This is a subjective plenitude, a kind of dialectical joy, one which conjoins in the same breath a materialist clarity and distinctness, a science without mastery or comfort, with a genuine over-brimming of the "spirit." The latter combines a hatred of injustice with a love of the future, a feeling of connectedness to everything that has happened and that will happen on the planet with an almost painful awareness of the specificity and limits of one's locale. When it is not linked into vibrant, activist networks, the congeniality of political connection and work, Marxism retains nevertheless unique theoretical pleasures that delight of the understanding so passionately expressed by Spinoza in the context of seventeenth-century science. Even Locke writes of the "constant delight" afforded by the work of knowing, a "sort of hawking and hunting, wherein the very pursuit makes a great part of the pleasure."[6] How much greater and intense this pleasure is in the context of an immanent encounter not with being or nature or even "society," but with the interesting and infuriating flesh of capital: concealed and intelligible at the same time, mappable yet infinitely complex there is a purely speculative, tinkerer's pleasure here, one represented perfectly by the thin, straining diagrams of finance made by conceptual artist Mark Lomardi or the organized chaos and texture of Andreas Gurski's photographs of visually exploding Chinese factories. This is that today rare sense that one is in touch with an essence of things, a "substance" composed out of nothing more than relations and forces, one that is entirely historical, contingent, and certainly very slippery, but which nevertheless has about it an utterly unforgettable expository weight, a power to reveal and to lay bare. This (provisional) conviction is precisely the same affective texture one experiences in the presence of others in the street during protest: though one encounter is ostensibly solitary and objective and the other subjective and crowded it would be impossible to divide this pleasure, this desire for knowledge and justice, which happens in the same breath.

We mention this unique Marxist *jouissance*, the self-sustaining pleasure of Marxist research and practice, because we are painfully aware that we are living, despite the shifts in the fortune of political Marxism mentioned above, in the ruins of the Left. This is in no way an inescapable fate and there are myriad reasons for hope, but the present nevertheless constitutes a miserable state of affairs for those taken by the possibilities of a different kind of world—a space in which the 1 percent has gained vastly at the expense of the 99 percent, in which we can expect an increase in global temperature of 4°C by the end of the century, and in which both unjust and damaging outputs of the present are as widely known as they are under-politicized. If the expository or analytic pertinence of Marx today is difficult to doubt—even the *New York Times* concedes this (though in the same register it reserves for "curiosities" of all kinds)—obvious strategic questions remain in the domain of politics. We live within tantalizing historical reach of a Left politics the corporeality, intensity, and scale of which dwarf our own or indeed that of past. We are not thinking here only of the so-called people's democracies, but all of the anarchisms, unionisms, antiimperialisms, feminisms, and social democratic movements that accompanied them across the long twentieth century. Living in the ruins does not mean living in the shadow of an absent perfection or harboring a desire to rebuild on the spot. It is, however, infuriatingly *lonely* in a way that constitutes an ever-present threat to the stamina and perseverance of a genuine politics. The theories anthologized here address in various ways a Marxism at once alive and dead, conjuncturally essential and nothing at the same time. For example, Badiou's philosophy is tailored to the maintenance of subjective organizational intensity in hard political times, an unambiguous philosophy of hope: it is the necessary spiritual fuel of the beleaguered (potentially universal) corpuscle. The autonomists have their own solution: communism is not, as Marx sometimes envisioned, a project 20, 30, 50 years in the making, but a project to be immanently produced in the interstices of the present, one that we should invent in the here and now rather than await in the form of a messianic future event. Although there are signs of a shift in the winds, we live (and should admit it) in the ruins, a context without guarantees of "progress" or redemption. Nothing in this political conjuncture, however, even remotely threatens the relevance and pleasure of Marxist theory and practice, just as the continuing existence of patriarchy has no effect at all on the relevance and pleasures of feminism. The fact that things may be difficult doesn't mean that the very real openings generated by the analytic rigor of Marxism, or the energetic way of being in the world produced by the connections and communities of Left practice, are unreal, or unnecessary, or aren't desperately needed. Indeed, Marxist thought is a necessary (though not sufficient) condition if there is to be any hope at all of creating a world in which human beings can at long last shape maximally their own possibilities in the just and lively company of those with whom they share the planet.

IV

Anthologies are uniquely irritating objects, which is not to say that we can do without them or that there aren't important differences between one kind of irritation and another. The question is not really *whether* but *how* an anthology fails. This one is no different, a tangle of awkward adjacencies and truncations. At the heart of the desire to anthologize are two irreconcilable injunctions. When grounded in a principle of inclusiveness—a kind of neutral scanning of the breadth and heterogeneity of a field—what is won in the domain of variety is often lost in thematic tightness or unity: pieces come to be incoherently tumbled together like items tossed into a laundry bag. When, however, the organizing principle isn't adequation, but a strong, coherent shaping of the field's structuring tensions and problems, the danger arrives in the form of exclusions and oversights of work and figures that everyone might think should be represented in an anthology. Where the first option gains a kind of panoramic, documentary breadth (while losing something like "spiritual" form), the latter gains coherence at the expense of the richness and depth of the field. The dangers are even more pronounced in a book of contemporary Marxist theory, one whose very title will be intelligible for many only as comedy or oxymoron. Isn't to utter the words Marx and Theory in the same sentence already to speak in contradiction? Marxism, of course, is regularly parodied as beneath the threshold of thought, a politics born of blind practice or psychopathology, just as its contemporaneity to anything but the nineteenth century is still by many called into question. We're confident that the texts included here are more than capable of de-mystifying both of these clichés.

This anthology has no interest in establishing the sanctity of a canon. Its exclusions are not passive aggressions, undeclared acts of war against unnamed schools or thinkers. We are tired of these rituals of faction, habits that are intellectually incurious and politically ruinous. We have excluded representatives from world-systems theory, Analytic Marxism, liberation theology, the New Dialectic, the UMass, and *Monthly Review* crews, as well as many other interesting clusters of contemporary Marxist research, not out of uninterest or suspicion, but out of an editorial commitment to using the word "theory" found in the title of this book not merely as a synonym for thought per se, but in the sense it has come to be used in North America as a byword for the transformation within philosophy enacted by the triple torsion of Marx, Nietzsche, and Freud. There are exceptions here: our choice to include Arif Dirlik's essay met what we thought was an urgent need to acknowledge the role played by "the rise of China" in the new conjuncture, while Alain Lipietz's work, though not conversant with the continental tradition, seemed pertinent in the context of the overwhelmingly productivist imperatives of contemporary capitalism.

What does it mean for a thought to be "Marxist?" What criteria or protocol legitimates this predicate? Is it a question of content, adherence to a package of empirical economic hypotheses or political tenets? Is there an axial Marxist hypothesis or position, one which when removed qualitatively changes the substance of a discourse? Or is it a matter of thresholds, a point reached in the complexion of a thought after which it simply ceases to be recognizably Marxian? Is it, instead a question of method or form? Here we might recall György Lukács's suggestion that if all of Marx's signature empirical hypotheses were proven false—the rate of profit to fall, the labor theory of value, and so on—the "truth" of Marxism would in no way be affected. What he meant of course was that the richness of dialectical materialism survives the failure of any given positive Marxian postulate, that a thought characterized by dialectical precision must by definition perpetually overcome and surpass itself. Ultimately, we have to confess to finding the question of just what it is that qualifies a thought as Marxist uninteresting, at least insofar as it envisions itself as anything beyond an intriguing specialist imbroglio. Certainly, we also experience all the categorical and definitional impulses of anyone caught up in the pleasures of theory, that desire to create and clarify differences and to defend logical attachments, and there may indeed be more at stake in these distinctions in the context of a discourse that actively insists on the inseparability of theory and practice. But we have to admit that we discern in the background of this question a tired paraphernalia of patrol, the specter of blindly guarded territory.

If pressed, however, we would offer the following. If the vocational destiny of feminism is that of rigorously safeguarding the capacity of the human to think itself beyond the limits imposed on thought and practice by patriarchy, then that of Marxism pertains to the need to equally contest the limits placed on thought and practice by the historical existence of capitalism. Both are arts and sciences of justice, which is to say, utterly essential analytic apparatuses *and* visionary political injunctions. The decisions that we made in bringing together the writers collected here was to offer an overview of the ways in which Marxism has responded to the complexities of our particular configuration of capitalism. It is a configuration in which capitalism reigns supreme, untouched, and unchallenged on the scale that would be needed to undo its logics and its structures, even as its self-certainties have been put into question and its ideologies no longer secure its future—a moment in which capitalism is undeniably powerful, constituting the very terrain of the quotidian, and yet stands all too ready to be jettisoned in favor of some other reality by the 99 percent for whom it doesn't even provide Keynesian comforts as it goes about rapidly making the planet uninhabitable.

Far from merely being characterized by tangential philosophical *interests*—something undertaken on the outskirts of the serious business of economics or politics—Marxist theory has functioned as an essential vector for the reinvigoration of philosophy itself. This is an improbable fate for a discourse often construed as fundamentally organized around a desire to escape or transcend the philosophical tradition. We have seen, precisely via the Marxisms of Étienne Balibar, Negri, Badiou, Žižek, and others, a tremendous resurgence of interest in the history of philosophy among a new generation of students and theorists. Balibar's recent comprehensive reevaluation of Locke, Negri's treatments of both Descartes and Spinoza, Žižek's Hegel and Schelling, Badiou's Plato: everywhere we discover Marxists scavenging essential theoretical bits and pieces from thinkers not just at a distance from their own tradition, but sometimes classically opposed to it. There are those for whom this pluralism will no doubt be the clearest symptom of revisionist decadence and confusion, a theory now so fully detached from practice (a further confirmation of Perry Anderson's famous argument about the character of Western Marxism) that it can risklessly drift, one enfeebled worldview among an infinity of others. However, we feel that this turn toward Marx within philosophy is not just another instance of the latter responding belatedly to exigent historical conditions, but a genuinely dialectical shift within its own disciplinary and normative space, one in some sense being grown from within the limits, exhaustions, and aporias of the tradition itself. We see this omnivorousness of contemporary Marxist thought as a mark of its strength, a desire to contend with diverse positions and to hybridize what it has learned with other strains of thought. By putting various strands of contemporary Marxist theory into dialogue within a single text, we hope to further those philosophical *and* political inquiries that promise to reshape the terrain on which we will live out our collective futures, a terrain filled to the brim with questions and dangers, but also unnervingly beautiful glints of reddish light.

Notes

1 The case of Deleuze, as seen below, is an ambivalent one. Although he makes certain to distinguish the passive, representational habits of tracing from the active qualities of the map, he is far more interested than Jacques Derrida or Maurice Blanchot in diagramming material assemblages. Nevertheless, the Marxism affirmed by Deleuze is less concerned with creating comprehensive maps of capitalism than it is with the task of subverting it.
2 Karl Marx, *The German Ideology*, ed. C. J. Arthur (New York: International Publishers, 1999), 42.
3 Michel Foucault, *Foucault Live*, ed. Sylvère Lotringer (New York: Semiotext(e), 1996), 378.
4 Žižek, *In Defense of Lost Causes* (London: Verso, 2008), 210.
5 Karl Marx, *Later Political Writings*, ed. Terrel Carver (Cambridge, MA: Cambridge University Press, 2004), 20.
6 *An Essay Concerning Human Understanding* (Indianapolis: Hackett, 1996), 1.

PART ONE

Notes on the Conjuncture

Introduction

Marxist theory has been at the forefront of attempts to comprehend and theorize the rapid, often violent processes that are currently reshaping human life on the planet—the developments, real and fictional, which collectively have been given the name of "globalization." The essays in this section represent attempts to identify the specificities of our present historical conjuncture, addressing structural issues including technological change, new geopolitical formations, new economics, post-industrialism, precarity, neoliberalization, and the demands of ecology, and raising the question of the challenges they pose for theory at the present time.

In "Capitalistic Systems, Structures and Processes," Félix Guattari and Eric Alliez address the relationship between two ways of understanding capitalism, one economic and one social. According to the first, the *semiotic system of capital*, capitalism is conceived as a "general function of semiotization of a certain mode of production, circulation and distribution:" capitalism is thus capital's "method" for the valorization of goods and services. According to the second, the *structure of segmentation*, capitalism is a "generator of a particular type of social relations" in which "regulations, laws, usages and practices come to the fore." This relationship is not one of simple opposition; the two go hand-in-hand.

Capitalism, they argue, is characterized by semiotic power—and what distinguishes it from earlier forms of exploitation is that this power is semiotically deterritorialized. It not only permits but also relies on "marginal freedoms, relative spaces for creativity," and what is historically specific to capitalism is that it seeks to exert control over these margins solely in order to maintain its own processual character. This criterion permits the distinction between different kinds of capitalism, neither effacing the differences between nor asserting their radical heterogeneity, and enables the delineation of the relative priority within each one of the market, production and the state. The current conjuncture—which they term Integrated World Capitalism—is characterized by the priority of production over the market, and the market over the state. Production for its own sake is accompanied by the pervasion of flexible, temporary labor, and by the deterritorialized, "mobile" or "minimum" state which, divested of its power within a national arena, can now only promote the increased participation in transnational processes of valorization—which raises the question of the potential limits of its integrative power, thus redefining the terms of the question of the horizon of a new collective response.

In "Rethinking Marx's Critical Theory," Moishe Postone argues that "the categories of Marx's mature critique are historically specific to modern, or capitalist, society," a claim from which it follows that this mature critique involves the historical relativization of all transhistorical notions. This relativization characterizes Postone's attempt to rethink Marx's critique, which he contrasts with the limitations of traditional Marxism, defined as "all analyses that understand capitalism essentially in terms of class relations structured by a market economy and private ownership of the means of production." Labor, for Postone, is thus not a transhistorical "activity mediating humans and nature that transforms matter in a goal-directed manner"—but an essentially capitalist process. This rethinking of Marx's critical theory develops from the work of Lukács and the theorists of the Frankfurt school, in whose work Postone identifies a theoretical tension between an adherence to a traditional understanding of capitalism in terms of private property, and an analysis that reveals such a conception as inadequate.

He observes that the shrinking and weakening of the state since the early 1970s—what Guattari and Alliez refer to as the "minimum" state—is, like the post-war expansion of the welfare state that took place under conservative and social-democratic administrations alike, a truly global, general phenomenon that is independent of politics, and that thus cannot adequately be grasped in terms of contingency. Postone's rethinking of Marx's critical theory nonetheless demonstrates strong affinities with poststructuralist critiques of totality, of the Subject, and of a dialectical logic of history, which, "grasped as the unfolding of an immanent necessity, should be understood as delineating a form of unfreedom." However, rather than denying these conceptions, Postone sees them as expressions of the reality of capitalist society. Heteronomous history, above all, is presented not as a narrative that can be dispelled discursively, but as an actually existing structure of domination that must be overcome.

Alan Lipietz's account of "The Impasses of Liberal Productivism" takes issue with what he identifies as the worldview that predominated at and after the late 1970s, according to which the world was undergoing a "technological revolution" which was prevented from developing fully by constraints imposed by the state and trade unions—"social provision, welfare state, anti-pollution laws and the like"—which starved firms of capital and prevented the supposedly "painful but necessary" changes that would allow the emerging society to flourish. The "societal paradigm" of this worldview—liberal productivism—is characterized by, first, the assertion of the "productivist techno-economic imperative" and the concomitant loss of the idea of real choice; secondly, the fragmentation that arises as firms increasingly take on the role of the "mother country;" thirdly, the integration of individuals into firms qua individuals rather than collectively; and fourthly the reduction of "national" administrative solidarity, with its former role taken on by "civil society" or the family.

Lipietz identifies four problems with this paradigm. The first is that the implementation of its political implications leads to exacerbated social polarization, and with it the return of the "problem of the dangerous classes" (not to mention the lucrative potential for employing poor people to protect the rich from other poor people). This polarization is then complemented by the second problem, which results from the fact that the "technological revolution" at all stages requires human input—sometimes highly skilled, sometimes unskilled. Lipietz foresees a situation in which "the upper echelons of the labor force retain Fordist social benefits . . . while the rest are condemned to neo-Taylorist casual employment." The third is the instability of recurrent crises of over-production, even when deferred by US deficit spending, for in the long term "a country cannot continue to drag others along by piling up debt." Finally, he presciently observes, nearly two decades before the onset of the financial crisis of 2008, that the insistence on free trade between countries without a common means of regulating growth results in "stagnation or at best spasmodic growth," the response to which (austerity) is barely tolerable in the North, but amounts in the debt-laden South to "misery, hunger and the agony of a whole people."

Paulin Hountondji's "Recapturing" addresses the relationship between economic production and knowledge production, and particularly the role and function of academic practice in "the economy of the entirety of scholarship, its place in the production of knowledge on a worldwide basis." Taking the concept of extraversion from development theory and applying it to a sociology of science, he shows that as long as the field of consideration is that of the research career of the individual scholar, the problems faced by scholars in Africa and the South can only ever appear as quantitative insufficiencies. Seen, however, from the perspective of the purpose served by research, its insertion into the society that produces it, and the extent to which it can be appropriated or expropriated, it becomes clear that the differences are not only quantitative but also qualitative, that African research "is extraverted, turned toward the exterior, ruled by and subordinate to outside needs instead of being self-centered and destined, first of all, to answer the questions posed by the African society itself."

Hountondji identifies a range of indices or indications of extraversion: the South's dependence on the North for both scientific equipment and infrastructure (including libraries, archives, publishers, and journals); that work produced in the South is better known in the North, while research on the periphery remains bound to the local context, for the European readership, and conditioned to the already extraverted export market; the focus on the center and the necessity of leaving the periphery, whether in the more overt form of the "brain drain" or the need to make temporary trips to the North to pursue a research project. Meanwhile, the converse movement from the North to the South is made in order to look "not . . . for science but only for the materials for science," a process that goes hand-in-hand with the erasure of traditional kinds of knowledge and language.

In "Immaterial Labor," in contrast, Maurizio Lazzarato considers the relationship between knowledge and production and its implications with respect to the phenomenon of immaterial labor, "the labor that produces the informational and cultural content of the commodity." The concept of immaterial labor refers both to changes in the labor process of traditional secondary and tertiary industries, "where the skills involved in direct labor are increasingly skills involving cybernetics and computer control (and horizontal and vertical communication)," and at the same time to the manifestation within the labor process of "activities that are not normally recognized as 'work'—in other words, the kinds of activities involved in defining and fixing cultural and artistic standards, fashions, tastes, consumer norms, and, more strategically, public opinion."

This involves rendering workers' subjectivity susceptible to organization and command, which brings about a shift in the relationship between capitalist and proletarian, at all levels of the labor process: "The capitalist needs to find an unmediated way of establishing command over subjectivity itself; the prescription and definition of tasks transforms into a prescription of subjectivities." Communication and co-operation become compulsory elements of labor—of the participation in a work team, a redefinition of workplace collectivity, or of its mediation through the requirements of capital. This, in turn, has implications for the cycle of capital, and in particular for the relationship between production and valorization. For the commodity produced by immaterial labor is not used up in the act of consumption. Consumption becomes a social process of communication, and "the process of the production of communication tends to become immediately the process of valorization," a tendency which reveals that "labor produces not only commodities, but first and foremost it produces the capital relation."

Silvia Federici's account of "Women, Land-Struggles, and Globalization" emphasizes and takes as its point of departure "the strategic importance that access to land has had for women and their communities, despite the ability of companies and governments to use it at times for their own ends," while pointing to—without romanticizing—a mode of sustaining life that is not oriented toward capital accumulation. Federici draws attention to the blending out of women's work, charting how unwaged work carried out by women, and subsistence farming in particular, tend to be ignored, despite the fact that women produce the bulk of the food that is consumed by their families.

In the light of the predication of capitalist development on the separation of agricultural producers from the land, the persistence of subsistence farming by women in particular, a persistence which depends on struggles worldwide for the reappropriation of land, represents not only a remarkable achievement, but also a lived struggle against the determination by market prices of who should live and who should die. This noncommercial use of natural resources provides "a practical model for the reproduction of life in a noncommercial way," and not only points but also contributes "to a noncompetitive, solidarity-centered mode of life that is crucial for the building of a new society," in which "reproducing ourselves does not come at the expense of other people nor presents a threat to the continuation of life on the planet."

Finally, Arif Dirlik investigates "The Idea of a 'Chinese Model',", which has frequently been contrasted, tacitly or explicitly, with the "neoliberal 'Washington consensus',", and has attracted particular attention as a result of the "enormous economic achievements of the last two decades, especially since the 2008 recession which seems to have caused relatively little damage to advances in the Chinese economy." Seeking to go beyond reductionist, economistic understandings, he asks what it means to talk of a "model" in the contemporary world, the features that would distinguish a "Chinese model," and the extent to which such a "model" might appeal to others as an alternative to the "neoliberal model of a market economy"—whether, that is, such a model is peculiar to China and to the particular circumstances of Chinese society, or whether it is open to emulation by others.

Dirlik criticizes the obliviousness in many discussions to China's unique historical trajectory, which distinguishes its development even from that of its "neighboring neo-authoritarian regimes:" in particular the Chinese Revolution's orientation toward "a socialist society that stressed egalitarianism, giving a voice to the people, and the creation of a new culture consistent with these goals," with the goal of "autonomous and self-reliant development." Recognizing the achievements of the Chinese Revolution in placing the social challenges of development on the agenda of Marxism, he suggests that it is premature to talk of a "Chinese model," less still of such a model as a socialist society, until the problems of environmental destruction and of the reliance of growth on real estate speculation and automobile manufacturing have been resolved.

CHAPTER ONE

Capitalistic Systems, Structures, and Processes

Félix Guattari and Eric Alliez

From Molecular Revolution. *New York: Penguin, 1984: 273–287.*

The question of capitalism can be envisaged from a number of angles, but those of the economy and the social constitute a necessary starting point.

First, capitalism can be defined as a general function of semiotization of a certain mode of production, circulation and distribution. Capitalism, the "method" of Capital, will be considered as a specific procedure of valorization of commodities, such as goods, activities and services, founded on index and symbolization systems drawn from a particular syntax and allowing the over-encoding and the control of the management running it.

This "formalist" definition can be sustained because, despite being indissociable from those of the technical and socio-economic arrangements (*agencement*) to which it is related, such a function of semiotization has no less an intrinsic coherence. From this point of view the styles (*modes*) of capitalistic "writings" (cf. Derrida) could be compared to the mathematical corpus whose axiomatic consistence is not called in question by the application which might be made in extra-mathematical fields. We propose to call this first level the *semiotic system* of capitalism, or the *semiotic of capitalistic valorization*.

Second, capitalism appears more as a generator of a particular type of social relations; here regulations, laws, usages and practices come to the fore. The procedures of economic writing may vary; what counts is the maintenance of a certain type of social *order* founded on the division of roles between those who monopolize power and those who are subject to it, and that just as much in the areas of work and economic life, as in those of life-styles, knowledge and culture. All these divisions, with those of sex, age-groups and race, end up by constituting "at the arrival-point" the concrete segments of the socius. This second level will be defined as the *structure of segmentation*, a level which seems also to maintain a certain degree of internal coherence whatever the transformations or the upheavals imposed upon it by history.

It is clear, however, that the "codage" of capitalism does not proceed from a "table of law" defining once and for all inter-human relations. The order which it imposes evolves just as does its own economic syntax. In this domain, as in many others, the influences are not unilateral, we are never confronted with a one-way causality. Neither is it a question of being satisfied with a simple opposition between semiotic system and segmentation system. These two aspects always go together, and their distinction will become pertinent only to the extent that it allows us to clarify the interactions which each has with a third, equally important, level: that of the process of production. Let us be clear straightaway that, in the present perspective, this lesser level should not be identified with what Marxists designate by the expression "relations of production" or "economic relations of the infrastructure." Doubtless our category of "process of production" subsumes the Marxist one, but it goes largely beyond it in the infinitely extensible domain of machines, both concrete and abstract. These components of the process have therefore to include material forces, human labor, social relations as well as investments of desire. In the cases where the *ordering* of these components leads to an enrichment of their potentialities—where the whole exceeds the sum of the parts—these process interactions shall be called diagrammatic—and we shall speak of mechanistic surplus-value.

Is it still legitimate, under these conditions, to continue to envisage capitalism as a general entity? Will not these formal definitions which are proposed for it be condemned to obliterate its diversity in time and space? What is the place of capitalism as mystery? The only element of historical continuity which seems capable of characterizing its various experiences seems to be precisely the process character of its sphere of production, in the very wide sense we have just proposed. One can "find" capitalism in all places and at all times, as soon as one considers it either from the point of view of the exploitation of proletarian classes, or from that of the setting-to-work of means of economic semiotization facilitating the rise of the great markets (paper money, money in circulation, credit, etc.). Nevertheless it remains true that the capitalisms of the last three centuries have really "taken off" only from the moment when the sciences, the industrial and commercial techniques and society have their futures together within a single process of generalized transformations (a process combined with de-territorialization). And everything leads us to believe that in the absence of such a "mechanical knot," of such a proliferation of the "mecanosphere," the societies in which capitalistic forms have developed would have been incapable of overcoming the major shocks which are brought about by world crises and wars and would certainly have ended up in the same sorts of blind alleys that were experienced by certain other great civilizations: an interminable agony or a sudden "inexplicable" death.

Capitalism would therefore represent a paroxystic form of the integration of not only different types of mechanisms, technical systems, economic systems, but also conceptual systems, religious systems, aesthetic systems, perceptual systems, systems of wants. Its work of semiotization—the method of *Capital*—would form at the same time a sort of collective computer[1] of society and production, and a "homing head" of innovations adapted to its internal pulsions. In these conditions, its raw material, its basic diet, would not be, directly, human labor or machine labor but the whole gamut of the *means of semiotic pilotage* relative to instrumentation, to the insertion in society, to the reproduction, to the circulation of many component parts concerned by this process of mechanical integration. What capitalizes capital is semiotic power. But not just any power—because in that case there would be no way of demarcating the earlier forms of exploitation—a semiotically de-territorialized power. Capitalism confers on certain social sub-systems a capacity for the selective control of society and production by means of a system of collective semiotization. What specifies it historically is that it only tries to control the different components which come together to maintain its processual character. Capitalism does not seek to exercise despotic power over all the wheels of society. It is even crucial to its survival that it manages to arrange marginal freedoms, relative spaces for creativity. What is of primary importance to it is the mastery of the semiotic wheels which are essential for the key productive arrangements and especially of those which are involved in changing machine processes (the adjustments of machine power). Doubtless it is obliged by the force of history to interest itself in all domains of the social—public order, education, religion, the arts etc. But, originally, this is not its problem; it is first of all and continuously a *mode of evaluation* and *technical means of control* of the power arrangements and their corresponding formulations.

All its "mystery" comes from the way it manages to articulate, within one and the same general system of enrolment and equivalence, entities which at first sight would seem radically different: of material and economic *goods*, of individual and collective human activities, and of technical, industrial and scientific processes. And the key to this mystery lies in the fact that it does not content itself with standardizing, comparing, ordering, informatizing these multiple domains but, with the opportunity offered by these diverse operations, it extracts from each of them one and the same *mechanical surplus-value* or *value of mechanical exploitation*. It is its capacity to re-order through a single system of semiotization the most diverse mechanical values which gives capitalism its hold, not only over material machines of the economic sphere (artisanal, manufacturing, industrial, etc.) but equally over the non-material machines working in the heart of human activities (productive-unproductive, public-private, real-imaginary, etc.).

Each "manifest" economic market thus displays in parallel different "latent" areas of mechanical values, values of desire, aesthetic values etc., which we could call values of content. The conscious and "flat" economic valorization is thus doubled by modes of "deep" valorization, relatively unconscious if compared to explicit systems of exchange valorizations. But the fact that these values of content are made, in the framework of the given relations of production, to give an account of themselves to the formal economic values is not without incidence on their internal organization. They find themselves, somehow in spite of themselves, brought within a framework of equivalence, brought into a generalized market of values and reference—and the whole problematic which turns around the division use value/exchange value is thus shown to be completely invalid by the fact that the setting-up of this framework of capitalist equivalence has as its effect to evacuate these forms of their social content. Use value is somehow drawn into the orbit of exchange value, thus eliminating from the surface of the capitalist process all that remained of naturalness, all spontaneity of "needs." Exit the unidimensional perspectives of revolutionary reappropriation of use value.

(Does this mean that the reign of exchange value is inevitable? Unless it means that we must rather imagine arrangements of desire which are so complex that they can express a subversive de-naturizing of human relations to exchange values? It being agreed that we shall speak here of value, or of *arrangements* of desire to mark ourselves off from any mythology of Otherness and of Absence which only takes up again, at another level, the project of "re-naturalization" or worldly relationships destroyed by capitalism.)

At the end of this process of integration, capitalistic valorization takes over based upon a double articulation with:

- the general market of formal economic values;
- the general market of mechanical values.

It is in this system of dual market that the essentially inegalitarian and manipulative character of exchange operations in a capitalistic context has its origin. It is in the nature of the mode of semiotization of capitalistic arrangements that, in the last instance, it always proceeds from a contradiction operation:

(1) of putting into communication and formal equivalence, asymmetric forces and powers from very different domains;

(2) of delimiting closed territories (rule of the laws of property) and of setting social divisions based on the programming of distribution of goods and rights, and similarly based on the definition of modes of feeling, of taste, of "unconscious" choices appropriate to different social groups.

(We are thus faced with another type of difficulty: threatened now with no longer being able to get out of a simple opposition between onomic form and mechanical content, we run the risk of hypostatizing a historical necessity in the generation of valorization processes, while the arrangements of pre-capitalist valorizations waiting to be over-encoded by a de-territorializing capitalist valorization, by their qualitative specificities, their heterogeneity, the unequal character of their relationships would appear as territorialized residues of an essentially quantifying movement of valorization, one that homogenizes and "equalizes.") If it is true, as Fernand Braudel has shown,[2] that the basically unequal character of capitalist markets was much more visible, much less "genteel," at the time of world economies centered around cities such as Venice, Antwerp, Genoa, Amsterdam, than all that of contemporary world markets, these latter have not as a result become translucent and neutral economic writing surfaces. On the contrary it is clear that the exploitation of the Third World does not belong to equal relationships, but rather to that of pillage "compensated" by the export of technological trinkets and a few luxury gadgets destined for consumption by a handful of privileged natives. All of which does not stop the "new economists" and "neo-liberals" from preaching the saving graces of the capitalist market, in all places and in all situations.

According to them, only this is capable of guaranteeing an optimum arbitration of cost and constraint.[3] The most reactionary economists seem thus to have interiorized an inverted dialectical vision of the progress of history. Since the worst aberrations are just part of historical necessity, one might just as well jump straight in without reservations. The market is thus alleged to be the only system which will ensure an optimal mobilization of all the information necessary to the regulation of complex societies. The market, explains Hayek,[4] is not only an anonymous mechanism allowing the exchange of goods and services or a "static mechanism for sharing of poverty," but, above all, a dynamic instrument for the production or diffusion of knowledge distributed to the social body. In short, it is the very idea of "freedom" which will be linked to the notion of information, and which finds itself taken in a "cybernetic" approach. Following Vera Lutz, it is "the imperfection of information which gives to capitalism its fundamental *raison d'être* as a system of social organization. If information were perfect, there would be no need for capitalists; we could all be, without any trouble, socialists."[5] Inequality of exchanges, according to the people who hold this theory, in the end depends only upon "imperfections" of the structures of *information cost* in these societies.[6] One more effort on the costs and everything will work out! However, it is clear that the Third World does not really "exchange" its labor and its riches for crates of Coca-Cola or even barrels of oil. It is aggressed and bled to death by the intrusion of dominant economies. And it is the same, though in different proportions, with the third and fourth worlds in the rich countries.

The unequal nature of capitalist markets really does not represent a streak of archaism, a historical residue. The pseudo-egalitarian presentation of "exchanges" on the world market no more results from a lack of information than from an ideological disguise of the processes of social subjection. It is the essential complement of the techniques of integration of the collective subjectivity in order to obtain from it an optimal libidinal consent, even an active submission to the relations of exploitation and of segregation. Compared with the mechanical values and the values of desire, the relevance of the distinction between goods and activities would seem likely to blur. In a particular type of structure, human activities, properly controlled and guided by the capitalistic society, generate active mechanical goods, while the evolution of other structures makes certain goods economically dated, and they thus find their "mechanical virulence" devalued. In the first case, a power of activity (a power asset) is transformed into a highly valuable *mechanical power*, in the second case a mechanical power (an Authority) tends to the side of *formal powers*.

(We have seen that if we satisfy ourselves with an opposition—economic semiotic system (for example, that of the market) and segmentary social structure—we are lacking the mechanical integrating factors. On the other hand, if we stop at an opposition semiotic system—for example, economic information—and mechanical process, we risk losing the territorialized collective investments, the effective structures of the economic and social ethology. In the former case, we get bogged down in formalistic sociological reductions, and in the latter we fly off into dialectical extrapolations which lead us away from historical realities. We therefore have to "hold" together the three components, systematic, structural and processual, of capitalism without granting anything but contingent priority to any one of them.)

The different evaluative formulae which economists generally present as mutually exclusive[7] have, in fact, always been closely linked—either in competition or in complementarity—in real economic history.[8] Is there not a case for seeking to qualify each of them more clearly? Their different forms of existence (commercial, industrial, financial, monopolistic, statist or bureaucratic valorization) are the result of placing in the foreground one or other of their fundamental components, "selected" from within the same range of basic components, which has thus been reduced here to three terms:

- the *processes* of mechanical production,
- the *structures* of social segmentation,
- the dominant economic semiotic *systems*.

From this minimum model—necessary, but hardly sufficient, because it is never a question of simple components themselves structured according to their own systems of priority—we now proceed to examine a sort of generative chemistry of structures of economic valorization resulting from the combination of contingent priorities between basic components.

In the following table of structures of capitalistic valorization:

(1) the structures of social segmentation shall only be considered from the point of view of the economic problematic of the *State* (the analysis of the consequences of centralist direction of an important part of economic movements—which can be observed in the national accounting—on the stratification of segmentary relations);

(2) the systems of economic semiotization will be considered only from the angle of the problematic of the *market* (in the widest sense, as referred to earlier, of markets of men, ideas, phantasmas, etc.);

(3) the productive processes will not be further specified.

The six formulae of structures of capitalistic valorization

(The priorities between components are indicated by arrows.)

	Order of priorities	Examples
(a)	State→production→market	*Asiatic mode of production*[9] *Nazi-type war economy*
(b)	Market→production→state	*Commercial proto-capitalism* *World economies* centered on a network of cities[10]
(c)	Market→state→production	*Liberal capitalism*
(d)	Production→state→market	*Colonial monopoly economy*
(e)	Production→market→state	*Integrated World Capitalism*
(f)	State→market→production	*State capitalism*

The object of this table, it should be emphasized, is not at all to present a general typology of historical forms of capitalism, but solely to show that *capitalism cannot be identified with a single formulation* (for example, market economy). One could make it more complex and refine it by introducing supplementary components or by differentiating the internal components of each cluster; the barriers are by no means watertight (there is "mechanical production" in the semiotic wheels of the market and at the level of the State—for example, in public buildings and in the media; there is "State power" at the heart of the most liberal economic systems; moreover these last-named always play a determinant role within the productive spheres). It is proposed here only to try to throw into relief, starting from certain correlations emerging from the second system of articulation which is found in each formula, certain correlations between systems which appear to be very distant the one from the other, but which go in the same historical direction.

In a general way:

(1) The capacity of certain structures to take on major historical upheavals or, to paraphrase a formula which is very dear to Ilya Prigogine, their capacity to direct "processes farm from historical equilibria" will depend on the primacy of productive components.

(2) The degree of resistance to change of the axioms of clan, ethnic, religious, urbanistic stratification, of castes, of classes, etc., depends on the primacy of the components of social segmentarity.

(3) On the more or less innovatory character of their semiotic valorization (the fact that these should be capable, or not, of adaptation, of growing richer by new procedures: their degree of "diagrammacity") will depend on their integrative power, their capacity to "colonize" not only economic life, but also social life, libidinal life, in other words, their possibility to transform society, to subjugate it to the mechanical phylums.

The fact that the "direction of history" should be related here to the evolutive phylum of production does not necessarily imply, it is worth noting, a finalization of history in transcendent objectives. The existence of a "mechanical direction" of history does not at all stop this from "going in all directions." The *mechanical phylum* inhabits and directs the *historical rhizome* (root) of capitalism, but without ever mastering its destiny which continues to be played out in an equal match between social segmentarity and the evolution of modes of economic valorization.

Let us look again at these different formulae of priorities.

Priorities of the market

Priority (b), relegating the question of the State to the third line, that, for example, of the *commercial proto-capitalism* of the thirteenth and fourteenth centuries (questions of the State came so far behind commercial interests for the merchants of the Dutch United Provinces of the seventeenth century that no one was really shocked by the fact that they provided arms for their Portuguese or French enemies).[11] It sets up a specific problem with the extension and consolidation of capitalism to the whole society through a sort of baroque flowering of all the productive cultural and institutional spheres.

The phenomenon of credit—via the trade in letters of change which thrusts its roots into international commerce—constituted the "clutch" of such a flowering. It should be noted that medieval law sought in vain to obstruct the free circulation of the effects of commerce; this practice ran into the hostility of public powers who wanted to stabilize exchanges and control monetary circulation. Hence the story of the "endorsement war," declared by these merchant bankers who, *de facto*, extended to the letter of exchange (bank-deposited money) what had already been admitted for the schedules (currency in circulation): the *right of transfer* (the schedules circulated by simple discount, while the letters of exchange were not—in law—freely transferable). The answer, though long awaited, was no less clear, without being decisive: in Venice, for example, the accountants of the Banco del Giro were forbidden, by the decree of July 6, 1652, to allow book transfers in order to pay endorsed letters of exchange. This fact would have remained marginal if it had not been symptomatic of the slowness and the incapacity of the (para-)statist structures to control the capitalistic monetary movements. In 1766 Accarias de Scrione was still able to write: "If ten or twelve first-class Amsterdam merchants got together for a banking operation, they could in a moment set into circulation throughout Europe more than two hundred millions of paper-money florins which were preferred to spot cash. There is no Sovereign who could do such a thing . . . Such credit is a power which these ten or twelve merchants wield in all the States of Europe with absolute independence of all authority."[12]

Priority (c), relegating the question of production to the third line, that, for example, of the *crude liberalism of the nineteenth-century capitalism*. It sets a specific historical problem with the constitution of modern territorialized States. Paradoxically, liberalism is always more preoccupied with the setting-up of a State apparatus than with a generalized growth of production. If one accepts Habermas's analysis that perhaps "no ideology, properly speaking, existed at that time"[13] then one understands more easily that, far from crowning the free-trading edifice, Say's Law—the theory of general equilibrium—represents rather its *juridical* formulation; it "throws the knife in the sea" and makes the body disappear in its fictional work. *Jurisdictio* of a linear, exclusive, algebraic representation; bring together therefore over-exploitation of the productive potential, general mobilization of the labor force, acceleration of the speed of circulation of goods, men and capital—and you will get an automatic equilibrium of supply and demand, thus verifying the self-regulation of the whole system . . . *"But on condition that there be no interference other than economic in the exchanges."*[14]

It can be seen what a unique historical conjunction was needed so that the liberal dream of a society free from any intervention from whatever authority could be set forth. Because the equilibrium of free competition is more or less that: *power without authority*. Without the affirmation (of the reality) of this distinction, Hobbes's formula would never have resulted in that terrible inversion—*veritas non auctoritas facit legem*. The truth of a power, England, which, through its industrial potential, is sufficiently in control of the market channels to play the game of putting the political aspects of material wealth in the background and still win more than that . . . (the repeal of the English Corn Laws dates, after all, only from the middle of the nineteenth century). In fact, the essence of liberalism is in the reverse movement, inseparable from that equivalence of content which translates the utopia of the absence of authority in terms of the affirmation of supreme power: *veritas* will only become *ratio* (the postulate of homogeneity, general equilibrium, henceforth drawing its legitimacy from the "national" order which they display) if it enters into the essential relationship with a constant *rationalization* of domination. Which, in plain terms, means that the State "has always been at least as strong as the social and political situation demanded."[15] Scarcely modified translation of the celebrated phrase of Hobbes: *Wealth is power and power is wealth . . .*

The existence of a large market implies central control—albeit a subtle one—which is absolutely necessary. The "teleguiding" of production based on an expanding market complements the interventions and arbitrages of territorialized States, without which the system would come up against its own limits. It would reveal itself, in particular, incapable of producing basic equipment (of the infrastructure, public services, collective facilities, military equipment, etc.).

Priorities of the state

Priority (a), which relegates the market to third place is, for example, the *Asiatic mode of production*, or the *Nazi type of war economy* (forced labor, relatively minor control of monetary economy, incarnation of the all-powerful nature of the State in the Pharaoh or the Führer, etc.). This sets us specific historical problems:

(1) With the control of the accumulation of capital. Surplus-value has to be accumulated as a matter of priority off the power of the State and its military machine; the growth of the economic and social power of diverse aristocratic strata has to be limited, otherwise it

would eventually threaten the ruling caste; it would eventually lead to the development of social classes. In the case of "Asiatic" empires, this regulation can be brought about by stopping production,[16] by massive sacrificial consumption, by sumptuous constructions, luxury consumption, etc. In the case of Nazi regimes, by internal exterminations and total war.

(2) With mechanical intrusion from outside, especially innovations in military techniques which they fail to adopt in time, because of their conservatism, and the difficulty they have in letting creative initiative develop. (Certain Asiatic empires have been liquidated in the space of a few years by nomadic war machines carrying some military innovation.)

Priority (f), which relegates the question of production to the third place is, for example, *State capitalism of the Soviet type* (Stalinist forms of planning, etc.), of which the affinities with the Asiatic mode of production have been many times underlined. (The Chinese model, at least that of the Maoist period, by its methods of massive enslavement of the collective labor force, belongs perhaps more to formula (a) than to formula (f).) This sets up a specific historical problem with the question of the instruments of economic semiotization, particularly with the setting-up of markets not only of economic values but also of prestige values, values of innovation, and of desires. In this sort of system, the disturbance of the market systems combined with a hyper-stratification of the social segments, is the correlate of an authoritarian control which can subsist only to the extent that its sphere of influence is not too exposed to outside influences, to competition from other branches of the mechanical productive phylum. Thus, in the end, the Gulag system is in tenable only insofar as the Soviet economy freezes, at least partially, innovative arrangements in the advanced technological, scientific, and cultural domains. This problematic is now prolonged by that of the demands for a democratization of the apparatus of social-semiotic control (the systems) (example: the Polish workers' struggle for "workers" control).

Priorities of production

Priority (d), which relegates the question of the market to third place, for example, *classical imperialist exploitation*, constitutes a supplementary form of accumulation for the great capitalist entities without significant mechanical involvement[17] and without thought of the effects of disorganization on the colonized society. The commercial monopolism of the periphery tended to favor the tendencies of monopoly capital in the metropolis and the strengthening of the authority of the State. It sets up a specific historical question with the reconstitution of the devastated colonial society, including the setting-up of a highly artificial State.

Priority (e), which relegates the question of the State to third place, for example, *Integrated World Capitalism*, sets itself up "above" and "below" the pre-capitalist and capitalist segmentary relations (that is to say, at one and the same time, at the world level and at the molecular level), and based upon semiotic means of evaluation and valorization of capital which are completely new and have an increased capacity for the mechanical integration of all human activities and faculties.

In principle, "the entire society becomes productive; the rhythm of production is the rhythm of life."[18] Considerably simplifying, we can say that this high point of the ascendancy of capital over society is established only on the conjunction between mechanical integration and social reproduction—this latter incidentally the result of a complex conservative mechanical re-territorialization if not of the exact terms of social segregation, at least of its essential axioms (hierarchical, racist, sexist, etc.). We shall speak here of *social-mechanical capital* and it is this which will lead us to take the rise of neo-liberal thought quite seriously, starting from the intrusion of information theory in the economic sphere. When information claims first place in the social machine, it would seem, in effect, that it ceases to be linked to the simple organization of the sphere of circulation to become, it its way, a factor of production. *Information as a factor of production . . .* here is the latest formula for decoding society through the formation of cybernetic capital. This is no longer the age of transcendental schematisim *à la* Keynes (finding a new space and a new rhythm of production based on an investment of statist mediation, as a function of the quest for equilibrium), and circulation will no longer be just a vector of the social validation of the profits of power; it becomes immediately production— re-territorialization—capitalization of mechanical profits, taking the form of manipulation and control of the segmentarized reproduction of society. Henceforth capital seems to operate on "a totality without origins, without contradictions, without criticism. Analytic of the totality where the totality is taken for granted"[19] and is itself indissociable from a totalitarian discourse which finds its form of expression in the cynicism of the "new economics." It should also be said that neo-liberal theory has no content outside this cynicism, which is all part of the will to affirm *production for production's sake, finally and in its most classic form* (it is in this context that we should place the unbelievable increase of American spending on military research). Hence the restructuration of productive space which will no longer be considered as it arises, in function the need to integrate new planetary "data": *permanent restructuration* has become the rule of the capitalist process itself, and crisis, the form itself of circulation. "Restructuration is not a rule for this phase, but an operation to develop in any phase, at all periods of the social process."[20] Only the crisis permits such a degree of integrative fusion between production and circulation, production and information, production and resegmentalization of society, and to realize the expansive "intension" of freed capital gaining a maximalized synergetic fluidity.

This fluidity can be verified at two levels:

- that of the mobile factory: it is indirectly through circulation that these "pseudo-commodities," which are now only indirectly products of labor, will be made (social conditions of production having fallen under the control of organization and information, the work process is now no more than a simple element in the process of valorization). For J. P. de Gaudemar "any productive unit thus tends to appear as a nodal point in a fluid network, a point of connections or of temporary breakdowns of fluidity, but which can only be analysed relative to the place it occupies in the network."[21] The management of productive space now becomes the arrangement of its optimal fluidity (temporary labor being, of course, an important part of this).

- from the territorial state to the "mobile" State (better known, in liberal terminology, under the name of "minimum" state); no longer conceiver and protector of an original national space of the valorization of capital, but promoter of increased participation in the trans-national space of valorization.[22] From contractual mechanics to thermo-dynamic balance—a long way from equilibrium.

The specific historical question which therefore arises with Integrated World Capitalism concerns the potential limits of its integrative power. It is by no means clear that it will indefinitely manage to innovate and to take over techniques and subjectivities. It is useful, once again, to underline here that Integrated World Capitalism is not a self-sufficient entity. Although it presents itself today as "the highest stage of capitalism," it is, after all, only one capitalist formula among others. It accommodates itself to the survival of large zones of archaic economy; it lives in symbiosis with liberal colonial economies of the classic type; it co-exists with Stalinist-type economies. Relatively progressive in the field of technico-scientific change, it is basically conservative in the social domain (not for ideological reasons, but for functional reasons). In addition one has the right to ask if we are not here dealing with one of its insurmountable contradictions. The capacity for adapting and reconversion shown by the economic structures of Integrated World Capitalism will perhaps find its limit with the renewal of the capacities of resistance of all social groups who refuse its "unidimensionalizing" ends. Certainly the internal contradictions of Integrated World Capitalism are not such that it must necessarily die of them. But its sickness is perhaps no less mortal: it results from the accumulation of all the *lateral* crises it throws up. The power of the productive process of Integrated World Capitalism seems inexorable, and its social effects incapable of being turned back; but it overturns so many things, comes into conflict with so many ways of life and social valorizations, that it does not seem at all absurd to anticipate that the development of new collective responses—new structures of declaration, evaluation and action—coming from the greatest variety of horizons, might finally succeed in bringing it down. (The appearance of new peoples' war machines as in Salvador; the struggle for workers' control in the countries of Eastern Europe; self-valorization of work struggles of the Italian style; a multitude of vectors of molecular revolution in all spheres of society.) As we see it, it is only through this sort of hypothesis that the definition of the objectives of the revolutionary transformation of society can be appreciated.

Translated by Brian Darling

Notes

1 Oskar Lange compares the capitalist market to a "proto-computer." Quoted by Fernand Braudel, *Civilisation matérielle, économie et capitalisme*, vol. 2 (Paris: Éditions Armand Colins, 1979), 192.
2 According to Fernand Braudel, the capitalist proto-markets were deployed in concentric zones starting from the metropolises which held economic keys allowing them to draw in most of the surplus value, while toward the peripheries they tended to a sort of zero point, because of the lethargy of exchanges and the low level of prices found there. Braudel considers that each economy-world is necessarily based on a single-city-world. But perhaps he is a bit too systematic on this point. Could one not imagine urban and capitalist processes which are not developed according to a mono-centered model, but according to a multi-polar stock of "archipelagoes of towns"?
3 Cf. Henri Lepage, *Demain le capitalism* (Paris: Livre de Poche, 1978), 419.
4 *Individualism and Economic Order* (London: Routledge & Kegan Paul, 1949).
5 Vera Lutz, *Central Planning for the Market Economy* (London: Longmans, 1969).
6 In contrast with what the theoreticians of "public choice" proclaim, the growth of information in this domain—in particular of mass media information controlled by the system—can only accentuate the unequalizing effects of these techniques of integration. The project which consisted of wanting to complete the theory of production and exchange of market goods or services with an equivalent theory which would be, as far as possible, compatible with the workings of the political equivalent markets (James Buchanan) perhaps started out with good intentions, but the least one can say is that it was incomplete and that it turned sour (cf. the devastating exploits in Pinochet's Chile, of the "Chicago Boys" of Milton Friedman). Economic, political and institutional markets are one thing, mechanical and libidinal markets are another. And it is only on the side of these latter that one can manage to seize the essential springs of social valorization and mechanical creativity.

7   On these modes of evaluation cf. Alain Cotta, *Théorie générale du capital, de la croissance et des fluctuations,* Paris, 1967, and *Encyclopaedia Univeralis,* entry "Capital."

8   Examples of complementarity: the fact that the proto-capitalism of the fifteenth and sixteenth centuries, although predominantly market and finance, should have become industrial in certain circumstances (cf. the recovery of Antwerp by industrialization, discussed by Fernand Braudel, *Civilisation matérial, économie et capitalisme,* vol. 3 (Paris: Éditions Armand Colins, 1979), 127); and the fact that a market economy, whatever its apparent "liberalism," should always carry a certain dose of State intervention or of "centralist" planning (Stalinist plans, for example), should have always preserved a minimum of market economy, either within its sphere of influence or in its relationship to the world market.

9   For instance China in the second and third centuries AD. Cf. *Sur le mode de production asiatique,* Sociales, 1969.

10   For instance Venice, Antwerp, Genoa, Amsterdam, between the thirteenth and seventeenth centuries.

11   Cf. Braudel, *Civilisation matérielle, économie et capitalisme,* vol. 3, 172–173.

12   Ibid., 207. And Fernand Braudel adds, magnanimously: "multi-national companies of today have, as we see, ancestors."

13   Jürgen Habermas, *L'Espace publique, archéologie de la publicité comme dimension constitutive de la société bourgeoise* (Paris: Payot, 1978), 98.

14   Habermas, *L'Espace publique,* 89. Michel Aglietta correctly relates classical (and neo-classical) economic theory to a theological construction "purely internal to the world of ideas, and the stricter it is the more cut off it is from any reality." Such would be the fate of the theory of general equilibrium, if "the end of theory is to express the essence in stripping it of all contingency; institutions, social interactions, conflicts . . . are the dross we must get rid of in order to find economic behavior in its pure state" (Michel Aglietta, *Réguation et crises du capitalisme* (Paris: Calmann-Lévy, 1976), 12).

15   Franz Neumann, *Der Funktionswandel des Gesetzes im Recht der Jürgerlichen Gesellschaft,* quoted by Habermas.

16   Étienne Balazs, *La Bureaucratie céleste* (Paris: Gallimard, 1968).

17   And, doubtless, slowing up the development of the productive mechanism in the metropolis cf. Fritz Sternberg, *Kapitalismus and Sozialismus vor dem Weltgericht* (1951): "The alliance between European imperialism and colonial feudalism . . . slowed down, in an extraordinary way, industrial development and in general the progressive development of the economy of the colonial empires" (quoted by Maximilien Rubel in *Marx,* Pléiade edn, vol. 1).

18   Antonio Negri, *Macchina Tempo* (Rome: Feltrinelli, 1982), 271.

19   Ibid., 278.

20   Ibid., 275.

21   Jean Paul de Gaudemar, *Naissance de l'usine mobile,* in *Usine et ouvrier, figure de nouvel ordre productif* (Paris: Maspero, 1980), 24.

22   This formulation, which we borrow in part from Pascal Arnaud, escapes in our view, the limits and restrictions which might be inherent in his frame of analysis (*Le Monétarisme appliqué aux économies chilienne et argentine,* cf. *Critiques de l'économie politique,* no. 18).

CHAPTER TWO

Rethinking Marx's Critical Theory

Moishe Postone

From History and Heteronomy. *Tokyo: University of Tokyo Center for Philosophy, 2009: 31–48.*

I would like to outline why, in my judgment, a critical theory of capitalism is indispensable for understanding the contemporary world. The historical developments of the twentieth century strongly suggest, however, that such a theory must be different from traditional critiques of capitalism if it is to be adequate to our social universe. In order to outline the basis for such an adequate theory, I shall interrogate some common understandings of the fundamental social relations of capitalism and outline a different understanding of those relations and, hence, of capitalism.

The fundamental historical transformations of the recent past—such as the rollback of welfare states in the capitalist West, the collapse or fundamental metamorphosis of bureaucratic party-states in the Communist East—more generally, the weakening of national states as economically sovereign entities—along with the apparently triumphant emergence of a new, neo-liberal, global capitalist order, and the possible development of rivalries among competing capitalist blocs—have reasserted the central importance of historical dynamics and large-scale global structural changes.

Because these changes have included the dramatic collapse of the Soviet Union and the fundamental metamorphosis of China, they have been interpreted as marking the historical end of Marxism and, more generally, of the theoretical relevance of Marx's social theory.

I wish to suggest a very different way of understanding the theoretical implications of recent historical transformations.

The past three decades can be viewed as marking the end of a period of the state-centered organization of social and economic life whose beginnings can be located in World War I and the Russian Revolution—a period characterized by the apparent primacy of the political over the economic. What is significant about this trajectory is its global character. It encompassed western capitalist countries and the Soviet Union, as well as colonized lands and decolonized countries. Differences in historical development did, of course, occur. But, viewed with reference to the trajectory as a whole, they were more a matter of different inflections of a common pattern than of fundamentally different developments. For example, the welfare state was expanded in all western industrial countries in the twenty-five years after the end of World War II and then limited or partially dismantled beginning in the early 1970s. These developments occurred regardless of whether conservative or social democratic ("liberal") parties were in power. Such general developments cannot be explained in terms of contingent political decisions, and strongly suggest the existence of general structural constraints and imperatives.

Consideration of such general historical patterns suggests, then, that positions, such as poststructuralism, that attempt to deal with history in terms of contingency are inadequate empirically to the history of capitalist society. Nevertheless, such considerations do not necessarily dispense with what might be regarded as the critical insight driving such attempts to deal with history contingently—namely, that history, grasped as the unfolding of an immanent necessity, should be understood as delineating a form of unfreedom.

That form of unfreedom is the object of Marx's critical theory of capitalism, which is centrally concerned with the imperatives and constraints that underlie the historical dynamics and structural changes of the modern world. That is, rather than deny the existence of such unfreedom by focusing on contingency, the Marxian critique seeks to uncover its basis and the possibility of its overcoming.

I am suggesting that, ironically, the very processes underlying the collapse of regimes of accumulation that had declared themselves heirs to Marx have reasserted the central importance of global historical dynamics, that those dynamics can be understood best within the framework of a critical theory of capitalism, and that approaches that do not engage this level of analysis are fundamentally inadequate to our social universe. That is, the historical transformations of recent decades point to the importance of a renewed encounter with Marx's critical analysis of capitalism.

As I noted above, however, the trajectory of the past century suggests that, if a critical theory of capitalism is to be adequate to the contemporary world, it must differ fundamentally from traditional Marxist critiques of capitalism. I would argue that Marx's mature social theory not only is the most rigorous and sophisticated theory we have of the historical dynamics of the modern world, but also provides the point of departure for precisely such a reconceptualized critical theory of capitalism. I shall outline a reinterpretation of Marx's mature social theory that rethinks his analysis of the basic nature of capitalism—its social relations, forms of domination, and historical dynamic—in ways that break fundamentally with traditional Marxist approaches. This reinterpretation could help illuminate the essential structuring elements and overarching historical dynamic of the contemporary world while providing a basic critique of traditional Marxism. It also recasts the relation of Marxian theory to other major currents of social theory.

By "traditional Marxism" I do not mean a specific historical tendency in Marxism, such as orthodox Second International Marxism, for example, but, more generally, all analyses that understand capitalism essentially in terms of class relations structured by a market economy and private ownership of the means of production. Relations of domination are understood primarily in terms of class domination and exploitation. Within this general interpretive framework, capitalism is characterized by a growing structural contradiction between that society's basic social relations (interpreted as private property and the market) and the forces of production (interpreted as the industrial mode of producing).

The unfolding of this contradiction gives rise to the possibility of a new form of society, understood in terms of collective ownership of the means of production and economic planning in an industrialized context—that is, in terms of a just and consciously regulated mode of distribution that is adequate to industrial production. Industrial production, in turn, is understood as a technical process, which is used by capitalists for their particularistic ends, but is intrinsically independent of capitalism and could be used for the benefit of all members of society.

This general understanding is tied to a determinate understanding of the basic categories of Marx's critique of political economy. The category of value, for example, has generally been interpreted as an attempt to show that social wealth is always and everywhere created by human labor. The theory of surplus-value, according to such views, seeks to demonstrate the existence of exploitation by showing that the surplus product is created by labor alone and, in capitalism, is appropriated by the capitalist class.

At the heart of this theory is a transhistorical—and commonsensical—understanding of labor as an activity mediating humans and nature that transforms matter in a goal-directed manner and is a condition of social life. Labor, so understood, is posited as the source of wealth in all societies and as that which constitutes what is universal and truly social. In capitalism, however, labor is hindered by particularistic and fragmenting relations from becoming fully realized. Emancipation, then, is realized in a social form where transhistorical "labor," freed from the fetters of the market and private property, has openly emerged as the regulating principle of society. (This notion, of course, is bound to that of socialist revolution as the "self-realization" of the proletariat.)

This basic framework encompasses a broad range of very different theoretical, methodological, and political approaches. Nevertheless, to the extent they all rest on the basic assumptions regarding labor and the essential characteristics of capitalism and of socialism outlined above, they remain bound within the framework of traditional Marxism.

And although powerful economic, political, social, historical, and cultural analyses have been generated within this traditional framework, its limitations have become increasingly evident in the light of twentieth-century developments such as the rise of state-interventionist capitalism and "actually existing socialism," the growing importance of scientific knowledge and advanced technology in the process of production, growing criticisms of technological progress and growth, and the increased importance of non-class-based social identities. Indeed classic social theorists such as Weber and Durkheim had already argued at the turn of the last century that a critical theory of capitalism—understood in terms of property relations—is too narrow to grasp fundamental features of modern society.

A number of theorists within the broader Marxist tradition—notably Georg Lukács as well as members of the Frankfurt School—attempted to overcome the traditional paradigm's limitations, and develop a critical social theory that would be more adequate to twentieth-century historical developments. These theorists proceeded on the basis of a sophisticated understanding of Marx's theory as a critical analysis of the cultural forms as well as the social structures of capitalist society, rather than as one of production and class structure alone, much less of economics. Moreover, they grasped such a theory as self-reflexive, that is, as a theory that attempts to analyze its own social context—capitalist society—in a way that reflexively accounts for the possibility of its own standpoint.

In their appropriation of Marx, these thinkers sought to respond theoretically to the historical transformation of capitalism from a market-centered form to a bureaucratic, state-centered form. Yet they were not able to fully realize this theoretical aim. On the one hand, their approaches tacitly recognized the inadequacies of a critical theory of modernity that defined capitalism solely in nineteenth-century terms—that is, in terms of the market and private ownership of the means of production. On the other hand, however, they remained bound to some of the assumptions of that very sort of theory.

This can be seen clearly in the case of Lukács's *History and Class Consciousness*, written in the early 1920s, which adopted Weber's characterization of modern society in terms of a historical process of rationalization, and embedded that analysis within the framework of Marx's analysis of the commodity form as the basic structuring principle of capitalism. By grounding the process of rationalization in this manner, Lukács sought to show that what Weber described as the "iron cage" of modern life is not a necessary concomitant of any form of modern society, but a function of capitalism—and, hence, could be transformed. At the same time, the conception of capitalism implied by his analysis is much broader than that of a system of exploitation based on private property and the market; it implies that the latter are not ultimately the central features of capitalism.

Yet when Lukács addressed the question of the possible overcoming of capitalism, he had recourse to the notion of the proletariat as the revolutionary Subject of history. This idea, however, is bound to a traditional conception of capitalism in terms of private property. It cannot illuminate the forms of bureaucratization and rationalization that Lukács himself had focused on. That is, Lukács's traditionalistic theory of the proletariat was in tension with the deeper and broader conception of capitalism implied by his analysis.

Lukács deeply influenced Frankfurt School theorists, whose approaches can also be understood in terms of a similar theoretical tension. This, however, is not a theme I shall further pursue here.

What I do wish to emphasize is that coming to terms with the inescapable and obvious centrality of capitalism in the world today requires a reconceptualization of capital, one that breaks fundamentally with the traditional Marxist frame.

It has become evident, considered retrospectively, that the social/political/economic/cultural configuration of capital's hegemony has varied historically—from mercantilism through nineteenth-century liberal capitalism and twentieth-century state-centric Fordist capitalism to contemporary neo-liberal global capitalism. Each configuration has elicited a number of penetrating critiques—of exploitation and uneven, inequitable growth, for example, or of technocratic, bureaucratic modes of domination. Each of these critiques, however, is incomplete; as we now see, capitalism cannot be identified fully with any of its historical configurations. This raises the question of the nature of capital, of the core of capitalism as a form of social life.

My work attempts to contribute to a critical understanding of that core of capitalism, one that is not limited to any of that social formation's epochs. I argue that at the heart of capitalism is a historically dynamic process, associated with multiple historical configurations, which Marx sought to grasp with the category of capital. This core feature of the modern world must be grasped if a critical theory of capitalism is to be adequate to its object. Such an understanding of capitalism can only be achieved on a very high level of abstraction. It could then serve as a point of departure for an analysis of epochal changes in capitalism as well as for the historically changing subjectivities expressed in historically determinate social movements.

In attempting to rethink Marx's analysis of capitalism's most basic relations, I try to reconstruct the systematic character of Marx's categorical analysis, rather than relying on statements made by Marx, without reference to their locus in the unfolding of his mode of presentation.

I argue that the categories of Marx's mature critique are historically specific to modern, or capitalist, society. This turn to a notion of historical specificity implicitly entailed a turn to a notion of the historical specificity of Marx's own theory. No theory—including that of Marx—has, within this conceptual framework, transhistorical validity.

This means that all transhistorical notions—including many of Marx's earlier conceptions regarding history, society and labor, as expressed in the idea of a dialectical logic underlying human history, for example— became historically relativized. In disputing their transhistorical validity, however, Marx did not claim that such notions were never valid. Instead, he restricted their validity to the capitalist social formation, while showing how that which is historically specific to capitalism, could be taken to be transhistorical. On this basis Marx criticized theories that project onto history or society in general, categories that, according to him, are valid only for the capitalist epoch.

If, however, such notions were valid only for capitalist society, Marx now had to uncover the grounds for their validity in the specific characteristics of that society. He sought to do so elucidating the most fundamental form of social relations that characterizes capitalist society and, on that basis, unfolding a theory with which he sought to explain the underlying workings of that society. That fundamental category is the commodity. Marx took the term "commodity" and used it to designate a historically specific form of social relations, one constituted as a structured form of social practice that, at the same time, structures the actions, worldviews and dispositions of people. As a category of practice, it is a form both of social subjectivity and objectivity.

What characterizes the commodity form of social relations, as analyzed by Marx, is that it is constituted by labor, it exists in objectified form and it has a dualistic character.

In order to elucidate this description, Marx's conception of the historical specificity of labor in capitalism must be clarified. Marx maintains that labor in capitalism has a "double character": it is both "concrete labor" and "abstract labor." "Concrete labor" refers to the fact that some form of what we consider laboring activity mediates the interactions of humans with nature in all societies. "Abstract labor" does not simply refer to concrete labor in general, but is a very different sort of category. It signifies that, in capitalism, labor also has a unique social function that is not intrinsic to laboring activity as such: it mediates a new form of social interdependence.

Let me elaborate: In a society in which the commodity is the basic structuring category of the whole, labor and its products are *not* socially distributed by traditional ties, norms, or overt relations of power and domination—that is, by manifest social relations—as is the case in other societies. Instead, labor itself replaces those relations by serving as a kind of quasi-objective means by which the products of others are acquired. A new form of interdependence comes into being where people do not consume what they produce, but where, nevertheless, their own labor or labor-products function as a quasi-objective, necessary means of obtaining the products of others. In serving as such a means, labor and its products in effect preempt that function on the part of manifest social relations.

In Marx's mature works, then, the notion of the centrality of labor to social life is not a transhistorical proposition. It does not refer to the fact that material production is always a precondition of social life. Nor should it be taken as meaning that material production is the most essential dimension of social life in general, or even of capitalism in particular. Rather, it refers to the historically specific constitution by labor in capitalism of a form of social mediation that fundamentally characterizes that society. On this basis, Marx tries to socially ground basic features of modernity, such as its overarching historical dynamic, and changes in its process of production.

Labor in capitalism, then, is both labor as we transhistorically and commonsensically understand it, according to Marx, and a historically specific socially mediating activity. Hence its objectifications—commodity, capital—are both concrete labor products and objectified forms of social mediation. According to this analysis, then, the social relations that most basically characterize capitalist society are very different from the qualitatively specific, overt social relations—such as kinship relations or relations of personal or direct domination— which characterize non-capitalist societies. Although the latter kind of social relations continue to exist in capitalism, what ultimately structures that society is a new, underlying level of social relations that is constituted by labor. Those relations have a peculiar quasi-objective, formal character and are dualistic—they are characterized by the opposition of an abstract, general, homogeneous dimension and a concrete, particular, material dimension, both of which appear to be "natural," rather than social, and condition social conceptions of natural reality.

The abstract character of the social mediation underlying capitalism is also expressed in the form of wealth dominant in that society. Marx's "labor theory of value" frequently has been misunderstood as a labor theory of wealth, that is, a theory that seeks to explain the workings of the market and prove the existence of exploitation by arguing that labor, at all times and in all places, is the only social source of wealth. Marx's analysis is not one of wealth in general, any more than it is one of labor in general. He analyzes value as a historically specific form of wealth, which is bound to the historically unique role of labor in capitalism; as a form of wealth, it is also a form of social mediation.

Marx explicitly distinguishes value from material wealth and relates these two distinct forms of wealth to the duality of labor in capitalism. Material wealth is measured by the quantity of products produced and is a function of a number of factors such as knowledge, social organization, and natural conditions, in addition to labor.

Value is constituted by human labor-time expenditure alone, according to Marx, and is the dominant form of wealth in capitalism. Whereas material wealth, when it is the dominant form of wealth, is mediated by overt social relations, value is a self-mediating form of wealth.

As I shall elaborate, Marx's analysis of capital is of a social system based on value that both generates and constrains the historical possibility of its own overcoming by a social order based on material wealth.

Within the framework of this interpretation, then, what fundamentally characterizes capitalism is a historically specific, abstract form of social mediation that is constituted by labor—by determinate forms of social practice—that becomes quasi-independent of the people engaged in those practices.

The result is a historically new form of social domination—one that subjects people to impersonal, increasingly rationalized, structural imperatives and constraints that cannot adequately be grasped in terms of class domination, or, more generally, in terms of the concrete domination of social groupings or of institutional agencies of the state and/or the economy. It has no determinate locus and, although constituted by determinate forms of social practice, appears not to be social at all. (I am suggesting that Marx's analysis of abstract domination is a more rigorous and determinate analysis of what Foucault attempted to grasp with his notion of power in the modern world.)

Significant in this regard is Marx's temporal determination of the magnitude of value. In his discussion of the magnitude of value in terms of socially necessary labor-time, Marx points to a peculiarity of value as a social form of wealth whose measure is temporal: increasing productivity increases the amount of use-values produced per unit time. But it results only in short-term increases in the magnitude of value created per unit time. Once that productive increase becomes general, the magnitude of value falls to its base level. The result is a sort of treadmill dynamic. On the one hand, increased levels of productivity result in great increases in use-value production. Yet increased productivity does not result in long-term proportional increases in value, the social form of wealth in capitalism.

Note that this peculiar treadmill dynamic is rooted in value's temporal dimension, and not in the way that pattern is generalized, e.g. through competition. The historically specific, abstract form of social domination intrinsic to capitalism's fundamental forms of social mediation is *the domination of people by time*. This form of domination is bound to a historically specific, abstract form of temporality—abstract Newtonian time—which is constituted historically with the commodity form.

This dynamic is at the core of the category of capital, which, for Marx, is a category of movement. It entails a ceaseless process of value's self-expansion, a directional movement with no external telos that generates large-scale cycles of production and consumption, creation and destruction.

Significantly, in introducing the category of capital, Marx describes it with the same language that Hegel used in the *Phenomenology* with reference to *Geist*—the self-moving substance that is the subject of its own process.[1] In so doing, Marx suggests that a historical Subject in the Hegelian sense does indeed exist in capitalism. Yet—and this is crucially important—he does not identify that Subject with the proletariat (as does Lukács), or even with humanity. Instead he identifies it with capital.

Marx's critique of Hegel in *Capital* suggests that capitalist relations are not extrinsic to the Subject, as that which hinders its full realization. Rather, he analyzes those very relations as constituting the Subject. In his mature theory, then, Marx does not posit a historical meta-subject, such as the proletariat, which will realize itself in a future society, but provides the basis for a critique of such a notion. This implies a position very different from that of theorists like Lukács, for whom the social totality constituted by labor provides the *standpoint* of the critique of capitalism, and is to be realized in socialism. In *Capital,* the totality and the labor constituting it have become the *objects* of critique. The historical Subject is the alienated structure of social mediation that is at the heart of the capitalist formation. The contradictions of capital point to the abolition, not the realization of the Subject.

In *Capital* Marx roots capitalism's historical dynamic ultimately in the double character of the commodity and, hence, capital. The treadmill dynamic that I have outlined is at the heart of this dynamic. It cannot be grasped if the category of surplus-value is understood only as a category of exploitation—as *surplus*-value—and not also as surplus-*value*—as the surplus of a temporal form of wealth. The temporality of this dynamic is not only abstract. Although changes in productivity, in the use-value dimension, do not change the amount of value produced per unit time, they do change the determination of what counts as a given unit of time. The unit of (abstract) time remains constant—and, yet, it is pushed forward, as it were, in (historical) time. The movement here is not the movement *in* (abstract) time, but the movement *of* time. Both abstract time and historical time are constituted historically as structures of domination.

This dialectic of value and use-value becomes historically significant with the emergence of relative surplus value and gives rise to a very complex, nonlinear historical dynamic underlying modern society. On the one hand, this dynamic is characterized by ongoing transformations of production, and more generally, of social life. On the other hand, this historical dynamic entails the ongoing reconstitution of its own fundamental condition as an unchanging feature of social life—namely that social mediation ultimately is effected by labor and, hence, that living labor remains integral to the process of production (considered in terms of society as a whole), regardless of the level of productivity. The historical dynamic of capitalism ceaselessly generates what is "new," while regenerating what is the "same." This dynamic both generates the possibility of another organization of social life and, yet, hinders that possibility from being realized.

Marx grasps this historical dynamic with his category of capital. As capital develops, it becomes less and less the mystified form of powers that "actually" are those of workers. Rather, the productive powers of capital increasingly become socially general productive powers that are historically constituted in alienated form and that no longer can be understood as those of immediate producers. This constitution and accumulation of socially general knowledge renders proletarian labor increasingly anachronistic; at the same time the dialectic of value and use-value reconstitutes the necessity of such labor.

One implication of this analysis of capital is that capital does not exist as a unitary totality, and that the Marxian notion of the dialectical contradiction between the "forces" and "relations" of production does not refer to a contradiction between "relations" that are intrinsically capitalist (e.g., the market and private property) and "forces" that purportedly are extrinsic to capital (labor). Rather, it is one between the two dimensions of capital. As a contradictory totality, capital is generative of the complex historical dynamic I began to outline, a dynamic that points to the possibility of its own overcoming.

The contradiction allowing for another form of life also allows for the possibility of imagining another form of life. That is, the theory grounds the possibility of itself by means of the same categories with which it grasps its object—and demands of all attempts at critical theory that they be capable of accounting for their own possibility.

Because the dynamic I have outlined is quasi-independent of its constituting individuals, it has the properties of an intrinsic historical logic. In other words, Marx's mature theory no longer hypostatizes history as a sort of force moving all human societies; it no longer pre-supposes that a directional dynamic of history in general exists. It does, however, characterize modern society in terms of an ongoing directional dynamic and seeks to explain that historical dynamic with reference to the dual character of the social forms expressed by the categories of the commodity and capital. The existence of a historical dynamic is now taken to be a manifestation of heteronomy.

In this evaluation, the critical Marxian position is closer to poststructuralism than it is to orthodox Second International Marxism. Nevertheless, it does not regard heteronomous history as a narrative, which can simply be dispelled discursively, but as a structure of domination that must be overcome. From this point of view, any attempt to rescue human agency by focusing on contingency in ways that bracket the existence of such historically specific structures of domination is—ironically—profoundly disempowering.

As an aside, it should be noted that, by grounding the contradictory character of the social formation in the dualistic forms expressed by the categories of the commodity and capital, Marx historicizes the notion of contradiction. The idea that reality or social relations in general are essentially contradictory and dialectical appears, in light of this analysis, to be one that can only be assumed metaphysically, not explained. This also suggests that any theory that posits an intrinsic developmental logic to history as such, whether dialectical or evolutionary, projects what is the case for capitalism onto history in general.

The understanding of capitalism's complex dynamic I have outlined allows for a critical, social (rather than technological) analysis of the trajectory of growth and the structure of production in modern society. The category of surplus-value not only indicates, as traditional interpretations would have it, that the surplus is produced by the working class—but it shows that capitalism is characterized by a determinate, runaway form of "growth." The problem of economic growth in capitalism, within this framework, is not only that it is crisis-ridden, as has frequently been emphasized by traditional Marxist approaches. Rather, the form of growth itself—one entailing the accelerating destruction of the natural environment—is problematic. The trajectory of growth would be different, according to this approach, if the ultimate goal of production were increased quantities of goods rather than of surplus value.

This approach also provides the basis for a critical analysis of the structure of social labor and the nature of production in capitalism. It indicates that the industrial process of production should not be grasped as a technical process that, although increasingly socialized, is used by private capitalists for their own ends. Rather, the approach I am outlining grasps that process as intrinsically capitalist. Capital's drive for ongoing increases in productivity gives rise to a productive apparatus of considerable technological sophistication that renders the production of material wealth essentially independent of direct human labor time expenditure. This, in turn, opens the possibility of large-scale socially general reductions in labor time and fundamental changes in the nature and social organization of labor. Yet these possibilities are not realized in capitalism. Although there is a growing shift away from manual labor, the development of technologically sophisticated production does not liberate most people from fragmented and repetitive labor. Similarly, labor time is not reduced on a socially general level, but is distributed unequally, even increasing for many. (The actual structure of labor and organization of production, then, cannot be understood adequately in technological terms alone; the development of production in capitalism must be understood in social terms as well.)

According to the reinterpretation I have outlined, then, Marx's theory extends far beyond the traditional critique of the bourgeois relations of distribution (the market and private property); it is not simply a critique of exploitation and the unequal distribution of wealth and power. Rather, it grasps modern industrial society itself as capitalist, and critically analyzes capitalism primarily in terms of abstract structures of domination, increasing fragmentation of individual labor and individual existence, and a blind runaway developmental logic.

This approach treats the working class as the crucial, most basic element of capitalism, rather than as the embodiment of its negation. It reconceptualizes post-capitalist society in terms of the overcoming of the proletariat and of the organization of production based on proletarian labor, as well as of the dynamic system of abstract compulsions constituted by labor as a socially mediating activity. That is, it conceptualizes the overcoming of capitalism in terms of a transformation of the general structure of labor and of time. In this sense, it differs both from the traditional Marxist notion of the realization of the proletariat, and from the capitalist mode of "abolishing" national working classes by creating an underclass within the framework of the unequal distribution of labor and of time nationally and globally.

By shifting the focus of analysis to the mode of mediation and away from the market and private property, this reinterpretation provides the basis for a critical theory of post-liberal society as capitalist and also could provide the basis for a critical theory of the so-called actually existing socialist countries as alternative (and failed) forms of capital accumulation, rather than as social modes that represented the historical negation of capital, in however imperfect a form.

Although the logically abstract level of analysis outlined here does not immediately address the issue of the specific factors underlying the structural transformations of the past thirty years, it can provide a framework within which those transformations can be grounded socially and understood historically. (It provides the basis for an understanding of the non-linear developmental dynamic of modern society that could incorporate many important insights of postindustrial theory while also elucidating the constraints intrinsic to that dynamic and, hence, the gap between the actual organization of social life and the way it could be organized—especially given the increasing importance of science and technology.)

Inasmuch as it seeks to ground socially, and is critical of, the abstract, quasi-objective social relations, and the nature of production, work, and the imperatives of growth in capitalism, this interpretation could also begin to address a range of contemporary concerns, dissatisfactions and aspirations in a way that could provide a fruitful point of departure for a consideration of the new social movements of recent decades and the sorts of historically constituted world views they embody and express. It might also be able to approach the global rise of forms of "fundamentalisms" as populist, fetishized forms of opposition to the differential effects of neo-liberal global capitalism.

Finally, this approach also has implications for the question of the social preconditions of democracy, inasmuch as it analyzes not only the inequalities of real social power that are inimical to democratic politics, but also reveals as socially constituted—and hence as legitimate objects of political debates—the systemic constraints imposed by capital's global dynamic on democratic self-determination.

By fundamentally rethinking the significance of value theory and reconceptualizing the nature of capitalism, this interpretation changes the terms of discourse between critical theories of capitalism and other sorts of social theory. It implicitly suggests that an adequate theory of modernity should be a self-reflexive theory capable of overcoming the theoretical dichotomies of culture and material life, structure and action, while grounding socially the overarching non-linear directional dynamic of the modern world, its form of economic growth, and the nature and trajectory of its production process.

In addressing such issues, the interpretation I have presented seeks to contribute to the discourse of contemporary social theory and, relatedly, to our understanding of the far-reaching transformations of our social universe.

Note

1　G. W. F. Hegel, Preface to the *Phenomenology of Spirit*, in *Hegel: Texts and Commentary*, ed. Walter Kaufmann (Garden City, NY: Doubleday Anchor, 1966), 28; *Capital*, vol. 1, 255–256.

CHAPTER THREE

The Impasses of Liberal Productivism

Alan Lipietz

From Towards a New Economic Order: Postfordism,
Ecology and Democracy. New York and Oxford:
Oxford University Press, 1992: 30–47.

Liberal-productivism can be defined as the world view (or "societal paradigm") which inspired the major turning point of the end of the 1970s, bringing to power Margaret Thatcher in Britain and Ronald Reagan in the United States. It came to dominate most international economic advisory and regulatory bodies (Organization for Economic Cooperation and Development [OECD], International Monetary Fund [IMF], the World Bank), was adopted by European socialists, and was behind the emergence (at least in outline) of a completely new development model in the 1980s. The model, as has already been said, is no longer very plausible, though it had a profound effect on the world order as well as on the reality facing a large number of countries. In France, liberal-productivism dominates the broad center ground stretching from the RPR[1] to the Socialist Party, since a paradigm always has a right and a left. This world view was founded on the ruins of Fordism in crisis, from whose downfall comes its major strength.

A new model

What liberal-productivism is more or less as follows: we are experiencing a "technological revolution"; propounds however, in the 1970s, constraints imposed by the state and trade unions—social provision, welfare state, anti-pollution laws and the like—stopped it developing freely, by starving firms of capital, and by preventing "painful but necessary changes." Therefore, the argument went, let us get rid of the constraints; stop subsidizing lame ducks and bureaucratic and inefficient public services, and raise interest rates to deter non-profitable activity. In this way, the free market would automatically establish a new development model in line with new technologies. These are essentially flexible because of the scope of their application, and therefore able to respond to varied and individualized demand, which the state cannot regulate. New technologies also need, because of the huge investment involved, direct deployment on a global scale, not amenable to control by even the largest states.

This kind of argument reflects the optimism of the triumphant nineteenth-century bourgeoisie—an unshakeable confidence in the virtues of the "development of productive forces," which could only be harmed by the constraints of outmoded legal rules and practices. This optimism embraced both the old liberals and the first Marxists, the only difference being that the former thought there was "too much state control" and the latter that there was "too much anarchy in the market."

It is important to stress, however, a major difference between nineteenth-century liberalism and contemporary liberal-productivism. The former tried to ensure the happiness of all by encouraging the citizen to seek individual enrichment. It was a "utilitarian," "hedonistic" liberalism, where the goal of technical progress and free enterprise was happiness through the enrichment of all.

Of course, the best exponents of the new liberalism, such as Ronald Reagan, do not ignore this aspect. However, very often and particularly in France, its language has been stripped of its appeal reduced to the cold necessity of the nature of things. Deregulation, free trade, technological change have come to dominate, like three mice chasing their tails, running round in a circle whose illogicality simply shows how impossible it is to stop. To the question "Why do we really need free trade and free enterprise?" the answer is "To modernize the productive system," and to the question "Why modernize the productive system?," the reply is "To cope with international competition." In other words, an unequivocal return to what in the past was unspoken: "Accumulate, accumulate, that is the Law and the prophets." "Productive modernization" becomes a categorical imperative, as philosophers would say, and free trade, free enterprise, flexibility and deregulation are its tools. There is no longer a need for higher justification of a political or moral nature.

This does not mean that liberal-productivism need no longer concern itself with justification, or with creating a social consensus. Building this cohesion, however, is no longer the priority of economic policy, and it is doubtful whether it is still an objective of policy as such. The "homeland," the collectivity to which the citizen has allegiance, becomes the firm or the market.

Within the firm, managers and workers constitute a community: everybody is in the same boat, as it were. They stand shoulder to shoulder— or tighten their belts—to weather the storm of competition. The task of trade unions—if there are any left—is no longer to protect workers' interests against employers' interest. The authority of the heads of businesses has to be respected; the most that can be done is to give them firm advice on improving collective efficiency in the interests of everybody—that is, of the members of the business threatened by the outside world.

The market gives everyone with enterprise and fighting spirit the chance to "win"; not to "win something," but simply to win, to beat other people. The Socialist Party slogan in the 1986 elections was *Vive la France qui gagne.* Of course, there have to be losers as well, but this is the cost of having the winners giving consumers the best services, the best products (here the tone of liberal-productivism becomes "progressist" again). Moreover, if you go to the wall, the success of others gives you a second chance; if you do not ask for too much, you can live on crumbs from rich people's tables, by being their servants, shining their shoes, showing them to their seats in high-class restaurants . . .

Who looks after the others—the ill, the handicapped, the permanently unemployed and unemployable? Not the state, or at least to the minimum degree, just enough to avoid "unrest"; let their relatives and neighbors look after them. Pierre Rosanvallon[2] called this "reintegrating solidarity into civil society." To hell with the bureaucratic ways of the welfare state; to hell with the administrative approach to solidarity! "Civil society" (that is, everything which is not the state) will take over. It amounts to a return to the oldest "welfare"—the voluntary sector—and to its "natural specialists" (women), who in their work and domestic duties bandage the wounds of the victims of the all-in struggle.

A rough attempt to define the "societal paradigm" of liberal-productivism would be as follows:

- greater emphasis on the productivist techno-economic imperative, now "categorical," and the disappearance of the very idea of an explicit choice of society deriving from democracy (invest because of the need to export, export because of the need to invest);

- fragmentation of social existence, with firms playing the role previously performed by the mother country (we must stand together against competitors), and the world market becoming the operating environment;

- a wide variety of ways to integrate the individual into the firm, from straightforward discipline to negotiated involvement, but all on the basis of the individual, not of collective individuality (class or job solidarity);

- an overall reduction of administrative-type solidarity based on belonging to a national collectivity, with "civil society" (meaning quite simply the family) supposed to take over responsibility for what the welfare state can no longer guarantee.

In the final analysis, it amounts to a hierarchical individualism, where first individuals' adherence to the collectivity is justified only if it is in their interest, and the collectivity does not concern itself with the interest of its individuals; and where secondly the collectivity acquires collective meaning only through the individualism of those who dominate it—that is, the "winners"—in whose interest it might be to take losers under their wing.

Any criticism of the impasses in this model must be preceded by an assessment of its rationality and effectiveness. It is a model which certainly stands up to analysis, and which can carry the day. By 1985, it appeared to be doing so, just as corporatism and its Fascist variants seemed destined to carry all before them around 1938. The liberal-productivist model offers a kind of stability which is questionable but real. In the past, feudal lords "offered" their peasants protection against attack by other lords, and also land in return for work. A particular social order was justified by the existence of generalized conflict, and the overall system remained stable for a long time. Naturally it was continually disturbed by wars and incursions and gratuitous revolts, but it was precisely this fact which made a feudal hierarchy acceptable as protection against the harsh conditions of the period.

Can liberal-productivism, however, be satisfied with this kind of overall stability based on permanent instability at the micro-level? It is precisely this which became open to doubt in the second half of the 1980s. The tensions in the model will now be analyzed.

A society torn apart

Above all, liberal-productivism leads to intense social polarization. The result can be described as a "two-tier society" or an "hourglass society," with people above and people below, and the center getting squeezed. This is what is happening with the spectacular "Latin-Americanization" (or "Brazilianization") of the United States. On top, the winners in the competition (the rich, the powerful, the decision makers, the bruisers) will benefit from the advantages of the technological revolution, in so far as there are any. In the middle, an increasingly smaller and more destabilized group of semi-skilled workers will no doubt benefit from a certain level of welfare protection, particularly in the employment field, but they cannot expect increases in real wages, as they could under Fordism. At the bottom, a mass of "job seekers" will be buffeted between casual work and unemployment. When unemployed, their lot will be more or less improved by public charity or help from their families, depending on how far local government authorities adopt a humanized version of the liberal model. As with feudalism, the fate of the poor depends on the "Christian spirit" of others.

The political implications of developments like this are obvious: we are back again to the famous nineteenth-century "problem of the dangerous classes," with the possibility of mass revolts destabilizing the system (the best possible result in my opinion), or the spread of individual crime. The latter case would be a return to the regulation principle of liberalism, when fear united the top two thirds of society, and even some of the lower third, against the "threat" of crime. The "law and order" issue as a political argument is all the more effective in that troublemakers can be isolated as "outsiders," as can those neatly summed up as "predelinquents"[3]—black people, young people from rundown housing complexes, and the like. One might even start a lucrative line of business by hiring some poor people as security guards to defend the rich against other poor people.

From Rio de Janeiro to Los Angeles, the model has shown it can work. It seems to have a great future: any collective action by the "lower third" which would, as before, allow the vicious circle to be broken by moving from individual action to the "class struggle," is now severely constrained by the collapse of collective secular ideals following the collapse of Fordism. Collective idealism very often takes refuge in archaic forms such as religious sects, fundamentalism, and the like. It is only through a progressive world view, different from Fordist-type progressive thinking (Marxist in Europe, developmentalist-nationalist in the Third World), that a struggle to free the oppressed and the marginalized can be started again. There is still a long way to go, but the fate of liberal-productivism depends on taking this major step, which could be a great risk or a major opportunity.

A false way out of Taylorism

Already, however, the model encounters another problem, concerned with production. Given the mode of regulation of the wage relation which usually prevails in neo-liberal thinking, there is quite simply no solution to the crisis of the Fordist labor-process model. In fact, by reducing as far as possible institutional links between the firm and its workers, and by encouraging casual work, there is a danger of an even greater gap between workers and the jobs they do—workers are even less consciously involved in the fight for productivity and quality.

Of course, it is in the famous "technological revolution" that the answer to this problem is sought. In car body shops or on printed circuit production lines, robots, by performing flawlessly 24 hours a day and never going on strike will solve the problem of workers slowing the pace of assembly lines or being no good at their work.

Unfortunately, "technology," even electronic, is not something which works on its own. It represents certain forms of cooperation between work already done to create machines, and the living work (on the line or not) of operatives, technicians and engineers. In theory, automated technology allows us to get rid of any conscious involvement, even informal and paradoxical, by line workers—it merely needs engineers to design the necessary machines and technicians to install and adjust them properly; then you simply let illiterate people feed the Beast with raw materials and reams of computerized data, and sweep up the debris afterwards! These unskilled people are easily replaced from the armies of unemployed waiting to take over. Relations such as these between the conception and execution of work are even easier to establish between large firms and subcontractors, on an inter-regional or international level. Large firms set up in urban areas with highly qualified, highly paid staff, monopolize the design of machines and the sale of end-products, and subcontract the actual manufacture to satellite firms operating in poorer areas with widespread unemployment.

A labor process model of this kind, which can be called "neo-Taylorist," is of course quite conceivable, and is the norm in the United States, Britain and France, in the service sector as well as manufacturing. Taken to the extreme, workshops would be like space exploration modules sent to Jupiter by engineers sitting behind their desks on Earth. Fine, but what if something goes wrong? In a space probe, each part has a back-up and a double back-up; in an automated workshop, you have to call out the after-sales or maintenance service of the firm supplying the machine, which brings us back to the main problem with Taylorism—there is a race to automate (and therefore to invest), and there are lower "on-the-spot" productivity gains because there are no people actually working on, adjusting and improving the machines on a permanent basis.

Why has the technology of automation been applied in this way rather than others? Basically for political reasons—the politics of production line and office. Whereas the original aim of Taylorism was to end the explicit and essential involvement of craftworkers' skills, neo-Taylorism tries to eliminate the residual, hidden and paradoxical involvement of the unskilled worker, of the supermarket cashier, of the office typist. It was natural that in the 1970s, neo-Taylorism triumphed in situations where operatives rejected this paradoxical involvement and showed this in absenteeism, work-to-rules, slowing the assembly line. In its Turin factory, the Fiat management set up the almost totally automated workshops of Robotgate, Digitron and LAM in order to have no workers present in the most troublesome sectors. The aim was to reestablish managerial authority; the cost of automation far exceeded the investment needed for optimal technical efficiency. At the beginning of the 1980s, after Fiat's "Fordist" workers had been defeated, the management had to admit that "the LAM system, designed at a time when industrial relations had broken down, is an interesting but one-off development. It is very expensive, takes up a huge amount of space and breaks down more frequently than a less sophisticated installation."[4]

The alternative, which I and many employers, including Italian ones, advocate, is obviously to go for systems which are "less sophisticated" but which mobilize the skills of line workers, in real time, at the actual point of production. Out goes "paradoxical" involvement; in comes dialogue between machine design, machine maintenance and line production; even, perhaps, amalgamation of the second and third functions. This would mean groups of workers, high skilled in more than one area, being able to adjust and repair their machines, and to advise and even cooperate with designers. This would have to go hand-in-hand with improved relations between firms involved in the same production process—continuous interaction and dialogue between those which design machines and those which use them. Subcontracting would be replaced by "partnership."

The 1980s showed that in countries where firms opted for this labor-process model, such as Japan, West Germany, Sweden and, in the end, Italy, the introduction of new technology was much more efficient; this is shown by the fact that this group of countries gained from the trade war. In other words, there are signs in the present day and age that we can turn on its head the age-old tendency of capitalism, pushed to its culmination by Taylorism, to separate the manual aspects of work from the intellectual ones.

However, what would be the cost of reuniting what Taylor separated? If employers recognize their employees' skill and initiative, how would they turn these to their own benefit, and what would they be prepared to pay for their employees' greater commitment to work? The immediate answer for many employers (particularly in France) trying to introduce the illusory Japanese concept of "quality circles" would be . . . nothing. "We are giving you greater job satisfaction. It is you who should thank us." Sometimes it works, for a time—with men, for example, who find it amusing for a short time. But women physically resent the fact that, while the new system might engage their attention and their intelligence, they have no time to think about their "second job"—shopping, planning meals, childcare. For the same wage, they would prefer flow-process work to working in "modules." Management is simply confirmed in its contempt for "manual workers."

What is worse is that "liberal" modes of regulation of the wage relation, by putting more emphasis on "flexibility" and casual work, mean it is virtually impossible for employees to feel consciously involved in improving the labor processes or ensuring quality products or services in "their" firm. To be "involved," employees must feel that their long-term interest is tied to that of their firm. The only solution is for them to get something in return; in other words, we need a new "grand compromise."

One possible approach to this is through individual negotiation, where, in return for involvement, workers receive bonuses, promotion or merit increases in pay; if they do not want to be involved, they can leave. This leads to bargaining in skills and involvement, inside and outside the firm— a kind of "institutionalized boot-licking." Workers sell to their employer not only their time, but also their readiness to cooperate more than their colleagues. This model, based on competition between skilled employees, has been called "Californian" by Philippe Messine,[5] a term based on the market in computer staff in the famous Silicon Valley. Unlike the "wage society" of the Fordist model, where even managing directors thought of themselves as employees, different from semi-skilled workers only in being further up the scale, what is happening is a "rebargaining" of the wage relation: employees are all individual entrepreneurs, but some sell their labor directly to others for a fee.

This model, quite different from neo-Taylorism as far as the labor process is concerned, is in fact perfectly compatible with it in the context of liberal-productivism, but it does not apply to the same segment of the labor force. It is quite possible to have, in the same factory or the same office, neo-Taylorism for the unskilled and semi-skilled, and an "individually negotiated involvement" for more qualified employees.

We can take this line of reasoning further: there can be guaranteed employment and collective bargaining in major firms, while neo-Taylorism is kept for women, immigrants and handicapped people in subcontracting firms and consumer services such as fast food. Japan, or the Germany described in Günter Wallraff's book *Lowest of the Low*,[6] are examples of this two-tier society, in which the upper echelons of the labor force retain Fordist social benefits from the past and are intimately involved in the fight for quality and productivity, while the rest are condemned to neo-Taylorist casual employment.

In this type of labor-process model, which Masahiko Aoki, a Japanese expert in labor economics, calls "workers' democracy,"[7] we are outside the scope of liberal-productivist principles *as far as the firm is concerned*. The "freedom of entrepreneurs" is in fact strictly limited by the contract which ties them to their employees, either implicitly by custom or explicitly by collective agreement. In exchange for employees' commitment, their jobs are guaranteed and they are continually involved in negotiations about technical changes and similar matters.

To call this "workers' democracy" is probably going too far, but Aoki stresses the "dilemma of workers' democracy": firms where the practice is to negotiate involvement collectively have to be careful because they operate in a liberal world. Their employees can be guaranteed something in return only to the extent that their commitment leads to higher sales, and this is not certain, since the market may collapse or a rival firm may out-perform them. Because of this, the collective compromise has to be limited to the smallest possible stable group of employees—a kind of wage-earners' *aristocracy,* fighting off "dangerous competitors"; that is, other employees. This is another example of the feudal model, except that some of the villains have become knights in league with the lord against the rest.

The compromise which I will propose will be much more advantageous for all employees; but it remains true that the Japanese compromise is far more attractive, even from the capitalist point of view, than Anglo-Saxon or French liberal-productivism . . .

The return of economic instability

The third major problem with liberal-productivism is macroeconomic—the recurrence of crises of overproduction, and periodic 1930s-style slumps in the social demand, as happened in Britain and the United States in the early 1980s and as will happen again (as in 1989–1990) when they bring down their trade deficit to manageable proportions.

In the case of Fordism, growth in demand is in a sense programmed. Entrepreneurs are guaranteed expanding markets, since all employers give their employees wage rises more or less in unison. It is therefore in their interest to invest, which in itself calls for more capital goods, spreads wages around, and so on. With regulation under liberalism, entrepreneurs get hints on market trends only by observing the behavior of other entrepreneurs. They invest if they think their neighbors' "investment mood" is on the upswing (economists call this "animal spirits"). The behavior of each entrepreneur therefore validates the guesses of the others, until a few bankers, wholesalers or entrepreneurs see that demand does not match recent investment, and the result is panic, stock market crashes and drop in output.

The classic solution to this lack of demand management, when there is no explicitly coordinated increase in total wages, is public spending on major investment projects or armaments. What a paradox! A liberal-productivist regime of accumulation only works well with a high-spending government which keeps taxes low! This is what happened in the United States from 1983 to 1988. By 1987 everybody had come to think that growth based on such a deficit could not go on, which led to the stock market crash. However, since the deficit remained high, US growth continued in 1988; and other countries, seeing the United States simply carrying on, carried on as well. As we shall see, this situation cannot last for ever, because of the balance of international payments—a country cannot continue to drag others along by piling up debts.

The great international disorder

The fourth problem facing liberal-productivism in its international dimension is free trade. As we have seen, the golden age of Fordism did not go down the road of an untrammeled open-market system, which was the favored grand design of the United States after World War II. In their long-term interest, they allowed the reconstruction of Japan and Western Europe to take place within a certain degree of protectionism. At the same time, independent Third World countries applied protectionism in their development policy, but they were not serious rivals. Things began to go wrong in the late 1960s, when first Western Europe and Japan and then the newly industrialized countries reached North American levels of competitiveness either by achieving comparable productivity or by having much lower wage levels. Markets and even production channels became internationalized, but at the international level there was still no regulatory mechanism to manage growth in demand that was comparable to Fordist compromises at national level.

The response of liberal-productivism to these problems was somewhat illogical—it called for even less organization, even fewer regulatory mechanisms. Free trade was supposed to work automatically to bring about both the "adjustment" of economies to each other, and the mutual encouragement of growth. Not only did neither happen, but what was worse, the only way in which free trade can "adjust" international imbalances (those which reduce deficits in countries with too many imports and too few exports, or allow them to attract capital investment and loans) has the effect of restricting growth world-wide. In fact, growth in the 1970s and 1980s was gained at the expense of greater imbalances.

It is useful to remind ourselves that imbalances were worse as a result of the oil shocks: nonoil-exporting countries had to increase exports of other commodities to pay for imported oil. As long as they paid "on credit"— that is, without reducing their deficit—things went reasonably well (the "first stage of the crisis"). Then the United States cut its deficit by reducing domestic demand (second stage), thereby dragging the rest of the world into recession. Then it went for growth again, pulling the rest with it, but . . . by increasing its deficit.

Basically, it is very logical. In the free-trade situation, trade deficits arise when certain countries expand too quickly for their capacity to produce competitively. And, as we have seen, the wrong choice of labor-process model ruined US competitiveness with Japan or West Germany. There are two possible responses to this situation. Either engineer a recession in the country in deficit; or allow it to borrow—that is, *not* to adjust. But if all countries in deficit go into recession by raising taxes or cutting government spending, who will take exports? Alternatively, if countries in deficit borrow, they need to raise interest rates to attract loans; and these high rates soon become the international norm. Entrepreneurs then find financial investments more profitable than producing goods, and stop investing in production.

In all these circumstances, if countries without the common means of regulating growth in demand are put together in a free-trade situation, the result is stagnation or at best spasmodic growth. As we shall see later, the European Community is a good example of this; but the Third World situation is even more dramatic because of the burden of debt from the past. Even a high-export country such as Brazil can have such a high debt burden that it must still continue to force its people to tighten their belts, export more and import less. But when the standard of living is already low, when distribution of wealth is very uneven with the poorest groups well below the national average, as in Brazil or India, and when the population is rising rapidly, what in other countries would be called "austerity" amounts in these cases to misery, hunger and the agony of a whole people.

When, in 1987, Brazil ended the price freeze which had significantly increased the purchasing power of the poorest groups but curtailed its ability to repay foreign borrowing, within just a few weeks whole families were priced out of their rented homes and had to move to the burgeoning shanty towns. Five years, before, recession in North America had jolted Brazil's export drive at a time when its Noreste province was hit by drought. Ground down by foreign debt, the Brazilian dictatorship rejected the idea of a small reduction in the comfortable living standards of the ruling classes to help the inhabitants of the affected areas. A million people died; I saw the dying crawl into the center of Recife, the provincial capital. That is what is meant by adjustment!

Reaganism, however, which was responsible in the final analysis for these catastrophes, did not remain unaffected by the impasse to which laissez-faire led. When the US trade deficit reached enormous proportions in the mid-1980s, the Reagan administration refused, of course, to impose on its electorate the IMF recipe of recession and huge devaluation. After a period when "everyone for themselves" was the guiding principle, Reaganism discovered the virtues of negotiation, multilateralism and partnership in international relations, and the active responsibility of the states in the regulation of demand. By the end of 1985, the United States suggested that Western Europe (in effect West Germany) and Japan should boost their domestic demand to attract American exports. More than that—they begged them and threatened them, and in the end deliberately weakened the dollar, as the most effective way to protect against imports and subsidize exports.

It did not work as well as expected, and the United States had to move to an increasingly explicit protectionism. The main point, however, for the present argument is that the policy of this intensely free-market government amounted to a return to the old "cooperative" doctrine of the OECD in the early 1970s; Stephen Marris, who had been the OECD's economic advisor at the time, took his cue from Cato in Ancient Rome and continually advocated such a move. To sum up: the responsibility for world growth lies on those countries with a trade surplus. It is up to them to boost home demand to attract others' exports. And it might be added that if they do not do this, it is perfectly legitimate for countries in deficit to have recourse to protectionism.

The American administration's new multilateralism, for which Bush's secretary of state, James Baker, was responsible, was as far removed from the free-market model as protectionism (one of its weapons) is from free trade. An explicit compromise between states is the only alternative to the all-out war which is at the heart of liberal-productivism. As in the case of the labor process, it is this kind of liberalism which is on the defensive, gradually giving way to a new grand design that is still being defined . . .

This is an important point in favor of the alternative compromise which I am proposing. But before coming to that, we need to look at a crisis common to both productivisms—to Fordism and to the liberalism which is trying to supplant it: in other words, the ecological crisis.

Notes

1 The *Rassemblement pour la République* was the party of Jacques Chirac, French prime minister from 1986 until 1988, when he unsuccessfully stood as the right-wing candidate against the socialist François Mitterrand in the second round of the presidential elections.
2 Ideologue of liberal-productivism (the left-wing version) and critic of the welfare state.
3 Jargon used by French social welfare departments to describe adolescents from rundown urban areas, "predestined" by their background to be delinquents.
4 Quoted by Giancarlo Santilli in his article "L'automatisation comme forme de contrôle social" (Automation as a Form of Social Control), *Travail*, 8, 1985.
5 Phillipe Messine, *Les Saturniens* (Paris: La Découverte, 1987).
6 Günter Wallraff, *Lowest of the Low* (Paris: Methuen, 1988); translation of *Ganz unten* (Cologne: Kiepenhauer & Witsch, 1985).
7 See Masahiko Aoki, "Intrafirm Mechanisms, Sharing and Employment," in *The Golden Age of Capitalism*, ed. Stephan Marglin and Juliet Schor (New York and London: Oxford University Press, 1990).

CHAPTER FOUR

Recapturing

Paulin Hountondji

From The Surreptitious Speech: Présence Africaine and the
Politics of Otherness 1947–1987, *ed. V. Y. Mudimbe. Chicago,
IL: University of Chicago Press, 1992: 238–248.*

It is from the economists that I borrow the notion of extraversion, as it
functions in the theory of development, in order to transfer it to another
terrain: that of a sociology of science.[1]

In fact, it seems urgent to me that the scientists in Africa, and perhaps
more generally in the Third World, question themselves on the meaning of
their practice as scientists, its real function in the economy of the entirety
of scholarship, its place in the process of production of knowledge on a
worldwide basis. "Are we satisfied or not with the lithe way it is going?" As
long as we look upon the problems of scientific research only from the angle
of the individual performance and career, we have nothing or almost nothing
to criticize about the present situation. We will only deplore, and that is
what we customarily do, the lack of equipment, the numerical weakness of
research groups compared to the importance that these groups have in the
industrialized nations, and other similar weaknesses. But these quantitative
insufficiencies are not really very worrisome. At most they would indicate
that scientific research is here still in its early stages, that it is relatively
young compared to that of the great industrial metropolitan centers, and
that with time the gap actually will be reduced, to the extent that scientific
and technological activity will be developed in Africa. Thus, one would
encourage a patience and greater efforts toward higher performance within

the framework of the present institutions and of the present production ration.

If we look more closely, however, the problem is less simple. For we must go beyond the quantitative parallels, beyond the performances of a given African scholar taken in isolation, or of a given research team; beyond the competitiveness of a given center or laboratory in order to examine, for example, the source of the equipment and other instruments used, the modalities of the choice of the subjects of research, the social needs and other practical demands from which the subjects chosen proceed, directly or indirectly; the geographical location in which these needs and demands first commanded attention, the real destination of the research results, the place where and the way in which these results are assigned, guarded, capitalized, the way in which they are applied, if need be; the complex links between this research and industry, this research and the economic activity in general—each time asking questions: What purpose does this research serve? Who will benefit from it? How does it insert itself in the very society that produces it? To what extent does this society manage to appropriate the results? To what extent, on the contrary, does it allow these to be taken away?

By considering things from this angle, one will readily notice that the difference (between scientific activity in Africa and that activity in the industrial metropolitan centers) is not only quantitative but qualitative as well, not only in degree or level of development but in orientation and in mode of operation. Research here is extraverted, turned toward the exterior, ruled by and subordinate to outside needs instead of being self-centered and destined, first of all, to answer the questions posed by the African society itself, whether directly or indirectly.

II

I will refer here to a study proposed elsewhere.[2] Scientific activity in the Third World seems to me to be characterized, globally, by its position of dependency. This dependency is of the same nature as that of the economic activity, which is to say that, put back in the context of its historical genesis, it obviously appears to be the result of the progressive integration of the Third World into the worldwide process of the production of knowledge, managed and controlled by the Northern countries.

It has been observed thousands of times before that, during the colonial period, the occupied territory functioned on the economic level as a warehouse for raw materials, destined to feed the factories of the metropolis. What has been less well observed is that it functioned also, with respect to metropolitan scientific activity, as a provider of raw materials. The colony was nothing other than an immense Storage place for new scientific facts, gathered in their crude state in order to be communicated to the urban laboratories and research centers, who took it upon themselves, and were the only ones who were able to do so, to treat them theoretically, to interpret them, to integrate them in their proper place in the system of the totality of the facts, both known and unknown to science. In other words, if the economic activity of the colony was characterized by a kind of industrial vacuum, scientific activity, too, was characterized by a crying theoretical vacuum. The colony lacked laboratories, as it lacked factories. It lacked laboratories in the broadest sense of the word, in the sense that every discipline, whether of the exact and natural sciences, of the social and human sciences, or of other sectors of knowledge, is by necessity developed in the laboratory. All the colony had to do, it was thought, was to build places especially organized and equipped for conceptual work, scholarly libraries or, if need be, that complicated technical apparatus necessary for the transformation of raw facts into verified knowledge—which is called experimentation. On the other hand, the metropolitan laboratories found, in the colony, a precious source of new information, an irreplaceable opportunity to enrich their stock of data and to step up one notch in their research, both through exhaustive and truly universal knowledge and through a practical mastery of the environment.

As a provider of raw materials, the colony was furthermore, as is known, one outlet among others, incidentally, for the products of the metropolitan industry. But what has been less well observed is that it functioned in the same manner with respect to the products of metropolitan scientific research. Thus, one used to find, and one still does, in the Dahomian market (Béninois, as it is called today), "Palmolive" soap made in France from palm oil (which Dahomey produced and still produces), as one found and still finds in another area textbooks of tropical geography, indeed, of the geography of Dahomey, produced in France from data gathered on the site, in Dahomey or in other tropical countries, and treated in the laboratories of the Institut National de Cartographie in Paris. Or in yet another sector there are locomotives, cars, various machinery and equipment that are the result of the technological application of the knowledge accumulated in the urban centers and of its industrial exploitation. The colony was, in its fashion, a consumer of science, as it was a consumer of industrial products, imported products in every case, and perceived as such; products whose origin and mode of "fabrication" the local population knew nothing about and that, therefore, could only appear to them as surreal and not to be mastered, miraculously placed on top of their daily reality like a veneer.

It would be interesting to examine the forms and modalities of this peripheral scientific "consumerism" in detail, to measure its importance, to calculate the relationship or, more precisely, the disproportion between the consumption and the more or less embryonic scientific production, which could provide a precise indication of the degree of scientific and technological dependency in the different countries, or in the different sectors of activity in the same country. It would, furthermore, be interesting to examine the nature and the relative importance of the facts and of the raw information "exported" from the colonies to the central laboratories of research, to compare these facts and this information with the raw materials proper exported from the same countries to the urban factories, and to establish criteria for a close approximate distinction between these two categories of "raw" materials. Such a distinction is not easily made, to the extent that even the raw materials of industry themselves sometimes undergo a "scientific" treatment in the urban center preceding their real transformation.

Finally, it would be interesting to appraise, from a historic and epistemological point of view, what European science owes to the Third World, to appraise the nature and the scope of the knowledge that came forth from the theoretical treatment of this new mass of data and information, to appraise the real working of the new disciplines based on these discoveries (tropical geography, tropical agriculture, African sociology, anthropology, etc.), and the alterations made in the older disciplines through these same discoveries.

This is not the place to resolve these complex problems. It suffices to have noted, at the very least, the real parallel between the functioning of the colony with respect to the metropolitan economic activity and its functioning with respect to the scientific activity; to have noted the very strong analogy between the applied strategies of removal in both cases, that is to say, on the one hand the draining of resource materials, and on the other the draining of information for the purpose of feeding the factories and the universities and urban research centers, all at the same time.

Undoubtedly, this analogy is far from perfect, since, for example, the "draining" of information does not deprive the colony that produced it of this information, while the removal of gold, ivory, and palm or peanut oil materially impoverishes the country that produces it. With respect to our problem, however, this difference is secondary.

There is more. Not only is this difference secondary, not only does the analogy remain very strong between the two forms of removal but, and this is the bottom line, it also concerns two complementary moments of one and the same process: accumulation on a worldwide scale. Scientific activity in general can, in fact, be thought of as a specific modality of economic activity; it is also an activity of production even if the objects produced here are those of knowledge, that is, concepts, intellectual and not material objects. Thus, it was natural that the annexation of the Third World, its integration in the worldwide capitalist system through trade and colonization, also comprise a "scientific" window, that the draining of material riches goes hand-in-hand with intellectual and scientific exploitation the extortion of secrets and other useful information, as it was natural, on a different level, that they go hand-in-hand with the extortion of works of art meant to fill the museums of the metropolitan areas.

III

The period of which we speak has certainly gone by, but it has left its traces. Economically (in the narrow sense of the word "economy,") one can no longer speak of an industrial vacuum, no more than one can speak of a theoretic vacuum in the field of science. The former colonies now have factories and an industrial activity that is sometimes intense, and on a different level they have universities, laboratories, and research centers that are at times very well equipped.

That multiplication of factories, however, has not led, as we know, to an authentic development but rather to a growth without development, to use Samir Amin's phrase. The establishment of assembly lines for automobiles and other industrial units of the same kind continues to obey a logic of extraversion. Neocolonial industry continues to be defined, on a massive scale, by the needs of the urban middle class: it aims to produce luxury consumer goods destined for the privileged few rather than consumer goods for the people. Therefore, it cannot provide the collective rise in the standard of living of the broadest layers of the population—which is what development would really be.

Mutatis mutandis, I personally hold that the peripheral multiplication of the structures of intellectual and scientific production (universities and research centers, libraries, etc.) far from ending extraversion have had as their essential role up until now the facilitating, therefore the reinforcement, of the draining of information, the violation of what is secret, the marginalization of "traditional" scholarship, the slow but sure integration of all useful information available in the South into the worldwide process of production of knowledge, managed and controlled by the North. In other words, these structures of scientific production are themselves also, for the same reason as the assembly lines, structures of import-substitution which, far from suppressing it, on the contrary, reinforce extraversion, reinforce the dependency of the periphery with respect to the center.

One can cite at least the following indications of this extraversion:

1. Scientific activity in our countries remains largely dependent upon the laboratory equipment made in the center. We have never produced a microscope; this holds all the more for the new equipment today, that is more and more sophisticated and necessary for today's research that is on the cutting edge. And so the first link in the chain, the making of the instruments of research, the production of the scientific means of production, already eludes us.

2. Our scientific practice remains largely dependent upon the libraries, archives, publishing houses, journals, and other scientific periodicals published in the North; more generally, dependent upon those holding places, locations on conservation and circulation of

the results of research, where the scientific memory of humanity takes shape, and which remain largely and essentially concentrated in the North. One must, without a doubt, recognize the enormous progress that has been made in this respect in the Southern countries for the last few dozen years. One should unquestionably appreciate, in all its merit, the intense activity of scientific publishing and editing that as materialized, here and there, through university annals, various Journals and periodicals, and more and more credible publishing houses. Still, the progress made in this area is far from having reversed the process. Proof for this is the simple fact that these publications continue to find their most numerous and most loyal readership in the Northern countries. Of course, it is not a question of complaint but rather of stating the fact, analyzing it, and sifting out the significance.

3. We are here touching upon theoretical extraversion in its true sense; the fact that the work of our scholars is always known and read more in the North than in the South: the still more serious fact that this circumstance, that at first sight could be considered as purely exterior, is, in fact, still interiorized by our scholars themselves, to the point where they curve the very orientation and the content of their works in determining the choice of the themes of their research as well as the theoretical models applied to their treatment. The Third World researcher, thus, has a tendency to let himself be guided in his scientific work by the expectations and the preoccupations of the European public to which his virtual assistantship belongs.

4. The result, among others, of this theoretical extraversion: research on the periphery bears most frequently on the immediate environment; it remains riveted to the local context, enclosed in the specific, incapable of and not very eager to rise to the universal. At first sight, one might find it contradictory that the centripetal orientation of the research is presented here as a sign of scientific extraversion. One would be more inclined to see, on the contrary, an indication there of a liberation for the researcher from the South with respect to the dominant themes of Northern research, the sign that this researcher gives priority to the questions that are of direct interest to his own society. But the truth is very different: for in the total movement of the history of the sciences, territorial specializations have, once again, been produced by Europe and responded, originally, to the theoretic and practical needs of Europe. The truth is that Africanism itself, both as practice and ideology, is once again an invention of Europe, and that by enclosing himself in it, the African researcher, in fact, accepts playing the subordinate role of a knowledgeable informer with

respect to European science. By becoming exclusive and badly mastered, the legitimate interest of the Southern researcher in his own milieu can thus generate dangerous traps. The obsession with the immediate future, the fear of breaking loose, then lead the researcher to scientific imprisonment and keep him away from an essential stage of the process of the totality of knowledge: the production of the theoretical models themselves, the elaboration of the conceptual schemas that thereafter permit the grasping of the specific as such.

5. But scientific extraversion can have a more immediately practical origin and reach: it can happen that the choice of the field of research is not conditioned only, that is, indirectly determined, by the preoccupations of the European readership, but that it is immediately dictated, without any deviations and any subtleties, by the demands of an economy that is itself extraverted. Until quite recently, agronomic research provided a fine example of this crass form of extraversion, since its work was aimed, essentially, at the improvement of export crops (palm trees [oil], coconut trees, coffee, cocoa, peanuts, cotton, etc.), destined for the factories of the North or the factories of "import-substitution," established here and there in the South, while the food crops, from which the great mass of the local populations lived, were being neglected. Things have certainly made progress since then, but the basic tendency remains: agronomic research often remains largely in the service of a trade economy.

6. The famous brain drain, the flight of the brains from the South toward the North, in this context, takes on a new significance: an accidental manifestation of the global extraversion of our economy and more particularly of our scientific activity, it should not be treated as an evil in itself but as the visible tip of an enormous iceberg that we must learn to take into consideration and, if possible, to raise in its entirety. Those who leave are not, in fact, the only ones: those who stay are indirectly caught up in the same movement. The brains of the Third World, all the intellectually and scientifically competent, are rigorously carried by the whole flow of worldwide scientific activity toward the center of the system. Some "settle" in the host countries; others go back and forth between the periphery and the center; still others, caught in the impossibility of managing a move, survive as best they can on the periphery, where they struggle every day, with varying degrees of success, against the demons of cynicism and discouragement, while their eyes remain turned toward the center, for it is essentially from there that come equipment and instruments of research, traditions, publications, theoretical and methodological models, and the entire parade of values and countervalues that accompany those.

7. A minor form of the *brain drain*, scientific South/North tourism, seems an important phenomenon to which little attention has been paid until now. In the normal routine of the researcher from the Third World, the journey remains unavoidable; the researcher must move physically, leave for the great industrial urban centers, either to perfect his scientific training, or, once his research project is launched, to pursue it beyond a certain threshold. The question is not whether such journeys are pleasant or not: undoubtedly, many find them pleasant, especially at the beginning of their careers; others, on the other hand, find them oddly repetitive, or experience them as a true wrenching. This is nothing but a question of personal appreciation that leaves the true question intact, that of the structural need for such journeys, of the objective constraints that render *this* form of scientific tourism inevitable, and that characterize the scientific activity in the Third World in a very particular way.

In saying that, naturally I do not claim to minimize the enormous scientific advantage one can take from such trips; on the contrary, I am focusing attention on the fact that these trips remain, under the present circumstances, the condition *sine qua non* of that kind of advantage. Under these circumstances, it would also be absurd, everything else being equal, to seek to put an end to scientific South/North "tourism," which is not a form of tourism at all, as I am trying to point out emphatically. The real demand lies elsewhere: it must be a question of changing, of profoundly transforming the present scientific relationships in the world, of promoting a self-centered scientific activity in those countries that are today peripheral.

I am, furthermore, not ignoring the fact that even in the center of the system today's researcher cannot remain altogether sedentary, under penalty of slow death, unless it be in the very heart of the center; there is the center of the center, the absolute pose: the United States of America which, to the detriment of Northern Europe and Japan, is attracting the "cream" of the international community of researchers more and more all the time. However, scientific "tourism" then no longer has the same significance: the flow of the researchers South/North is not the result of an internal imbalance in scientific activity in the secondary capitalist countries; each one of them develops, and very well at that, an independent, self-centered activity, in principle capable of surviving by itself. The exodus of its men of science toward the United States, or for certain disciplines toward Japan, for this reason, comes from their seeking something "more." With respect to the exodus South/North, it represents a luxury rather than a vital necessity.

8. To make this complete, another form of scientific "tourism" should be examined: the mover North/South. The movement that brings a researcher from the industrialized nation to a nation

of the periphery never has the same function as the opposite movement. The European or American scholar is not going to Zaire or the Sahara looking for science but only for the materials for science and, if need be, for a terrain to apply his discoveries. He is not going to look there for his paradigms, his theoretical and methodological models, but on the one hand for new information and facts that might enrich his paradigms, and on the other hand for distant territories where, with the least possible risk to his own society, he can perform his nuclear experiments or other types of experiments postulating various degrees of danger.

Entire portions of contemporary knowledge were born from this scientific investment in the South by the North. Out of this have come new disciplines, such as social and cultural anthropology, and different specializations within the previous disciplines. The knowledge thus collected, the knowledge on Africa and the Third World, completely escapes Africa and the Third World but is systematically returned to Europe, repatriated, capitalized, accumulated in the center of the system. Consequently, there is no extraversion in the movement North/South, but a simple tactical detour in the service of a self-sufficiency and of a strengthened technological mastery.

9. Under these conditions, what becomes of the traditional knowledge and know how? It is a fact that, in our oral cultures, there exist bodies of knowledge, sometimes very elaborate ones, faithfully transmitted from one generation to the next and often enriched in the course of this transmission. These knowledges of plants, animals, health, and illness, this knowledge of agriculture and the artisans, instead of developing, of gaining in precision and in vigor through the contact with foreign science, have more of a tendency to turn in upon themselves, subsisting in the best cases *side by side* with the new knowledge in a relationship of simple juxtaposition, and in the worst cases possibly disappearing completely and being erased from the collective memory. The integration into the worldwide process of the production of knowledge thus has the effect of marginalizing the old wisdom, indeed, in the worst of cases, of driving them out of the conscious memory of the peoples who, at a given time, produce them.

10. Scientific extraversion shows itself as well by using merely Western languages as languages of science, obliging the Third World researcher to accept the humiliating terms of these languages of foreign origin in order to have access to knowledge and, even more so, to reproduce and extend it. Without a doubt, one must be careful not to exaggerate the inconveniences that result from this situation, or to fall into the extremes of a Romanticism that would

have each language already be, in itself and through itself, the expression of a determined vision of the world, and consequently have the mother tongue be the only one in which any person can express his true identity. Without a doubt, language should be brought back to its instrumental role and made to comply with the modern demands of a widened community, in a world where no one, under penalty of asphyxiation, can entirely turn in upon himself any longer. Equally to be recognized is the antinatural character of the real relationships that presently exist in certain Third World countries, and particularly in Black Africa, between the native languages and the imported languages: the factual marginalization of the former to the exclusive advantage of the latter, the relegation of native languages to substandard languages, indeed "dialects" or "patois," barely good enough to express the platitudes of everyday life, the absence of a daring project of generalized literacy and the use of native languages as vehicles for teaching and for research at the highest level, with a real democratization of knowledge as an end.

I will not go any further. These remarks have no other goal than to indicate a direction of research and to ground its legitimacy with respect to the existing research. They come forth from a well-known discipline: the sociology of science. But contrary to the usual work in this field, the study envisioned here could not stop at examining the functioning of science in the industrialized societies. On the contrary, it will question specific traits of scientific and technological activity in the Third World, at the periphery of the worldwide capitalist system. The final objective is to establish a new scientific and technological politics that, in the end, would allow the collective appropriation of knowledge and of the entire scientific heritage available in the world by the peoples who, until now, have constantly been dispossessed of the fruits of their labor in this area as in all others.

Notes

1 This text was delivered as three papers at the Sixth General Assembly of the Conseil pour Ie Dévelopement de la Rechcrehe Economique et Sociale en Afrique (CODESRIA) in Dakar, December 5–10, 1988, under the title "Recherche et extraversion: Eléments pour une sociologie de la science dans les pays de la périphérie."

2 Paulin J. Hountondji, "Situation de l'anthropologue africain: Note critique sur unc forme d'extraversion scientifique" (paper delivered at a colloquium around Georges Balandier on Les Nouveaux Enjeux de l'Anthropologie, in Cérisy, France, June 1988. To be published in a collective work under the direction of Gabriel Gosselin.

CHAPTER FIVE

Immaterial Labor

Maurizio Lazzarato

From Radical Thought in Italy: A Potential Politics,
*ed. Paolo Virno and Michael Hardt. Minneapolis, MN:
University of Minnesota Press, 1996: 133–150.*

A significant amount of empirical research has been conducted concerning the new forms of the organization of work. This, combined with a corresponding wealth of theoretical reflection, has made possible the identification of a new conception of what work is nowadays and what new power relations it implies.

An initial synthesis of these results—framed in terms of an attempt to define the technical and subjective-political composition of the working class—can be expressed in the concept of *immaterial labor*, which is defined as the labor that produces the informational and cultural content of the commodity. The concept of immaterial labor refers to *two different aspects* of labor. On the one hand, as regards the "informational content" of the commodity, it refers directly to the changes taking place in workers' labor processes in big companies in the industrial and tertiary sectors, where the skills involved in direct labor are increasingly skills involving cybernetics and computer control (and horizontal and vertical communication). On the other hand, as regards the activity that produces the "cultural content" of the commodity, immaterial labor involves a series of activities that are not normally recognized as "work"—in other words, the kinds of activities involved in defining and fixing cultural and artistic standards, fashions, tastes, consumer norms, and, more strategically, public opinion. Once the privileged domain of the bourgeoisie and its children, these activities have since the end of the 1970s become the domain of what we have come to define as "mass intellectuality." The profound changes in these strategic sectors have radically modified not only the composition, management, and regulation of the workforce—the organization of production—but also, and more deeply, the role and function of intellectuals and their activities within society.

The "great transformation" that began at the start of the 1970s has changed the very terms in which the question is posed. Manual labor is increasingly coming to involve procedures that could be defined as "intellectual," and the new communications technologies increasingly require subjectivities that are rich in knowledge. It is not simply that intellectual labor has become subjected to the norms of capitalist production. What has happened is that a new "mass intellectuality" has come into being, created out of a combination of the demands of capitalist production and the forms of "self-valorization" that the struggle against work has produced. The old dichotomy between "mental and manual labor," or between "material labor and immaterial labor," risks failing to grasp the new nature of productive activity, which takes this separation on board and transforms it. The split between conception and execution, between labor and creativity, between author and audience, is simultaneously transcended within the "labor process" and reimposed as political command within the "process of valorization."

The restructured worker

Twenty years of restructuring of the big factories has led to a curious paradox. The various different post-Fordist models have been constructed both on the defeat of the Fordist worker and on the recognition of the centrality of (an ever increasingly intellectualized) living labor within production. In today's large restructured company, a worker's work increasingly involves, at various levels, an ability to choose among different alternatives and thus a degree of responsibility regarding decision-making. The concept of "interface" used by communications sociologists provides a fair definition of the activities of this kind of worker—as an interface between different functions, between different work teams, between different levels of the hierarchy, and so forth. What modern management techniques are looking for is for "the worker's soul to become part of the factory." The worker's personality and subjectivity have to be made susceptible to organization and command. It is around immateriality that the quality and quantity of labor are organized. This transformation of working-class labor into a labor of control, of handling information, into a decision-making capacity that involves the investment of subjectivity, affects workers in varying ways according to their positions within the factory hierarchy, but it is nevertheless present as an irreversible process. Work can thus be defined as the capacity to activate and manage productive cooperation. In this phase, workers are expected to become "active subjects" in the coordination of the various functions of production, instead of being subjected to it as simple command. We arrive at a point where a collective learning process becomes the heart of productivity, because it is no longer a matter of finding different ways of composing or organizing already existing job functions, but of looking for new ones.

The problem, however, of subjectivity and its collective form, its constitution and its development, has immediately expressed itself as a clash between social classes within the organization of work. I should point out that what I am describing is not some utopian vision of recomposition, but the very real terrain and conditions of the conflict between social classes.

The capitalist needs to find an unmediated way of establishing command over subjectivity itself; the prescription and definition of tasks transforms into a prescription of subjectivities. The new slogan of Western societies is that we should all "become subjects." Participative management is a technology of power, a technology for creating and controlling the "subjective processes." As it is no longer possible to confine subjectivity merely to tasks of execution, it becomes necessary for the subject's competence in the areas of management, communication, and creativity to be made compatible with the conditions of "production for production's sake." Thus the slogan "become subjects," far from eliminating the antagonism between hierarchy and cooperation, between autonomy and command, actually re-poses the antagonism at a higher level, because it both mobilizes and clashes with the very personality of the individual worker. First and foremost, we have here a discourse that is authoritarian: one *has* to express oneself, one *has* to speak, communicate, cooperate, and so forth. The "tone" is that of the people who were in executive command under Taylorization; all that has changed is the content. Second, if it is no longer possible to lay down and specify jobs and responsibilities rigidly (in the way that was once done with "scientific" studies of work), but if, on the contrary, jobs now require cooperation and collective coordination, then the subjects of that production must be capable of communication—they must be active participants within a work team. The communicational relationship (both vertically and horizontally) is thus completely predetermined in both form and content; it is subordinated to the "circulation of information" and is not expected to be anything other. The subject becomes a simple relayer of codification and decodification, whose transmitted messages must be "clear and free of ambiguity," within a communications context that has been completely normalized by management. The necessity of imposing command and the violence that goes along with it here take on a normative communicative form.

The management mandate to "become subjects of communication" threatens to be even more totalitarian than the earlier rigid division between mental and manual labor (ideas and execution), because capitalism seeks to involve even the worker's personality and subjectivity within the production of value. Capital wants a situation where command resides within the subject him- or herself, and within the communicative process. The worker is to be responsible for his or her own control and motivation within the work group without a foreman needing to intervene, and the foreman's role is redefined into that of a facilitator. In fact, employers are extremely worried by the double problem this creates: on one hand, they are forced to recognize the autonomy and freedom of labor as the only possible form of cooperation in production, but on the other hand, at the same time, they are obliged (a life-and-death necessity for the capitalist) not to "redistribute" the power that the new quality of labor and its organization imply. Today's management thinking takes workers' subjectivity into consideration only in order to codify it in line with the requirements of production. And once again this phase of transformation succeeds in concealing the fact that the individual and collective interests of workers and those of the company are not identical.

I have defined working-class labor as an abstract activity that nowadays involves the application of subjectivity. In order to avoid misunderstandings, however, I should add that this form of productive activity is not limited only to highly skilled workers; it refers to a use-value of labor power today, and, more generally, to the form of activity of every productive subject within postindustrial society. One could say that in the highly skilled, qualified worker, the "communicational model" is already given, already constituted, and that its potentialities are already defined. In the young worker, however, the "precarious" worker, and the unemployed youth, we are dealing with a pure virtuality, a capacity that is as yet undetermined but that already shares all the characteristics of postindustrial productive subjectivity. The virtuality of this capacity is neither empty nor ahistoric; it is, rather, an opening and a potentiality that have as their historical origins and antecedents the "struggle against work" of the Fordist worker and, in more recent times, the processes of socialization, educational formation, and cultural self-valorization.

This transformation of the world of work appears even more evident when one studies the social cycle of production: the "diffuse factory" and decentralization of production on the one hand and the various forms of tertiarization on the other. Here one can measure the extent to which the cycle of immaterial labor has come to assume a strategic role within the global organization of production. The various activities of research, conceptualization, management of human resources, and so forth, together with all the various tertiary activities, are organized within computerized and multimedia networks. These are the terms in which we have to understand the cycle of production and the organization of labor. The integration of scientific labor into industrial and tertiary labor has become one of the principal sources of productivity, and it is becoming a growing factor in the cycles of production that organize it.

"Immaterial Labor" in the classic definition

All the characteristics of the postindustrial economy (both in industry and society as a whole) are highly present within the classic forms of "immaterial" production: audiovisual production, advertising, fashion, the production of software, photography, cultural activities, and so forth. The activities of this kind of immaterial labor force us to question the classic definitions of *labor* and *labor power*,[1] because they combine the results of various different types of work skill: intellectual skills, as regards the cultural-informational content; manual skills for the ability to combine creativity, imagination, and technical and manual labor; and entrepreneurial skills in the management of social relations and the structuring of that social cooperation of which they are a part. This immaterial labor constitutes itself in forms that are immediately collective, and we might say that it exists only in the form of networks and flows. The organization of the cycle of production of immaterial labor (because this is exactly what it is, once we abandon our factoryist prejudices—a cycle of production) is not obviously apparent to the eye, because it is not defined by the four walls of a factory. The location in which it operates is outside in the society at large, at a territorial level that we could call "the basin of immaterial labor." Small and sometimes very small "productive units" (often consisting of only one individual) are organized for specific ad hoc projects, and may exist only for the duration of those particular jobs. The cycle of production comes into operation only when it is required by the capitalist; once the job has been done, the cycle dissolves back into the networks and flows that make possible the reproduction and enrichment of its productive capacities. Precariousness, hyperexploitation, mobility, and hierarchy are the most obvious characteristics of metropolitan immaterial labor. Behind the label of the independent "self-employed" worker, what we actually find is an intellectual proletarian, but who is recognized as such only by the employers who exploit him or her. It is worth noting that in this kind of working existence it becomes increasingly difficult to distinguish leisure time from work time. In a sense, life becomes inseparable from work.

This labor form is also characterized by real managerial functions that consist in (1) a certain ability to manage its social relations and (2) the eliciting of social cooperation within the structures of the basin of immaterial labor. The quality of this kind of labor power is thus defined not only by its professional capacities (which make possible the construction of the cultural-informational content of the commodity), but also by its ability to "manage" its own activity and act as the coordinator of the immaterial labor of others (production and management of the cycle). This immaterial labor appears as a real mutation of "living labor." Here we are quite far from the Taylorist model of organization.

Immaterial labor finds itself at the crossroads (or rather, it is the interface) of a new relationship between production and consumption. The activation of both productive cooperation and the social relationship with the consumer is materialized within and by the process of communication. The role of immaterial labor is to promote continual innovation in the forms and conditions of communication (and thus in work and consumption). It gives form to and materializes needs, the imaginary, consumer tastes, and so forth, and these products in turn become powerful producers of needs, images, and tastes. The particularity of the commodity produced through immaterial labor (its essential use-value being given by its value as informational and cultural content) consists in the fact that it is not destroyed in the act of consumption, but rather it enlarges, transforms, and creates the "ideological" and cultural environment of the consumer. This commodity does not produce the physical capacity of labor power; instead, it transforms the person who uses it. Immaterial labor produces first and foremost a "social relationship" (a relationship of innovation, production, and consumption). Only if it succeeds in this production does its activity have an economic value. This activity makes immediately apparent something that material production had "hidden," namely, that labor produces not only commodities, but first and foremost it produces the capital relation.

The autonomy of the productive synergies of immaterial labor

My working hypothesis, then, is that the cycle of immaterial labor takes as its starting point a social labor power that is independent and able to organize both its own work and its relations with business entities. Industry does not form or create this new labor power, but simply takes it on board and adapts it. Industry's control over this new labor power presupposes the independent organization and "free entrepreneurial activity" of the labor power. Advancing further on this terrain brings us into the debate on the nature of work in the post-Fordist phase of the organization of labor. Among economists, the predominant view of this problematic can be expressed in a single statement: immaterial labor operates within the forms of organization that the centralization of industry allows. Moving from this common basis, there are two differing schools of thought: one is the extension of neoclassical analysis; the other is that of systems theory.

In the former, the attempt to solve the problem comes through a redefinition of the problematic of the market. It is suggested that in order to explain the phenomena of communication and the new dimensions of organization one should introduce not only cooperation and intensity of labor, but also other analytic variables (anthropological variables? immaterial variables?) and that on this basis one might introduce other objectives of optimization and so forth. In fact, the neoclassical model has considerable difficulty in freeing itself from the coherence constraints imposed by the theory of general equilibrium. The new phenomenologies of labor, the new dimensions of organization, communication, the potentiality of spontaneous synergies, the autonomy of the subjects involved, and the independence of the networks were neither foreseen nor foreseeable by a general theory that believed that material labor and an industrial economy were indispensable. Today, with the new data available, we find the microeconomy in revolt against the macroeconomy, and the classical model is corroded by a new and irreducible anthropological reality.

Systems theory, by eliminating the constraint of the market and giving pride of place to organization, is more open to the new phenomenology of labor and in particular to the emergence of immaterial labor. In more developed systemic theories, organization is conceived as an ensemble of factors, both material and immaterial, both individual and collective, that can permit a given group to reach objectives. The success of this organizational process requires instruments of regulation, either voluntary or automatic. It becomes possible to look at things from the point of view of social synergies, and immaterial labor can be taken on board by virtue of its global efficacy. These viewpoints, however, are still tied to an image of the organization of work and its social territory within which effective activity from an economic viewpoint (in other words, the activity conforming to the objective) must inevitably be considered as a surplus in relation to collective cognitive mechanisms. Sociology and labor economics, being systemic disciplines, are both incapable of detaching themselves from this position.

I believe that an analysis of immaterial labor and a description of its organization can lead us beyond the presuppositions of business theory—whether in its neoclassical school or its systems theory school. It can lead us to define, at a territorial level, a space for a radical autonomy of the productive synergies of immaterial labor. We can thus move against the old schools of thought to establish, decisively, the viewpoint of an "anthropo-sociology" that is constitutive.

Once this viewpoint comes to dominate within social production, we find that we have an interruption in the continuity of models of production. By this I mean that, unlike the position held by many theoreticians of post-Fordism, I do not believe that this new labor power is merely functional to a new historical phase of capitalism and its processes of accumulation and reproduction. This labor power is the product of a "silent revolution" taking place within the anthropological realities of work and within the reconfiguration of its meanings. Waged labor and direct subjugation (to organization) no longer constitute the principal form of the contractual relationship between capitalist and worker. A polymorphous self-employed autonomous work has emerged as the dominant form, a kind of "intellectual worker" who is him- or herself an entrepreneur, inserted within a market that is constantly shifting and within networks that are changeable in time and space.

The cycle of immaterial production

Up to this point I have been analyzing and constructing the concept of immaterial labor from a point of view that could be defined, so to speak, as "microeconomic." If now we consider immaterial labor within the globality of the production cycle, of which it is the strategic stage, we will be able to see a series of characteristics of post-Taylorist production that have not yet been taken into consideration.

I want to demonstrate in particular how the process of valorization tends to be identified with the process of the production of social communication and how the two stages (valorization and communication) immediately have a social and territorial dimension. The concept of immaterial labor presupposes and results in an enlargement of productive cooperation that even includes the production and reproduction of communication and hence of its most important contents: subjectivity. If Fordism integrated consumption into the cycle of the reproduction of capital, post-Fordism integrates communication into it. From a strictly economic point of view, the cycle of reproduction of immaterial labor dislocates the production–consumption relationship as it is defined as much by the "virtuous Keynesian circle" as by the Marxist reproduction schemes of the second volume of *Capital*. Now, rather than speaking of the toppling of "supply and demand," we should speak about a redefinition of the production–consumption relationship. As we saw earlier, the consumer is inscribed in the manufacturing of the product from its conception. The consumer is no longer limited to consuming commodities (destroying them in the act of consumption). On the contrary, his or her consumption should be productive in accordance to the necessary conditions and the new products. Consumption is then first of all a consumption of information. Consumption is no longer only the "realization" of a product, but a real and proper social process that for the moment is defined with the term *communication*.

Large-scale industry and services

To recognize the new characteristics of the production cycle of immaterial labor, we should compare it with the production of large-scale industry and services. If the cycle of immaterial production immediately demonstrates to us the secret of post-Taylorist production (that is to say, that social communication and the social relationship that constitutes it become productive), then it would be interesting to examine how these new social relationships innervate even industry and services, and how they oblige us to reformulate and reorganize even the classical forms of "production."

Large-scale industry

The postindustrial enterprise and economy are founded on the manipulation of information. Rather than ensuring (as nineteenth-century enterprises did) the surveillance of the inner workings of the production process and the supervision of the markets of raw materials (labor included), business is focused on the terrain outside of the production process: sales and the relationship with the consumer. It always leans more toward commercialization and financing than toward production. Prior to being manufactured, a product must be sold, even in "heavy" industries such as automobile manufacturing; a car is put into production only after the sales network orders it. This strategy is based on the production and consumption of information. It mobilizes important communication and marketing strategies in order to gather information (recognizing the tendencies of the market) and circulate it (constructing a market). In the Taylorist and Fordist systems of production, by introducing the mass consumption of standardized commodities, Ford could still say that the consumer has the choice between one black model T5 and another black model T5. "Today the standard commodity is no longer the recipe to success, and the automobile industry itself, which used to be the champion of the great 'low price' series, would want to boast about having become a neoindustry of singularization"—and quality.[2] For the majority of businesses, survival involves the permanent search for new commercial openings that lead to the identification of always more ample or differentiated product lines. Innovation is no longer subordinated only to the rationalization of labor, but also to commercial imperatives. It seems, then, that the postindustrial commodity is the result of a creative process that involves both the producer and the consumer.

Services

If from industry proper we move on to the "services" sector (large banking services, insurance, and so forth), the characteristics of the process I have described appear even more clearly. We are witnessing today not really a growth of services, but rather a development of the "relations of service." The move beyond the Taylorist organization of services is characterized by the integration of the relationship between production and consumption, where in fact the consumer intervenes in an active way in the composition of the product. The product "service" becomes a social construction and a social process of "conception" and innovation. In service industries, the "back-office" tasks (the classic work of services) have diminished and the tasks of the "front office" (the relationship with clients) have grown. There has been thus a shift of human resources toward the outer part of business. As recent sociological analyses tell us, the more a product handled by the service sector is characterized as an immaterial product, the more it distances itself from the model of industrial organization of the relationship between production and consumption. The change in this relationship between production and consumption has direct consequences for the organization of the Taylorist labor of production of services, because it draws into question both the contents of labor and the division of labor (and thus the relationship between conception and execution loses its unilateral character). If the product is defined through the intervention of the consumer, and is therefore in permanent evolution, it becomes always more difficult to define the norms of the production of services and establish an "objective" measure of productivity.

Immaterial labor

All of these characteristics of postindustrial economics (present both in large-scale industry and the tertiary sector) are accentuated in the form of properly "immaterial" production. Audiovisual production, advertising, fashion, software, the management of territory, and so forth are all defined by means of the particular relationship between production and its market or consumers. Here we are at the furthest point from the Taylorist model. Immaterial labor continually creates and modifies the forms and conditions of communication, which in turn acts as the interface that negotiates the relationship between production and consumption. As I noted earlier, immaterial labor produces first and foremost a social relation—it produces not only commodities, but also the capital relation.

If production today is directly the production of a social relation, then the "raw material" of immaterial labor is subjectivity and the "ideological" environment in which this subjectivity lives and reproduces. The production of subjectivity ceases to be only an instrument of social control (for the reproduction of mercantile relationships) and becomes directly productive, because the goal of our postindustrial society is to construct the consumer/communicator—and to construct it as "active." Immaterial workers (those who work in advertising, fashion, marketing, television, cybernetics, and so forth) satisfy a demand by the consumer and at the same time establish that demand. The fact that immaterial labor produces subjectivity and economic value at the same time demonstrates how capitalist production has invaded our lives and has broken down all the oppositions among economy, power, and knowledge. The process of social communication (and its principal content, the production of subjectivity) becomes here directly productive because in a certain way it "produces" production. The process by which the "social" (and what is even more social, that is, language, communication, and so forth) becomes "economic" has not yet been sufficiently studied. In effect, on the one hand, we are familiar with an analysis of the production of subjectivity defined as the constitutive "process" specific to a "relation to the self" with respect to the forms of production particular to knowledge and power (as in a certain vein of poststructuralist French philosophy), but this analysis never intersects sufficiently with the forms of capitalist valorization. On the other hand, in the 1980s a network of economists and sociologists (and before them the Italian postworkerist tradition) developed an extensive analysis of the "social form of production," but that analysis does not integrate sufficiently the production of subjectivity as the content of valorization. Now, the post-Taylorist mode of production is defined precisely by putting subjectivity to work both in the activation of productive cooperation and in the production of the "cultural" contents of commodities.

The aesthetic model

But how is the production process of social communication formed? How does the production of subjectivity take place within this process? How does the production of subjectivity become the production of the consumer/communicator and its capacities to consume and communicate? What role does immaterial labor have in this process? As I have already said, my hypothesis is this: *the process of the production of communication tends to become immediately the process of valorization.* If in the past communication was organized fundamentally by means of language and the institutions of ideological and literary/artistic production, today, because it is invested with industrial production, communication is reproduced by means of specific technological schemes (knowledge, thought, image, sound, and language reproduction technologies) and by means of forms of organization and "management" that are bearers of a new mode of production.

It is more useful, in attempting to grasp the process of the formation of social communication and its subsumption within the "economic," to use, rather than the "material" model of production, the "aesthetic" model that involves author, reproduction, and reception. This model reveals aspects that traditional economic categories tend to obscure and that, as I will show, constitute the "specific differences" of the post-Taylorist means of production.[3] The "aesthetic/ideological" model of production will be transformed into a small-scale sociological model with all the limits and difficulties that such a sociological transformation brings. The model of author, reproduction, and reception requires a double transformation: in the first place, the three stages of this creation process must be immediately characterized by their social form; in the second place, the three stages must be understood as the articulations of an actual productive cycle.[4]

The "author" must lose its individual dimension and be transformed into an industrially organized production process (with a division of labor, investments, orders, and so forth), "reproduction" becomes a mass reproduction organized according to the imperatives of profitability, and the audience ("reception") tends to become the consumer/communicator. In this process of socialization and subsumption within the economy of intellectual activity the "ideological" product tends to assume the form of a commodity. I should emphasize, however, that the subsumption of this process under capitalist logic and the transformation of its products into commodities does not abolish the specificity of aesthetic production, that is to say, the creative relationship between author and audience.

The specific differences of the immaterial labor cycle

Allow me to underline briefly the *specific differences* of the "stages" that make up the production cycle of immaterial labor (immaterial labor itself, its "ideological/commodity products," and the "public/consumer") in relation to the classical forms of the reproduction of "capital."

As far as immaterial labor being an "author" is concerned, it is necessary to emphasize the radical autonomy of its productive synergies. As we have seen, immaterial labor forces us to question the classical definitions of labor and labor power, because it results from a synthesis of different types of know-how: intellectual skills, manual skills, and entrepreneurial skills. Immaterial labor constitutes itself in immediately collective forms that exist as networks and flows. The subjugation of this form of cooperation and the "use value" of these skills to capitalist logic does not take away the autonomy of the constitution and meaning of immaterial labor. On the contrary, it opens up antagonisms and contradictions that, to use once again a Marxist formula, demand at least a "new form of exposition."

The "ideological product" becomes in every respect a commodity. The term *ideological* does not characterize the product as a "reflection" of reality, as false or true consciousness of reality. Ideological products produce, on the contrary, new stratifications of reality; they are the intersection where human power, knowledge, and action meet. New modes of seeing and knowing demand new technologies, and new technologies demand new forms of seeing and knowing. These ideological products are completely internal to the processes of the formation of social communication; that is, they are at once the results and the prerequisites of these processes. The ensemble of ideological products constitutes the human ideological environment. Ideological products are transformed into commodities without ever losing their specificity; that is, *they are always addressed to someone, they are "ideally signifying,"* and thus they pose the problem of "meaning."

The general public tends to become the model for the consumer (audience/client). The public (in the sense of the user—the reader, the music listener, the television audience) whom the author addresses has as such a double productive function. In the first place, as the addressee of the ideological product, the public is a constitutive element of the production process. In the second place, the public is productive by means of the reception that gives the product "a place in life" (in other words, integrates it into social communication) and allows it to live and evolve. *Reception is thus, from this point of view, a creative act* and an integrative part of the product. The transformation of the product into a commodity cannot abolish this double process of "creativity"; it must rather assume it as it is, and attempt to control it and subordinate it to its own values.

What the transformation of the product into a commodity cannot remove, then, is the *character of event*, the open process of creation that is established between immaterial labor and the public and organized by communication. If the innovation in immaterial production is introduced by this open process of creation, the entrepreneur, in order to further consumption and its perpetual renewal, will be constrained to draw from the "values" that the public/consumer produces. These values presuppose the modes of being, modes of existing, and forms of life that support them. From these considerations there emerge two principal consequences. First, values are "put to work." The transformation of the ideological product into a commodity distorts or deflects the social imaginary that is produced in the forms of life, but at the same time, commodity production must recognize itself as powerless as far as its own production is concerned. The second consequence is that the forms of life (in their collective and cooperative forms) are now the source of innovation.

The analysis of the different "stages" of the cycle of immaterial labor permits me to advance the hypothesis that what is "productive" is the whole of the social relation (here represented by the author-work-audience relationship) according to modalities that directly bring into play the "meaning." The specificity of this type of production not only leaves its imprint on the "form" of the process of production by establishing a new relationship between production and consumption, but it also poses a problem of legitimacy for the capitalist appropriation of this process. This cooperation can in no case be predetermined by economics, because it deals with the very life of society. "Economics" can only appropriate the forms and products of this cooperation, normalizing and standardizing them. The creative and innovative elements are tightly linked to the values that only the forms of life produce. Creativity and productivity in postindustrial societies reside, on the one hand, in the dialectic between the forms of life and values they produce and, on the other, in the activities of subjects that constitute them. The legitimation that the (Schumpeterian) entrepreneur found in his or her capacity for innovation has lost its foundation. Because the capitalist entrepreneur does not produce the forms and contents of immaterial labor, he or she does not even produce innovation. For economics there remains only the possibility of managing and regulating the activity of immaterial labor and creating some devices for the control and creation of the public/ consumer by means of the control of communication and information technologies and their organizational processes.

Creation and intellectual labor

These brief considerations permit us to begin questioning the model of creation and diffusion specific to intellectual labor and to get beyond the concept of creativity as an expression of "individuality" or as the patrimony of the "superior" classes. The works of Simmel and Bakhtin, conceived in a time when immaterial production had just begun to become "productive," present us with two completely different ways of posing the relationship between immaterial labor and society. The first, Simmel's, remain completely invested in the division between manual labor and intellectual labor and give us a theory of the creativity of intellectual labor. The second, Bakhtin's, in refusing to accept the capitalist division of labor as a given, elaborate a theory of social creativity. Simmel, in effect, explains the function of "fashion" by means of the phenomenon of imitation or distinction as regulated and commanded by class relationships. Thus the superior levels of the middle classes are the ones that create fashion, and the lower classes attempt to imitate them. Fashion here functions like a barrier that incessantly comes up because it is incessantly battered down. What is interesting for this discussion is that, according to this conception, the immaterial labor of creation is limited to a specific social group and is not diffused except through imitation. At a deeper level, this model accepts the division of labor founded on the opposition between manual and intellectual labor that has as its end the regulation and "mystification" of the social process of creation and innovation. If this model had some probability of corresponding to the dynamics of the market of immaterial labor at the moment of the birth of mass consumption (whose effects Simmel very intelligently anticipates), it could not be utilized to account for the relationship between immaterial labor and consumer-public in postindustrial society. Bakhtin, on the contrary, defines immaterial labor as the superseding of the division between "material labor and intellectual labor" and demonstrates how creativity is a social process. In fact, the work on "aesthetic production" of Bakhtin and the rest of the Leningrad circle has this same social focus. This is the line of investigation that seems most promising for developing a theory of the social cycle of immaterial production.

Translated by Paul Colilli and Ed Emery

Notes

1 The editors of this anthology have changed "work" and "workforce" to "labor" and "labor power."
2 Yves Clot, "Renouveau de l'industrialisme et activité philosophique," *Futur antérieur* 10 (1992): 22.
3 Both the creative and the social elements of this production encourage me to venture the use of the "aesthetic model." It is interesting to see how one could arrive at this new concept of labor by starting either from artistic activity (following the situationists) or from the traditional activity of the factory (following Italian workerist theories), both relying on the very Marxist concept of "living labor."
4 Walter Benjamin has already analyzed how since the end of the nineteenth century both artistic production and reproduction, along with its perception, have assumed collective forms. I cannot pause here to consider his works, but they are certainly fundamental for any genealogy of immaterial labor and its forms of reproduction.

CHAPTER SIX

Women, Land Struggles, and Globalization: An International Perspective

Silvia Federici

From Journal of Asian and African Studies *39 (1–2)*
(April 2004): 47–62

How can we ever get out of poverty if we can't get a piece of land to work? If we had land to plant, we wouldn't need to get food sent to us all the way from the United States. No. We'd have our own. But as long as the government refuses to give us the land and other resources we need, we'll continue to have foreigners running our country.

ELVIA ALVARADO (BENJAMIN 1987: 104)

Introduction: Women keep the world alive

Until not long ago, issues relating to land and land struggles would have failed to generate much interest among North Americans, unless they were farmers or descendants of the American Indians for whom the importance of land as the foundation of life is still paramount, culturally at least. For the rest of the population, the land question seemed to have receded into a distant past, as in the aftermath of a prolonged urbanization and industrialization process, land no longer appeared as the fundamental means of reproduction, and new technologies claimed to provide the power, self-reliance, and creativity that people once associated with agriculture.

This has been a great loss because this amnesia has led to a world where the basic questions concerning our existence—where our food comes from, whether it nourishes or poisons our bodies—remain unanswered and are often unasked. This indifference to land among urban dwellers is coming to an end, however. Concern for the genetic engineering of agricultural crops and the ecological impact of the destruction of the tropical forests, together with the struggles of indigenous people, like the Zapatistas who have risen up in arms to oppose land privatization, have created a new awareness about the importance of the "land question," not long ago still identified as a "Third World" issue.

There has also been a conceptual shift, in the last twenty years, concerning our understanding of the relation between land and capitalism. This shift has been promoted by the work of activist-scholars like Maria Mies (1986), Vandana Shiva (1989), Veronika Bennholdt-Thomsen, Nicholas Faraclas, and Claudia von Werlhof (2001), who have shown that land is the material basis for women's subsistence work, and the main source of "food security" for millions of people across the planet. Maria Mies also views this subsistence work as the paradigm of a new social perspective, providing a realistic alternative to capitalist globalization.

It is against this political and conceptual background that I examine the struggles that women are making worldwide to gain access to land, boost subsistence farming, and counter the expanding commercialization of natural resources. I argue that these efforts are extremely important. Thanks to them, billions of people are able to survive, and they point in the direction of the changes we have to make if we are to regain control over the means of production, and construct a society where our reproduction does not threaten the survival of other people, nor threatens the continuation of life on the planet.

Women and land: A historical perspective

It is an indisputable fact, though one difficult to measure, that women are the subsistence farmers of the planet. That is, women are responsible for and produce the bulk of the food that is consumed by their families (immediate or extended) or that is sold at the local markets for consumption. This is especially true in Africa, even though across the continent women's right to own land is often denied, and women's access to land, in some countries, is possible only through the intervention and mediation of male kins (Wanyeki 2003).[1]

Subsistence farming is difficult to measure because it is unwaged work; thus its status is similar to that of housework. Even the women who are subsistence farmers often do not consider it as work and, despite attempts to measure its significance in quantitative terms, we do not have reliable estimates concerning the number of hours or number of workers involved, and the value of their work.

International agencies like FAO (Food and Agriculture Association), the ILO (International Labor Organization), and the United Nations have generally overlooked the difficulties posed by the measurement of subsistence work. But they have recognized that much depends on the definition we use. Thus they have noted that:

> In Bangladesh, [the] labor force participation of women was 10 percent according to the Labor Force Survey of 1985/86. But when, in 1989, the Labor Force Survey included in the questionnaire specific activities such as threshing, food-processing and poultry-rearing the economic activity rate went up to 63 percent. (UN 1995: 114)[2]

It is not easy, then, on the basis of the few statistics available, to assess how many people, and in particular how many women are involved in subsistence farming; but clearly it is a substantial number. In the case of sub-Saharan Africa, according to FAO (2002), "women produce up to 80 percent of all the basic foodstuffs for household consumption and for sale." Given that the population of sub-Saharan Africa is about three-quarters of a billion people, with a large percentage of children, this means that more than a hundred million African women must be subsistence farmers.[3] Indeed, women hold up more than half the sky!

We should also recognize that the persistence of subsistence farming is an astounding phenomenon considering that capitalist development has been premised on the separation of agricultural producers, women above all, from the land. This reality can only be explained on the basis of a tremendous struggle women have made to resist the commercialization of agriculture.

Evidence for this struggle is found throughout the history of colonization, from the Andes to Africa. In response to land expropriation by the Spaniards (assisted by local chiefs), women in Mexico and Peru, in the 16th and 17th centuries, ran to the mountains, rallied the population to resist the foreign invaders, and became the staunchest defenders of the old cultures and religions, which were centered on the worship of nature-gods (Silverblatt 1987; Federici 2004). Later, in the nineteenth century, in Africa and Asia, women defended the traditional female farming systems against the systematic attempts made by the European colonialists to dismantle them and redefine agricultural work as a male job.

As Ester Boserup (among others) has shown, with reference to West Africa, not only did colonial officers, missionaries and, later, agricultural developers impose commercial crops at the expense of food production; though African women did most of the farming, they excluded women from the study of modern farming systems and denied them technical assistance. They also privileged men with regard to land assignment, even when the men were absent from their homes (Boserup 1970: 53–55, 59–60). Thus, in addition to eroding women's "traditional" rights, as participants in communal land-systems and independent cultivators, the colonialists and developers alike introduced new divisions between women and men. They imposed a new sexual division of labor, based upon women's subordination to men and their confinement to unpaid household labor, which, in the colonialists' schemes, included unpaid cooperation with their husbands in the cultivation of cash-crops.

Women, however, did not accept this deterioration in their social position without protest. In colonial Africa, whenever they feared that the government might sell their land or might appropriate their crops, they revolted. Exemplary is the protest that women mounted against the colonial authorities in Kedjom Keku and Kedjom Ketinguh, in Northwestern (then British) Cameroon, in 1958. Angered by rumors claiming that the government was going to put their land up for sale, 7,000 women repeatedly marched to Bamenda, the provincial capital at the time, and, in their longest stay, camped for two weeks outside the British colonial administrative buildings, "singing loudly and making their rumbustious presence felt" (Diduk 1989: 339–340).

In the same region, women fought against the destruction of their subsistence farms by foraging cattle owned by either members of the local male elite or the nomadic Fulani to whom the colonial authorities had granted seasonal pasturage rights expecting to collect a herd tax. In this case too, the women's boisterous protest defeated the plan, forcing the authorities to sanction the offending pasturalists. As Susan Diduk writes:

> In the protests women perceived themselves as fighting for the survival and subsistence needs of family and kin. Their agricultural labor was and continues to be indispensable to daily food production. Kedjom men also emphasise the importance of these roles in the past and present. Today they are frequently heard to say, "Don't women suffer for farming and for carrying children for nine months? Yes, they do good for the country." (Diduk 1989: 343)[4]

There were many similar struggles, in the 1940s and 1950s, throughout Africa, by women resisting the introduction of cash crops, to which the most fertile lands were being allocated, and the extra work it imposed on them, which took them away from their subsistence farming.

How productive women's subsistence farming continued to be, from the viewpoint of the survival of the colonized communities, can be seen from the contribution it made to the anti-colonial struggle and specifically to the maintenance of liberation fighters in the bush (e.g., in Algeria, Kenya, and Mozambique) (Davidson 1981: 76–78, 96–98, 170). Similarly, in the post-independence period, women fought against being recruited into agricultural development projects as unpaid "helpers" of their husbands. The best example of this resistance is the intense struggle women made in the Senegambia to refuse to cooperate in the commercial cultivation of rice crops, which came at the expense of their subsistence food production (Carney and Watts 1991).

It is because of these struggles—which are now recognized as the main reason for the failure of agricultural development projects through the 1960s and 1970s (Moser 1993)—that women continue to be the world's main subsistence farmers; and a sizable subsistence sector has survived in many regions of the world, despite the commitment of pre- and post-independence governments to promote "economic development" along capitalist lines. The determination of millions of women in Africa, Asia, and the Americas to not abandon subsistence farming must be emphasized to counter the tendency, present even among radical social scientists, to interpret the survival of subsistence work only as a consequence of international capital's need to cheapen the cost of the reproduction of labor and "liberate" male workers for the cultivation of cash crops and other form of waged labor.

Claude Meillassoux (1981), the main Marxist proponent of this theory, has argued that female subsistence-oriented production, or the "domestic economy," as he calls it, has ensured a supply of cheap workers for the capitalist sector at home and abroad and, as such, it has subsidized capitalist accumulation. As his argument goes, thanks to the work of the "village," the laborers who migrated to Paris or Johannesburg have provided a "free" commodity to the capitalist who hired them; since the employers did not have to pay for their upbringing nor had to continue to support them with unemployment benefits when their work was no longer needed.

From this perspective, women's labor in subsistence farming would be a bonus for governments, companies, and development agencies, enabling them to more effectively exploit waged workers and transfer wealth from the rural to the urban areas, in effect degrading the quality of the lives of female farmers and their communities (Meillassoux 1981: 110–111). To his credit, Meillassoux acknowledges the efforts made by international agencies and governments to "underdevelop" the subsistence sector. He sees the constant draining of its resources, and recognizes the precarious nature of this system of labor-reproduction, anticipating that it may soon undergo a decisive crisis.[5] But overall, he too has failed to recognize the struggle underpinning the survival of subsistence work and its continuing importance—despite the attacks waged upon it—from the viewpoint of the community's capacity to resist the encroachment of capitalist relations.

As for liberal economists—their view of "subsistence work" degrades it to the level of an "uneconomic," "unproductive" activity (in the same way as liberal economics refuses to see women's unpaid domestic labor in the home as work). As an alternative, liberal economists propose "income generating projects," the universal remedy to poverty in the neoliberal agenda,[6] and presumably the key to women's emancipation.

What these different perspectives ignore is the strategic importance that access to land and food production has had for women and their communities, despite the ability of companies and governments to use it at times for their own ends. An analogy can be made with the situation that developed during slavery in Jamaica, where the plantation owners gave the slaves small plots of land ("provision grounds") to cultivate for their own support. The owners took this measure to save on food imports and reduce the cost of reproducing their workers. But the slaves were able to take advantage of it, as it gave them more mobility and independence such that—according to some historians—even before emancipation, a proto-peasantry had formed in the island, possessing a remarkable freedom of movement, and already deriving some income from the sale of its own products (Bush 1990; Morrissey 1989).[7]

Extending this analogy to illustrate the post-colonial capitalist use of subsistence labor we can say that subsistence agriculture has been an important means of support for billions of workers, giving wage laborers the possibility to contract better conditions of work and survive labor strikes and political protests, so that in several countries the wage sector has acquired an importance disproportionate to its small numerical size (Federici 1992).[8]

The "village"—a metaphor for subsistence farming in a communal setting—has been a crucial site also for women's struggle, providing a base from which to reclaim the wealth the state and capital were removing from it. It is a struggle that has taken many forms, often being directed as much against men as against government, but always strengthened by the fact that women had access to land and could also support themselves and their children directly through the production of food and through the sale of their surplus product. Even after becoming urbanized, women have continued to cultivate any patch of land they could gain access to in order to feed their families and maintain a certain degree of autonomy from the market (Bryceson 1993: 105–117).

To what extent the village has been a source of power for female and male workers across the former colonial world can be measured by the attack that from the early 1980s through the 1990s the World Bank, the International Monetary Fund (IMF), and the World Trade Organization

(WTO) have waged against it under the guise of Structural Adjustment and "globalization."[9]

The World Bank has made the destruction of subsistence agriculture and the commercialization of land the centerpiece of its ubiquitous structural adjustment programs (Federici 1992; Caffentzis 1995; Faraclas 2001; Turner and Brownhill 2001). As a consequence, large tracts of communal land have been taken over by agribusiness and devoted to export crops, while "cheap" (i.e. subsidized) imported foods, from Europe and North America, have flooded the liberalized economies of Africa and Asia (which are forbidden to subsidize their farmers), further displacing women farmers from the local markets. War has completed the task, terrorizing millions into flight from their homelands (Federici 2000).

What has followed has been a *reproduction crisis* of proportions not seen even in the colonial period. Even in regions famous for their agricultural productivity, like southern Nigeria, food is now scarce or too expensive to be within reach of the average person who, after the implementation of structural adjustment programs, has to contend simultaneously with price hikes, frozen wages, devalued currency, widespread unemployment, and cuts in social services.[10]

This is where the importance of women's struggles for land stands out. Women have been the main buffer for the world proletariat against starvation imposed by the World Bank's neo-liberal regime. They have been the main opponents of the neo-liberal demand that "market prices" determine who should live and who should die, and they are the ones who have provided a practical model for the reproduction of life in a non-capitalist way.

Struggles for subsistence and against "Globalization" in Africa, Asia, and the Americas

Faced with a renewed drive toward land privatization, the extension of cash crops, and the rise in food prices due to economic adjustment and globalization, women have resorted to many strategies to continue to support their families, pitting them against the most powerful institutions on the planet.

One of the primary strategies women have adopted to defend their communities from the impact of economic adjustment and dependence on the global market has been the expansion of subsistence farming also in the urban centers.

Exemplary is the case of Guinea Bissau studied by Galli and Funk (1995) which shows that, since the early 1980s, women have planted small gardens with vegetables, cassava, and fruit trees around most houses in the capital city of Bissau and other towns; and in time of scarcity they have preferred to forfeit the earnings they might have made selling their produce to ensure their families would not go without food.[11] Still with reference to Africa, this picture is confirmed by Christa Wichterich who describes women subsistence farming and urban gardening as "cooking pot economics." She too notes that in the 1990s, it was revived in many Africa's cities; the urban farmers being mostly women from the lower class:

> There were onions and papaya trees, instead of flower-borders, in front of the housing estates of underpaid civil servants in Dar-es-Salaam; chickens and banana plants in the backyards of Lusaka; vegetables on the wide central reservations of the arterial roads of Kampala, and especially of Kinshasa, where the food supply system had largely collapsed . . . In [Kenyan] towns [too] . . . green roadside strips, front gardens and wasteland sites were immediately occupied with maize, plants, sukum wiki, the most popular type of cabbage. (Wichterich 2000: 73)

However, in order to expand food production women have had to battle to expand their access to land, which the international agencies' drives to privatize land and commercialize agriculture have further jeopardized.

This may be the reason why, in the case of Guinea Bissau, many women have chosen to remain in the rural area, while most of the men have migrated, with the result that there has been a "feminization of the rural areas, many villages now consisting of women farming alone or in women's coops" (Galli and Funk 1995: 23).

Regaining or expanding land for subsistence farming has been one of the main battles also for rural women in Bangladesh, leading to the formation of the Landless Women Association that has been carrying on land occupations since 1992. During this period, the Association has managed to settle 50,000 families, often confronting landowners in pitched confrontations. According to Shamsun Nahar Khan Doli, a leader of the Association to whom I owe this report, many occupations are on "chars," low-lying islands formed by soil deposits in the middle of a river.[12] Such new lands should be allocated to landless farmers, according to Bangladeshi law, but because of the growing commercial value of land, big landowners have increasingly seized them. Women are now organizing to stop them, defending themselves with brooms, spears of bamboo, and even knives. Women have also set up alarm systems to gather other women when boats with the landowners or their goons approach, and push the attackers off or stop them from landing.

Similar land struggles are being fought in South America. In Paraguay, for example, the Peasant Women's Commission (CMC) was formed in 1985 in alliance with the Paraguayan Peasant's Movement (MCP) to demand land distribution (Fisher 1993: 86). As Jo Fischer points out, the CMC was the first peasant women's movement that went into the streets in support of its demands, and incorporated in its program women's concerns, also condemning "their double oppression, both as peasants and as women" (Fisher 1993: 87).

The turning point for the CMC came when the government granted large tracts of land to the peasant movement in the forests close to the Brazilian border. The women took these grants as an opportunity to organize a model community joining together to collectively farm their strips of land. As Geraldina, an early founder of CMC pointed out:

> We work all the time, more now than ever before, but we've also changed the way we work. We're experimenting with communal work to see if it gives us more time for other things. It also gives us a chance to share our experiences and worries. This is a very different way of living for us. Before, we didn't even know our neighbors. (Fisher 1993: 98)

Women's land struggles have included the defense of communities threatened by commercial housing projects constructed in the name of "urban development." "Housing" has often involved the loss of "land" for food production historically. An example is the struggle of women in the Kawaala neighborhood of Kampala (Uganda) where the World Bank, in conjunction with the Kampala City Council (KCC), in 1992–1993, sponsored a large housing project that would destroy much subsistence farm land around or near people's homes. Not surprisingly, it was women who most strenuously organized against it, through the formation of an Abataka (Residents) Committee, eventually forcing the Bank to withdraw from the project. According to one of the women leaders:

> While men were shying away, women were able to say anything in public meetings in front of government officials. Women were more vocal because they were directly affected. It is very hard for women to stand without any means of income . . . . most of these women are people who basically support their children and without any income and food they cannot do it . . . You come and take their peace and income and they are going to fight, not because they want to, but because they have been oppressed and suppressed. (Tripp 2000: 183)

Aili Mari Tripp points out that the situation in the Kawaala neighborhood is far from unique.[13] Similar struggles have been reported from different parts of Africa and Asia, where peasant women's organizations have opposed the development of industrial zones threatening to displace them and their families and contaminate the environment.

Industrial or commercial housing development often clashes, today, with women's subsistence farming, in a context in which more and more women even in urban centers are gardening (in Kampala women grow 45 percent of the food for their families). It is important to add that in defending land from assault by commercial interests and affirming the principle that "land and life are not for sale," women again, as in the past against colonial invasion, are defending their peoples' history and their culture. In the case of Kawaala, the majority of residents on the disputed land had been living there for generations and had buried their kin there—for many in Uganda the ultimate evidence of land ownership. Tripp's reflections on this land struggle are pertinent to my thesis:

> Stepping back from the events of the conflict, it becomes evident that the residents, especially the women involved, were trying to institutionalize some new norms for community mobilization, not just in Kawaala but more widely in providing a model for other community projects. They had a vision of a more collaborative effort that took the needs of women, widows, children, and the elderly as a starting point and recognized their dependence on the land for survival. (Tripp 2000: 194)

Two more developments need to be mentioned in conjunction with women's defense of subsistence production. First, there has been the formation of regional systems of self-sufficiency aiming to guarantee "food security" and maintain an economy based on solidarity and the refusal of competition. The most impressive example in this respect comes from India where women formed the National Alliance for Women's Food Rights, a national movement made of thirty-five women's groups. One of the main efforts of the Alliance has been the campaign in defense of the mustard seed economy that is crucial for many rural and urban women in India. A subsistence crop, the seed has been threatened by the attempts of multinational corporations based in the United States to impose genetically engineered soybeans as a source of cooking oil.[14] In response, the Alliance has built "direct producer-consumer alliances" to "defend the livelihood of farmers and the diverse cultural choices of consumers," as stated by Vandana Shiva (2000), one of the leaders of the movement. In her words: "We protest soybean imports and call for a ban on the import of genetically-engineered soybean products. As the women from the slums of Delhi sing, 'Sarson Bachao, Soya Bhagaa,' or, 'Save the Mustard, Dump the Soya'" (Shiva 2000).

Second, across the world, women have been leading the struggle to prevent commercial logging and save or rebuild forests, which are the foundation of people's subsistence economies, providing nourishment as well as fuel, medicine, and communal relations. Forests, Shiva writes, echoing testimonies coming from every part of the planet, are "the highest expression of earth's fertility and productivity" (Shiva 1989: 56). Thus, when forests come under assault it is a death sentence for the tribal people who live in them, especially the woman. Therefore, women do everything to stop the loggers. Shiva often cites, in this context, the Chikpo movement—a movement of women, in Garhwal, in the foothills of the Himalaya who, beginning in the early 1970s, embrace the trees destined to fall and put their bodies between them and the saws when the loggers come (Shiva 1989).

While women in Garhwal have mobilized to prevent forests from being cut down, in villages of Northern Thailand they have protested the Eucalyptus plantation forcibly planted on their expropriated farms by a Japanese paper-making company with the support of the Thai military government (Matsui 1996: 88–90). In Africa, an important initiative has been the "Green Belt Movement," which under the leadership of Wangari Maathai is committed to planting a green belt around the major cities and, since 1977, has planted tens of millions of trees to prevent deforestation, soil loss, desertification, and fuel-wood scarcity (Maathai 1993).

But the most striking struggle for the survival of the forests is taking place in the Niger Delta, where the mangrove tree swamps are being threatened by oil production. Opposition to it has mounted for twenty years, beginning in Ogharefe, in 1984, when several thousand women from the area laid siege to Pan Ocean's Production Station demanding compensation for the destruction of the water, trees, and land. To show their determination, the women also threatened to disrobe should their demands be frustrated—a threat they put in action when the company's director arrived, so that he found himself surrounded by thousands of women naked, a serious curse in the eyes of the Niger Delta communities, which convinced him at the time to accept the reparation claims (Turner and Oshare 1994: 140–141).

The struggle over land has also grown since the 1970s in the most unlikely place—New York City—in the form of an urban gardening movement. It began with the initiative of a women-led group called the "Green Guerrillas," who began cleaning up vacant lots in the Lower East Side. By the 1990s, eight hundred and fifty urban gardens had developed in the city and dozens of community coalitions had formed, such as the Greening of Harlem Coalition that was begun by a group of women who wanted "to reconnect with the earth and give children an alternative to the streets." Now it counts more than twenty-one organizations and thirty garden projects (Wilson and Weinberg 1999: 36).

It is important to note here that the gardens have been not only a source of vegetables and flowers, but have served community-building and have been a stepping stone for other community struggles (like squatting and homesteading). Because of this work, the women came under attack during Mayor Giuliani's regime, and for some years now one of the main challenges this movement has faced has been stopping the bulldozers. Over last decade, a hundred gardens have been lost to "development," more than forty have been slated for bulldozing, and the prospects for the future seem gloomy (Wilson and Weinberg 1999: 61). Since his appointment, in fact, the mayor of New York City, Michael Bloomberg, like his predecessor, has declared war on these gardens.

The importance of the struggle

As we have seen, in cities across the world at least a quarter of the people depend on food produced by women's subsistence labor. In Africa, for example, a quarter of the people living in towns say they could not survive without subsistence food production. This is confirmed by the UN Population Fund, which claims that "some two hundred million city dwellers are growing food, providing about one billion people with at least part of their food supply" (UN 2001). When we consider that the bulk of the food subsistence producers are women we can see why the men of Kedjom, Cameroon would say, "Yes, women subsistence farmers do good for humanity." Thanks to them, the billions of people, rural and urban, who earn one or two dollars a day do not go under, even in time of economic crisis.

Equally important, women's subsistence production counters the trend by agribusiness to reduce cropland—one of the causes of high food prices and starvation—while ensuring control over the quality of food and protecting consumers against manipulation of crops and poisoning by pesticides. Further, women subsistence production represents a safe way of farming, a crucial consideration at a time when the effects of pesticides on agricultural crops is causing high rates of mortality and disease among peasants across the world, starting with women (see, for example, Settimi et al. 1999). Thus, subsistence farming gives women an essential means of control over their health and the health and lives of their families (Bennholdt-Thomsen and Mies 1999).

Most important, we can also see that subsistence production is contributing to a noncompetitive, solidarity-centered mode of life that is crucial for the building of a new society. It is the seed of what Veronika Bennholdt-Thomsen and Maria Mies call the "other" economy which "puts life and everything necessary to produce and maintain life on this planet at the center of economic and social activity and not the never-ending accumulation of dead money" (Bennholdt-Thomsen and Mies 1999: 5).

Notes

1 A detailed description of the land tenure system and women's property rights in seven African countries—Cameroon, Ethiopia, Mozambique, Nigeria, Rwanda, Senegal, Uganda is found in *Women and Land in Africa* (2003) by Muthoni L.Wanyeki. The author found that in general women control food crop production (in some countries like Uganda up to 90%) and control the benefits resulting from the sale of surplus crops. However, their right to own and inherit land is generally limited or denied especially in patrilineal cultures. African women have access to land according to customary laws, but they have

users' rights through their relations with men, through marriage or inheritance. In Latin America as well women's land ownership rights have been extremely restricted, by means of "legal, cultural, and institutional" mechanisms rooted in a patriarchal ideology and patriarchal division of labor. On this subject see Deere and Léon (2001) 2–3.

2   In 1988, the International Labor Organization (ILO) defined subsistence workers in agriculture and fishing as those who "provide food, shelter and a minimum of cash income for themselves and their households" (UN 1995: 114)—a fuzzy definition depending on which notion of "minimum cash income" and "provision" one uses. Moreover, its operative meaning is derived from intentions, for example, the subsistence workers' lack of "market orientation," and deficiencies they experience, such as having no access to formal credit and advanced technology.

3   The social and economic impact of colonialism varied greatly, depending (in part) on the duration of direct colonial control. We may even interpret the present differences in women's participation in subsistence and cash-crop agriculture as a measure of the extent of colonial appropriation of land. Using the UN-ILO labor force participation statistics, and remembering the measurement problem concerning subsistence farming, we see that sub-Saharan Africa has the highest percentage of the female labor force in agriculture (75 percent); while in Southern Asia it is 55 percent; South-East Asia, 42 percent; and East Asia, 35 percent. By contrast, South and Central America have low women's participation rates in agriculture similar to those found in "developed" regions like Europe between 7 and 10 percent. That is, the participation rates roughly correlate with the duration of formal colonialism in the regions.

4   On the struggles of women farmers in Western Cameroon in the 1950s, see also Margaret Snyder and Mary Tadesse who write: "Women continued to persist in their economic activities during colonial times, despite the formidable odds they faced. One example is the way they mobilized to form corn mill societies in western Cameroon in the 1950s. Over time 200 such societies were formed with a total membership of 18,000. They used grinding mills that were owned in common, fenced their fields, and constructed water storage units and co-operative stores . . . In other words, 'for generations women established some form of collective actions to increase group productivity, to fill-in socio-economic gaps wherever the colonial administration failed, or to protest policies that deprived them of the resources to provide for their families' " (Snyder and Tadesse 1995: 23).

5   The crisis consists in the fact that if the domestic economy becomes too unproductive, it then fails to reproduce the immigrant worker, but if it becomes too productive, it drives up the costs of labor, as the worker in this case can avoid wage labor.

6   Exemplary here is Caroline Moser, a "World Bank feminist" who executes a very sophisticated analysis of the work of women and whose approach to women is, in her terms, "emancipatory." After presenting a careful analysis of the many theoretical approaches to women's labor (Marxist included), the case studies she examines are two "income generating" projects and a "food for work" scheme (Moser 1993: 235–238).

7 However, as soon as the price of sugar on the world market went up, the plantation owner cut the time allotted to the slave for cultivation of their provision grounds.

8 See, for example, what Michael Chege (1987: 250) writes of African wage workers and the land: ". . . most African laborers maintain a foothold in the country side; the existence of labor totally alienated from land ownership is yet to happen." One of the consequences of this "lack of alienation" is that the African worker can rely on a material basis of solidarity (especially the provision of food) from the village whenever s/he decides to strike.

9 The attack waged by the World Bank through Structural Adjustment falsifies Meillassoux's claim that the domestic economy is functional to capitalism, but verifies his prediction that a "final" crisis of capitalism looms because of its inability to preserve and control the domestic economy (Meillassoux 1981: 141).

10 Witness the dramatic decline in the "real wage" and the increase in the rate of poverty in Nigeria. Once considered a "middle income" country, Nigeria now has 70 percent of its population living on less than one US dollar a day, and 90 percent on less than two US dollars a day (cf., UN Development Program statistics from its website).

11 In Bissau, women planted rice during the rainy season in plots on the peripheries of town. During the dry season more enterprising women try to get access to nearby plots in order to plant irrigated vegetables not only for domestic consumption but for sale (Galli and Funk 1995: 20).

12 This report is based on an oral testimony at the Prague "Countersummit" of 2000.

13 Tripp concludes that ". . . the Kawaala struggle is in many ways a microcosm of some of the changes that are occurring in Uganda" (Tripp 2000: 194). Similar struggles have been waged throughout the Third World, where peasant women's organizations have opposed the development of industrial zones threatening to displace them and their families and contaminate the environment.

14 This attempt was given a boost in 1998 when the mustard seed cooking oil locally produced and distributed was mysteriously found to be adulterated to such a point that 41 people died after consuming it. The government then banned its production and sale. The National Alliance responded by taking the case to court and calling on producers and consumers not to cooperate with the government's ban (Shiva 2000: 54).

Bibliography

Benjamin, Medea, ed. *Don't be Afraid Gringo: A Honduran Woman Speaks from the Heart: The Story of Elvia Alvarado*. New York: Harper Perennial, 1987.

Bennholdt-Thomsen, Veronika, Nicholas Faraclas, and Claudia von Werlhof, eds. *There is an Alternative: Subsistence and Worldwide Resistance to Corporate Globalization*. London: Zed, 2001.

Bennholdt-Thomsen, Veronika, Nicholas Faraclas, and Maria Mies. *The Subsistence Perspective: Beyond the Globalised Economy*. London: Zed, 1999.

Boserup, Ester. *Women's Role in Economic Development*. London: George Allen and Unwin Ltd, 1970.

Bryceson, Deborah Fahy. *Liberalizing Tanzania's Food Trade. Private and Public Faces of Urban Marketing Policy. 1930–1988*. London: Zed Books, 1993.

Bush, Barbara. *Slave Women in Caribbean Society, 1650–1838*. Bloomington, IN: Indiana University Press, 1990.

Caffentzis, George. "The Fundamental Implications of the Debt Crisis for Social Reproduction in Africa." In *Paying the Price: Women and the Politics of International Economic Strategy*, ed. M. Dalla Costa and G. F. Dalla Costa. London: Zed Books, 1995.

Carney, Judith and Watts, Michael. "Disciplining Women? Rice, Mechanization, and the Evolution of Mandinka Gender Relations in Senegambia." *Signs* 16(4) 1991: 651–681.

Chege, Michael. "The State and Labor in Kenya." In *Popular Struggles for Democracy in Africa*, ed. Peter Anyang' Nyong'o. London: Zed Books, 1987.

Davidson, Basil. *The People's Cause: A History of Guerillas in Africa*. London: Longman, 1981.

Deere, Carmen Diana and Magdalena Léon. *Empowering Women. Land and Property Rights in Latin America*. Pittsburg, PA: University of Pittsburg, 2001.

Diduk, Susan. "Women's Agricultural Production and Political Action in the Cameroon Grassfields." *Africa* 59(3) 1989: 338–355.

FAO. 2002. *Gender and Agriculture*. Retrieved March 18, 2002. http://www.fao.org/Gender/agrib4-e.htm

Faraclas, Nicholas. "Melanesia, the Banks, and the BINGOs: Real Alternatives Are Everywhere (Except in the Consultants' Briefcases)." In *There is an Alternative: Subsistence and Worldwide Resistance to Corporate Globalization*, ed. Veronika Bennholdt-Thomsen, Nicholas Faraclas, and Claudia von Werlhof. London: Zed, 2001.

Federici, Silvia. "The Debt Crisis, Africa, and the New Enclosures." In *Midnight Oil: Work, Energy, War, 1973–1992*, ed. Midnight Notes. New York: Autonomedia, 1992.

— "Reproduction and Feminist Struggle in the New International Division of Labor." In *Women, Development and Labor of Reproduction. Struggles and Movements*, ed. M. Dalla Costa and G. F. Dalla Costa. Trenton, NJ: Africa World Press, 1999.

— *Caliban and the Witch: Women, the Body, and Primitive Accumulation*. Brooklyn, NY: Autonomedia, 2004.

Fisher, Jo. *Out of the Shadows: Women, Resistance and Politics in South America*. London: Latin American Bureau, 1993.

Galli, Rosemary and Ursula Frank. "Structural Adjustment and Gender in Guinea Bissau." In *Women Pay the Price: Structural Adjustment in Africa and the Caribbean*, ed. Gloria T. Emeagwali. NJ: Africa World Press, 1995.

Maathai, Wangari. "Kenya's Green Belt Movement." In *Africa, Fifth Edition*, ed. F. Jeffress Ramsay. Guilford, CT: The Dushkin Publishing Group, 1993.

Matsui, Yayori. *Women in the New Asia: From Pain to Power*. London: Zed Books, 1996.

Meillassoux, Claude. *Maidens, Meal and Money: Capitalism and the Domestic Community*. Cambridge, MA: Cambridge University Press, 1981.

Mies, Maria. *Patriarchy and Accumulation on a World Scale: Women in the International Division of Labor.* London: Zed Books, 1986.

Mies, Maria and Vandana Shiva. *Ecofeminism.* London: Zed, 1996.

Morrisey, Marietta. *Slave Women in the New World.* Lawrence, KS: University Press of Kansas, 1989.

Moser, Caroline O. N. *Gender Planning and Development: Theory, Practice and Training.* London: Routledge, 1993.

Scott, James C. *Weapons of the Weak: Everyday Forms of Peasant Resistance.* New Haven, CT: Yale University Press, 1985.

Settimi, L. et al. "Cancer Risk among Female Agricultural Workers: A Multi-Center Case-Control Study." *American Journal of Industrial Medicine* 36 (1989): 135–141.

Shiva, Vandana. *Staying Alive: Women, Ecology and Development.* London: Zed Books, 1989.

— *Stolen Harvest: Hijacking of the Global Food Supply.* Boston, MA: South End Press, 2000.

Silverblatt, Irene. *Moon, Sun, and Witches: Gender Ideologies and Class in Inca and Colonial Peru.* Princeton, NJ: Princeton University Press, 1987. Print.

Tripp, Aili Mari. *Women and Politics in Uganda.* Oxford: James Currey, 2000.

Turner, Terisa E. and Leigh S. Brownhill, eds. *Gender, Feminism and the Civil Commons. A Special Issue of Canadian Journal of Development Studies.* Volume XXII (2001).

— "African Jubilee: Mau Mau Resurgence and the Fight for Fertility in Kenya, 1986–2001." In *Gender, Feminism and the Civil Commons. A Special Issue of Canadian Journal of Development Studies Volume XXII* (2001b), ed. Terisa E. Turner and Leigh S. Brownhill.

Turner, Terisa E. and M. O. Oshare. "Women's Uprisings against the Nigerian Oil Industry." In *Arise! Ye Mighty People!: Gender, Class and Race in Popular Struggles,* ed. Terisa Turner. Trenton, NJ: Africa World Press, 1994.

United Nations. *The World's Women 1995: Trends and Statistics.* New York: United Nations, 1995.

United Nations Population Fund. *State of the World Population 2001.* New York: United Nations, 2001.

Wanyeki, Muthoni L. *Women and Land in Africa. Culture, Religion and Realizing Women's Rights.* London: Zed Books, 2003.

Wichterich, Christa. *The Globalized Woman: Reports from a Future of Inequality.* London: Zed, 2000.

Wilson, Peter Lamborn and Bill Weinberg. *Avantgardening. Ecological Struggles in the City and the World.* New York: Autonomedia, 1999.

CHAPTER SEVEN

The Idea of a "Chinese Model"

Arif Dirlik

From International Critical Thought 1 (2) (August 2011): 129–137.

I would like to take up in this discussion some questions thrown up by the idea of a "Chinese model." The term itself has appeared with increasing frequency over the last decade among both Chinese scholars and foreign observers of the People's Republic of China (PRC). Against the continued economic difficulties faced by the United States, Europe and Japan, the seeming success of the PRC in weathering the world recession since 2008 has enhanced the significance of the "model."

There is a suggestion in the term of a model that is not only superior to the reigning neoliberal orthodoxy, promoted most enthusiastically by the United States and United Kingdom, but also, given the remarkably rapid development of the PRC over the last three decades, to the development path pioneered by Euro/American societies since the origins of capitalist modernization in the eighteenth century.[1] Yet, what this model consists of, and how it may be translated into different social and political contexts remains quite vague.

Three questions are of particular interest in this discussion. First, what significance do we attribute to the idea of a "model" in the contemporary world, especially with respect to the deployment of the idea of model within a Chinese political discourse? Secondly, what might be the features of a so-called Chinese model? And, finally, in what sense might this "model" be appealing to others, especially over the neoliberal model of a market economy theoretically unfettered by social and political intervention but also in its own right, as a socialist path of development?

Global modernity and the Chinese model

The idea of a "Chinese model" may refer to a model of development that is peculiar to China, appropriate to the particular circumstances of Chinese society. Or it may be understood in more universalistic terms, as a model open to emulation by others, in which case its relevance transcends the boundaries of Chinese society.

The distinction is an important one, even if it is ignored in most references to the "Chinese model." If the model is a product of the particular circumstances of Chinese society, the implication is that it may not be emulated by others, or may be emulated only with adjustment to different circumstances and needs. This is indeed the way the Chinese experience as an example for others has been understood in Chinese political discourse going back to the 1940s. Within Marxism and the history of socialist revolutions, the Chinese Revolution was the first (if not the only) one to insist on the necessity of articulating the universalist discourse of theory to concrete local circumstances, as is clearly implied by principles encapsulated in such phrases as "making Marxism Chinese" (*Makesi Zhuyi de Zhongguohua*), "Chinese style socialism" (*Zhongguo Shi de Shehuizhuyi*), or, most recently, "socialism with Chinese characteristics" (*you Zhongguo Tese de Shehuizhuyi*). The strategy of revolution or development expressed by these phrases distinguished the Chinese path not only from capitalist societies but also from other socialisms, most importantly that of the Soviet Union while it existed. There has been a sense all along that the experience of the Chinese Revolution was relevant to all societies placed similarly to China in global politics, so-called semi-feudal and semi-colonial societies, which in an earlier day made China a part of both the second and the third worlds. But throughout, the Chinese experience provided not a path to be followed but an example of articulating the universal to the particular, or translating the global to the local, which called upon others to find their own paths by following a similar procedure. This idea of a revolutionary practice that necessarily integrated universal principles with concrete local circumstances distinguished the path of revolution not only from one national context to another but also applied to different localities within the same nation. The "vernacularization" of Marxism has been one of the significant contributions of the Chinese Revolution to Marxist theory. Despite significant transformations over the years, it has characterized Chinese Marxism throughout, in Maoist as well as post-Maoist Marxism. This attitude toward the Chinese Revolution has been extended in Chinese Marxism to revolutions and development elsewhere.[2]

This distinction between a universal model and a model that is derivative of local circumstances is more important than ever under the regime of global modernity, characterized by an insistence on national or local particularity within the context of a globalized capitalism. We have witnessed over the last two decades a proliferation of calls for "alternative modernities" even as the globalization of capitalism has restricted, if not abolished, spaces within which to imagine and construct such alternatives. One important consequence has been a simultaneous proliferation of "models." There are no longer just two or three models as in the days of the Cold War, but an increasing number of them. We encounter daily references to the "Iranian model," the "Turkish model," the "Indonesian model," and many others, as changing circumstances around the world call attention to one or another example of development deemed relevant by various constituencies.

It is possible that the "Chinese model" was responsible at least in part for the stress on particular modernities, and it continues to inspire faith in the possibility of alternatives. It is more difficult to judge its significance. It may be suggested that there were always significant differences between societies, and that no two capitalisms or socialisms are entirely alike. The difference between the present and the past may lie not in the novelty of difference but in a heightened consciousness of and will to difference. The Cold War no doubt disguised the many differences of the day by subordinating them to a binary or tripartite division of the world. So did the hegemonic discourse of modernization, capitalist or socialist, with its own binarisms of progressive and traditional, or advanced and backward. The globalization of modernity ironically has brought to the surface a consciousness of difference that also has set off a search for different paths of development, especially in those societies empowered by success in the global economy. And there seems to be no shortage of models for development, even if they do not command equal degrees of attention. Still, if there is a Chinese model, it is one of many.

In light of these considerations, would it make more sense to speak of a "Chinese paradigm" (*Moshi* or *Fanshi*) rather than a "Chinese model" (*Mofan*, *Moshi*), which would shift attention from an example to be emulated to an example that provides not only inspiration but also procedural principles, central to which is attentiveness to the possibilities and limitations of concrete local circumstances as well as location in the world? This is not only consistent with the legacies of the Chinese Revolution and socialist thinking, but responds more closely to the ideological tendencies of global modernity. It would also avoid the ambiguities of the idea of a "Chinese model," with its implications of an established pattern, that hardly does justice to what may be but a work in progress, a subject itself of experimentation.

Is there a "Chinese model"?

The question I would like to raise here is whether the idea of a "Chinese model" is based on a substantial set of norms and practices, or derives its meaning primarily from its contrasts with liberalism or neoliberalism, much as the similar idea of a "Beijing consensus" (*Beijing Gongshi*) acquired a hearing some years back for its supposed contrasts to the "Washington consensus."[3] If that is indeed the case, secondly, do we need a further specification of its goals, and whether or not those goals pertain simply to issues of economic development, or include social and political goals as well? After all, simply being different from neoliberalism does not tell us much about whether or not the "model" points toward socialism, or other, possibly more conservative goals as another variant of authoritarian developmentalism, associated in the late 1980s with so-called new authoritarianism (*Xin Quanwei Zhuyi*).

This latter idea, traceable to the inspiration of Samuel P. Huntington's 1969 publication, *Political Order in Changing Societies*, was associated early on with the developmental paths followed most effectively by a number of Eastern Asian societies, namely, Japan, South Korea, Taiwan, Singapore, and Hong Kong under British colonial rule.[4] Following World War II, especially from the 1960s, these regimes achieved rapid development under a combination of political authoritarianism (or dictatorship) and sub-contractual economic development, beginning with the creation of export zones, that would serve as the pioneering moments in the emergence of "a new international division of labor," neoliberal assaults on national economic boundaries and, ultimately, what has come to be known as globalization. In the traditionalism which underwrote their authoritarianism, these regimes also pointed to the cultural resurgences that would come with globalization, challenging the Eurocentric assumptions of an earlier modernization discourse. The result was also the stripping down of modernity to its technologies, which served different social, political and cultural trajectories, with success dependent on historical circumstances, with cultural legacies allegedly playing a crucial role.[5] It was the developmental success of Eastern Asian societies that empowered the Confucian revival of the 1980s that since then has served as an explanation of their success.[6]

The so-called Chinese model may be considered one more variant of authoritarian development that in its origins owed much to these societies both for inspiration and for triggering its take-off. Contemporary discussions display a remarkable "forgetfulness" concerning the part that the Japanese, South Korean, Taiwanese, but especially the Singaporean "models" played in inspiring policy in the initial phase of "reform and opening" (*gaige kaifang*) in the 1980s and through the 1990s. But their significance goes beyond the inspiration they provided. The flourishing economies of Eastern Asia provided a context for the development of the PRC in which they played a strategically crucial part. It may be no exaggeration to say that investments and technological input from these societies, as well as from overseas Chinese in Southeast Asia were responsible for bringing the Chinese economy to its take-off stage. This context is also one of the particularities of Chinese development that call into question its emulation by others.

There are two important historical differences, nevertheless, that distinguish China's development from that of these neighboring neo-authoritarian regimes, which also receive little attention these days, especially among commentators outside of China. The PRC when it launched its modernization program after 1978 was the product of one of the most important revolutions of the century, heralding the reemergence of the colonial, "semi-colonial and feudal" worlds through movements for national liberation. In this case, it was a national liberation movement imbued with socialist goals. The liberation of the nation was to be grounded in a social and cultural revolution. It may be noted that other societies of the region also went through social transformations of one kind or another as a condition of development, from the reconstitution of Japanese society after World War II to land reform in Taiwan to anti-colonial movements in Singapore, Korea, and Hong Kong. Unlike in these societies where the transformations created new social hierarchies consistent with developments within the capitalist system, the Chinese Revolution sought a social and cultural transformation toward the creation of a socialist society that stressed egalitarianism, giving a voice to the people, and the creation of a new culture consistent with these goals. Another very significant difference was also the goal and a by-product of the revolution: autonomous and self-reliant development. Transformations in the rest of the societies of the region were accomplished under the aegis of imperial powers, most importantly after World War II the United States. In the case of the PRC, avoiding foreign domination of the economy (capitalist or socialist) was a fundamental premise and goal of the revolution.

What is remarkable about discussions of the "Chinese model" idea is the obliviousness to this historical trajectory that makes China unique and, therefore, difficult if not impossible to emulate. China as we know it today is a product of this revolution, which unfortunately is often beclouded by the claims to continuity with a so-called 5,000 years of tradition of a resurgent traditionalism that covers over the revolution (which, I understand, is described in the new Museum of History in Beijing to a "period of rejuvenation"). More often than not, that same revolution has been rendered into a "negative example" for its failures, which were real but only part of the story. Deploying the revolution as a foil against which to claim legitimacy for the present has covered over its legacies to the present, both positive and negative. Thus it is hardly mentioned that during the revolutionary years before 1978 the Chinese economy developed rapidly, registering annual growth rates that match the much touted rates of the post-1978 period (Prime 1989). While occasions of ill-considered enthusiasm had disastrous consequences for the people, and self-reliant development required extraction of all surplus from the people, especially in rural areas, there was nevertheless ongoing improvement in people's lives from education and health care to increases in life-expectancy (Bramall 1993). The social transformation that the revolution sought may have been less than perfect, but it came with an organizational transformation that unified and integrated the country, laying the infrastructure that would serve well after 1978. These changes also created a new culture of politics and work, the significance of which for later development is yet to be analyzed. On the other hand, while the organizational achievements of the revolution lay the foundation for subsequent development, they also stand in the way of further changes necessitated by development in a new direction.[7]

There is also a tendency to downplay the national liberation aspects of the struggle, more its economic and cultural than its political aspects. China's economic "globalization" is now extended back over time, erasing the problematic relationship with the outside world that marked the last two centuries. Culture has been nationalized, but now it is continuity with the past that is stressed rather than the dialectical discontinuity called for by the revolution. Political colonialism is remembered in the stress on past "national humiliation," but it is accompanied also by its erasure, as for instance in the literature on the Shanghai Expo which by-passed the humiliations China had suffered in early twentieth-century fairs.[8]

The point here is not that these things should be remembered to foster continued suspicion and hostility, but because they are important to assessing the meaning of "the Chinese model" beyond its reductionist economistic understanding. Divorced from the legacies of the revolution, the "Chinese model" becomes one more version of authoritarian development, seeking ideological and cultural compliance with the demands of development as a participant in the global capitalist economy, without any concerns beyond success in this economy. This is how it is widely perceived in China, and by admirers of Chinese development abroad. To cite one recent convert from neoliberalism to the "Chinese model" by Francis Fukuyama (2011):

> The most important strength of the Chinese political system is its ability to make large, complex decisions quickly, and to make them relatively well, at least in economic policy. This is most evident in the area of infrastructure, where China has put into place airports, dams, high-speed rail, water and electricity systems to feed its growing industrial base. Contrast this with India, where every new investment is subject to blockage by trade unions, lobby groups, peasant associations and courts. India is a law-governed democracy, in which ordinary people can object to government plans; China's rulers can move more than a million people out of the Three Gorges Dam flood plain with little recourse on their part.

Nonetheless, the quality of Chinese government is higher than in Russia, Iran, or the other authoritarian regimes with which it is often lumped—precisely because Chinese rulers feel some degree of accountability towards their population. That accountability is not, of course, procedural; the authority of the Chinese Communist party is limited neither by a rule of law nor by democratic elections. But while its leaders limit public criticism, they do try to stay on top of popular discontents, and shift policy in response.

Fukuyama's observations may be exemplary of most discussions of the "China model." What makes it work is its deficit of democracy. Authoritarianism makes possible the rapid and efficient mobilization of resources not possible in a democratic society, exemplified by India, another so-called developing economy. The Party-state may be repressive in other ways, but it is a force for innovation and efficiency economically. It is also superior to other authoritarian regimes because it relatively responsive to crisis and the population. In neither case is there any reference to the organizational and cultural legacies of the revolution—whether with regard to repressiveness or responsiveness. There is no hint either that legacies of the revolution, however weakened, may still be powerful ideological forces in shaping both people's demands and leaders' responses. Little noticed also is the continued anxiety about self-reliance and autonomy in the midst of participation in a neoliberal global capitalist economy of which China has become an integral part. The model appears as just a more efficient authoritarianism of uncertain origin. And it is more common than not these days to find the explanation in the pre-revolutionary past, most importantly Confucianism of both state and people. In the end, what remains of a "Chinese model" open to emulation by others are authoritarianism, organizational efficiency, and innovativeness. What is glossed over are the social goals that continue to be an important constituent of the model, or the paradigm, as I suggest.

The appeals of the model

Among the competing "models" of a post-Eurocentric global modernity, the Chinese model receives the greatest attention because of the enormous economic achievements of the last two decades, especially since the 2008 recession which seems to have caused relatively little damage to advances in the Chinese economy. It is also the one that is tacitly or explicitly contrasted with the US economy in its resonance with the "Beijing consensus" idea set against the neoliberal "Washington consensus." There is some sense that as the Chinese economy overtakes its rivals, the model, too, may achieve global hegemony. Authoritarianism is integral to the model, whether or not it is always recognized as such. A recent discussion observes that:

> . . . today's emerging markets are increasingly drawn to a new and compelling doctrine of state-managed capitalism. They are learning to combine market economics with traditional autocratic or semiautocratic politics in a process that signals an intellectual rejection of the Western economic model. According to this doctrine, the government maintains control over a partly liberalized economy and the people accept a very non-Western kind of civic bargain: political oppression in the public square in return for relative economic freedom and a rising quality of life. Both of these trends have a powerful cheerleader in Beijing. (Harper 2010: 3)

How convincing are such views? The assessment cited above that the Chinese model is superior not only to contemporary alternatives but even to the economies that initiated global economic modernization is to be approached critically because of its obliviousness to historical circumstances, as well to problems that await solution that are the products of development. Judging by railroads and automobiles, China is a society on the move, which contrasts sharply with stagnation elsewhere. But the problems are equally impressive. I am referring here to commonly recognized problems, such as the unprecedented social and spatial inequalities resulting from development over the last three decades, reversing the achievements of the revolution, enormous ecological problems that threaten further development, corruption, social instability arising from these problems, and a deficit of democracy, however conceived, that is the other face of authoritarianism along with issues of free speech and legal due process. Above all, however, is the question of the direction of development, which is another crucial aspect of the notion of an "alternative." China's developmental success has been achieved within the parameters set by existing models of development, most importantly in the United States, with a heavy emphasis on urbanization, the provision of consumer goods internally and externally, and a corresponding concentration of resources. While it is widely recognized that such a model of development may not be any more sustainable in China than in the United States, so far the corrections to it seem to have been mostly of a cosmetic nature. The destruction of the countryside and the depletion of natural resources continue apace. So do reliance on real estate speculation and automobile manufacturing to keep the engine of growth in motion.[9] These are problems readily acknowledged by the leadership, and yet there is no plausible "alternative" in sight.

It seems premature to speak of a "Chinese model" until these problems have been resolved, let alone a model as a socialist society. It also seems that those abroad who are most taken with the "Chinese model" are those who place economic and technological development ahead of all other social and political concerns, admirers of authoritarianism seeking escape from the problems of democratic societies, or, simply groupies of China cultivated by Confucian institutes who seem to perceive China as a mélange of an exotic but suddenly accessible culture and much needed commercial opportunities for the future.[10] The success of the PRC in alleviating poverty is a powerful source of attraction. So is the seeming vitality of Chinese society, which disguises that it suffers from the same problems that afflict liberal corporate economies, especially problems of deep inequality, cultural disorientation, and ecology. China's problems are not exceptional. Currently available "models" all suffer from more or less similar problems which diminish their claims to serve as models for others. This is part of the crisis of our times. I think it is fair to say in the case of China that however satisfying it may be from a nationalistic perspective, little of the admiration is fostered by hopes in movement toward socialist goals of social justice, equality, and democratic practices based on those ideals. The "Chinese model" in its success or as competitor can even be put to use in some advanced societies such as the United States as an excuse for curtailing democracy and redirecting education toward corporate goals.[11]

There is also a perception, that of a minority unfortunately, that if it is indeed possible to speak of a "Chinese model," it is as a model in the process of formation, a work in progress with a still uncertain future. It is quite obvious that even the leadership in China is deeply divided over solutions to these problems, which are crucial to the formulation of development strategies. As is evident once again from the most recent National People's Congress, and the new five-year plan, resolving the social challenges of development remains a priority. Whether or not these concerns in the long run overcome the fetishism of development, and redirect it toward socialist ends, remains an open question. Even if socialist policies are rejuvenated, moreover, questions will persist concerning their implementation over obstacles presented by conflicting economic and political interests. It is also important to remember that as times have changed, so has the understanding of socialism as necessarily people-based rather than state-centered. The Chinese Revolution of the twentieth century played an important part in placing some of these questions on the political agenda of Marxism and socialism. Whether or not they remain on the development agenda will have important consequences for the future.

The "Chinese model" and Marxism

I would like to conclude with a brief glance at Marxism in light of questions concerning the "Chinese model." While the legacies of revolution and socialism are quite important in my opinion for understanding the forces that continue to shape Chinese society and politics, it would be intellectually self-deceptive to ignore, as noted above, that what most commentators in and out of China find attractive about contemporary China is not "socialism" but "capitalism with Chinese characteristics," made possible by repudiating the revolutionary socialism of the past. While the leadership has made an effort to rejuvenate Marxism through the "Marxism project" (*Makesi Zhuyi Gongcheng*), sponsored by President Hu Jintao, Marxism is no more a concern for the population at large in China than it is elsewhere. It is impossible, in other words, to ignore a widely shared impression of disconnect between ideology, theory and practice.

This situation raises serious questions not just about the course of China's development but Marxism as well. The discussion above has focused on the first question, the question of China's development, which I have suggested remains structurally and historically under-theorized. But what does the same situation say about Marxism? Are the theoretical premises of Marxism sufficient to grasp a historical situation that in its social and cultural proclivities and needs is significantly different from those which gave rise to the theory in the first place? If the theory could be modified sufficiently to account for these new challenges and still retain its theoretical identity, what political solutions would it offer, if any, given that the theoretical analysis and political practice are necessarily mediated by ideological orientations and cultural desires that do not permit a straightforward translation of theory into politics? What are the limits placed on Marxist theoretical premises and propositions by changes in state–society relations due to economic globalization, transformations in social relations that arise from changes in gender and ethnic relations, as well as people's movements, transnationalization of class relations and cultural practices, cultural fragmentation under global modernity, and ecological constraints on development? Marxism, while it has been critical of economic organization under capitalism, nevertheless has shared in the developmental goals of capitalism as a condition of socialism. Does a thoroughgoing critique of capitalism at the present, when we have a far more comprehensive understanding of the consequences of unbridled development, require also a critique of the fetishization of development—developmentalism—in order to imagine a substantial alternative to capitalism that also recognizes the social and ecological limits to development? What would be the social and political configuration appropriate to an economic organization that gives priority to human welfare and survival? Finally, Marxism has assumed national form in the past in response to the demands of national revolutionary politics. Does globalization require that it return to the internationalist goals and transnational practices that initially informed the theory, and mark the practices presently of global social movements? If Marxism is to retain its credibility and relevance not simply as theoretical discourse but also as meaningful political practice, these questions call for urgent confrontation.

Notes

1   Karon (2011) for a discussion by the conservative scholar, Francis Fukuyama. See, also, Huang (2011), discussing the annual Yellow Paper released by CASS.
2   For an extensive discussion, see Dirlik (2005).
3   The terms are in a basic sense interchangeable. For example, see Yu, Keping, Huang Ping, Xie Shuguang, and Gao Jian (2005).
4   See Huntington (1968). For a sampling of discussions in China in the late 1980s, see Rosen and Zou (1990–1991).
5   See Berger and Huntington (2002). We might remember that Berger's was a major voice authorizing the Confucian revival beginning in the late 1970s, and Huntington played a leading intellectual role over four decades as an advocate of authoritarian development as well as of cultural (civilizational) "uniqueness" and homogeneity in shaping developmental trajectories. A prominent Chinese scholar who advocates similar ideas is He Chuanqi. See China Development Gateway (2009).
6   For a critical discussion see Dirlik (2011).
7   The historical circumstances of the last three decades of development include, according to a recent piece, the leadership of Deng Xiaoping, the role of Chinese overseas, and China's location in Eastern Asia, a region of immense economic vitality for the last half century. See Etienne (2011). While the discussion is brief, the stress on concrete structural circumstances is fundamental to discussions that rely on generalities about culture and innovation. On the other hand, the author is also oblivious to historical context, possibly out of an expressed hostility to the revolutionary past.
8   For "national humiliation," see Callahan (2010). For world's fairs, see, for an example of Fairs histories published in connection with the Shanghai Expo, Yu (2009). For a more critical perspective on the Fairs, see Rydell (1984).
9   For an interesting discussion of the new automobile culture, see Waldmeir, Patti, John Reed, and Shirley Chen (2011). For the crisis brewing in real estate development (or, better, maldevelopment), see the recent report by the Daily Mail Reporter (2011).
10 See, for example, Bell (2008). For a recent discussion of the Confucius institutes, see Louie (2011).
11 For a recent analysis that suggests that authoritarianism may be a source of appeal of the "Chinese model," especially in developing societies, see Palmer (2010).

Bibliography

Bell, Daniel A. *China's New Confucianism: Politics and Everyday Life in a Changing society*. Princeton, NJ: Princeton University Press, 2008.

Berger, Peter L. and Huntington P. Samuel. *Many Globalizations: Cultural Diversity in the Contemporary World*. Oxford: Oxford University Press, 2002.

Bramall, Chris. *In Praise of Maoist Economic Planning: Living Standards and Economic Development in Sichuan since 1931*. New York: Oxford University Press, 1993.

Callahan, William A. *The Pessoptimist Nation*. New York: Oxford University Press, 2010.

China Development Gateway. *China Modernization Report 2009: The Study of Cultural Modernization*, 2009. http://en.chinagate.cn/dateorder/2009-02/24/content_17327414.htm.

Dirlik, Arif. "Mao Zedong and 'Chinese Marxism'." In *Marxism in the Chinese revolution*, ed. Arif Dirlik, 75–104. Boulder, CO: Rowman and Littlefield, 2005.

— "Confucius in the Borderlands: Global Capitalism and the Reinvention of Confucianism." In *Culture and Society in Postrevolutionary China: The Perspective of Global Modernity: The Liang Qichao Memorial Lectures*, ed. Arif Dirlik, 97–156. Hong Kong: Chinese University Press, 2011.

Etienne, Gilbert. "Exploding the Myth of the 'Beijing Consensus.'" *Business Standard*, March 19, 2011. http://www.business-standard.com/india/news/gilbert-etienne-explodingmyththe-beijing-consensus/429110/.

Fukuyama, Francis. "Democracy in America has Less than Ever to Teach China." January 20, 2011. http://www.ftchinese.com/story/001036584/en/?print=y.

"The Ghost Towns of China: Amazing Satellite Images Show Cities Meant to be Home to Millions Lying Deserted." *Mailonline*, December 18, 2002. http://www.dailymail.co.uk/news/article-1339536/Ghost-towns-China-Satellite-images-cities-lying-completely-deserted.html.

Huang Jingjing. "China's Success Attributed to Socialism Model." *Global Times*, March 2, 2011. http://china.globaltimes.cn/chinanews/2011-03/628936.html.

Huntington, Samuel P. *Political Order in Changing Societies*. New Haven: Yale University Press, 1968.

Karon, Tony. "Why China does Capitalism Better than the U.S." *Time*, January 20, 2011. www.time.com/time/world/article/0,8599,2043235,00.html.

Louie, Kam. "Confucius the Chameleon: Dubious Envoy for 'Brand China.'" *Boundary 2* 38(1) (2011): 77–100.

Palmer, Stefan. *The Beijing Consensus: How China's Authoritarian Model will Dominate the Twenty-First Century*. New York: Basic Books, 2010.

Prime, Penelope B. "Socialism and Economic Development: The Politics of Accumulation in China." In *Marxism and the Chinese Experience: Issues in Contemporary Chinese Socialism*, ed. Dirlik Arif and Meisner Maurice, 136–151. Armonk, NY: ME Sharpe, 1989.

Rosen, Stanley, and Gary Zou, eds. "The Chinese Debate on the New Authoritarianism." *Chinese Sociology and Anthropology* 23(2) (1990–1991).

Rydell, Robert W. *All the World's a Fair: Visions of Empire at American International Expositions, 1876–1916*. Chicago, IL: University of Chicago Press, 1984.

Waldmeir, Patti, John Reed, and Shirley Chen. "The Dragon Wagon: A New Paradigm." *gufnews.com*, March 27, 2011. http://gulfnews.com/business/features/the-dragon-wagon-a-new-paradigm-1.783247.

Yu Keping, Huang Ping, Xie Shuguang, and Gao Jian, eds. *Zhongguo moshi yu "Beijing gongshi": chaoyue 'huashengdun gongshi'* [*China model and the Beijing consensus: Beyond the Washington consensus*]. Beijing: Social Sciences Publishing Press, 2005.

Yu Li, ed. *Lishide huimou: Zhongguo canjia shibohuide gushi, 1851–2008* [*History staring back: The story of China's participation in world expos, 1851–2008*]. Shanghai: Dongfang chuban zhongxin, 2009.

PART TWO

Shapes of the Social

Introduction

One of the most significant contributions Marxism has made to social, cultural, and political theory has been the materialist theory of social forms. Thinkers across the political spectrum now accept the fact that the character and nature of economic systems give shape to the social, even if they don't always follow through with the full implications of what this suggests for how we think and map social life. As productive systems have changed and societies have become more variegated and complex, new theories examining the contemporary shape of the social have had to be developed. The essays in this section explore the interconnections between class, social hierarchies, gender, race, and ethnicity in the in the context of new economic and social configurations, developing different ways of understanding the relationships of categories of identity to the social formation of capitalism, to capitalist production, and to the horizon of the emancipation from capital.

In "Is there a 'Neo-Racism'?" Étienne Balibar addresses the contemporary upsurge of racist movements and policies, and asks if the phenomenon is "a *new* racism, irreducible to earlier 'models'," or "a mere tactical adaptation?" He insists on the importance of inquiry into the function of the theory-building of academic racism (which finds its prototype in the evolutionist anthropology of "biological" races), and argues that this function does not reside either in the organizing capacity of intellectual rationalizations or in the image of community or original identity. "It resides, rather, in the fact that the theories of academic racism mimic scientific discursivity by basing themselves upon visible 'evidence' (whence the essential importance of the stigmata of race and in particular of bodily stigmata), or, more exactly, they mimic the way in which scientific discursivity articulates 'visible facts' to 'hidden causes' and thus connect up with a spontaneous process of theorization inherent in the racism of the masses."

Observing the tendency of racist discourse to ape and mimic the discursive patterns of scientific observation, explanation and theorization, Balibar contends that "the racist complex inextricably combines a crucial function of *misrecognition* (without which the violence would not be tolerable to the very people engaging in it) and a 'will to know', a violent *desire* for immediate *knowledge of* social relations." The key to comprehending neo-racism is the substitution of immigration for race in racist discourse, a substitution which is not simply a camouflaging, but fits rather within a framework of "racism without races." What emerges is "a racism whose dominant theme is not biological heredity but the insurmountability of cultural differences, a racism which, at first sight, does not postulate the superiority of certain groups or peoples in relation to others but 'only' the harmfulness of abolishing frontiers, the incompatibility of life-styles and traditions." The prototype of this racism without races is modern anti-Semitism, which emerges as an already "culturalist" and "differentialist" phenomenon, and carries with it the demand for assimilation in order to attain even a precarious integration.

In "Marx after Marxism," Dipesh Chakrabarty sets out a subaltern's perspective on history, subalterneity and difference. Acknowledging that "to be a Marxist is to work within European traditions of thought anyway," he develops his argument from and proceeds in the light of his observation that "Marx places the question of subjectivity right at the heart of his category 'capital' when he posits the conflict between 'real labor' and 'abstract labor' as one of its central contradictions." The central question is whether Marx's categories efface or enable the recognition or even illumination of that which they necessarily cannot enclose. "In other words, are there ways of engaging with the problem of 'universality' of capital that do not commit us to a bloodless liberal pluralism that only subsumes all difference(s) within the Same?"

Chakrabarty acknowledges that much in Marx is "truly 19th-century, gender-blind and obviously Eurocentric," and sees the contemporary relevance of Marxism not only in the fact that the problem of Indian modernity cannot be separated from the question of European imperialism, but also in the potential to make Marx's categories "speak to what we have learnt from the philosophers of 'difference' about 'responsibility' to the plurality of the world." He identifies within Marx's account of the commodity a "built-in openness to 'difference'," the gap between abstract labor and real labor, that which both inheres within the commodity but cannot be enclosed by the commodity as sign, and argues that unconcealing this tension is central to the practice of subaltern history of taking "history to its limits in order to make its unworking visible."

Maya Gonzales and Jeanne Neton's account of "The Logic of Gender" is a rethinking of Marxist feminism that seeks "to understand why humanity is still powerfully inscribed with one or the other gender." They chart the systematic dialectic of gender, which is understood as a "real abstraction" that consists in the assignment of individuals to separate spheres, which are defined not as separate and distinct spaces, but rather "as *concepts* that take on a materiality." In doing so they rethink and reinvigorate the "imprecise, theoretically deficient and sometimes even misleading" categories with which gender tends to be understood—the binaries of productive and reproductive, paid and unpaid, public and private, sex and gender—with the aim of developing "categories that are as specific to capitalism as 'capital' itself."

Central to their analysis is the frequent conflation of the concepts of the reproduction of the commodity of labor power, and the reproduction of the social totality. The key to the relationship between the two is the peculiar commodity of labor power, which is "neither a person nor *just* a commodity"—at the heart of which lies the distinction between use value and (exchange) value. Understanding the reproduction of gender relies on differentiating "reproduction that is commodified, monetised, or mass produced from that which is not." Unwaged activities are "*the non-social of the social*: they are not socially validated but are nonetheless part of the capitalist mode of production," and the ascription of individuals to this sphere is carried out by means of the juridical categories of men and women. Opposing the glorification of women's self-organization of activities that are not directly mediated by the market, Gonzales and Neton see this fate of being compelled to deal with the abject as a lens through which gender is revealed as a powerful constraint.

In "Class Struggle or Postmodernism? Yes, please!" Slavoj Žižek considers a different manifestation of the binary distinction between public and private: the relationship between democracy and its other—not only its political other of various forms of alternatives to democracy, but "primarily that which the very definition of political democracy tends to exclude as 'non-political' (private life and economy in classical liberalism, etc.)." While accepting that the act of drawing such a distinction is "a political gesture *par excellence*," he inverts the argument by asking "what if the political gesture *par excellence*, at its purest, is precisely the gesture of separating the Political from the non-Political, of excluding some domains from the Political?"

Endorsing Butler's understanding of the reflexivity of desire (and of the connection between the reflexivity of psychoanalysis and that of German idealism) and Laclau's "notion of *antagonism* as fundamentally different from the logic of symbolic/structural difference," Žižek reconsiders the relationship between universality and exclusion and its consequences for the relationship between class struggle and identity politics. He identifies a resistance against any act that fundamentally alters the political terrain, a liberal-democratic resistance which he finds shared across a wide spectrum including Derrida, Habermas, Rorty and Dennett, and suggests that today's task might be to break with these shared presuppositions.

Central to Théorie Communiste's "Communisation in the Present Tense" is the distinction of communization from socialization, a mode of managing the economy predicated on a change in ownership of the material means of production. Communization, in contrast, consists in the immediate establishment of a human community directly constituted by immediately social individuals (the establishment, that is, of communism), and is characterized by the fact that it contains no distinction between the seizure of the means of subsistence (in the broadest sense) and this transformation of proletarians into immediately social individuals. Communization is thus not the establishment of the rule of the proletariat, but the immediate abolition of classes (including of the proletariat).

Communization thus implies the negation rather than the affirmation of the working class, which implies the rejection both of proletarian identity and of an orientation toward workers' autonomy: "To abolish capital is at the same time to negate oneself as a worker and not to self-organize as such." The very existence of the proletariat, its definition in relation to and distinction from capital, is thus the limit of its own action. It follows that communization is not a transition; communist measures "are not embryos of communism, but rather they are its production." The horizon of communization can only ever be a present of the direct production of communism.

In "Patriarchy and Commodity Society," Roswitha Scholz foregrounds the centrality of gender to the development of capitalism to develop a Marxist-Feminist theoretical framework that can account both for developments since the end of actually existing socialism and for the current economic crisis. Her point of departure is the insistence that the object of critique should not be the expropriation of surplus value and the resulting inequality or relationship of exploitation, but rather the "social character of the commodity-producing system and thus . . . the form of activity particular to abstract labor."

Scholz finds at the heart of this system "a core of female-determined reproductive activities" that are "dissociated from value and abstract labor."

Capitalism, then, reveals itself as structurally and constitutively gendered as male, a gendering that effaces itself in its emergence. This gendering, and the dissociation from value of the activities of the reproduction of humanity, is not a consequence of capitalism, but rather a necessary precondition of value production. It thus becomes necessary to speak of the emergence of a commodity-producing patriarchy that determines the historical development of modernity and postmodernity. Indeed, the universalization of gender relations under the principle of value dissociation as part of the development of the capitalist value form is revealed as an instrumental aspect of the rise of modernity.

CHAPTER EIGHT

Is there a Neo-Racism?

Étienne Balibar

From Race, Nation, Class: Ambiguous Identities. *London: Verso,*
1991: 17–28.

To what extent is it correct to speak of a neo-racism? The question is forced upon us by current events in forms which differ to some degree from one country to another, but which suggest the existence of a transnational phenomenon. The question may, however, be understood in two senses. On the one hand, are we seeing a new historical upsurge of racist movements and policies which might be explained by a crisis conjuncture or by other causes? On the other hand, in its themes and its social significance, is what we are seeing only a *new* racism, irreducible to earlier "models," or is it a mere tactical adaptation? I shall concern myself here primarily with this second aspect of the question.[1]

First of all, we have to make the following observation. The neo-racism hypothesis, at least so far as France is concerned, has been formulated essentially on the basis of an internal critique of theories, of discourses tending to legitimate policies of exclusion in terms of anthropology or the philosophy of history. Little has been done on finding the connection between the newness of the doctrines and the novelty of the political situations and social transformations which have given them a purchase. I shall argue in a moment that the theoretical dimension of racism today, as in the past, is historically essential, but that it is neither autonomous nor primary. Racism—a true "total social phenomenon"—inscribes itself in practices (forms of violence, contempt, intolerance, humiliation and exploitation), in discourses and representations which are so many intellectual elaborations of the phantasm of prophylaxis or segregation (the need to purify the social body, to preserve "one's own" or "our" identity from all forms of mixing, interbreeding or invasion) and which are articulated around stigmata of otherness (name, skin color, religious practices). It therefore organizes affects (the psychological study of these has concentrated upon describing their obsessive character and also their "irrational" ambivalence) by conferring upon them a stereotyped form, as regards both their "objects" and their "subjects." It is this combination of practices, discourses and representations in a network of affective stereotypes which enables us to give an account of the formation of a racist community (or a community of racists, among whom there exist bonds of "imitation" over a distance) and also of the way in which, as a mirror image, individuals and collectivities that are prey to racism (its "objects") find themselves constrained to see themselves as a community.

But however absolute that constraint may be, it obviously can never be cancelled out as constraint *for its victims*: it can neither be interiorized without conflict (see the works of Memmi) nor can it remove the contradiction which sees an identity as community ascribed to collectivities which are simultaneously denied the right to define themselves (see the writings of Frantz Fanon), nor, most importantly, can it reduce the permanent excess of actual violence and acts over discourses, theories and rationalizations. From the point of view of its victims, there is, then, an essential dissymmetry within the racist complex, which confers upon its acts and "actings out" undeniable primacy over its doctrines, naturally including within the category of actions not only physical violence and discrimination, but words themselves, the violence of words in so far as they are acts of contempt and aggression. Which leads us, in a first phase, to regard shifts in doctrine and language as relatively incidental matters: should we attach so much importance to justifications which continue to retain the same structure (that of a denial of rights) while moving from the language of religion into that of science, or from the language of biology into the discourses of culture or history, when in practice these justifications simply lead to the same old acts?

This is a fair point, even a vitally important one, but it does not solve all the problems. For the destruction of the racist complex presupposes not only the revolt of its victims, but the transformation of the racists themselves and, consequently, *the internal decomposition of the community created by racism*. In this respect, the situation is entirely analogous, as has often been said over the last twenty years or so, with that of sexism, the overcoming of which presupposes both the revolt of women and the break-up of the community of "males." Now, racist theories are indispensable in the formation of the racist community. There is in fact no racism without theory (or theories). It would be quite futile to inquire whether racist theories have emanated chiefly from the elites or the masses, from the dominant or the dominated classes. It is, however, quite clear that they are "rationalized" by intellectuals. And it is of the utmost importance that we enquire into the function fulfilled by the theory-building of academic racism (the prototype of which is the evolutionist anthropology of "biological" races developed at the end of the nineteenth century) in the crystallization of the community which forms around the signifier, "race."

This function does not, it seems to me, reside solely in the general organizing capacity of intellectual rationalizations (what Gramsci called their "organicity" and Auguste Comte their "spiritual power") nor in the fact that the theories of academic racism elaborate an image of community, of original identity in which individuals of all social classes may recognize themselves. It resides, rather, in the fact that the theories of academic racism mimic scientific discursivity by basing themselves upon visible "evidence" (whence the essential importance of the stigmata of race and in particular of bodily stigmata), or, more exactly, they mimic the way in which scientific discursivity articulates "visible facts" to "hidden causes" and thus connect up with a spontaneous process of theorization inherent in the racism of the masses.[2] I shall therefore venture the idea that the racist complex inextricably combines a crucial function of misrecognition (without which the violence would not be tolerable to the very people engaging in it) and a "will to know," a violent desire for immediate knowledge of social relations. These are functions which are mutually sustaining since, both for individuals and for social groups, their own collective violence is a distressing enigma and they require an urgent explanation for it. This indeed is what makes the intellectual posture of the ideologues of racism so singular, however sophisticated their theories may seem. Unlike for example theologians, who must maintain a distance (though not an absolute break, unless they lapse into "gnosticism") between esoteric speculation and a doctrine designed for popular consumption, historically effective racist ideologues have always developed "democratic" doctrines which are immediately intelligible to the masses and apparently suited from the outset to their supposed low level of intelligence, even when elaborating elitist themes. In other words, they have produced doctrines capable of providing immediate interpretative keys not only to what individuals are experiencing but to what they are in the social world (in this respect, they have affinities with astrology, characterology and so on), even when these keys take the form of the revelation of a "secret" of the human condition (that is, when they include a secrecy effect essential to their imaginary efficacity: this is a point which has been well illustrated by Leon Poliakov).[3]

This is also, we must note, what makes it difficult to *criticize* the content and, most importantly, the influence of academic racism. In the very construction of its theories, there lies the presupposition that the "knowledge" sought and desired by the masses is an elementary knowledge which simply justifies them in their spontaneous feelings or brings them back to the truth of their instincts. Bebel, as is well known, called anti-Semitism the "socialism of fools" and Nietzsche regarded it more or less as the politics of the feeble-minded (though this in no way prevented him from taking over a large part of racial mythology himself). Can we ourselves, when we characterize racist doctrines as strictly demagogic theoretical elaborations, whose efficacity derives from the advance response they provide for the masses' desire for knowledge, escape this same ambiguous position? The category of the "masses" (or the "popular") is not itself neutral, but communicates directly with the logic of a naturalization and racization of the social. To begin to dispel this ambiguity, it is no doubt insufficient merely to examine the way the racist "myth" gains its hold upon the masses; we also have to ask why other sociological theories, developed within the framework of a division between "intellectual" and "manual" activities (in the broad sense), are unable to fuse so easily with this desire to know. Racist myths (the "Aryan myth," the myth of heredity) are myths not only by virtue of their pseudo-scientific content, but in so far as they are forms of imaginary transcendence of the gulf separating intellectuality from the masses, forms indissociable from that implicit fatalism which imprisons the masses in an allegedly natural infantilism.

We can now turn our attention to "neo-racism." What seems to pose a problem here is not the *fact* of racism, as I have already pointed out—practice being a fairly sure criterion (if we do not allow ourselves to be deceived by the denials of racism which we meet among large sections of the political class in particular, which only thereby betrays the complacency and blindness of that group)—but determining to what extent the relative novelty of the language is expressing a *new* and lasting articulation of social practices and collective representations, academic doctrines and political movements. In short, to use Gramscian language, we have to determine whether something like a hegemony is developing here.

The functioning of the category of *immigration* as a substitute for the notion of race and a solvent of "class consciousness" provides us with a first clue. Quite clearly, we are not simply dealing with a camouflaging operation, made necessary by the disrepute into which the term "race" and its derivatives has fallen, nor solely with a consequence of the trans formations of French society. Collectivities of immigrant workers have for many years suffered discrimination and xenophobic violence in which racist stereotyping has played an essential role. The interwar period, another crisis era, saw the unleashing of campaigns in France against "foreigners," Jewish or otherwise, campaigns which extended beyond the activities of the fascist movements and which found their logical culmination in the Vichy regime's contribution to the Hitlerian enterprise. Why did we not at that period see the "sociological" signifier definitively replace the "biological" one as the key representation of hatred and fear of the other? Apart from the force of strictly French traditions of anthropological myth, this was probably due, on the one hand, to the institutional and ideological break which then existed between the perception of immigration (essentially European) and colonial experience (on the one side, France "was being invaded," on the other it "was dominant") and, on the other hand, because of the absence of a new model of articulation between states, peoples and cultures on a world scale.[4] The two reasons are indeed linked, the new racism is a racism of the era of "decolonization," of the reversal of population movements between the old colonies and the old metropolises, and the division of humanity within a single political space. Ideologically, current racism, which in France centers upon the immigration complex, fits into a framework of "racism without races" which is already widely developed in other countries, particularly the Anglo-Saxon ones. It is a racism whose dominant theme is not biological heredity but the insurmountability of cultural differences, a racism which, at first sight, does not postulate the superiority of certain groups or peoples in relation to others but "only" the harmfulness of abolishing frontiers, the incompatibility of life-styles and traditions; in short, it is what P. A. Taguieff has rightly called a *differentialist racism*.[5]

To emphasize the importance of the question, we must first of all bring out the political consequences of this change. The first is a destabilization of the defences of traditional anti-racism in so far as its argumentation finds itself attacked from the rear, if not indeed turned against itself (what Taguieff excellently terms the "*turn-about effect*" of differentialist racism). It is granted from the outset that races do not constitute isolable biological units and that in reality there are no "human races." It may also be admitted that the behavior of individuals and their "aptitudes" cannot be explained in terms of their blood or even their genes, but are the result of their belonging to historical "cultures." Now anthropological culturalism, which is entirely orientated toward the recognition of the diversity and equality of cultures—with only the polyphonic ensemble constituting human civilization—and also their transhistorical *permanence*, had provided the humanist and cosmopolitan anti-racism of the post-war period with most of its arguments. Its value had been confirmed by the contribution it made to the struggle against the hegemony of certain standardizing imperialisms and against the elimination of minority or dominated civilizations— "ethnocide." Differentialist racism takes this argumentation at its word. One of the great figures in anthropology, Claude Lévi-Strauss, who not so long ago distinguished himself by demonstrating that all civilizations are equally complex and necessary for the progression of human thought, now in "Race and Culture" finds himself enrolled, whether he likes it or not, in the service of the idea that the "mixing of cultures" and the suppression of "cultural distances" would correspond to the intellectual death of humanity and would perhaps even endanger the control mechanisms that ensure its biological survival.[6] And this "demonstration" is immediately related to the "spontaneous" tendency of human groups (in practice national groups, though the anthropological significance of the political category of nation is obviously rather dubious) to preserve their traditions, and thus their identity. What we see here is that biological or genetic naturalism is not the only means of naturalizing human behavior and social affinities. At the cost of abandoning the hierarchical model (though the abandonment is more apparent than real, as we shall see), *culture can also function like a nature*, and it can in particular function as a way of locking individuals and groups a priori into a genealogy, into a determination that is immutable and intangible in origin.

But this first turn-about effect gives rise to a second, which turns matters about even more and is, for that, all the more effective: if insurmountable cultural difference is our true "natural milieu," the atmosphere indispensable to us if we are to breathe the air of history, then the abolition of that difference will necessarily give rise to defensive reactions, "interethnic" conflicts and a general rise in aggressiveness. Such reactions, we are told, are "natural," but they are also dangerous. By an astonishing volte-face, we here see the differentialist doctrines themselves proposing to *explain racism* (and to ward it off).

In fact, what we see is a general displacement of the problematic. We now move from the theory of races or the struggle between the races in human history, whether based on biological or psychological principles, to a theory of "race relations" within society, *which naturalizes not racial belonging but racist conduct*. From the logical point of view, differentialist racism is a meta-racism, or what we might call a "second position" racism, which presents itself as having drawn the lessons from the conflict between racism and anti-racism, as a politically operational theory of the causes of social aggression. If you want to avoid racism, you have to avoid that "abstract" anti-racism which fails to grasp the psychological and sociological laws of human population movements; you have to respect the "tolerance thresholds," maintain "cultural distances" or, in other words, in accordance with the postulate that individuals are the exclusive heirs and bearers of a single culture, segregate collectivities (the best barrier in this regard still being national frontiers). And here we leave the realm of speculation to enter directly upon political terrain and the interpretation of everyday experience. Naturally, "abstract" is not an epistemological category, but a value judgment which is the more eagerly applied when the practices to which it corresponds are the more concrete or effective: programs of urban renewal, anti-discrimination struggles, including even positive discrimination in schooling and jobs (what the American New Right calls "reverse discrimination"; in France too we are more and more often hearing "reasonable" figures who have no connection with any extremist movements explaining that "it is anti-racism which creates racism" by its agitation and its manner of "provoking" the mass of the citizenry's national sentiments).[7]

It is not by chance that the theories of differentialist racism (which from now on will tend to present itself as the *true anti-racism* and therefore the true humanism) here connect easily with "crowd psychology," which is enjoying something of a revival, as a general explanation of irrational movements, aggression and collective violence, and, particularly, of xenophobia. We can see here the double game mentioned above operating fully: the masses are presented with an explanation of their own "spontaneity" and at the same time they are implicitly disparaged as a "primitive" crowd. The neo-racist ideologues are not mystical heredity theorists, but "realist" technicians of social psychology . . .

In presenting the turn-about effects of neo-racism in this way, I am doubtless simplifying its genesis and the complexity of its internal variations, but I want to bring out what is strategically at stake in its development. Ideally one would wish to elaborate further on certain aspects and add certain correctives, but these can only be sketched out rudimentarily in what follows.

The idea of a "racism without race" is not as revolutionary as one might imagine. Without going into the fluctuations in the meaning of the word "race," whose historiosophical usage in fact predates any reinscription of "genealogy" into "genetics," we must take on board a number of major historical facts, however troublesome these may be (for a certain anti-racist vulgate, and also for the turn-abouts forced upon it by neo-racism).

A racism which does not have the pseudo-biological concept of race as its main driving force has always existed, and it has existed at exactly this level of secondary theoretical elaborations. Its prototype is anti-Semitism. Modern anti-Semitism—the form which begins to crystallize in the Europe of the Enlightenment, if not indeed from the period in which the Spain of the *Reconquista* and the Inquisition gave a statist, nationalistic inflexion to theological anti-Judaism—is already a "culturalist" racism. Admittedly, bodily stigmata play a great role in its phantasmatics, but they do so more as signs of a deep psychology, as signs of a spiritual inheritance rather than a biological heredity.[8] These signs are, so to speak, the more revealing for being the less visible and the Jew is more "truly" a Jew the more indiscernible he is. His essence is that of a cultural tradition, a ferment of moral disintegration. Anti-Semitism is supremely "differentialist" and in many respects the whole of current differentialist racism may be considered, from the formal point of view, *as a generalized anti-Semitism*. This consideration is particularly important for the interpretation of contemporary Arabophobia, especially in France, since it carries with it an image of Islam as a "conception of the world" which is incompatible with Europeanness and an enterprise of universal ideological domination, and therefore a systematic confusion of "Arabness" and "Islamicism."

This leads us to direct our attention toward a historical fact that is even more difficult to admit and yet crucial, taking into consideration the

French national form of racist traditions. There is, no doubt, a specifically French branch of the doctrines of Aryanism, anthropometry and biological geneticism, but the true "French ideology" is not to be found in these: it lies rather in the idea that the culture of the "land of the Rights of Man" has been entrusted with a universal mission to educate the human race. There corresponds to this mission a practice of assimilating dominated populations and a consequent need to differentiate and rank individuals or groups in terms of their greater or lesser aptitude for—or resistance to—assimilation. It was this simultaneously subtle and crushing form of exclusion/inclusion, which was deployed in the process of colonization and the strictly French (or "democratic") variant of the "White man's burden." I return in later chapters to the "paradoxes of universalism and particularism in the functioning of racist ideologies or in the racist aspects of the functioning of ideologies."[9]

Conversely, it is not difficult to see that, in neo-racist doctrines, the suppression of the theme of hierarchy is more apparent than real. In fact, the idea of hierarchy, which these theorists may actually go so far as loudly to denounce as absurd, is reconstituted, on the one hand, in the practical application of the doctrine (it does not therefore need to be stated explicitly), and, on the other, in the very type of criteria applied in thinking the difference between cultures (and one can again see the logical resources of the "second position" of meta-racism in action).

Prophylactic action against racial mixing in fact occurs in places where the established culture is that of the state, the dominant classes and, at least officially, the "national" masses, whose style of life and thinking is legitimated by the system of institutions; it therefore functions as an undirectional block on expression and social advancement. No theoretical discourse on the dignity of all cultures will really compensate for the fact that, for a "Black" in Britain or a "*Beur*" in France, the assimilation demanded of them before they can become "integrated" into the society in which they already live (and which will always be suspected of being superficial, imperfect or simulated) is presented as progress, as an emancipation, a conceding of rights. And behind this situation lie barely reworked variants of the idea that the historical cultures of humanity can be divided into two main groups, the one assumed to be universalistic and progressive, the other supposed irremediably particularistic and primitive. It is not by chance that we encounter a paradox here: a "logically coherent" differential racism would be uniformly conservative, arguing for the fixity of *all* cultures. It is in fact conservative, since, on the pretext of protecting European culture and the European way of life from "Third Worldization," it utopianly closes off any path toward real development. But it immediately reintroduces the old distinction between "closed" and "open," "static" and "enterprising," "cold" and "hot," "gregarious" and "individualistic" societies—a distinction which, in its turn, brings into play all the ambiguity of the notion of culture (this is particularly the case in French!).

The difference between cultures, considered as separate entities or separate symbolic structures (that is, "culture" in the sense of *Kultur*), refers on to cultural inequality within the "European" space itself or, more precisely, to "culture" (in the sense of *Bildung*, with its distinction between the academic and the popular, technical knowledge and folklore and so on) as a structure of inequalities tendentially reproduced in an industrialized, formally educated society that is increasingly internationalized and open to the world. The "different" cultures are those which constitute obstacles, or which are established as obstacles (by schools or the norms of international communication) to the acquisition of culture. And, conversely, the "cultural handicaps" of the dominated classes are presented as practical equivalents of alien status, or as ways of life particularly exposed to the destructive effects of mixing (that is, to the effects of the material conditions in which this "mixing" occurs).[10] This latent presence of the hierarchic theme today finds its chief expression in the priority accorded to the individualistic model (just as, in the previous period, openly inegalitarian racism, in order to postulate an essential fixity of racial types, had to presuppose a differentialist anthropology, whether based on genetics or on *Völkerpsychologie*): the cultures supposed implicitly superior are those which appreciate and promote "individual" enterprise, social and political individualism, as against those which inhibit these things. These are said to be the cultures whose "spirit of community" is constituted by individualism.

In this way, we see how the *return of the biological theme* is permitted and with it the elaboration of new variants of the biological "myth" within the framework of a cultural racism. There are, as we know, different national situations where these matters are concerned. The ethological and sociobiological theoretical models (which are themselves in part competitors) are more influential in the Anglo-Saxon countries, where they continue the traditions of Social Darwinism and eugenics while directly coinciding at points with the political objectives of an aggressive neo-liberalism.[11] Even these tendentially biologistic ideologies, however, depend fundamentally upon the "differentialist revolution." What they aim to explain is not the constitution of races, but the vital importance of cultural closures and traditions for the accumulation of individual aptitudes, and, most importantly, the "natural" bases of xenophobia and social aggression. Aggression is a fictive essence which is invoked by all forms of neo-racism, and which makes it possible in this instance to displace biologism one degree: there are of course no "races," there are only populations and cultures, but there are biological (and biophysical) causes and effects of culture, and biological reactions to cultural difference (which could he said to constitute something like the indelible trace of the "animality" of man, still bound as ever to his extended "family" and his "territory"). Conversely, where pure culturalism seems dominant (as in France), we are seeing a progressive drift toward the elaboration of discourses on biology and on culture as the external regulation of "living organisms," their reproduction, performance and health. Michel Foucault, among others, foresaw this.[12]

It may well be that the current variants of neo-racism are merely a transitional ideological formation, which is destined to develop toward discourses and social technologies in which the aspect of the historical recounting of genealogical myths (the play of substitutions between race, people, culture and nation) will give way, to a greater or lesser degree, to the aspect of psychological assessment of intellectual aptitudes and dispositions to "normal" social life (or, conversely, to criminality and deviance), and to "optimal" reproduction (as much from the affective as the sanitary or eugenic point of view), aptitudes and dispositions which a battery of cognitive, sociopsychological and statistical sciences would then undertake to measure, select and monitor, striking a balance between "hereditary and environmental factors." In other words, that ideological formation would develop toward a "post-racism," I am all the more inclined to believe this since the internationalization of social relations and of population movements within the framework of a system of nation–states will increasingly lead to a rethinking of the notion of frontier and to a redistributing of its modes of application; this will accord it a function of social prophylaxis and tie it into more individualized statutes, while technological transformations will assign educational inequalities and intellectual hierarchies an increasingly important role in the class struggle within the perspective of a generalized techno-political selection of individuals. In the era of nationenterprises, the true "mass era" is perhaps upon us.

Translated by Chris Turner

Notes

1 It was only after writing this article that Pierre-André Taguieffs book, *La Force du préjugé. Essai sur Ie racisme et ses doubles* (Paris: La Découverte, 1988), became known to me. In that book he considerably develops, completes, and nuances the analyses to which I have referred above, and I hope, in the near future, to be able to devote to it the discussion it deserves.

2 Colette Guillaumin has provided an excellent explanation of this point, which is, in my opinion, fundamental: "The activity of categorization is *also* a *knowledge activity*. . . . Hence no doubt the ambiguity of the struggle against stereotypes and the surprises it holds in store for us. Categorization is pregnant with knowledge as it is with oppression" (*L'Idéologie raciste. Genèse et langage actuel*, Mouton, Paris & TheHague, 1972, 183 *et seq.*).

3 L. Poliakov. *The Aryan Myth: A History of Racist and Nationalist Ideas in Europe.* trans. E. Howard (Brighton: Sussex University Press, 1974); *La Causalité diabolique: essais sur l'origine des persécutions.* Paris: Calmann-Lévy, 1980.

4 Compare the way in which, in the United States, the "Black problem" remained separate from the "ethnic problem" posed by the successive waves of European immigration and their reception. until, in the 1950s and 1960s, a new "paradigm of ethnicity" led to the latter being projected on to the former (cf. Michael Omi and Howard Winant, *Racial Formation in the United States*. London: Routledge & Kegan Paul, 1986).

5 See in particular his "Les Présuppositions dèfinitionnelles d'un indéfinissable; Ie racisme," *Mots* 8, 1984; "L'Identité nationale saisie par les logiques de racisation. Aspects, figures et problèmes du racisme différentialiste," *Mots* 12, 1986; "L'ldentité française au miroir du racisme différentialiste," *Espaces* 89, *L'identité française* (Paris: Editions Tierce, 1985). The idea is already present in the studies by Colette Guillaumin. See also Véronique de Rudder, "L'Obstacle culturel: la différence et la distance," *L'Homme et la société*, January 1986. Compare, for the Anglo-Saxon world, Martin Barker, *The New Racism: Conservatives and the Ideology of the Tribe* (London: Junction Books, 1981).

6 This was a lecture written in 1971 for UNESCO, reprinted in *The View from Afar*, trans. J. Neugroschel and P. Hoss (New York: Basic Books, 1985); cf. the critique by M. O'Callaghan and C. Guillaumin, "Race et race . . . la mode 'naturelle' en sciences humaines," *L'Homme et la société* 3(1–2), 1974. From a quite different point of view, Lévi-Strauss is today attacked as a proponent of "anti-humanism" and "relativism" (cf. T. Todorov, "Lévi-Strauss entre universalisme et relativisme," *Le Débat* 42, 1986; A. Finkielkraut, *La Défaite de la pensée*, Paris: Gallimard, 1987). Not only is the discussion on this point not closed, it has hardly begun. For my own part, I would argue not that the doctrine of Lévi-Strauss "is racist," but that the racist theories of the nineteenth and twentieth centuries have been constructed within the conceptual field of humanism: it is therefore impossible to distinguish between them on the basis suggested above (see my "Racism and Nationalism," *Race, Nation, Class: Ambiguous Identities* [London: Verso, 1991]: 37–67).

7 In Anglo-Saxon countries, these themes are widely treated by "human ethology" and "sociobiology." In France, they are given a directly culturalist basis. An anthology of these ideas, running from the theorists of the New Right to more sober academics, is to be found in A. Béjin and J. Freund (eds) *Racismes, antiracismes* (Paris: Méridiens-Klincksieck, 1986). It is useful to know that this work was simultaneously vulgarized in a mass circulation popular publication, *J'ai tout compris* 3, 1987 ('Dossier choc: *Immigrés: demain fa haine*' edited by Guillame Faye).

8 Ruth Benedict, among others, pointed this out in respect of H. S. Chamberlain: "Chamberlain, however, did not distinguish Semites by physical traits or by genealogy; Jews, as he knew, cannot be accurately separated from the rest of the population in modern Europe by tabulated anthropomorphic measurements. But they were enemies because they had special ways of thinking and acting. 'One can very soon become a Jew' . . . etc." (*Race and Racism*, [London: Routledge & Kegan Paul, 1983], 132 *et seq.*). In her view, it was at once a sign of Chamberlain's "frankness" and his "self-contradiction." This self-contradiction became the rule, but in fact it is not a self-contradiction at all. In anti-Semitism, the theme of the inferiority of the Jew is, as we know, much less important than that of his irreducible otherness. Chamberlain

even indulges at times in referring to the "superiority" of the Jews, in matters of intellect, commerce, or sense of community, making them all the more "dangerous." And the Nazi enterprise frequently admits that it is an enterprise of *reduction of the Jews* to "subhuman status" rather than a consequence of any de facto subhumanity: this is indeed why its object cannot remain mere slavery, but must become extermination.

9 See "Racism and Nationalism."

10 It is obviously this subsumption of the "sociological" difference between cultures beneath the institutional hierarchy of Culture, the decisive agency of social classification and its naturalization, that accounts for the keenness of the "radical strife" and resentment that surrounds the presence of immigrants in schools, which is much greater than that generated by the mere fact of living in close proximity. Cf. S. Boulot and D. Boyson-Fradet, "L'Echec scolaire des enfants de travailleurs immigrés," *Les Temps modernes*, special number: "L'Immigration maghrébine en France," 1984.

11 Cf. Barker, *The New Racism.*

12 Michel Foucault, *The History of Sexuality*, vol. 1, *An Introduction*, trans. Robert Jurley (London: Peregrine, 1978).

CHAPTER NINE

Marx after Marxism: A Subaltern Historian's Perspective

Dipesh Chakrabarty

From Economic and Political Weekly *28 (22) (May 29, 1993):*
1094–1096.

The old certitudes which once made Marxists feel like they belonged to one international tribe have to be rethought. But this rethinking has to issue from our own positions as intellectuals who think out of a real or imaginary base in India, and its tasks cannot be deduced from contemporary European and Anglo-American theory in any formulaic manner. An attempt at outlining a possible approach to this question.

At the outset I should make it clear that my remarks do not in any way implicate the *Subaltern Studies* collective. What follows are my own reflections on some current problems of Marxist historiography as they appear to me, and they arise from an interest in writing histories of subaltern classes and of the phenomena of subordination and domination in general. But they also arise at a particular time when Marxism is being seriously questioned in avant-garde western theorizing. Since to be a Marxist is to work within European traditions of thought anyway, one can ignore the challenge of what generally pass under names like "post-structuralism" or "deconstruction" only at one's peril. The old certitudes that once made Marxists feel like they belonged to one international tribe have to be rethought. (This at any rate is one of the assumptions on which this short intervention is based.) But this rethinking has to issue from our own positions as intellectuals who think out of a real or imaginary base in India, and its tasks cannot be deduced from contemporary European and Anglo-American theory in any formulaic manner. What follows is an attempt at outlining a possible approach to this question.

Many readers will recall that *Subaltern Studies* began as an argument within Indian Marxism and in particular against the teleologies that colonialist and nationalist-Marxist narratives had promoted in the 1970s in the field of Indian history. Initially, we wanted to oppose the methodological elitism of both varieties, but our aim was also to produce "better" Marxist histories. It soon had become clear, however, as our research progressed, that a critique of this nature could hardly afford to ignore the problem of universalism/Eurocentrism that was inherent in Marxist (or for that matter liberal) thought itself. This realization made us receptive to the critiques of Marxist historicism—in particular to the message advocating an attitude of "incredulity toward grand narratives"—that French poststructuralist thinkers increasingly made popular in the English-language academic world in the 1980s. But there have always remained important and crucial differences. Unlike in the Paris of the poststructuralists, there was never any question in Delhi, Calcutta or Madras of a wholesale rejection of Marx's thought. Foucault's scathing remark in *The Order of Things* that "Marxism exists in nineteenth-century thought as a fish in water, that is, it is unable to breathe anywhere else," may have its point (however exaggerated) but it never resonated with us with anything like the energy that anti-Marxism displays in the writings of some post-modernists.

This was so not because we believed in any Habermasian project of retrieving Enlightenment reason from the clutches of an all-consuming instrumental rationality. Our attachment to Marx's thought has different roots. They go back to the question of European imperialism from which the problem of Indian modernity cannot be separated. (The question of colonial modernity, or I might say the question of colonialism itself, remains an absent problem in much poststructuralist/postmodern writing.) However, for a modern Indian intellectual—that is, someone who engages in serious commerce with the thought-products of the European Enlightenment and with their inheritances and legacies but someone who is also aware, from the cultural practices of Indian society, of there always being other possibilities of "wording" that now exist in uneven and often subordinate relationship to "Western metaphysics" (forgive this summary expression)—it is difficult to trash Marx's thought quite in the manner of a Foucault. Again, not because it is difficult to sympathize with the intellectual criticisms of historicism. (I will in fact go on to argue here that these criticisms have to be made central to our reading of Marx.) It is because critical narratives of imperialism are constitutive of our collective origin-myths. The story of becoming an "Indian" academic-intellectual and having to (because there is no other realistic option!) deal in and with thoughts that never fail to remind you of their European origins, does not make sense without there being a concomitant narrative locating the emergence of such an intellectual class in the history of capitalist/European imperialism. To say this is not to claim the privileges of the "victim." Imperialism enables as much as it victimises. Without English imperialism in India and a certain training in Anglo-Euro habits of thought, there would not have been any *Subaltern Studies*. The story of "capital" and that of the emergence of the market-society in Europe—undeniably a historicist narrative in the most popular recensions—have a central place in our collective self-fashioning. It follows then that Marx's critique of capital and commodity will be indispensable for any critical understanding we might want to develop of ourselves. How can a critique of modernity in India ignore the history of commodification in that society? But, at the same time, this relationship to Marx cannot any longer be the straightforward one that the Indian communist parties once encouraged, where the scripting of our histories on the lines of some already-told European drama posed no intellectual problems for self-understanding.

As deconstructive political philosophy increasingly ponders the intractable problem of genuinely "non-violative" relationship between the Self ("the West") and its Other, and turns to questions of difference and ethics—questions made urgent by the current globalization of capital, information, and technology—the task for students of Marx in my part of the world does not seem to be one of improving "Marxism" in order to make it impregnable against further assault from the postmodernists. Much in Marx is truly 19th-century, gender-blind and obviously Eurocentric. A post-colonial reading of Marx, it seems to me, would have to ask if and how, and which of, his categories could be made to speak to what we have learnt from the philosophers of "difference" about "responsibility" to the plurality of the world. The age of multinational capital devolves on us this responsibility to think "difference" not simply as a theoretical question but as a tool for producing practical possibilities for action.

The talk of "difference" often elicits hostile response from Marxists. There appear to be a couple of things at stake. There is, first of all, the long-ingrained habit of thinking the world through the common, and seemingly universal and solidarity-producing, language of Marxist prose. Secular history itself is a master-code implicit in modern political thought. Historians are comfortable with the talk of difference so long as the talk does not threaten the very idea of history itself. This produces a second-order problem to which there is no quick and readymade solution and which therefore looks to many like an intellectual dead-end. How would conversation proceed between two historians if "differences" could not be contained within the sameness of the very code (i.e., history) that made the conversation possible in the first place? One may legitimately ask: How can one write/think/talk the non-West in the academia without in some sense anthropologizing it? Most historians would prefer to stop at this point and simply get on with the job. Progressive historians would perhaps even endorse the strategy of "anthropologizing": it is part and parcel, they would in effect argue, of the struggle to make the world more democratic. After all, what material benefits can the subaltern classes gain from imaginations in which gods, spirits, humans and animals cohabit the same world? Pointing out that a secular and modern historical consciousness is itself part of the problem of "colonization of the mind" for many "traditions" such as those of the "Hindus" I am not making a universal claim and I have put the word Hindu in quotes to indicate its socially constructed and contingent nature is often of no help to these historians.

Yet, as an Indian historian, this is where I think we confront an almost insoluble problem in writing subaltern history. The problem is also of some critical urgency in India given the current wave of Hindutva. Let me explain the problem of method by referring this group we have called "Hindus." For most Hindus, gods, spirits and the so-called supernatural have a certain "reality." They are as real as "ideology" is—that is to say, after Žižek, they are embedded in practices. The secular calendar is only one of the many time-worlds we travel. The bringing together of these different time-worlds in the construction of a modern public life in India has always had something to do with all the major crises modern India has had to endure, the most recent being the current upsurge of a fascistic Hindu movement that has already caused enormous sufferings to the Muslims. The usual vocabulary of political science in India, which discusses this problem in terms of Europe and categories of the secular and the sacred and makes this into a question (recycled from European history) of "religion" in public life, is pathetically inadequate in its explanatory capacity. The word religion, everybody agrees, captures nothing of the spirit of all the heterodox Hindu practices it is meant to translate. For however cynical one may be in one's analysis of the "reasons" why the Hindu political parties may want to use the "Hindu" card, one still has to ask questions about the many different meanings that divine figures (such as the god-king Rama) assumes in our negotiations of modernity. But this is where I return to the dilemma I posed in the previous paragraph: Do we, in the already universal language of Marxist prose, simply anthropologize these meanings, or do we, in developing a Marxist prose suited to our struggles (i.e., the struggles that arise for modern Indian intellectuals from their being situated in a colonial modernity) also struggle to inscribe into the visions of Marx's critique of capital, horizons of radical otherness?

I cannot pretend to escape these problems any more than other Marxists can, nor do I aspire to do so. The very limited question I can deal with in this short space is: Do Marx's categories allow us to trace the marks of what must of necessity remain unenclosed by these categories themselves? In other words, are there ways of engaging with the problem of "universality" of capital that do not commit us to a bloodless liberal pluralism that only subsumes all difference(s) within the Same?

Looking back at some work I did on (Indian) "working class" history a few years ago, I only seem to have half-thought the problem. I documented a history whose narrative(s) produced several points of friction with the teleologies of "capital." In my study of the jute mill workers of colonial Bengal I tried to show how the production relations in these mills were structured from the inside as it were by a whole series of relations that could only be considered "pre-capitalist." The coming of "capital" and "commodity" did not appear to lead to the politics of equal rights that Marx saw as internal to the categories. I refer herein particular to the critical distinction Marx draws between "real" and "abstract" labor in explaining the production and form of the commodity. This is how I then read the distinction (with enormous debt to Michel Henry and I. I. Rubin):

> Marx places the question of subjectivity right at the heart of his category "capital" when he posits the conflict between "real labor" and "abstract labor" as one of its central contradictions. "Real labor" refers to the labor power of the actual individual, labor power "as it exists in the personality of the laborer"—that is, as it exists in the "immediate exclusive individuality" of the individual. Just as personalities differ, similarly the labor power of one individual is different from that of another. "Real labor" refers to the essential heterogeneity of individual capacities. "Abstract" or general labor, on the other hand, refers to the idea of uniform, homogeneous labor that capitalism imposes on this heterogeneity, the notion of a general labor that underlies "exchange value." It is what makes labor measurable and makes possible the generalised exchange of commodities. It expresses itself . . . in capitalist discipline, which has the sole objective of making every individual's concrete labor—by nature heterogeneous—"uniform and homogeneous" through supervision and technology employed in labor process . . . Politically,. . . the concept of "abstract labor" is an extension of the bourgeois notion of the "equal rights" of "abstract individuals": whose political life is reflected in the ideals and practice of "citizenship." The politics of "equal rights" is thus precisely the "politics" one can read into the category "capital" . . . (Chakrabarty, *Rethinking Working-Class History: Bengal 1890–1940*, Princeton University Press, 1989, 225–226)

It now seems to me that Marx's category of "commodity" has a certain built-in openness to "difference" that I did not fully exploit in my exposition. My reading of the term "pre-capital" remained, in spite of my efforts, hopelessly historicist, and my narrative never quite escaped the (false) question: Why did the Indian working class fail to sustain a long-term sense of class-consciousness, the meta-problem of "failure" itself arising from the well-known Marxist tradition of positing the working class as a transhistorical subject? Besides, it is also clear from the above quote that my reading took the ideas of the "individual" and "personality" as unproblematically given, and read the word "real" (in "real labor") to mean something primordially natural (and therefore not social).

But my larger failure lay in my inability to see that if one reads the "real" as socially/culturally produced—and not as a Rousseauvian "natural," something that refers simply to the naturally different endowments of different, and ahistorical, individuals—other possibilities open up, among them the one of writing "difference" back into Marx. For the "real" then (in his reading) must refer to different kinds of "social" and hence to different orders of temporality. It should in principle even allow for the possibility of these temporal horizons being mutually incommensurable. The transition from "real" to "abstract" is thus also a question of transition from many and possibly incommensurable temporalities to the homogeneous time of abstract labor, the transition from "non-history" to "history." "Real" labor, therefore, is precisely that which cannot not be enclosed by the sign, commodity, while it constantly inheres in the latter. The gap between real and abstract labor and the force constantly needed to close it, is what introduces the movement of "difference" into the very constitution of the commodity and thereby eternally defers its achievement of its true/ideal character.

The sign "commodity," as Marx explains will always carry as parts of its internal structure certain universal emancipatory narratives. If one overlooked the tension Marx situated at the heart of this category, these narratives could indeed produce the standard teleologies one normally encounters in Marxist historicism: that of citizenship, the juridical subject of Enlightenment thought, the subject of political theory of rights, etc. I do not mean to deny the practical utility of these narratives in modern political structures. The more interesting problem for the Marxist historian, it seems to me, is the problem of temporality that the category "commodity," constituted through the tension between "real" and "abstract" labor, invites us to think of. If "real" labor, as we have said, belongs to a world of heterogeneity whose various temporalities—Michael Taussig's work on Bolivian tin miners clearly shows that they are not even all "secular" (i.e., bereft of gods and spirits)—cannot be enclosed in the sign History, then I can find a place in a historical narrative of capitalist transition (or commodity production) only as a Derridean trace of something that cannot be enclosed, an element that constantly challenges from within capital's and commodity's—and by implication, History's—claims to unity and universality.

The prefix "pre" in "pre-capital," it could be said similarly, is not a reference to what is simply chronologically prior on an ordinal, homogeneous scale of time. "Pre-capitalist" is a hyphenated identity, it speaks of a particular relationship to capital marked by the tension of difference in horizons of time. The "pre-capitalist" can only exist within the temporal horizon of capital and is yet something that disrupts the continuity of this time precisely by suggesting another time that is not on the same, secular, homogeneous calendar (which is why what is pre-capital is not chronologically prior to capital). This is another time which, theoretically, could be entirely incommensurable with the godless, spiritless time of what we call "history."

Subaltern histories, thus conceived in relationship to the question of difference, will have a split running through them. On the one hand, they are "histories" in that they are constructed within the mastercode of secular History and use the accepted academic codes of history writing (and thereby perforce anthropologize all other forms of memory). On the other hand, they cannot ever afford to grant this master-code its claim of being a mode of thought that comes to all human beings naturally, or even to be treated as something that exists cut there in nature itself (remember the tell-tale title of J. B. S. Haldane's book, *Everything Has A History?*). Subaltern histories are therefore constructed within a particular kind of historicized memory, one that remembers History itself as a violation, an imperious code that accompanied the civilizing process that the European Enlightenment inaugurated in the 18th century as a world-historical task. This memory does not have the character of nostalgia for it bespeaks a pain that is in no sense historical in our parts of the world.

Of course, the empirical historian who writes these histories is not a peasant or a tribal (and often not even a woman) himself. He produces History—as distinct from other forms of memory—precisely because he has been transposed and inserted—in our case, by England's work in India—into the global narratives of citizenship and socialism. He writes history, that is, only after his own labor has entered the process of being made abstract in the world-market for ideational commodities. The subaltern, then, is not the empirical peasant or tribal in any straightforward sense that a populist program of history-writing may want to imagine. The figure of the subaltern is necessarily mediated by problems of representation. In terms of the analysis that I have been trying to develop here, one might say that, subaltern is what fractures from within the signs that tell of the insertion of the historian (as a speaking subject) into the global narratives of capital. It is what gathers itself under "real" labor in Marx's critique of capital, the figure of difference that governmentality—in Foucault's sense of the term—all over the world has to subjugate and civilize.

There are implications that follow: subaltern histories written with an eye to difference cannot constitute yet another attempt—in the long and universalistic tradition of "socialist" histories—to help erect the subaltern as the subject of modern democracies, that is, to expand the history of the modern in such a way as to make it more representative of society as a whole. This is a laudable objective on its own terms and has undoubted global relevance. But thought does not have to stop at political democracy or the concept of egalitarian distribution of wealth (though the aim of achieving these ends will legitimately fuel many immediate political struggles). But, fundamentally, this thought is insensitive to philosophical questions of difference and can acknowledge difference only as a practical problem. Subaltern histories will engage philosophically with questions of difference which are elided in the dominant traditions of Marxism. At the same time, however, just as "real" labor cannot be thought outside of the problematic of "abstract" labor, the subaltern cannot be thought outside of the global narrative of capital though it does not belong to this narrative. Stories about how this or that group in Asia, Africa or Latin America resisted the "penetration" of capitalism do not constitute "subaltern" history for subaltern histories do not refer to a resistance prior and exterior to capital. *Subaltern Studies*, as I think of it, can only situate itself theoretically at the juncture where we give up neither Marx nor "difference," for the resistance it speaks of is something that can happen only within the time-horizon of capital and yet disrupts the unity of that time. Unconcealing the tension between real and abstract labor ensures that capital/commodity has heterogeneities and incommensurabilities inscribed in its core.

Or, to put it differently, the practice of subaltern history would aim to take history to its limits in order to make its unworking visible.

CHAPTER TEN

The Logic of Gender: On the Separation of Spheres and the Process of Abjection

Maya Gonzalez and Jeanne Neton

From Endnotes 3 (September 2013): 56–91.

Within marxist feminism we encounter several sets of binary terms to analyze gendered forms of domination under capitalism.[1] These include: productive and reproductive, paid and unpaid, public and private, sex and gender. When considering the gender question, we found these categories imprecise, theoretically deficient and sometimes even misleading. This article is an attempt to propose categories which will give us a better grasp of the transformation of the gender relation since the 1970s and, more importantly, since the recent crisis.

The account that follows is strongly influenced by systematic dialectics, a method that tries to understand social forms as interconnected moments of a totality.[2] We therefore move from the most abstract categories to the most concrete, tracing the unfolding of gender as a "real abstraction." We are only concerned with the form of gender specific to capitalism, and we assume from the outset that one can talk about gender without any reference to biology or prehistory. We begin by defining gender as a separation between spheres. Then, having done so, we specify the individuals assigned to those spheres. Importantly, we do not define spheres in spatial terms, but rather in the same way Marx spoke of the two separated spheres of production and circulation, as *concepts* that take on a materiality.

The binaries listed above appear to limit one's grasp of the ways in which these spheres function at present, as they lack historical specificity and promote a transhistorical understanding of gendered "domination" which takes patriarchy as a feature of capitalism *without making it historically specific to capitalism*. We hope to delineate categories that are as specific to capitalism as "capital" itself. We argue that these binaries depend on category errors whose faults become clear once we attempt to illuminate the transformations within capitalist society since the 1970s. Forms of domestic and so-called reproductive activities have become increasingly marketized, and while these activities may occupy the "sphere" of the home, just as they did before, they no longer occupy the same structural positions within the capitalist totality, despite exhibiting the same concrete features. For this reason, we found ourselves forced to clarify, transform, and redefine the categories we received from marxist feminism, not for the sake of theory, but to understand why humanity is still powerfully inscribed with one or the other gender.

Production/Reproduction

Whatever the form of the process of production in a society, it must be a continuous process, must continue to go periodically through the same phases. A society can no more cease to produce than it can cease to consume. When viewed, therefore, as a connected whole, and as flowing on with incessant renewal, every social process of production is, at the same time, a process of reproduction.[3]

When Marx speaks of reproduction he does not refer to the production and reproduction of any commodity in particular; rather, he is concerned with the reproduction of the social totality. However, when marxist feminists speak of reproduction, what they often aim to specify is the production and reproduction of the commodity labor-power. This is because, in Marx's critique, the relationship between the reproduction of labor-power and the reproduction of the capitalist totality is incomplete.

When Marx speaks of labor-power, he claims it is a commodity with a distinctive character, unlike any other

Although Marx speaks of the specificities of the commodity labor-power,[4] there are some aspects of this specification which require more attention.

First, let us investigate the separation between labor-power and its bearer. The exchange of labor-power presupposes that this commodity is brought to the market by its bearer. However, in this particular case, labor-power and its bearer are one and the same living person. Labor-power is the living, laboring capacity of this person, and as such, it cannot be detached from the bearer. Thus the particularity of labor-power poses an ontological question.

Going back to *Capital*, at the outset of Chapter One we encounter the commodity, and it is only a few chapters later that we will fully discover its most peculiar manifestation, that is to say, labor-power. In accord with Marx, it is correct to begin with the naturalised and self-evident realm of commodity circulation, in order to render the commodity a curious and unnatural thing indeed. We will not, however, enquire only about what organises these "things," these objects; but rather—in terms of a gender analysis—we will enquire into these *other bodies*, human objects, which bumble about in their own "natural" way, and who, like the fetishised commodity, appear to have no history. Yet they surely do.

For at the heart of the commodity form is the dual character of labor—both abstract and concrete—and accordingly, Chapter One of *Capital* introduces the contradiction between use-value and (exchange) value. This is the contradiction which unfolds from the first pages of Marx's critique to the very end. Indeed, the split between these two irreconcilable aspects of the commodity form is the guiding thread that allows Marx to trace and disclose all the other contradictory forms that constitute the capitalist mode of production.

Let us summarise briefly this contradiction. On the one hand, the commodity in its aspect as use-value stands, in all its singularity, as a particular object differentiated from the next. It has a definite use which, as Marx claims, is necessary for its production as exchange-value. In addition, because it is singular, it is a single unit, one of many which add up to a sum, a quantity of individual things. It does not amount to a sum of homogeneous labor-time in the abstract, but a sum of concrete individual and separable labors. On the other hand, in its aspect as exchange-value, it represents an aliquot portion of the "total social labor" within society—a quantum of socially necessary labor time, or the average time required for its reproduction.

This contradiction, *the* contradiction—far from being specific only to "things"—is fundamentally the very condition of being in the world for a proletarian. From this standpoint, the proletarian confronts the world in which the capitalist mode of production prevails as an accumulation of commodities; the proletarian does this *as* a commodity—and therefore this confrontation is at once a chance meeting between one commodity and another, and at the same time an encounter between subject and object.

This ontological split exists because labor-power is neither a person nor *just* a commodity. As Marx tells us, the commodity labor-power is peculiar and unlike any other. The peculiarity of the commodity labor-power is what gives it a central place in a mode of production based on value, as the very use-value of labor-power (or living labor capacity) is *the* source of (exchange-) value. Furthermore, the contradiction between use-value and (exchange-) value has additional implications, when we consider the very production and reproduction of labor-powers. This peculiar "production" is specific enough to deserve extra attention, for, as far as we know, *at no time does a labor-power roll off an assembly line.*

How then is labor-power produced and reproduced? Marx identifies the particularity of the use-value of labor-power. But does he adequately distinguish the production of labor-power from the production of other commodities? He writes:

> the labor-time requisite for the production of labor-power reduces itself to that necessary for the production of [its] means of subsistence.[5]

When raising the problem of the value of labor-power, Marx concludes that it is equal to the labor-time necessary for its production, as is the case for any other commodity. However, in this case, it is mysteriously reduced to the labor-time necessary for the production of the worker's means of subsistence. But a cart full of "means of subsistence" does not produce labor-power as a ready-made commodity.

If we were to compare the production of labor-power with the production of any other commodity, we would see that the "raw materials" used for this production process, i.e. the means of subsistence, transmit their value to the end product, while the new labor needed to turn these commodities into a functioning labor-power adds no value to this commodity. If we were to push this analogy further, we could say that—in terms of value—labor-power consists only of *dead labor.*

In the above quote, Marx reduces the necessary labor required to produce labor-power to the "raw materials" purchased in order to accomplish its (re)production. Any labor necessary to turn this raw material, this basket of goods, into the commodity labor-power, is therefore not considered living labor by Marx, and indeed, in the capitalist mode of production it is not deemed necessary labor at all. This means that however necessary these activities are for the production and reproduction of labor-power, *they are structurally made non-labor.* This necessary labor is not considered as such by Marx because the activity of turning the raw materials equivalent to the wage into labor-power takes place *in a separate sphere from the production and circulation of values.* These necessary non-labor activities do not produce value, not because of their concrete characteristics, but rather, because they take place in a sphere of the capitalist mode of production which is not directly mediated by the form of value.

There must be an exterior to value in order for value to exist. Similarly, for labor to exist and serve as the measure of value, there must be an exterior to labor (we will return to this in Part Two). While the autonomist feminists would conclude that every activity which reproduces labor-power produces value,[6] we would say that, for labor-power to have a value, some of these activities have to be cut off or dissociated from the sphere of value production.[7]

Therefore, the reproduction of labor-power presupposes the separation of two different spheres

As articulated above, there is a sphere of non-labor or extra-necessary labor which envelops the process of transforming dead labor, that is commodities purchased with the wage, into the living labor capacity found on the market. We must now look at the specificities of this sphere.

Terms like the "reproductive sphere" are insufficient for identifying this sphere, because what we are trying to name cannot be defined as a specific set of activities according to their use-value or concrete character. Indeed, the same concrete activity, like cleaning or cooking, can take place in either sphere: it can be value-producing labor in one specific social context and non-labor in another. Reproductive tasks such as cleaning can be purchased as services, and prefab meals can be bought in place of time spent preparing meals. However, to fully appreciate how—beyond labor-power—gender is reproduced, it will be necessary to differentiate reproduction that is commodified, monetised, or mass produced from that which is not.

Because the existing concepts of production and reproduction are themselves limited, we need to find more precise terms to designate these two spheres. From now on we will use two very descriptive (and therefore rather clunky) terms to name them: (a) the *directly market-mediated* sphere (DMM); and (b) the *indirectly market-mediated* sphere (IMM). Rather than coming up with jargonistic neologisms, our aim is to use these as placeholders and to concentrate on the structural characteristics of these two spheres. In the course of our presentation (see Part Two) we will have to add another set of descriptive terms (waged/unwaged) to sufficiently elaborate the nuanced characteristics of these spheres.

The production and reproduction of labor-power necessitates a whole set of activities; some of them are performed in the directly market-mediated or DMM sphere (those that are bought as commodities, either as product or service), while others take place in that sphere which is not directly mediated by the market—the IMM sphere. The difference between these activities does not lie in their concrete characteristics. Each of these concrete activities—cooking, looking after children, washing/mending clothes—can sometimes produce value and sometimes not, depending upon the "sphere," rather than the actual place, in which it occurs. The sphere, therefore, is not necessarily the home. Nor is this sphere defined by whether or not the activities taking place within it consist of those that reproduce labor-power. It is defined by the relationship of these reproductive tasks to exchange, the market and the accumulation of capital.

This conceptual distinction has material consequences. Within the directly market-mediated sphere, reproductive tasks are performed under directly capitalist conditions, that is, with all the requirements of the market, whether they are performed within the manufacturing or the service sector. Under the constraints and command of capital and the market, the production of goods and services, regardless of their content, must be performed at competitive levels in terms of productivity, efficiency and product uniformity. The index of productivity is temporal, while that of efficiency pertains to the ways in which inputs are economically utilised. Furthermore, the uniformity of the product of labor requires the uniformity of the laboring process, and of the relationship of those who produce to what they produce.

One can immediately see the difference between tasks performed in this sphere, and that outside of it. In the DMM sphere, the rate of return on a capitalist investment is paramount and therefore all activities performed— even if they are "reproductive" in their use-value character—must meet or exceed the going rate of exploitation and/or profit. On the other hand, outside the DMM sphere, the ways in which the wage is utilised by those who reproduce the use-value labor-power (via the reproduction of its bearer) is not subject to the same requirements. If those ways are uniform at all, they are nevertheless highly variable in terms of the necessary utilization of time, money and raw materials. Unlike in the DMM sphere, there is no direct market-determination of every aspect of the reproduction process. (In Part Two we will address the indirectly market-mediated sphere of state-organised reproduction).

The indirectly market-mediated sphere has a different temporal character. The 24-hour day and 7-day week[8] still organise the activities within this sphere, but "socially necessary labor time" (SNLT) is never *directly* a factor in that organization. SNLT applies to the process of abstraction occurring through the mediation of the market, which averages out the amount of time required within the labor process to competitively sell a product or service. Bankruptcy and the loss of profit are factors weighing on this process; likewise the innovative use of machinery in order to decrease the time required to produce goods. Thus, the increase of profit or market share dominates the DMM sphere. Of course, mechanization is also possible in the IMM sphere, and there have been many innovations of that sort. In this case, however, the aim is not to allow the production of more use-values in a given amount of time, but to reduce the time spent on a given activity, usually so that more time can be dedicated to another IMM activity. When it comes to the care of children, for example, even if some activities can be performed more quickly, they have to be looked after the *whole day*, and this amount of time is not flexible (we will return to this in Part Five).

In addition, different forms of domination characterise these spheres respectively. Market dependency, or impersonal abstract domination, organises DMM relations of production and reproduction, through the mechanism of value-comparison in terms of socially necessary labor time. The kind of "direct market-mediation" within this sphere is abstract domination, and as such, it is a form of indirect compulsion determined on the market ("behind the backs of the producers"). Hence, there is no structural necessity toward direct violence, or planning, in order to allocate labor *per se*.

In contrast, there is no such mechanism comparing the various performances of the concrete activities occurring in the IMM sphere— which is to say, as being socially determined. They cannot be dictated by abstract market domination and the objective constraints of SNLT, except in an indirect way such that the requirements of production transform the requirements of labor-power's maintenance outside of the DMM sphere. Instead, other mechanisms and factors are involved in the division of IMM activities, from direct domination and violence to hierarchical forms of cooperation, or planned allocation at best.[9] There is no impersonal mechanism or way to objectively quantify, enforce or equalise "rationally" the time and energy spent in these activities or to whom they are allocated. When an "equal and just" sharing of these activities is attempted, it must be constantly negotiated, since there is no way to quantify and equalise "rationally" the time or energy spent. What does it mean to clean the kitchen, what does it mean to look after a child for one hour: is your hour of childcare the same as my hour of childcare? This allocation cannot but remain a conflictual question.

Paid/Unpaid

Marxist feminists have often added to the distinction between production and reproduction another one: that between paid and unpaid labor. Like many before us, we find these categories imprecise and we prefer to use the waged/unwaged distinction. As we further explicate the spheres of DMM and IMM in relation to that which is waged or unwaged, we elucidate the overlapping of these spheres through the principle of *social validation*. En route we will explore the ways in which the activities in question can be called labor or not; that is, if they *qualify* as labor or not in this mode of production.

The difference between paid/unpaid on the one side, and waged/unwaged on the other is blurred by the form of the wage, by what we must name *the wage fetish*. The wage itself is not the monetary equivalent to the work performed by the worker who receives it, but rather the price for which a worker sells their labor-power, equivalent to a sum of value that goes one way or another into the process of their reproduction, as they must reappear the next day ready and able to work.[10] However, it appears that those who work for a wage have fulfilled their social responsibility for the day once the workday is over. What is *not* paid for by the wage appears to be a world of non-work. Therefore, all "work" appears to be paid tautologically as that which is work, since one does not appear to get paid for that which one does when not "at work." However, it is imperative to remember that Marx demonstrated that no actual living labor is ever paid for in the form of the wage.

Obviously, this does not mean that the question of whether an activity is waged or not is irrelevant. Indeed, she who does not go to work does not get a wage. Wage-labor is the only way the worker can have access to the means necessary for their own reproduction and that of their family. Moreover, validation by the wage qualitatively affects the activity itself. When an activity that was previously unwaged becomes waged, even when it is unproductive, it takes on some characteristics that resemble those of abstract labor. Indeed, the fact that labor-power is exchanged for a wage makes its performance open to rationalizations and comparisons. In return, what is expected from this labor-power is at least the socially average performance—including all its characteristics and intensity—regulated and corresponding to the social average *for this kind of labor* (clearly the absence of value makes it impossible to compare it with any other kind of labor). An individual who cannot deliver a proper performance in the necessary amount of time will not be able to sell their labor-power in the future. Therefore, the wage validates the fact that labor-power has been employed adequately, whilst universally recognizing it as social labor, whatever the concrete activity itself might have been, or whether it was "productively" consumed.

Now we must consider this distinction between the waged and unwaged, insofar as it intersects with that between the IMM and DMM spheres. When we consider those activities which are waged, we are referring to those which are social[11]; those which are unwaged are *the non-social of the social*: they are not socially validated but are nonetheless part of the capitalist mode of production. Importantly, however, these do not map directly onto the spheres of IMM and DMM.

We see that within the interplay of these four terms there are some waged activities which overlap with those of the IMM sphere: those organised by the state (the state sector). Within this imbricated set of categories, the sphere of IMM activities intersects with the sphere of waged labor. These waged and IMM activities are forms of state-organised reproduction that are not directly market-mediated (see Figure 10.1). These activities reproduce the use-value of labor-power but are waged and thus socially validated. Nevertheless, these activities are not productive of value, nor are they subject to the same criteria of direct market-mediation (see above). They are social because they are remunerated through the social form of value. Because they are not productive of value, they are the forms of reproduction which are a collective cost to capital: they are paid indirectly through deductions from collective wages and surplus-value in the form of taxes.

Let us now turn things round one more time and look at what the wage *buys*; that is, what is an element of the wage, what constitutes the exchange-value of labor-power. The wage buys the commodities necessary for the reproduction of labor-power, and it also buys services which participate in this reproduction, whether directly (by paying a private nanny, for example) or indirectly (for example, by paying taxes for state-expenditure on education, which is part of the indirect wage). These services, whether they are productive of value or not,[12] have a cost that is reflected in the exchange-value of labor-power: they imply, in one way or another, a deduction from surplus-value.

What remains are the activities that are non-waged, and that therefore do not increase the exchange-value of labor-power. These are the non-social of the social, the non-labor of labor (see Addendum 1). They are cut off from social production; they must not only *appear as*, but also *be* non-labor, that is, they are *naturalized*.[13] They constitute a sphere whose dissociation is necessary to make the production of value possible: the *gendered sphere*.

In the next part we will finally turn to the individuals who have been assigned to this sphere. However, we should first consider another binary: public/private.

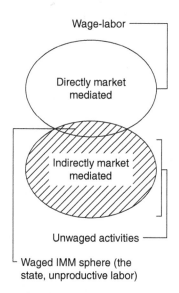

FIGURE 10.1 *A graphical representation of the relation between the DMM/IMM and waged/unwaged spheres.*

Addendum 1: On labor

For us, labor will be defined, in its opposition to non-labor, as an activity that is socially validated as such, because of its specific function, its specific social character in a given mode of production. Other bases for definitions of labor are also possible, to cite a few: exchange between man and nature, expense of energy, distinction between pleasant/unpleasant activities. However, we think that none of these definitions can help us understand anything about the character of unwaged IMM activities. These definitions only take into account their concrete characteristics, and in the case of unwaged IMM activities, this leads to banal or absurd descriptions. Is comforting a child an exchange with nature? Is sleeping a labor that reproduces labor-power? Is brushing one's teeth labor? Brushing somebody else's teeth? We think that our definition of labor, while it may seem banal at first glance, is the only one capable of passing over these meaningless questions, and that it constitutes the right starting-point for research into the specific character of these activities.

Public/Private

Many people use the category "public" to designate the state sector. And marxist feminists often use the concept of the "private" sphere to designate everything within the sphere of the home. We find it necessary to hold fast to the traditional dichotomy of private/public as that which separates the economic and the political, civil society and the state, bourgeois individual and citizen.[14] Prior to capitalism the term "private" referred to the household, or *oikos*, and it was considered *the* sphere of the economic. With the advent of the capitalist era the private sphere moved outward beyond the household itself.

Here we begin to see the inadequacy of the concept of "the private sphere" as a place outside of "the public sphere" that includes the economy, as for example in feminist theory. For the private is not merely that which is located in the domestic sphere, and associated with domestic activities. Rather, it is the totality of activities inside and outside of the home. As a result of the structural separation between the economic and the political (political economy)—corresponding to the spread of capitalist social (production) relations—the private sphere becomes increasingly diffuse, rendering the home only one amongst many moments of "the economic" or "the private". Therefore, contrary to most feminist accounts, it was *only* within the context of pre-modern relations—prior to the separation of the political and the economic under capitalism—that the private sphere constituted the household. In contrast, in the modern capitalist era, the scope of private exploitation spans the entire social landscape.

Where then is "the public" if the private is the totality of productive and reproductive activities? Marx claims that the public is an abstraction from society in the form of the state. This sphere of the political and the juridical is the real abstraction of *Right* separated from the actual divisions and differences constituting civil society. For Marx, this abstraction or separation must exist in order to attain and preserve the formal equality (accompanied, of course, by class inequality) necessary for self-interested private owners to accumulate capital in a manner uninhibited rather than controlled or dictated by the state. This is what distinguishes the modern state, which is adequate to capitalist property relations, from other state systems corresponding to other modes of production, whether monarchical or ancient democratic.

This means that the modern capitalist state and its "public sphere" is not an actually existing place, but an abstract "community" of "equal citizens." Hence, the differentiation between the sphere of economic relations and that of the political—including relations between unequals mediated by relations between "abstract equal citizens"—renders "citizens" only *formally* equal according to the state and civil rights. As a result, these "individuals" appear as equals on the market—even though in "real life" (the private sphere of civil society) they are anything but.[15] This abstraction, "the public," must exist precisely because the directly market-mediated sphere is mediated by the market, a space of mediation between private labors, produced independently from one another in private firms owned and operated by private (self-interested) individuals.

What then is the relationship between on the one hand, the spheres of public/private, political/economic, state/civil society, and on the other hand, the spheres of direct and indirect market-mediation? The meeting-point of these spheres marks the moment of their constitutive separation, and defines those anchored to one as distinct from the other, as *different*. This difference is determined by whether those individuals defined by the state directly exchange the labor-power commodity they bear within their person as their own property, or—if that exchange is mediated indirectly— through those with formal equality.

Now we are ready to look at the individuals who have been assigned to each sphere. What we see at first, when we look at the dawn of this mode of production, is individuals who have different rights, which are defined by the law as two different juridical beings: *men and women*. We will be able to see how this juridical difference was inscribed on the "biological" bodies of these individuals when we come to analyze the sex/gender binary. For now, we must see how the dichotomy between public and private does the initial work of anchoring individuals as men and women to the different spheres reproducing the capitalist totality through their differential right not merely to private property, but to *that property which individuals own in their persons.*

This peculiar form of property is necessary to generalised wage-relations because value presupposes formal equality between the owners of commodities so that "free" exchange (capital and labor-power) can occur despite the fact that there is a structural "real" inequality between two different classes: those possessing the means of production and those dispossessed of that form of property. However, "free exchange" can only occur through a disavowal of that class difference, through its deferral to another binary: *citizen* and *other*, not between members of opposed classes but between those within each class. In order to found the bourgeois mode of production, it was not necessary for all workers to be given equality under the sign of "the citizen." Historically, "citizen" only names a specific category to which both property owners and certain proletarians are able to belong. As capitalist juridical relations disavow class through the reconstitution of the difference between citizen and other, the historical conditions under which the bourgeois mode of production was itself constituted were various forms of unfreedom. For this reason we have citizen and other as mapping onto: *male (white)/non-(white) male.*

For instance, under the conditions of slavery in North America, the classification of white was necessary to maintain the property of masters over slaves. Women were also classified as other, but for different reasons, as we shall see. One factor worth mentioning here is that within this relation of white/person of color/woman, the preservation of the purity of the "white master," as opposed to the "black slave" is of the utmost importance—as well as the strict preservation of the dominant master signifier of equality ("white blood" and therefore "white mothers") across future generations of the bourgeoisie. Therefore the division between white and non-white women was also closely regulated in order to preserve such a taxonomy, within the mixed context of both plantation-based commodity production in the New World and the rise of industrial capitalism.[16]

However, what constitutes the citizen/other binary in this mode of production is not based upon a negative definition of slavery but rather upon "free" labor, consisting of those with, as opposed to without, the same formal freedom. "Free labor" as Marx identified it—that is, the technical definition of freedom for the wage laborer—requires what we might call "double freedom":

> For the conversion of his money into capital, therefore, the owner of money must meet in the market with the free laborer, free in the double sense, that as a free man he can dispose of his labor-power as his own commodity, and that on the other hand he has no other commodity for sale, is short of everything necessary for the realisation of his labor-power.[17]

Nevertheless, haven't women always been wage-laborers? Of course, since the origin of capitalism, women have been bearers of labor-power, and their capacity to labor has been utilised by capital; but they have only quite recently become the *owners* of their labor-power, with "double freedom." Prior to the last quarter century, women were indeed free *from the means of production*, but they were not free to sell their labor-power *as their own*.[18] The freedom of ownership, which includes mobility between lines of work, was historically only for some at the expense of others. Those struggling for political and "public" freedom, or double freedom, were caught in a double-bind. They were forced to make arguments on behalf of their ("but-different") equality, while at the same time having interests in contradiction with those of others who identified with the same fight for equality on different terms.[19]

This is especially true in the case of women, who were caught between demanding freedom as the ideal, equal human, and freedom *as different*. This is because their "real difference" under capitalism is not ideal or ideological but embodied, and structurally reproduced through the practices which define women as different. This "real difference" is entangled within a web of mutually constitutive and reinforcing relations which necessarily presuppose the citizen, state and public sphere to which women might appeal for human and civil rights on the one hand, and reproductive rights on the other.

Therefore, even if it is true that formal freedom itself was a precondition for value production and exchange, nevertheless, what it organised—the civil society of bourgeois individuals—was necessary for the continuing reproduction of the public or legal sphere. The right to "be equal" and thus equally free, does not itself reorganise the distribution of property, nor as we shall see, the conditions of possibility for capital accumulation. These spheres work in concert. If this were not the case, it would be possible to abolish the actually existing forms of historically specific "difference" through legal and "political" actions, *within* the state. This would amount to the abolition of the private through the public sphere—a revolution through reform which is structurally impossible.

"Equality" as double-freedom is the freedom to be structurally dispossessed. This is not to say that it is not *worthwhile*. The question is, can it also become "worthwhile" to capital, the state and its attendant apparatuses of domination? As most of us will have experienced first-hand, the gender distinction has persisted long after differential freedom was abolished for the majority of women. If this differential freedom was in fact what anchored women to the indirectly market-mediated sphere, why did its abolition not "free" women from the category "woman" and the gendered sphere of reproduction?

Double-freedom and the sex-blind market

When looking at the history of the capitalist mode of production, it is striking that, in many cases, once inequalities have been secured by juridical mechanisms, they can take on a life of their own, making their own basis in law superfluous. As women in many countries slowly but surely received equal rights in the public sphere, the mechanism that reinforced this inequality in the "private sphere" of the economic—of the labor-market— was already so well established that it could appear as the enactment of some mysterious natural law.

Ironically, the reproduction of dual spheres of gender and the anchoring of women to one and not the other is perpetuated and constantly re-established by the very mechanism of the "sex-blind" labor-market, which obtains not for the man/woman distinction directly but rather for the price distinction, or the exchange-value of their labor-power. Indeed, labor markets, if they are to remain markets, must be "sex-blind." Markets, as the locus of exchanges of equivalents, are supposed to blur concrete differences in a pure comparison of abstract values. How then can this "sex-blind" market reproduce the gender difference?

Once a group of individuals, women, are defined as "those who have children" (see Addendum 2) and once this social activity, "having children," is structurally formed as constituting a handicap,[20] women are defined as *those who come to the labor-market with a potential disadvantage*. This systematic differentiation—through the market-determined risk identified as childbearing "potential"—keeps those who embody the signifier "woman" anchored to the IMM sphere. Therefore, because capital is a "sex-blind" abstraction, it concretely punishes women for having a sex, even though that "sexual difference" is produced by capitalist social relations, and absolutely necessary to the reproduction of capitalism itself. One could imagine a hypothetical situation in which employers did not enquire about the gender of an applicant, but only rewarded those who have "the most mobility" and those who are "the most reliable, 24/7"; even in this case gender bias would reappear as strong as ever. As an apparent contradiction, once sexual difference becomes structurally defined and reproduced, woman as a bearer of labor-power with a higher social cost becomes its opposite: the commodity labor-power with a cheaper price.

Indeed, the better-remunerated jobs—that is, those which can tendentially pay for more than the reproduction of a single person—are those for which a certain degree of skill is expected. In those skilled sectors, capitalists are ready to make an investment in the worker's skills, knowing that they will benefit from doing so in the long term. They will therefore privilege the labor-power that is likely to be the most reliable over a long period. If the worker is potentially going to leave, then she will not be as good an investment, and will get a lower price. This lower price tag, fixed to those who look like the kind of people who "have children," is not determined by the sorts of skills that are formed in the IMM sphere. Even though the sphere a woman is relegated to is full of activities which require lifelong training, this does not increase the price of her labor-power, because no employer has to pay for their acquisition. As a result, capital can use women's labor-power in short spurts at cheap prices.

In fact, the general tendency toward "feminization" is not the gendering of the sex-blind market, but rather the movement by capital toward the utilization of cheap short-term flexibilised labor-power under post-Fordist, globalized conditions of accumulation, increasingly deskilled and "just-in-time." We must take this definition of feminization as primary, before we attend to the rise of the service sector and the increasing importance of care and affective labor, which is part and parcel of the "feminization turn." This turn comes about through the dynamic unfolding of capitalist social relations historically, a process that we will see in the last two parts of the text. But first we must summarise what we have learned about gender until now, and attempt a definition. This requires analysis and criticism of another common binary: sex and gender.

Addendum 2: On women, biology and children

The definition of women as "those who have children" presupposes a necessary link between 1) the fact of having a biological organ, the uterus 2) the fact of bearing a child, of being pregnant 3) the fact of having a specific relation to the result of this pregnancy. Conflating the three obscures:

1) On the one side, the mechanisms that prevent, favor, or impose the fact that somebody with a uterus will go through pregnancy, and how often that will occur.[21] These mechanisms include: the institution of marriage, the availability of contraceptives, the mechanisms that enforce heterosexuality as a norm, and (at least for a long time and still in many places) the interdiction/shame associated with forms of sex that do not risk leading to pregnancy (oral/anal sex, etc.).

2) On the other side, the changing definition of what a child is and what level of care a child necessitates. While there was a period in which children were considered as half-animal, half-human creatures who only had to be cleaned and fed until they became small adults—that is, able to work—the modern reality of childhood and its requirements often make "having children" a never-ending business.

Sex/Gender

We are now prepared to address the gender question. What then is gender? For us, it is the *anchoring* of a certain group of individuals in a specific sphere of social activities. The result of this anchoring process is at the same time the continuous reproduction of two separate genders.

These genders concretise themselves as an ensemble of ideal characteristics, defining either the "masculine" or the "feminine." However, these characteristics themselves, as a list of behavioral and psychological qualities, are subject to transformation over the course of the history of capitalism; they pertain to specific periods; they correspond to certain parts of the world; and even within what we might call the "West" they are not necessarily ascribed in the same way to all people. As a binary however, they exist in relation to one another, regardless of time and space, even if their mode of appearance is itself always in flux.

Sex is the flip side of gender. Following Judith Butler, we criticise the gender/sex binary as found in feminist literature before the 1990s. Butler demonstrates, correctly, that both sex and gender are socially constituted and furthermore, that it is the "socializing" or pairing of "gender" with culture, that has relegated sex to the "natural" pole of the binary nature/culture. We argue similarly that they are binary social categories which simultaneously de-naturalise gender while naturalizing sex. For us, sex is the naturalization of gender's dual projection upon bodies, aggregating biological differences into discrete naturalised semblances.

While Butler came to this conclusion through a critique of the existentialist ontology of the body,[22] we came to it through an analogy with another social form. Value, like gender, necessitates its other, "natural" pole (i.e. its concrete manifestation). Indeed, the dual relation between sex and gender as two sides of the same coin is analogous to the dual aspects of the commodity and the fetishism therein. As we explained above, every commodity, including labor-power, is both a use-value and an exchange-value. The relation between commodities is a social relation between things and a material relation between people.

Following this analogy, sex is the material body, which, as use-value to (exchange-) value, attaches itself to gender. *The gender fetish* is a social relation which acts upon these bodies so that it appears as a natural characteristic of the bodies themselves. While gender is the abstraction of sexual difference from all of its concrete characteristics, that abstraction transforms and determines the body to which it is attached—just as the real abstraction of value transforms the material body of the commodity. Gender and sex combined give those inscribed within them a natural semblance ("with a phantomlike objectivity"), as if the social content of gender was "written upon the skin" of the concrete individuals.

The transhistoricization of sex is homologous to a foreshortened critique of capital, which contends that use-value is transhistorical rather than historically specific to capitalism. Here, use-value is thought to be that which positively remains after revolution, which is seen as freeing use-value from the integument of exchange-value. In terms of our analogy with sex and gender, we would go one step further and say that both gender and sex are historically determined. Both are entirely social and can only be abolished together—just as exchange-value and use-value will both have to be abolished in the process of communization. In this light, our feminist value-theoretical analysis mirrors Butler's critique in so far as we both view the sex/gender binary as being socially determined and produced through social conditions specific to modernity.

The denaturalization of gender

But gender is not a static social form. The abstraction of gender becomes increasingly denaturalised, making sex appear all the more concrete and biological. In other words, if sex and gender are two sides of the same coin, the relation between gender and its naturalised counterpart is not stable. There is a potential discrepancy between them, which some have called a "troubling," and we term "denaturalization."

Over time gender is ever more abstracted, defining sexuality more and more arbitrarily. The marketization and commodification of gender appears increasingly to *de-naturalise* gender from *naturalised* biological concerns. One might say that capitalism itself deconstructs gender and denaturalises it. Nature—whose increasing superfluity is in juxtaposition to gender's ongoing necessity—appears as the presupposition of gender rather than its effect. In more familiar terms, reflecting capital's "problem" with labor: "nature" (the "natural" side of the sex/gender binary) becomes increasingly superfluous to the generational reproduction of the proletariat, while the "cost" assigned to "female" bodies—or the counter-pole to sex—becomes increasingly imperative to capital accumulation as the tendency toward feminization. Hence, the reproduction of gender is of utmost importance, as labor-power with a lower cost, while a reserve army of proletarians as surplus population is increasingly redundant.

What the female gender signifies — that which is socially inscribed upon "naturalised," "sexuated" bodies—is not only an array of "feminine" or gendered characteristics, but essentially a price tag. Biological reproduction has a social cost which is *exceptional* to average (male) labor-power; it becomes the burden of those whose cost it is assigned to—regardless of whether they can or will have children. It is in this sense that an abstraction, a *gendered average*, is reflected back upon the organization of bodies in the same way exchange-value, a blind market average, is projected back upon production, molding and transforming the organization of the character of social production and the division of labor. In this sense, the transformation of the condition of gender relations goes on behind the backs of those whom it defines. And in this sense, gender is constantly reimposed and *re-naturalised*.

The history of gender within capitalism: From the creation of the IMM sphere to the commodification of gendered activities

To understand this dialectical process of de-naturalization and re-naturalization we first have to retrace the transformations within the gender relation over the course of the capitalist mode of production, and attempt a periodization. At this more concrete level, there are many possible points of entry to take, and we opt for a periodization of the family, since it is the economic unit that brings together the indirectly market-mediated (IMM) and the directly market-mediated (DMM) spheres which delimit the aspects of proletarian reproduction. We must try to figure out whether changes in the family form correspond to transformations in the process of labor's valorization.

Primitive accumulation and the extended family

During the era of primitive accumulation, a major problem facing the capitalist class was how to perfectly calibrate the relationship between the IMM and DMM spheres such that workers would, on the one hand, be forced to survive only by selling their labor-power, and on the other, be allotted only enough personal property to continue self-provisioning without bringing up the cost of labor-power.[23] Indeed, at the moment when the IMM was constituted, it had to take on as much as possible of the reproduction of labor-power, to be as big as possible, but *just enough* so that the proportion of self-provisioning allowed nevertheless required the habitual re-emergence of labor-power on the market. Therefore, the sphere of IMM supplementing the wage was subordinated to the market as a necessary presupposition of wage-relations and capitalist exploitation, and as its immediate result.

In the course of the transition from the 18th to the 19th century, the family—centered in the home as a unit of production—became *the* economic unit mediating between the IMM and DMM spheres of labor-power's reproduction. However, for the first part of the 19th century, as long as no retirement benefits existed and as long as it was also the case that children were expected to go to work before they even reached puberty, the family comprised several generations residing in one home. In addition, the activities of the IMM sphere were not carried out by married women alone; indeed they were done with the participation of children, grandmothers and other female relatives, even lodgers. If it was the case that only the "singly free" adult male members of the family could legally be owners of the wage, this did not mean that adult women and young children did not also work outside the home.

Indeed, at the beginning of industrialization, women represented one-third of the workforce. Like children, they did not decide if or where they would take employment, or which job they would perform; they were more or less subcontracted by their husbands or fathers. (Marx even compared it with some forms of the slave trade: the male head of the family bargained the price of the labor-power of his wife and children and chose to accept or decline. And let us not forget that in some countries, such as France and Germany, women only got the right to work without the authorization of their husbands in the 1960s or 1970s). Far from being a sign of the emancipation of women, or of the modern views of the husband, women working outside the home was a blatant indicator of poverty. Even if married women were generally expected to stay at home when the family could afford it (where they often did home-based production, especially for the textile industry), many women never married—for it was an expensive business—and some were not supposed to become pregnant, forming their own family. Younger daughters were often sent to become servants or helpers in other families, remaining "officially" single. Therefore, even if those responsible for the IMM sphere were always women, and those responsible for the wage were always men (one could say, by definition), the two genders and the two spheres did not map one to one in that period.

The nuclear family and Fordism

In the second part of the 19th century, what some call the second industrial revolution, there was a progressive move toward the nuclear family as we think of it today. First, after decades of labor struggles, the state stepped in to limit the employment of women and children, partly because it was faced with a crisis in the reproduction of the work force. Labor-power was expected to become more skilled (for example literacy increasingly became a skill required to access a job), and increasing attention was given to the education of children. A new category emerged, that of childhood, with its specific needs and phases of development. Looking after children became a complicated business, which could no longer be provided by elder siblings.[24]

This process culminated with Fordism, and its new standards of consumption and reproduction. With the generalization of retirement benefits and retirement homes, generations came to be separated from each other in individual houses. The allocation of family responsibilities between husband and wife became strictly defined by the separation between the spheres. IMM activities that used to be carried out together with other women (such as washing clothes) became the individual responsibility of one adult woman per household. The married woman's life often came to be entirely confined to the IMM sphere. It became the fate of most women, and their entire lives (including their personality, desires, etc.) were shaped by this fate.

It was therefore with the nuclear family (in a specific period of capitalism, and importantly, in a specific area of the world) that gender became a rigid binary, mapping one to one with the spheres. It became a strict norm, which does not mean everyone fitted into it. Many feminists who refer to gender as a set of characteristics that define "femininity" and "masculinity" have the norms of that period in mind. From this point on, individuals identified as women were born with different life-destinies than individuals defined as men—they lived "on two different planets" (some on Mars . . .), and were socialised as two distinct kinds of subjects. This distinction cut across all classes.

No longer helped by other members of the family, doing the IMM activities isolated behind four walls, married women were made to bear the entire burden of IMM activities on their own. This isolation would not have been possible without the introduction of household appliances turning the most extreme physical tasks into chores that could be carried out alone. The washing-machine, the indoor water-tap, the water heater—these helped to dramatically reduce the time spent on some IMM activities. But every minute gained was far from increasing the housewife's leisure time. Every spare moment had to be used to increase the standards of reproduction: clothes were washed more often, meals became ever more varied and healthy, and most importantly, childcare became an all-consuming IMM activity from infant care to the facilitation of children's leisure activities.

The 1970s: Real subsumption and the commodification of IMM activities

The commodification of IMM activities is clearly not a new phenomenon. From the beginning of capitalism it was possible to buy ready-made meals instead of cooking them, to buy new clothes instead of mending them, to pay a servant to look after the children or to do the housework. However, those were privileges of the middle and upper classes. Indeed, each time an IMM activity is turned into a commodity, it has to be paid for in the wage. Therefore, the mass-consumption of these commodities would only have been likely in periods of steady wage increases, since these services, as long as they were only formally subsumed, increased the exchange-value of necessary labor in an inverse ratio to surplus-value.

However, as a result of the possibilities opened by real subsumption, the value of some of these commodities can decrease at the same time as they are mass-produced. Advances in productivity make these commodities more and more affordable, and some of them—particularly ready-made meals and household appliances—slowly but surely became affordable with the wage. Nevertheless, some IMM activities are more difficult to commodify at a price low enough to be paid for by every wage. Indeed, even if it is possible to commodify childcare, it is not possible to make advances in productivity that would allow its cost to become ever cheaper. Even if the nourishing, washing of clothes, and so on, can be done more efficiently, the time for childcare is never reduced. You cannot look after children *more quickly*: they have to be attended to 24 hours a day.

What is possible is to rationalise childcare, for example, by having the state organise it and thereby reducing the adult-to-child ratio. However, there are limits to how many children one adult can possibly handle, especially if, in that process, this adult has to impart a specific standard of socialization, knowledge and discipline. This work can also be performed by the cheapest labor possible; that is, by women whose wage will be lower than the wage of a working mother. But in this case, IMM activities are simply deferred to the lowest-paid strata of the total population. Therefore the problem is not reduced. Rather, its negative effects are redistributed, often to poor immigrants and women of color.

So we see that all these possibilities are limited: there is always a remainder, which we will refer to as *the abject*,[25] that is, what cannot be subsumed or is not worth subsuming. It is obviously not abject *per se*—it exists as abject because of capital, and it is shaped by it. There is always this remainder that has to remain outside of market-relations, and the question of who has to perform it in the family will always be, to say the least, a conflictual matter.

Crisis and austerity measures: The rise of the abject

With the current crisis, all signs indicate that the state will be increasingly unwilling to organise IMM activities, since they are a mere cost. Expenses in childcare, elderly-care and healthcare are the first to be cut, not to mention education and after-school programs. These will become DMM for those who can afford it (privatization), or lapse into the sphere of unwaged indirect market-mediation—therefore increasing the abject.

The extent of this remains to be seen, but the trend in countries affected by the crisis is already clear. In the US, and in most countries of the Eurozone (with the notable exception of Germany), governments are cutting their spending to reduce their debt-to-GDP ratios.[26] Countries like Greece, Portugal and Spain, but also the UK, are drastically scaling down their expenses in healthcare and childcare. In Greece and Portugal public kindergartens are closing down. Infringements on the rights of pregnant women to maternity leave and benefits, or to resume their jobs after maternity, have been reported in Greece, Portugal, Italy, and the Czech Republic.[27] In the UK, where state-run nurseries are closing one by one, the situation is described by an anti-capitalist feminist group involved in the Hackney nurseries campaign, Feminist Fight Back:

> All over the UK local authorities have begun to announce significant reductions of funding to social services, from libraries and healthcare to playgrounds and art groups, from rape crisis centres to domestic violence services. Of particular relevance to women are the profound effects that will be felt in children's services, both in council and community nurseries and in New Labor's flagship Sure Start Centres, which provide a variety of services to parents on a "one-stop" basis.[28]

In a country where the Prime Minister himself advocates the organization of community services on a "voluntary basis," under the central policy idea of the "Big Society," a culture "where people, in their everyday lives, in their homes, in their neighborhoods, in their workplace . . . feel both free and powerful enough to help themselves and their own communities,"[29] anti-state feminists are faced with a dilemma:

> Our aim is for provision "in and against the state". This raises a core question in the struggle over public goods and shared resources and labor: how are we to ensure that our autonomous efforts to reproduce our own communities do not simply create Cameron's Big Society for him?—thereby endorsing the logic that if the state will no longer provide for us we will have to do it ourselves?[30]

The struggle around kindergartens which took place in Poznan (Poland) in 2012 also reflects this dilemma. The municipality is slowly transferring all the public kindergartens to private institutions to save costs. When the workers of one of the nurseries protested with parents and activists, against privatization, the local authorities came up with the option of letting the workers organise the nursery, but without providing them with any subsidies or guarantees. This made it a very dim option that was eventually rejected by the workers and parents.[31]

However, some marxist feminists seem to glorify the self-organization of IMM activities by women as a necessary step in the creation of an alternative society. For example Silvia Federici, in her 2010 text "Feminism and the Politics of the Common in an Era of Primitive Accumulation":

> If the house is the *oikos* on which the economy is built, then it is women, historically the house-workers and house-prisoners, who must take the initiative to reclaim the house as a center of collective life, one traversed by multiple people and forms of cooperation, providing safety without isolation and fixation, allowing for the sharing and circulation of community possessions, and above all providing the foundation for collective forms of reproduction. . . . It remains to clarify that assigning women this task of commoning/collectivizing reproduction is not to concede to a naturalistic conception of "femininity". Understandably, many feminists would view this possibility as "a fate worse than death." . . . But, quoting Dolores Hayden, the reorganisation of reproductive work, and therefore the reorganisation of the structure of housing and public space is not a question of identity; it is a labor question and, we can add, a power and safety question.[32]

Silvia Federici is right—we do consider this possibility worse than death. And her answer to this objection, which quotes Dolores Hayden rather freely, misses the point: the labor question *is* an identity question.[33] Even if we might, in the crisis, have no choice but to self-organise these reproductive activities—and even though, most likely, abject reproduction will in the end mainly be foisted upon women—we must fight against this process which reinforces gender. We must treat it as it is: a self-organization of the abject, of what no one else is willing to do.

It is important here to state that, even if unwaged IMM activities and the abject might refer to the same concrete activities, these two concepts must be differentiated. Indeed, the category of the abject refers specifically to activities that became waged at some point but are in the process of returning into the unwaged IMM sphere because they've become too costly for the state or capital. While IMM is a purely structural category, independent of any dynamic, the concept of the abject grasps the specificities of these activities and the process of their assignment in our current period. Indeed, we can say that, if many of our mothers and grandmothers were caught in the sphere of IMM activities, the problem we face today is different. It is not that we will have to "go back to the kitchen," if only because *we cannot afford it*. Our fate, rather, is *having to deal with the abject*. Contrary to the IMM activities of the past, this abject has already been to a large extent denaturalised. It does not appear to those performing it as some unfortunate natural fate, but more like an extra burden that one must deal with alongside wage-labor.[34] Being left to deal with it is the ugly face of gender today, and this helps us to see gender as it is: a powerful constraint.[35]

Indeed, the process of de-naturalization creates the possibility of gender appearing as *an external constraint*. This is not to say that the constraint of gender is less powerful than before, but that it can now be seen as a constraint, that is, as something outside oneself that it is possible to abolish.

A last thought, to conclude: if it happens to be true that the present moment allows us to see both our class-belonging and our gender-belonging as external constraints, this cannot be purely accidental. Or can it? This question is critical for an understanding of the struggle which leads to the abolition of gender, that is, to the reproduction by non-gendered individuals of a life in which all separate spheres of activity have been abolished.

Notes

1 In the broadest strokes, marxist feminism is a perspective which situates gender oppression in terms of social reproduction, and specifically the reproduction of labor-power. Often it considers the treatment of such topics in Marx and in subsequent marxist accounts of capitalism deficient, and in light of the "unhappy marriage" and "dual systems" debates, it generally supports a "single system" thesis. It is also worth noting that this article is meant to continue a conversation from the 1970s, the "domestic labor debate," which turns on the relationship between value and reproduction, and which deploys Marxist categories in order to consider whether "domestic" and "reproductive" labor are productive.

2 See "Communisation and Value-Form Theory," *Endnotes* 2 (April 2010).

3 Marx, *Capital*, vol. 1 (MECW 35), 565.

4 Ibid., Chapter 6.

5 Ibid., 181.

6 Such as Leopoldina Fortunati: see *The Arcane of Reproduction* (Autonomedia 1981).

7 On this point, we are very much influenced by Roswitha Scholz's value-dissociation theory, even if there remain major differences in our analyses, especially when it comes to the dynamics of gender. See Roswitha Scholz, *Das Geschlecht des Kapitalismus* (Bad Honnef: Horleman 2000).

8 That is, homogeneous time. See Moishe Postone, *Time, Labor and Social Domination* (Cambridge, MA: Cambridge University Press 1993), Chapter 5, "Abstract Time."

9 The gendered internalization of this allocation of IMM activities, what we will call "naturalization," obviously plays a large role in this. We will look closer at this mechanism in Part Four.

10 The fact that the wage itself does not come with a training manual is interesting. One may do with it "as one pleases"—particularly those who are its direct recipients—and so it is not distributed according to the specificities of the IMM sphere, i.e. the size of one's family, standard of living or the responsible/economical use of a particular income stream. This point would require more attention, but for now it will suffice to say: it is just not the capitalist's responsibility.

11 Clearly, all activities taking place in the capitalist mode of production are social, but certain reproductive activities are rejected by its laws as non-social, as they form *an outside within the inside of the totality of the capitalist mode of production*. This is why we use the social/unsocial binary, sometimes found in feminist accounts, with caution. A problem with the term is that it can imply that "reproductive labor" occurs in a "non-social sphere" outside of the capitalist mode of production, in either a domestic mode of production (see Christine Delphy, *Close to Home: A Materialist Analysis of Women's Oppression* [Hutchinson 1984]), or as a vestige of a previous mode of production. It can even sometimes be used to argue that it is another mode of production left unsocial because of its lack of rationalization and that what is needed is the socialization of this sphere. We think it is less confusing, and far more telling, to focus on the process of social validation itself.

12 Services that are paid from revenue are unproductive, and, in this sense, are part of the waged IMM sphere.

13 Marx provides a useful insight into the process of naturalization: "Increase of population is a natural power of labor for which nothing is paid. From the present standpoint, we use the term *natural power* to refer to *social power*. All *natural powers of social labor* are themselves historical products." Marx, *Grundrisse* (MECW 28), 327.

14 For Marx, civil society—or what in most political theory is considered "natural" society—stands *opposed* to the state.

15 See Marx, On the Jewish Question (MECW 3).

16 See Chris Chen's "The Limit Point of Capitalist Equality," *Endnotes* 3 (September 2013): 202–23.

17 Marx, *Capital*, vol. 1, (MECW 35), 179.

18 In France, before 1965, women could not engage in wage-labor without the authorization of their husband. In West Germany, that was not before 1977—see Part Five below.

19 We find the need for a class analysis which can cut through this thicket of intra-class disparities, while attending to the disparities of each with regard to their own particular and differential relation to capitalist domination. In short, proletarian identity, as an abstraction based upon a common form of unfreedom, was *never* going to account for everyone, even at the most abstract level. Another more nuanced analysis would be needed—one which would come up against the problematic of workers' identity itself.

20 Because the creation of a future generation of workers who are for a period of their life non-workers is a cost to capital which it disavows, and because this activity is posited as a *non-labor that steals time away from labor*.

21 See Paola Tabet, "Natural Fertility, Forced Reproduction", in Diana Leonard and Lisa Adkins (eds) *Sex in Question: French Materialist Feminism* (London: Taylor & Francis 1996).

22 See her critique of Simone de Beauvoir's "uncritical reproduction of the Cartesian distinction between freedom and the body." Judith Butler, *Gender Trouble* (New York: Routledge 1990), Chapter 1: "Subjects of Sex/Gender/Desire."

23 See Michael Perelman, *The Invention of Capitalism: Classical Political Economy and the Secret History of Primitive Accumulation* (Durham: Duke University Press 2000).

24 For the effects of compulsory education on working-class families see Wally Seccombe, *Weathering the Storm: Working-class Families from the Industrial Revolution to the Fertility Decline* (London: Verso 1993).

25 We take this term in its etymological sense: *ab-ject*, that which is cast off, thrown away, but *from something that it is part of.*

26 See "The Holding Pattern," *Endnotes* 3 (September 2013): 12–54.

27 Francesca Bettio, "Crisis and Recovery in Europe: The Labor Market Impact on Men and Women," 2011.

28 Feminist Fightback Collective, "Cuts are a Feminist Issue." *Soundings* 49 (Winter 2011).

29 Speech by David Cameron on "The Big Society," Liverpool, July 19, 2010.

30 Feminist Fightback, "Cuts are a Feminist Issue."

31 Women with Initiative (from Inicjatywa Pracownicza-Workers' Initiative), "Women Workers Fight Back against Austerity in Poland," *Industrial Worker* 1743, March 2012.

32 Silvia Federici, *Revolution at Point Zero, Housework, Reproduction, and Feminist Struggle* (New York: Common Notions 2012), 147.

33 This is obviously not to say that we don't value the whole of Federici's contribution to the marxist feminist debate. Along with Dalla Costa and James's, *The Power of Women and the Subversion of the Community*, Silvia Federici's texts are surely the most interesting pieces from the "domestic labor debate" of the 1970s. What we want to criticise here is a position that is currently influential within the "commons" debate, and that we consider highly problematic.

34 "A massive and sudden emergence of uncanniness, which, familiar as it might have been in an opaque and forgotten life, now harries me as radically separate, *loathsome*. Not me. Not that. But not nothing, either. A 'something' that I do not recognize as a thing. A weight of meaninglessness, about which there is nothing insignificant, and which curses me." Julia Kristeva, *Power of Horrors: An Essay on Abjection* (New York: Columbia University Press 1982), 2.

35 Obviously there are nowadays some men, even if few, who do a considerable part of the abject. And they get to know what many women experience: *that the abject sticks to one's skin.* Many of these men, especially when they end up having to do most of the childcare, seem somehow to be undergoing a process of *social castration.*

CHAPTER ELEVEN

Postmodernism or Class?
Yes, Please

Slavoj Žižek

From Judith Butler, Ernesto Laclau and Slavoj Žižek, Contingency, Hegemony, Universality. *London: Verso, 2000: 90–135.*

The realization of the world as global market, the undivided reign of great financial conglomerates, etc., all this is an indisputable reality and one that conforms, essentially, to Marx's analysis. The question is, where does politics fit in with all this? What kind of politics is really heterogeneous to what capital demands?—that is today's question.

ALAIN BADIOU

In a well-known Marx Brothers joke Groucho answers the standard question "Tea or coffee?" with "Yes, please!"—a refusal of choice. The basic underlying idea of this essay is that one should answer in the same way the false alternative today's critical theory seems to impose on us: either "class struggle" (the outdated problematic of class antagonism, commodity production, etc.) or "postmodernism" (the new world of dispersed multiple identities, of radical contingency, of an irreducible ludic plurality of struggles). Here, at least, we can have our cake and eat it—how?

To begin with, I would like to emphasize my closeness to both my partners in this endeavor: in both Judith Butler's and Ernesto Laclau's work, there is a central notion (or, rather, two aspects of the same central notion) that I fully endorse, finding it extraordinarily productive. In Judith Butler's work, this notion is that of the fundamental *reflexivity* of human desire,[1] and the notion (concomitant to the first one, although developed later) of "passionate attachments," of traumatic fixations that are unavoidable and, simultaneously, inadmissible—in order to remain operative, they have to be repressed; in Laclau, it is, of course, the notion of *antagonism* as fundamentally different from the logic of symbolic/structural difference, and the concomitant notion of the hegemonic struggle filling out the empty place of universality as necessary/impossible. In both cases, we are thus dealing with a term (universality, "passionate attachment") which is simultaneously impossible and necessary, disavowed and unavoidable. So where is my difference with the two of them? To define it is more difficult than it may appear: any direct attempt to formulate it via a comparison between our respective positions somehow misses the point.[2] I have dealt in more detail with the task of providing the "cognitive mapping" for tracing these differences in my latest book;[3] so, to avoid repetition, this essay is conceived as a supplement to that book, focusing on a specific topic: that of universality, historicity and the Real.

Another introductory remark: it is quite probable that a counterclaim could sometimes be made that in my dialogue with Butler and Laclau I am not actually arguing against their position but against a watered-down popular version which they would also oppose. In such cases I plead guilty in advance, emphasizing two points: first—probably to a much greater degree than I am aware—my dialogue with them relies on shared presuppositions, so that my critical remarks are rather to be perceived as desperate attempts to clarify my *own* position via its clear delimitation; secondly, my aim—and, as I am sure, the aim of all three of us—is not to score narcissistic points against others, but—to risk an old-fashioned expression—to struggle with the Thing itself which is at stake, namely, the (im)possibilities of radical political thought and practice today.

I

Let me begin with Laclau's concept of *hegemony*, which provides an exemplary matrix of the relationship between universality, historical contingency and the limit of an impossible Real—one should always bear in mind that we are dealing here with a distinct concept whose specificity is often missed (or reduced to some vague proto-Gramscian generality) by those who refer to it. The key feature of the concept of hegemony lies in the contingent connection between intrasocial differences (elements within the social space) and the limit that separates society itself from non-society (chaos, utter decadence, dissolution of all social links)—the limit between the social and its exteriority, the non social, can articulate itself only in the guise of a difference (by mapping itself on to a difference) between elements of social space. In other words, radical antagonism can be represented only in a distorted way, through the particular differences internal to the system.[4] Laclau's point is thus that external differences are always-already also internal and, furthermore, that the link between the two is ultimately contingent, the result of political struggle for hegemony, not inscribed into the very social Being of agents.

In the history of Marxism, the tension that defines the concept of hegemony is best exemplified by its oscillation between the radical revolutionary logic of equivalence (Us against Them, Progress against Reaction, Freedom against Tyranny, Society against Decadence), which had to have recourse to different contingent groups to realize the universal task of global social transformation (from working class to colonized peasants; see also Sorel's oscillation from Leftist Syndicalism to Fascism), and the "revisionist" reduction of the progressive agenda to a series of particular social problems to be resolved gradually via compromises. More generally, we are suspended between a pure corporate vision of society as a Body with each part occupying its proper place, and the radical revolutionary vision of antagonism between society and antisocial forces ("the people is split into friends and enemies of the people")—and, as Laclau emphasizes, both these extremes ultimately coincide: a pure corporate vision has to eject forces that oppose its organic notion of the social Body into pure externality (the Jewish plot, etc.), thus reasserting radical antagonism between the social Body and the external force of Decadence; while radical revolutionary practice has to rely on a *particular* element (class) which embodies universality (from Marxist proletariat to Pol Pot's peasants). The only solution to this deadlock seems to be to accept it as such—to accept that we are condemned to the unending struggle between particular elements to stand in for the impossible totality:

> If hegemony means the representation, by a particular social sector, of an impossible totality with which it is incommensurable, then it is enough that we make the space of topological substitutions fully visible, to enable the hegemonic logic to operate freely. If the fullness of society is unachievable, the attempts at reaching it will necessarily fail, although they will be able, in the search for that impossible object, to solve a variety of partial problems.[5]

Here, however, a series of questions arises from my perspective. Does not this solution involve the Kantian logic of the infinite approach to the impossible Fullness as a kind of "regulative Idea"? Does it not involve the resigned/

cynical stance of "although we know we will fail, we should persist in our search"—of an agent which knows that the global Goal toward which it is striving is impossible, that its ultimate effort will necessarily fail, but which nonetheless accepts the need for this global Specter as a necessary lure to give it the energy to engage in solving partial problems? Furthermore (and this is just another aspect of the same problem), is not this alternative—the alternative between achieving "fullness of society" and solving "a variety of partial problems"—too limited? Is it not that—here, at least—there is a Third Way, although definitely not in the sense of the Risk Society theorists? What about changing the very fundamental *structural principle* of society, as happened with the emergence of the "democratic invention"? The passage from feudal monarchy to capitalist democracy, while it failed to reach the "impossible fullness of society," certainly did more than just "solve a variety of partial problems."

A possible counter-argument would be that the radical break of the "democratic invention" consists in the very fact that what was previously considered an *obstacle* to the "normal" functioning of power (the "empty place" of power, the gap between this place and the one who actually exerts power, the ultimate indeterminacy of power) now becomes its positive *condition*: what was previously experienced as a threat (the struggle between more subjects-agents to fill in the place of power) now becomes the very condition of the legitimate exercise of power. The extraordinary character of "democratic invention" thus consists in the fact that—to put it in Hegelian terms—the contingency of power, the gap between power *qua* place and its place-holder, is no longer only "in itself," but becomes "for itself," is acknowledged explicitly "as such," reflected in the very structure of power.[6] What this means is that—to put it in the well-known Derridan terms—the condition of impossibility of the exercise of power becomes its condition of possibility: just as the ultimate failure of communication is what compels us to talk all the time (if we could say what we want to say directly, we would very soon stop talking and shut up for ever), so the ultimate uncertainty and precariousness of the exercise of power is the only guarantee that we are dealing with a legitimate democratic power.

The first thing to add here, however, is that we are dealing with a series of breaks: within the history of modernity itself, one should distinguish between the break of the "first modernity" ("democratic invention": the French Revolution, the introduction of the notion of the sovereignty of the people, of democracy, of human rights . . .) and the contemporary break of what Beck, Giddens and others call the "second modernity" (the thorough reflexivization of society).[7] Furthermore, is not already the "first modernity" already characterized by the inherent tension between the "people's democracy" (People-as-One, General Will) with its potentially "totalitarian" outcome, and the liberal notion of individual freedom, reducing state to a "night watchman" of civil society.

So the point is that, again, we are dealing with the multitude of configurations of the democratic society, and these configurations form a kind of Hegelian "concrete universality"—that is to say, we are not dealing simply with different subspecies of the genus of Democracy, but with a series of breaks which affect the very universal notion of Democracy: these subspecies (early Lockeian liberal democracy, "totalitarian" democracy . . .) in a way explicate ("posit," are generated by) the inherent tension of the very universal notion of political Democracy. Furthermore, this tension is not simply internal/inherent to the notion of Democracy, but is defined by the way Democracy relates to its Other: not only its political Other—non-Democracy in its various guises—but primarily that which the very definition of political democracy tends to exclude as "non-political" (private life and economy in classical liberalism, etc.). While I fully endorse the well-known thesis that the very gesture of drawing a clear line of distinction between the Political and the non-Political, of positing some domains (economy, private intimacy, art . . .) as "apolitical," is a political gesture *par excellence*, I am also tempted to turn it around: what if the political gesture *par excellence*, at its purest, is precisely the gesture of separating the Political from the non-Political, of excluding some domains from the Political?

II

Let me, then, take a closer look at Laclau's narrative which runs from Marxist essentialism (the proletariat as the universal class whose revolutionary mission is inscribed into its very social being and thus discernible via "objective" scientific analysis) to the "postmodern" recognition of the contingent, tropological, metaphorico-metonymic, link between a social agent and its "task." Once this contingency is acknowledged, one has to accept that there is no direct, "natural" correlation between an agent's social position and its tasks in the political struggle, no norm of development by which to measure exceptions say, because of the weak political subjectivity of the bourgeoisie in Russia around 1900, the working class had to accomplish the bourgeois-democratic revolution itself . . .[8] My first observation here is that while this standard postmodern Leftist narrative of the passage from "essentialist" Marxism, with the proletariat as the unique Historical Subject, the privileging of economic-class struggle, and so on, to the postmodern irreducible plurality of struggles undoubtedly describes an actual historical process, its proponents, as a rule, leave out the resignation at its heart—the acceptance of capitalism as "the only game in town," the renunciation of any real attempt to overcome the existing capitalist liberal regime.[9] This point was already made very precisely in Wendy Brown's perspicuous observation that "the political purchase of contemporary American identity politics would seem to be achieved in part *through* a certain renaturalization of capitalism."[10] The crucial question to be asked is thus:

> to what extent a critique of capitalism is foreclosed by the current configuration of oppositional politics, and not simply by the "loss of the socialist alternative" or the ostensible "triumph of liberalism" in the global order. In contrast with the Marxist critique of a social whole and Marxist vision of total transformation, to what extent do identity politics require a standard internal to existing society against which to pitch their claims, a standard that not only preserves capitalism from critique, but sustains the invisibility and inarticulateness of class—not incidentally, but endemically? Could we have stumbled upon one reason why class is invariably named but rarely theorized or developed in the multiculturalist mantra, "race, class, gender, sexuality"?[11]

One can describe in very precise terms this reduction of class to an entity "named but rarely theorized": one of the great and permanent results of the so-called "Western Marxism" first formulated by the young Lukács is that the class-and-commodity structure of capitalism is not just a phenomenon limited to the particular "domain" of economy, but the structuring principle that overdetermines the social totality, from politics to art and religion. *This* global dimension of capitalism is suspended in today's multiculturalist progressive politics: its "anti-capitalism" is reduced to the level of how today's capitalism breeds sexist/racist oppression, and so on. Marx claimed that in the series production-distribution-exchange-consumption, the term "production" is doubly inscribed: it is simultaneously one of the terms in the series and the structuring principle of the entire series. In production as one of the terms of the series, production (as the structuring principle) "encounters itself in its oppositional determination,"[12] as Marx put it, using the precise Hegelian term. And the same goes for the postmodern political series class-gender-race . . .: in class as one of the terms in the series of particular struggles, class *qua* structuring principle of the social totality "encounters itself in its oppositional determination."[13] In so far as postmodern politics promotes, in effect, a kind of "politicization of the economy," is not this politicization similar to the way our supermarkets—which fundamentally exclude from their field of visibility the actual production process (the way vegetables and fruit are harvested and packed by immigrant workers, the genetic and other manipulations in heir production and display, etc.)—stage within the field of the displayed goods, as a kind of ersatz, the spectacle of a pseudo-production (meals prepared in full view in "food courts," fruit juices freshly squeezed before the customers' eyes, etc.)?[14] An authentic Leftist should therefore ask the postmodern politicians the new version of the old Freudian question put to the perplexed Jew: "Why are you saying that one should politicize the economy, when one should in fact politicize the economy?"[15]

So inso-far as postmodern politics involves a "[t]heoretical retreat from the problem of domination within capitalism,"[16] it is *here*, in this silent suspension of class analysis, that we are dealing with an exemplary case of the mechanism of ideological displacement: when class antagonism is disavowed, when its key structuring role is suspended, "other markers of social difference may come to bear an inordinate weight; indeed, they may bear all the weight of the sufferings produced by capitalism in addition to that attributable to the explicitly politicized marking."[17] In other words, this *displacement* accounts for the somewhat "excessive" way the discourse of postmodern identity politics insists on the horrors of sexism, racism, and so on—this "excess" comes from the fact that these other "-isms" have to bear the surplus-investment from the class struggle whose extent is not acknowledged.[18]

Of course, the postmodernists' answer would be that I am "essentializing" class struggle: there is, in today's society, a series of particular political struggles (economic, human rights, ecology, racism, sexism, religious . . .), and no struggle can claim to be the "true" one, the key to all the others . . . Usually, Laclau's development itself (from his first breakthrough work, *Politics and Ideology in Marxist Theory*, to his standard classic, co-authored with Chantal Mouffe, *Hegemony and Socialist Strategy*) is presented as the gradual process of getting rid of the "last remnants of essentialism":[19] in the first book following the classic Marxist tradition—the economy (the relations of production and economic laws) still serves as a kind of "ontological anchorage point" for the otherwise contingent struggles for hegemony (i.e. in a Gramscian way, the struggle for hegemony is ultimately the struggle between the two great classes for which of them will occupy-hegemonize a series of other "historical tasks"—national liberation, cultural struggle, etc.); it is only in the second book that Laclau definitely renounces the old Marxist problematic of infra- and superstructure, that is, the objective grounding of the "super structural" hegemonic struggle in the economic "infrastructure"—economy itself is always-already "political," a discursive site (one of the sites) of political struggles, of power and resistance, "a field penetrated by pre-ontological undecidability of irrevocable dilemmas and aporias."[20]

In their *Hegemony* book, Laclau and Mouffe clearly privilege the *political struggle for democracy*,—that is to say, they accept Claude Lefort's thesis that the key moment in modern political history was the "democratic invention" and all other struggles are ultimately the "application" of the principle of democratic invention to other domains: race (why should other races not also be equal?), sex, religion, the economy . . . In short, when we are dealing with a series of particular struggles, is there not always one struggle which, although it appears to function as one in the series, effectively provides the horizon of the series as such? Is this not also one of the consequences of the notion of hegemony? So, insofar as we conceive radical plural democracy as "the promise that plural democracy, and the struggles for freedom and equality it engenders, should be deepened and extended to all spheres of society,"[21] is it possible simply to extend it to the economy as another new terrain? When Brown emphasizes that "if Marxism had any analytical value for *political* theory, was it not in the insistence that the problem of freedom was contained in the social relations implicitly declared 'unpolitical'—that is, naturalized—in liberal discourse,"[22] it would be too easy to accept the counter-argument that postmodern politics, of course, endorses the need to denaturalize/repoliticize the economy, and that its point is precisely that one should also denaturalize/repoliticize a series of other domains (relations between the sexes, language, etc.) left "undeconstructed" by Marx. Postmodern politics definitely has the great merit that it "repoliticizes" a series of domains previously considered "apolitical" or "private"; the fact remains, however, that it does not in fact repoliticize capitalism, because *the very notion and form of the "political" within which it operates is grounded in the "depoliticization" of the economy.* If we are to play the postmodern game of plurality of political subjectivizations, it is formally necessary that we do not ask certain questions (about how to subvert capitalism as such, about the constitutive limits of political democracy and/or the democratic state as such . . .). So, again, apropos of Laclau's obvious counter-argument that the Political, for him, is not a specific social domain but the very set of contingent decisions that ground the Social, I would answer that the postmodern emergence of new multiple political subjectivities certainly does not reach this radical level of the political act proper.

What I am tempted to do here is to apply the lesson of Hegelian "concrete universality" to "radical democracy": Laclau's notion of hegemony is in fact close to the Hegelian notion of "concrete universality," in which the specific difference overlaps with the difference constitutive of the genus itself; as in Laclau's hegemony, in which the antagonistic gap between society and its external limit, non-society (the dissolution of social links), is mapped on to an intra-social structural difference. But what about the infamous Hegelian "reconciliation" between Universal and Particular rejected by Laclau on account of the gap that forever separates the empty/impossible Universal from the contingent particular content that hegemonizes it?[23] If we take a closer look at Hegel, we see that—insofaras every particular species of a genus does not "fit" its universal genus—when we finally arrive at a particular species that fully fits its notion, *the very universal notion is transformed into another notion.* No existing historical shape of state fully fits the notion of State—the necessity of dialectical passage from State ("objective spirit," history) into Religion ("Absolute Spirit") involves the fact that the only existing state that effectively fits its notion is a *religious community*—which, precisely, is no longer a state. Here we encounter the properly dialectical paradox of "concrete universality" qua historicity: in the relationship between a genus and its subspecies, one of these subspecies will always be the element that negates the very universal feature of the genus. Different nations have different versions of soccer; Americans do not have soccer, because "baseball is their soccer." This is analogous to Hegel's famous claim that modern people do not pray in the morning, because reading the newspaper is their morning prayer. In the same way, in disintegrating socialism, writers' and other cultural clubs did act as political parties. Perhaps, in the history of cinema, the best example is the relationship between Western and sci-fi space operas: today, we no longer have "substantial" Westerns, because space operas have *taken their place*, that is, *space operas are today's Westerns*. So, in the classification of Westerns, we would have to supplement the standard subspecies with space opera as today's non-Western stand-in for the Western. Crucial here is this intersection of different genuses, this partial overlapping of two universals: the Western and space opera are not simply two different genres, they *intersect*—that is, in a certain epoch, space opera becomes a subspecies of the Western (or, the Western is "sublated" in the space opera). . . In the same way, "woman" becomes one of the subspecies of man, Heideggerian *Daseinsanalyse* one of the subspecies of phenomenology, "sublating" the preceding universality; and—back to a "radical democracy"—in the same way, "radical democracy" that was actually "radical" in the sense of politicizing the sphere of economy would, precisely, no longer be a "(*political*) *democracy*."[24] (This, of course, does not mean that the "impossible fullness" of Society would in fact be actualized: it simply means that the limit of the impossible would be transposed on to another level.) And what if the Political itself (the radically contingent struggle for hegemony) is also split/barred in its very notion? What if *it can be operative only insofar as it "represses" its radically contingent nature, insofar as it undergoes a minimum of "naturalization"*? What if the essentialist lure is irreducible: we are never dealing with the Political "at the level of its notion," with political agents who fully endorse their contingency—and the way out of this deadlock via notions like "strategic essentialism" is definitely condemned to fail?

My conclusion would thus be to emphasize that the impossibility at work in Laclau's notion of antagonism is *double*: not only does "radical antagonism" mean that it is impossible adequately to represent/articulate the *fullness* of Society—on an even more radical level, *it is also impossible adequately to represent/articulate this very antagonism/negativity that prevents Society from achieving its full ontological realization*. This means that ideological fantasy is not simply the fantasy of the impossible fullness of Society: not only is Society impossible, this impossibility itself is distortedly represented-positivized within an ideological field—*that* is the role of ideological fantasy (say, of the Jewish plot).[25] When this very *impossibility* is represented in a positive element, inherent impossibility is changed into an external obstacle. "Ideology" is also the name for the guarantee that *the negativity which prevents Society from achieving its fullness does actually exist*, that it has a positive existence in the guise of a big Other who pulls the strings of social life, like the Jews in the anti-Semitic notion of "the Jewish plot." In short, the basic operation of ideology is not only the dehistoricizing gesture of transforming an empirical obstacle into the eternal condition (women, Blacks . . . are by nature subordinated, etc.), but also the *opposite* gesture of transposing the a priori closure/impossibility of a field into an empirical obstacle. Laclau is well aware of this paradox when he denounces as ideological the very notion that after the successful revolution, a non-antagonistic self-transparent society will come about. However, this justified rejection of the fullness of post-revolutionary Society does not *justify* the conclusion that we have to renounce any project of a global social transformation, and limit ourselves to partial problems to be solved: the jump from a critique of the "metaphysics of presence" to anti-utopian "reformist" gradualist politics is an illegitimate short circuit.

III

Like Laclau's notion of universality as impossible/necessary, Butler's elaboration of universality is much more refined than the standard historicist denouncing of each universality as "false," that is, secretly privileging some particular content, while repressing or excluding another. She is well aware that universality is unavoidable, and her point is that—while, of course, each determinate historical figure of universality involves a set of inclusions/exclusions—universality simultaneously opens up and sustains the space for questioning these inclusions/exclusions, for "renegotiating" the limits of inclusion/ exclusion as part of the ongoing ideologico-political struggle for hegemony. The predominant notion of "universal human rights," for instance, precludes—or, at least, reduces to a secondary status—a set of sexual practices and orientations; and it would be too simplistic to accept the standard liberal game of simply insisting that one should redefine and broaden our notion of human rights to include also all these "aberrant" practices—what standard liberal humanism underestimates is the extent to which such exclusions are *constitutive* of the "neutral" universality of human rights, so that their actual inclusion in "human rights" would radically rearticulate, even undermine, our notion of what "humanity" in "human rights" means. Nonetheless, the inclusions/exclusions involved in the hegemonic notion of universal human rights are not fixed and simply consubstantial with this universality but the stake of the continuous ideologico-political struggle, something that can be renegotiated and redefined, and the reference to universality can serve precisely as a tool that stimulates such questioning and renegotiation ("If you assert universal human rights, why are we [gays, Blacks . . .] not also part of it?").

So when we criticize the hidden bias and exclusion of universality, we should never forget that we are already doing so *within* the terrain opened up by universality: the proper critique of "false universality" does not call it into question from the standpoint of pre-universal particularism, it mobilizes the tension inherent to universality itself, the tension between the open negativity, the disruptive power, of what Kierkegaard would have called "universality-in-becoming," and the fixed form of established universality. Or—if I may interpret Butler in Hegelian terms—we have, on the one hand, the "dead," "abstract" universality of an ideological notion with fixed inclusions/exclusions and, on the other, "living," "concrete" universality as the permanent process of the questioning and renegotiation of its own "official" content. Universality becomes "actual" precisely and only by rendering thematic the exclusions on which it is grounded, by continuously questioning, renegotiating, displacing them, that is, by assuming the gap between its own form and content, by conceiving itself as unaccomplished in its very notion. This is what Butler's notion of the politically salient use of "performative contradiction" is driving at: if the ruling ideology performatively "cheats" by undermining—in its actual discursive practice and the set of exclusions on which this practice relies—its own officially asserted universality, progressive politics should precisely openly practise performative contradiction, asserting on behalf of the given universality the very content this universality (in its hegemonic form) excludes.

Here I should just like to emphasize two further points:

- the exclusionary logic is always redoubled in itself: not only is the subordinated Other (homosexuals, non-white races . . .) excluded/repressed, but hegemonic universality itself also relies on a disavowed "obscene" particular content of its own (say, the exercise of power that legitimizes itself as legal, tolerant, Christian . . . relies on a set of publicly disavowed obscene rituals of violent humiliation of the subordinated[26]). More generally, we are dealing here with what one is tempted to call the *ideological practice of disidentification.* That is to say, one should turn around the standard notion of ideology as providing a firm identification to its subjects, constraining them to their "social roles": what if, on a different—but no less irrevocable and structurally necessary—level, ideology is effective precisely by constructing a space of *false disidentification,* of false distance toward the actual co-ordinates of those subjects' social existence?[27] Is not this logic of disidentification discernible from the most elementary case of "I am not only an American (husband, worker, democrat, gay . . .), but, beneath all these roles and masks, a human being, a complex unique personality" (where the very distance toward the symbolic feature that determines my social place guarantees the efficiency of this determination), up to the more complex case of cyberspace playing with one's multiple identities? The mystification operative in the perverse "just playing" of cyberspace is therefore double: not only are the games we are playing in it more serious than we tend to assume (is it not that, in the guise of a fiction, of "it's just a game," a subject can articulate and stage features of his symbolic identity—sadistic, "perverse," and so on—which he would never be able to admit in his "real" intersubjective contacts?), but the opposite also holds, that is, the much-celebrated playing with multiple, shifting personas (freely constructed identities) tends to obfuscate (and thus falsely liberate us from) the constraints of social space in which our existence is trapped.

- Let me evoke another example: why did Christa Wolf's *The Quest for Christa T* exert such a tremendous impact on the GDR public in the 1960s? Because it is precisely a novel about the failure—or, at least, the vacillation—of ideological interpellation, about the failure of fully recognizing oneself in one's socio-ideological identity:

> When her name was called: "Christa T.!"—she stood up and went and did what was expected of her; was there anyone to whom she could say that hearing her name called gave her much to think about: Is it really me who's meant? Or is it only my name that's being used? Counted in with other names, industriously added up in front of the equals sign? And might I just as well have been absent, would anyone have noticed?[28]

Is not this gesture of "Am I that name?," this probing into one's symbolic identification so well expressed by Johannes R. Becher's quote which Wolf put at the very beginning of the novel: "This coming-to-oneself—what is it?," hysterical provocation at its purest? And my point is that such a self-probing attitude, far from effectively threatening the predominant ideological regime, is what ultimately makes it "livable"—this is why her West German detractors were in a way paradoxically right when, after the fall of the Wall, they claimed that Christa Wolf, by expressing the subjective complexities, inner doubts and oscillations of the GDR subject, actually provided a realistic literary equivalent of the ideal GDR subject, and was as such much more successful in her task of securing political conformity than the open naive propagandist fiction depicting ideal subjects sacrificing themselves for the Communist Cause.[29]

- The theoretical task is not only to unmask the particular content of inclusions/exclusions involved in the game, but also to account for the enigmatic emergence of the space of universality itself.

Furthermore—and more precisely—the real task is to explore the fundamental shifts in the very logic of the way universality works in the socio-symbolic space: premodern, modern, and today's "post-modern" notion and ideological practice of universality do not, for example, differ only with regard to the particular contents that are included/excluded in universal notions—somehow, on a more radical level, the very underlying notion of universality functions in a different way in each of these epochs. "Universality" as such does not mean the same thing since the establishment of bourgeois market society in which individuals participate in the social order not on behalf of their particular place within the global social edifice but *immediately*, as "abstract" human beings.

Let me return to the notion of universal human rights. The Marxist symptomal reading can convincingly demonstrate the particular content that gives the specific bourgeois ideological spin to the notion of human rights: "universal human rights are in effect the right of white male property owners to exchange freely on the market, exploit workers and women, and exert political domination . . .." This identification of the particular content that hegemonizes the universal form is, however, only half the story; its other, crucial half consists in asking a much more difficult supplementary question about the *emergence of the very form of universality*: how, in what specific historical conditions, does abstract universality itself become a "fact of (social) life"? In what conditions do individuals experience themselves as subjects of universal human rights? That is the point of Marx's analysis of "commodity fetishism": in a society in which commodity exchange predominates, individuals themselves, in their daily lives, relate to themselves, as well as to the objects they encounter, as to contingent embodiments of abstract-universal notions. What I am, my concrete social or cultural background, is experienced as contingent, since what ultimately defines me is the "abstract" universal capacity to think and/or to work. Or: any object that can satisfy my desire is experienced as contingent, since my desire is conceived as an "abstract" formal capacity, indifferent toward the multitude of particular objects that may—but never fully do—satisfy it. Or take the already mentioned example of "profession": the modern notion of profession implies that I experience myself as an individual who is not directly "born into" his social role—what I will become depends on the interplay between contingent social circumstances and my free choice; in this sense, today's individual has the profession of electrician or professor or waiter, while it is meaningless to claim that a medieval serf was a peasant by profession. The crucial point here is, again, that in certain specific social conditions (of commodity exchange and a global market economy), "abstraction" becomes a direct feature of actual social life, the way concrete individuals behave and relate to their fate and to their social surroundings.

Here Marx shares Hegel's insight into how universality becomes "for itself" only insofar as individuals no longer fully identify the kernel of their being with their particular social situation, only in so far as they experience themselves as forever "out of joint" with regard to this situation: the concrete, effective existence of the universality is the individual without a proper place in the global edifice—in a given social structure, Universality becomes "for itself" only in those individuals who lack a proper place in it. The mode of appearance of an abstract universality, its entering into actual existence, is thus an extremely violent move of disrupting the preceding organic balance.

My claim is thus that when Butler speaks of the unending political process of renegotiating the inclusions/exclusions of the predominant ideological universal notions, or when Laclau proposes his model of the unending struggle for hegemony, *the "universal" status of this very model is problematic*: are they providing the *formal* co-ordinates of *every* ideologico-political process, or are they simply elaborating the notional structure of *today's* ("postmodern") *specific* political practice which is emerging after the retreat of the classical Left?[30] They (more often than not, in their explicit formulations) *appear* to do the first (for Laclau, say, the logic of hegemony is somewhat unambiguously articulated as a kind of Heideggerian *existential structure* of social life), although one can also argue that they are merely theorizing a very specific historical moment of the "postmodern" Left. . . .[31] In other words, the problem for me is *how to historicize historicism itself*. The passage from "essentialist" Marxism to postmodern contingent politics (in Laclau), or the passage from sexual essentialism to contingent gender-formation (in Butler), or—a further example—the passage from metaphysician to ironist in Richard Rorty, is not a simple epistemological progress but part of the global change in the very nature of capitalist society. It is not that before, people were "stupid essentialists" and believed in naturalized sexuality, while now they know that genders are performatively enacted; one needs a kind of metanarrative that explains this very passage from essentialism to the awareness of contingency: the Heideggerian notion of the epochs of Being, or the Foucauldian notion of the shift in the predominant *épistème,* or the standard sociological notion of modernization, or a more Marxist account in which this passage follows the dynamic of capitalism.

IV

So, again, crucial in Laclau's theoretical edifice is the paradigmatically Kantian co-dependency between the "timeless" existential a priori of the logic of hegemony and the *historical narrative* of the gradual passage from the "essentialist" traditional Marxist class politics to the full assertion of the contingency of the struggle for hegemony—just as the Kantian transcendental a priori is co-dependent with his anthropologico-political evolutionary narrative of humanity's gradual progression toward enlightened maturity. The role of this evolutionary narrative is precisely to resolve the above-mentioned ambiguity of the formal universal frame (of the logic of hegemony)—implicitly to answer the question: is this frame really a non-historical universal, or simply the formal structure of the specific ideologico-political constellation of Western late capitalism? The evolutionary narrative mediates between these two options, telling the story of how the universal frame was "posited as such," became the explicit structuring principle of ideologico-political life. The question none the less persists: is this evolutionary passage a simple passage from error to true insight? Is it that each stance fits its own epoch, so that in Marx's time "class essentialism" was adequate, while today we need the assertion of contingency? Or should we combine the two in a proto-Hegelian way, so that the very passage from the essentialist "error" to "true" insight into radical contingency is historically conditioned (in Marx's time, the "essentialist illusion" was "objectively necessary," while our epoch enables the insight into contingency)? This proto-Hegelian solution would allow us to combine the "universal" scope or "validity" of the concept of hegemony with the obvious fact that its recent emergence is clearly linked to today's specific social constellation: although sociopolitical life and its structure were always-already the outcome of hegemonic struggles, it is nonetheless only today, in our specific historical constellation—that is to say, in the "postmodern" universe of globalized contingency—that the radically contingent-hegemonic nature of the political processes is finally allowed to "come/return to itself," to free itself of the "essentialist" baggage . . .

This solution, however, is problematic for at least two reasons. First, Laclau would probably reject it as relying on the Hegelian notion of the necessary historical development that conditions and anchors political struggles. Second, from my perspective, today's postmodern politics of multiple subjectivities is precisely not political enough, in so far as it silently presupposes a non-thematized, "naturalized" framework of economic relations. Against the postmodern political theory which tends increasingly to prohibit the very reference to capitalism as "essentialist," one should assert that the plural contingency of postmodern political struggles and the totality of Capital are not opposed, with Capital somehow "limiting" the free drift of hegemonic displacements—today's capitalism, rather, provides *the very background and terrain for the emergence of shifting-dispersed-contingent-ironic-and so on, political subjectivities*. Was it not Deleuze who in a way made this point when he emphasized how capitalism is a force of "deterritorialization"? And was he not following Marx's old thesis on how, with capitalism, "all that is solid melts into air"?

So, ultimately, my key point apropos of Butler and Laclau is the same in both cases: the need to distinguish more explicitly between contingency/substitutability *within* a certain historical horizon and the more fundamental exclusional foreclosure that *grounds this very horizon.* . . .

V

This notion of the subject as the "answer of the Real" finally allows me to confront Butler's standard criticism of the relationship between the Real and the Symbolic in Lacan: the determination of the Real as that which resists symbolization is itself a symbolic determination, that is, the very gesture of excluding something from the Symbolic, of positing it as beyond the prohibitive Limit (as the Sacred, Untouchable), is a symbolic gesture (a gesture of symbolic exclusion) *par excellence* . . . In contrast to this, however, one should insist on how the Lacanian Real is strictly *internal* to the Symbolic: it is nothing but its inherent limitation, the impossibility of the Symbolic fully to "become itself." As we have already emphasized, the Real of sexual difference does not mean that we have a fixed set of symbolic oppositions defining masculine and feminine "roles," so that all subjects who do not fit into one of these two slots are excluded/rejected into the "impossible Real"; it means precisely that every attempt at its symbolization fails—that sexual difference cannot be adequately translated into a set of symbolic oppositions. However, to avoid a further misunderstanding: the fact that sexual difference cannot be translated into a set of symbolic oppositions in no way implies that it is "real" in the sense of some pre-existing external substantial Entity beyond the grasp of symbolization: precisely as real, sexual difference is *absolutely internal* to the Symbolic—it is its point of inherent failure.

It is in fact Laclau's notion of antagonism that can exemplify the Real: just as sexual difference can articulate itself only in the guise of the series of (failed) attempts to transpose it into symbolic oppositions, so the antagonism (between Society itself and the non-Social) is not simply external to the differences that are internal to the social structure, since, as we have already seen, it can articulate itself only in the guise of a difference (by mapping itself on to a difference) between elements of social space.[32] If the Real were to be directly external to the Symbolic, then Society definitely *would* exist: for something to exist, it has to be defined by its external limit, and the Real would have served as this externality guaranteeing the inherent consistency of Society. (This is what anti-Semitism does by way of "reifying" the inherent deadlockimpossibility-antagonism of the Social in the external figure of the Jew—the Jew is the ultimate guarantee that society exists. What happens in the passage from the position of strict class struggle to Fascist anti-Semitism is not just a simple replacement of one figure of the enemy [the bourgeoisie, the ruling class] with another [the Jews], but the shift from the logic of antagonism which makes Society impossible to the logic of external Enemy which guarantees Society's consistency.) The paradox, therefore, is that Butler is, in a way, right: yes, the Real *is* in fact internal/inherent to the Symbolic, not its external limit, but *for that very reason*, it cannot be symbolized. In other words, the paradox is that the Real as external, excluded from the Symbolic, is in fact a symbolic determination—what eludes symbolization is precisely the Real as the *inherent point of failure* of symbolization.[33]

Precisely because of this internality of the Real to the Symbolic, it is possible to touch the Real through the Symbolic—that is the whole point of Lacan's notion of psychoanalytic treatment; this is what the Lacanian notion of the psychoanalytic *act* is about—the act as a gesture which, by definition, touches the dimension of some impossible Real. This notion of the act must be conceived of against the background of the distinction between the mere endeavor to "solve a variety of partial problems" within a given field and the more radical gesture of subverting the very structuring principle of this field. An act does not simply occur within the given horizon of what appears to be "possible" it redefines the very contours of what is possible (an act accomplishes what, *within* the given symbolic universe, appears to be "impossible," yet it changes its conditions so that it creates retroactively the conditions of its own possibility). So when we are reproached by an opponent for doing something unacceptable, an act occurs when we no longer defend ourselves by accepting the underlying premiss that we hitherto shared with the opponent; in contrast, we fully accept the reproach, changing the very terrain that made it unacceptable—an act occurs when our answer to the reproach is "Yes, *that* it is precisely what I am doing!"

In film, a modest, not quite appropriate recent example would be Kevin Kline's blurting out "I'm gay" instead of "Yes!" during the wedding ceremony in *In and Out*: openly admitting the truth that he is gay, and thus surprising not only us, the spectators, but even himself.[34] In a series of recent (commercial) films, we find the same surprising radical gesture. In *Speed*, when the hero (Keanu Reeves) is confronting the terrorist black-mailer partner who holds his partner at gunpoint, he shoots not the blackmailer, but *his own partner in the leg*—this apparently senseless act momentarily shocks the blackmailer, who lets go of the hostage and runs away. . . . In *Ransom*, when the media tycoon (Mel Gibson) goes on television to answer the kidnappers request for two million dollars as a ransom for his son, he surprises everyone by saying that he will offer two million dollars to anyone who will give him any information about the kidnappers, and announces that he will pursue them to the end, with all his resources, if they do not release his son immediately. This radical gesture stuns not only the kidnappers—immediately after accomplishing it, Gibson himself almost breaks down, aware of the risk he is courting . . . And finally, the supreme case: when, in the flashback scene from *The Usual Suspects*, the mysterious Keyser Soeze (Kevin Spacey) returns home and finds his wife and small daughter held at gunpoint by the members of a rival mob, he resorts to the radical gesture of shooting his wife and daughter themselves dead—this act enables him mercilessly to pursue members of the rival gang, their families, parents, friends, killing them all. . . .

What these three gestures have in common is that, in a situation of the forced choice, the subject makes the "crazy," impossible choice of, in a way, *striking at himself*, at what is most precious to himself. This act, far from amounting to a case of impotent aggressivity turned on oneself, rather changes the co-ordinates of the situation in which the subject finds himself: by cutting himself loose from the precious object through whose possession the enemy kept him in check, the subject gains the space of free action. Is not such a radical gesture of "striking at oneself" constitutive of subjectivity as such? Did not Lacan himself accomplish a similar act of "shooting at himself" when, in 1979, he dissolved the *École freudienne de Paris*, his *agalma*, his own organization, the very space of his collective life? Yet he was well aware that only such a "self-destructive" act could clear the terrain for a new beginning.

In the domain of politics proper, most of today's Left succumbs to ideological blackmail by the Right in accepting its basic premises ("the era of the welfare state, with its unlimited spending, is over," etc.)—ultimately, this is what the celebrated "Third Way" of today's social democracy is about. In such conditions, an authentic act would be to counter the Rightist agitation apropos of some "radical" measure ("You want the impossible; this will lead to catastrophe, to more state intervention . . .") not by defending ourselves by saying that this is not what we mean, that we are no longer the old Socialists, that the proposed measures will not increase the state budget, that they will even render state expenditure more "effective" and give a boost to investment, and so on and so forth, but by a resounding "Yes, that is *precisely* what we want!"[35] Although Clinton's presidency epitomizes the Third Way of today's (ex-) Left succumbing to Rightist ideological blackmail, his healthcare reform program would nonetheless amount to a kind of *act*, at least in today's conditions, since it would be based on the rejection of the hegemonic notions of the need to curtail Big State expenditure and administration—in a way, it would "do the impossible." No wonder, then, that it failed: its failure—perhaps the only significant, albeit negative, *event* of Clinton's presidency—bears witness to the material force of the ideological notion of "free choice." That is to say: although the great majority of so-called ordinary people were not properly acquainted with the reform program, the medical lobby (twice as strong as the infamous defence lobby!) succeeded in imposing on the public the fundamental idea that with universal healthcare, free choice (in matters concerning medicine) would be somehow threatened—against this purely fictional reference to "free choice," any enumeration of "hard facts" (in Canada, healthcare is less expensive and more effective, with no less free choice, etc.) proved ineffectual.

As for the subject's (agent's) identity: in an authentic act, I do not simply express/actualize my inner nature—rather, I redefine myself, the very core of my identity. To evoke Butler's often-repeated example of a subject who has a deep homosexual "passionate attachment," yet is unable openly to acknowledge it, to make it part of his symbolic identity:[36] in an authentic sexual act, the subject would have to change the way he relates to his homosexual "passionate attachment"—not only in the sense of "coming out," of fully identifying himself as gay. An act does not only shift the limit that divides our identity into the acknowledged and the disavowed part more in the direction of the disavowed part, it does not only make us to accept as "possible" our innermost disavowed "impossible" fantasies: it transforms the very coordinates of the disavowed phantasmic foundation of our being. An act does not merely redraw the contours of our public symbolic identity, it also transforms the spectral dimension that sustains this identity, the undead ghosts that haunt the living subject, the secret history of traumatic fantasies transmitted "between the lines," through the lacks and distortions of the explicit symbolic texture of his or her identity.

Now I can also answer the obvious counter-argument to this Lacanian notion of the act: if we define an act solely by the fact that its sudden emergence surprises/transforms its agent itself and, simultaneously, that it retroactively changes its conditions of (im)possibility, is not Nazism, then, an act *par excellence*? Did Hitler not "do the impossible," changing the entire field of what was considered "acceptable" in the liberal democratic universe? Did not a respectable middle-class *petit bourgeois* who, as a guard in a concentration camp, tortured Jews, also accomplish what was considered impossible, in his previous "decent" existence and acknowledge his "passionate attachment" to sadistic torture? It is here that the notion of "traversing the fantasy," and—on a different level—of transforming the constellation that generates social symptoms becomes crucial. An authentic act disturbs the underlying fantasy, attacking it from the point of "social symptom" (let us recall that Lacan attributed the invention of the notion of symptom to Marx!). The so-called Nazi revolution, with its disavowal/displacement of the fundamental social antagonism ("class struggle" that divides the social edifice from within)—with its projection/externalization of the cause of social antagonisms into the figure of the Jew, and the consequent reassertion of the corporatist notion of society as an organic Whole—clearly *avoids* confrontation with social antagonism: the "Nazi revolution" is the exemplary case of a pseudo-change, of a frenetic activity in the course of which many things did change—"something was going on all the time"—so that, precisely, something—that which *really matters*—would *not* change; so that things would fundamentally "remain the same."

In short, an authentic act is not simply external with regard to the hegemonic symbolic field disturbed by it: an act is an act only *with regard to some symbolic field*, as an intervention into it. That is to say: a symbolic field is always and by definition in itself "decentered," structured around a central void/impossibility (a personal life-narrative, say, is a *bricolage* of ultimately failed attempts to come to terms with some trauma; a social edifice is an ultimately failed attempt to displace/obfuscate its constitutive antagonism); and an act disturbs the symbolic field into which it intervenes not out of nowhere, but precisely *from the standpoint of this inherent impossibility, stumbling block, which is its hidden, disavowed structuring principle.* In contrast to this authentic act which intervenes in the constitutive void, point of failure—or what Alain Badiou has called the "symptomal torsion" of a given constellation[37]—the inauthentic act legitimizes itself through reference to the point of substantial fullness of a given constellation (on the political terrain: Race, True Religion, Nation . . .): it aims precisely at obliterating the last traces of the "symptomal torsion" which disturbs the balance of that constellation.

One palpable political consequence of this notion of the act that has to intervene at the "symptomal torsion" of the structure (and also a proof that our position does not involve "economic essentialism") is that in each concrete constellation, there is *one* touchy nodal point of contention which decides where one "truly stands." For example, in the recent struggle of the so-called democratic opposition in Serbia against the Milošević regime, the truly touchy topic is the stance toward the Albanian majority in Kosovo: the great majority of the "democratic opposition" unconditionally endorse Milošević's anti-Albanian nationalist agenda, even accusing him of making compromises with the West and "betraying" Serb national interests in Kosovo. In the course of the student demonstrations against Milošević's Socialist Party falsification of the election results in the winter of 1996, the Western media which closely followed events, and praised the revived democratic spirit in Serbia, rarely mentioned the fact that one of the demonstrators' regular slogans against the special police was "Instead of kicking us, go to Kosovo and kick out the Albanians!." So—and this is my point—it is theoretically as well as politically wrong to claim that, in today's Serbia, "anti-Albanian nationalism" is simply one among the "floating signifiers" that can be appropriated either by Milošević's power bloc or by the opposition: the moment one endorses it, no matter how much one "reinscribes it into the democratic chain of equivalences," one already accepts the terrain as defined by Milošević, one—as it were—is already "playing his game." In today's Serbia, the absolute *sine qua non* of an authentic political act would thus be to reject absolutely the ideologico-political topos of the Albanian threat in Kosovo.

Psychoanalysis is aware of a whole series of "false acts": psychotic-paranoiac violent *passage à l'acte*, hysterical acting out, obsessional self-hindering, perverse self-instrumentalization—all these acts are not simply wrong according to some external standards, they are *immanently wrong*, since they can be properly grasped only as reactions to some disavowed trauma that they displace, repress, and so on. What we are tempted to say is that the Nazi anti-Semitic violence was "false" in the same way: all the shattering impact of this large-scale frenetic activity was fundamentally "misdirected," it was a kind of gigantic *passage à l'acte* betraying an inability to confront the real kernel of the trauma (the social antagonism). So what we are claiming is that anti-Semitic violence, say, is not only "factually wrong" (Jews are "not really like that," exploiting us and organizing a universal plot) and/or "morally wrong" (unacceptable in terms of elementary standards of decency, etc.), but also "untrue" in the sense of an inauthenticity which is simultaneously epistemological and ethical, just as an obsessional who reacts to his disavowed sexual fixations by engaging in compulsive defence rituals acts in an inauthentic way. Lacan claimed that even if the patient's wife is really sleeping around with other men, the patient's jealousy is still to be treated as a pathological condition; in a homologous way, even if rich Jews "really" exploited German workers, seduced their daughters, dominated the popular press, and so on, *anti-Semitism is still an emphatically "untrue," pathological ideological condition*—why? What makes it pathological is the *disavowed subjective libidinal investment* in the figure of the Jew—the way social antagonism is displaced-obliterated by being "projected" into the figure of the Jew.[38]

So—back to the obvious counter-argument to the Lacanian notion of the act: this second feature (for a gesture to count as an act, it must "traverse the fantasy") is not simply a further, additional criterion, to be added to the first ("doing the impossible," retroactively rewriting its own conditions): if this second criterion is not fulfilled, the first is not really met either—that is to say, we are not actually "doing the impossible," traversing the fantasy toward the Real.

* * *

The problem of today's philosophico-political scene is ultimately best expressed by Lenin's old question "What is to be done?"—how do we reassert, on the political terrain, the proper dimension of the act? The main form of the resistance against the act today is a kind of unwritten *Denkverbot* (prohibition to think) similar to the infamous *Berufsverbot* (prohibition to be employed by any state institution) from the late 1960s in Germany—the moment one shows a minimal sign of engaging in political projects that aim seriously to change the existing order, the answer is immediately: "Benevolent as it is, this will necessarily end in a new Gulag!"

The "return to ethics" in today's political philosophy shamefully exploits the horrors of Gulag or Holocaust as the ultimate bogey for blackmailing us into renouncing all serious radical engagement. In this way, conformist liberal scoundrels can find hypocritical satisfaction in their defence of the existing order: they know there is corruption, exploitation, and so on, but every attempt to change things is denounced as ethically dangerous and unacceptable, recalling the ghosts of Gulag or Holocaust . . .

And this resistance against the act seems to be shared across a wide spectrum of (officially) opposed philosophical positions. Four philosophers as different as Derrida, Habermas, Rorty and Dennett would probably adopt the same left-of-center liberal democratic stance in practical political decisions; as for the political conclusions to be drawn from their thought, the difference between their positions is negligible. On the other hand, already our immediate intuition tells us that a philosopher like Heidegger on the one hand, or Badiou on the other, would definitely adopt a different stance. Rorty, who made this perspicacious observation, concludes from it that philosophical differences do not involve, generate or rely on political differences—politically, they do not really matter. What, however, if philosophical differences *do* matter politically, and if, as a consequence, this *political* congruence between philosophers tells us something crucial about their pertinent *philosophical* stance? What if, in spite of the great passionate public debates between deconstructionists, pragmatists, Habermasians and cognitivists, they nonetheless share a series of philosophical premises— what if there is an unacknowledged proximity between them? And what if the task today is precisely to break with this terrain of shared premisses?

Notes

1   More precisely, the idea, already present in her first book, *Subjects of Desire* (New York: Columbia University Press, 1987), of connecting the notion of reflexivity at work in psychoanalysis (the reversal of the regulation of desire into the desire for regulation, etc.) with the reflexivity at work in German Idealism, especially in Hegel.

2   To begin with, one would have to question (or "deconstruct") the series of preferences accepted by today's deconstructionism as the indisputable background for its endeavor: the preference of difference over sameness, for historical change over order, for openness over closure, for vital dynamics over rigid schemes, for temporal finitude over eternity . . . For me, these preferences are by no means self-evident.

3   See Slavoj Žižek, *The Ticklish Subject: The Absent Centre of Political Ontology* (London and New York: Verso, 1999), especially chapters 4 and 5.

4   It is worth mentioning here that the first to formulate the problematic that underlies this notion of hegemony (a One which, within the series of elements, holds the place of the impossible Zero, etc.) was Jacques-Alain Miller, in his

"Suture," intervention at Jacques Lacan's seminar on February 24, 1965, first published in *Cahiers pour l'analyse* 1 (1966): 37–49.

5 Ernesto Laclau, "The Politics of Rhetoric," intervention at the conference "Culture and Materiality," (Davis: University of California April 23–25, 1998), published in *Material Events: Paul De Man and the Afterlife of Theory*, ed. Tom Cohen, Barbara Cohen, J. Hillis Miller, and Andrzej Warminski (Minneapolis: University of Minnesota Press, 2000).

6 This shift is analogous to the series of shifts that characterize the emergence of modern society as reflexive society: we are no longer directly "born into" our way of life; rather, we have a "profession," we play certain "social roles" (all these terms denote an irreducible contingency, the gap between the abstract human subject and its particular way of life); in art, we no longer directly identify certain artistic rules as "natural," we become aware of a multitude of historically conditioned "artistic styles" between which we are free to choose.

7 Let me take Francis Fukuyama's half-forgotten thesis about the End of History with the advent of the global liberal democratic order. The obvious choice seems to be: either one accepts the allegedly Hegelian thesis of the End of History, of the finally found rational form of social life, or one emphasizes that struggles and historical contingency go on, that we are far from any End of History. . . . My point is that neither of the two options is truly Hegelian. One should, of course, reject the naive notion of the End of History in the sense of achieved reconciliation, of the battle already won in principle; however, with today's global capitalist liberal democratic order, with this regime of "global reflexivity," we *have* reached a qualitative break with all history hitherto; history in a way, *did* reach its end; in a way we actually *do* live in a post-historical society. Such globalized historicism and contingency are the definitive indices of this "end of history." So, in a way, we should really say that today: although history is not at its end, the very notion of "historicity" functions in a different way from before.

8 The opposite case is even more crucial and fateful for the history of Marxist politics: not when the proletariat takes over the (democratic) task left unaccomplished by the "preceding" class, the bourgeoisie, but when the very revolutionary task of the proletariat itself is taken over by some "preceding" class—say; by the *peasants* as the very opposite of the proletariat, as the "substantial" class *par excellence*, as in revolutions from China to Cambodia.

9 Is it not, then, that in today's opposition between the dominant forms of the political Right and Left, what we actually have is what Marco Revelli called "the two Rights": that the opposition is actually the one between the "populist" Right (which calls itself "Right") and the "technocratic" Right (which calls itself the "New Left")? The irony is that today, because of its populism, the Right is much closer to articulating the actual ideological stance of (whatever remains of) the traditional working class.

10 Wendy Brown, *States of Injury*, Princeton, NJ: Princeton University Press, 1995, 60.

11 Ibid., 61.

12 Karl Marx, *Grundrisse*, Harmondsworth: Penguin, 1972, 99.

13 On a more general level—and well beyond the scope of this essay—one should again today make thematic the status of (*material*) *production* as opposed to

participation in symbolic exchange (it is the merit of Fredric Jameson that he insists on this point again and again). For two philosophers as different as Heidegger and Badiou, material production is not the site of "authentic" Truth-Event (as are politics, philosophy, art . . .); deconstructionists usually start with the statement that production is also part of the discursive regime, not outside the domain of symbolic culture—and then go on to ignore it and focus on culture. . . . Is not this "repression" of production reflected within the sphere of production itself, in the guise of the division between the virtual/symbolic site of "creative" planning-programming and its execution, its material realization, carried out more and more in Third World sweatshops, from Indonesia or Brazil to China? This division—on the one hand, pure "frictionless" planning, carried out on research "campuses" or in "abstract" glass-covered corporate high-rises; on the other, the "invisible" dirty execution, taken into account by the planners mostly in the guise of "environmental costs," etc.—is more and more radical today—the two sides are often even geographically separated by thousands of miles.

14 On this spectacle of pseudo-production, see Susan Willis, *A Primer for Daily Life* (New York: Routledge, 1991), 17–18.

15 Am I not thereby getting close to Richard Rorty's recent attack on "radical" Cultural Studies elitism (see Richard Rorty, *Achieving Our Country*, Cambridge, MA: Harvard University Press, 1998)? The difference nonetheless is that Rorty seems to advocate the Left's participation in the political process as it is in the United States, in the mode of resuscitating the progressive Democratic agenda of the 1950s and early 1960s (getting involved in elections, putting pressure on Congress . . .), not "doing the impossible," that is, aiming at the transformation of the very basic co-ordinates of social life. As such, Rorty's (political, not philosophical) "engaged pragmatism" is ultimately the complementary reverse of the "radical" Cultural Studies stance, which abhors actual participation in the political process as an inadmissible compromise: these are two sides of the same deadlock.

16 Brown, *States of Inquiry*, 14.

17 Ibid., 60. In a more general way, political "extremism" or "excessive radicalism" should always be read as a phenomenon of ideologico-political *displacement*: as an index of its opposite, of a limitation, of a refusal actually to "go to the end." What was the Jacobins' recourse to radical "terror" if not a kind of hysterical acting out bearing witness to their inability to disturb the very fundamentals of economic order (private property, etc.)? And does not the same go even for the so-called excesses of Political Correctness? Do they also not betray the retreat from disturbing the actual (economic, etc.) causes of racism and sexism?

18 An example of this suspension of class is the fact, noticed by Badiou (see Alain Badiou, *L'abrégé du métapolitique*, Paris: Editions du Seuill, 1998, 136–137) that in today's critical and political discourse, the term "worker" has disappeared from the vocabulary, substituted and/or obliterated by "immigrants [immigrant workers: Algerians in France, Turks in Germany, Mexicans in the United States]." In this way, the *class* problematic of workers' exploitation is transformed into the *multiculturalist* problematic of racism, intolerance, etc.—and the multiculturalist liberals' excessive investment in

protecting immigrants' ethnic, etc., rights clearly derives its energy from the "repressed" class dimension.

19 Jacob Torfing, *New Theories of Discourse* (Oxford: Blackwell, 1999), 36.
20 Ibid., 38.
21 Ibid., 304.
22 Brown, *States of Inquiry*, 14.
23 In other words, "concrete universality" means that every definition is ultimately circular, forced to include/repeat the term to be defined among the elements providing its definition. In this precise sense, all great progressive materialist definitions are circular, from Lacan's "definition" of the signifier ("a signifier is what represents the subject or the chain of all other signifiers") up to the (implicit) revolutionary definition of man ("man is what is to be crushed, stamped on, mercilessly worked over, in order to produce a new man"). In both cases, we have the tension between the series of "ordinary" elements ("ordinary" signifiers, "ordinary" men as the "material" of history) and the exceptional "empty" element (the "unary" Master-Signifier, the socialist "New Man," which is also at first an empty place to be filled up with positive content through revolutionary turmoil). In an authentic revolution, there is no a priori positive determination of this New Man—that is, a revolution is not legitimized by the positive notion of what Man's essence, "alienated" in present conditions and to be realized through the revolutionary process, is: the only legitimization of a revolution is negative, a will to break with the Past. So, in both cases, the subject is the "vanishing mediator" between these two levels, that is, this twisted/curved tautological structure in which a subspecies is included, counted, in the species as its own element, is the very structure of subjectivity. (In the case of "man," the revolutionary subject—Party—is the "vanishing mediator" between "normal" corrupted men and the emerging New Man: it represents the New Man for the series of "ordinary" man.)
24 As such, concrete universality is linked to the notion of symbolic *reduplicatio*, of the minimal gap between a "real" feature and its symbolic inscription. Let us take the opposition between a rich man and a poor man: the moment we are dealing with *reduplicatio*, it is no longer enough to say that the species of man can be subdivided into two subspecies, the rich and the poor, those with money and those without it—it is quite meaningful to say that there are also "rich men without money" and "poor men with money," that is, people who, in terms of their symbolic status, are identified as "rich," yet are broke, have lost their fortune; and people who are identified as "poor" in terms of their symbolic status yet have unexpectedly struck it rich. The species of "rich men" can be thus subdivided into rich men *with* money and rich men *without* money, that is, the notion of "rich men" in a way includes itself as its own species. Along the same lines, is it not true that in the patriarchal symbolic universe, "woman" is not simply one of the two subspecies of humankind, but "a *man* without a penis"? More precisely, one would have to introduce here the distinction between phalus and penis, because phalus qua signifier is precisely the symbolic *reduplicatio* of penis, so that in a way (and this is Lacan's notion of symbolic castration), *the very presence of the penis indicates the absence of the phallus*—man has it (the penis), and is not it (the phallus), while woman who does not have it (the

penis), is it (the phallus). So, in the male version of castration, the subject *loses, is deprived of, what he never possessed in the first place* (in perfect opposition to love which, according to Lacan, means giving what one does not have). Perhaps this also shows us the way—one of the ways—to redeem Freud's notion of *Penisneid* what if this unfortunate "penis envy" is to be conceived as a *male* category, what if it designates the fact that the penis a man actually has is never *that*, the *phallus*, that it is always deficient with regard to it (and this gap can also express itself in the typical male phantasmic notion that there always is at least one *other* man whose penis "really is the phallus," who really embodies full potency)?

25 I draw here on Glyn Daly's paper "Ideology and Its Paradoxes" (forthcoming in *The Journal of Political Ideologies*).

26 I elaborated the logic of this "obscene supplement of power" in detail in Chapter I of *The Plague of Fantasies* (London and New York: Verso, 1997).

27 I draw here on Peter Pfaller, "Der Ernst der Arbeit ist vom Spiel gelernt," in *Work and Culture* (Klagenfurt: Ritter Verlag, 1998), 29–36.

28 Christa Wolf, *The Quest for Christa T.* (New York: Farrar, Straus & Giroux, 1970), 55.

29 In a strictly symmetrical way, the Soviet literary critics were right in pointing out that John le Carré's great spy novels—in depicting the Cold War struggle in all its moral ambiguity, with Western agents like Smiley, full of doubts and incertitudes, often horrified at the manipulations they were forced to effect—were much more potent literary legitimizations of Western anti-Communist democracy than vulgar anti-Communist spy thrillers in the mode of Ian Fleming's James Bond series.

30 This is also why *Gender Trouble* is by far Butler's "greatest hit," and *Hegemony and Socialist Strategy* (co-authored with Chantal Mouffe) Laclau's "greatest hit": on top of their timely and perspicacious intervention into the theoretical scene, both books were identified with a specific political practice, serving as its legitimization and/or inspiration—*Gender Trouble* with the anti-identitarian turn of queer politics toward the practice of performative displacement of the ruling codes (cross-dressing, etc.); *Hegemony* with the "enchainment" of the series of particular (feminist, anti-racist, ecological . . .) progressive struggles as opposed to the standard leftist domination of the economic struggle. (Judith Butler, *Gender Trouble: Feminism and the Subversion of Identity* (New York: Routledge, 1990); Ernesto Laclau and Chantal Mouffe, *Hegemony and Socialist Strategy: Towards a Radical Democratic Politics* (London and New York: Verso, 1985).

31 And, along the same lines, is not the opposition between the impossible actualization of the fullness of Society and the pragmatic solving of partial problems—rather than being a non-historical a priori—also the expression of a precise historical moment of the so-called breakdown of large historico-ideological narratives?

32 As the reader may have noticed, my manipulative strategy in this essay is to play one of my partners against the other—what are friends for, if not to be manipulated in this way? I (implicitly) rely on Butler in my defence of Hegel against Laclau (let us not forget that Butler vindicated even Hegelian Absolute Knowledge, that ultimate *bête noire* of anti-Hegelians: see her brilliant

intervention "Commentary on Joseph Flay's 'Hegel, Derrida, and Battaille's Laughter'," in William Desmond, ed., *Hegel and His Critics* [Albany, NY: SUNY Press 1989], 174–178), and now on Laclau's notion of antagonism in order to defend the Lacanian Real against Butler's criticism.

33 For the Lacanians *cognoscenti*, it is clear that I am referring here to his "formulas of sexuation": the Real as external is the exception that grounds symbolic universality, while the Real in the strict Lacanian sense—that is, as inherent to the Symbolic—is the elusive, entirely non-substantial point of failure that makes the Symbolic forever "non-all." On these "formulas of sexuation," see Jacques Lacan, *Le Séminaire, livre XX: Encore* (Paris: Éditions du Seuil, 1975), chapters VI, VII.

34 However, the film turns into social kitsch by staging the easy conversion of the small-town community from horror of the fact that the teacher of their children is gay into tolerant solidarity with him—in a mocking imitation ofRanciereian metaphoric universalization, they all proclaim: "We are gay!."

35 When the status quo cynics accuse alleged "revolutionaries" of believing that "everything is possible," that one can "change everything," what they really mean is that *nothing at all is really possible*, that we cannot *really* change anything, since we are basically condemned to the world the way it is.

36 Many people feel that who they are as egos in the world, whatever imaginary centers they have, would be radically dissolved were they to engage in homosexual relations. They would rather die than engage in homosexual relations. For these people homosexuality represents the prospect of the psychotic dissolution of the subject (Judith Butler's interview with Peter Osborne, in *A Critical Sense*, ed. Peter Osborne, London: Routledge, 1966, 120).

37 See Alain Badiou, *L'être et l'événement* (Paris: Editions du Seuil, 1988), 25.

38 And is this not strictly analogous to False Memory Syndrome? What is problematic here is not only the fact that "memories" unearthed through the suggestive help of the all-too-willing therapist are often revealed to be fake and fantasized—the point, rather, is that *even if they are factually true* (that is, even if the child was actually molested by a parent or a close relative), *they are "false,"* since they allow the subject to assume the neutral position of a passive victim of external injurious circumstances, obliterating the crucial question of his or her *own libidinal investment* in what happened to him or her.

CHAPTER TWELVE

Communization in the Present Tense

Théorie Communiste

From Communization and Its Discontents, *ed. Benjamin Noys.*
New York: Minor Compositions, 2011: 41–60.

In the course of revolutionary struggle, the abolition of the state, of exchange, of the division of labor, of all forms of property, the extension of the situation where everything is freely available as the unification of human activity—in a word, the abolition of classes—are "measures" that abolish capital, imposed by the very necessities of struggle against the capitalist class. The revolution is communization; it does not have communism as a project and result, but as its very content.

Communization and communism are things of the future, *but it is in the present that we must speak about them.* This is the content of the revolution to come that these struggles signal—in this cycle of struggles—each time that the very fact of acting as a class appears as an external constraint, a limit to overcome. *Within itself, to struggle as a class has become the problem*—it has become its own limit. Hence the struggle of the proletariat as a class signals and produces the revolution as its own supersession, as communization.

Crisis, restructuring, cycle of struggle: On the struggle of the proletariat as a class as its own limit

The principal result of the capitalist production process has always been the renewal of the capitalist relation between labor and its conditions: in other words it is a process of self-presupposition.

Until the crisis of the late 1960s, the workers' defeat and the restructuring that followed, there was indeed the self-presupposition of capital, according to the latter's concept, but the contradiction between proletariat and capital was located at this level through the production and confirmation, within this very self-presupposition, of a working class identity through which the cycle of struggles was structured as the competition between two hegemonies, two rival modes of managing and controlling reproduction. This identity was the very substance of the workers' movement.

This workers' identity, whatever the social and political forms of its existence (from the Communist Parties to autonomy; from the Socialist State to the workers' councils), rested entirely on the contradiction which developed in this phase of real subsumption of labor under capital between, on the one hand, the creation and development of labor-power employed by capital in an ever more collective and social way, and on the other, the forms of appropriation by capital of this labor-power in the immediate production process, and in the process of reproduction. This is the conflictual situation which developed in this cycle of struggles as workers' identity—an identity which found its distinguishing features and its immediate modalities of recognition in the "large factory," in the dichotomy between employment and unemployment, work and training, in the submission of the labor process to the collectivity of workers, in the link between wages, growth and productivity within a national area, in the institutional representations that all this implied, as much in the factory as at the level of the state—i.e. in the delimitation of accumulation within a national area.

The restructuring was the defeat, in the late 1960s and the 1970s, of this entire cycle of struggles founded on workers' identity; the content of the restructuring was the destruction of all that which had become an impediment to the fluidity of the self-presupposition of capital. These impediments consisted, on the one hand, of all the separations, protections and specifications that were erected in opposition to the decline in value of labor-power, insofar as they prevented the working class as a whole, in the continuity of its existence, of its reproduction and expansion, from having to face as such the whole of capital. On the other hand, there were all the constraints of circulation, turnover, and accumulation, which impeded the transformation of the surplus product into surplus-value and additional capital. Any surplus product must be able to find its market anywhere, any surplus-value must be able to find the possibility of operating as additional capital anywhere, i.e. of being transformed into means of production and labor power, without any formalization of the international cycle (such as the division into blocs, East and West, or into center and periphery) predetermining this transformation. Financial capital was the architect of this restructuring. With the restructuring that was completed in the 1980s, the production of surplus-value and the reproduction of the conditions of this production coincided.

The current cycle of struggles is fundamentally defined by the fact that the contradiction between classes occurs at the level of their respective reproduction, which means that the proletariat finds and confronts its own constitution and existence as a class in its contradiction with capital. From this flows the disappearance of a worker's identity confirmed in the reproduction of capital—i.e. the end of the workers' movement and the concomitant bankruptcy of self-organization and autonomy as a revolutionary perspective. Because the perspective of revolution is no longer a matter of the affirmation of the class, it can no longer be a matter of self-organization. To abolish capital is at the same time to negate oneself as a worker and not to self-organize as such: it's a movement of the abolition of enterprises, of factories, of the product, of exchange (whatever its form).

For the proletariat, to act as a class is currently, on the one hand, to have no other horizon than capital and the categories of its reproduction, and on the other, for the same reason, it is to be in contradiction with and to put into question its own reproduction as a class. This conflict, this *rift* in the action of the proletariat, is the content of class struggle and what is at stake in it. What is now *at stake* in these struggles is that, for the proletariat, to act as a class is the limit of its action as a class—this is now an objective situation of class struggle—and that the limit is constructed as such in the struggles and becomes *class belonging as an external constraint*. This determines the level of conflict with capital, and gives rise to internal conflicts within the struggles themselves. This transformation is a determination of the current contradiction between classes, but it is in every case the particular practice of a struggle at a given moment and in given conditions.

This cycle of struggles is the action of a recomposed working class. It consists, in the core areas of accumulation, in the disappearance of the great workers' bastions and the proletarianization of employees; in the tertiarization of employment (maintenance specialists, equipment operators, truck drivers, shippers, stevedores, etc.—this type of employment now accounts for the majority of workers); in working in smaller companies or sites; in a new division of labor and of the working class with the outsourcing of low value-added processes (involving young workers, often temporary, without career prospects); in the generalization of lean production; in the presence of young workers whose education has broken the continuity of generations succeeding each other and who overwhelmingly reject factory work and the working class condition in general; and in offshoring.

Large concentrations of workers in India and China form part of a global segmentation of the labor force. They can neither be regarded as a renaissance elsewhere of what has disappeared in "the West" in terms of their global definition, nor in terms of their own inscription in the national context. It was a social system of existence and reproduction that defined working-class identity and was expressed in the workers' movement, and not the mere existence of quantitative material characteristics.[1]

From daily struggles to revolution, there can only be a rupture. But this rupture is signalled in the daily course of the class struggle each time that class belonging appears, within these struggles, as an external constraint which is objectified in capital, in the very course of the proletariat's activity as a class. Currently, the revolution is predicated on the supersession of a contradiction which is constitutive of the class struggle: for the proletariat, being a class is the obstacle that its struggle as a class must get beyond. With the production of class belonging as an external constraint, it is possible to understand *the tipping point of the class struggle*—its supersession—as a produced supersession, on the basis of current struggles. In its struggle against capital, the class turns back against itself, i.e. it treats its own existence, everything that defines it in its relation to capital (and it is nothing but this relation), as the limit of its action. Proletarians do not liberate their "true individuality," which is denied in capital: revolutionary practice is precisely the coincidence between the change in circumstances and that in human activity or self-transformation.

This is the reason why we can currently speak of communism, and speak of it in the present as a real, existing movement. It is now a fact that revolution is the abolition of all classes, insofar as *action as a class of the proletariat is, for itself, a limit*. This abolition is not a goal that is set, a definition of revolution as a norm to be achieved, but a current content in what the class struggle is itself. To produce class belonging as an external constraint is, for the proletariat, to enter into conflict with its previous situation; this is not "liberation," nor is it "autonomy." This is the "hardest step to take" in the theoretical understanding and practice of contemporary struggles.

The proletariat does not thereby become a "purely negative" being. To say that the proletariat only exists as a class in and against capital, that it produces its entire being, its organization, its reality and its constitution as a class in capital and against it, is to say that it is the class of surplus-value producing labor. What has disappeared in the current cycle of struggles, following the restructuring of the 1970s and 1980s, is not this objective existence of the class, but is rather the confirmation of a proletarian identity in the reproduction of capital.

The proletariat can only be revolutionary by recognizing itself as a class; it recognizes itself as such in every conflict, and it has to do so all the more in the situation in which its existence as a class is that which it has to confront in the reproduction of capital. We must not be mistaken as to the content of this "recognition." For the proletariat to recognize itself as a class will not be its "return to itself" but rather a total extroversion (a self-externalization) *as it recognizes itself as a category of the capitalist mode of production*. What we are as a class is immediately nothing other than our relation to capital. For the proletariat, this "recognition" will in fact consist in a practical cognition, in conflict, not of itself for itself, but of capital—i.e. its de-objectification. The unity of the class can no longer constitute itself on the basis of the wage- and demands-based struggle, as a prelude to its revolutionary activity. The unity of the proletariat can only be the activity in which it abolishes itself in abolishing everything that divides it.

From struggles over immediate demands to revolution, there can only be a rupture, a qualitative leap. But this rupture is not a miracle, it is not an alternative; neither is it the simple realization on the part of the proletariat that there is nothing else to do than revolution in the face of the failure of everything else. "Revolution is the only solution" is just as inept as talk of the revolutionary dynamic of demands-based struggles. This rupture is produced positively by the unfolding of the cycle of struggles which precedes it; it is *signalled* in the multiplication of *rifts* within the class struggle.

As theorists we are on the look-out for, and we promote, these rifts within the class struggle of the proletariat through which it calls itself into question; in practice, we are actors in them when we are directly involved. We exist in this rupture, in this rift in the proletariat's activity as a class. There is no longer any perspective for the proletariat on its own basis as class of the capitalist mode of production, other than the capacity to supersede its class existence in the abolition of capital. There is an absolute identity between being in contradiction with capital and being in contradiction with its own situation and definition as a class.

It is through this *rift* within action as a class itself that *communization* becomes a question in the present. This rift within the class struggle, in which the proletariat has no other horizon than capital, and thus simultaneously enters into contradiction with its own action as a class, is the dynamic of this cycle of struggles. Currently the class struggle of the proletariat has identifiable elements or activities which signal its own supersession in its own course.

Struggles producing theory[2]

The theory of this cycle of struggle, as it has been presented above, is not an abstract formalization which will then prove that it conforms to reality through examples. It is its practical existence, rather than its intellectual veracity, that it proves in the concrete. It is a particular moment of struggles which themselves are already theoretical (in the sense that they are productive of theory), insofar as they have a critical relation vis-à-vis themselves.

Most often, these are not earthshaking declarations or "radical" actions but rather all the practices of the proletariat of flight from, or rejection of, its own condition. In current strikes over layoffs, workers often no longer demand to keep their jobs, but increasingly they fight for substantial redundancy payments instead. *Against capital, labor has no future.* It was already strikingly evident in the so-called "suicidal" struggles of the Cellatex firm in France, where workers threatened to discharge acid into a river and to blow up the factory, threats which were not carried out but which were widely imitated in other conflicts over the closure of firms, that the proletariat is nothing if it is separated from capital and that it bears no future within itself, *from its own nature*, other than the abolition of that by which it exists. It is the de-essentialization of labor which becomes the very activity of the proletariat: both tragically, in its struggles without immediate perspectives (i.e. its suicidal struggles), and as demand for this de-essentialization, as in the struggles of the unemployed and the precarious in the winter of 1998 in France.

Unemployment is no longer clearly separated from employment. The segmentation of the labor force; flexibility; outsourcing; mobility; part-time employment; training; internships; and informal work have blurred all the separations.

In the French movement of 1998, and more generally in the struggles of the unemployed in this cycle of struggles, *it was the definition of the unemployed which was upheld as the point of departure for the reformulation of waged employment.* The need for capital to measure everything in labor time and to posit the exploitation of labor as a matter of life or death for it is simultaneously the de-essentialization of living labor relative to the social forces that capital concentrates in itself. This contradiction, inherent in capitalist accumulation, which is a contradiction in capital-in-process, takes the very particular form of the definition of the class vis-à-vis capital; the unemployment of the class claims for itself the status of being the starting-point for such a definition. In the struggles of the unemployed and the precarious, the struggle of the proletariat against capital makes this contradiction its own, and champions it. The same thing occurs when workers who have been sacked don't demand jobs but severance pay instead.

In the same period, the Moulinex employees who had been made redundant set fire to a factory building, thus inscribing themselves in the dynamic of this cycle of struggles, which makes the existence of the proletariat as a class the limit of its class action. Similarly, in 2006, in

Savar, 50 km north of Dhaka, Bangladesh, two factories were torched and a hundred others ransacked after workers had not been paid for three months. In Algeria, minor wage demands turned into riots, forms of representation were dismissed without new ones being formed, and it was the entirety of the living conditions and reproduction of the proletariat, which came into play beyond the demands made by the immediate protagonists of the strike. In China and India, there's no prospect of the formation of a vast *workers' movement* from the proliferation of various types of demands-based action affecting all aspects of life and the reproduction of the working class. These demands-based actions often turn paradoxically on the destruction of the conditions of labor, i.e. of their own *raison d'être*.

In the case of Argentina, people self-organized as the unemployed of Mosconi, as the workers of Brukman, as slum-residents . . . but in self-organizing they immediately came up against what they were as an obstacle, which, in the struggle, became that which had to be overcome, and which was seen as such in the practical modalities of these self-organized movements. The proletariat cannot find within itself the capacity to create other inter-individual relations, without overturning and negating what it is itself in this society, i.e. without entering into contradiction with autonomy and its dynamic. Self-organization is perhaps the first act of revolution, but all the following acts are directed against it (i.e. against self-organization). In Argentina it was the determinations of the proletariat as a class of this society (i.e. property, exchange, the division of labor, the relation between men and women . . .) which were effectively undermined by the way productive activities were undertaken, i.e. in the actual modalities of their realization. It is thus that the revolution as communization becomes credible.

In France in November 2005, in the *banlieues*, the rioters didn't demand anything, they attacked their own condition, they made everything that produces and defines them their target. Rioters revealed and attacked *the proletarian situation now*: the worldwide precarization of the labor force. In doing so they immediately made obsolete, in the very moment in which such a demand could have been articulated, any desire to be an "ordinary proletarian."

Three months later, in spring 2006, still in France, as a demands-based movement, the student movement against the *contrat première embauche* (CPE [first employment contract]) could only comprehend itself by becoming the general movement of the precarious; but in doing so it would either negate its own specificity, or it would inevitably be forced to collide more or less violently with all those who had shown in the riots of November 2005 that the demand to be an "ordinary proletarian" was obsolete. To achieve the demand through its expansion would in effect be to sabotage it. What credibility was there in a link-up with the November rioters on the basis of a stable job for all? On the one hand, this link-up was objectively inscribed in the genetic code of the movement; on the other hand, the very necessity of this link-up induced an internal love–hate dynamic, just as objective, within the movement. *The struggle against the CPE was a movement of demands, the satisfaction of which would have been unacceptable to itself as a movement of demands.*

In the Greek riots, the proletariat didn't demand anything, and didn't consider itself to be opposed to capital as the foundation of any alternative. But if these riots were a movement of the class, they didn't constitute a struggle in what is the very matrix of classes: *production*. It is in this way that these riots were able to make the key achievement of producing and targeting class belonging as a constraint, but they could only reach this point by confronting this *glass floor* of production as their limit. And the ways in which this movement produced this external constraint (the aims, the unfolding of the riots, the composition of the rioters . . .) was intrinsically defined by this limit: the relation of exploitation as coercion pure and simple. Attacking institutions and the forms of social reproduction, taken in themselves, was on the one hand what constituted the movement, and what constituted its force, but this was also the expression of its limits.

Students without a future, young immigrants, precarious workers, these are all proletarians who every day live the reproduction of capitalist social relations as coercion; coercion is *included* in this reproduction because they are proletarians, but they experience it every day as *separated* and aleatory (accidental and non-necessary) in relation to production itself. At the same time as they struggle in this moment of coercion which they experience as separated, they only conceive of and live this separation as a lack in their own struggle against this mode of production.

It is in this way that this movement produced class belonging as an exterior constraint, but only in this way. It is in this way that it locates itself at the level of this cycle of struggles and is one of its determining historical moments.

In their own practice and in their struggle, proletarians called themselves into question as proletarians, but only by autonomizing the moments and the instances of social reproduction in their attacks and their aims. Reproduction and production of capital remained foreign to each other.

In Guadeloupe, the importance of unemployment, and of the part of the population that lives from benefits and/or from an underground economy, means that wage-demands are a contradiction in terms. This contradiction structured the course of events between, on the one hand, the *Liyannaj Kont Pwofitasyon* (LKP), which was centered on permanent workers (essentially in public services) but which attempted to hold the terms of this contradiction together through the multiplication and the infinite diversity of demands, and, on the other, the absurdity of central wage-demands for the majority of people on the barricades, in the looting, and in the attacks on public buildings. The demand was destabilized in the very course of the struggle; it was contested, as was its form of organization, but the specific forms of exploitation of the entire population, inherited from its colonial history, were able to prevent this contradiction from breaking out more violently at the heart of the movement (it is important to note that the only death was that of a trade-unionist killed on a barricade). From this point of view, the production of class belonging as an external constraint was more a sociological state, more a sort of schizophrenia, than something at stake in the struggle.

In general, with the outbreak of the current crisis, the wage demand is currently characterized by a dynamic that wasn't previously possible. It is an *internal* dynamic which comes about as a result of the *whole* relation between proletariat and capital in the capitalist mode of production such as it emerged from the restructuring and such as it is now entering into crisis. The wage demand has changed its meaning.

In the succession of financial crises which for the last twenty years or so have regulated the current mode of valorization of capital, the sub-prime crisis is the first to have taken as its point of departure not the financial assets that refer to capital investments, but household consumption, and more precisely that of the poorest households. In this respect it inaugurates a specific crisis of the wage relation of restructured capitalism, in which the continual decrease in the share of wages in the wealth produced, both in the core countries and in the emerging ones, remains definitive.

The "distribution of wealth," from being essentially conflictual in the capitalist mode of production, has become *taboo*, as was confirmed in the recent movement of strikes and blockades (October–November 2010) following the reform of the pensions system in France. In restructured capitalism (the beginnings of the crisis of which we are currently experiencing), the reproduction of labor power was subjected to a *double decoupling*. On the one hand a decoupling between the valorization of capital and the reproduction of labor power and, on the other, a decoupling between consumption and the wage as income.

Of course, the division of the working day into necessary and surplus labor has always been definitive of the class struggle. But now, in the struggle over this division, it is paradoxically in the proletariat's definition to the very depth of its being as a class of this mode of production, *and as nothing else*, that it is apparent in practice, and in a conflictual way, that its existence as a class is the limit of its own struggle as a class. This is *currently* the central character of the wage demand in class struggle. In the most trivial course of the wage demand, the proletariat sees its own existence as a class objectify itself as something which is alien to it to the extent that the capitalist relation itself places *it in its heart* as something *alien*.

The current crisis broke out because proletarians could no longer repay their loans. It broke out on the very basis of the wage relation which gave rise to the financialization of the capitalist economy: wage cuts as a requirement for "value creation" and global competition within the labor force. It was this functional necessity that returned, but in a negative fashion, within the historical mode of capital accumulation with the detonation of the subprime crisis. It is now the wage relation that is at the core of the current crisis.[3] The current crisis is the beginning of the phase of reversal of the determinations and dynamic of capitalism as it had emerged from the restructuring of the 1970s and 1980s.

Two or three things we know about it

It is because the proletariat is not-capital, because it is the dissolution of all existing conditions (labor, exchange, division of labor, property), that it finds here the content of its *revolutionary action* as *communist measures*: the abolition of property, of the division of labor, of exchange and of value. Class belonging as external constraint is thus *in itself* a content, that is to say a practice, which supersedes itself in communizing measures when the limit of the struggle as a class is manifested. *Communization* is nothing other than *communist measures* taken as simple *measures of struggle* by the proletariat against capital.

It is the paucity of surplus-value relative to accumulated capital which is at the heart of the crisis of exploitation: if, at the heart of the *contradiction* between the proletariat and capital there was not the question of labor which is productive of *surplus-value*; if there was only a problem of distribution, i.e. if the contradiction between the proletariat and capital wasn't a contradiction for the very thing, namely the capitalist mode of production, whose dynamic it constitutes; i.e. if it was not a "game which produces the abolition of its own rule," the revolution would remain a pious wish. Hatred of capital and the desire for another life are only the necessary ideological expressions of this contradiction for-itself which is exploitation.

It is not through an attack on the side of the nature of labor as productive of surplus-value that the demands-based struggle is superseded (which would always devolve back to a problem of distribution), but through an attack on the side of the means of production as capital. The attack against the capitalist nature of the means of production is their abolition as value-absorbing labor in order to valorize itself; it is the extension of the situation where everything is freely available, the destruction (perhaps physical) of certain means of production, their abolition as the factories in which it is defined what it is to be a product, i.e. the matrices of exchange and commerce; it is their definition, their absorption in individual, inter-subjective relations; it is the abolition of the division of labor such as it is inscribed in urban zoning, in the material configuration of buildings, in the separation between town and country, in the very existence of something which is called a factory or a point of production. Relations between individuals are fixed in things, because exchange value is by nature material.[4] The abolition of value is a concrete transformation of the landscape in which we live, it is a new geography. The abolition of social relations is a very material affair.

In communism, appropriation no longer has any currency, because it is the very notion of the "product" which is abolished. Of course, there are objects which are used to produce, others which are directly consumed, and others still which are used for both. But to speak of "products" and to pose the question of their circulation, their distribution or their "transfer," i.e. to conceive a moment of appropriation, is to presuppose points of rupture, of "coagulation" of human activity: the market in market societies, the de-pot where goods are freely available in certain visions of communism. The "product" is not a simple thing. To speak of the "product" is to suppose that a result of human activity appears as *finite* vis-à-vis another such result or the sphere of other such results. It is not from the "product" that we must proceed, but from activity.

In communism, human activity is infinite because it is indivisible. It has concrete or abstract results, but these results are never "products," for that would raise the question of their appropriation or of their transfer under some given mode. If we can speak of *infinite human activity* in communism, it is because the capitalist mode of production already allows us to see—albeit contradictorily and not as a "good side"—human activity as a continuous global social flux, and the *"general intellect"* or the "collective worker" as the dominant force of production. The social character of production does not prefigure anything: it merely renders the basis of value contradictory.

The destruction of exchange means the workers attacking the banks which hold their accounts and those of other workers, thus making it necessary to do without; it means the workers communicating their "products" to themselves and the community directly and without a market, thereby abolishing themselves as workers; it means the obligation for the whole class to organize itself to seek food in the sectors to be communized, etc. There is no measure which, in itself, taken separately, is "communism." What is communist is not "violence" in itself, nor "distribution" of the shit that we inherit from class society, nor "collectivization" of surplus-value sucking machines: it is the nature of the movement which connects these actions, underlies them, renders them the moments of a process which can only communize ever further, or be crushed.

A revolution cannot be carried out without taking communist measures: dissolving wage labor; communizing supplies, clothing, housing; seizing all the weapons (the destructive ones, but also telecommunications, food, etc.); integrating the destitute (including those of us who will have reduced ourselves to this state), the unemployed, ruined farmers, rootless drop-out students.

From the moment in which we begin to consume freely, it is necessary to reproduce that which is consumed; it is thus necessary to seize the means of transport, of telecommunications, and enter into contact with other sectors; so doing, we will run up against the opposition of armed groups. The confrontation with the state immediately poses the problem of arms, which can only be solved by setting up a distribution network to support combat in an almost infinite multiplicity of places. Military and social activities are inseparable, simultaneous, and mutually interpenetrating: the constitution of a front or of determinate zones of combat is the death of the revolution. From the moment in which proletarians dismantle the laws of commodity relations, there is no turning back. The deepening and extension of this social process gives flesh and blood to new relations, and enables the integration of more and more non-proletarians to the communizing class, which is simultaneously in the process of constituting and dissolving itself. It permits the abolition to an ever greater extent of all competition and division between proletarians, making this the content and the unfolding of its armed confrontation with those whom the capitalist class can still mobilize, integrate, and reproduce within its social relations.

This is why all the measures of communization will have to be a vigorous action for the dismantling of the connections which link our enemies and their material support: these will have to be rapidly destroyed, without the possibility of return. Communization is not the peaceful organization of the situation where everything is freely available and of a pleasant way of life amongst proletarians. The dictatorship of the social movement of communization is the process of the integration of humanity into the proletariat which is in the process of disappearing. The strict delimitation of the proletariat in comparison with other classes and its struggle against all commodity production are at the same time a process which *constrains* the strata of the salaried *petite-bourgeoisie*, the class of social (middle-) management, to join the communizing class. Proletarians "are" not revolutionaries like the sky "is" blue, merely because they "are" waged and exploited, or even because they are the dissolution of existing conditions. In their self-transformation, *which has as its point of departure what they are*, they constitute themselves as a revolutionary class. The movement in which the proletariat is defined in practice as the movement of the constitution of the human community is the reality of the abolition of classes. The social movement in Argentina was confronted by, and posed, the question of the relations between proletarians in employment, the unemployed, and the excluded and middle strata. It only provided extremely fragmentary responses, of which the most interesting is without doubt that of its territorial organization. The revolution, which in this cycle of struggles can no longer be anything but communization, supersedes the dilemma between the Leninist or democratic class alliances and Gorter's "proletariat alone": two different types of defeat.

The only way of overcoming the conflicts between the unemployed and those with jobs, between the skilled and the unskilled, is to carry out measures of communization which remove the very basis of this division, right from the start and in the course of the armed struggle. This is something which the occupied factories in Argentina, when confronted by this question, tried only very marginally, being generally satisfied (cf. Zanon) with some charitable redistribution to groups of *piqueteros*. In the absence of this, capital will play on this fragmentation throughout the movement, and will find its Noske and Scheidemann amongst the self-organized.

In fact, as already shown by the German revolution, it is a question of dissolving the middle strata by taking concrete communist measures which compel them to begin to join the proletariat, i.e. to achieve their "proletarianization." Nowadays, in developed countries, the question is at the same time simpler and more dangerous. On the one hand a massive majority of the middle strata is salaried and thus no longer has a material base to its social position; its role of management and direction of capitalist cooperation is essential but ever rendered precarious; its social position depends upon the very fragile mechanism of the subtraction of fractions of surplus value. On the other hand, however, and for these very same reasons, its formal proximity to the proletariat pushes it to present, in these struggles, national or democratic alternative managerial "solutions" which would preserve its own positions.

The essential question which we will have to solve is to understand how we extend communism, before it is suffocated in the pincers of the commodity; how we integrate agriculture so as not to have to exchange with farmers; how we do away with the exchange-based relations of our adversary to impose on him the logic of the communization of relations and of the seizure of goods; how we dissolve the block of fear through the revolution.

To conclude, capital is not abolished for communism but through communism, more precisely through its production. Indeed, communist measures must be distinguished from communism: they are not embryos of communism, but rather they are its production. This is not a period of transition, it is the revolution: communization is only the *communist production of communism*. The struggle against capital is what differentiates communist measures from communism. The revolutionary activity of the proletariat always has as its content the mediation of the abolition of capital through its relation to capital: this is neither one branch of an alternative in competition with another, nor communism as immediatism.

Translated by Endnotes

Notes

1   For China and India to manage to constitute themselves as their own internal market would depend on a veritable revolution in the countryside (i.e. the privatization of land in China and the disappearance of small holdings and tenant farming in India) but also and above all on a reconfiguration of the global cycle of capital, supplanting the present globalization (i.e. this would mean a renationalization of economies, superseding/preserving globalization, and a definancialization of productive capital).

2   These examples are mostly French; publication of this text in Britain and the United States provides an opportunity to test the theses that are defended here.

3   It is a crisis in which the identity of overaccumulation and of under-consumption asserts itself.

4   "(T)hat thing [money] is an objectified relation between persons . . . it is objectified exchange value, and exchange value is nothing more than a mutual relation between people's productive activities." Marx, *Grundrisse* (Harmondsworth: Penguin, 1973), 160.

CHAPTER THIRTEEN

Patriarchy and Commodity Society: Gender without the Body

Roswitha Scholz

From Marxism and the Critique of Value, *ed. Neil Larsen, Mathias Nilges, Josh Robinson, and Nicholas Brown Chicago and Alberta: MCM', 2014: 115–132.*

In the 1980s, after the collapse of the Eastern Bloc, culturalism and theories of difference became especially prominent in women's studies courses, a discipline which has since largely developed into gender studies. Marxist feminism, which, until the end of the 1980s, had determined the debates in this field, retreated into the background. Recently, however, the increasing de-legitimization of neoliberalism connected to the current economic crisis has produced a resurgence and increasing popularity of a diverse set of Marxisms. To date, however, these developments have barely had an impact on the fields of feminist theory or gender studies—aside from some critical globalization debates and area studies interrogating the themes of labor and money. Deconstruction is still the lead vocalist in the choir of universal feminism, especially in gender theory. Meanwhile, assertions of the necessity of a new feminism (in particular a feminism that once again includes a materialist plane of analysis) have become commonplace. The popular argument of the 1980s and 1990s that claims that we are confronted with a "confusion of the sexes" is being rapidly deflated. Instead, it is becoming clear that neither the much-professed equalization of genders nor the deconstructivist play with signifiers has yielded convincing results.

The "rediscovery" of Marxist theory on one hand and the insight that feminism is in no way anachronistic or superfluous on the other, even if it can no longer be continued in those forms that have become characteristic of the past few decades, lead me to consider a new Marxist-Feminist theoretical framework, one which is able to account for recent developments since the end of actually existing socialism and the current global economic crisis. It should, of course, be clear that one cannot seamlessly connect traditional Marxist concepts and analysis with twenty-first-century problematics. Without critical innovation, a direct application is similarly impossible for those theoretical frameworks from which I will draw in what follows, such as Adorno's critical theory, even if his examinations provided us with an important basis for a patriarchy-critical theory of the present. Those feminist debates of the last twenty years that have been based on Adorno and critical theory can provide inspiration, but they must also be modified. I cannot elaborate on this here.[1] Instead, I would like to forward a few facets of my theory of gender relations, or value-dissociation theory, which I have developed via the engagement with some of the theories alluded to above. As I will show, asymmetrical gender relations today can no longer be understood in the same sense as "classical" modern gender relations; however, it is essential to base their origins in the history of modernization. Similarly, one has to account for postmodern processes of differentiation and the relevance of cultural-symbolic levels, which have emerged since the 1980s. The cultural-symbolic order should here be understood as an autonomous dimension of theory. Yet, this autonomous dimension is to be thought simultaneously with value dissociation as a basic societal principle without understanding Marxian theory as purely materialist. Such a theory is much better equipped to grasp the totality, insofar as the cultural-symbolic as well as the socio-psychological levels are included in the context of a social whole. Economy and culture are, therefore, neither identical (as "identity logic" that violently aims to subjugate differences to the same common denominator would suggest), nor can they be separated from each other in a dualistic sense. Rather, their identity and non-identity must be conceived as the conflictual incompatibility that shapes the commodity-producing patriarchy as such: the self-contradictory basic principle of the social form of value dissociation.

Value as societal base principle

Besides the above-mentioned critical theory of Adorno, the primary theoretical benchmarks are a new, fundamental critical theory of "value" and of "abstract labor" as enhancements of the Marxist critique of political economy, whose most prominent theorists in the last decade are Robert Kurz and Moishe Postone.[2] I intend to give their texts a feminist twist.

According to this new value-critical approach, it is not surplus value itself—that is, it is not the solely externally determined exploitation of labor by capital qua legal relations of property—which stands at the center of critique. Instead, such a critique begins at an earlier point, namely with the societal character of the commodity-producing system and thus with the form of activity particular to abstract labor. Labor as abstraction develops for the first time under capitalism alongside the generalization of commodity production and must, therefore, not be ontologized. Generalized commodity production is characterized by a key contradiction: under the obligation of the valorization of value, the individuals of capitalist enterprise are highly integrated into a network while nevertheless paradoxically engaging in non-societal production, as socialization (*Vergesellschaftung*) proper is only established via the market and exchange. As commodities, products represent past abstract labor and, therefore, value. In other words, commodities represent a specific quantity of expenditure of human energy, recognized by the market as socially valid. This representation is, in turn, expressed by money, the universal mediator and simultaneous end in itself of the form of capital. In this way, people appear unsocial and society appears to be constituted through things, which are mediated by the abstract quantity of value. The result is the alienation of members of society, as their own sociability is only bestowed upon them by commodities, dead things, thus, emptying sociability in its social form of representation entirely of its concrete, sensual content. This relation can, for the time being, be expressed via the concept of fetishism, keeping in mind that this concept itself is as-of-yet incomplete.

Opposed to this stand premodern societies, in which goods were produced under different relations of domination (personal as opposed to reified by the commodity form). Goods were produced in the agrarian field and in trades primarily for their use, determined by specific laws of guilds that precluded the pursuit of abstract profit. The very limited premodern exchange of goods was not carried out in markets and relations of competition in the modern sense. It was, therefore, not possible at this point in history to speak of a social totality in which money and value have become abstract ends in themselves. Modernity is consequently characterized by the pursuit of surplus value, by the attempt to generate more money out of money, yet not as a matter of subjective enrichment but instead as a tautological system determined by the relation of value to itself. It is in this context that Marx speaks of the "automatic subject."[3] Human needs become negligible and labor power itself is transformed into a commodity. This means that the human capacity for production has become externally determined—yet not in the sense of personal domination but in the sense of anonymous, blind mechanisms. And it is only for that reason that productive activities in modernity have become forced into the form of abstract labor. Ultimately, the development of capitalism marks life globally by means of money's motility, and abstract labor, which emerged only under capitalism and appears unhistorically as an ontological principle. Traditional Marxism only problematizes a part of this system of correlations, namely the legal appropriation of surplus value by the bourgeoisie, thus focusing on unequal distribution rather than commodity fetishism. The critique of capitalism and imaginations of postcapitalist societies consequently are limited to the goal of equal distribution within the commodity-producing system in its non-sublated forms. Such critiques fail to see that the suffering resulting from capitalism emerges from its very formal relations of which private property is merely one of many results. Accordingly, the Marxisms of the workers' movements were limited to an ideology of legitimization of system-immanent developments and social improvements. Today, this form of thought is inappropriate for a renewed critique of capitalism, as it has absorbed (and made its own) all basic principles of capitalist socialization, in particular the categories of value and abstract labor, misunderstanding these categories as transhistorical conditions of humanity. In this context, a radical value-critical position regards past examples of actually existing socialism as the value-producing system of state-bureaucratically determined processes of recuperative modernization (*nachholende Modernisierung*) in the global East and South, which, mediated by global economic processes and the race of the development of productive forces against the West, had to collapse in the post-Fordist stage of development of capitalist development at the end of the 1980s. Since then, the West has been engaged in the process of withdrawing social reforms in the context of crises and globalization.

Value dissociation as societal base principle

The concepts of value and abstract labor, I argue, cannot sufficiently account for capitalism's basic form as a fundamentally fetishistic relation. Similarly, we have to account for the fact that under capitalism reproductive activities emerge that are primarily carried out by women. Accordingly, value dissociation means that capitalism contains a core of female-determined reproductive activities and the affects, characteristics, and attitudes (emotionality, sensuality, and female or motherly caring) which are dissociated from value and abstract labor. Female relations of existence, that is female reproductive activities under capitalism, therefore are of a different character than abstract labor, which is why they cannot be straightforwardly subsumed under the concept of labor. Such relations constitute a facet of capitalist societies that cannot be captured by Marx's conceptual apparatus. This facet is a necessary aspect of value, yet it also exists outside of it and is (for this very reason) its precondition. In this context I borrow from Frigga Haug the notion of a "logic of time-saving" that determines one side of modernity that is generally associated with the sphere of production, what Kurz calls the "logic of utilization [*Vernutzung*] of business administration," and a "logic of time-expenditure" that corresponds to the field of reproduction. Value and dissociation therefore stand in a dialectical relation to each other. One cannot simply be derived from the other. Rather, both simultaneously emerge out of each other. In this sense, value dissociation can be understood as the macro-theoretical framework within which the categories of the value form function micro-theoretically, allowing us to examine fetishistic societization in its entirety instead of value alone. One must stress here, however, that the sensitivity that is usually falsely perceived as an unmediated a priori in the fields of reproduction, consumption, and its related activities, as well as needs that are to be satisfied in this context, emerged historically before the backdrop of value dissociation as total process (*Gesamtprozess*). These categories must not be misunderstood as unmediated or natural, despite the fact that eating, drinking, and loving are not solely connected to symbolization (as vulgar constructivisms might claim). The traditional categories available to us to critique political economy, however, are also lacking in another regard. Value dissociation implies a particular socio-psychological relation. Certain undervalued qualities (sensitivity, emotionality, deficiencies in thought and character, etc.) are associated with femininity and are dissociated from the masculine-modern subject. These gender-specific attributes are a fundamental characteristic of the symbolic order of the commodity-producing patriarchy. Such asymmetrical gender relations should, I believe, as far as theory is concerned, be examined by focusing only on modernity and postmodernity. This is not to say that these relations do not have a premodern history but that their universalization endowed them with an entirely new quality. The universalization of such gender relations at the beginning of modernity meant that women were now primarily responsible for the lesser-valorized (as opposed to the masculine, capital-producing) areas of reproduction, which cannot be represented monetarily. We must reject the understanding of gender relations under capitalism as a precapitalist remainder. The small, nuclear family as we know it, for example, only emerged in the eighteenth century, just as the public and private spheres as we understand them today only emerged in modernity. What I claim here, therefore, is that the beginning of modernity not only marked the rise of capitalist commodity production, but it also saw the emergence of a social dynamism that rests on the basis of the relations of value dissociation.

Commodity-producing patriarchy as civilizational model

With Frigga Haug, I assume that the notion of a commodity-producing patriarchy is to be regarded as a civilizational model, yet I would like to modify her propositions by taking into account the theory of value dissociation.[4] As is generally well known, the symbolic order of the commodity-producing patriarchy is characterized by the following assumptions: politics and economics are associated with masculinity; male sexuality, for example, is generally described as individualized, aggressive, or violent, while women often function as pure bodies. The man is therefore regarded as human, man of intellect, and body-transcendent, while women are reduced to non-human status, to the body. War carries a masculine connotation, while women are seen as peaceful, passive, devoid of will and spirit. Men must strive for honor, bravery, and immortalizing actions. Men are thought of as heroes and capable of great deeds, which requires them to productively subjugate nature. Men stand at all times in competition with others. Women are responsible for the care for the individual as well as for humanity itself. Yet their actions remain socially undervalued and forgotten in the process of the development of theory, while their sexualization is the source of women's subordination to men and underwrites their social marginalization.

This notion also determines the idea of order underlying modern societies as a whole. Moreover, the ability and willingness to produce and the rational, economical, and effective expenditure of time also determines the civilizational model in its objective structures as a totality of relations—its mechanisms and history as much as the maxims of individual agency. A provocative formulation of all this might suggest that the male gender should be understood as the gender of capitalism, keeping in mind that such a dualist understanding of gender is of course the dominant understanding of gender in modernity. The commodity-producing civilizational model this requires has its foundation in the oppression and marginalization of women and the simultaneous neglect of nature and the social. Subject and object, domination and subjugation, man and woman are thus typical dichotomies, antagonistic counterparts within the commodity-producing patriarchy.[5]

Yet, it is important to prevent misunderstandings in this respect. Value dissociation is in this sense also to be understood as a metaconcept, since we are concerned with theoretical exegesis on a high level of abstraction. This means for the single empirical units or subjects that they are neither able to escape the socio-cultural patterns, nor able to become part of these patterns. Additionally, as we shall see, gender models are subject to historical change. It is, therefore, important to avoid simplified interpretations of value dissociation theory resembling, for instance, the idea of a "new femininity" associated with the difference-feminism of the 1980s or even the "Eve principle" currently propagated by German conservatives.[6] What we must foreground in all of this is that abstract labor and domestic labor along with the known cultural patterns of masculinity and femininity determine each other simultaneously. The old "chicken or egg" question is nonsensical in this regard. Yet, such a non-dialectical approach is characteristic of deconstructivist critics who insist that masculinity and femininity initially must be produced culturally before a gendered distribution of actions can take place.[7] Frigga Haug, too, proceeds from the ontologizing assumption that cultural meaning attaches itself over the course of history to a previously gendered division of labor.[8]

Within the commodity-producing modern patriarchy develops, as shown above, a public sphere, which itself comprises a number of spheres (economy, politics, science, etc.), and a private sphere. Women are primarily assigned to the private sphere. These different spheres are on one hand relatively autonomous, and on the other hand mutually determined—that is, they stand in dialectical relation to each other. It is important, then, that the private sphere is not misunderstood as an emanation of value but instead as a dissociated sphere. What is required is a sphere into which actions such as caring and loving can be deported and that stands opposed to the logic of value and time saving and its morality (competition, profit, performance). This relation between private sphere and the public sector also explains the existence of male bonds and institutions that found themselves, by means of an affective divide, against all that which is female. As a consequence, the very basis of the modern state and politics, along with the principles of liberty, equality, and fraternity, rests since the eighteenth century upon the foundation of male bonds. This is not to say, however, that patriarchy resides in the spheres created by this process of dissociation. For example, women have always to an extent been active in the sphere of accumulation. Nevertheless, dissociation becomes apparent here as well, since, despite the success of Angela Merkel and others, women's existence in the public sphere is generally determined by lesser valorization and women largely remain barred from upward mobility. All this indicates that value dissociation is a pervasive social formal principle that is located on a correspondingly high level of abstraction and which cannot be mechanistically separated into different spheres. This means that the effects of value dissociation pervade all spheres, including all levels of the public sphere.

Value dissociation as societal base principle and the critique of identity logic

Value dissociation as critical practice disallows identity-critical approaches. That is, it does not allow for approaches that reduce analyses to the level of structures and concepts that subsume all contradictions and the non-identical, in regard to both the transmission of mechanisms, structure, and characteristics of the commodity-producing patriarchy to societies that do not produce commodities and to the homogenization of different spheres and sectors within the commodity-producing patriarchy itself, disregarding qualitative differences. Instead, the (historically mobile) relation or degree of value dissociation is to be understood as a societal base principle, which corresponds to androcentric-universalist thought, and not merely as a set of relations related to the production of value. After all, what is important here is not simply that it is average labor time or abstract labor that determines money as equivalent form. More important is the observation that value itself must define as less valuable and dissociate domestic labor, the non-conceptual, and everything related to non-identity, the sensuous, affective, and emotional. Dissociation, however, is not congruent with the non-identical in Adorno. More accurately, the dissociated represents the dark underbelly of value itself. Here, dissociation must be understood as a precondition, which ensures that the contingent, the irregular, the non-analytical, that which cannot be grasped by science, remains hidden and unilluminated, perpetuating classifying thought that is unable to register and maintain particular qualities, inherent differences, ruptures, ambivalences, and non-contemporaneity.

Inversely, this means for the "socialized society" of capitalism, to appropriate Adorno's phrase, that these levels and sectors cannot be understood in relation to each other as irreducible elements of the real, but that they also have to be examined in their objective, internal relations corresponding to the notion of value dissociation as societal form principle of the social totality that constitutes a given society on the level of ontology and appearance in the first place. Yet, at every moment, value dissociation is also aware of its own limitations as theory. The self-interrogation of value dissociation theory here must go far enough to prevent positioning it as an absolute, societal form principle. That which corresponds to its concept can, after all, not be elevated to the status of main contradiction, and the theory of value dissociation can, like the theory of value, not be understood as a theory of the logic of the one. In its critique of identity logic, therefore, value dissociation theory remains true to itself and can only persist insofar as it relativizes and at times even disclaims itself. This also means that value dissociation theory must leave equal space for other forms of social disparity (including economic disparity, racism, and anti-Semitism).[9]

Value dissociation as historical process

According to the epistemological premises of the formation of value dissociation theory, we cannot resort to linear analytical models when examining developments in a variety of global regions. Developments generally determined by the commodity form and the associated form of patriarchy did not take place in the same fashion and under the same circumstances in all societies (especially in societies that were formerly characterized by symmetrical gender relations, which have, to this day, not entirely adopted modernity's gender relations). Additionally, we must foreground alternative paternalistic structures and relations, which, while largely overwritten by modern, Western patriarchy in the context of global economic developments, have not entirely lost their idiosyncrasies. Further, we have to account for the fact that throughout the history of Western modernity itself ideas of masculinity and femininity have varied. Both the modern conception of labor and dualist understandings of gender are products of, and thus go hand-in-hand with, the specific developments that led to the dominance of capitalism. It was not until the eighteenth century that the modern "system of dual genderedness" (Carol Hagemann-White) emerged that led to a "polarization of gendered characteristics" (Karin Hausen). Prior to this, women were largely regarded as just another variant of being-man, which is one of the reasons that the social and historical sciences have throughout the last fifteen years stressed the pervasiveness of the single-gender model upon which pre-bourgeois societies were based. Even the vagina was in the context of this model frequently understood as a penis, inverted and pushed into the lower body.[10] Despite the fact that women were largely regarded as inferior, prior to the development of a large-scale modern public, there still existed for them a variety of possibilities for gaining social influence. In premodern and early modern societies, man occupied a largely symbolic position of hegemony. Women were not yet exclusively confined to domestic life and motherhood, as has been the case since the eighteenth century. Women's contribution to material reproduction was in agrarian societies regarded equally as important as the contributions of men.[11] While modern gender relations and their characteristic polarization of gender roles were initially restricted to the bourgeoisie, they rapidly spread to all social spheres with the universalization of the nuclear family in the context of Fordism's rise to dominance in the 1950s.

Value dissociation is, therefore, not a static structure, as a series of sociological structuralist models claim, but should instead be understood as a process. In postmodernity, for example, value dissociation acquires a new valence. Women are now widely regarded as "doubly socialized" (Regina Becker-Schmidt), which means that they are similarly responsible for both family and profession. What is new about this, however, is not this fact itself. After all, women have always been active in a variety of professions and trades. The characteristic particular to postmodernity in this regard is that the double socialization of women throughout the last few years highlighted the structural contradictions that accompany this development. As indicated above, an analysis of this development must begin with a dialectical understanding of the relation between individual and society. This means that the individual is at no point entirely subsumed within the objective structural and cultural patterns, nor can we assume that these structures stand in a purely external relation to the individual. This way, we are able to see clearly the contradictions of double socialization that are connected to the increasing differentiation of the role of women in postmodernity that emerges alongside postmodernity's characteristic tendencies toward individualization. Current analyses of film, advertising, and literature, too, indicate that women are no longer primarily seen as mothers and housewives.

Consequently, it is not only unnecessary but in fact highly suspect to suggest that we must deconstruct the modern dualism of gender, as queer theory and its main voice, Judith Butler, claim. This strand of theory sees the internal subversion of bourgeois gender dualism via repeated parodying practice that can be found in gay and lesbian subcultures as an attempt to reveal the "radical incredulity" of modern gendered identity.[12] The problem with such an approach, however, is that those elements that are supposed to be parodied and subverted have in the capitalist sense already become obsolete. For a while now, we have been witnessing actually existing deconstruction, which becomes legible in the double socialization of women, but also when examining fashion and the changed habitus of women and men. Yet, this has happened without fundamentally eradicating the hierarchy of genders. Instead of critiquing both classically modern and the modified, flexible postmodern gendered imaginary, Butler ultimately merely affirms postmodern (gender) reality. Butler's purely culturalist approach cannot yield answers to current questions, and indeed presents to us the very problem of hierarchic gender relations in postmodernity in progressive disguise as a solution.

The dialectic of essence and appearance and the feralization of commodity-producing patriarchy in the era of globalization

In the attempt to analyze postmodern gender relations, it is important to insist upon the dialectic of essence and appearance. This means that changes in gender relations must be understood in relation to the mechanisms and structures of value dissociation, which determine the form principle of all social planes. Here, it becomes apparent that in particular the development of productive forces and the market dynamic, which also rely upon value dissociation, undermine their own precondition insofar as they encourage woman's development away from her traditional role. Since the 1950s, an increasing number of women were integrated into abstract labor, the process of accumulation, accompanied by a range of processes rationalizing domestic life, increased options for birth control, and the gradual equalization of access to education compared to men.[13] Consequently, the double socialization of women also underwent a change, and now resides on a higher level in the social hierarchy and similarly generates higher levels of self-valorization for women. Even though a large percentage of women have now been integrated into "official" society, they remain responsible for domestic life and children, they must struggle harder than men to rise up in the professional hierarchy, and their salaries are on average significantly lower than those of men. The structure of value dissociation has therefore changed, but in principle still very much exists. In this context, it may not be surprising to suggest that we appear to experience a return to a single-gender model, however with the same, familiar content: women are men, only different. Yet, since this model also moved through the classic modern process of value dissociation, it manifests itself differently than in premodern times.[14]

Traditional bourgeois gender relations are no longer appropriate for today's "turbo-capitalism" and its rigorous demands for flexibility. A range of compulsory flexible identities emerge, which are, however, still represented differently as regards gender.[15] The old image of woman has become obsolete and the doubly socialized woman has become the dominant role. Even more, recent analyses of globalization and gender relations suggest that after a period in which it seemed as though women were finally able to enjoy greater, system-immanent freedoms, we also witnessed an increasing feralization of patriarchy. Of course, in this case, too, we have to consider a variety of social and cultural differences corresponding to a variety of global regions. Similarly, we have to note the differently situated position of women in a context in which a logic of victors and vanquished still dominates, even as the victors threaten to disappear into the abyss opened up by the current destruction of the middle class.[16] Since, for example, well-situated women are able to afford the services of underpaid female immigrant laborers, we are witnessing a redistribution of, for example, personal care and nursing within the female plane of existence.

For a large part of the population, the "feralization of patriarchy" means that we can expect conditions similar to black ghettoes in the United States or the slums of Third World countries: women will be similarly responsible for money and survival. Women will be increasingly integrated into the world market without being given an opportunity to secure their own existence. They raise children with the help of female relatives and neighbors (another example of the redistribution of personal care and related fields of labor), while men come and go, move from job to job and from woman to woman, who may periodically have to support them. The man no longer occupies the position of provider due to the increasing precarity of employment relations and the erosion of traditional family structures.[17] Increasing individualization and atomization of social relations proceeds before the backdrop of unsecured forms of existence, and continue even in times of great economic crisis without principally eradicating the traditional gender hierarchy along with the widespread eradication of the social welfare state and compulsory measures of crisis management.

Value dissociation as societal form principle consequently merely removes itself from the static, institutional confines of modernity (in particular, the family and labor). The commodity-producing patriarchy, therefore, experiences increasing feralization without leaving behind the existing relations of value, abstract, and dissociated elements of reproduction. We must note here, too, that we are currently experiencing a related escalation of masculine violence, ranging from domestic violence to suicide bombers. In regards to the latter, we must further note that it is not only fundamentalist Islam that attempts to reconstruct "authentic" religious patriarchal gender relations. Indeed, it is the Western patriarchal model of civilization that should constitute the focus of our critique. Simultaneously, we are also confronted with a transition on the psychological level. In postmodernity, a "gendered code of affect" emerges that corresponds to the traditional male code of affect.[18] Nevertheless, old affective structures necessarily continue to play an important role as well, since they ensure that, even in times of postmodern single-gender relations, women continue to assume dissociated responsibilities, making possible the pervasiveness of the mother with several children who still manages to be a doctor, scientist, politician, and much more. This may occur in the form of the return to traditional female roles and ideals, particularly prevalent in times of great crisis and instability.

While turbo-capitalism demands gender-specific flexible identities, we cannot assume that corresponding postmodern gender models, such as the model of the doubly socialized woman, are permanently able to stabilize reproduction in the context of today's crisis capitalism. After all, the current stage of capitalism is characterized by the "collapse of modernization" and an associated inversion of rationalism into irrationalism.[19] The double socialization of the individualized woman should in this regard (seemingly paradoxical) be understood as serving an important, functional role for the commodity-producing patriarchy, even as the latter is slowly disintegrating. Organizations dedicated to crisis management in Third World countries, for example, are frequently led by women (while one also has to recognize that reproductive activities in general are increasingly playing a subordinate role). Exemplary of the development within the West in this regard is Frank Schirrmacher (conservative publicist and coeditor of the *Frankfurter Allgemeine Zeitung*)'s 2006 book *Minimum*, which describes the "fall and re-birth of our society," in the context of which Schirrmacher wants to assign women the role of crisis managers, believing that they fulfill an important function as *Trümmerfrauen*[20] and as cleaning and decontamination personnel.[21] In order to justify such claims, Schirrmacher mobilizes crude biological and anthropological lines of argumentation in order to account for the widespread collapse of social and gender relations and to offer so-called solutions carried out on the backs of women. In order to avoid such pseudo-solutions, it is necessary to analyze current social crises in relation to their social and historical contexts, as value dissociation theory emphasizes. From this basis, it is then also possible to ask which important theoretical and practical conclusions need to be drawn from the dilemmas of the socialization of value-dissociation that today increasingly reduces man and nature to the most basic levels of existence and that can no longer be addressed with Old Left or Keynesian reform programs. Likewise, deconstructivist and postcolonial approaches, which for example interpret racism purely culturally, are unable to address the current crisis, as are post-operatist approaches that altogether refuse to address the general problem of the socialization of value dissociation and instead seek refuge in movement-religious notions of the multitude and act as though the latter concept includes answers to racism and sexism.[22] What is required here, therefore, is a new turn toward a critique of political economy. Such a critique, however, can no longer be carried out in its traditional form that focuses on labor-ontological and androcentric-universalist methodology and must instead include a turn toward a radical value-dissociation theory and its epistemological consequences.

Conclusion

What I have attempted to show schematically in this essay is the need to think economy and culture in its contradictory identity and non-identity from the (itself contradictory) perspective of value dissociation as social base principle. Value dissociation, then, must also be understood not as a static structure but instead as a historically dynamic process. This approach refuses the identity-critical temptation to forcefully subsume the particular within the general. Instead, it addresses the tension between concept and differentiation (without dissolving the concept into the non-distinct, the infinite) and is thus able to speak to current processes of homogenization and differentiation in ways that can also address connected conflicts, including male violence. It is important to note that the theory of value dissociation, as far as it constitutes a societal base principle (and therefore is not solely concerned with gender relations in a narrow sense), must at times deny itself, insofar as it must allot next to sexism equal space to analyses of racism, anti-Semitism, and economic disparities, avoiding any claim toward universality. Only by relativizing its own position and function in this manner is value dissociation theory able to exist in the first place.

Translated by Mathias Nilges

Notes

1   See, for instance, Roswitha Scholz, *Das Geschlecht des Kapitalismus.*
    Feministische Theorie und die postmoderne Metamorphose des Patriarchats
    (Unkel: Horlemann, 2000), 61 and following, 107 and following, 184 and
    following, and Scholz, "Die Theorie der geschlechtlichen Abspaltung und die
    Kritische Theorie Adornos," *Der Alptraum der Freiheit. Perspektiven radikaler*
    Gesellschaftskritik, ed. Robert Kurz, Roswitha Scholz, and Jörg Ulrich
    (Blaubeuren: Verlag Ulmer Manuskripte, 2005).

2   Robert Kurz, *Der Kollaps der Modernisierung* (Leipzig: Reclam, 1994); Kurz,
    Schwarzbuch Kapitalismus: ein Abgesang auf die Marktwirtschaft (Frankfurt
    am Main: Eichborn Verlag, 1999); Moishe Postone, "Anti-Semitism and
    National Socialism," *Germans and Jews since the Holocaust*, ed. Anson
    Rabinbach and John David Zipes (New York: Holmes and Meier, 1986);
    Postone, *Time, Labor, and Social Domination: A Reinterpretation of Marx's*
    Critical Theory (Cambridge, MA: Cambridge University Press, 1993).

3   See Karl Marx, *Capital* Vol. I, Chapter 4: "The General Formula for Capital,"
    esp. 255 (eds).

4   Frigga Haug, *Frauen-Politiken* (Berlin: Argument, 1996), 229 and following.

5   Ibid.

6   Eva Herman, *Das Eva-Prinzip* (München: Pendo, 2006).

7   Regine Gildmeister and Angelika Wetterer, "Wie Geschlechter gemacht werden.
    Die soziale Konstruktion der Zwei-Geschlechtlichkeit und ihre Reifizierung
    in der Frauenforschung," *Traditionen Brüche. Entwicklungen feministischer*
    Theorie (Freiburg: Kore, 1992), 214 and following.

8   Haug, *Frauen-Politiken*, 127 and following.

9   Since the focus of the examination at hand is on modern gender relations, I
    am unable to discuss these other forms of social disparity in detail. For a more
    substantial analysis, see Scholz, *Differenzen der Krise—Krise der Differenzen.*
    Die neue Gesellschaftskritik im globalen Zeitalter und der Zusammenhang
    von "Rasse," Klasse, Geschlecht und postmoderner (Unkel: Horlemann, 2005).

10 Thomas Laqueur, *Making Sex: Body and Gender from the Greeks to Freud*
    (Cambridge, MA: Harvard University Press, 1990), 25 and following.

11 Bettina Heintz and Claudia Honegger, "Zum Strukturwander weiblicher
    Widerstandsformen," *Listen der Ohnmacht. Zur Sozialgeschichte weiblicher*
    Widerstandsformen, ed. Bettina Heintz and Claudia Honegger (Frankfurt am
    Main: Europäische Verlagsanstalt, 1981), 15.

12 Judith Butler, *Gender Trouble* (London: Routledge, 1991), 208.

13 Ulrich Beck, *Risikogesellschaft: Auf dem Weg in eine andere Moderne*
    (Frankfurt: Suhrkampf, 1986), 174 and following.

14 Kornelia Hauser, "Die Kulturisierung der Politik. 'Anti-Political-Correctness'
    als Deutungskämpfe gegen den Feminismus," *Bundeszentrale für politische*
    Bildung: Aus Politik und Zeitgeschichte (Bomm: Beilage zur Wochenzeitung
    Das Parlament, 1996), 21.

15 Compare Irmgard Schultz, *Der erregende Mythos vom Geld. Die neue*
    Verbindung von Zeit, Geld und Geschlecht im Ökologiezeitalter (Frankfurt
    am Main: Campus Verlag, 1994), 198 and following, and Christa Wichterich,

Die globalisierte Frau. Berichte aus der Zukunft der Ungleichheit (Reinbek: Rowohlt, 1998).

16 Compare Robert Kurz, "Der letzte Stadium der Mittelklasse. Vom klassischen Kleinburgertum zum universellen Humankapital," *Der Alptraum der Freiheit, Perspectiven radikaler Gesellschaftskritik*, see n1, 133.

17 Compare Schultz, *Der erregende Mythos vom Geld*, 198 and following.

18 Compare Hauser, *Bundeszentrale für politische Bildung*, 21.

19 For a more detailed account of the current stage of capitalism and its departure from the classic forms of modernity, as well as for the origins of the term "collapse of modernization," see Kurz, *Kollaps*.

20 Women who helped clear debris after World War II—literally: "rubblewomen" (eds).

21 See also Christina Thürmer-Rohr, "Feminisierung der Gesellschaft. Weiblichkeit als Putz- und Entseuchungsmittel," *Vagabundinnen. Feministische Essays*, ed. Christina Thürmer-Rohr (Berlin: Orlanda Frauenverlag, 1987).

22 See Michael Hardt and Antonio Negri, *Empire* (Cambridge, MA: Harvard University Press, 2001), and Scholz, *Differenzen*, 247 and following.

PART THREE

Vicissitudes of Truth

Introduction

Marxism is as much a philosophical project as it is a political orientation or a set of economic concerns. Even the Marx of *Capital* is as concerned with unraveling the contradictions immanent in concepts like "value" as he is with the fate of the working class or the historical tendencies of capitalist development. Indeed, and this is the point, those three axes are in *Capital* rigorously inseparable. Two of Marx's formulations have inscribed themselves as unavoidable—as ideas that must be either embraced, modified, or carefully quarantined—within Marxist discourse. The first is his well-known eleventh thesis on Feuerbach: "The philosophers have merely interpreted the world in various ways; the point is to change it." It would be a mistake to read this thesis as though interpreting the world and changing it were to be understood as opposites; Marx's "merely" [*nur*] calls for something more, not something other, and "changing the world" has to take place at the level of thought as much as that of action in the everyday sense. What is the form appropriate to a philosophy that would construe the world as radically mutable, that would produce new points of potential within the actual—and in so doing, would have already changed it? *Capital* is one answer to this question, which has nonetheless not ceased to be asked within the Marxist sequence.

The second formulation is equally well known, but more complex than it initially appears: Marx's claim, in an afterword to the first volume of *Capital*, to have set the Hegelian dialectic, hitherto "standing on its head," back on its feet. In effect this claim contains two theses. The first, implicit thesis is entailed by the embrace of the Hegelian dialectic as a philosophical form. At the most general level, we might refer to this form as the "historical suture"—the idea that philosophy is the history of philosophy, and that ideas only take on their full dimensions when placed within a historical sequence. Fredric Jameson's "always historicize" is an embrace of the historical suture in just this sense, rather than a call to multiply contextual accretions. It is also an embrace of Marx's second, explicit claim, that the Hegelian dialectic is "standing on its head"—which is to say that in Hegel the philosophical sequence is derived purely from its own immanent self-overcoming—and must be restored to its feet. Marx's second claim produces what we might call the "materialist suture," the attempt to understand the intellectual sequence in a mutually determining relationship with the process of the production and reproduction of human life. These two philosophical interventions (the historical and materialist sutures) along with their corollary (the imperative to produce a form of theory that would also be a form of practice, and vice versa) form the core of the Marxist philosophical problematic: a generative orientation toward incoherence—between theory and practice, thought and history—that each of the thinkers in this section encounters in particular ways.

The first two entries in this section confront an historical crisis within the Marxist philosophical sequence, namely its confrontation with a French poststructuralist thought that seemed to threaten its foundations, and that did indeed expose certain short-circuits within Marxian thought. In "Scattered Speculations on the Question of Value," Gayatri Spivak undertakes to continue Marx's critique of the concept of value from a feminist and deconstructive standpoint "after Derrida," which is to say after some of the certitudes of a certain historical Marxism had been put radically in question. Rather than "deconstruct" Marx, however, Spivak here understands the dialectical Marx to be already less interested in producing a stable foundation for value than he is invested in discontinuities, contradictions, and incoherences—Spivak's word for these, "textuality," appears here as more period than technical terminology—within the concept of value itself. Already suggesting the standpoint of Kojin Karatani, Spivak understands Marx's exploration of value to outline a set of incoherences without sublating them into a coherent theory of value. But this does not mean that the labor theory of value can be summarily dismissed; in effect, the labor theory of value, suitably destabilized, emerges as a kind of repressed truth of capitalism itself, which can only be successfully contained at the cost of ignoring the geographical and gendered division of labor.

Pierre Macherey's "Philosophy as Operation," arises from an impulse not far removed from Spivak's: to re-write the Marxist sequence after a certain interpretation of it had been rendered naïve. Macherey's aim here might be summed up by his re-translation of Hegel's scandalous "What is rational is actual, and what is actual is rational" from *Philosophy of Right*. This dictum would seem to represent the height of conservatism, and indeed the poet Heinrich Heine confronted Hegel with precisely that accusation. But as careful readers of Hegel know well, "actual" [*wirklich*] is in Hegel a complex term, designating not mere factual existence but rather a kind of potentiality. Macherey then insists that "everything rational is operative, everything operative is rational." Philosophy is then not an "inoperative" reflection on what exists or what is true, but an active production of truth: Marx's radical eleventh thesis on Feuerbach is already inchoately present in the "conservative" Hegel of *Philosophy of Right*. But if Marx stands Hegel on his feet, Macherey turns him around. For if there is undeniably a materialist Hegel, it is a Hegel that understands theory as being a kind of practice. Macherey also understands what is implicit in Hegel but not developed, namely that practice is also a kind of theory. But this version of materialism shatters Hegelian totality from the inside, since the totality of practices is not to be unified into a single framework.

Kojin Karatani, though roughly the contemporary of Spivak and Macherey, is by the time of "What is Transcritique," which serves as an introduction to a much larger project, no longer inspired by such anxieties. Nonetheless, the project of "transcritique" can be seen as continuous with these earlier pieces in its impulse to think inconsistency consistently (Slavoj Žižek, represented elsewhere in this volume, is another key figure in this sequence). In the overall movement of Marx's *Capital*, there can be no question that the trajectory is not, as it is in Hegel's *Phenomenology of Spirit*, toward some ultimate synthesis, but toward the sharpening of contradiction to the point where it becomes crisis. Karatani, counterintuitively, produces Kant rather than Hegel as the formal inspiration behind this movement. Marx is then not so much invested in dialectical contradiction as he is in the play of antinomies, which in Kant's *Critique of Pure Reason* are contradictory positions that each make equal claim to reason: time and space are finite, time and space are infinite. Rather than the sublation of these contradictory positions, Karatani privileges the shuttling back and forth between them, which substitutes for the dialectic the influential concept of "parallax." For Karatani, a key moment is Marx's encounter with the positions of David Ricardo, who held economic value to be produced by labor, and Samuel Bailey, who held economic value to be determined by its position in a system of exchange. Marx does not sublate these positions into a more ample conception of value, but rather leaves them in contradiction: the sphere of circulation and the sphere of production are equally necessary to the production of value, but the two spheres do not cohere. Indeed, the worker herself is, in aggregate, also the consumer, and occupies these incompatible spheres at one and the same time. The recognition of this "identity of identity and difference" (a Hegelian rather than a Kantian formulation) then presents novel political possibilities.

Alain Badiou represents an anomalous yet indispensable figure within this sequence. A dialectician by disposition and a Maoist by filiation, as well as a philosopher who has endorsed Marx's economic analyses without qualification, Badiou nonetheless rejects both the historical and materialist sutures. The reasons for these rejections have to do with the implications of his ontology, founded on the transfinite set theory of Georg Cantor. Here, in "The Idea of Communism," Badiou provides an admirable introduction to his own system, which is too complex to enter into in detail here. Briefly, one can say that Badiou rejects the historical suture because there is no coherence to history as such, and he rejects the materialist suture because that would prioritize elements that in his system must remain unhierarchized and merely multiple. One can make objections to this orientation, but the point to make for the moment is that these rejections are made in the name of a perfect identification of theory and practice, a kind of absolutization of Marx's eleventh thesis. Indeed, "truth" for Badiou is not a referential or logical truth, but rather a "truth procedure," which is to say a practice, a sequence assembled by subjects in fidelity to an "event," which is the irruption into a given state of affairs of what exceeds that state of affairs and is indistinguishable within it. These procedures take place in one of four realms: art, love, science, and politics. In the last realm, Badiou names the French Revolution (1792–1794), the People's War of Liberation in China (1927–1949), Bolshevism (1902–1917), and the Great Cultural Revolution (1965–1968) as examples of truth procedures. The "communist idea" is the name of the regime of belief that incorporates an individual into a genuinely political truth procedure.

As Badiou points out, "the victory of the communist Idea is not at issue," as it was, "far too dangerously and dogmatically," for much of the twentieth century. Boris Groys begins his analysis at precisely that point where a Marxist project, far from presenting the impossible of a given a state of affairs, assumes the mantle of the state itself. The privileged figure under which incoherence is made comprehensible is neither subsumption nor discontinuity nor parallax nor multiplicity, but rather metanoia, the enclosure of one perspective within another. This is, of course, one figure for the dialectic, and Groys's contention is that we only understand the Soviet Union by understanding that it understood itself as the dialectic incarnate: in Groys's terms, as the "administration of metanoia," the constant internal pressure to re-revolutionize the revolution. The Soviet Union was, in other words, committed to the unity of theory and practice: "Lenin and Stalin and later Mao used all their power constantly to re-ignite the revolution and to administer it anew. They wished always to be more dialectical than history itself, to pre-empt time." Thus, counter-intuitively, the breakup of the Soviet Union, initially an attempt (and by no means the first) by communism to harness capitalism, must be understood not as a defeat in a metaphorical "cold" war, but rather as a self-abolition quite in line with earlier Soviet self-overcoming impulses. More importantly, it is precisely the closure of the Soviet moment that renders it "completed . . . and thus free for repetition."

Finally, Nicholas Brown's and Imre Szeman's "Twenty-Five Theses on Philosophy in the Age of Finance Capital" returns to the form of Marx's theses on Feuerbach, as well as that of Adorno's *Minima Moralia* and, reaching further back, the philosophical fragments of Friedrich Schlegel and his circle. The idea is not to produce a coherent or complete account of the contemporary condition of thought, but rather to present points of departure that connect substantially to those conditions. In particular, the legacy of Hegel and Hegelian, "classical" Marxism, having been treated as an embarrassing ancestry in the poststructuralist period, and as (as Marx said of Hegel in an earlier period) a "dead dog" in the neoliberal era, is re-opened as a space of possibility and as a standpoint from which to critique other Left positions—even as the historical ironies entailed in thinking through a Hegelian Marx in the twenty-first century are clearly registered.

CHAPTER FOURTEEN

Scattered Speculations on the Question of Value[1]

Gayatri Spivak

From Diacritics *15 (4) (Winter 1985): 73–93.*

One of the determinations of the question of value is the predication of the subject. The modern "idealist" predication of the subject is consciousness. Labor-power is a "materialist" predication. Consciousness is not thought, but rather the subject's irreducible intendedness toward the object. Correspondingly, labor-power is not work (labor), but rather the irreducible possibility that the subject be more than adequate—super-adequate—to itself, labor-power: "it distinguishes itself [*unterscheidet sich*] from the ordinary crowd of commodities in that its use creates value, and a greater value than it costs itself" [Karl Marx, *Capital*, Vol. 1, 342; translation modified].

The "idealist" and the "materialist" are both exclusive predications. There have been attempts to question this exclusivist opposition, generally by way of a critique of the "idealist" predication of the subject: Nietzsche and Freud are the most spectacular European examples. Sometimes consciousness is analogized with labor-power as in the debates over intellectual and manual labor. Althusser's notion of "theoretical production" is the most controversial instance [*For Marx* 173–193]. The anti-Oedipal argument in France seems to assume a certain body without predication or without predication-function. (The celebrated "body without organs" is one product of this assumption—see Gilles Deleuze and Felix Guattari, *Anti-Oedipus*:

Capitalism and Schizophrenia.) I have not yet been able to read this as anything but a last-ditch metaphysical longing. Since I remain bound by the conviction that subject-predication is methodologically necessary, I will not comment upon this anti-Oedipal gesture. The better part of my essay will concern itself with what the question of value becomes when determined by a "materialist" subject-predication such as Marx's.[2] This is a theoretical enterprise requiring a certain level of generality whose particular political implications I have tabulated in passing and in conclusion. Here it is in my interest to treat the theory-politics opposition as if intact.

Before I embark on the generalized project, I will set forth a practical deconstructivist-feminist-Marxist position on the question of value in a narrow disciplinary context. The issue of value surfaces in literary criticism with reference to canon-formation. From this narrowed perspective, the first move is a counter-question: *why* a canon? What is the ethico-political agenda that operates a canon? By way of a critique of phallocentrism, the deconstructive impulse attempts to decenter the desire for the canon. Charting the agenda of phallocentrism involves the feminist, that of logocentrism the Marxist interested in patterns of *domination*. Yet for a deconstructivist critic it is a truism that a full undoing of the canon-apocrypha opposition, like the undoing of any opposition, is impossible. ("The impossibility of a full undoing" is the curious definitive prediction of deconstruction.) When we feminist Marxists are ourselves moved by a desire for alternative canon-formations, we work with varieties of and variations upon the old standards. Here the critic's obligation seems to be a scrupulous declaration of "interest."

We cannot avoid a kind of historico-political standard that the "disinterested" academy dismisses as "pathos." That standard emerges, mired in overdeterminations, in answer to the kinds of counter-questions of which the following is an example: what subject-effects were systematically effaced and trained to efface themselves so that a canonic norm might emerge? Since, considered from this perspective, literary canon-formation is seen to work within a much broader network of successful epistemic violence, questions of this kind are asked not only by feminist and Marxist critics, but also by anti-imperialist deconstructivists. Such counter-questions and declarations are often seen as constituting *the* new Marxist (feminist-deconstructivist) point of view on literary value. Since I share the point of view they subtend, I place them on the threshold of my essay as I move into my more generalized (more abstract?) concerns.

The first distinction to make, then, is that the point of view above focuses on *domination*. Concentrating on the desire for the canon, on the complicity with old standards, and on epistemic violence, the practical perspective of the discipline in the narrow sense need do no more than persistently clean up (or muddy) the "idealist" field as it nourishes the question of value. Any consideration of the question of value in its "materialist" predication must, however, examine Marx's investigation of *exploitation*.

On the level of intellectual-historical gossip, the story of Marx's investigation of exploitation is well-known. Around 1857, Marx set out to unpack the concept-phenomenon money in response to the analyses and crisis-managerial suggestions of Frederic Bastiat and Henry Charles Carey, and to the utopian socialist projects endorsed by Proudhon. It is our task to suggest that, by lifting the lid of that seemingly unified concept-phenomenon, Marx uncovered the economic *text*. Sometimes it seems that cooking is a better figure than weaving when one speaks of the text, although the latter has etymological sanction. Lifting the lid, Marx discovers that the pot of the economic is forever on the boil. What cooks (in all senses of this enigmatic expression) is Value. It is our task also to suggest that, however avant-gardist it may sound, in this uncovering Value is seen to escape the onto-phenomenological question. It is also our task to emphasize that this is not merely asking ourselves to attend once again to the embarrassment of the final economic determinant but that, if the subject has a "materialist" predication, the question of value necessarily receives a textualized answer.[3]

Let us first deal with the continuist version of Marx's scheme of value.[4] Here is a crude summary: use-value is in play when a human being produces and uses up the product (or uses up the unproduced) immediately. Exchange-value emerges when one thing is substituted for another. Before the emergence of the money-form, exchange-value is ad hoc. Surplus-value is created when some value is produced for nothing. Yet even in this continuist version value seems to escape the onto-phenomenological question: what is it (*ti esti*). The usual answer—value is the representation of objectified labor begs the question of use-value.

. . .

In opening the lid of Money as a seemingly unitary phenomenon, Marx discovers a forever-seething chain in the pot: Value-Money-Capital. As in Hegel—of course Marx is not always a Hegelian but he seems to be here—those arrows are not irreversible. Logical schemes are not necessarily identical with chronological ones. But for purposes of philosophical cogitation and revolutionary agitation, the self-determination of the concept capital can be turned backward and forward and every which way. (Perhaps it was the relative ease of the former and the insurmountable difficulties of the latter that led Marx to question philosophical justice itself.) Keeping this in mind, let us flesh the seething chain with names of relationships:

$$\text{Value} \xrightarrow{\text{representation}} \text{Money} \xrightarrow{\text{transformation}} \text{Capital}$$

(My account here is a rough summary of "The Chapter on Money," and section 1 of "The Chapter on Capital" in the *Grundrisse*.) This chain is "textual" in the general sense on at least two counts.[5] The two ends are open, and the unified names of the relationships harbor discontinuities.

Exigencies of space will not permit elaboration of what is at any rate obvious—from the details of everyday life, through the practical mechanics of crisis-management, to the tough reasonableness of a book like *Beyond the Waste Land* (ed. Samuel Bowles et al.)—that the self-determination of capital as such is to date open-ended at the start. That moment is customarily sealed off in conventional Marxist political economic theory by extending the chain one step:

$$\text{Labor} \xrightarrow{\text{Representation}} \text{Value} \xrightarrow{\text{representation}} \text{Money} \xrightarrow{\text{transformation}} \text{Capital}$$

In fact, the basic premise of the recent critique of the labor theory of value is predicated on the assumption that, according to Marx, Value represents Labor.[6]

Yet the definition of Value in Marx establishes it as not only a representation but also a differential. What is represented or represents itself in the commodity-differential is Value: "In the exchange-relation of commodities their exchange-value appeared to us as totally independent of their use-value. But if we abstract their use-value from the product of labor, we obtain their value, as it has just been defined. The common element that represents itself (*sich darstellt*) in the exchange-relation of the exchange-value of the commodity, is thus value" [*Capital* I 128; translation modified]. Marx is writing, then, of a differential representing itself or being represented by an agency ("we") no more fixable than the empty and ad hoc place of the investigator or community of investigators (in the fields of economics, planning, business management). Only the continuist urge that I have already described can represent this differential as representing labor, even if "labor" is taken only to "imply" as objectified in the "commodity." It can be justly claimed that one passage in *Capital* I cannot be adduced to bear the burden of an entire argument. We must, however, remember that we are dealing here with the definitive passage on Value upon which Marx placed his imprimatur. For ease of argument and calculation, it is precisely the subtle open-endedness at the origin of the economic chain or text seen in this passage that Marx must himself sometimes jettison; or, for perspectivizing the argument, must "transform." (For a consideration of the "transformation" problem in this sense, see Richard D. Wolff et al., "Marx's (Not Ricardo's) 'Transformation Problem': A Radical Conceptualization," *History of Political Economy* 14, no. 4 [1982].)

I will presently go on to argue that the complexity of the notion of use-value also problematizes the origin of the chain of value. Let us now consider the discontinuities harbored by the unified terms that name the relationships between the individual semantemes on that chain. Such resident discontinuities also textualize the chain.

First, the relationship named "representation" between Value and Money. Critics like Goux or Marc Shell comment on the developmental narrative entailed by the emergence of the Money-form as the general representer of Value and establish an adequate analogy between this narrative on the one hand and narratives of psycho-sexuality or language-production on the other. (See Marc Shell, *Money, Language, and Thought: Literary and Philosophical Economies from the Medieval to the Modern Era.* It should be remarked that Shell's narrative account of the history of money is less subtle than Marx's analysis of it.) My focus is on Marx's effort to open up the seemingly unified phenomenon of Money through the radical methodology of the dialectic—opening up, in other words, the seemingly positive phenomenon of money through the work of the negative. At each moment of the three-part perspective, Marx seems to indicate the possibility of an indeterminacy rather than stop at a contradiction, which is the articulative driving force of the dialectical morphology. Here is the schema, distilled from the *Grundrisse*:

Position: The money commodity—the precious metal as medium of universal exchange—is posited through a process of separation from its own being as a commodity exchangeable for itself: "From the outset they represent superfluity, the form in which wealth originally appears [*ursprünglich erscheint*]" [*Grundrisse* 166; translation modified]. As it facilitates commodity exchange "the simple fact that the commodity exists doubly, in one aspect as a specific product whose natural form of existence ideally contains (latently contains) its exchange value, and in the other aspect as manifest exchange value (money), in which all connection with the natural form of the product is stripped away again—this double, *differentiated* existence must develop into a *difference*" [147]. When the traffic of exchange is in labor-power as commodity, the model leads not only to difference but to indifference: "In the developed system of exchange . . . the ties of personal dependence, of distinctions, of education, etc. are in fact exploded, ripped up . . . ; and individuals seem independent (this is an independence which is at bottom merely an illusion, and it is more correctly called indifference [*Gleichgültigkeit—im Sinne der Indifferenz*—Marx emphasizes the philosophical quality of indifference]" [163].

Negation: Within circulation seen as a constantly repeated circle or totality, money is a vanishing moment facilitating the exchange of two commodities. Here its independent positing is seen as "a negative relation to circulation," for, "cut off from all relation to [circulation], it would not be money, but merely a simple natural object" [217]. In this moment of appearance its positive identity is negated in a more subtle way as well: "If a fake £ were to circulate in the place of a real one, it would render absolutely the same service in circulation as a whole as if it were genuine" [210]. In philosophical language: the self-adequation of the idea, itself contingent upon a negative relationship, here between the idea of money and circulation as totality, works in the service of a functional *in*-adequation (fake = real).

Negation of negation: Realization, where the actual quantity of money matters and capital accumulation starts. Yet here too the substantive specificity is contradicted (as it is not in unproductive hoarding). For, "to dissolve the things accumulated in individual gratifications is to realize them" [234]. In other words, logical progression to accumulation can only be operated by its own rupture, releasing the commodity from the circuit of capital production into consumption in a simulacrum of use-value.

I am suggesting that Marx indicates the possibility of an indeterminacy rather than only a contradiction at each of these three moments constitutive of the chain:

$$\text{Value} \xrightarrow{\text{representation}} \text{Money} \xrightarrow{\text{transformation}} \text{Capital}$$

This textualization can be summarized as follows: the utopian socialists seemed to be working on the assumption that money is the root of all evil: a positive origin. Marx applies the dialectic to this root and breaks it up through the work of the negative. At each step of the dialectic something seems to lead off into the open-endedness of textuality: indifference, inadequation, rupture. (Here Derrida's implied critique of the dialectic as organized by the movement of semantemes and by the strategic exclusion of syncategoremes ["White Mythology" 270] would support the conduct of Marx's text.)

Let us move next to the relationship named "transformation between Money and Capital," a relationship already broached in the previous link. (This is not identical with the "transformation problem" in economics.) An important locus of discontinuity here is the so-called primitive or originary accumulation. Marx's own account emphasizes the discontinuity in comical terms, and then resolves it by invoking a process rather than an origin:

We have seen how money is transformed into capital; how surplus-value is made through capital, and how more capital is made from surplus-value. But the accumulation of capital presupposes surplus-value; surplus-value presupposes capitalist production; capitalist production presupposes the availability of considerable masses of capital and labor-power in the hands of commodity producers. The whole movement, therefore, seems to turn around in a never-ending circle, which we can only get out of by assuming a "primitive" [*ursprünglich*: originary] accumulation . . . which precedes capitalist accumulation; an accumulation which is not the result of the capitalist mode of production but its point of departure. This primitive accumulation plays approximately the same role in political economy as original sin does in theology. Adam bit the apple, and thereupon sin fell on the human race. [*Capital* I 873]

Marx's resolution:

The capital-relation presupposes a complete separation between the workers and the ownership of the conditions for the realization of their labor. . . . So-called primitive accumulation, therefore, is nothing else than the historical process of divorcing the producer from the means of production. [*Capital* I 874–875]

This method of displacing questions of origin into questions of process is part of Marx's general Hegelian heritage, as witness his early treatment, in the *Economic and Philosophical Manuscripts*, of the question: "Who begot the first man, and nature in general?" [*Early Writings* 357].

When, however, capital is fully developed—the structural moment when the process of extraction, appropriation, and realization of surplus-value begins to operate with no extra-economic coercions—capital logic emerges to give birth to capital as such. This moment does not arise either with the *coercive* extraction of surplus-value in pre-capitalist modes of production, or with the accumulation of interest capital or merchant's capital (accumulation out of buying cheap and selling dear). The moment, as Marx emphasizes, entails the *historical* possibility of the definitive predication of the subject as labor-power. Indeed, it is possible to suggest that the "freeing" of labor-power may be a description of the social possibility of this predication. Here the subject is predicated as structurally super-adequate to itself, definitively productive of surplus-labor over necessary labor. And because it is this necessary possibility of the subject's definitive super-adequation that is the origin of capital as such, Marx makes the extraordinary suggestion that Capital consumes the use-value of labor-power. If the critique of political economy were simply a question of restoring a society of use-value, this would be an aporetic moment. "Scientific socialism" contrasts itself to a "utopian socialism" committed to such a restoration by presupposing labor outside of capital logic or wage-labor. The radical heterogeneity entailed in that presupposition was dealt with only very generally by Marx from the early *Economic and Philosophical Manuscripts* onwards. Indeed, it may perhaps be said that, in revolutionary practice, the "interest" in social justice "unreasonably" introduces the force of illogic into the good use-value fit—*philosophical* justice—between Capital and Free Labor. If pursued to its logical consequence, revolutionary practice must be persistent because it can carry no theoretico-teleological justification. It is perhaps not altogether fanciful to call this situation of open-enddedness an insertion into textuality. The more prudent notion of associated labor in maximized social productivity working according to "those foundations of the forms that are common to all social modes of production" is an alternative that restricts the force of such an insertion [*Capital* III 1016].

In the continuist romantic anti-capitalist version, it is precisely the place of use-value (and simple exchange or barter based on use-value) that seems to offer the most secure anchor of social "value" in a vague way, even as academic economics reduces use-value to mere physical co-efficients. This place can happily accommodate word-processors (of which more later) as well as independent commodity production (hand-sewn leather sandals), our students' complaint that they read literature for pleasure not interpretation, as well as most of our "creative" colleagues' amused contempt for criticism beyond the review, and mainstream critics' hostility to "theory." In my reading, on the other hand, it is use-value that puts the entire textual chain of Value into question and thus allows us a glimpse of the possibility that even textualization (which is already an advance upon the control implicit in linguistic or semiotic reductionism) may be no more than a way of holding randomness at bay.

For use-value, in the classic way of deconstructive levers, is both outside and inside the system of value-determinations (for a discussion of deconstructive "levers," see Derrida, *Positions* 71). It is outside because it cannot be measured by the labor theory of value—it is outside of the circuit of exchange: "A thing can be a use-value without being a value" [*Capital* I 131]. It is, however, not *altogether* outside the circuit of exchange. Exchange-value, which in some respects is the species-term of Value, is also a superfluity or a parasite of use-value: "This character (of exchange) does not yet dominate production as a whole, but concerns only its superfluity and is hence itself more or less *superfluous* . . . an accidental enlargement of the sphere of satisfactions, enjoyments. . . . It therefore takes place only at a few points originally at the borders of the natural communities, in their contact with strangers" [*Grundrisse* 204].

The part–whole relationship is here turned inside out. (Derrida calls this "invagination." See "The Law of Genre," *Glyph* 7 [1980]. My discussion of "invagination" is to be found in *Displacement: Derrida and after*, ed. Mark Krupnick 186–189.) The parasitic part (exchange-value) is also the species term of the whole, thus allowing use-value the normative inside place of the host as well as banishing it as that which must be subtracted so that Value can be defined. Further, since one case of use-value can be that of the worker wishing to consume the (affect of the) work itself, that necessary possibility renders indeterminate the "materialist" predication of the subject as labor-power or super-adequation as calibrated and organized by the logic of capital. In terms of that necessarily possible "special case," this predication can no longer be seen as the excess of surplus labor over *socially* necessary labor. The question of *affectively* necessary labor brings in the attendant question of desire and thus questions in yet another way the mere philosophical justice of capital logic without necessarily shifting into utopian idealism.

If a view of *affectively* necessary labor (as possible within the present state of socialized consumer capitalism) as *labor* as such is proposed without careful attention to the international division of labor, its fate may be a mere political avant-gardism. This, in spite of its sincere evocations of the world economic system, is, I believe, a possible problem with Antonio Negri's theory of zerowork.[7] The resistance of the syncategoremes strategically excluded from the system so that the great semantemes can control its morphology (Derrida) can perhaps be related to the *heterogeneity* of use-value as a private grammar. For Derrida, however, capital is generally interest bearing commercial capital. Hence surplus-value for him is the super-adequation of *capital* rather than a "materialist" predication of the *subject* as super-adequate to itself. This restricted notion can only lead to "idealist" analogies between capital and subject, or commodity and subject.

The concept of socially necessary labor is based on an identification of subsistence and reproduction. Necessary labor is the amount of labor required by the worker to "reproduce" himself in order to remain optimally useful for capital in terms of the current price-structure. Now if the dynamics of birth-growth-family-life reproduction is given as much attention as, let us say, the relationship between fixed and variable capitals in their several moments, the "materialist" predication of the subject as labor-power is rendered indeterminate in another way, without therefore being "refuted" by varieties of utopianism and "idealism." This expansion of the textuality of value has often gone unrecognized by feminists as well as mainstream Marxists, when they are caught within hegemonic positivism or orthodox dialectics.[8] They have sometimes tried to close off the expansion, by considering it as an opposition (between Marxism and feminism), or by way of inscribing, in a continuist spirit, the socializing or ideology-forming functions of the family as direct means of producing the worker and thus involved in the circuit of the production of surplus-value for the capitalist. They have also attempted to legitimize domestic labor within capital logic. Most of these positions arise from situational exigencies. My own involvement with them does not permit critical distance, as witness in the last page of this essay. That these closing off gestures are situationally admirable is evident from the practical difficulty of offering alternatives to them.

Let us consider the final item in the demonstration of the "textuality" of the chain of value. We have remarked that in circulation as totality, or the moment of negation in Marx's reading of money, money is seen as in a negative relation to circulation because, "cut off from all relation to (circulation) it would not be money, but merely a simple natural object." Circulation as such has the morphological (if not the "actual") power to insert Money back into *Nature*, and to *banish* it from the textuality of Value. Yet it is also circulation that bestows textuality upon the Money-form. Textuality as a structural description indicates the work of differentiation (both plus and minus) that opens up identity-as-adequation. Circulation in the following passage does precisely that with the restricted circuit of adequation within the money form itself: "You may turn and toss an ounce of gold in any way you like, and it will never weigh ten ounces. But here in the process of circulation one ounce practically does weigh ten ounces." Marx describes this phenomenon as the "*Dasein*" of the coin as "value sign" [*Wertzeichen*]. "The circulation of money is an outer movement [*äußere Bewegung*] . . . In the friction with all kinds of hands, pouches, pockets, purses . . . the coin rubs off . . . By being used it gets used up" [*A Contribution to the Critique of Political Economy* 108; the translation of "*Dasein*" as "the work it performs" seems puzzling].

If in its first dialectical "moment," circulation has the morphological potential of canceling Money back into Nature, in its third "moment" it is shown to run the risk of being itself sublated into *Mind*: "The continuity of production presupposes that circulation time has been sublated [*aufgehoben*]. The nature of capital presupposes that it travels through the different phases of circulation not as it does in the idea-representation [*Vorstellung*] where one concept turns into the other at the speed of thought [*mit Gedankenschnelle*], in no time, but rather as situations which are separated in terms of time" [*Grundrisse* 548; translation modified]. By thus sublating circulation into Mind, production (of Value) as *continuous* totality would annul Value itself. For Value would not be value if it were not realized in consumption, strictly speaking, outside of the circuit of production. Thus capital, as the most advanced articulation of value "presupposes that it travels through different phases." The scheme is made problematic by the invagination of use-value, as discussed earlier in this essay.

Has circulation time of capital been sublated into the speed of Mind (and more) within telecommunication? Has (the labor theory of) Value become obsolete in micro-electronic capitalism? Let us mark these tantalizing questions here. I shall consider them at greater length below.

The consideration of the textuality of Value in Marx, predicated upon the subject as labor-power, does not answer the onto-phenomenological question "What is Value?" although it gives us a sense of the complexity of the mechanics of evaluation and value-formation. It shows us that the Value-form in the general sense and in the narrow—the economic sphere as commonly understood being the latter—are irreducibly complicitous. It implies the vanity of dismissing considerations of the economic as "reductionism." I have already indicated various proposed formulations that have the effect of neutralizing these suggestions: to find in the development of the money-form an adequate analogy to the psychoanalytic narrative; to see in it an analogy to metaphor or language; to subsume domestic or intellectual labor into a notion of the production of value expanded within capital logic. What narratives of value-formation emerge when consciousness itself is subsumed under the "materialist" predication of the subject?

If consciousness within the "idealist" analogy is seen as necessarily super-adequate to itself by way of intentionality, we can chart the emergence of ad hoc universal equivalents that measure the production of value in what we may loosely call "thought." Like the banishment of the money-commodity from the commodity-function, these equivalents can no longer themselves be treated as "natural examples." (Because these analogies are necessarily loose, one cannot be more specific in that last phrase.) One case of such a universal equivalent is "universal humanity"—both psychological and social—as the touchstone of value in literature and society. It is only half in jest that one would propose that the "credit" of certain "major" literatures is represented by capital-accumulation in terms of the various transformations of this universal equivalent. "Pure theory," within the Althusserian model of "theoretical production," may be seen as another case of a universal equivalent. The relativization of Value as a regression into the narrative stage where any commodity could be "cathected" as the value-form is, to follow Goux's analogy, the Freudian stage of polymorphous perversion, and can be channeled into aesthetics as varied as those of symbolism and postmodernism.

. . . Nietzsche in *The Genealogy of Morals* gives us two moments of the separation and transformation of an item from within the common circuit of exchange. They are worth mentioning because *The Genealogy of Morals* is Nietzsche's systematic attempt at a "critique of moral values," a "put[ting]in question [*in Frage stellen*]" of "the value of these values" [*Grundrisse* 348; translation modified]. The Nietzschean enterprise is not worked out on what I call a "materialist" subject-predication as labor-power, but rather by way of a critique of the "idealist" subject—predication as consciousness, through the double determinants of "philology" and "physiology" [Nietzsche, *On the Genealogy of Morals and Ecce Homo* 20]. Because it is a reinscription of the history of value as obliterated and discontinuous semiotic chains—ongoing sign-chains—disconnected references to money (guilt and punishment as systems of exchange), and to the inscription of coins, abound. The more crucial moment, the *separation* of the money-commodity, is touched upon once at the "beginning" and once at the inauguration of the "present," as the separation of the scapegoat and the sublation of that gesture into mercy respectively. That sublation is notoriously the moment of the creditor sacrificing himself for the debtor in the role of God's son in the Christ story [*On the Genealogy of Morals and Ecce Homo* 77, 72]. (Any notions of "beginning" and "present" in Nietzsche are made problematic by the great warning against a successful genealogical method: "All concepts in which an entire process is semiotically concentrated elude definition; only that which has no history is definable" [ibid. 80].)

I think there can be no doubt that it is this separation rather than inscription or coining that is for Marx the philosophically determining moment in the discourse of value. Attention to Marx's concept-metaphor of the foreign language is interesting here. Often in our discussion of language the word seems to retain a capital "L" even when it is spelled in the lowercase or rewritten as *parole*. Using a necessarily pre-critical notion of language, which suggests that in the mother tongue "word" is inseparable from "reality," Marx makes the highly sophisticated suggestion that the development of the value-form separates "word" and "reality" (signifier and signified), a phenomenon that may be appreciated only in the learning of a foreign language: "To compare money with language is . . . erroneous. . . . Ideas which have first to be translated out of their mother tongue into a foreign language in order to circulate, in order to become exchangeable, offer a *somewhat better* analogy; but the analogy then lies not in language, but in the foreignness of language" [*Grundrisse* 163. If this were a technical discussion where it was necessary to respect the specificity of the vocabulary of linguistics, I would not, of course, equate word/reality and signifier/signified.] It is certainly of interest that, using a necessarily post-monetary notion of Value-in-exchange, which must suggest that "political economy [is] . . . concerned with a system of equivalence [*systeme d'équivalence*] . . . [between a specific] labor and [aspecific] wage [*un travail et un salaire*]," Saussure shows us that, even in the mother tongue, it is the work of difference that remains originary, that even as it is most "native," language is always already "foreign," that even in its "incorporeal essence," "the linguistic signifier . . . [is] constituted not by its material substance but only [*uniquement*] by the differences that separate its acoustic image from all others" [*Course in General Linguistics* 79, 118–119].

The binary opposition between the economic and the cultural is so deeply entrenched that the full implications of the question of Value posed in terms of the "materialist" predication of the subject are difficult to conceptualize. One cannot foresee a teleological moment when these implications are catastrophically productive of a new evaluation. The best one can envisage is the persistent undoing of the opposition, taking into account the fact that, first, the complicity between cultural and economic value-systems is acted out in almost every decision we make; and, secondly, that economic reductionism is, indeed, a very real danger. It is a paradox that capitalist humanism does indeed tacitly make its plans by the "materialist" predication of Value, even as its official ideology offers the discourse of humanism as such; while Marxist cultural studies in the First World cannot ask the question of Value within the "materialist" predication of the subject, since the question would compel one to acknowledge that the text of exploitation might implicate Western cultural studies in the international division of labor.[9] Let us, if somewhat fancifully, invoke the word—process or again. It is an extremely convenient and efficient tool for the production of writing. It certainly allows us to produce a much larger quantity of writing in a much shorter time and makes fiddling with it much easier. The "quality" of writing—the "idealist" question of value—as well as the use-value of manual composition—affectively necessary labor—are rendered irrelevant here. (It is of course not to be denied that the word-processor might itself generate affective use-value.) From within the "idealist" camp, one can even say, in the wake of a trend that runs from Professor A. B. Lord to Father Walter J. Ong, the following: we were not in on the "inception" of writing, and can copiously deplore the harm it did to the orality of the verbal world; we are, however, present at the inception of telecommunication, and, being completely encompassed by the historical ideology of efficiency, we are unable to reckon with the transformations wrought by the strategic exclusions of the randomness of *bricolage* operated by programming (see A. B. Lord, *The Singer of Tales*; Walter J. Ong, *Orality and Literacy*).

These are not the objections that I emphasize. I draw attention, rather, to the fact that, even as circulation time attains the apparent instantaneity of thought (and more), the continuity of production ensured by that attainment of apparent coincidence must be broken up by capital: its means of doing so is to keep the labor reserves in the comprador countries outside of this instantaneity, thus to make sure that multinational investment does not realize itself fully there through assimilation of the working class into consumerist-humanism.[10] It is one of the truisms of *Capital* I that technological inventions open the door to the production of relative rather than absolute surplus-value. [*Capital* I 643–654. "Absolute surplus-value" is a methodologically irreducible theoretical fiction.] Since the production and *realization* of relative surplus-value, usually attendant upon technological progress *and* the socialized growth of consumerism, increase capital expenditure in an indefinite spiral, there is the contradictory drive within capitalism to produce more absolute and less relative surplus-value as part of its crisis management. In terms of this drive, it is in the "interest" of capital to preserve the comprador theater in a state of relatively primitive labor legislation and environmental regulation. Further, since the optimal relationship between fixed and variable capital has been disrupted by the accelerated rate of obsolescence of the former under the rapid progress within telecommunications research and the attendant competition, the comprador theater is also often obliged to accept scrapped and out-of-date machinery from the post-industrialist economies. To state the problem in the philosophical idiom of this essay: as the subject as super-adequation in labor-power seems to negate itself within telecommunication, a negation of the negation is continually produced by the shifting lines of the international division of labor. This is why any critique of the labor theory of value, pointing at the unfeasibility of the theory under post-industrialism, or as a calculus of economic indicators, ignores the dark presence of the Third World.[11]

It is a well-known fact that the worst victims of the recent exacerbation of the international division of labor are women. They are the true surplus army of labor in the current conjuncture. In their case, patriarchal social relations contribute to their production as the new focus of super-exploitation (see June Nash and Maria Patricia Fernandez-Kelly (eds) *Women, Men, and the International Division of Labor*). As I have suggested above, to consider the place of sexual reproduction and the family within those social relations should show the pure (or free) "materialist" predication of the subject to be gender-exclusive.

The literary academy emphasizes when necessary that the American tradition at its best is one of individual Adamism and the loosening of frontiers.[12] In terms of political activism within the academy, this free spirit exercises itself at its best by analyzing and calculating predictable strategic effects of specific measures of resistance: boycotting consumer items, demonstrating against investments in countries with racist domestic politics, uniting against genocidal foreign policy. Considering the role of telecommunication in entrenching the international division of labor *and* the oppression of women, this free spirit should subject its unbridled passion for subsidizing computerized information retrieval and theoretical production to the same conscientious scrutiny. The "freeing" of the subject as super-adequation in labor-power entails an absence of extra-economic coercion. Because a positivist vision can only recognize the latter, that is to say, *domination*, within post-industrial cultures like the U.S., telecommunication seems to bring nothing but the promise of infinite liberty for the subject. Economic coercion as *exploitation* is hidden from sight in "the rest of the world."

These sentiments expressed at a public forum drew from a prominent U.S. left is the derisive remark: "She will deny the workers their capuccino!" I am not in fact suggesting that literary critics should be denied word-processors. My point is that the question of Value in its "materialist" articulation must be asked as the capuccino-drinking worker and the word-processing critic actively forget the actual price-in-exploitation of the machine producing coffee and words. This is certainly not required of every literary critic. But if the literary critic in the U.S. today decides to ask the question of Value only within the frame allowed by an unacknowledged "nationalist" view of "productivity," she cannot be expected to be taken seriously everywhere. (The real problem is, of course, that she *will* be taken seriously, and the work of multinational ideology-reproduction will go on.) If my position here is mistaken for an embarrassing economic determinism, the following specification may be made: "There is a short-of and beyond of [economic determinism]. To see to it that the beyond does not become the within is to recognize . . . the need of a communicating pathway (*parcours*). That pathway has to leave a wake (*sillage*) in the text. Without that wake or track, abandoned to the simple content of its conclusions, the ultra-transcendental text"—the discourse of textuality in the economic that I have been at pains to explicate and disclose—"will so closely resemble the pre-critical text"— economic determinism—"as to be indistinguishable from it. We must now meditate upon the law of this resemblance" [Derrida, *Of Grammatology* 61]. I have done no more in this essay than to encourage such a meditation, to suggest that, following Marx, it is possible to put the economic text "under erasure," to see, that is, the unavoidable and pervasive importance of its operation and yet to question it as a concept of the last resort. (Incidentally, this also emphasizes that putting "under erasure" is as much an affirmative as a negative gesture.) In 1985, Walter Benjamin's famous saying, "there has never been a document of *culture* which was not at one and the same time a document of barbarism" [*Illuminations* 256] should be a starting rather than a stopping-point for Marxist axiological investigations. A "culturalism" that disavows the economic in its global operations cannot get a grip on the concomitant production of barbarism.

If, on the other hand, the suggestion is made that in the long run, through the multinationals, *everyone* will have word-processors *and* capuccino (not to mention guns and butter), the *evaluating* critic must be prepared to enter the debate between Samir Amin and the late Bill Warren, some of the broad strokes of which I have outlined above [see Warren, *Imperialism: Pioneer of Capitalism*; Amin, "Expansion or Crisis of Capitalism?"]. She must be prepared to admit that the unification churches being projected by the mechanisms of Euro-currency and "the globalization of markets" (we read it as "global crisis") do not lend much credibility to this uninstructed hope.

. . .

In "Marx's (not Ricardo's) 'Transformation Problem,'" Richard A. Wolff, Bruce Brothers, and Antonino Collari suggest that when "Marx . . . considers a social object in which the processes of circulation constitute effective preconditions for the process of production,. . . the relevant magnitude must be the price of production of the consumed means of production and not the abstract labor time physically embodied in them" [Wolff et al., "Marx's 'Transformation Problem,'" 574]. I have so far been arguing, among other things, that to set the labor theory of value aside is to forget the textual and axiological implications of a materialist predication of the subject. The passage I quote, however, seems to be an appropriate description of the perspectival move which provisionally must set that theory aside. As a result of this move, "the equivalence of exchange *must be constructed* out of the processes specific to competitive capitalism which tend to establish a proportional distribution of un-paid labor time in the form of an average rate of profit on total capital, *no longer assumed* as in volume 1" ["Marx's 'Transformation Problem'" 572; italics mine, and I have conflated three sentences]. Thus the authors situate the specific arena of the labor theory of value but go on to suggest that, since "Marx's focus [was] on class relations as his object of discourse . . . simultaneously, however, the concept of value remains crucial to the quantification of prices of production. Price on production, as an absolute magnitude of labor time, *can be conceived only as a specific deviation from value*" ["Marx's 'Transformation Problem'" 575; italics mine].

I have not touched the topic of the value-price relationship in these pages. Further, I have questioned the mechanics of limiting the definition of value to the physical embodiment of abstract labor time. I would in fact argue that the premises of *Capital* I are themselves dependent upon a gesture of reduction that may be called a construction [*Capital* I 135]. Generalizing from Wolff's and his co-authors' position, I would find that Marx's focus on class (mode of production) must be made to accommodate his reach on crisis (world system). Yet Wolff and his co-authors' perspectival situation of the labor theory of value and concurrent definition of price of production as deviation or differential seem to us admirably just. Within the discipline of economics, which must keep any textualized notion of use-value out, it seems crucial to suggest that "Marx . . . affirms the interdependence of value and value-form ([understood as] price of production), an interdependence which cannot be expressed by treating the relation between the two concepts as merely a functional relation between dependent and independent variables."[13] As I move more conclusively into the enclosure of my own disciplinary discourse, perhaps it might not be inappropriate to suggest that this essay does no more than point at the confused ideological space of some varieties of such an interdependence.

I will now appropriate yet another item on the threshold of this essay: the Derridian concept of "interest" as in "scrupulous declaration of interest." Derrida's own understanding of surplus-value as capital-appreciation or interest is, as I have suggested above, restricted. I simply wrest it back from that "false" metaphor and "literalize" it.[14] If and when we ask and answer the question of value, there seems to be no alternative to declaring one's "interest" in the text of the production of Value.

I offer this formula because the problem of "how to relate a critique of 'foundationalism,' which like its object is interminable and may always go astray, to a critique of ideology that allows for at least provisional endings and ends in research and 'political' practice" remains with us [Dominick La Capra, Lecture given at Wesleyan University, 1984]. The early Derrida assured us that "deconstruction falls a prey to its own critique" and went largely unheeded [*Of Grammatology* 24]. The later

Derrida, miming this precaution interminably, has been written off as, at best, a formal experimentalist or, at worst, uninteresting and repetitive. It should be clear from the last few pages that I can endorse Jean-François Lyotard's benevolent "paganism" as an axiological model as little as I can Jürgen Habermas's Europocentric rationalism. [Jean-François Lyotard, *Instructions païennes; Rudiments païens* with Jean-Loup Thébaud, *Au juste.* Jürgen Habermas, *Communication and the Evolution of Society.*] One of the more interesting solutions offered is Dominick La Capra's "historiography as transference." Yet there, too, there are certain desires to appropriate the workings of the unconscious of which we should beware. For "repetition-displacement of the past into the present" (La Capra's version of transferential historiography) may be too continuist and harmless a version of the transactions in transference. And it might not be enough simply to say that "it is a useful critical fiction to believe that the texts or phenomena to be interpreted may answer back and even be convincing enough to lead one to change one's mind" [La Capra, *History and Criticism* 73]. Given Lacan's elaborate unfolding of the relationship between transference and the ethical moment, I can do no better here than to reiterate an earlier doubt, expressed not in terms of historiography but rather of literary criticism:

> Nor will the difference between text and person be conveniently effaced by refusing to talk about the psyche, by talking about the text as part of a self-propagating mechanism. The disjunctive, discontinuous metaphor of the subject, carrying and being carried by its burden of desire, does systematically misguide and constitute the machine of text, carrying and being carried by its burden of "figuration." One cannot escape it by dismissing the former as the residue of a productive cut, and valorizing the latter as the only possible concern of a "philosophical" literary criticism. This opposition too, between subject "metaphor" and text "metaphor," needs to be in-definitely deconstructed rather than hierarchized. [Spivak, "The Letter as Cutting Edge," *Literature and Psychoanalysis: Reading Otherwise* 225]

The formula—"scrupulous declaration of interest in the text of the production of Value"—that I offer comes out of the most problematic effect of the sovereign subject, the so-called deliberative consciousness. Thus, there is no guarantee in deconstruction for freezing this imperative into a coercive theoretical universal, though it is of course subject to all the constraints of ethico-logical grounding. The encroachment of the fictive (related, of course, to the textual) upon this operation cannot be appreciated without passing through the seemingly deliberative, which, even in the most self-conscious transferential situation, can, at any rate, only be resisted rather than fully avoided.

In closing, I will invoke the very threshold, the second paragraph of this essay, where I write: "The 'idealist' and the 'materialist' are both exclusive predications." *All* predications are exclusive and thus operate on the metonymic principle of a part standing for the putative whole: "As soon as one retains only a predicate of the circle (for example, return to the point of departure, closing off the circuit), its signification is put into the position of a trope, of metonymy if not metaphor" [Derrida, "White Mythology" 264]. In this sense, the "idealist" and the "materialist" predications of the subject are metonyms of the subject. Writing of the constitution of the subject as such, Lacan writes: "The double-triggered mechanism of metaphor is the very mechanism by which the symptom . . . is determined. And the enigmas that desire seems to pose for a 'natural philosophy' . . . amount to no other derangement of instinct than that of . . . metonymy" ["The Agency of the Letter in the Unconscious" *Ecrits* 166–167]. Insofar as the two predications are *concepts* of the subject, they are unacknowledged metaphoric substitute-presentations of the subject. Between metaphor and metonymy, symptom and desire, the political subject distances itself from the analyst-in-transference by declaring an "interest" by way of a "wild" rather than theoretically grounded practice. Lest I seem, once again, to be operating on an uncomfortable level of abstraction, let me choose a most non-esoteric source. Here is the *McGraw-Hill Dictionary of Modern Economics* on the encroachment of the fictive upon the deliberative in the operation of the economic text:

> Originally the Dow-Jones averages represented the average (arithmetical mean) price of a share of stock in the group. As stocks split, the substitution of issues in the averages, and other factors occurred, however, a formula was devised to compensate for these changes. Although the Dow-Jones averages no longer represent the actual average prices of these stocks in the groups, they still represent the levels and changes in the stock-prices reasonably well. [178]

I say above that "the full implications of the question of Value posed within the 'materialist' predication of the subject cannot yet be realized." I must now admit what many Marxist theoreticians admit today: that in any theoretical formulation, the horizon of full realization must be indefinitely and irreducibly postponed. On that horizon it is not utopia that may be glimpsed [see Jameson, *The Political Unconscious: Narrative as a Socially Symbolic Act* 103f.]. For utopias are historical attempts at topographic descriptions that must become dissimulative if attempts are made to represent them adequately in actual social practice. The complicity between idealisms and materialisms in the production of theory is better acknowledged, even as one distances oneself from idealism, if one designates this open end by the name of the "apocalyptic tone."[15] This tone announces the pluralized apocalypse of the practical moment, in our particular case the set or ensemble of ideology-critical, aesthetic-troping, economically aware performative, or operational value-judgment. My careful language here should make clear that the practical moment is not a "fulfillment." In the pluralized apocalypse, the body does not rise. There is no particular need to see this as the thematics of castration. Why not affirm as its concept-metaphor the performative and operational evaluation of the repeated moves of the body's survival and comfort, historically named woman's work or assigned to domestic labor when it is minimally organized? Why appropriate the irreducible non-fit between theory and practice (here in the grounding and making of Value judgments) into Oedipus's hobble?

I offer, then, no particular apology for this *deliberate* attempt to show the difference between pre-critical economism and the role of the economic text in the determination of Value; and, further, to plot some of the "interests" in its foreclosure.

Notes

1 I am deeply grateful to Professor John Fekete for a thorough criticism of this piece.
2 Any serious consideration of this question must take into account Georg Simmel's monumental *Philosophy of Money*, trans. Tom Bottomore and David Frisby (London: Routledge and Kegan Paul, 1978). My differences with Simmel are considerable. He writes in a brilliantly analogical vein that cannot acknowledge the discontinuity between "idealist" and "materialist" predications. Although he is technically aware of the argument from surplus-value, he is basically interested in value-in-exchange. His anti-socialism is thus directed against a pre-Marxian socialism. His few references to Marx, as the translators note in their admirable introduction, do not betray knowledge of the Marxian text. Yet I have also been deeply influenced by his meditations upon the relationship between money and individualism and upon the beginnings of what Volosinov later called "behavioral ideology"; in a certain way even by his cogitation upon woman as commodity. In these respects, he should be distinguished from both the Engels of the *Origin of the Family* and the Weber of *The Protestant Ethic and the Spirit of Capitalism*.
3 I am obliged here to admit that the "answer" that follows in this essay can in no way be considered definitive. This is my third attempt at working over these questions. The first, "Marx after Derrida," is to be found in William E. Cain, ed., *Philosophical Approaches to Literature: New Essays on Nineteenth- and Twentieth-Century Texts* (Lewisburg: Bucknell University Press, 1984). The second, an extended version of "the same piece," is forthcoming in Derek Attridge, Geoff Bennington, and Robert Young (eds) *Post-Structuralism and the Question of History* (Cambridge, MA: Cambridge University Press).
4 If we think of Marx, Freud, Nietzsche (Derrida includes Heidegger) as the crucial Western thinkers of discontinuity, betrayed or obliged by their method

to unbridgeable gaps and shifts in planes, a deconstructivist reading shows their texts to be a battle ground between the intimations of discontinuity and the strong pull toward constructing a continuous argument with a secure beginning (archē), middle (historical enjambement), and end (telos). By and large, scholarship attempts to establish the continuity of the argument. It is therefore the continuist versions that are generally offered as the real Marx, the real Freud, and the real Nietzsche.

5 Textual criticism of this sort assumes, (a) in the narrow sense, that even "theoretical" texts are produced in language, and, (b) that "reality" is a fabrication out of discontinuities and constitutive differences with "origins" and "ends" that are provisional and shifting. "One no longer has a tripartition between a field of reality, the world, a field of representation, the book, and a field of subjectivity, the author. But an arrangement [*agencement*] puts in connection certain multiplicities drawn in each of these orders, so much that a book does not have its continuation in the following book nor its object in the world, nor yet its subject in one or more authors" [Deleuze and Guattari, *Mille plateaux* 34; translation mine].

6 I refer to this critique at greater length below. Here a brief checklist will suffice: Piero Sraffa, *Production of Commodities by Means of Commodities* (Cambridge, MA: Cambridge University Press, 1960); Samir Amin, *The Law of Value and Historical Materialism* (New York: Monthly Review Press, 1978); Diane Elson, ed., *Value: The Representation of Labor in Capitalism Atlantic Highlands*, NJ: Humanities Press, 1979); lan Steedman, *Marx after Sraffa* (London: Verso Edition, 1981); lan Steedman, *The Value Controversy* (London: Verso Edition, 1981).

7 For excellent elaborations of this theory, see the "Introduction"s and indeed the entire issues of *Zerowork: Political Materials 1 & 2* (December 1975 and Fall 1977). One of the most revolutionary suggestions of this thought is that the working class includes the unwaged as well as the waged. I am suggesting that the unwaged under socialized capital has a different status and definition from the unwaged in the peripheral capitalisms.

8 One striking exception is Diane Elson, "The Value Theory of Labor," in Elson, ed., *Value*. I propose something similar in "Feminism and Critical Theory," forthcoming in *For Alma Mater*, Paula Treichler (Urbana, IL: University of Illinois Press).

9 Hazel Carby and the Centre for Contemporary Cultural Studies (eds) *The Empire Strikes Back: Race and Racism in 70s Britain* (London: Hutchinson, 1982) is a significant exception. Not only are the authors aware of the connection between racism in Britain and the international division of labor; they are also aware that a study of race relations in Britain cannot pretend to be a general study of the Third World.

10 There is a steadily growing body of work dealing with this phenomenon, a glimpse of which may be found in journals such as *NACLA, The Bulletin of Concerned Asian Scholars*, and *Economic and Political Weekly*. A bibliographical starting point would be Kathleen Cough and Hari P. Sharma (eds) *Imperialism and Revolution in South Asia* (New York: Monthly Review Press, 1973), Part 1; Samir Amin, *Unequal Development: An Essay on the Social Formations of Peripheral Capitalism*, trans. Brian Pearce (New York: Monthly Review Press, 1976); and Cheryl Payer, *The Debt Trap: The IMF and*

the Third World (New York: Monthly Review Press, 1974), and *The World Bank: A Critical Analysis* (New York: Monthly Review Press, 1982).

11 See Deborah Fahy Bryceson, "Use Value, the Law of Value and the Analysis of Non-Capitalist Production," *Capital & Class* 20 (Summer 1983). (I have differences of theoretical detail with Bryceson, which are immaterial to my argument here.) My account of the "Third World" here is of the predominant "peripheral capitalist model of development," which works through "an alliance of imperialism with the local exploiting classes" (Samir Amin, *The Future of Maoism*, trans. Norman Finkelstein [New York: Monthly Review Press, 1982], 9–10).

12 In spite of necessary qualifications, this argument underlies much of the criticism relating to the U.S. nineteenth century and a certain twentieth century. A general line may be traced from F. O. Matthiessen, *American Renaissance: Art and Expression in The Age of Emerson and Whitman* (London: Oxford University Press, 1941), through R. W. B. Lewis, *The American Adam: Innocence, Tragedy and Tradition in the 19th Century* (Chicago, IL: University of Chicago Press, 1955), to, say, Sherman Paul's *The Lost America of Love* (Baton Rouge: Louisiana State University Press, 1981).

13 "Marx's Transformation Problem," 576. This, incidentally, also reveals the mistake of the layperson who "refutes" the labor theory of value because "you cannot deduce prices from it." Marx's theory is one where politics, economics, and ideology are relatively autonomous in the determination of class relations in the broadest sense. The point, therefore, is not to reduce value to a calculus of price, especially within models of general equilibrium. Wolff, et al. do produce equations that take this into account. They are, however, aware that the more important issue is that the practical moment in Marx questions abstract economic rigor; even as I argue in the body of this essay that the axiological moment in Marx questions mere philosophical justice.

14 The most powerful development of this conception is the mysterious *Spurs: Nietzsche's Styles*, trans. Barbara Harlow (Chicago, IL: University of Chicago Press, 1978). Part of the mystery lies, I think, in that Derrida is here trying to make "woman his subject" (his "interest"?) and hint enigmatically at "affirmative deconstruction." As I will soon explain, my notion of interest must take the risk of being related to the deliberative consciousness. Over a year after the writing of this essay, at the point of implementing the final editorial suggestions, I begin to realize how astutely Paul de Man had predicted this move from "false" metaphor to "literalization" in the field of political practice. It would take a careful elaboration of de Man's entire complex argument in *Allegories of Reading* to establish the parallel between my move here and grammar and "figure" in the following definition of "textuality." "We call text any entity that can be considered from . . . a double perspective: as a generative, open-ended, non-referential grammatic system and as a figural system closed off by a transcendental system that subverts the grammatical code to which the text owes its existence" [Paul de Man, *Allegories of Reading* 270; italics mine]. Suffice it here to consolidate the parallel by pointing out that, toward the bottom of the same page, de Man aphoristically describes the necessity of this subversion, this closing off, in the following way: ". . . and if a text does not *act*, it cannot state what it knows" (italics mine).

15   "On An Apocalyptic Tone Recently Adopted in Philosophy," trans. John P. Leavey, Jr, Semeia 23 (1982). I believe it is possible to read in this obscure text a practical politics of the open end. I hope to write in detail of it in my forthcoming book on Derrida. I will content myself with quoting a relatively less aphoristic sentence: "To raise or set the tone higher . . . is to . . . make the inner voice delirious, the inner voice that is the voice of the other in us" [71].

Bibliography

Althusser, Louis. *Lenin and Philosophy.* Trans. Ben Brewster. New York: Monthly Review Press, 1971.

— *For Marx.* Trans. Ben Brewster. London: New Left Books, 1977.

Benjamin, Walter. "Theses on the Philosophy of History." *Illuminations.* Trans. Harry Zohn. Ed. Hannah Arendt. New York: Schocken, 1969, 253–264.

— "The Author as Producer." *Reflections: Essays, Aphorisms, Autobiographical Writings.* Trans. Edmund Jephcott. Ed. Peter Demetz. New York: Harvest, 1978.

Bowles, Samuel, et al., eds. *Beyond the Waste Land: A Democratic Alternative to Economic Decline.* Garden City, NY: Anchor, 1983.

Deleuze, Gilles and Felix Guattari. *Anti-Oedipus: Capitalism and Schizophrenia.* Trans. Robert Hurley, et al. New York: Viking, 1977.

— *Mille Plateaux.* Paris: Minuit, 1980.

de Man, Paul. *Allegories of Reading.* New Haven, CT: Yale University Press, 1979.

Derrida, Jacques. *Of Grammatology.* Trans. Gayatri Chakravorty Spivak. Baltimore, MD: Johns Hopkins University Press, 1976.

— "The Law of Genre." *Glyph* 7 (1980): 202–229.

— *Positions.* Trans. Alan Bass. Chicago, IL: University of Chicago Press, 1981.

— "White Mythology: Metaphor in the Text of Philosophy." *Margins of Philosophy.* Trans. Alan Bass. Chicago, IL: University of Chicago Press, 1982, 209–271.

Freud, Sigmund. *The Standard Edition of the Complete Psychological Works.* Volume IV. Trans. James Strachey, et al. London: Hogarth Press, 1961.

Goux, Jean-Joseph. "Numismatiques I." *Tel Quel* 35 (Autumn 1968): 64–89.

— "Numismatiques II." *Tel Quel* 36 (Winter 1969): 54–74.

CHAPTER FIFTEEN

Philosophy as Operation

Pierre Macherey

From In a Materialist Way, *ed. Warren Montag.*
London: Verso, 1998: 28–41.

To present philosophy as operation is to affirm its practical orientation, by detaching it from purely theoretical speculation; but it is also to connect it with a determinate mode of practice. For all practices are not of the same kind or value. To recognize this, it suffices to consider the opposite, completely classical, conception of an inoperative philosophy, which takes place by means of a disinterested inquiry, aiming exclusively at ideal values of the true and good outside of every technical consideration: wisdom without works, literally "disworked" *(désoeuvrée)*, idle, inoperative but not at all inactive, all the more active because it puts into play, if not to work, this kind of practice of leisure, eternally dissident because it is severed from every connection to objective realizations, is realized in an absolute activity which takes itself for an end, because it avoids a confrontation with external results which would limit its scope.

Under the heading of a "praxis" opposed more to a "poiesis"—that is, precisely to an operation—than a "theory," Aristotle established the concept of this inoperative activity. One must return to it, in order to bring out the opposite characteristics of operation, and thus to discover the issues raised by a presentation of philosophy as operation. Operation, "poiesis," amounts to a production of a work, that is, it is a technical activity exercised with a view to a goal external to the procedure that it pursues, and hence without intrinsic or immanent finality, because "its origin is in the producer and not in the product."[1] In this case, action, considered in itself, because it depends on the decision of its artisan, is only an arbitrary, artificial intrigue; it remains foreign to the elements it utilizes and which for it are only means to be exploited, outside of its characteristic ends; it consists in an artificial production, which is essentially distinct from a natural genesis, the latter proceeding, on the contrary, through the internal development of a principle or power which is actualized, without external break or intervention, in its completed form. Let us take some classical examples from Aristotle to illustrate this distinction. To build a house—this is the very model of a "poietic" operation—is a finite activity which is accomplished in the goal that limits it: the "finished" house, that is, the terminated house, apart from which it would remain deprived of meaning, because it would be useless. What would be the art of a builder who endlessly pursued his manipulations and did not lead to the production of any actual construction? Here activity is exhausted, disappears, one might say it is "reified" in its result, with a view to which alone it has taken place. To live, on the contrary, is *par excellence* the form of a "praxis," because this activity completely finds its end in itself, without having produced an external effect capable of being isolated from the process that accomplishes it, and responding to a motivation which would be foreign to it: the significance of this activity is natural, irreducible to any kind of artifice, because its subject coincides with its object, and it finds its sole justification in this identity. Thus, if health cures, and not the doctor, it is because the art of treating does not amount to a technical procedure but consists in a way of living based on nature, in a "regime" based on a correct apprehension of causes and ends.

This conception of "praxis," as its very name indicates, belongs to classical antiquity; and Aristotle only systematized its expression. It is to the "divine Plato" that Freud traced back the discovery of the fact that the erotic drive has value in itself and exists independently of its objects and its goals, a thesis he takes up in his tum in order to place it at the foundation of his own theory of sexuality; and, in a general way, Freud credited ancient civilization for thus having practiced the drive for itself, in its unlimited movement, before submitting it to a final destination.[2] Yet what characterizes this "use of pleasures" and makes it a privileged example of practice is that it displaces the interest of the object toward the subject, whose diverse activities only reveal the intimate power, the intention. To live one's practice in this way is to make it depend on a relationship to the self whose purity must not be altered and whose depth must not be limited by anything. Socrates, through the myth given to him by Plato, discovers in the art of questions, and not in that of answers, the form *par excellence* of amorous provocation and the perfect image of philosophy, it is indeed because the intention is what matters most of all, along with the appeal it makes to the soul to fold back onto itself in order to discover in itself the infinity of the idea. The ancient Greeks did not, as the standard version would have it, establish an exclusive relation between practice and theory, which separates and opposes them: on the contrary, they invented the concept of a practice whose vocation is primarily theoretical, since it guarantees a relation to the truth which is also the foundation of every authentic knowledge.

This invention was to have a great future. Let us offer only one example: what one finds at the basis of the Kantian notion of practical reason, entirely opposed to that of a pragmatic reason, that is, a technical reason which "acts" by adjusting means to ends, the latter remaining independent of one another. From this perspective, an operative reason, which privileges content over form, must necessarily remain impure: it is pathologically affected by the material interests that become its functioning. Practical reason, on the contrary, tries to realize itself in a form of activity which is pure, free in relation to every determination imposed from the outside. Here again, it is a question of an objectless practice, because it finds its complete destination in its subject, with which it is completely identified. And this is why it is also an intentional activity: it takes place in the fact of being willed, without being connected to the conditions that would be required for its execution. For if reason not only *can* but *must* act, it can do so only provided that it frees itself from every hypothetical imperative which would subject it to other interests, under the pretext of ensuring the success of its undertakings: establishing itself from a truly anti-Machiavellian perspective, it renounces every search for mediations, every ruse of reason.

If the question of practice is the occasion of a crucial choice for philosophy, this choice does not amount to an elementary decision that would make it opt for or against practice, but depends on an investigation bearing on practice itself, and trying to dissociate the diverse forms that the latter assumes, in relation to the stakes that qualify it. Thus, there would be an essentially philosophical practice, centered on the subject and showing the latter its destination, which would have to be privileged in relation to the degenerated forms of material practices inscribed in a world of necessity where no freedom is even possible. The philosopher, a practitioner who is spontaneous and conscious of himself, whom no objective determination separates from his intimate vocation, is then in a position to decide sovereignly on all things, at least in a negative way: without attachments, his attitude is that of universal critique, which carries out an unlimited requestioning of the ordinary forms of obligation and belief. His function is one of interrogation, of provocation: through his presence alone, he calls forth scandalous evidence of the state of facts, whose right he denies in his name alone, completely exposing himself in this defiance. Here philosophy unconditionally devotes itself to practice; one might even say that it frees itself from every theoretical obligation, its primary concern being not to know but to act, in the name of principles so absolute that they do not even have to be put to the test of a speculative examination which would scrutinize them and technically delimit their content.

This figure of philosophy is the one Hegel precisely included under the rubric of the "spiritual animal kingdom": this ironic formula he himself implicitly applied to those intellectual circles which had begun to proliferate in Germany, and particularly at Jena, at the beginning of the nineteenth century, and which appear quite similar to those Marx would himself cruelly mock in *The German Ideology* by also placing them within the context of a degenerated Hegelian filiation. It is worthwhile to take the trouble to linger over this description, for it has lost nothing of its topicality. What is an intellectual animal? And first of all what is animal in this form of intellectuality? It is the conviction of having naturally its value in itself, all the rest existing only according to the necessity of supporting it and putting it to good use as its "element."

> The original determinateness of the nature is, therefore, only a simple principle, a transparent universal element, in which the individuality remains as free and self-identical as it is unimpeded in unfolding its different moments, and in its realization is simply in a reciprocal relation with itself; just as in the case of indeterminate animal life, which breathes the breath of life, let us say, into the element of water, or air or earth, and within these again into more specific principles, steeping its entire nature in them, and yet keeping that nature under its own control, and preserving itself as a unity, in spite of the limitation imposed by the element, and remaining in the form of this particular organization the same general animal life.[3]

Just as fish flap their fins or birds display their feathers, in conformity with their essential nature that they seek only to make appear, the intellectual animal is devoted to the pure practice of his capacities, his talents, which he removes from the test of external conditions because they would ruin his appearance. "In this way, the entire action does not go outside itself, either as circumstances, or as End, or means, or as a work done."[4] For this figure is precisely that of the inoperative intellectual, and here we find our point of departure.

The intellectuals Hegel is talking about, and whose image remains for us quite present, are all the more interrogative, questioning, and critical because they remain without works. Their non-productive practice completely draws its certainty from the end with which it is so identified that it refuses to be separated from it: although they are without works, they are not at all without causes, or rather with a Cause to which they are devoted with impunity. Exclusive defenders of a right, they claim its universal nature to the point that they do not consent to determine its concept, nor differentiate the domains of its application, nor rank its levels of validity. Specialists of amalgamation, if one may put it that way, spiritual animals are rather cool and without commitments: to the extent that they shy away from the limitation of a point of view, of a position, they do not at all aim at a certain result, depending on concrete occasions and perspectives that the latter lead to reality, but rather at an abstract totality and global ends, whose fiction would be annulled by being subordinated to effective arguments, or to the simple consideration of facts. Here we have the representation of a perfect "engagement": so perfect that no concrete approach nor any concrete content has really engaged it. And the freedom thus offered for our admiration is the freedom of the void, which vanishes in the myth of an indeterminate, inaugural Action, claiming only a value of spontaneity, innocent of all knowledge. As a fable puts it: in the beginning was the action.

Yet to this ineffective conception of practice Hegel opposes another conception, which is that of practice as labor and as process: the latter is not that absolute action which finds its end in itself, pure "praxis" in the original sense of the word, but an operation which produces objective effects and works. If there is an activity of reason, being exercised within the very limits of reality, it consists in such an operation, for it finds its realization, its *Wirklichkeit*, in it. One knows that in this last instance, Hegel intends another word: *wirklich* is only that which results from the movement of a *wirken*, that is, literally, from a production of works. Thus, is something actual only if it is operative? One can say: everything rational is operative, everything operative is rational. We find here literally the idea that philosophy is to be considered as an operation.

What distinguishes this operation from an action in general? It is the fact that it is inserted into a process, that it proceeds from an intervention that, as such, presupposes intermediaries and a point of view: in order to produce works, one must adopt the point of view of a position, one must take a position, for without doing so it is not possible to enter into a relation with a determinate content. To the unlimited form of an objectless—but not subjectless—praxis, the point of view of operation opposes the necessity of submitting to the conditions of an actual and no longer fictitious engagement. Yet these conditions are limitative: *determinatio negatio est*—which means not that the productivity of a point of view is tied to the restrictive choices on which it relies, by virtue of a kind of law of compensation, but that the share of negativity it includes constitutes it in its very order, inside and not outside the unfolding of the "operations" whose linkage it authorizes. The result is that between the agent and the end that it pursues one must interpose a third element—Hegel speaks of a third term—in order to indicate, as in a syllogism, the rationality intrinsically characteristic of every operative process. The fictitious action of which we previously spoke is spontaneous: it is immediate and without mediations. Actual operation, which depends on a determinate taking of a position, is, on the contrary, necessarily mediated.

The Aristotelian conception of activity, which brought back activity to the transition from power to action, or from the virtual to the real according to a dual schema, formed the economy of such a mediating element. By considering activity as foreign to the nature of movement, to which it does violence and deviates in the sense of something artificial and arbitrary, the Aristotelian conception excluded activity from its internal rationality. Now by substituting for this binary representation a ternary, properly "dialectical" representation—a substitution that illustrates the metaphor of the "labor of the negative"—Hegel not only adds a term to the enumeration of the moments that constitute practice, but he completely overturns their internal disposition, so as to establish their concrete, actual unity, no longer in the form of a succession or adjustment. In fact, if the middle term appears as the practical syllogism's motor of development, it is because this term is not injected from outside in its unfolding, through an artificial and abstract violence, but because it coincides with the necessity of its own operation.

The change thus introduced into the theoretical constitution of practice is not formal but also modifies the content of practice. The pure activity of "praxis," as we have seen, amounts to an essentially subjective practice: its end is to explain the potentialities given in the existence of a subject-substance, that is, of a subject without process, which in its action, never has anything but a relation to itself. On the contrary, insofar as it is thought of within the conceptual field of an immanent negativity, and no longer that of an extrinsic negation, which disqualifies it by restricting it to the consideration of strictly technical ends, operation becomes an objective practice, determined as a process which is no longer that of the exposition of a subject. What is an objective practice? It is not a practice subservient to objects, and by the fact of this submission enclosed within a finite perspective. It is a practice that, in its own movement—insofar as the latter returns negatively onto itself, and thereby is inserted into a much vaster movement which includes it, the latter in its turn growing beyond its apparent limits in order to be inscribed within a context of still larger development, etc.—ends up producing its objects. It "produces" them not in the sense of a material fabrication, carried out completely externally—and from this point of view it must be said that the usual critiques of Hegelian "idealism" are off the mark—but in the sense of a manifestation or a revelation, which emphasize them within their own finite limits, by cutting them off on the basis of an overall organization, simultaneously natural and historical, within which all aspects of reality tend to be in play.

One can say that such an objective practice is a "process without a subject," in the sense that here the process is to itself its own subject: it produces itself rather than being produced, inside the movement that determines it, in relation to the totality of its conditions. It is not a question of a spontaneous production, dependent on some isolated initiative, but of a labor which is collective in the strongest sense of the word, since in its own constitution it requires no less than all of reality, caught up in the differential chain of its moments. This means that operation, if it refers to an operator, does not rely on it as if on an autonomous principle, which could be detached, *tamquam imperium in imperio*, from the activity in which it takes part; it encounters it instead as a moment in the development of the order to which it itself belongs. Does this imply that operation as such is subordinate to the functioning of a structure? No, if one thinks of this subordination as a subjection and of this structure itself as a finite arrangement of elements, as a system in the mechanistic sense of the word, already constituted prior to the practices in which it takes place: such an account would deprive the concept of operation of its content by removing its internal negativity, that is, the faculty that belongs to a determinate activity: reconsidering onto itself, or transforming itself and modifying its conditions at the same time that it carries out its effects. For an operation is by no means prefigured and somehow preestablished in the system of its conditions, of which it would be only an application or a particular case. But it effectuates itself, in the active sense of this expression, in relation to works whose realization, in return, overturns the objective field inside which they are produced.

To operate is thus to take part, in the sense that making a commitment is to carry out activities which require the limitation of a point of view, so as to displace these limits inside the movement that governs them, instead of accepting them as given, and as such unsurpassable, limits. Basically, one will say: to operate is to take risks, including the risk of making a mistake. In fact, by producing works one exposes oneself to the test of a necessarily antagonistic confrontation through which the meaning of what one does must be intrinsically altered, because it cannot escape a resumption which, connecting it with new presuppositions, modifies its initial constitution. Operation is not finished in its outcomes, for the latter never have a definitive, "finished" form; instead, their accomplishment is inseparable from their contestation, which from particular effects gradually gives rise to the general system of conditions on the basis of which they have been produced. "And even at the end of each truth we must add that we are bearing the opposite truth in mind."[5] Nothing takes place which does not divide, by the same token splitting up the field of its realization and revealing its internal contradictions.

To consider philosophy as operation, and not as the creation of ideas or the defence and illustration of well-known causes, whatever the nature of those ideas and causes, is to know that neither thought nor action exhausts itself in its manifest content but behind itself pursues a secret destination, a destination that no totality or destiny decrees. While seeking his father and mother Oedipus blinds himself by awaiting them where he believes them to be. One is seized, surprised, deciphered by one's sources instead of inventing or even interpreting them. An operation is simultaneously a diversion and a detour, no a priori form of correctness directs it; instead, a ruse of reason is at work in it, a ruse so conducted that one knows neither who leads it nor who is led by it. This indecision, this uncertainty, finally open up, on the basis of a limited point of view at first, a global field of investigation, in which enters into play more than simply its stated pretext, but which is only its factual origin. They pertain to that "knowledge of the union that the thinking mind has with all of nature,"[6] whose possession constitutes, according to Spinoza, the sovereign good. This is why one must set aside a specialized conception of operation which would erase these backgrounds and, enclosing them in the false alternative of intentions and works, would freeze their specificity, by ignoring the fact that the series of determinations in which it is inscribed is, in fact as well as by right, unlimited. No one knows what a body can do, nor what a mind knows.

In order to express its nature as operation, it might be said again that philosophy is a "theoretical practice," provided that this formula does not merely suggest a formal equivalence between a theory and a practice, the latter taking the place of the former and vice versa, so that by being confused they would both lose their own natures. "Theoretical practice" is not the magical formula that would guarantee that the identity of theory and practice could be given initially: rather, it indicates a process in which operations are produced, inside which theory and practice take shape concurrently, against each other, with each other, in the sense that they are reciprocally put to work, in a movement in which it appears that there is never pure theory, whose meaning would be limited to its stated results, nor any pure practice, innocent because it would elude the confrontation of its intentions with its effects. If philosophy is operation, it is because it is penetrated by that contradiction of theory and practice which is also the condition of their concrete unity, the latter consisting in the actual development of their antagonism instead of in their final, ideal reconciliation—the end is after all only another beginning.

To the ritualistic question "What is an intellectual?" the following response will be proposed: an intellectual is one who, whatever might also be the domain of his particular activities, expresses himself in works whose meaning goes beyond their immediate justification and in order to be recognized necessitates not only the effort of an interpretation, by explaining his intentions, but a testing of their immediate results, that is, their transformation. In fact, an authentic theory is one that, rejecting as illusory the criteria of truth guaranteed inside of its own order, takes shape in the form of its own practice, which is not its simple application, since it tends to modify its internal constitution. And a consistent practice is one that, not being limited to imperatives of execution, which directly attach to it the norms of its success, encounters, or rather generates, the theory in which it reflects on itself in order to place itself in a new perspective which, at the same time that it indicates other means to it, also changes its orientations. This is why intellectuality does not belong, like private property, to a specialized and talkative caste, assembling in a closed order the holders of true knowledge, the knowers of good language, or the masters of the most just causes: intellectuality is instead found in all domains of activity, provided that they do not give way to mechanistic tasks accomplished without principles, or to the pure illustration of self that transforms every practice into an exhibition, a spectacle.

But if philosophy is, in this sense, operation, one is bound to wonder: what kind of operation is it? What are the materials, means, and stakes that distinguish it? Or else must one say that philosophy, belonging to all domains of activity, is based in them and mixed up with them? Doesn't philosophy then risk being diluted in an abstract and unanimous form of activity in general, a form that would only be so enlarged because it would also be deprived of content? If philosophy is everywhere, and if everyone is a philosopher, philosophical operation loses its determination, thus ceasing to be, in the strict sense, an operation. To an operating philosophy, or one claiming this characteristic, one must ask the following question, then: what are its works? Do they consist in a general methodology applied indifferently to all practices so as to govern their functioning by attaching criteria and ends to them? One could then wonder from where philosophy itself would derive the criteria and ends authorizing it to produce such a model. Above all, one would be astonished to see philosophy bring back its relation to practice in the form of an application, that is, of an external and mechanistic relation entirely opposed to the conditions we have recognized as being those of an actual implementation.

But philosophy is not the undifferentiated practice of all practices, a kind of common Operation, which would include all the forms of operation in the field, then purely theoretical, of its observation. Nor is philosophy a single practice defined by the limits of a domain of objects, in which are attached to it the obligations of productivity characteristic of a definite enterprise, and which terminates, more or less, in its immediately noticeable effects. As operation, philosophy is practice itself, in all sectors of its intervention, insofar as it puts back into question the limits inside which its activities are carried out, and thus discovers the tendentially unlimited power of its processes. This can also be said in the following way: every practice is philosophical, or in relation with philosophical ulterior motives, which strives to go beyond the goals that directly inspire it, in order to reflect the global content and universal requisites that inevitably put its simplest procedures into play. In every practice, philosophy is that which incites it to think about itself, not in terms of a preestablished knowledge, but by relying on the development of its own operations, in so far as the latter are all, in their way, images of the absolute.

From this point of view, the traditional project consisting in making all the approaches of philosophy enter into the framework of a Theory which would rigorously systematize their unfolding, by making them enter into the limits of an order, which—by right if not in fact—is finished, appears more derisory than insane. Philosophy, which is this movement of going past limits, of reflecting the immediate in the mediated, a movement all of whose modes of activity can find the incentive in themselves, provided that they strive for it, cannot enclose its pretensions within the boundaries of any domain, or of any discourse, whatever prestige is attached to it. This is why philosophy's universality genuinely arises not from theory but from practice: philosophy is not the universality of a knowledge which would include everything, and would substitute its determinations for reality once and for all; rather, it is the potential universality of an operation which, without being enclosed within the fiction of a general form, pursues inside itself the movement that leads it beyond its given limits, and thus carries out the encounter of its truth.

Philosophy finds its truth in practice, for the latter provides it with the conditions of its actual implementation: thus, this truth is not a separate, exclusive truth, relying only on the authority of its stated principles, in the form of a self-sufficient discourse. Philosophy is, instead, truth as it stands out from the development of a process which, without requiring the guarantee of any external authority, expresses its relation with reality considered in its totality, and thereby, in practice, justifies itself and demonstrates the correctness of its approach. To philosophize is perhaps, according to a very ancient conception, to identify oneself with the totality. But if this formula can be retained, it is with the qualification that it cannot be a question of a given identity, whose models an actual thought must reject. The identity pursued by philosophy takes shape through the movement that tends to connect philosophy with all of reality: it is the identity of philosophy's operation.

Remarks on practice

1. To think practice is not to think of practice, or to think about practice, from outside, from a point of view not its own, without taking part in practice. One must instead think practice within practice.

2. Practice, first of all: one must start with practice, one must rest on practice. But what does practice start with? On what does practice rest? Practice starts with practice. Practice rests on practice.

   Thus, the primacy of practice is the primacy of practice over itself.

3. Where does practice go? Nowhere but into practice, that is, into other practices. Practice does not constitute its actions as complete totalities, with clear-cut contours, but continues them into others, then into still others, without ever reaching definitive results.

   To begin, practice. To end, still practice. Everywhere and always, there is practice, that is, diverse forms of practice, which are connected with one another and act on one another.

4. If practice is instructive, it is because it is a permanent reconsideration of its own effects: thus, there is always something new to learn from it. Practice is not doomed to the destination of a single meaning which would be its law, its only law.

   This is why it is futile to seek guarantees in practice: practice can make all guarantees; it can also break all guarantees.

   Practice traces and effaces limits: its element is the limit; and its signification is beyond limits.

5. To be put back into practice: it is always practice that decides. But its criteria do not have a uniform function: practice does not constitute a homogeneous order in which all practices are mixed together because they conform to a single model which is that of Practice.

   In practice, within practice: these formulas have an objective value of determination only if they refer to a differentiated content, to a network of articulated practices, which are sustained by opposing one another.

6. There exists no Practice as such. There are only materially, historically, socially determined practices.

7. To think practice is to grasp the infinity of its processes, their complexity, their tendential nature, the necessity of a movement which always continues—in excess, or in default—on itself. Not in order to absorb practice or enclose it within the limits of a complete theory, but in order to accompany it, if possible to inflect its development, and thus, provisionally, to master it.

8. Where do correct ideas come from? From practice. But where do false ideas come from? Also from practice. From practice come, together and concurrently, correct and false ideas.

   If practice, in the last instance, distinguishes correct ideas, it is because it is divided in itself, causing several instances, unequal and antagonistic levels of decision, to appear.

   Practice develops in the midst of contradiction: it is impossible to think practice without contradiction.

9. "In the beginning was the action." But it does not suffice that an action begin for it really to produce effects. An action must continue beyond from its beginning, it must "leave" its beginning behind. An actual action is not only the positive and continuous deployment of what was given at its point of departure: by being linked to other actions which compete with and complete it, it also enters into a negative relation with itself.

   Practice never amounts to a single and simple action: instead, it develops by means of contradiction through a complex ensemble of various actions.

10. Ideas come from practice: let us say instead that they come within practice, from which they emerge without ever truly escaping, for they are also always brought back to it. They are formed at the knots of practice, wherever its different moments intersect, interconnect, and break.

    Wherever practice divides, a knowledge appears, which articulates it.

11. "It is necessary to act, not to allow something to be done, but to do something." These formulas, which one often hears, betray an impatience and an embarrassment: they express an indetermination instead of a determination. How to determine oneself to act? How to determine the content of one's action?

    To intervene is literally to come between, interpose, or be interposed, that is, also, "to find a means," an intermediary which, by resting on the internal contradictions of a situation, provides practice with its actual impetus.

    To know (savoir) is to discover those mediations which give every practice the principle of its development: to recognize (connaître) is to extract the middle term.

12. One proves movement by walking. One recognizes the taste of a pear by eating it. Our forms of knowledge are submitted to the law of facts. But this law is not external to them, nor are they foreign to it. The law of facts is also the knowledge they carry with them, which is discovered in practice.

    A blind practice, which does not generate its forms of reflection and control, is an illusion. A formal knowledge (connaissance), which makes its truth foreseen independently of the conditions of its production, is a game.

13. No practice is without knowledge (savoir), whether explicit or implicit.

    No knowledge (savoir) is without practice, whether concerted or involuntary.

14. "The proof of the pudding is in the eating." No: this proves much more that one is tasting something believed to be pudding. What teaches the consumer about his daily experience is that things are not necessarily as they seem to him or as their name indicates to him.

    The proof of the pudding is instead that one makes it: only then does one knows what one has put in it. The truth of facts cannot be found by consuming it, but by producing it.

15. We say that something is practice when it seems to agree with our usage: it is as if it were made for us, or us for it. A practical mind, likewise, fits situations or occasions. Practice is a matter of adjustment: correctness is the form of its truth.

    But this correctness is not the undifferentiated exactness of an external, mechanistic adaptation: it presupposes an evaluation and the choice of an orientation, the implementation of a perspective, reconsidering itself in such a way as to produce its own transformation. It is the correctness of an engagement. Correctness is also the result of a labor, and this labor is costly.

    Nothing is given by practice. Practice does not give without compensation, that is, without a commitment: one must take part in it, that is, expose oneself to the risk of a permanent readjustment, which modifies the subject of the practice as well as its object.

16. To be pragmatic is to recognize the sovereignty of practice, to stick to experience as closely as possible and to embrace detours, to bow to the facts, to adapt oneself to them. But to follow—and only to follow practice is to yield to the illusion that practice constitutes an autonomous order and is self-sufficient; basically, it is to believe that, full of itself and free of lacunae, proceeding straight ahead toward its goals, practice decrees laws which only remain to be applied, without itself being implicated in them, without discussing or seeking to modify them. It is therefore to remain external to practice, by renouncing participation in its incessant self-transformation.

    It is not enough to submit to practice, one must concretely connect oneself with it, by being engaged in it and by reflecting on it. It is not enough to apply the lessons of practice, one must really put them into practice.

17. Can one speak of a practical truth and say: it is correct in practice, hence, it is true in theory? One can, provided that one considers this correctness in the sense of an adjustment, that is, of a tendential movement, which never leads to definitive results. And also provided that one consider this truth as one moment in a process of knowledge (*connaissance*), whose production is carried out without ever escaping practice.

18. To be engaged is to be engaged with or in something, from a point of view which at the beginning is delimited and definite, hence, determinate. To be absolutely engaged, in an unlimited way, is to engage only one's responsibility, by being enclosed in an intimate relationship of self to self, which seems free only because it is indeterminate: it is not to be engaged with nothing, nor in nothing.

    To be engaged is thus to adjust oneself to certain conditions so as to be able, in return, to act on and transform them.

19. A practice is first of all a position, going well beyond its stated goals, or certain goals that it admits to itself. The perspective to which practice is tied is imposed on it by the objective conditions of its operation, outside of which it would be ineffective. But those conditions also lead it to go beyond its immediate intention: thus, they open up a much larger domain of investigation to it, a domain not tied to simple tasks of execution.

    No practice is free at the origin: rather, it is inside its process that a practice discovers and produces the forms through which, negatively reconsidering itself, it grows in a new and unforeseen sense.

20. No practice is entirely free or entirely constrained. Tied to a perspective whose limits oblige it, every practice is a reconsideration, reflection, enlargement or reversal of this perspective. One invents one's practice by consciously accepting its conditions so as to go beyond them.

21. A practice which does not question its rootedness in order to transform it would no longer be a practice. Without roots, it could not carry out this modification.

Notes

1 Aristotle, *Nicomachean Ethics* VI/4. Trans. Terrence Irwin. Indianapolis: INL Hackett Publishing Company, 1985.
2 Sigmund Freud, *Three Essays on the Theory of Sexuality* (preface to the fourth edition and note added in 1910 to the first essay). Trans. James Strachey. New York, NY: Basic Books, 1962.
3 Georg Wilhelm Friedrich Hegel, *Phenomenology of Spirit*. Trans. A. V. Miller. Oxford: Oxford University Press, 1977, 238.
4 Ibid., 241.
5 Blaise Pascal, *Pensées* Trans. A. J. Krailsheimer. New York, NY: Penguin Books, 1966, 576, 224.
6 Spinoza, *Tractatus de Intellectus Emendatione*, 5.

CHAPTER SIXTEEN

What is Transcritique?

Kojin Karatani

From Transcritique. *London: MIT Press, 2003: 1–26.*

Kantian philosophy is called transcendental, as distinct from transcendent. Simply stated, the transcendental approach seeks to cast light on the unconscious structure that precedes and shapes experience. And yet, can't it be said that from its very inception, philosophy itself has always taken just such an introspective approach? If that is the case, then what distinguishes Kantian reflection? Kant's unique way of reflection appeared in his early work, *Dreams of a Visionary*. Kant wrote, "Formerly, I viewed human common sense only from the standpoint of my own; now I put myself into the position of another's reason outside of myself, and observe my judgments, together with their most secret causes, from the point of view of others. It is true that the comparison of both observations results in pronounced parallax, but it is the only means of preventing the optical delusion, and of putting the concept of the power of knowledge in human nature into its true place." What Kant is saying here is not the platitude that one should see things not only from one's own point of view, but also from the point of view of others. In fact, it is the reverse. If one's subjective view is an optical delusion, then the objective perspective or the viewpoint of others cannot but be an optical delusion as well. And if the history of philosophy is nothing but the history of such reflections, then the history of philosophy is itself nothing but optical delusion. The reflection that Kant brought about is the kind that reveals that reflections in the past were optical delusions. This Kantian reflection as a critique of reflection is engendered by "pronounced parallax" between the subjective viewpoint and the objective viewpoint. To explain, take an example of a technology that did not exist in Kant's time.

Reflection is often spoken of by way of the metaphor of seeing one's image in the mirror. In the mirror, one sees one's own face from the perspective of the other. But in today's context, photography must also be taken into consideration. Compare the two. Although the mirror image can be identified with the perspective of the other, there is still certain complicity with regard to one's own viewpoint. After all, people can see their own image in the mirror as they like, while the photograph looks relentlessly "objective." Of course, the photograph itself is an image (optical delusion) as well. What counts then is the "pronounced parallax" between the mirror image and photographic image. At the time photography was invented, it is said that those who saw their own faces in pictures could not help but feel a kind of abhorrence—just like hearing a tape recording of one's own voice for the first time. People gradually become accustomed to photographs. In other words, people eventually come to see the image in the photograph as themselves. The crux here is the pronounced parallax that people presumably experience when they "first" see their photographic image.

Philosophy begins with introspection as mirror, and that is where it ends. No attempt to introduce the perspective of the other can change this essential fact. In the first place, philosophy began with Socrates's "dialogue." But the dialogue itself is trapped within the mirror, so to speak. People alternately criticize Kant for having remained in a subjectivist self-scrutiny, or search for a way out of that in the *Critique of Judgment*'s introduction of plural subjects. But the truly revolutionary event in philosophy had already occurred in *Critique of Pure Reason*, where Kant attempted to obliterate the complicity inherent in introspection precisely by confining himself to the introspective framework. Here one can observe the attempt to introduce an objectivity (qua otherness) that is totally alien to the conventional space of introspection—mirror. Kant has been criticized for his subjective method, lacking in the other. But in fact, his thought is always haunted by the perspective of the other. *Critique of Pure Reason* is not written in the self-critical manner of *Dreams of a Visionary*. And yet, "the pronounced parallax" has not disappeared. This emerged in the form of antinomy, which exposes the fact that both thesis and antithesis are nothing more than "optical delusions."

. . . in *The German Ideology* Marx criticized the young Hegelians—a group to which he himself had belonged just months before, when he was exiled to France. To Engels, this book presented a new view of history that replaced German idealism with an economic purview. German ideology was nothing more than the discourse of a backward nation, attempting to realize conceptually that which had already become a reality in the advanced nation of England. But for Marx, it was by stepping outside of Germany's ideology for the first time that he was able to experience an awakening, accompanied by a certain shock. This was to see things neither from his own viewpoint, nor from the viewpoint of others, but to face the reality that is exposed through difference (parallax). When he moved to England, Marx devoted himself to the critique of classical economics, which was then dominant. In Germany, Marx had already carried out the critique of capitalism and classical economics. What was it that endowed Marx with the new critical perspective that came to fruition in *Capital*? It was an occurrence that, according to the discourse of classical economics, could only be an accident or mistake: the economic crisis, or more precisely, the pronounced parallax brought about by it.

What is important is the fact that Marx's critique was always born from migration and the pronounced parallax that results from it. Hegel criticized Kant's subjectivism and emphasized objectivity. But in Hegel, the pronounced parallax discovered by Kant is extinguished. Likewise, the pronounced parallax discovered by Marx was extinguished by Engels and other Marxists. As a result, one is left with an image of Kant and Marx as thinkers who constructed solid, immovable systems. A closer reading, however, reveals that they were in fact practicing constant transposition, and that the move to different discursive systems was what brought about the pronounced parallax. This is obvious in the case of the exiled Marx, but the same thing can be observed in Kant as well. Kant was not an exile in spatial terms—he never moved away from his hometown of Königsberg. Rather, it was his stance that made him a kind of exile, a man independent from the state: Kant rejected a promotion to a post in Berlin, the center of state academia, instead insisting on cosmopolitanism. Kant is generally understood to have executed the transcendental critique from a place that lies between rationalism and empiricism. However, upon reading his strangely self-deprecating *Dreams of a Visionary Explained by Dreams of Metaphysics*, one finds it impossible to say that he was simply thinking from a place between these two poles. Instead, it is the "parallax" between positions that acts. Kant, too, performed a critical oscillation: He continuously confronted the dominant rationalism with empiricism, and the dominant empiricism with rationalism. The Kantian critique exists within this movement itself. The transcendental critique is not some kind of stable third position. It cannot exist without a transversal and transpositional movement. It is for this reason that I have chosen to name the dynamic critiques of Kant and Marx—which are both transcendental and transversal—"transcritique."

According to Louis Althusser, Marx made an epistemological break in *The German Ideology*. But in my transcritical understanding, the break did not occur once, but many times, and this one in particular was not the most significant. It is generally thought that Marx's break in *The German*

Ideology was the establishment of historical materialism. But in fact that was pioneered by Engels, who wrote the main body of the book. One must therefore look at Marx as a latecomer to the idea; he came to it because of his obsession with a seemingly outmoded problem (to Engels)—the critique of religion. Thus Marx says: "For Germany the *criticism of religion* is in the main complete, and criticism of religion is the premise of all criticism."[1] He conducted a critique of state and capital as an extension of the critique of religion. In other words, he persistently continued the critique of religion under the names of state and capital. (And this was not merely an application of the Feuerbachian theory of self-alienation that he later abandoned.)

The development of industrial capitalism made it possible to see previous history from the vantage point of production. So it is that Adam Smith could already pose a stance akin to historical materialism by the mid-eighteenth century. But historical materialism does not have the potency to elucidate the capitalist economy that created it. Capitalism, I believe, is nothing like the economic infrastructure. It is a certain force that regulates humanity beyond its intentionality, a force that divides and recombines human beings. It is a religio-generic entity. This is what Marx sought to decode for the whole of his life. "A commodity appears at first sight an extremely obvious, trivial thing. But its analysis brings out that it is a very strange thing, abounding in metaphysical subtleties and theological niceties."[2] Here Marx is no longer questioning and problematizing metaphysics or theology in the narrow sense. Instead, he grasps the knotty problematic as "an extremely obvious, trivial thing." Thinking this way about Marx, one realizes that an equivalent of historical materialism—or even what is known as Marxism for that matter—could have existed without Marx, while the text *Capital* could not have existed if not for him.

The 'Marxian turn'—the kind that is truly significant and that one cannot overlook—occurred in his middle career, in the shift from *Grundrisse* or *A Contribution to the Critique of Political Economy* to *Capital*: it was the introduction of the theory of "value form." What provoked Marx's radical turn, which came after he finished writing *Grundrisse*, was his initiation to skepticism: It was Bailey's critique of Ricardo's labor theory of value. According to David Ricardo, exchange value is inherent in a commodity, which is expressed by money. In other words, money is just an illusion (*Schein* in Kant). Based upon this recognition, both Ricardian Leftists and Proudhon insisted on abolishing currency and on replacing it with the labor money or the exchange bank. Criticizing them as he did, however, Marx was still relying on the labor theory of value (akin to Ricardo). On the other hand, Bailey criticized the Ricardian position by claiming that the value of a commodity exists only in its relationship with other commodities, and therefore the labor value that Ricardo insists is inherent in a commodity is an illusion.

Samuel Bailey's skepticism is similar to Hume's criticism that there is nothing like a Cartesian ego cogito; there are just many egos. To this position, Kant responded that yes, an ego is just an illusion, but functioning there is the transcendental apperception X. But what one knows as metaphysics is that which considers the X as something substantial. Nevertheless, one cannot really escape from the drive [*Trieb*] to take it as an empirical substance in various contexts. If so, it is possible to say that an ego is not just an illusion, but a transcendental illusion. Kant achieved this position later in his life; but first his dogmatic slumber had to be interrupted by Hume's skepticism. And in this precise manner, Marx must have been severely stricken by Bailey's skepticism. But, again, like Kant, Marx developed this thought into another dimension, which I would like to call the "transcendental reflection on value."

Classical economics held that each commodity internalizes a labor value. But, in reality, commodities can have values only after their relationship is synthesized by money, and each one of them is given its value. In reality only prices exist as the indicators of the mutual relations between commodities. Thus Bailey stressed that the value of a commodity exists only thanks to its relationship with other commodities. But Bailey did not question what expresses price: money. In other words, he did not question what relates commodities to each other and composes the system: that is, money as the general equivalent. Money in this sense is totally irrelevant to money as substance like gold or silver; rather, it is like a Kantian transcendental apperception X, as it were. The stance to see it in relation to its materiality is what Marx called fetishism. After all, money as substance is an illusion, but more correctly, it is a transcendental illusion in the sense that it is hardly possible to discard it.

For mercantilists and bullionists—the predecessors of classical economics—money was an object to be revered. This was evidently the fetishism of money. Scorning this, classical economists posited the substance of value in labor in and of itself. But this so-called labor theory of value did not resolve the enigma of money; rather, it reinforced and sustained it. Both Ricardo—the advocate of the labor theory of value—and Bailey—its radical critic (and the unacknowledged primogenitor of neoclassical economics)—managed to erase money *only superficially*. As Marx said, in times of crisis, people still want money suddenly, going back to bullionism. The Marx of *Capital* stands on the side of the mercantilist, rather than Ricardo or Bailey. By criticizing both Ricardo and Bailey on such a premise, his critique elucidated a *form* that constitutes the commodity economy. In other words, what Marx focused on was not the objects themselves but the relational system in which the objects are placed.

According to Marx, if gold becomes money, that is not because of its immanent material characteristics, but because it is placed in the value form. The value form—consisting of relative value form and equivalent form—makes any object that is placed in it money. Anything—*anything*—that is exclusively placed in the general equivalent form becomes money; that is, it achieves the right to attain anything in exchange (i.e., its owner can attain anything in exchange). People consider a certain thing (i.e., gold) as sublime, only because it fills the spot of general equivalent. Crucially, Marx begins his reflections on capital with the miser, the one who hoards the right to exchange—in the strict sense, the right to stand in the position of equivalent form—at the expense of use. The desire for money or the right to exchange is different from the desire for commodities themselves. I would call this 'drive [*Trieb*]' in the Freudian sense, to distinguish it from 'desire'. To put it another way, the drive of a miser is not to own an object, but to stand in the position of equivalent form, even at the expense of the object. The drive is metaphysical in nature; the misers' goal is to 'accumulate riches in heaven', as it were.

One tends to scorn the drive of the miser. But capital's drive to accumulate is essentially the same. Capitalists are nothing but "rational misers" to use Marx's term. Buying a commodity from someone somewhere and selling it to anyone anywhere, capitalists seek to reproduce and expand their position to exchange, and the purpose is not to attain many 'uses'. That is to say that the motive drive of capitalism is not in people's desire. Rather, it is the reverse; for the purpose of attaining the right to exchange, capital has to create people's desire. This drive of hoarding the right to exchange originates in the precariousness inherent in exchange among others.

Historical materialists aim to describe how the relationships between nature and humans as well as among humans themselves transformed/developed throughout history. What is lacking in this endeavor is any reflection upon the capitalist economy that organizes the transformation/development. And to this end, one must take into consideration the dimension of exchange, and why the exchange inexorably takes the form of value. Physiocrats and classical economists had the conviction that they could see all aspects of social relations transparently from the vantage point of production. The social exchange, however, is consistently opaque and thus appears as an autonomous force which we can hardly abolish. Engels's conviction that we should control the anarchic drive of capitalist production and transform it into a planned economy was little more than an extension of classical economists' thought. And Engels's stance was, of course, the source of centralist communism.

One of the most crucial transpositions/breaks in Marx's theory of value form lies in its attention to use-value or the process of circulation. Say, a certain thing becomes valuable only when it has use-value to other people; a certain thing—no matter how much labor time is required to make it—has no value if not sold. Marx technically abolished the conventional division between exchange-value and use-value. No commodity contains exchange-value as such. If it fails to relate to others, it will be a victim of "sickness unto death" in the sense of Kierkegaard. Classical economists believe that a commodity is a synthesis between use-value and exchange-value. But this is only an ex post facto recognition. Lurking behind this synthesis as event is a "fatal leap [*salto mortale*]." Kierkegaard saw the human being as a synthesis between finity and infinity, reminding us that what is at stake in this synthesis is inevitably 'faith'. In commodity exchange, the equivalent *religious* moment appears as 'credit'. Credit, the treaty of presuming that a commodity can be sold in advance, is an institutionalization of postponing the critical moment of selling a commodity. And the commodity economy, constructed as it is upon credit, inevitably nurtures crisis.

Classical economics saw all economic phenomena from the vantage point of production, and insisted that it had managed to demystify everything (other than production) by reasoning that it was all secondary and illusory. As a result, it is mastered by the circulation and credit that it believes itself to have demystified, and thus it can never elucidate why crisis occurs. Crisis is the appearance of the critical moment inherent in the commodity economy, and as such it functions as the most radical critique of the political economy. In this light, it may be said that pronounced parallax brought by crisis led Marx to *Capital*.

In the preface to the second edition of *Capital*, Marx "openly avowed [himself] to be the pupil of that mighty thinker" Hegel.[3] In fact, Marx sought to describe the capitalist economy as if it were a self-realization of capital qua the Hegelian Spirit. Notwithstanding the Hegelian descriptive style, however, *Capital* distinguishes itself from Hegel's philosophy in its motivation. The end of *Capital* is never the "absolute Spirit." *Capital* reveals the fact that capital, though organizing the world, can never go beyond its own limit. It is a Kantian critique of the ill-contained drive of capital/reason to self-realize beyond its limit.

And all the enigmas of capital's drive are inscribed in the theory of value form. The theory of value form is not a historical reflection that follows *exchange* from barter to the formation of money. Value form is a kind of form that people are not aware of when they are placed within the monetary economy; this is the form that is discovered only *transcendentally*. In the reverse of his descriptive order—from form of value, money form to miser to merchant capital to industrial capital—one has to read Marx's retrospective query from the latter to the former. Classical economists rebuked the businesses of bullionists, mercantilists, and merchant capitalists of the previous age and denounced their economic role. They argued that while they earn profit from the difference of unequal exchange, industrial capital makes money from fair, equal exchange: it derives profit from the division of labor and cooperative work. In contrast, Marx thought of capital by returning to the model of merchant capital. He saw capital in the general formula: Money-Commodity-Money'. This is to see capital essentially as merchant capital. Capital under this light is a self-increasing, self-reproductive money. This is the movement M-C-M' itself. The case of industrial capital—which is usually considered to be totally different—differs only in that the role of C is a complex that consists of raw material, means of production, and labor-power commodity. And this last, labor-power commodity, is truly inherent in industrial capital. For industrial capital earns surplus value not only by making workers work, but also by making them buy back—in totality—what they produce.

Classical economists' claim that merchant capital (or mercantilism) conducts unequal exchange misses the point. The fact is, when merchant capital attains surplus value from the exchange between different value systems, each trade—either M-C or C-M—is strictly based upon equal exchange. Merchant capital attains surplus value from spatial difference. Meanwhile, industrial capital attains surplus value by incessantly producing new value systems *temporally*—that is, with technological innovation. This categorical division does not prevent industrial capital from attaining surplus value from the activity of merchant capital. Whatever the kind, capital is not choosy in how it attains surplus value; it always attains surplus value from the difference of value systems by equal exchange within each deal. But, one of the points I want to pose is that how surplus value is earned—in contrast to how profit is earned—is strictly invisible, and the whole mechanism remains in a black box, as it were. Thus invisibility is also a condition for the struggle within the process of circulation.

It is troubling that many Marxists posit surplus value only in the 'exploitation' of the production process rather than in the differences between value systems. These Marxists see the relationship between capitalists and wage workers as a (disguised) extension of that between feudal lord and serfs and they believe that this was Marx's idea. But it originated in the Ricardian Socialists, who drew from Ricardo's theory of profit the idea that profit making is equal to the exploitation of surplus labor. This became the central theory of the English labor movement in the early nineteenth century. Though it is true that Marx himself said a similar thing time and again and it may entertain a vulgar ear, it should be distinguished from that aspect of Marx that actually elucidated the enigma of surplus value. The best it can do is to explain absolute surplus value (achieved by the elongation of the labor day), but not relative surplus value (achieved by the improvement of labor productivity)—the particular characteristic of industrial capitalism. What is more, seeing the relationship between capitalist and wage worker in comparison with the relationship between feudal lord and serf is seriously misleading: first, it results in envisioning the abolishment of the capitalist economy from the vantage point of the master/slave dialectic; and second, it leads to centralizing the struggle in production process by ignoring the circulation process.

The Marx of *Capital*, in contrast, stresses the priority of the circulation process. In the manner of Kant, Marx points out an antinomy: He says, on the one hand, that surplus value (for industrial capital) cannot be attained in the process of production *in itself*, and, on the other hand, that it cannot be attained in the process of circulation *in itself*. Hence, "Hic Rhodus, hic salta!" Nevertheless, this antinomy can be undone, that is, only by proposing that the surplus value (for industrial capital) comes from the difference of value systems in the *circulation process* (like in merchant capital), and yet that the difference is created by technological innovation in the *production process*. Capital has to discover and create the difference incessantly. This is the driving force for the endless technological innovation in industrial capitalism; it is not that the productionism comes from people's hope for the progress of civilization as such. It is widely believed that the development of the capitalist economy is caused by our material desires and faith in progress; so it is that it would always seem possible to change our mentality and begin to control the reckless development rationally; and further, it would seem possible to abolish capitalism itself, when we wish. The drive of capitalism, however, is deeply inscribed in our society and culture; or more to the point, our society and culture are created by it; it will never stop by itself. Neither will it be stopped by any rational control or by state intervention.

Marx's *Capital* does not reveal the necessity of revolution. As the Japanese Marxian political economist, Kozo Uno (1897–1977) pointed out, it only presents the necessity of crisis.[4] And crisis, even though it is the peculiar illness of the capitalist economy, is the catalyst for its incessant development; it is part of the whole mechanism. The capitalist economy cannot eradicate the plague, yet neither will it perish because of it. Environmentalists warn that the capitalist economy will cause unprecedented disasters in the future, yet it is not that these disasters will terminate the capitalist economy. Also, it is impossible that capitalism will collapse by the reverse dynamic, when, in the future, commodification is pushed to its limit—it is impossible that it would die a natural death.

Finally, the only solution most of us can imagine today is state regulation of capital's reckless movement. But we should take notice of the fact that the state, like capital, is driven by its own certain *autonomous* power—which won't be dissolved by the globalization of capitalism. This autonomy should nevertheless be understood in distinction from the sense of historical materialism's doctrine that state and nation assume superstructure in relationship with economic base; they are relatively autonomous to, though determined by, it. First of all, as I have suggested, the very notion that the capitalist economy is base or infrastructure is itself questionable. As I have tried to elucidate in the book, the world organized by money and credit is rather one of illusion, with a peculiarly religious nature. Saying this from the opposite view, even though state and nation are composed by communal illusion, precisely like capitalism, they inevitably exist, thanks to their necessary grounds. Simply put, they are founded on *exchanges* that are different from the commodity exchange. So it is that no matter how many times one stresses their nature of being "imagined communities,"[5] it is impossible to dissolve them. As young Marx pointed out vis-à-vis another bind: "To abolish religion as the *illusory* happiness of the people is to demand the *real* happiness. The demand to give up illusions about the existing state of affairs is the *demand to give up a state of affairs which needs illusions*. The criticism of religion is therefore *in embryo the criticism of the value of tears*, the *halo* of which is religion."[6] The same can be said of state and nation.

After reflecting upon "value form," the Marx of *Capital* seems to explicate the historical genesis of commodity exchange in the chapter "Process of Exchange." There he stresses that it began in between communities: "The exchange of commodities begins where communities have their boundaries, at their points of contact with other communities, or with members of the latter. However, as soon as products have become commodities in the external relations of a community, they also, by reaction, become commodities in the internal life of the community."[7] Despite its appearance, this depiction is not strictly of a historical situation, but the form of exchange that is discovered and stipulated only by a transcendental retrospection. Furthermore, Marx's statement, which I quoted earlier, is in fact based upon the premise that there are other forms of exchange. Commodity exchange is a peculiar form of exchange among other exchanges. First, there is exchange within a community—a reciprocity of gift and return. Though based upon mutual aid, it also imposes the community's code—if one does not return, one will be ostracized—and exclusivity. Second, the original exchange between communities is plunder. And rather it is this plunder that is the basis for other exchanges: For instance, commodity exchange begins only at the point where mutual plunder is given up. In this sense, plunder is deemed a type of exchange. For instance, in order to plunder continuously, it is necessary to protect the plundered from other plunderers, and even nurture economico-industrial growth. This is the prototype of the state. In order to keep on robbing, and robbing more and more, the state guarantees the protection of land and the reproduction of labor power by redistribution. It also promotes agricultural production by public undertakings such as regulating water distribution through public water works. It follows that the state does not appear to be abetting a system of robbery: Farmers think of paying tax as a return (duty) for the protection of the lord; merchants pay tax as a return for the protection of their exchange and commerce. Finally, the state is represented as a supra-class entity of reason.

Plunder and redistribution are thus forms of exchange. Inasmuch as human social relations entail the potential of violence, these forms are inevitably present. And the third form is what Marx calls the commodity exchange between communities. As I analyze in detail in the book, this exchange engenders surplus value or capital, though with mutual consent;

and it is definitively different from the exchange of plunder/redistribution. Furthermore, and this is the final question of this book, a fourth kind of exchange exists: association. This is a form of mutual aid, yet neither exclusive nor coercive like community. Associationism can be considered as an ethicoeconomic form of human relation that can appear only after a society once passes through the capitalist market economy. It is thought that Proudhon was the first to have theorized it; according to my reading, however, Kant's ethics already contained it.

In his famous book, *Imagined Communities*, Benedict Anderson said that the nation–state is a marriage between nation and state that were originally different in kind. This was certainly an important suggestion. Yet it should not be forgotten that there was another marriage between two entities that were totally heterogeneous—the marriage between state and capital. In the feudal ages, state, capital, and nation were clearly separated. They existed distinctively as feudal states (lords, kings, and emperors), cities, and agrarian communities, all based upon different principles of exchange. States were based upon the principle of plunder and redistribution. The agrarian communities that were mutually disconnected and isolated were dominated by states; but, within themselves, they were autonomous, based upon the principle of mutual aid and reciprocal exchange. Between these communities, markets or cities grew; these were based upon monetary exchange relying on mutual consent. What crumbled the feudal system was the total osmosis of the capitalist market economy. But the economic process was realized only in the political form, of the absolutist monarchy. The absolutist monarchical states conspired with the merchant class, monopolized the means of violence by toppling feudal lords (aristocracy), and finally abolished feudal domination (extra-economic domination) entirely. This was the very story of the wedding between state and capital. Protected by the absolutist state, merchant capital (bourgeoisie) grew up and nurtured the identity of the nation for the sake of creating a unified market. Yet this was not all in terms of the formation of the nation. The agrarian communities, that were decomposed along with the permeation of the market economy and by the urbanized culture of enlightenment, had always existed on the foundation of the nation. While individual agrarian communities that had been autarkic and autonomous were decomposed by the osmosis of money, their communalities—mutual aid and reciprocity—themselves were recovered *imaginarily* within the nation. In contradistinction from what Hegel called the state of understanding (lacking spirit), or the Hobbesian state, the nation is grounded upon the empathy of mutual aid descending from agrarian communities. And this emotion consists of a feeling of indebtedness toward the gift, indicating that it comes out of the relation of exchange.

It was amid the bourgeois revolution that these three were legally married. As in the trinity intoned in the French Revolution—liberty, equality, and fraternity—capital, state, and nation copulated and amalgamated themselves into a force forever after inseparable. Hence to be strict the modern state must be called the capitalist nation–state. They were made to be mutually complementary, reinforcing each other. When economic liberty becomes excessive and class conflict is sharpened, the state intervenes to redistribute wealth and regulate the economy, and at the same time, the emotion of national unity (mutual aid) fills up the cracks. When facing this fearless trinity, undermining one or the other does not work. If one attempts to overthrow capitalism alone, one has to adapt statism, or one is engulfed by nationalist empathy. It goes without saying that the former appeared as Stalinism and the latter as fascism. Seeing capitalist commodity exchange, nation, and state as forms of exchange is possible only from an *economic stance*. If the concept of economic infrastructure has significance, it is only in this sense.

In the modern period, among the three principles of exchange, it was the commodity exchange that expanded and overpowered the others. Inasmuch as it operated within the trinity, however, it is impossible that the capitalist commodity exchange could monopolize the whole of human relationality. With respect to the reproduction of humans and nature, capital has no choice but to rely on the family and agrarian community; in this sense capital is essentially dependent upon the precapitalist mode of production. Herein exists the ground of the nation. On the other hand, while absolutist monarchs disappeared by bourgeois revolutions, the state itself has remained. The state can never be dissolved and subsumed into the representatives of national sovereignty (i.e., government). For the state, no matter what kind, always exists as the bare sovereign vis-à-vis other states (if not always to its nation); in crises (wars), a powerful leader (the subject of determination) is always called for, as evidenced in Bonapartism and fascism.

One frequently hears today that the nation–state will be gradually decomposed by the globalization of capitalism (neo–liberalism). This is impossible. When individual national economies are threatened by the global market, they demand the protection (redistribution) of the state and/ or bloc economy, at the same time as appealing to national cultural identity. So it is that any counteraction to capital must also be one targeted against the state and nation (community). The capitalist nation–state is fearless because of its makeup. The denial of one ends up being reabsorbed into the ring of the trinity by the power of the other two. Countermovements in the past, such as corporatism, welfare society, and social democracy, resulted in the perfection of the ring rather than its abolition.

Marx thought that the socialist revolution would be possible only in the most advanced country, England, because socialism was supposed to be possible only in the stage where bourgeois society was fully ripe, ripe enough to decompose. Nonetheless, in reality it could not have seemed less likely to him that it would occur. In the particular situation where universal suffrage was installed and labor unions strengthened, revolution seemed like it had receded even farther into the distance. What really receded, however, was the revolution that was imagined from the vantage point of and as an extension of bourgeois revolution; the fact was that from that juncture on, a different kind of revolution came to be called for. One should not forget that it was under such circumstances that Marx came to grips with the task of writing *Capital*. His recognition that a criticism of capitalism would no longer suffice made him write such a monumental piece.

After Marx's death, as the social democratic party in Germany made remarkable advances, Engels came to abandon the classical concept of violent revolution and believe in the possibility of revolution via parliamentary means. This was the path to social democracy, in which the state manages the capitalist economy and redistributes the wealth to the working class. Next, Engels's disciple Bernstein eliminated the last dregs of the "revolution" fantasy that were still present in Engels. Meanwhile, Marxism was established along the line of Leninism, which rejects such visions of social democracy. However, at the end of the twentieth century, the left has ultimately returned to Bernstein's way of thinking. Clearly, this is to completely lose sight of the critical need to supersede (*aufheben*) the capitalist nation–state. In World War I, social democrats not only failed to prevent the war, but also got involved in the frenzy of nationalism. And it is quite possible that they will repeat the same faux pas in the future. Yet, as all of us know well by now, Leninism cannot replace it. Is there an alternative? I would posit that it can be found in *Capital*, the book Marx wrote as he deliberately remained in England where the possibility of classical revolution was fading away. As I have explained, the trinity of capital, nation, and state is rooted in the necessary forms that human exchange could assume, and therefore, it is nearly impossible to get out of the ring. Marx in *Capital*, however, discovered an exit, the fourth type of exchange: association.

The Marxists of the late nineteenth century overlooked the communism of later Marx, the idea that an association of associations would replace the Capital–Nation–State. In *The Civil War in France*—written as an address to the general council of the international working men's association—Marx wrote: "If united co-operative societies are to regulate national production upon a common plan, thus taking it under their own control, and putting an end to the constant anarchy and periodical convulsions, which are the fatality of capitalist production—what else, gentlemen, would it be but Communism, 'possible' Communism?"[8] The association of producers'/consumers' cooperatives has been conceptualized and practiced by socialists since Robert Owen, and by Proudhonist anarchists. In *Capital*, too, Marx considers cooperatives in comparison with stock companies and highly appreciates them: While stock companies are only passive abolition [*aufhebung*] of the capitalist system, the positive abolition is discovered in the cooperative of which stockholders are workers themselves.[9] But Marx saw their limits as well. They are destined either to fail in the fierce competition with capital, or to turn themselves into stock companies. For this reason, both Lenin and Engels ignored them or, at best, marginalized them as subordinate to labor movements. On the other hand, and notwithstanding the limits, it was precisely in them that Marx saw the possibility of communism.

Bakunin attacked Marx as a centralist thinker by associating him with the state socialist Lassalle. He either did not know or ignored the fact that Marx was critical of Lassalle's direction (the Gotha Programme) to have the state protect and foster cooperative production. Marx was clear: "That the workers desire to establish the conditions for co-operative production on a social scale, and first of all on a national scale, in their own country, only means that they are working to transform the present conditions of production, and it has nothing in common with the foundation of co-operative societies with state aid. But as far as the present co-operative societies are concerned, they are of value *only* insofar as they are the independent creations of the workers and not protégés either of the government or of the bourgeois."[10] In other words, Marx is stressing that the association of cooperatives itself must take over the leadership from the state, in the place of state-led cooperative movements, whereby capital and state will wither away. And this kind of proposition of principle aside, Marx never said anything in particular about future prospects.

All in all, communism for Marx was nothing but associationism, but inasmuch as it was so, he had to forge it by critiquing. Marx's thinking fell between that of Lassalle and Bakunin. This oscillation allowed later generations to draw either stance from Marx's thought. But what we should see here is less contradiction or ambiguity than Marx's transcritique. What was clear to Marx was that it is impossible to counter the autonomous powers of the trinity by simply denouncing them. Based as they are upon certain necessities, they have autonomous powers. In other words, functioning as they are as transcendental apperception, not only are they irresolvable but also even revive stronger. To finally abolish the trinity, a deep scrutiny into (and critique of) them is required. Where can we find the clue to form the countermovement? This, I believe, is in the theory of value form in *Capital*. In the preface, Marx clarified his stance as follows:

> To prevent possible misunderstandings, let me say this. I do not by any means depict the capitalist and landowner in rosy colors. But individuals are dealt with here only in so far as they are the personifications of economic categories, the bearers [*Träger*] of particular class-relations and interests. My standpoint, from which the development of the economic formation of society is viewed as a process of natural history, can less than any other make the individual responsible for relations

whose creature he remains, socially speaking, however much he may subjectively raise himself above them.[11]

The "economic categories" mentioned here signify the forms of value. Who are capitalists and proletariats is determined by where the individuals are placed: in either relative form of value or equivalent form. This is totally irrespective of what they think. This structuralist view was a necessity. Here Marx did not suffice with simply accusing capitalism of immorality; this is the essence of Marxian ethics. In *Capital*, there is no subjectivity. Even capitalists—especially those in stock companies—are agents of capital's movement, but not subjects. The same is true of workers. So it is that people either read in *Capital* the (natural historical) law of history whereby a capitalist society gradually yet apodictically turns into a communist society, or sought motives of revolutionary acts in pre-*Capital* texts. As is evident, however, neither method worked. Concerning the former, it is totally impossible to assume that capitalism will end autotelically. In principle there cannot be a telos as such in natural history. Concerning the latter, what was discovered in those texts was, more or less, subsumed into a narrative of the Hegelian dialectic of master and slave: that is, proletariat qua slave will finally rebel against bourgeoisie qua master at the extremity of alienation and impoverishment. In this narrative, a workers' rebellion is supposed to take place in the production process as a general strike, and this would lead to their seizure of state power. I cannot believe that Marx's position at the time of writing *Capital* was such. If *Capital* has been rather shunned by Marxists themselves, it is more because of the difficulty in finding a prospect of revolution therein. And the new revolution would have to be different from those which could happen in various places of the world outside England and North America. Then, how is a revolution possible in the world where there seems to be no moment for subjective intervention to appear?

The fact that in value form place determines the nature of the subject who occupies it nevertheless does not prevent capitalists from being subjective. Since capital itself is the subject of a self-reproductive movement, the agents—capitalists—can be active, and this activity is precisely that of money or the position of purchaser (the equivalent form). On the other hand, those who sell the labor-power commodity—workers—have no other choice but to be passive. In this relationality, it is only natural that they can only engage in an economic struggle wherein they negotiate with capitalists over their own commodity price. It is absolutely impossible to expect workers to stand up under such conditions. If this has occurred historically, it has been thanks to social chaos resulting from war, or a situation where employers were particularly villainous. But it is not that workers resistance against capital is totally hopeless. The movement of capital M-C-M'—namely, the realization of surplus value—is dependent upon whether or not products are sold. And surplus value is realized in principle only by workers *in totality* buying back what they produce. In the production process, the relationship between capitalist and workers is certainly like that between master and slaves. But the process of capital's metamorphosis (or transubstantiation) is not so one-dimensional as to be defined by that. Because at the end of the cycle, capital, too, has to stand in the position of selling (the relative form of value), and it is precisely at this moment and this moment only that workers are in the subjective position. This is the place where the commodities of capitalist production are sold— the place of *consumption*. This is the only place where workers in totality with purchasing power are in the buying position. Marx articulated this: "What precisely distinguishes capital from the master-slave relation is that the *worker* confronts him as consumer and possessor of exchange values, and that in the form of the *possessor of money*, in the form of money he becomes a simple center of circulation—one of its infinitely many centers, in which his specificity as worker is extinguished."[12] For capital, consumption is the place where surplus value is finally realized, and for this objective precisely, the only place where it is subordinated to the will of consumers/ workers.

In the monetary economy, buying and selling as well as production and consumption are separated. This introduces a split in the workers' subject: as workers (the sellers of labor-power commodity) and consumers (the buyers of capitalist commodities). In consequence, it comes to appear as if corporations and consumers were the only subjects of economic activities. It also segregates the labor and consumers' movements. In recent history, while labor movements have been stagnant, consumers' movements have flourished, often incorporating issues of environmental protection, feminism, and minorities. Generally, they take the form of civil acts, and are not connected to, or are sometimes even antagonistic to, the labor movement. After all, though, consumers' movements are laborers' movements in *transposition*, and are important only inasmuch as they are so. Conversely, the labor movement could go beyond the bounds of its "specificity" and become universal inasmuch as it self-consciously acts as a consumers' movement. For, in fact, the process of consumption as a reproduction of labor-power commodity covers a whole range of fronts of our life-world, including child care, education, leisure, and community activities. But what is at stake here is obviously related to, yet clearly different from, the process of reproduction in the sense of Gramsci: the cultural ideological apparati such as family, school, church, and so forth. In this context, it is first and foremost the process of the reproduction of labor-power as a topos of ordeal for capital's self-realization, and hence the position in which workers can finally be the subject.

Marxists failed to grasp the transcritical moment where workers and consumers intersect. And in this sense, the anarcho-sandicalists, who opposed them, were the same. They both saw the specific class relation in the capitalist economy (capitalist and wage workers) as a version of that of feudal lord and serfs. They both believed that what had been evident in the feudal system came to be veiled under the capitalist commodity economy; therefore, the workers are supposed to stand up and overthrow the capitalist system according to the dialectic of master and slave. But in reality, workers do not stand up at all, because, *they believe*, the workers' consciousness is reified by the commodity economy, and *their* task as the vanguard is to awaken workers from the daydream. *They believe* that the reification is caused by the seduction of consumerist society and/or manipulation by cultural hegemony. Thus, to begin with, what *they* should and can do is to critically elucidate the mechanism. Or to say it outright, that is the only business left for *them* today. What Fredric Jameson calls "the cultural turn" is a form of "despair" inherent in the Marxist practice. There are various forms of the despair, but they are, more or less, all the result of production-process centrism.

What about civil acts that overlap the consumption front? In keeping a distance from labor movements, they lack a penetrating stance toward the capitalist relation of production. They tend to be absorbed into the social democracy that, approving the market economy, seeks to correct its shortcomings through state regulations as well as redistribution of wealth.

I said that Marx of *Capital* did not present an easy way out of capitalism. But, from the beginning, there is no way for *Capital*, the scrutiny of money that transforms into capital, to present a direct procedure for abolishing/sublating it. The Marxists after Engels, who read the theory of value form merely as an introduction, did not develop any account of money themselves. They imagined that the state regulation and planned economy would abolish the capitalist market economy, brushing aside the fact that abolishing the market economy would be equal to abolishing free exchanges of individuals. Their stance was based totally on the labor theory of value (of classical economics), that is, their vision totally belonged to the domain of the value system of capitalist economy. From this stance, the best we got was the vision of a society where everyone gets what he or she earns. They were blinded to the autonomous dimension of money that Marx tackled in *Capital*. As I have said, money is not merely a denominator of value, but a mediating function through which all individual commodities are exchanged, and through which the value-relation among all commodities is constantly adjusted and readjusted. For this precise reason, money exists as an organizer of the system of commodities, namely, a transcendental apperception X of human exchange. Certainly in the everyday market economy, money qua illusion is hypostatized. Due to fetishism, the movement of capital occurs as an auto-multiplication of money. Bourgeois economists stress the superiority of the market economy by veiling the aspect of capital's movement. Yet one cannot abandon the market economy in general. It would result in a total loss. And again, there is no prospect of abolishing capital and state in social democracy that acknowledges but controls the capitalist market economy.

The ultimate conclusion of *Capital* is the antinomy: money should exist; money should not exist. To supersede (*aufheben*) money equals the creation of a money that would fulfill the conflicting conditions. Marx said nothing about this possible money. All he did was critique Proudhon's ideas of labor money and exchange bank. Proudhon, too, was based upon the labor theory of value; he sought to make a currency that purely valorizes labor time. Here there was a blind spot: Labor value is conditioned by the social exchanges via money; it is formed as value only after the fact of the exchange. That is to say, the social labor time qua substance of value is formed via money, which thus cannot replace money. Labor money would tacitly rely on the existing monetary economy; even if it tried to challenge the existing system, it would just be exchanged with the existing money for the difference in price with the market value. What it could do at best would be to neutralize money.

. . .

In the movement of capital M-C-M', capital has to confront two critical moments: buying labor-power commodity and selling products to workers. Failure in either moment disables capital from achieving surplus value. In other words, it fails to be capital. That is to say that in these moments workers can counter capital. The first moment is expressed by Antonio Negri as "Don't Work!" This really signifies, in our context, "Don't Sell Your Labor-Power Commodity!" or "Don't Work as a Wage Laborer!" The second moment says, like Mahatma Gandhi, "Don't Buy Capitalist Products!" Both of them can occur in the position in which workers can be the subject. But in order for workers/consumers to be able "not to work" and "not to buy," there must be a safety net whereupon they can still work and buy to live. This is the very struggle *without* the capitalist mode of production: the association consisting of the producers'/consumers' cooperatives and Local Exchange Trading Systems (LETS). The struggle *within* inexorably requires these cooperatives and LETS as an extra-capitalist mode of production/consumption; and furthermore, this can accelerate the reorganization of capitalist corporation into cooperative entity. The struggle immanent in and the one ex-scendent to the capitalist mode of production/consumption are combined only in the circulation process, the topos of consumers = workers. For it is only there that the moment for individuals to become subject exists. Association cannot exist without the subjective interventions of individuals, and such is possible only having the *circulation* process as an axis.

Karl Polanyi likened capitalism (the market economy) to cancer.[13] Coming into existence in the interstice between agrarian communities and feudal states, capitalism invaded the internal cells and transformed their predispositions according to its own physiology. If so, the transnational network of workers qua consumers and consumers qua workers is a culture of anticancer cells, as it were. In order to eliminate capital, it is imperative to eliminate the conditions by which it was produced in the first place. The counteractions against capitalism *within* and *without*, having their base in the circulation front, are totally legal and nonviolent; none of the three can interrupt them. According to my reading, Marx's *Capital* offers a logical ground for the creation of this culture/movement. That is, the asymmetric relationship inherent in the value form (between commodity and money) produces capital, and it is also here where the transpositional moments that terminate capital can be grasped. And it is the task of transcriticism to make full use of these moments.

Notes

1 Karl Marx, "A Contribution to the Critique of Hegel's Philosophy of Law: Introduction" [1844], in Karl Marx and Friedrich Engels, *Collected Works*, vol. 3 (New York: International Publishers, 1976), 175.
2 Karl Marx, *Capital: A Critique of Political Economy*, vol. 1, trans. Ben Fowkes (Harmondsworth: Penguin Books, 1976), 163.
3 Marx, *Capital*, vol. 1, 102–103.
4 See Kozo Uno, *Principles of Political Economy*, trans. Thomas T. Sekine (Atlantic Highlands, NJ: Humanities Press, 1980).
5 Benedict Anderson, *Imagined Communities* (London: Verso, 1983).
6 Marx, *Capital*, vol. 1, 176.
7 Ibid., 182.
8 Karl Marx, "The Civil War in France," in Karl Marx and Friedrich Engels, *Collected Works*, vol. 22 (New York: International Publishers, 1976), 335.
9 See Marx, *Capital*, vol. 3, 567.
10 Karl Marx, "Critique of the Gotha Programme," in Karl Marx and Friedrich Engels, *Collected Works*, vol. 24 (New York: International Publishers, 1976), 93–94.
11 Marx, *Capital*, vol. 1, 92.
12 Karl Marx, *Grundrisse*, Notebook IV, trans. Martin Nicolaus (Harmondworth: Penguin Books, 1993), 420–421.
13 See Karl Polanyi, *The Great Transformation* (Boston: Beacon Press, 1944).

CHAPTER SEVENTEEN

The Idea of Communism

Alain Badiou

From The Idea of Communism, ed. Costas Douzinas and Slavoj Žižek. London: Verso, 2010: 1–14.

My aim today is to describe a conceptual operation to which, for reasons that I hope will be convincing, I will give the name "the Idea of communism." No doubt the trickiest part of this construction is the most general one, the one that involves explaining what an Idea is, not just with respect to political truths (in which case the Idea is that of communism) but with respect to any truth (in which case the Idea is a modern version of what Plato attempted to convey to us under the names *eidos*, or *idea*, or, even more precisely, the Idea of the Good). I will leave a good deal of this generality implicit,[1] in order to be as clear as possible regarding the Idea of communism.

Three basic elements—political, historical and subjective—are needed for the operation of "the Idea of communism."

First, the political element. This concerns what I call a truth, a political truth. Regarding my analysis of the Chinese Cultural Revolution (a political truth if ever there was one), one reviewer for a British newspaper remarked— merely from noting my positive account of this episode of Chinese history (which *he* of course regards as a sinister, bloody catastrophe)—that it was "not hard to feel a certain pride in workaday Anglo-Saxon empiricism, which inoculates us [the readers of the *Observer*] against the tyranny of pure political abstraction."[2] He was basically taking pride in the fact that the dominant imperative in the world today is "Live without any Idea." So, to please him, I will begin by saying that a political truth can, after all, be described in a purely empirical way: it is a concrete, time-specific sequence in which a new thought and practice of collective emancipation arise, exist and eventually disappear.[3] Some examples of this can even be given: the French Revolution, from 1792 to 1794; the People's War of Liberation in China, from 1927 to 1949; Bolshevism in Russia, from 1902 to 1917; and—unfortunately for the *Observer*'s critic, although he probably won't like my other examples all that much either—the Great Cultural Revolution, at any rate from 1965 to 1968. That said, formally, that is, philosophically, I am speaking about a truth procedure here, in the sense that I have been giving this term since *Being and Event*. I'll come back to this shortly. But let's note right away that every truth procedure prescribes a Subject of this truth, a Subject who—even empirically—cannot be reduced to an individual.

Now for the historical element. As the timeframe of political sequences clearly shows, a truth procedure is inscribed in the general becoming of Humanity, in a local form whose supports are spatial, temporal, and anthropological. Designations such as "French" or "Chinese" are the empirical indices of this localization. They make it clear why Sylvain Lazarus (cf. note 3) speaks of "historical modes of politics," not simply of "modes." There is in fact a historical dimension of a truth, although the latter is in the final analysis universal (in the sense that I give this term in my *Ethics* book, for example, or in my *Saint Paul: The Foundation of Universalism*) or eternal (as I prefer to put it in *Logics of Worlds* or in my *Second Manifesto for Philosophy*). In particular, we will see that, within a given type of truth (political, but also amorous, artistic, or scientific), the historical inscription encompasses an interplay between types of truth that are different from one another and are therefore situated at different points in human time in general. In particular, there are retroactive effects of one truth on other truths that were created before it. All this requires a transtemporal availability of truths.

And finally, the subjective element. What is at issue is the possibility for an individual, defined as a mere human animal, and clearly distinct from any Subject, to decide[4] to become part of a political truth procedure. To become, in a nutshell, a militant of this truth. In *Logics of Worlds*, and in a simpler manner in the *Second Manifesto for Philosophy*, I describe this decision as an incorporation: the individual body and all that it entails in terms of thought, affects, potentialities at work in it, and so forth, becomes one of the elements of another body, the body-of-truth, the material existence of a truth in the making in a given world. This is the moment when an individual declares that he or she can go beyond the bounds (of selfishness, competition, finitude . . .) set by individualism (or animality—they're one and the same thing). He or she can do so to the extent that, while remaining the individual that he or she is, he or she can also become, through incorporation, an active part of a new Subject. I call this decision, this will, a subjectivation.[5] More generally speaking, a subjectivation is always the process whereby an individual determines the place of a truth with respect to his or her own vital existence and to the world in which this existence is lived out.

I call an "Idea" an abstract totalization of the three basic elements: a truth procedure, a belonging to history, and an individual subjectivation. A formal definition of the Idea can immediately be given: an Idea is the subjectivation of an interplay between the singularity of a truth procedure and a representation of History.

In the case that concerns us here, we will say that an Idea is the possibility for an individual to understand that his or her participation in a singular political process (his or her entry into a body-of-truth) is also, in a certain way, a *historical* decision. Thanks to the Idea, the individual, as an element of the new Subject, realizes his or her belonging to the movement of History. For about two centuries (from Babeuf's "community of equals" to the 1980s), the word "communism" was the most important name of an Idea located in the field of emancipatory, or revolutionary, politics. To be a communist was of course to be a militant of a Communist Party in a given country. But to be a militant of a Communist Party was also to be one of millions of agents of a historical orientation of all of Humanity. In the context of the Idea of communism, subjectivation constituted the link between the local belonging to a political procedure and the huge symbolic domain of Humanity's forward march toward its collective emancipation. To give out a flyer in a marketplace was also to mount the stage of History.

So it is clear why the word "communism" cannot be a purely political name: for the individual whose subjectivation it supports, it effectively connects the political procedure to something other than itself. Nor can it be a purely historical term. This is because, lacking the actual political procedure, which, as we shall see, contains an irreducible element of contingency, History is but empty symbolism. And finally, it cannot be a purely subjective, or ideological, word either. For subjectivation operates "between" politics and history, between singularity and the projection of this singularity into a symbolic whole and, without such materialities and symbolizations, it cannot attain the status of a decision. The word "communism" has the status of an Idea, meaning that, once an incorporation has taken place, hence from within a political subjectivation, this term denotes a synthesis of politics, history and ideology. That is why it is better understood as an operation than as a concept. The communist Idea exists only at the border between the individual and the political procedure, as that element of subjectivation that is based on a historical projection of politics. The communist Idea is what constitutes the becoming-political Subject of the individual as also and at the same time his or her projection into History.

If only so as to move toward the philosophical turf of my friend Slavoj Žižek,[6] I think it might help to clarify things by formalizing the operation of the Idea in general, and of the communist Idea in particular, in the register of Lacan's three orders of the Subject: the Real, the Imaginary and the Symbolic. First, we will posit that the truth procedure itself is the Real on which the Idea is based. Next, we will allow that History exists only symbolically. In effect, it cannot appear. In order to appear, belonging to a world is necessary. However, History, as the alleged totality of human becoming, has no world that can locate it in an actual existence. It is a narrative constructed after the fact. Finally, we will grant that subjectivation, which projects the real into the symbolic of a History, can only be imaginary, for one major reason: no real can be symbolized as such. The real exists, in a given world, and under very specific conditions that I will come back to later. However, as Lacan said over and over, it is unsymbolizable. So the real of a truth procedure cannot be "really" projected into the narrative symbolism of History. It can be so only imaginarily, which doesn't mean— far from it—that this is useless, negative or ineffective. On the contrary, it is in the operation of the Idea that the individual finds the capacity to consist "as a Subject."[7] We will therefore assert the following: the Idea exposes a truth in a fictional structure. In the specific case of the communist Idea, which is operative when the truth it deals with is an emancipatory political sequence, we will claim that "communism" exposes this sequence (and consequently its militants) in the symbolic order of History. In other words, the communist Idea is the imaginary operation whereby an individual subjectivation projects a fragment of the political real into the symbolic narrative of a History. It is in this sense that one may appropriately say that the Idea is (as might be expected!) ideological.[8]

It is essential today to understand that "communist" can no longer be the adjective qualifying a politics. An entire century of experiences both epic in scope and appalling was required to understand that certain phrases produced by this short-circuiting between the real and the Idea were misconceived, phrases such as "communist party" or "communist state"—an oxymoron that the phrase "socialist state" attempted to get around. The long-term effects of the Hegelian origins of Marxism are evident in this short-circuiting. For Hegel, in fact, the historical exposure of politics was not an imaginary subjectivation, it was the real as such. This was because the crucial axiom of the dialectic as he conceived of it was: "The True is the process of its own becoming" or—what amounts to the same—"Time is the being-there of the concept." As a result, in line with the Hegelian philosophical heritage, we are justified in thinking that, under the name of "communism," the historical inscription of revolutionary political sequences or of the disparate fragments of collective emancipation reveals their truth: to move forward according to the meaning of History. This latent subordination of truths to their historical meaning entails that we can speak "in truth" of communist politics, communist parties and communist militants. It is clear, however, that we need to avoid any such adjectivation today. To combat such a thing, I have many times had to insist that History does not exist, which is in keeping with my conception of truths, namely, that they have no meaning, and especially not the meaning of History. But I need to clarify this verdict. Of course, there is no real of History and it is therefore true, transcendentally true, that it cannot exist. Discontinuity between worlds is the law of appearance, hence of existence. What *does* exist, however, under the real condition of organized political action, is the communist Idea, an operation tied to intellectual subjectivation and that integrates the real, the symbolic and the ideological at the level of the individual. We must bring this Idea back, by uncoupling it from any predicative usage. We must rescue the Idea, but also free the real from any immediate fusion with it. Only political sequences that it would ultimately be absurd to label as communist can be recovered by the communist Idea as the potential force of the becoming-Subject of individuals.

So we must begin with truths, with the political real, in order to define the Idea in terms of the threefold nature of its operation: politics-real, history-symbolic and ideology-imaginary.

Let me begin by reminding you of a few of my usual concepts, in a very abstract, simple form.

I call an "event" a rupture in the normal order of bodies and languages as it exists for any particular situation (if you refer to *Being and Event* [1988] or *Manifesto for Philosophy* [1989]) or as it appears in any particular world (if you refer instead to *Logics of Worlds* [2006] or the *Second Manifesto for Philosophy* [2009]). What is important to note here is that an event is not the realization of a possibility that resides within the situation nor is it dependent on the transcendental laws of the world. An event is the creation of new possibilities. It is located not merely at the level of objective possibilities but at the level of the possibility of possibilities. Another way of putting this is: with respect to a situation or a world, an event paves the way for the possibility of what—from the limited perspective of the make-up of this situation or the legality of this world—is strictly impossible. If we keep in mind here that, for Lacan, the real = the impossible, the intrinsically real aspect of the event will be readily seen. We might also say that an event is the occurrence of the real as its own future possibility.

I call a "State" or "state of the situation" the system of constraints that limit the possibility of possibilities. By the same token, we will say that the State is that which prescribes what, in a given situation, is the impossibility specific to that situation, from the perspective of the formal prescription of what is possible. The State is always the finitude of possibility, and the event is its infinitization. For example, what is the State comprised today with regard to its political possibilities? Well, the capitalist economy, the constitutional form of government, the laws (in the juridical sense) concerning property and inheritance, the army, the police . . . Through all these systems, all these apparatuses, including, of course, those that

Althusser called "ideological State apparatuses," which could be defined by their one common goal—preventing the communist Idea from designating a possibility—we can see how the State organizes and maintains, often by force, the distinction between what is possible and what isn't. It follows clearly from this that an event is something that can occur only to the extent that it is subtracted from the power of the State.

I call a "truth procedure" or a "truth" an ongoing organization, in a given situation (or world), of the consequences of an event. It will be noted at once that a fundamental randomness, that of its eventual origins, partakes in every truth. I call "facts" the consequences of the existence of the State. It will be observed that intrinsic necessity is always on the side of the State. So it is clear that a truth cannot be made up of pure facts. The non-factual element in a truth is a function of its orientation, and this will be termed subjective. We will also say that the material "body" of a truth, insofar as it is subjectively oriented, is an exceptional body. Making unabashed use of a religious metaphor, I will say that the body-of-truth, as concerns what cannot be reduced to facts within it, can be called a glorious body. With respect to this body, which is that of a new collective Subject in politics, of an organization composed of individual multiples, we will say that it shares in the creation of a political truth. In the case of the State of the world in which this creation is at work, we will speak of historical facts. History as such, made up of historical facts, is in no way subtracted from the power of the State. History is neither subjective nor glorious. History should instead be said to be the history of the State.[9]

So we can now return to our subject, the communist Idea. If, for an individual, an Idea is the subjective operation whereby a specific real truth is imaginarily projected into the symbolic movement of a History, we can say that an Idea presents the truth as if it were a fact. In other words, the Idea presents certain facts as symbols of the real of truth. This was how the Idea of communism allowed revolutionary politics and its parties to be inscribed in the representation of a meaning of History the inevitable outcome of which was communism. Or how it became possible to speak of a "homeland of socialism," which amounted to symbolizing the creation of a possibility—which is fragile by definition—through the magnitude of a power. The Idea, which is an operative mediation between the real and the symbolic, always presents the individual with something that is located between the event and the fact. That is why the endless debates about the real status of the communist Idea are irresolvable. Is it a question of a regulative Idea, in Kant's sense of the term, having no real efficacy but able to set reasonable goals for our understanding? Or is it an agenda that must be carried out over time through a new post-revolutionary State's action on the world? Is it a utopia, perhaps a plainly dangerous, and even criminal, one? Or is it the name of Reason in History? This type of debate can never be concluded, for the simple reason that the subjective operation of the

Idea is not simple but complex. It involves real sequences of emancipatory politics as its essential real condition, but it also presupposes marshalling a whole range of historical facts suitable for symbolization. It does not claim that the event and its organized political consequences are reducible to facts, as this would amount to subjecting the truth procedure to the laws of the State. But neither does it claim that the facts are unsuitable for any historical transcription (to make a Lacanian sort of play on words) of the distinctive characters of a truth. The Idea is an historical anchoring of everything elusive, slippery and evanescent in the becoming of a truth. But it can only be so if it admits as its own real this aleatory, elusive, slippery, evanescent dimension. That is why it is incumbent upon the communist Idea to respond to the question "Where do just ideas come from?" the way Mao did: "Just ideas" (and by this I mean what constitutes the path of a truth in a situation) come from practice. "Practice" should obviously be understood as the materialist name of the real. It would thus be appropriate to say that the Idea that symbolizes the becoming "in truth" of just (political) ideas in History, that is to say, the Idea of communism, therefore comes itself from the idea of practice (from the experience of the real) in the final analysis, but nevertheless cannot be reduced to it. This is because it is the protocol not of the existence but rather of the *exposure* of a truth in action.

All of the foregoing explains, and to a certain extent justifies, why it was ultimately possible to go to the extreme of exposing the truths of emancipatory politics in the guise of their opposite, that is to say, in the guise of a State. Since it is a question of an (imaginary) ideological relationship between a truth procedure and historical facts, why hesitate to push this relationship to its limit? Why not say that it is a matter of a relationship between event and State? *State and Revolution* is the title of one of Lenin's most famous texts. The State and the Event are indeed what are at stake in it. Nevertheless, Lenin, following Marx in this regard, is careful to say that the State in question after the Revolution will have to be the State of the withering away of the State, the State as organizer of the transition to the non-State. So let's say the following: the Idea of communism can project the real of a politics, subtracted as ever from the power of the State, into the figure of "another State," provided that the subtraction lies within this subjectivating operation, in the sense that the "other State" is also subtracted from the power of the State, hence from its own power, insofar as it is a State whose essence is to wither away.

In this context that it is necessary to think and endorse the vital importance of proper names in all revolutionary politics. Their importance is indeed both spectacular and paradoxical. On the one hand, in effect, emancipatory politics is essentially the politics of the anonymous masses; it is the victory of those with no names,[10] of those who are held in a state of colossal insignificance by the State. On the other hand, it is distinguished all along the way by proper names, which define it historically, which represent it, much more forcefully than is the case for other kinds of politics. Why is there this long series of proper names? Why this glorious Pantheon of revolutionary heroes? Why Spartacus, Thomas Münzer, Robespierre, Toussaint-L'Ouverture, Blanqui, Marx, Lenin, Rosa Luxemburg, Mao, Che Guevara, and so many others? The reason is that all these proper names symbolize historically—in the guise of an individual, of a pure singularity of body and thought—the rare and precious network of ephemeral sequences of politics as truth. The elusive formalism of bodies-of-truth is legible here as empirical existence. In these proper names the ordinary individual discovers glorious, distinctive individuals as the mediation for his or her own individuality, as the proof that he or she can force its finitude. The anonymous action of millions of militants, rebels, fighters, unrepresentable as such, is combined and counted as one in the simple, powerful symbol of the proper name. Thus, proper names are involved in the operation of the Idea, and the ones I just mentioned are elements of the Idea of communism at its various stages. So let us not hesitate to say that Khrushchev's condemnation of "the cult of personality," apropos Stalin, was misguided, and that, under the pretence of democracy, it heralded the decline of the Idea of communism that we witnessed in the ensuing decades. The political critique of Stalin and his terrorist vision of the State needed to be undertaken in a rigorous way, from the perspective of revolutionary politics itself, and Mao had begun to do as much in a number of his writings.[11] Whereas Khrushchev, who was in fact defending the group that had led the Stalinist State, made no inroads whatsoever as regards this issue and, when it came to speaking of the Terror carried out under Stalin, merely offered an abstract critique of the role of proper names in political subjectivation. He himself thereby paved the way for the "New Philosophers" of reactionary humanism a decade later. Whence a very precious lesson: even though retroactive political actions may require that a given name be stripped of its symbolic function, this function as such cannot be eliminated for all that. For the Idea—and the communist Idea in particular, because it refers directly to the infinity of the people—needs the finitude of proper names.

Let's recapitulate as simply as possible. A truth is the political real. History, even as a reservoir of proper names, is a symbolic place. The ideological operation of the Idea of communism is the imaginary projection of the political real into the symbolic fiction of History, including in its guise as a representation of the action of innumerable masses via the One of a proper name. The role of this Idea is to support the individual's incorporation into the discipline of a truth procedure, to authorize the individual, in his or her own eyes, to go beyond the Statist constraints of mere survival by becoming a part of the body-of-truth, or the subjectivizable body.

We will now ask: why is it necessary to resort to this ambiguous operation? Why do the event and its consequences also have to be exposed in the guise of a fact—often a violent one—that is accompanied by different versions of the "cult of personality"? What is the reason for this historical appropriation of emancipatory politics?

The simplest reason is that ordinary history, the history of individual lives, is confined within the State. The history of a life, with neither decision nor choice, is in itself a part of the history of the State, whose conventional mediations are the family, work, the homeland, property, religion, customs, and so forth. The heroic, but individual, projection of an exception to all the above—as is a truth procedure—also aims at being shared with everyone else; it aims to show itself to be not only an exception but also a possibility that everyone can share from now on. And that is one of the Idea's functions: to project the exception into the ordinary life of individuals, to fill what merely exists with a certain measure of the extraordinary. To convince my own immediate circle—husband or wife, neighbors and friends, colleagues—that the fantastic exception of truths in the making also exists, that we are not doomed to lives programmed by the constraints of the State. Naturally, in the final analysis, only the raw, or militant, experience of the truth procedure will compel one or another person's entry into the body of truth. But to take him or her to the place where this experience is to be found—to make him or her a spectator of, and therefore partly a participant in, what is important for a truth—the mediation of the Idea, the sharing of the Idea, are almost always required. The Idea of communism (regardless of what name it might otherwise be given, which hardly matters: no Idea is definable by its name) is what enables a truth procedure to be spoken in the impure language of the State, and thereby for the lines of force by virtue of which the State prescribes what is possible and what is impossible to be shifted for a time. In this view of things, the most ordinary action is to take someone to a real political meeting, far from their home, far from their predetermined existential parameters, in a hostel of workers from Mali, for example, or at the gates of a factory. Once they have come to the place where politics is occurring, they will make a decision about whether to incorporate or withdraw. But in order for them to come to that place, the Idea—and for two centuries, or perhaps since Plato, it has been the Idea of communism—must have already shifted them in the order of representations, of History and of the State. The symbol must imaginarily come to the aid of the creative flight from the Real. Allegorical facts must ideologize and historicize the fragility of truth. A banal yet crucial discussion among four workers and a student in an ill-lit room must momentarily be enlarged to the dimensions of Communism and thus be both what it is and what it will have been as a moment in the local construction of the True. Through the enlargement of the symbol, it must become visible that "just ideas" come from this practically invisible practice. The five-person meeting in an out-of-the-way suburb must be eternal in the very expression of its precariousness. That is why the real must be exposed in a fictional structure.

The second reason is that every event is a surprise. If this were not the case, it would mean that it would have been predictable as a fact, and so would be inscribed in the history of the State, which is a contradiction in terms. The problem can thus be formulated in the following way: how can we prepare ourselves for such surprises? And this time the problem really exists, even if we are already currently militants of a previous event's consequences, even if we are included in a body-of-truth. Granted, we are proposing the deployment of new possibilities. However, the event to come will turn what is still impossible, even for us, into a possibility. In order to anticipate, at least ideologically or intellectually, the creation of new possibilities, we must have an Idea. An Idea that of course involves the newness of the possibilities that the truth procedure of which we are the militants has brought to light, which are real-possibilities, but an Idea that also involves the formal possibility of *other* possibilities, ones as yet unsuspected by us. An Idea is always the assertion that a new truth is historically possible. And since the forcing of the impossible into the possible occurs via subtraction from the power of the State, an Idea can be said to assert that this subtractive process is infinite. It is always formally possible that the dividing line drawn by the State between the possible and the impossible may once again be shifted, however radical its previous shifts—including the one in which we as militants are currently taking part—may have been. That is why one of the contents of the communist Idea today—as opposed to the theme of communism as a goal to be attained through the work of a new State—is that the withering away of the State, while undoubtedly a principle that must be apparent in any political action (which is expressed by the formula "politics at a distance from the State" as an obligatory refusal of any direct inclusion in the State, of any request for funding from the State, of any participation in elections, etc.), is also an infinite task, since the creation of new political truths will always shift the dividing line between Statist, hence historical, facts and the eternal consequences of an event.

With this in mind, I will now conclude by turning to the contemporary inflections of the Idea of communism.[12] In keeping with the current reassessment of the Idea of communism, as I mentioned, the word's function can no longer be that of an adjective, as in "communist party," or "communist regimes." The party-form, like that of the socialist State, is no longer suitable for providing real support for the Idea. This problem moreover first found negative expression in two crucial events of the 1960s and 1970s: the Cultural Revolution in China and the amorphous entity called "May '68" in France. Later, new political forms, all of which are of the order of politics without a party, were—and are still being—tried out.[13] Overall, however, the modern, so-called democratic form of the bourgeois State, of which globalized capitalism is the cornerstone, can boast of having no rivals in the ideological field. For three decades now, the word "communism" has been either totally forgotten or practically equated with criminal enterprises. That is why the subjective situation of politics has everywhere become so incoherent. Lacking the Idea, the popular masses' confusion is inescapable.

Nevertheless, there are many signs—this book, and the conference on which it is based, for example—suggesting that this reactionary period is coming to an end. The historical paradox is that, in a certain way, we are closer to problems investigated in the first half of the nineteenth century than we are to those we have inherited from the twentieth century. Just as in around 1840, today we are faced with an utterly cynical capitalism, which is certain that it is the only possible option for a rational organization of society. Everywhere it is implied that the poor are to blame for their own plight, that Africans are backward, and that the future belongs either to the "civilized" bourgeoisies of the Western world or to those who, like the Japanese, choose to follow the same path. Today, just as back then, very extensive areas of extreme poverty can be found even in the rich countries. There are outrageous, widening inequalities between countries, as well as between social classes. The subjective, political gulf between Third World farmers, the unemployed, and poor wage-earners in our so-called developed countries, on the one hand, and the "Western" middle classes on the other, is absolutely unbridgeable and tainted with a sort of indifference bordering on hatred. More than ever, political power, as the current economic crisis with its single slogan of "rescue the banks" clearly proves, is merely an agent of capitalism. Revolutionaries are divided and only weakly organized, broad sectors of working-class youth have fallen prey to nihilistic despair, the vast majority of intellectuals are servile. In contrast to all this, though just as isolated as Marx and his friends were at the time when the retrospectively famous *Manifesto of the Communist Party* came out in 1848, there are nonetheless more and more of us involved in organizing new types of political processes among the poor and working masses and in trying to find every possible way to support the re-emergent forms of the communist Idea in reality. Just as at the beginning of the nineteenth century, the victory of the communist Idea is not at issue, as it would later be, far too dangerously and dogmatically, for a whole stretch of the twentieth century. What matters first and foremost is its existence and the terms in which it is formulated. In the first place, to provide a vigorous subjective existence to the communist hypothesis is the task those of us gathered here today are attempting to accomplish in our own way. And it is, I insist, a thrilling task. By combining intellectual constructs, which are always global and universal, with experiments of fragments of truths, which are local and singular, yet universally transmissable, we can give new life to the communist hypothesis, or rather to the Idea of communism, in individual consciousnesses. We can usher in the third era of this Idea's existence. We can, so we must.

Translated by Andrew Gibson

Notes

1   The theme of the Idea appears gradually in my work. It was no doubt already present in the late 1980s from the moment when, in *Manifesto for Philosophy*, I designated my undertaking as a "Platonism of the Multiple," which would require a renewed investigation into the nature of the Idea. In *Logics of Worlds*, this investigation was expressed as an imperative: "true life" was conceived of as life lived in accordance with the Idea, as opposed to the maxim of contemporary democratic materialism, which commands us to live without any Idea. I examined the logic of the Idea in greater detail in *Second Manifesto for Philosophy*, in which the notion of ideation, and thus of the operative, or working, value of the Idea is introduced. This was backed up by a multifaceted commitment to something like a renaissance of the use of Plato. For example: my seminar, which for the past two years has been titled "For Today: Plato!"; my film project, *The Life of Plato*; and my complete translation (which I call a "hypertranslation") of *The Republic*, renamed *Du Commun(isme)* and divided into nine chapters, which I hope to complete and publish in 2010.

2   Rafael Behr, "A Denunciation of the 'Rat Man,'" *Observer*, March 1, 2009. *Translator's note*.

3   The rarity of politics, in the guise of sequences destined for an immanent end, is very powerfully argued by Sylvain Lazarus in his book *Anthropologie du nom* (Paris: Seuil, 1996). He calls these sequences "historical modes of politics," which are defined by a certain type of relationship between a politics and its thought. My philosophical elaboration of a truth procedure would appear to be very different from this (the concepts of event and genericity are completely absent from Lazarus's thought). I explained in *Logics of Worlds* why my philosophical enterprise is nevertheless compatible with Lazarus's, which puts forward a thought of politics elaborated from the standpoint of politics itself. Note that for him, too, obviously, the question of the timeframe of the modes is very important.

4   This aspect of decision, of choice, of the Will, in which the Idea involves an individual commitment, is increasingly present in the works of Peter Hallward. It is telling that, as a result, references to the French and Haitian Revolutions, in which these categories are the most visible, should now haunt all his work.

5   In my *Théorie du sujet*, published in 1982, the couple formed by subjectivation and the subjective process plays a fundamental role. This is an additional sign of my tendency, as Bruno Bosteels contends in his work (including his English translation of the book, published by Continuum, 2009), to return little by little to some of the dialectical intuitions of that book.

6   Slavoj Žižek is probably the only thinker today who can simultaneously hew as closely as possible to Lacan's contributions and argue steadfastly and vigorously for the return of the Idea of communism. This is because his real master is Hegel, of whom he offers an interpretation that is completely novel, inasmuch as he has given up subordinating it to the theme of Totality. There are two ways of rescuing the Idea of communism in philosophy today: either by abandoning Hegel, not without regret, incidentally, and only after repeated considerations of his writings (which is what I do), or by putting forward a different Hegel, an unknown Hegel, and that is what Žižek does, based on

Lacan (who was a magnificent Hegelian—or so Žižek would claim—at first explicitly and later secretly, all along the way).

7 To live "as a Subject" can be taken in two ways. The first is like "to live as an Immortal," a maxim translated from Aristotle. "As" means "as if one were." The second way is topological: incorporation in effect means that the individual lives "in" the subject-body of a truth. These nuances are clarified by the theory of the body-of-truth on which *Logics of Worlds* concludes, a decisive conclusion but, I must admit, one that is still too condensed and abrupt.

8 Basically, if you really want to understand the tired-out word "ideology," the simplest thing to do is to stay as close as possible to its derivation: something can be said to be "ideological" when it has to do with an Idea.

9 That history is the history of the State is a thesis introduced into the field of political speculation by Sylvain Lazarus, but he has not yet published all its consequences. Here, too, one could say that my ontologico-philosophical concept of the State, as it was introduced in the mid-1980s, is distinguished by a different (mathematical) point of departure and a different (metapolitical) destination. However, its compatibility with Lazarus's is confirmed in one major regard: no political truth procedure can be confused, in its very essence, with the historical actions of a State.

10 Those who have "no name," those who have "no part" and ultimately, in all current political actions, the organizing role of the workers "without papers" are all part of a negative, or rather stripped down, view of the human terrain of emancipatory politics. Jacques Rancière, starting in particular with his in-depth study of these themes in the nineteenth century, has specifically highlighted, in the philosophical field, the implications for democracy of not belonging to a dominant societal category. This idea actually goes back at least as far as to the Marx of the *Manuscripts of 1844*, who defined the proletariat as generic humanity, since it does not itself possess any of the properties by which the bourgeoisie defines (respectable, or normal, or "well-adjusted," as we would say today) Man. This idea is the basis of Rancière's attempt to salvage the word "democracy," as is evident in his essay *The Hatred of Democracy* (London: Verso, 1996). I am not sure that the word can so easily be salvaged, or, at any rate, I think that making a detour through the Idea of communism is unavoidable. The debate has begun and will go on.

11 Mao Zedong's writings on Stalin were published in the short book *Mao Tsé-toung et la construction du socialisme*, clearly subtitled "Modèle soviétique ou voie chinoise," translated and presented by Hu Chi-hsi (Paris: Le Seuil, 1975). Guided by the idea of the eternity of the True, I wrote a commentary on this book, in the preface to *Logics of Worlds*.

12 On the three stages of the Idea of communism, especially the one (the second stage) during which the Idea of communism attempted to be overtly political (in the sense of the program, of both the party and the State), see the final chapters of my *Circonstances 4*, published in English as *The Meaning of Sarkozy* (London: Verso, 2008).

13 There have been numerous, fascinating experiments with new political forms over the past three decades. The following could be mentioned: the Solidarity movement in Poland in 1980–1981; the first sequence of the Iranian Revolution; the *Organisation Politique* in France; the Zapatista movement in Mexico; the Maoists in Nepal. This list is not intended to be exhaustive.

CHAPTER EIGHTEEN

The Kingdom of Philosophy: The Administration of Metanoia

Boris Groys

From The Communist Postscript. *London: Verso, 2009: 103–127.*

Why did the Communist parties of the East—first and foremost the Soviet and the Chinese Communist Parties—cease work on the communist project and instead switch their countries to the development of capitalism? This question can only be answered properly when examined in the context of the materialist dialectic. As has been stated, the materialist dialectic thinks the unity of A and not-A. If A is a project, then not-A is the context of this project. To impel project A ever onwards is to act one-sidedly, because the context of this project, namely not-A, is then ignored forever. Moreover, the context of such a project becomes its fate, for this context dictates the conditions within which the project is to be realized. Passing from the project to its context is a necessity for anyone who seeks to grasp the whole. And because the context of Soviet communism was capitalism, the next step in the realization of communism had to be the transition from communism to capitalism. The project of building communism in a single country is not refuted by this transition, but is instead confirmed and definitively realized. For communism is thus given a historical location not just in space but also in time; that is to say, it becomes a complete historical formation with the possibility of even being reproduced or repeated.

The principal problem of a society that understands itself as an open society is that of limiting its projects, of bringing them to an end. In such a society it is well-nigh impossible to consider a project as finite. In an open society, economic growth, scientific research and the struggle for social justice can only be conceived of as infinite; so too desire, and the work of difference. Whatever limits are set for the realization of these projects are dictated solely by the "objective" conditions within which they are developed and made real. In an open society, projects are thus realized only to the extent that they are interrupted at some point from outside. . . . [U]nder-financing is the primary cause for projects being halted at some point and thereby finally receiving a form, that is, being realized. Generational change is the other reason for the cessation of projects: the protagonists of a project die out, the new generation loses interest and the project falls out of fashion. Projects are constantly becoming "outdated" in this sense instead of being realized. The life of an open modern society has a rhythm that is determined almost entirely by biology. Each generation has a certain period of time at its disposal, generally around a decade, in which to formulate and develop its projects. Of course work on these projects may subsequently continue. But all that is thought and done in such cases will be regarded as outdated and irrelevant by definition. In an open society, economics and biology thus discharge the function of limiting, bringing to an end and incarnating projects that would otherwise never receive a form, a body.

Hence limits to the projective infinity of thought—to what Hegel termed bad infinity—are set in open societies as well. So the question is not whether closure actually occurs, for it occurs in every case, but rather when and how this closure occurs. In an open capitalist society, closure is predominantly administered by capital. By contrast, philosophy has always aimed to appropriate and administer this event of closure, limitation, interruption and transition itself, and not to allow it to be externally dictated. A project can also be brought to an end by a deliberate shift of perspective from the project itself to the context of this project. In the philosophical tradition, such a change of perspective is termed metanoia. The term metanoia can be used to describe the transition from an individual subjective perspective to a general perspective, to a metaposition. Metanoia is also used in the sense of a conversion to the Christian faith, which similarly changes the perspective from which the world is regarded. Husserl's call for a phenomenological reduction, in which the "natural attitude" is replaced by the "phenomenological attitude," is likewise a call for metanoia. The famous formula of McLuhan, "the medium is the message" is also a de facto demand for metanoia—a shift of attention from the message to its medium. However, metanoia need not be performed in only one direction. Having attained the universal perspective of the good as such, Plato posed the question of how ideas of the good could be embodied in the intramundane state. Husserl asks how the disposition for the phenomenological is to be located historically. If metanoia is the transition from the object to its context, then there is also a reversed metanoia, which asks about the context of that context, thus leading back to the earlier perspective at a different level of reflection.

It is often claimed nowadays that the conquest of a metaposition is impossible, and that metanoia is thus similarly impossible: one's original perspective cannot be changed at will. The possibility of metanoia appears to be based solely in metaphysics, that is, in the privileging of the soul in relation to the body. But if there is no immortal soul that can transcend the finite body, then obtaining a metaposition also appears to be impossible, for the body always has a particular structure and location in the world that dictate a person's perspective and cannot be changed arbitrarily. This argument was advanced with particular vehemence by Nietzsche, and it has subsequently almost acquired the status of a self-evident proposition, so that whenever anyone speaks today, he is afterwards asked first about where he comes from and from which perspective he speaks. Race, class and gender serve as the standard coordinates of this space in which each speaker is inherently positioned. The concept of cultural identity also serves this same goal of initial positioning. The effectiveness of these parameters is barely diminished even when they are interpreted not as "natural" determinants but as social constructions. For while social constructions can be deconstructed, they cannot be abolished, altered or exchanged at will. Hence the only options available to the subject are those either of infinitely cultivating the cultural identity pregiven by his body (or by the social codification of this body), or of infinitely deconstructing this identity. In Hegelian terms, however, both infinities are bad infinities, for it is not known how they can be limited and brought to an end. One can only hope that this reflection on one's own perspective ceases at some point because the money required for continuing it any further has run out. Or alternatively, hope that death will finally arrive some day, and one will no longer be bothered by questions of the type "where do you come from," because another question will have become more important, that of where we have gone.

But there is no such thing as a perfect synchronization of body and soul. Classical metaphysics anticipated the life of the soul after the end of the body. Metanoia, understood as the transition from the usual, worldly "natural" perspective to an alternative, universal and metaphysical perspective, entailed the abstraction from one's own worldly perspective in expectation of the continued life of the soul following the death of the body. Today, metanoia functions as the anticipation of the continued life of the body as a corpse following the death of the soul. Hence, even given the presuppositions of the most rigorous materialism, it is possible to alter one's perspective through metanoia prior to the change of perspective being externally dictated by economics or biology. Metanoia, that is, is not only possible when humans are understood as being under-incarnated— i.e., not only when one's soul is supposed to outlast the body—but also when humans are understood as being over-incarnated, as is the case in the modern era—i.e., when it is thought that the soul lives more briefly than the body. Following the end of the soul, the body is transported to a different place from the one in which it was located during its life—namely, to the cemetery. Foucault quite rightly includes the cemetery along with the museum, the clinic, the prison and the ship (and one could also add the rubbish heap) amongst those other places, the heterotopias. Thus a human can experience metanoia by imagining his or her body as a corpse during life, thereby acquiring a heterotopian perspective.

Deconstruction can also be understood as an effect of such an "other" metanoia—as the thematization of a postmortal decomposition that has "always already" begun in life. The same can be said of the Deleuzian "body without organs," which is likewise best envisaged as a corpse in an advanced state of decomposition. And this also holds true for the mass-cultural interest in figures that symbolize the continued life of the body after the death of the soul: vampires, zombies and so on. For our purposes, what is most important to emphasize here is that metanoia, which is indispensible for gaining access to the whole, does not stand in contradiction to the principal thesis of materialism concerning the impossibility of the continued life of the soul after death. Metanoia not only anticipates the limiting and ending of bad infinity by nature or economics; it simultaneously accelerates this process of bringing to an end. This acceleration of the transition, compared to the "natural" or "economic" transition, is of decisive importance for any politics. The administration of metanoia establishes the possibility of being quicker than time. It involves a type of asceticism of time: one gives oneself less time than nature or the economy would have placed at one's disposal.

Asceticism generally consists in allowing oneself less than is allowed by external factors. In no sense does this entail internalizing from a feeling of weakness those limits that have been set externally. In describing asceticism as such an act of internalization, Nietzsche overlooked its most important dimension. Asceticism does not consist in passively accepting the limits that are forced on us from outside; it consists rather in drawing those limits much closer than is necessary. Only by imposing these more narrow limits on one's own possibilities can sovereignty, authorship and autonomy be won. Modern art is often characterized as a series of broken taboos, as a constant expansion of the possibility of making art. In fact, the situation is precisely the reverse. New taboos and new reductions were constantly being introduced in modern art. For no obvious reason, artists imposed on themselves the obligation to use only abstract geometric figures, or only ready-mades, or only words. The forms of modern art are due solely to this self-imposed ascetic creation of taboos, restrictions and reductions. This example demonstrates that newness arises not from expansion but rather from reduction, from a new mode of asceticism. Metanoia leads to a renunciation—namely the renunciation of always doing the same thing, of always following the same path, always seeking to ride out further in the same bad infinity. Badiou speaks about fidelity to the revolutionary event.[1] But fidelity to revolution is fidelity to infidelity. The asceticism of time entails the duty of being unfaithful, of bringing about the transition, the change, the metanoia even when—indeed precisely when—there are no external circumstances that compel this metanoia upon us.

An insight central to Hegel is relevant here: thinking is defined by the incessant alternation of thoughts. It was on this basis that Hegel regarded with extreme skepticism the intention of remaining faithful to one's own ideas and thoughts. And indeed, even if someone represents a political viewpoint so consistently that he never expresses or accepts a contrary view, this still does not entail that he always remains faithful to his political viewpoint. For sometimes he will also think about other things, such as eating, sleeping, or other everyday activities. But then he is thinking of what is other to his political ideas, of the not-A, of the context within which he articulates his views. Hence he also accepts the status quo, and this itself includes a political dimension—and indeed, a political dimension that possibly contradicts de facto the political viewpoint to which he wishes to remain faithful. To think means nothing other than constantly to alter the thoughts one has "in one's head." Not by chance, Hegel discusses how the revolutionary guillotine is a true portrayal of thinking because it causes heads to roll approximately as fast as thoughts rotate in those heads.[2] Hegel sought to introduce a logic—dialectical logic, to be precise—into this process of the alternation of thoughts, but we can agree with Kierkegaard that such a logic is ultimately arbitrary. There is simply no unequivocal criterion for determining if a project or an ideology or a religion "has outlived itself," "is historically superseded." We remain trapped in paradox and cannot merely rely on the course of time to resolve it for us. Metanoia remains ultimately groundless, purely performative, revolutionary.

For Hegel, the world is the way it is as the product of this dialectical reversal, the repeated metanoia of the absolute spirit. But at some point this constant self-renunciation of the absolute spirit must itself have become absolute, compelling the spirit to be silent, to stop. For Hegel, reality has been abandoned by spirit: it is what is left over after the history of spirit. When spirit is no longer present, the dialectic also appears to stop, and relations stabilize. By contrast, dialectical materialism has relocated the contradictions into the things themselves, into bodies, into what is material. Even when the soul has abandoned the body, the body's exchanges with its environment do not cease—they merely take on a different form. The quantitative becomes the qualitative—but the whole dialectical process does not thereby stop. Where the soul once was has now become corpse. But the difference, if this difference is considered dialectically, is not so great as it may appear at first glance.

The Soviet regime was above all the administration of metanoia, of constant transition, of constant endings and new beginnings, of self-contradiction. Lenin's corpse, which was and remains exhibited in a mausoleum, is the immutable icon of materialist metanoia, of the permanent change practiced by the Soviet communist leadership. Change is antiutopian: if utopia is understood to be a definitive, perfectly rational order, then change is a betrayal of utopia. But when change ceases to be blind change driven by nature or by the forces of capitalism, then it acquires a dimension of grace. Change is thereby linguistified, becoming metanoia—and in consequence the possibility arises of speaking to this change, of criticizing it, of addressing complaints to it. Both Lenin and Stalin and later Mao all used their power constantly to re-ignite the revolution and administer it anew. They wished always to be more dialectical than history itself, to pre-empt time. Their greatest fear was of being too late, of missing the moment that calls for change. This desire for the turning point, for the new beginning, also gripped the Soviet Union following the death of Stalin, shortly after which massive de-Stalinization commenced. Even public reference to the name of Stalin was forbidden, or at least reduced to a minimum; Stalin's writings became inaccessible; his deeds were expunged from the history books. Then came the Brezhnev era of so-called stagnation. This period was basically the Soviet version of the *belle époque*; people began to grow bored. The Party reacted to this growing boredom with the Stalinist slogans of reconstruction and acceleration (*perestroika i uskorenie*). As in the Stalin era, reconstruction, change or metanoia was understood and practiced as the path to acceleration. Once again, the intention was to be faster than history, faster than time.

Although the self-abolition of communism at the initiative and under the direction of the leadership of the Communist Party is a historically unique event, it is often trivialized because it is still consistently styled as a defeat in a war—in this instance, the Cold War—or as the result of the struggle for freedom by the people subjugated by communism. But neither of these very familiar explanations is accurate. The Cold War was not a war, but only a metaphor of a war: it was therefore a war that could only be lost metaphorically. In military terms, the Soviet Union was unassailable. And all those groups that had spoken out for their freedom had been entirely pacified prior to the transition to capitalism. The Russian dissident movement had been wholly finished off, until the mid-1980s. The *Solidarność* movement in Poland had been brought to an end just as promptly by the Polish security forces. The unrest in Beijing was successfully suppressed, and order was restored. It was precisely this total defeat of every internal opposition and this complete immunity with regards to any possible external intervention that led the Soviet and the Chinese leaderships to undertake the transition to capitalism. If either leadership had not felt absolutely secure, it would never have undertaken such immense reconstruction and acceleration.

The fact that the Soviet Union disintegrated in the course of this reconstruction has sometimes contributed to this perception of a defeat. The Soviet Union was regarded from outside predominantly as the "Russian empire," and its disintegration is consequently often interpreted as the defeat of Russia in its struggle against the efforts of other nations for independence. Somehow it is forgotten here that it was in fact Russia that dismantled the Soviet Union, when the Russian government—at the time under Yeltsin—withdrew from the Soviet Union in an agreement with the Ukraine and Belorussia. Independence was thus imposed on the other Soviet Republics. It was a turning point that was induced from above, from the center, at the initiative of a leadership that had been raised in the conviction that its task consisted in shaping history dialectically, not in suffering it passively. Marxists have always believed that capitalism represents the best mechanism for economic acceleration. Marx frequently emphasized this, and employed it as an argument against "utopian communism." The proposal to tame capitalism, to instrumentalize it, to set it to work within the frame of a socialist order and under the control of the Communist Party for communist victory—this had been on the agenda from the October Revolution on. It was a possibility that was much discussed, and had even been tested from time to time, although only very inconsistently. However, the idea had never been finally translated into action because the communist leadership had never felt secure enough, and feared losing power through this experiment. In the 1980s and 90s, it felt strong enough, and risked the experiment. It is still too soon to judge whether this experiment has failed. In China, the Communist Party is still firmly in control. In Russia, central control is continually being strengthened, rather than being weakened. The model will be tested further—and may yet prove entirely successful.

In this context, it is worth recalling that both the conditions and the juridical process for the disintegration of the Soviet Union were actually designed and created by Stalin. In the so-called "Stalinist Constitution" of 1936, Article 17 states: "Each Union Republic shall retain the right freely to secede from the USSR." This formulation was later adopted without any alteration in the final Soviet Constitution of 1977 as Article 72. The significance of this Article is made sufficiently clear when it is recalled that the only civil war in the history of the USA was sparked by this question of whether the individual states were free to leave the union. The individual Republics, by contrast, were constitutionally guaranteed the right to withdraw without any restrictions or conditions. This shows that the Soviet Union was conceived by Stalin from the outset not as a unified state but as a loose union of independent states. The objection that such a constitution pre-programs a potential disintegration of the Soviet Union was already raised at the time by certain experts in international law. Stalin, however, was steadfast in his decision to retain the Article in question unchanged.

The reason for this could only be that Stalin wanted to define the Soviet Union dialectically—as at once state and non-state.

No doubt, the Stalinist constitution inherited this definition from still earlier documents of union. But its retention can only be interpreted as a response to criticism directed against Stalin's thesis of the possibility of building socialism in one country—most notably, criticism by Trotsky. This country, in which socialism was to be built, was therefore presented as a federation of nations, as a collection of countries—more of a socialist community of states, standing in opposition to the capitalist community of states, than a single, unitary and isolated state. In the Soviet Union this conception of a community of states was also carried out consistently in everyday life. Each Republic had its government, its parliament, its administration, its language. There were official visits of party and state functionaries from one Republic to another; conferences of writers were organized, as were cultural festivals, exchanges of experts, and so on. The internal life of the state was performed as if on an international stage. But the decisive role in all this was played by the category "nationality" in the passport of every Soviet citizen. The function of this category was and remains a mystery to foreigners, who understand nationality to mean citizenship of a state. But it played an important role for all citizens of the Soviet Union—and indeed, in all spheres of their lives. There, nationality meant membership of a people, ethnic origin. One could choose one's nationality only if one's parents were of different nationalities. Otherwise, the nationality of the parents was inherited. In every practical matter—and above all when looking for work—one was asked about one's nationality, and often about the nationality of one's parents. Thus Soviet internationalism did not mean a one-sided universalism that would overcome and efface ethnic differences. To the contrary, in the construction of the Soviet Union as a socialist and internationalist community of states, none of its citizens were allowed ever to forget where they came from. Only the Communist Party, embodying dialectical reason, could decide where nationality ended and where internationalism began, and vice versa.

The process of privatization, through which the transition from communism to capitalism was organized, was no less dialectical. The complete abolition of the private ownership of the means of production was seen by the theoreticians and practitioners of Soviet communism as the crucial precondition for constructing first a socialist and subsequently a communist society. Only the total state-socialization of all private property could bring about the total social plasticity necessary if the Communist Party were to obtain completely new and unparalleled formative power over society. The abolition of private property entailed a radical break with the past, and even with history as such, for this was understood as the history of private property relations. But above all, this abolition meant that art was granted precedence over nature—over human nature and over nature as such. If the "natural rights" of humans, including the right to private property, are abolished, and their "natural" bonds to their ancestry, their heritage and their "innate" cultural tradition are also broken off, then humanity can invent itself anew and in complete freedom. Only the human who no longer possesses anything is freely available for every social experiment. The abolition of private property therefore represents the transition from the natural to the artificial, from the kingdom of necessity to the kingdom of (politically formative) freedom, from the traditional state to the total artwork.

On this basis, the re-introduction of private property forms an equally decisive precondition for ending the communist experiment, at least at first glance. The disappearance of a communist-governed state accordingly does not represent a merely political event. We know from history that governments, political systems and relations of power have often been altered without rights to private property being essentially affected. In these cases, social and economic life remains structured according to private law even as political life undergoes a radical transformation. By contrast, following the abdication of the Soviet Union there was no longer any social contract in force. Giant territories became abandoned and lawless wastelands, which, as in the period of the American Wild West, had to be newly structured. That is to say, they had to be parcelled out, distributed, and released for private appropriation—and in accordance with rules that were in fact dictated by the state leadership itself. Clearly, there is no possibility of completely returning by this route to a condition that existed prior to the state-socialization of goods, prior to the abolition of inheritance, prior to the break with the origin of private wealth.

Privatization ultimately proves to be just as artificial a political construct as socialization was before it. The same state that had once socialized in order to build communism now privatized in order to build capitalism. In both cases private property is equally subordinated to a *raison d'état*, and is thus manifestly an artifact, a product of a statecraft of deliberate planning. Privatization as the (re-)introduction of private property therefore does not lead back to nature—to natural inheritance and to natural law. Like its communist precursor, the postcommunist state is a constitutive and not merely an administrative power. Thus the postcommunist situation is distinguished by the fact that it reveals the artificiality of capitalism, in that it presents the emergence of capitalism as a purely political project of social reorganization, and not as the result of a "natural" process of economic development.

The construction of capitalism in the Eastern European countries, pre-eminently in Russia, is not a consequence of economic or political necessity, nor an unavoidable and "organic" historical transition. Rather, a political decision was taken to convert society from the construction of communism to the construction of capitalism, and to this end (and in complete accordance with classical Marxism) artificially to produce a class of private property owners in order to then make them the pillars of this construction. This involved the violent dismemberment and private appropriation of the dead body, the corpse of the socialist state, reminiscent of those bygone sacred feasts when members of a people or a tribe communally consumed the dead totemic animal. On the one hand, such a feast meant a privatization of the totemic animal, for each person received a little private piece of it; on the other hand, however, through precisely this privatization, these feasts formed the basis of the tribe's supra-individual and supra-private community. The materialist dialectic of the corpse here demonstrates its enduring effectiveness.

The real effrontery of Stalinist-style socialism consisted in its anti-utopianism, that is, in its assertion that utopia was basically already realized in the Soviet Union. The really existing place in which the socialist camp had been established was proclaimed to be the non-place of utopia. No special effort or insight is required—nor was any needed back then—to prove that this assertion is counterfactual, that the official idyll was manipulated by the state, and that conflict and struggle continued, whether as the struggle for individual survival, as the struggle against repression and manipulation, or as permanent revolution. And nonetheless, it is just as impossible to dismiss the famous claim "it is done" from the world once and for all simply by referring to factual injustices and shortcomings, as it is to dispel the no less famous dogmas "atman is brahman" or "samsara is nirvana," for it involves a paradoxical identity of anti-utopia and utopia, hell and paradise, damnation and salvation. The no less paradoxical metanoia of re-privatization finally gave the event of communism its historical form. And with that, communism was in fact no longer utopia—its earthly incarnation was completed. Completed here means finished, and thus set free for repetition.

Such repetition certainly does not mean a return to Soviet communism, which is a historically unique and definitively concluded phenomenon. But further attempts to establish rule through language, that is to say, to establish the kingdom of philosophy, are very probable—indeed, are inevitable. Language is more universal and more democratic than money. It is, moreover, a more effective medium than money, for more can be said than can be bought and sold. But above all, the linguistification of social power relations gives to every individual human the possibility of contradicting power, fate and life—of criticizing them, accusing them, cursing them. Language is the medium of equality. When power becomes linguistic, it is compelled to operate under the conditions of the equality of all speakers— whether it wishes to or not. Admittedly, the equality of language is distorted and even destroyed if it is demanded that all speakers construct arguments of formal-logical validity. But the task of philosophy is precisely that of freeing humans from oppression by formal-logically valid language. Philosophy is a type of desire, for it is defined as the unfulfilled and unfulfillable love of wisdom. But it is a desire that has been totally linguistified, and its paradoxicality has thus been made transparent. Philosophy is an institution that offers humans the chance to live in self-contradiction without having to hide this fact. On this basis, the wish to expand this institution to the whole of society can never be wholly suppressed.

Notes

1 Alain Badiou, *Metapolitics*, trans. Jason Barker (London and New York: Verso, 2005), 127ff.
2 Georg Wilhelm Friedrich Hegel, *Phenomenology of Spirit*, trans. A. V. Miller (Oxford: Clarendon Press, 1977), 359ff.

CHAPTER NINETEEN

Twenty-Five Theses on Philosophy in the Age of Finance Capital

Imre Szeman and Nicholas Brown

From A Leftist Ontology, *ed. Carsten Strathausen. Minneapolis: University of Minnesota Press, 2009: 33–55.*

. . .

Nihil humani a me alienum puto. De omnibus dubitandum.
(Marx's favorite maxims: Nothing human is alien to me.
Everything should be doubted.)

We present here a set of theses that might help to imagine the role and scope of philosophy in the age of finance capitalism. The sources of these theses are as eclectic as a music collection: they bear with them the traces of broken relationships, misdirected enthusiasms, the inevitable, short-lived fascination with new, the enduring influence of old favorites that one cannot get past (about a final category—"things that sounded good drunk"—we'll say no more). These theses should not be taken as prescriptive. They might be read in the light of Friedrich Schlegel's conception of his philosophical fragments, as scraps or remnants of a total system that could never really exist.

Fredric Jameson has described his own critical practice as a "translation mechanism," a theoretical machine that makes it possible to convert other discourses into the central political problematic that animates Marxism

(Zhang 1998: 365–66). We conceive these theses in much the same spirit: as grasping toward a mediating code rather than presenting a set of truth-claims. The utility of these theses will thus be determined by their ability to help produce a philosophy politically rather than conceptually adequate to finance capitalism—a philosophy that takes up the political challenge of the present without thereby failing to become anything more than an expression of (an adequation of) the dynamism of finance capitalism itself.

1   *A theft*—Relativism is the dialectic for idiots.

2   *Hegel is dead*—One is always coming up against reminders that we have "moved beyond" teleological, Eurocentric Hegel. Sometimes these reminders come in the imperative. But how do we know something is beyond something else, rather than behind it or beside it, above it or below it, without reference to a vanishing point? And isn't the presumption of a vanishing point in time what we call teleology? Never mind: teleology and Eurocentrism—the dominion of the Same—are bad ideas and they should be avoided. Hegel, bless his 18th-century soul, didn't always manage to do so. But why this fixation on Hegel? Let us rather say that the method he invented, but which even he did not always fully understand, has nothing to do with these. Anyone who can muster the strength to read Hegel with both sympathy and skepticism—in other words, to read Hegel like we read everyone else—can see that teleology is the thinnest veneer, even if diligently applied; a last-ditch attempt to save the dialectic from its own deepest implication: the perpetual deferral of Utopia, the impossibility of recuperating contradiction once and for all. Far from being a philosophy of the Same, the dialectic elevates antagonism into an ontology—and in so doing turns the very fiber of being into a tissue of fissures, contradictions, frustration, and carnage. The violence of this gesture—visible, above all, in Hegel's brutal contempt for Kant and the often deadpan irony brought to bear on anything that resembles a unitary conception of Being—is lost on us today, due in no small part to Hegel's own rhetoric. But like those Victorian novels where social upheaval is prevented how? by staging a marriage!—the flimsiness of the ultimate reconciliation gives the clue to its falsity. As with the "cosmological constant"— which Einstein briefly introduced into general relativity to silence what his own theory said about the history of the universe—so with teleology: the dialectic gets along better without it. It has been said that every competent student of physics today knows far more about general relativity than Einstein ever did. Perhaps we are in a position to understand the dialectic better than Hegel.

3   *American Hegelians*—Critical common sense in North America still gets itself worked up into a lather about the evils of the

dialectic. But even during the heyday of the most recent orthodoxy, it wasn't always easy to see what it was fighting against. Once upon a time, in a land far, far away, the dialectic meant Kojève, or Sartre, or Stalinist pseudo-philosophy. Enemies worth fighting! But we literalminded North Americans largely missed the point, and developed a hatred for a Hegelian orthodoxy that we never really experienced. Who were the American Hegelians? There were some, not in the last century but the one before that. One ran a shoe factory and lived for a time with the Creek in Oklahoma. Another was a superintendent of schools and believed the dialectic could be used to show that history would end in St. Louis, Missouri. These were the American Hegelians. And then there's Francis Fukuyama—another Midwesterner, by the way. So what's the panic? See thesis #2.

4 *A bad penny for your thoughts*—The best critics of the dialectic are practical dialecticians. As for the rest of us, we must beware lest we find ourselves, in our relation to thought, in the position of Milton's Abdiel, rushing to God with his discovery, only to find "Already known what he for news had thought/To have reported."

5 *As easy as 1, 2, 3*—The thought of the One goes around creating an awful mess, but it's not terribly common among metropolitan intellectuals. Call it fundamentalism, call it narrow nationalism, call it ethnic chauvinism—or call it the philosophy of Being: the idea is that totality should conform to a single rule. The thought of the Three effectively means the thought of infinity; it is always perfectly correct—and perfectly banal. Multiplicity is easy to find, Difference is indeed everywhere—and very useful, too, for playing whack-a-mole with the thought of the One. But a concept as universal as Difference necessarily lacks all specificity. It is empty as to content. How then, without content, can there be any difference? Are we not back to the thought of the One? This is not mere logic chopping. The point is not that there is no difference between the Same and the Different—that would be absurd—it is rather that they share a Ground—that every mere difference exists by virtue of a field that stamps it with the imprint of the Same. The most innovative thinker of the Three is Alain Badiou, who adds it to the thought of the Zero—and in so doing produces, in the antagonism between Situation and Void, a brilliant version of the thought of the Two. So what is the thought of the Two, the structuring antagonism? Here's an ontological version of it. We all know that the subject's object doesn't coincide with that same object in itself because if it did, the subject would be God. In other words, knowledge is imperfect. But here's the part that's easy to forget: the subject is not a fool, and knows this. The "object in itself," then, is

also the subject's object. Both are real; the object is not, so to speak, simultaneous with itself. It is split: not between what is known of it and what is beyond knowledge, but between the object that exists for us and the object that exists (for us) independently of us. But if the subject knows the same object in two different and incompatible ways, then neither is the subject simultaneous with itself. This should make it clear that the subject–object split is misnamed. The split is within the object itself—or if you prefer, within the subject. This restlessness within the object (or the subject) is called History.

The choice among these three options—or is it two?—is not trivial.

6   *Three classes or two?*—The existence of classes in our age is not a factual question, but a political one. Nobody will deny that wealth is distributed unevenly. Those who want to do something about this live in a world that consists of two strata, the poorer and larger of which must struggle against the domination of the richer and smaller. Those who benefit, or think they benefit, from the status quo live in a world with three classes or, what is the same thing, with none, since the notion of the "middle class" can encompass everyone who does not belong purely to Labor or Capital in the classical sense—which is to say virtually everyone. The question is not whether, empirically, there are two classes or three or a thousand or none. The question is rather: is there class antagonism, or isn't there? Here, the distinction between the descriptive and the political—perhaps always a spurious distinction—disappears.

7   *More haste, less speed*—Though it belongs to a different era, *Minima Moralia* is a handbook for conducting philosophy in the age of finance capitalism. One cannot avoid reflecting on the temptations and limitations of bourgeois intellectual thought, and indeed, of the temptations of reflecting on these temptations. The concept of "reflexive modernity" lately championed in the social scientists by Ulrich Beck and the architect of the Third Way, Anthony Giddens, seems to represent an advance over a modernity that has no prefacing adjective. But just as being against capitalism doesn't imply that one is a socialist, so being reflexive doesn't mean the problems of modernity are magically solved. Adorno reminds us again and again of the institutional settings out of which thought grows, and the constraints and expectations these settings produce. "Since there are no longer, for the intellectual, any given categories, even cultural, and bustle endangers concentration with a thousand claims, the effort of producing something in some measure worthwhile is now so great as to be beyond almost everybody" (1974: 29). Is it possible that Totality has been rejected not because it is specious or Eurocentric but because to think it takes too much time? It might as well be

admitted: far from having been slowly co-opted by a shift from a university of culture to a university of excellence (as Bill Readings suggests [1996]), intellectual labor is the very model for production in the age of finance capital. Long before high-tech firms plopped pool tables down in the middle of their high-ceiling, reconverted factory-buildings, the professoriate was working twelve-hour flex-time days on gothic campuses and hanging out at the faculty club.

As for us: guilty as charged. The lesson here is to leave behind even the lingering idea of intellectual purity vis-à-vis the contaminated state of the rest of the world. And to think with less speed, but more urgency.

8   *Aura after Aura*—There is no longer anything threatening or dangerous about Walter Benjamin's reflections on the significance of mechanical reproduction for "a number of outmoded concepts, such as creativity and genius, eternal value and mystery" (1968: 218). It is often forgotten that Benjamin positions his reflections as coming at the end of a fifty year process of social transformation that was only beginning to be expressed symptomatically in culture in the 1920s and 30s. Benjamin's work on mechanical reproduction is thus belated; indeed, Benjamin was writing at the dawn of the age of electronic circulation, an age that Debord (also belatedly) sketched in *Society of the Spectacle.*

What kinds of things are born in and destroyed by electronic circulation? It would be wrong to suggest that this is a question that no one has yet taken up. However, it seems to us that when it has been addressed, the question is taken too literally. The attempt to think about the social significance of images and visuality at the present time seems to be stuck in the to and fro of the epistemologies of idealism. The problem of mediation has not got beyond certain very basic notions in Hegel—perhaps because Hegel is not to be got beyond. Whatever the case, contemporary thought has tended to conceive the history of representation as a very un-dialectical intensification of a more or less eternal dynamic.

Ours is an age that imagines the visual to have a specific and exceptional force and power. The idea of American cultural imperialism (itself a stand-in for globalization) is often imagined as synonymous with the spread of the visual signs emanating from the United States: advertising, the design of consumer packaging, Hollywood. Nevertheless, for all its vaunted power, our theories of electronic circulation amount to undertheorized ideas about cultural diffusion (any visual image will expand to fill the existing global space), osmosis (it seeps into you), and contamination (it poisons you). More needs to be said.

9   *The world is not legible, but audible*—As for the other side of
global culture, the flow of musical form across the surface of
the globe, things look even less promising. Both disciplinary
musicology and cultural-studies approaches to music are—
somebody has to say it—stupidly empirical in the absence of any
sort of remotely adequate theory of the object. But music is an
activity by means of which bodies are synchronized into a social
body, and a genuine theory of music may one day be able to do
more to explain the modalities of global culture than any theory
of the image. The global trajectory of musical forms, subterranean
and unpredictable compared with the colonization of the world
by the Image, may be the very substance in which new social
relationships are registered. The job of theory, in that case, would
be to cognize (interpret does not seem quite the right word) the
non-cognitive (unconscious does not seem quite the right word)
performance of musical being-in-the-world. Could it be, as Jacques
Attali proposed, that "the world . . . is not legible, but audible"?
(1985). Unfortunately, Attali's thesis remains in the realm of
science fiction: Music predicts the future! The missing term that
would make this intelligible is desire. Can we say more reasonably
that music embodies a social desire? Sometimes this desire dies
and nothing is born. But if the desire is realized in social form, the
musical form that nurtured it appears prescient.

10 *Nobody knows, everyone is in the know*—Simultaneously, two
contradictory theses about that most alien of creatures, the mass,
have been emerging in globalization. On the one hand, there is
a sense that globalization institutes an era in which, belatedly,
mass culture critiques hit their mark. Now that global media
monopolies have anxiously consolidated their hold on every
aspect of leisure, we can safely skip over the more optimistic
pronouncements of some theorists of mass culture and go straight
to Horkheimer and Adorno: "Fun is a medicinal bath" (1998:
140). On the other hand, globalization is also the era of the end
of ideology and of the universality of cynical reason (in Žižek's
famous formulation, "they know what they are doing but they
are doing it anyway"). What philosophy in the age of finance
capitalism needs to explain is how both of these phenomena
can not only occur together, but are in fact produced out of the
same historical conditions of possibility (and contradiction).
Elsewhere Žižek writes that "a direct reference to extra-ideological
coercion (of the market, for example) is an ideological gesture
par excellence: the market and (mass) media are dialectically
interconnected" (1994: 15). In other words, whatever explanation
one produces must come from the *inside* rather than the *outside*.

It is not only, as Hardt and Negri (2000) suggest, that the outside has disappeared: for philosophy, it was *always* a mistake to conceive of an outside. But that's history for you.

11 *The eclipse of the so-called tradition*—For Gramsci, "traditional" intellectuals are connected to one another across time. Since "traditional intellectuals experience through an '*esprit de corps*' their uninterrupted historical continuity and their special qualification, they put themselves forward as autonomous and independent of the dominant social group" (1971: 7). It is this simultaneous autonomy vis-à-vis the present and filiation to the past that still fires the imagination of critical theorists, even though we are now suspicious of both this separation and this connection. But what if we imagined ourselves first and foremost as "organic" intellectuals? Shouldn't we more properly see ourselves as part of that strata of intellectuals that, *especially* in the age of finance capitalism, give contemporary capital "homogeneity and an awareness of its function not only in the economic but also in the social and political fields?" (1971: 5). The exemplary organic intellectual in the age of factories and production is the engineer. Like it or not, the exemplary organic intellectuals in the age of finance capitalism are intellectuals and cultural workers—otherwise known as "content providers."

12 *Ex Nihilo*—You can't start from scratch. If the unruly spirit of Adorno must energize one part of philosophy in the age of finance capitalism, the caution of Raymond Williams should animate the other. The technological euphoria that pervades the official discourses of finance capitalism all too often finds its equivalent in the enthusiasm of theory for all manner of techno-theories (from Debord's spectacle to Haraway's cyborgs) that contemplate a present that has made an absolute break with the past. Williams reminds us that things are far messier than that. Every social formation is the product of more than a single class, and the product of more than a single age. Academics who theorize the present in the manner of science-fiction films (the ones that imagine the future as so absolutely future that not even the practice of eating real food remains) have a predilection for nineteenth-century houses.

It is an open question whether futurity can be positively conceived at all. The future is no more than a lack in the present—as the Mozambiquan writer Mia Couto puts it in his story "Os mastros do Paralém" ("The Flags of Beyondward"), "o destino de um sol é nunca ser olhado" (1998: 185): the destiny of a sun is never to be beheld. Positive visions of the future like the cyber-Utopias of our own very recent past or the popular futurisms of the 1950s—or for that matter Plato's *Republic*—cannot think the future; they can only re-articulate the actual in futuristic form.

13   *Without a base*—The base/superstructure model has had a rough ride since it was taken all too literally by those Marxists who followed Marx. By now, everyone agrees that what is fundamentally missing from this model is, as Williams has said, "any adequate recognition of the indissoluble connections between material production, political and cultural institutions and activity, and consciousness" (1977: 57). Paulin Hountondji (1990, 1992) and others have described the ways in which the cultural is finally collapsed into the economic, and the economic into the cultural, in such a manner that one must go beyond what is implied in Williams's criticism. There needs to be a whole new model of causality in the age of finance capitalism, since one of the things that distinguishes this period from all others is that it no longer makes sense to comprehend the social totality through the lens of even a highly developed and complicated idea of base/superstructure. John Tomlinson writes that "the complexity of the linkages established by globalization extends to phenomena which social scientists have labored to separate out into the categories in which we now, familiarly, break down human life: the economic, the political, the social, the interpersonal, the technological, the environmental, the cultural and so forth. Globalization arguably confounds such taxonomy" (1999: 13). What this means is that we have to take seriously the fact that material explanations may require increasing reference to immaterial forces and entities.

At any rate, one need not be ashamed to maintain that, precisely to the extent—not necessarily great—that humanity controls its own destiny, any intervention in history's course has to take place at the level of thought. This is not the same as idealism. No doubt an infinity of determinations come before thought; no doubt, even, the truth of thought lies outside itself. But if nothing can happen until it becomes possible, possibility cannot be understood in purely materialist way. Conception, too, is a condition of possibility.

14   *We refute us thus*—Every materialism is vulgar, ripe with unexamined presuppositions to be sneered at by any philosopher who happens to pass by. Every philosophy is an idealism susceptible to some version of Johnson's boot. What if both these statements are true? Perhaps then the only way out is to occupy the antagonism between them: not by "refuting" one to champion the other, but rather by engaging in the intimate and perpetual

struggle against one's own idealism. How many people have tried this? We can think of one, anyway.

15 *Worstward, ho!*—"We" and "Ours." Such words embolden polemics such as these. Fear not: we imagine neither a universal subject nor a unitary community. But we also refuse to imagine a "West" that has long founded not only the unreflective "we"s and "our"s of the Eurocentric academy, but also their critique. Indeed, we assert that there is no West, there is no Westernization; for that matter, there is no modernity or modernization. There is Capital, and there is its limit, as expressed both in its internal contradictions and in active resistance to it (which is also, in a different way, internal). There is therefore no such thing as multiculturalism. The instant something becomes a culture—the moment that it ceases to be a world—it belongs to Capital or, what is more rare, resistance to Capital. What we call the "West" names this culturalizing machine, an aspect of Capital. Perhaps especially, of capitalism now.

16 *Capitalism always comes from elsewhere*—It is well known that the disequilibrium intrinsic to the function of capital can be kept under control only by the expansion of capital itself: as Marx put it in the *Grundrisse*, "the tendency to create the world market is directly given in the concept of capital itself. Every limit appears as a barrier to be overcome" (1973: 408). This is from the perspective of Capital. But it should not be thought that any place is originally capitalist and therefore free from the encroachment of capital. From any human perspective, Capital is always encroaching. The privatization of government, the "corporatization" of the arts, of higher education, of sports, of heretofore un-rationalized industries like cattle ranching, continues in the dominant countries today a process that has gone by many names, among them colonialism yesterday, and enclosure before that.

17 *Capitalism is indigenous everywhere*—Marx's pages in the *Grundrisse* on "pre-capitalist" modes of production, problematic though they are in so many respects, are important for suggesting that every social formation tends to produce inequalities that can easily give rise to a pool of free labor—a suggestion, it should be noted, which is corroborated by any number of fictional narratives of the colonial encounter. Capitalism is not simply another, particularly voracious, social formation, but rather, as Deleuze and Guattari claimed in *Anti-Oedipus* (1983) the specific nightmare of *every* social formation, the secret possibility, always repressed, of recoding existing social inequalities as the capital–labor relation.

To confuse "Capitalism" with the "West" is to elevate the latter, a merely heuristic category, to a causal level where it has no place.

18   *Ex hybridis, libertinis servisque conscripserat*—It is finally
recognized that hybridity, one of the dominant terms of the last
decade, presupposed its opposite. This incoherence cannot be
removed simply by asserting, as the most advanced thinkers of
hybridity did, that hybridity goes "all the way down," that the
essence which inheres in the concept can be deferred infinitely—
any more than the fable to which this phrase refers can explain the
suspension of the Earth in space by resting it on an infinite series
of turtles. At some point both theories presuppose a ground. If
hybridity really went "all the way down," it would annihilate itself
as a concept. This is not to argue for authenticity; indeed, if by
"hybridity" one means simply "lack of essence," it does indeed go
"all the way down." But, in order to maintain its distinctness as a
concept, hybridity must also mean a "combination of essences."
There is no way out of this contradiction except to return the word
to its origins in a class distinction. In Latin, *hibrida* refers to the
child of slave and freeborn. "Hybridity," then, would come to refer
to something like the complicity of homologous class fractions in
dominant and dominated regions of the globe. But no doubt we
have better words for this.

19   *Same difference*—It is becoming clear that the hegemonic concept
of Difference is at one and the same time the most universal and
(therefore) the most empty concept, virtually synonymous with
Being since both name the very medium of experience. In fact it is
Difference (as slogan and as concept), not Totality, that reduces the
complexity of the world to the monotonous Same, since the truly
different (i.e. what refuses to be seen as merely different—what
goes, for example, by the ideological names of "totalitarianism,"
"fundamentalism," "communism," and "tribalism," to name just a
few examples) is excluded from the field of difference. The primacy
of "difference" in fact outlines an identity—the unacknowledged
frame of the monoculture, global capitalism.

20   *Fear of error or fear of truth?*—A position of permanent critique
can itself become yet another kind of metaphysics. Suspicion about
the strategic function of the signified, for example, is a powerful
demystifying tool, but in its chronic form it produces a delimitation
of the domain of truth more crippling than any naïveté.

21   *The good, the bad, and the ugly; or, the baby and the bathwater*—
It has been said that the essence of liberalism is a facile separation
of the good from the bad, as though systems—economic,
philosophical, whatever—could be simply carved up and the
undesirable elements discarded: Competition is good but poverty
is bad, so let's just get rid of poverty (while retaining the dynamic

that sustains it); Marx is good but revolution is bad, so let's forget about revolution (while educating undergraduates in the poetry of Capital). Totality, incidentally, is the name for the rejection of this tendency, which is as common as ever—it is virtually the editorial policy of the *New York Times*—but a seemingly contrary tendency is equally insidious. This is to conflate a philosophical concept not with its dialectically necessary other but with an ideological cognate. Utopia is a case in point: the construction of Utopias is a transparently ideological operation, but the notion of Utopia—that is, the reservation within thought of an horizon that is not merely the present—is essential to any genuine politics. Indeed, the failure to think Utopia in the strong sense leads directly to Utopia in the first sense—in particular, to the Utopia (never called that) of a market without poverty. This corresponds to Hegel's "bad infinity" of infinite approximation as opposed to the properly infinite judgment. The same goes for Totality—the denigration of which in current thought serves to discredit the dialectic by associating it with the thematics of the eradication of difference, with which it has nothing in common.

22 *And the truth shall set you free*—"In any case, the death of metaphysics or the overcoming of philosophy has never been a problem for us: it is just tiresome, idle chatter. Today it is said that systems are bankrupt, but it is only the concept of system that has changed. So long as there is a time and a place for creating concepts, the operation that undertakes this will always be called philosophy, or will be indistinguishable from philosophy, even if it is called something else" (Deleuze and Guattari 1994: 9). This is true, and yet Deleuze and Guattari's description of this ceaseless activity of invention called philosophy can't help but send the wrong message in an age that has grown accustomed to language of invention—inventing communities, inventing identities, inventing ideas . . . hey, no problem! But the generation of concepts does not occur willy-nilly. If philosophy's truth originates outside itself (as Lenin taught us), so does it finally reside. The real truth of all thinking, its effective truth, is of a fundamentally different order than the truth it claims for itself. In Christian allegory, the anagogic Truth that it seeks is only an alibi for its real truth, which is the production of faith and a community of believers. So too with thought. If the intellectual wants to change the world, so much the better. But here there are no shortcuts; St. Augustine could not just order his congregation to believe. There are other, perhaps better, ways to change the world. But for the intellectual, however naïve it may seem, the only path is responsibility to Truth.

23   *What is to be done?*—This is the question that is not being asked
today. Let us call one possible position the politics of immanence.
Better yet, let us call it Michael Hardt and Antonio Negri (2000).
There is to be no revolution, certainly no Party; the world to
come will arrive through a plurality of struggles which, taken as
a whole, express the desire of the multitude. What desire? The
desire that was so effortlessly coopted during the Cold War by
high wages in the first world and (relatively) generous development
aid in the third? Or the desire which, after the disintegration of
actually existing socialism, exists only to be brutally crushed
in the name of the Market? For the secret of the story of the
immanent desire of the multitude is that it quietly relied on a
prior transcendent revolution. Once the revolution (or at least its
vestige) disappears as Capital's threat and horizon, the desire of
the multitude has no recourse. And surely we do not need to be
reminded that in the wrong circumstances the Utopian desire of
the multitude can be channeled toward the most obscene ends.
The other position might be called the politics of transcendence;
or better yet Slavoj Žižek (2002a, 2002b) and Alain Badiou
(2001). There is to be a revolution, even a revolutionary party,
but revolution is fundamentally a decision, a risky experiment
never guaranteed to succeed, and therefore an untheorizable
particularity. Yes, yes, yes—and a resounding no. Lenin had a
theory of revolution, a very precise understanding of the historical
conjuncture in which revolution was a possible decision. But our
situation, in which no merely national revolution will have much
significance (the dilemmas faced by the few national governments
genuinely on the Left are evidence enough of this), is immeasurably
more complex than Lenin's. We remember Lenin because his
revolution succeeded. How many failed? The potential cost of not
asking "What is to be done?" is a period of bloody and ineffective
rebellions, some of them deeply reactionary. Neither is invoking
"Seattle" much help; the protests against our current mode of
globalization are a sign and a slogan, but not an organizing
principle. And waiting for a Messiah will only waste time. What
we face instead is the hard work, the collective work, of theorizing
the possibilities that inhere in our current conjuncture and possible
ways to proceed. The only thing worse than picking the wrong
moment would be missing the right one, and it may come sooner
than we think.

24   *What is the multitude?*—Since the moment of its appearance,
we have been enchanted with the poetry of the multitude. But
before we get too carried away, it's worth asking what it is. How
can it both resolutely refuse being reduced to a unity and at the

same time explode in a political project? Isn't a positive political project—as opposed to political drift, the average of all political projects, or to "the multitude against," a unity imposed negatively from without—a concrete unity? Hardt and Negri (2004) invoke neuroscience to explain the apparent contradiction. The brain doesn't have a center of command, but it manages to make "decisions" without ever being a real unity. What feels in our daily life like a subjective decision is just the outcome of innumerable parallel processes. So far so good: in some sense this is no more than obvious. But allow us to ask the dialectical question of the "reality of the appearance": What if the illusion were taken away? Isn't the illusion of a subject itself a necessary part of the functioning of this decentered system that is not a subject? But in this case, the "illusion" is not simply an illusion but also real. Can we then read Hardt and Negri's analogy back again into political subjecthood? Is the illusion of transcendent unity essential to the functioning of a real immanent multiplicity? Does someone have to come up with a project and sell everyone else on it? Does the political subjectivity of the multitude require—gasp!—a political vanguard to bring it into being? Somehow, we're not too keen on that idea, either.

25 *Project(ions)*—Writing philosophy in the age of finance capitalism is neither the most self-indulgent (and thus useless) practice possible, nor is it the sole space in which it is possible to fan the flames of aesthetico-utopian imaginings. As Fredric Jameson reminds us, "Capitalism itself has no social goals" (2000: 62). It is through philosophy that such goals can be imagined.

Works cited

Adorno, Theodor (1974) *Minima Moralia: Reflections from Damaged Life.* Trans. E.F.N. Jephcott. London: New Left Books.
— (1990) *Negative Dialectics*. Trans. E.B. Ashton. London: Routledge.
Attali, Jacques (1985) *Noise: The Political Economy of Music*. Trans. Brian Massumi. Minneapolis: University of Minnesota Press.
Badiou, Alain (2001) *Ethics: An Essay on the Understanding of Evil*. Trans. Peter Hallward. London: Verso.
Beck, Ulrich (2000) *What is Globalization?* Trans. Patrick Camillier. Oxford: Blackwell.
Benjamin, Walter (1968) "The Work of Art in the Age of Mechanical Reproduction." In *Illuminations*. Trans. Harry Zohn. New York: Shocken Books, 217–51.

Bolter, Jay David and Grusin, Richard (1999) *Remediation: Understanding New Media*. Cambridge, MA: MIT Press.

Chakrabarty, Dipesh (2000) *Provincializing Europe: Postcolonial Thought and Historical Difference*. Princeton, NJ: Princeton University Press.

Comaroff, Jean and Comaroff, John L. (2000) "Millennial Capitalism: First Thoughts on a Second Coming." *Public Culture* 12(2), 291–343.

Couto, Mia Cada (1998) *Homem É uma Raça*. Rio de Janeiro: Nova Fronteira.

Crary, Jonathan (1999) *Suspensions of Perception: Attention, Spectacle, and Modern Culture*. Cambridge, MA: MIT Press.

— (1992) *Techniques of the Observer: On Vision and Modernity in the Nineteenth Century*. Cambridge, MA: MIT Press.

Deleuze, Gilles and Guattari, Felix (1983) *Anti-Oedipus: Capitalism and Schizophrenia*. Trans. Robert Hurley, Mark Seem, and Helen R. Lane. Minneapolis, MN: University of Minnesota Press.

— (1994) *What is Philosophy?* Trans. Hugh Tomlinson and Graham Burchill. New York: Verso.

Falk, Richard (1999) *Predatory Globalization*. Oxford: Blackwell.

Gramsci, Antonio (1971) *Selections from the Prison Notebooks*. Ed. and Trans. Quintin Hoare and Geoffrey Nowell Smith. New York: International Publishers.

Hardt, Michael and Negri, Antonio (2000) *Empire*. Cambridge, MA: Harvard University Press.

— (2004). *Multitude: War and Democracy in the Age of Empire*. New York: Penguin.

Held, David (1995) *Democracy and the Global Order: From the Modern State to Cosmopolitan Governance*. Palo Alto, CA: Stanford University Press.

Horkheimer, Max and Adorno, Theodor (1998) *Dialectic of the Enlightenment*. Trans. John Cumming. New York: Continuum.

Hountondji, Paulin J. (1990). "Scientific Dependency in Africa Today." *Research in African Literatures* 21.3, 5–15.

— (1992) "Recapturing," in *The Surreptitious Speech: Présence Africaine and the Politics of Otherness 1947–1987*, ed. Valentin-Yves Mudimbe. Chicago: University of Chicago Press, 238–256.

Jameson, Fredric (2000) "Globalization and Political Strategy." *New Left Review* 4, 49–68.

Marx, Karl (1973) "The German Ideology." In *Karl Marx and Friedrich Engels, The Marx-Engels Reader*. Ed. Robert C. Tucker. New York: W.W. Norton & Company, 146–200.

— (1973) *Grundrisse*. Trans. Martin Nicolaus. New York: Vintage.

Miyoshi, Masao (1996) "A Borderless World? From Colonialism to Transnationalism to the Decline of the Nation-State." In Rob Wilson and Wimal Dissanayake (eds) *Global/Local: Cultural Production and the Transnational Imaginary*. Durham, NC: Duke University Press, 78–106.

Readings, Bill (1996) *The University in Ruins*. Cambridge, MA: Harvard University Press.

Spivak, Gayatri Chakravorty (1999) *A Critique of Postcolonial Reason*. Cambridge, MA: Harvard University Press.

Tomlinson, John (1999) *Globalization and Culture*. Chicago: University of Chicago Press.

Williams, Raymond (1983) *Culture and Society 1780–1950*. New York: Columbia University Press.

— (1977) *Marxism and Literature*. Oxford: Oxford University Press.

Zhang, Xudong (1998) "Marxism and the Historicity of Theory: An Interview with Fredric Jameson." *New Literary History* 29(3), 353–83.

Žižek, Slavoj (1994) "Introduction: The Spectre of Ideology." In Slavoj Žižek, ed. *Mapping Ideology*. New York: Verso, 1–33.

— (2002a) *Revolution at the Gates*. New York: Verso.

— (2002b) *Welcome to the Desert of the Real*. New York: Verso

PART FOUR

Theories of Culture

Introduction

Marxist cultural study has in recent decades been focused by two intimately related sets of phenomena, namely the consequences for cultural production of the intensive and extensive completion of the global dominance of capitalism. The intensive dominance of capitalism is registered most obviously in the core economies (but increasingly elsewhere) as the final commodification of culture; the disappearance of amateur, "popular" in the older sense, and high-art fields alike; the dominance of advertising and commercial culture; the cultural saturation of consumer culture under the sign of good design; and so on. The extensive dominance of capital is registered most obviously in the peripheral and semi-peripheral economies (but also elsewhere) as colonialism and imperialism and later "globalization," weaponized Keynesianism, and neo-colonialism, and is registered in culture as the prestige accorded Northern cultural forms and the commercial dominance of American consumer culture. In other words, contemporary Marxist cultural study will articulate its aims along two axes: a temporal axis concerned with the relation between inherited forms, categories, and distinctions and altered economic and political circumstances; and a spatial axis concerned with the relationships among cultural forms that are suddenly universally seen to take their place in a newly global space. As Roberto Schwarz has formulated this problematic: "Where are we? And what time is it?"

In "Misplaced Ideas," Schwarz describes the world of the novels of Machado de Assis, where the dominant ideology, which reigns precisely because of its more or less effective functioning in the dominant economies, nonetheless fails to function in Brazil, or rather functions differently. The "real conditions of existence" in nineteenth-century Brazil are not those of nineteenth-century Europe, being rather governed by the institution of latifundia, slaveholding and its immediate legacy, and the peculiar relations of personal favor that emerge between landowners and clients. In this situation an ideology built around the idea of free labor obviously cannot function "properly"; that is, it cannot be expected to establish an imaginary grid onto which real relations can be mapped. But neither can it be ignored, as is one of the prestigious ruling ideas of the epoch. In Machado's Brazil, what is false consciousness in Europe is merely decorative—i.e. obviously false—in Brazil. This makes nineteenth-century Brazil look in a measure ridiculous, and this precisely what is so funny about Machado. But the joke really works the other way, because what is false in Brazil must be false everywhere. Since Machado's characters don't believe in the world view they proclaim, this world view is saturated with cynicism, an absolute cynicism which then extends back to the European metropole itself, where, from this perspective, the dominant ideology appears as what it is and nothing more, a technique of domination. The second, more materialist reason, is that Brazil itself is not external to Europe, but rather part of the same world economy; and so the social relations that falsify Enlightenment ideology in Brazil also pertain, though invisibly, to a European life world that consumes coffee, sugar, and rubber.

Chidi Amuta's analysis also necessarily takes place on both axes, but most fundamentally concerns the problem of literary form under a neo-colonial regime, one in which formal political dependence is accompanied by economic dependency on the core economies. Amuta takes on dominant critical trends within the Nigerian literary field at the moment when a post-Marxist "literary decolonization" rhetoric had taken hold. Amuta's essay is not so much a refinement of Marxist literary analysis as a demonstration of the extent to which an orthodox set of coordinates can serve an extraordinary demystifying function in the hands of a perceptive critic. Amuta's framework adopts a base-superstructure dynamic that presents an embarrassment for some Marxists and a whipping post for anti-Marxist critique. But the questions such a framework raise for cultural anti-imperialism are substantial. Is cultural liberation a path to economic liberation (if so, how?) or an alibi for continued economic subservience? Neither is class conceived by Amuta in any conspicuously sophisticated way. And yet the introduction of class within putative "Afrocentric" and "Eurocentric" world views—dated terms but ones with plenty of contemporary analogues—opens up these categories considerably. What is really at stake in the conflict between two sets of literary values? Do they stand for continental worldviews—do they stand for (racial, ethnic, gendered, class, sexual) worldviews at all—or do they rather represent the more or less arbitrary positions of class fractions struggling for hegemony over the conferral of literary value?

Fredric Jameson's "The Antinomies of Postmodernity" draws out some of the implications of his pathbreaking work on postmodernism, which is understood by Jameson as the incorporation of cultural production into the sphere of commodity circulation generally: the becoming-economic of the cultural and the becoming-cultural of the economic and the drawing to a close of a modernist period in which these two zones enjoyed a semi-autonomy that was both ideological and real. Here we are unexpectedly returned to Kantian antinomies rather than Hegelian contradictions, and indeed the primary categories—space and time—refer to the Kantian a priori representations, as well as to the axes of extensive and intensive commodification we began with above. In postmodern thought the investment in change is overwhelming, even as the category of change—what would come after capitalism?—becomes impossible to think. Along the spatial axis as well—and here Jameson echoes Amuta—homogeneity and difference become impossible to distinguish. On one hand, a proliferation of identities, subject positions, and putative worldviews; on the other, a system that subsumes all of these differences as a diversity within a modernity (which is, once we are all modern, postmodernity) that is identified with the market as the ultimate horizon of human history. For the point is that in postmodern thought—as was the case with Lukács's "antinomies of bourgeois thought"—these antinomies are not to be resolved. Their sublation is performed, if at all, by a form of thought which somehow subsists as a foreign body within postmodern reason: namely a "spatial dialectic" whose most immediate referent may be Roberto Schwarz.

Imre Szeman returns us to an apparently more modest register, asking what distinguishes "Marxist Criticism, Then and Now." Szeman argues that, despite the fact that Marxism has at least since Lukács privileged literature as an object of analysis and critique, there is no unitary methodology or set of considerations that distinguish a Marxist approach to literature from others. He does, however, provide an historicization and structural analysis of what he identifies as the three primary modes of Marxist literary criticism. The first accepts the discipline of literary studies as it is, and attempts to refigure from the inside what literary criticism can do. The second is the study of the literary field itself in its relationship with other fields and other cultural practices. A third, to which the essays in this section largely belong, pursues both dimensions, understanding the work of literature as both ideological (enmeshed in relations of power) and utopian (in some sense free from these same relations of power). Szeman argues that these two positions do not represent a dialectical contradiction to be resolved by a more expansive understanding of literature or of institutional structures, but rather (again) an antinomy that literary theory cannot resolve. The essay then points to a fourth, as yet unnamed possibility, emerging from the very resistance of Marxist literary theory to being absorbed into the various post-Marxist revisionisms. When, due to its very extensive and intensive dominance, capitalism is put back in question, Marxist criticism is, in however modest a way, there to ask it.

From the same terrain of contemporary literary theory, Carolyn Lesjak draws rather different conclusions. Rather than beginning from Marxist theory, Lesjak surveys contemporary literary theory and finds it alarmingly conformist. From recent coinages—"the new formalism," "the new Darwinism," "strategic formalism," and the like—to slightly older tendencies like new historicism and the return to beauty in the late 1990s, to the proliferation of anti-hermeneutic "reading" slogans of the day before yesterday, contemporary literary criticism is, on a first approximation, deliberately free of negativity, which is to say deeply cynical. On a second approximation, however, we realize that "surface" and "symptomatic" approaches exhaust a certain ideological terrain and as such, like superstition and the enlightenment in Hegel, imply and require each other. Antinomies once again! Lesjak, however, argues for "reading dialectically," which here involves placing a "surface reading" of textual proximities, modeled on the lines of Eve Sedgwick's *Touching Feeling*, alongside Fredric Jameson's more classically dialectical juxtaposition of temporal sequences. In other words, the dialectic of essence and appearance is not to be resolved in favor of either term—neither depth nor surface—but the relationship between the two is to become the object of analysis. The relationship between surface and depth becomes a figure for Marxist analysis itself: the spatial dialectic, the relationship between the texture of everyday life and the movement of capital that both determines it—in some sense *is* it—and at the same time withholds itself from it.

If Lesjak's intervention takes place primarily along the axis of space— the near space of textual proximity and the disjunctive space of a spatial dialectic—Sarah Brouillette's "Creative Labor" is fundamentally concerned with time: namely, the always ideological time of eternity. Brouillette begins by identifying the proudly conformist creative-class theorist Richard Florida with Left theorists of immaterial labor such as Michael Hardt, Antonio Negri, Maurizio Lazzarato, and Paolo Virno. As Brouillette is well aware, these two sets of theorists have more or less diametrically opposed political views, and these views are on the part of neither party fantastically misconceived. But both conceptions of labor share an ahistorical conception of good (creative, virtuosic) labor as opposed to bad (managed, rote) labor. Both conceptions are then more symptoms than diagnoses, understanding creativity both ahistorically—as the unalienated essence of human labor— and contradictorily—as the unique source of value under capital yet romantically honorable and free. Neither set of conceptions, then, pays any heed to the "contradictory, material, and constitutive histories of artists' labor," rather turning labor itself into an act of self-expression that is, under capitalism, precisely what labor is not.

Nicholas Brown's "The Work of Art in the Age of its Real Subsumption under Capital," obviously indebted to Jameson's work on postmodernism, is at the same time a response to Szeman's invocation of a fourth Marxist criticism that would account for, rather than simply assert, culture's contradictory status as both ideological and utopian, and to Brouillette's call for a criticism that would take into account "the contradictory relationship between artists and the markets for their work" and the specificity of aesthetic labor. Brown attempts to produce a Jamesonian "translation mechanism" that would mediate between a Marxist account of the end of modernism—Jamesonian postmodernism—and a formalist one—the bad "objecthood" decried by Michael Fried. But another term must first be introduced, namely the Bourdieusian concept of the "restricted field," whose overrunning by the market is the secret referent of Jamesonian postmodernism and Friedian objecthood alike. The presumed autonomy of the work of art in the modernist period is then understood to have an institutional and para-institutional basis that conditions its autonomy rather than determining its content: ideology and utopia are, for the modernist period, both accounted for. But what happens in the contemporary moment, when institutional and para-institutional protections from the anonymous market have tendentially disappeared? Brown asks instead what the consequences would be if works of art were indeed produced under conditions of pure heteronomy to the market—as commodities without intrinsic excess, like wallpaper. Such a set of conditions is hardly inconceivable, but Brown, like Szeman, understands that under such conditions the utopian aspect of culture would be derisory, and criticism as we know it would be incoherent. Brown spends the end of the essay exploring possible technologies by which a work of art might successfully assert its autonomy against the anonymous market: an assertion whose politics, in a neoliberal moment where the market is imagined as the very horizon of human experience and history, are not as parochial as they might appear.

CHAPTER TWENTY

Misplaced Ideas: Literature and Society in Late-Nineteenth-Century Brazil

Roberto Schwarz

From Misplaced Ideas: Essays on Brazilian Culture.
London: Verso, 1992: 19–32.

Every science has principles on which its system is based. Free labor is one of the principles of Political Economy. Yet in Brazil the "unpolitical and abominable" fact of slavery reigns.

This argument—the summary of a liberal pamphlet, by a contemporary of Machado de Assis[1]—places Brazil outside the system of science. We fell short of the reality to which science refers; we were rather an "unpolitical and abominable" moral fact. All this was a degradation, when we think that science was Enlightenment, Progress, Humanity, etc. As for the arts, Joaquim Nabuco expresses a comparable feeling when he protests against the subject of slavery in the plays of Alencar: "If it is horrible to the foreigner, how much more does it humiliate the Brazilian!"[2] Other authors of course came to opposite conclusions. Since the science of economy and other liberal ideologies did not concern themselves with our reality, they are what is abominable, irrelevant to political life, foreign and foolish. "Better have good Negroes from the African coast, for our happiness and theirs, notwithstanding the Briton, with his morbid philanthropy, which makes him forget his own home and allows his poor white brother to die from hunger, a slave without a master to pity him; the hypocritical and stupid Briton, who weeps over the destiny of our happy slave and thus exposes himself to the ridicule of true philanthropy."[3]

These authors, each in his own way, reflect the disparity between the slave society of Brazil and the principles of European liberalism. Shaming some, irritating others who insist on their hypocrisy, these principles in which neither one nor the other of the opposing parties can recognize Brazil—are the unavoidable frame of reference for everybody. In sum, an ideological comedy is set up, *different from the European.* Of course, free labor, equality before the law and, more generally, universalism were also an ideology in Europe; but there they corresponded to appearances and hid the essential—the exploitation labor. Among us, the same ideas would be false in a different sense, so to speak, in an original way. The Declaration of the Rights of Man, for instance, transcribed in part in the Brazilian Constitution of 1824, since it did not even correspond to appearances, could not deceive, and indeed cast the institution of slavery into a sharper light.[4] This professed universality of principles throws the same sharp light on the general practice of *favor* and transforms it into scandal. Under these conditions, what was the value of the grand bourgeois abstractions that we used so often? They didn't describe life—but ideas do not live by that alone. Thinking in a similar direction, Sérgio Buarque remarks: "By bringing from distant lands our forms of life, our institutions, and our vision of the world and by striving to maintain all that in an environment sometimes unfavorable and hostile, we were exiles in our own land."[5] This inadequacy in our thinking, no accident as we shall see, was in fact continually present, impregnating and rendering awkward the ideological life of the Second Reign, even down to its smallest detail. Sometimes inflated, sometimes trivial, very seldom on the right note, the literary prose of the time is one of the many witnesses of this fact.

Although the causes of this state of affairs are commonplaces of our historiography, their cultural effects have been insufficiently studied. As is well known, we were an agrarian and independent country, divided into latifundia, whose productivity depended on the one hand on slave labor and on the other on a foreign market. The peculiarities we have already mentioned arise more or less directly from this. For instance, bourgeois economic thinking—the priority of profit with all its social implications— was inevitable for us, since it prevailed in international trade, toward which our economy was directed. The constant practice of such trade taught this way of thought to more than a few. Moreover, we had become independent not long ago in the name of French, English and American liberal ideas, which were therefore part of our national identity. On the other hand, with equal necessity, this ideological ensemble had to be at war with slavery and its defenders and yet live with them.[6] In the realm of belief, the incompatibility between slavery and liberalism is clear, as we have seen. But at the practical level it could also be felt. Inasmuch as he was property, a slave could be sold, but not fired. In this respect, the free worker gave more freedom to his employer, and immobilized less capital. This is one reason, among others, why slavery set limits to the rationalization of production. Commenting on what he saw on a plantation, a traveller wrote: "there is no specialization of labor because they try to make economic use of their hands." After quoting this passage, F. H. Cardoso remarks that here "economic" does not stand for reducing work to a minimum, but for stretching it to a maximum amount of time. Work had to be made to fill and discipline the day of the slave. In short, the opposite of what was modern. Based on violence and military discipline, slave production could not be ordered around the idea of efficiency.[7] The rational study and continual modernization of the processes of production, with all the prestige that went with the revolution they were causing in Europe, made no sense in Brazil. To make things more complex, the slave latifundium had been an enterprise of commercial capital from the very beginning, and therefore profit had always been its pivot. However, profit as a subjective priority is common to early forms of capitalism and to more modern ones. So that, up to the time when slave labor became less profitable than wage labor, the "uncultivated and abominable" slaveowners who sought profit were in fact more thoroughly capitalistic than our defenders of Adam Smith, as capitalism for the latter meant only freedom. In short, the lines of intellectual life were bound to be hopelessly entangled. In matters of rationality, roles were shuffled: economic science became fantasy and morality, obscurantism equalled realism and responsibility, technical considerations were not practical, and altruism sought to bring about the exploitation of labor, etc. And, more generally, in the absence of the point of view of the slaves, who were not organized, the confrontation between humanity and inhumanity, in which no doubt there was a question of justice, ended up in a more earthbound way as a conflict between two modes of investment. Of course, one of the parties found the more spiritual version of this opposition more suitable.[8]

Challenged at every turn by slavery, the liberal ideology—the ideology of the newly emancipated nations of America—was derailed. It would be easy to deduce the resulting incongruities, many of which stirred the mind and conscience of nineteenth-century Brazil. We have already seen some examples. However, they remained oddly inessential. The test of reality did not seem important. It was as if the coherence and generality of thought was of little importance, or rather as if the criteria by which culture was judged were different—but in what way? By its sheer presence, slavery revealed the inadequacy of liberal ideas; but this does not mean to say that they affected or changed their orientation. Slavery was indeed the basic productive relationship, and yet it was not the social relation directly at work in ideological life. The key lay elsewhere. To find it, we must take up again the country as a whole. To schematize, we can say that colonization, based on the monopoly of the land, produced three classes of population: the proprietor of the latifundium, the slave and the "free man," who was in fact dependent. Between the first two, the relation is clear. Our argument will hinge on the situation of the third. Neither proprietor, nor proletarian, the free man's access to social life and its benefits depended, in one way or another, on the favor of a man of wealth and power.[9] The caricature of this "free man" was the *agregado*.[10] Favor was, therefore, the relationship by which the class of free men reproduced itself, a relationship in which the other member was the propertied class. The field of ideological life is formed by these two classes, and it is governed, therefore, by this relationship.[11] Thus, under a thousand forms and names, favor formed and flavored the whole of the national life, excepting always the basic productive relationship which was secured by force. Favor was present everywhere, combining itself with more or less ease to administration, politics, industry, commerce, the life of the city, the court, and so on. Even professions, such as medicine, or forms of skilled labor, such as printing, which in Europe were on the whole free of favor, were among us governed by it. As the professional depended on favor to exercise his profession, so the small proprietor depended on it for the security of his property, and the public servant for his position. Favor was our quasi-universal social mediation—and being more appealing than slavery, the other relationship inherited from colonial times, it is understandable that our writers based their interpretation of Brazil upon it, thereby unwittingly disguising the violence that had always been essential to the sphere of production.

Slavery gives the lie to liberal ideas; but favor, more insidiously, uses them, for its own purposes, originating a new ideological pattern. The element of arbitrariness, the fluid play of preferences to which favor subjects whatever it touches, cannot be fully rationalized. In Europe, when attacking such irrationalities, universalism had its sights on feudal privilege. In opposing this, bourgeois civilization had postulated the autonomy of the individual, universality of law, culture for its own sake, a day's pay for a day's work, the dignity of labor, etc., against the prerogatives of the *Ancien Régime*. Favor in turn implies the dependency of the individual, the exception to the rule, ornamental culture, arbitrary pay and the servility of labor. However, Brazil was not to Europe as feudalism was to capitalism. On the contrary, we were a function of European capitalism, and moreover, had never been feudal, for our colonization was the deed of commercial capital. In face of the European achievement, no Brazilian could have had the idea nor the strength to be, let us say, the Kant of favor, giving universality to this social form.[12] In this confrontation, the two principles were not of equal strength: in the sphere of reasoning, principles the European bourgeoisie had developed against arbitrariness and slavery were eagerly adopted; while in practice, sustained by the realities of plantation life, favor continually reasserted itself, with all the feelings and notions that went with it. The same is true of institutions, bureaucracy and justice, for example, which although ruled by patronage affirmed the forms and theories of the modern bourgeois state. As well as the predictable debates, therefore, this antagonism produced a stable coexistence between the two views which is of interest to study. *Once the European ideas and motives took hold, they could serve, and very often did, as a justification, nominally "objective," for what was unavoidably arbitrary in the practice of favor.* Real as it was, the antagonism vanished into thin air, and the opposing positions walked hand in hand. The effects of this displacement of function were many, and deeply touched our literature, as we will see. Liberalism, which had been an ideology well grounded in appearances, came to stand for the conscious desire to participate in a reality that appearances did not sustain. When he justified arbitrariness by means of some "rational" reason, the beneficiary consciously exalted himself and his benefactor, who, in turn, had no motive to contradict him, rationality being the highest value of the modern world. Under these conditions, which side believed in the justification? To what appearance did it correspond? But this was not a problem, for what was important was the commendable intention which governed both patronage and gratitude. The symbolic compensation was perhaps a little out of tune, but not ungrateful. Or, we might say, this use of justification was out of harmony with liberalism, but quite in tune with favor, which was, of course, all important. And how better to give luster to individuals and to the society they establish, than through the most illustrious ideas of their time, which in this case were European? In this context, ideologies do not describe reality, not even falsely, and they do not move according to a law of their own; we shall therefore call them "ideologies of the second degree." Their law of movement is a different one, not the one they name; it honors prestige, rather than a desire for system and objectivity. The reasons for this were no secret: the inevitable "superiority" of Europe, and the demands of the moment of expression, of self-esteem and fantasy, which are essential to favor. In this way, as we have said before, the test of reality and coherence did not seem to be decisive, notwithstanding its continuous presence as a requirement, recalled or forgotten according to circumstances. Thus, one could methodically call dependence independence, capriciousness utility, exceptions universality, kinship merit, privilege equality, and so on. By linking itself to the practice of what, in principle, it should criticize, liberalism caused thought to lose its footing. Let us not forget, however, the complexity of this step: inasmuch as they became preposterous, these ideas also ceased to mislead.

That was not the only way in which favor and liberalism could meet. However, it was the most complex, all-embracing, and striking of the possible combinations, and in our ideological climate, decisive. For the moment, let us consider but a few aspects of it. We have seen that in this combination, the ideas of the bourgeoisie, ideas whose sober grandeur goes back to the civic and rational spirit of the Enlightenment, take on the function of providing . . . ornament and aristocratic style; they attest and celebrate participation in a majestic sphere, in this case the European world in the process of . . . industrialization. There could not be a stranger relation between name and function. The historical novelty lies not in the ornamental character of knowledge and culture, part of the colonial and Iberian tradition, but in the extraordinary dissonance created when "modern" culture is used to this purpose. Is it as impractical as a trinket? Or does it confer distinction upon those who wear it? Could it be our panacea? Should it shame us before the eyes of the world? What is for sure is that in the comings and goings of argument and interest, all these aspects would show up, so that in the minds of the more attentive they were inextricably linked and mixed. Ideological life degraded and elevated its participants all at once, and this was often well known. For this reason, it was an unstable combination which could easily degenerate into the most bitter and hostile criticism. In order to maintain itself, it needed a permanent complicity, a complicity which the practice of favor tended to guarantee. At the moment of the exchange of favors, with its aspect of mutual personal recognition, it was not in the interest of either party to denounce the other, although both had the wherewithal to do so. This ever-renewed complicity had, moreover, heavy implications of class: in the Brazilian context, favor assured both parties, especially the weaker one, that neither was a slave. Even the most miserable of those given favor saw his freedom recognized in this act. All this transformed these exchanges, even if very modest, into a ceremony conferring social superiority, and therefore valued in itself. Ballasted by the infinite duress and degradation of slavery which it seeks to conjure away, this recognition sustains an extraordinary complicity, made even worse by the adoption of the bourgeois vocabulary of equality, merit, labor and reason. Machado de Assis will be the master of these complexities. Yet there is another side to it. Immersed as we are, still today, in the universe of capital, which did not take classical form in Brazil, we tend to see this combination as being only disadvantage. It may well not have had any advantage, but in order to appreciate it in its complexity, we should keep in mind that the ideas of the European bourgeoisie, initially aimed at privilege, had become apologetic from 1848 on: the wave of social struggles in Europe showed that universality hid class antagonisms.[13] Therefore, to catch its peculiar tone, we must consider that our improper discourse was hollow even when used properly. We can note in passing that this pattern will be repeated in the twentieth century, when we have several times sworn fealty to its most bankrupt ideologies on the world stage—in full belief that we are quite up-to-date. In literature, as we shall see, something singular results, an emptying out of what is already hollow. Here again, Machado will be the master.

In short, if we insist upon the extent to which slavery and favor twisted the ideas of the times, it is not in order to dismiss them, but to describe them *qua* twisted—not in line with their own demands. They are recognizably Brazilian in their peculiar distortion. Hence, stepping back from the search for causes, we are still left with that experience of incongruity which was our point of departure: the impression that Brazil gives of ill-assortedness—unmanageable contrasts, disproportions, nonsense, anachronisms, outrageous compromises and the like—the sort of combination which the art of Brazilian Modernism, and later on, Tropicalism, as well as political economy, have taught us to appreciate.[14] Examples abound. Let us look at some, not for the purpose of analysis but to suggest the ubiquity of what we have described and the variation of which it is capable. In the magazines of the time; the statement of purpose in the first issue, whether serious or bantering, is written for bass and falsetto: first, the redeeming purpose of the press is asserted, in the combative tradition of the Enlightenment; the great sect founded by Gutenberg calls for action in the face of indifference; at the heights, youth and the condor, rejecting the past and its prejudices, look toward the future, while the purifying torch of the press banishes the darkness or corruption. Second, accommodating themselves to circumstances, the magazines declare their goodnaturedness, their eagerness to "provide all classes, and particularly honest families, a means of delightful instruction and agreeable recreation." The redeeming intention joins with puzzles, calls for the unity of all Brazilians, dress patterns, practical hints and serial, novels.[15] The light verse that serves as the epigraph to *The Marmot in the Court* [During the Empire, the city of Rio was known as the "Court"] is an unintended caricature of this sequence: "Here is the marmot/In his variety/ He is ever-liked/And by all/He speaks the truth/Says what he feels/Loves and respects/Everyone." If, in another realm, we scrape our walls a little, we find the same conjunction: "The change in architecture was superficial. European wallpaper was pasted or hung on slave-built walls of earth, or paintings were hung, in order to create the illusion of modern interiors, like those of industrial Europe. In some cases, the pretence reached the absurd: The painting of Greco-Roman architectural motifs—pilasters, architraves, colonnades, friezes, etc., often done to deceive, suggested a neoclassic setting that could never have been built with the techniques and materials available in Brazil. In other cases, windows were painted on the walls with views of Rio de Janeiro or Europe, suggesting an exterior world quite distant from the real one of slave quarters and slave labor."[16] This text describes rural homes in the Province of São Paulo in the second half of the nineteenth century. As for the Court: "Here changes responded to new habits, which included the use of objects of greater refinement—crystal, china and porcelain and in the adoption of more formal behavior, as in the serving of meals. At the same time these architectural changes gave an appearance of veracity to the whole, which tried to reproduce the life of

European homes. The social strata that benefited the most from a slave-system exclusively based on agricultural production attempted to create an illusion for their own use of an ambience with urban and European characteristics thus everything or almost everything had to be imported."[17] This comedy lives in the remarkable opening chapters of *Quincas Borba*. Under the pressure of opinion, Rubião, a recent heir, must exchange his black slave for a French cook and a Spanish servant, with whom he is not at ease. Besides gold and silver, the metals that speak to his heart, he now buys statuettes of bronze as well—a Faust and a Mephistopheles. A graver matter, but equally under the imprint of the times, is the wording of our hymn to the Republic, written in 1890 by Medeiros e Albuquerque, a self-proclaimed "decadent" poet. It was progressive and altogether unconvincing. "We cannot believe that of yore/slaves could have existed in our noble land." ("Of yore" was but two years before, abolition having occurred in 1888.) A declaration of the revolutionary government of Pernambuco made many years earlier (1817), sounds just as off, but for opposite reasons: "Patriots, your properties, even those most repugnant to the ideals of justice, will be held sacred."[18] It refers to rumors of emancipation, which had to be denied to reassure the owners. The life of Machado de Assis is an example as well; in it, the militant journalist (enthusiastic about "the workingman's intelligence"), the author of a humorous column and of serious quatrains (the latter commemorating the wedding of the imperial princesses), and the Chevalier of the Order of the Rose follow one another in rapid succession.[19] Against all this Silvio Romero will take the field. "It is necessary to lay the foundations of a national spirit, conscious of its merits and defects, of its strength and its infirmities, and not concoct a pastiche, a kind of stuffed puppet, which only serves to shame us in the eyes of the foreigner. There is but one way to achieve this desideratum, we must immerse ourselves in the life-giving current of naturalistic and monistic ideas which are transforming the old world."[20] From afar, this substitution of one pastiche for another is so obvious it makes us smile. But it is also dramatic, since it points out to what extent our desire for authenticity had to express itself in an alien language. The romantic pastiche was only superseded lay another, this time Naturalism. In sum, in the magazines, in behavior, in the setting of the home, in national symbols, in revolutionary proclamations, in theory and in everything else, always the same "harlequin" composition, to use Mario de Andrade's word: the dissonance between representations, and what, upon consideration, we know to be their context.

The combination of latifundia and unfree labor, given durability by its important role in the international market, and later, by internal politics, stood firm through Colony, Emperors and Regencies, through Abolition, the First Republic, and even now is a matter of debate and bullets.[21] Our ideological life, no less determined by national dependency, did vary: at a distance, it followed in the steps of Europe. (Let us point out that it is only the ideology of independence which turns this into a problem; foolishly when it insists on an impossible cultural autonomy; profoundly, when it reflects upon what was truly possible.) The tenacity of the basic social relationships and the ideological volatility of the "elite" were both a part of the dynamics of capitalism as an international system, the part that it was ours to live out. The latifundia, little changed, saw the baroque, neoclassic, romantic, naturalist and modernist cultures pass by, cultures which in Europe reflected immense transformations in its social order. We could well suppose that here they would lose their point, which in part did occur. But this loss, to which we were condemned by the working of the international system of colonialism, condemned the working of that very system itself. We say this to indicate its more-than-national significance.

All this was no secret, although not worked out theoretically. For the arts, as opposed to theory, making something of it was easier since there was always a way to adore, quote, ape, sack, adapt or devour these manners and fashions, so that they would reflect, in their defectiveness, a cultural embarrassment in which we would recognize ourselves. Let us go back for a moment. Liberal ideas could not be put into practice, and yet they could not be discarded. They became a part of a special practical situation, which would reproduce itself and not leave them unchanged. Therefore, it does not help to insist on their obvious falsehood. We should rather observe their dynamics, of which this falsehood was a true component. Faced with these ideas, Brazil, the outpost of slavery, was ashamed—for these were taken to be ideas of the time—and resentful, for they served no purpose. But they were also adopted with pride, in an ornamental vein, as a proof of modernity and distinction. And, of course, they were revolutionary when put in the service of Abolitionism. Subordinate to the demands of place, and not losing their original claims, they circled, governed by a peculiar rule whose merits and faults, ambiguities and deceptions were peculiar as well. To know Brazil was to know these displacements, experienced and practiced by everyone as a sort of fate, for which, however, there was no proper name, since the improper use of names was part of its nature. Widely felt to be a defect, well-known but little reflected upon, this system of displacement certainly did debase ideological life and diminished the chances for genuine thought. However, it made for a skepticism in matters of ideology which could be both thorough and effortless, and compatible, besides, with a good deal of talk. Pushed a bit further, it will produce the astonishing force of Machado de Assis' vision. Now, the ground of this skepticism surely lies not in the reflective exploration of the limits of liberal thought. It rather lies in an intuitive starting point, which spared us this effort. Embedded in a system they did not describe, even in appearance, the ideas of the bourgeoisie saw everyday life invalidate their pretension to universality from the very beginning. If they were accepted, they were so for reasons they themselves could not accept. Instead of functioning as the horizon of thought, they appeared on a vaster background which rendered them relative: the back-and-forth of arbitrariness and favor. The ground of its claims to universality was shaken. Thus, what in Europe was a great critical feat, could among us be ordinary incredulity. Utilitarianism, egoism, formalism, and the like, were clothes to be worn on occasion, perhaps fashionable, but uncomfortably tight. Thus we see that this world is of consequence to the history of culture: when in its peculiar orbit, the most prestigious ideology of the West was bound to cut the ludicrous figure of a mania among manias. In such wise, our national oddities became world-historical. Perhaps this is comparable to what happened in Russian literature. Faced with the latter, even the greatest novels of the French realism seem naive. And why? In spite of their claims to universality, the psychology of rational egoism and the ethics of Enlightenment appeared in the Russian Empire as a "foreign" ideology, and therefore, a localized and relative one. Sustained by its historical backwardness, Russia forced the bourgeois novel to face a more complex reality. The comic figure of the Westernizer, Francophile or Germanophile (frequently under an allegorical or ridiculous name), the ideologies of progress, of liberalism, of reason, all these were ways of bringing into the foreground the modernization that came with Capital. These enlightened men proved themselves to be lunatics, thieves, opportunists, cruel, vain and parasitical. The system of ambiguities growing out of the local use of bourgeois ideas—one of the keys to the Russian novel—is not unlike the one we described for Brazil. The social reasons for this similarity are clear. In Russia, too, modernization would lose itself in the infinite extent of territory and of social inertia, and would clash with serfdom or its vestiges—a clash many felt as a national shame, although it gave others the standard by which to measure the madness of the individualism and progressomania that the West imposed and imposes on the world. The extreme form of this confrontation, in which progress is a disaster and backwardness a shame, is one of the springs of Russian literature. Whatever the difference in stature, there is in Machado—for the reasons that I have pointed out—something similar, something of Gogol, Dostoyevsky, Goncharov and Chekhov.[22] Let us say, then, that the very debasement of thought among us, of which we were so bitterly aware, and which today stifles the student of our nineteenth century, was a sore spot of the world-historical process and for this reason a valuable clue to it.[23]

In the process of reproducing its social order, Brazil unceasingly affirms and reaffirms European ideas, always improperly. In their quality of being improper, they will be material and a problem for literature. The writer may well not know this, nor does he need to, in order to use them. But he will be off-key unless he feels, notes, and develops—or wholly avoids—this aspect. And although there is an indefinite number of solutions to the problem, violations are palpable and definite. Their non-artistic names are ingenuousness, loquacity, narrow-mindedness, aping, provinciality, etc., the specific and local effects of an alienation with long arms—the consequences of the lack of social transparency, imposed, first, by our colonial situation and later on by our dependency. For all that, the reader has learned very little about Brazilian history, literary or general, and we have not placed Machado de Assis. What is then the use of what has been said so far? Instead of a literary history set within a social "panorama," a construction always suggestive and true to a certain extent, but necessarily vague, I have tried a different solution. I have sought to specify a social mechanism in the form in which it became an internal and active element of our culture: the inescapable difficulty which Brazil forced upon its cultivated men in the very process of its social reproduction. In other words, an analysis of the ground of intellectual experience. I have tried to see in the movement of our ideas something that made us singular, starting from the common observation, almost a feeling, that in Brazil ideas were off-center in relation to European usage. And I have presented a historical explanation for this displacement, an explanation which brought in relations of production and parasitism in Brazil, our economic dependency and its counterpart, the intellectual hegemony of Europe, revolutionized by capital. In short, in order to analyze a national peculiarity, sensed in everyday life, we have been driven to reflect on the colonial process, which was international. The constant interchange of liberalism and favor was the local and opaque effect of a planetary mechanism. Now, the everyday movement of ideas and practical perspectives was the obvious and natural material for literature, once the fixed forms had lost their validity in the arts. It was, therefore, the point of departure for the novel, even more so, the realistic novel. Thus, what we have described is the manner in which the movement of world history, in its cryptic and local results, repeated again and again, passes into writing, which it now determines from the inside—whether or not the writer knows or wills it. In other words, we have defined a vast and heterogeneous, but structured, field, which is a historical *consequence*, and can be an artistic origin. While studying it, we saw that it differs from the European field, although using the same vocabulary. Therefore, difference, comparison and distance are part of its very definition: sometimes reason is on our side, sometimes it belongs to others, but it always appears in an ambiguous light. The result is an equally singular chemistry the affinities and antipathies of which we have described to some extent. It is only natural that such material should propose original problems to the literature that depends on it. As a final observation, let us only say that, contrary to what is generally thought, the material of the artist turns out not to be shapeless: it is historically shaped and in some way registers the social process to which it owes its existence. In shaping it, in turn, the writer superimposes form upon form, and the depth, force, and complexity of the artistic results will depend upon the success of this operation, of this relation to the preformed material in which the energies of history lie. The match of forms is not obvious. And, one more variation of the same theme, let us conclude by saying that even when dealing with the most modest matters of everyday life, the subject matter of our novelists has always been world-historical. This they shaped as well as they could, but it would not have been their subject, had they dealt with it directly.

Translated by Edmund Leites and Roberto Schwarz

Notes

1 A. R. de Torres Bandeira, "A liberdade do trabalho e a concorréncia, seu efeito, so prejudiciais ã classe operéria?" *O Futuro*, January 1863. Machado was a frequent contributor to this magazine.

2 *A Polêmica Alencar-Nabuco*, ed. Afrãno Coutinho (Rio de Janeiro: Tempo Brasileiro, 1965): 106.

3 Deposition of a commercial firm, M. Wright & Cia, regarding the financial crisis of the 1850. Quoted in Joaquim Nabuco, *Um Extadista do Império* 1 (1936): 188. And again in Sérgio Barque de Holanda, *Raizes do Brasil* (Rio de Janeiro: J. Olympio, 1956): 96.

4 Emília Viotti da Costa, "Introdução ao estudo da Emancipação politica," ed. Carlos Guilherme Mota, *Brasil em Perspectiva* (São Paulo: Difusão Européia do Livro, 1963).

5 Holanda, *Raizes do Brasil*, 15.

6 Emília Viotti da Costa, "Introdução."

7 Fernando Henrique Cardoso, *Capitalismo e Escravidão* (São Paulo: Difusão Européia do Livro, 1962): 189–191 and 198.

8 As Felipe de Alencastro remarks in an as-yet unpublished work, the true national question of our nineteenth century was the defence of the slave traffic in the face of English pressure. A question that could not be less attractive to intellectual enthusiasm.

9 For a more complete discussion of the subject, see Maria Sylvia de Carvalho Franco, *Homens Lives na Ordem Escravocat* (São Paulo: Instituto de Estudos Brasileiros, 1969).

10 *Agregado* roughly means a man of no property, totally dependent upon a family with property, but still not a slave.

11 On the ideological effects of latifundia, see Chapter III of *Raizes do Brasil*, "A herança rural."

12 As Machado de Assis remarks in 1879, "the external impact determines the direction of our movement; for the time being in our environment, the force necessary for the creation of new doctrines is lacking." See "A nova geração," *Obra Completa* 3 (1959): 826–27.

13 Georg Lukács, "Marx und das Problem des Ideologischen Verfalls," *Probleme des Realismus*, 4 (1938).

14 Dealt with in a different manner, the same observation can be found in Sérgio Barque: "We may construct excellent works, enrich our humanity with new and unforeseen aspects, bring to perfection the type of civilization we

represent: still, what is certain is that the consequences of both our efforts and of our laziness seems to take part in a system proper to another climate and a different landscape," *Raizes do Brasil* (São Paulo: Companhia dos Letras, 1936), 15.

15 See the "prospecto" in "Typographia de F. de Paula Brito, R. J.," in *O Espelho*, no. 1 (1859): 1, a weekly magazine of literature, fashion, crafts and the arts; "Introdução," in *Revista Fluminense* 1, no. 1 (1868): 1–2, a weekly for news, literature, science, pastimes, etc.; "Typographia de Paula Brito," in *A Marmota na Corte*, no. 1 (1840): 1; *Revista Illustrada*, no. 1 (1876), published by Angelo Agostini; "Apresentação," in *O Bezouro*, 1, no. 1 (1878), a humorous and satiric periodical; "Cavaco," in *O Cabriflo*, no. 1 (1866): 2.

16 Nestor Goulart Reis Filho, *Arquitetura Residenciul Brasileira no Século XIX*, manuscript, 14–15.

17 Ibid., 8.

18 Emília Viotti da Costa, "Introdução."

19 Jean-Michel Massa (ed.), *A juventude de Machado de Assis* (Rio de Janeiro: Civilização Brasileira, 1971): 265, 435, 568.

20 Sílvio Romero, *Ensaios de Crítica Parlamentar* (Rio de Janeiro Moreira: Maximino & Cia, 1883): 15.

21 For the reasons for this inertia, see Celso Furtado, *Formação econômica do Brasil* (São Paulo: Companhia Editora Nacional, 1971).

22 For an exacting analysis of our ideological problems, in a manner somewhat different from my own, see Paula Beiguelman, *Teoria e Ação no Ponsamento Abolicionista*, Vol. 1, in (ed.) *Formação Política do Brasil* (São Paulo: Livraria Pioneira, 1967). In her book there are several quotations which seem to come from Russian novels. For example, the following from Pereira Barreto: "On one side are the abolitionists, riding upon a sentimental rhetoric and armed with a revolutionary metaphysics, pursuing abstract types in order to turn them into social formulas; on the other side are the land-owners, silent and humiliated, in the attitude of those who recognize their guilt or meditate an impossible revenge." Pereira Barreto was the proponent of a scientific agriculture—in the avant-garde of coffee cultivation—and he believed that abolition should be an automatic consequence of agricultural progress. Besides, he considered Negroes to be an inferior race; it was a disgrace to depend upon them (Paula Beiguelman, *Teoria e Ação no Ponsamento Abolicionista*, Vol. 1, in (ed.) *Formação Politica do Brasil* [São Paulo: Livraria Pioneira, 1967]: 159).

23 Antonio Candido offers suggestive ideas on this matter. He tries to identify a tradition rooted in the social type we call "Malandro" (rogue) in our literature. See his "Dialética da Malandragem," in *Revista do Instituto de Estudos Brasileiros*, no. 8 (1970), and the paragraphs on "anthropology," an ironic theory of the 1920s concerning Brazil's incorporation of foreign cultures, in "Digressão sentimental sobre Oswald de Antrade," in *Vários Escritos* (São Paulo: Livraria Duas Cidades, 1970): 84 et seq.

CHAPTER TWENTY ONE

Traditionalism and the Quest for an African Literary Aesthetic

Chidi Amuta

From The Theory of African Literature. *London: Zed Books and Institute for African Alternatives, 1989: 33–50.*

It is important that we understand that cultural imperialism in its era of neo-colonialism is a more dangerous cancer because it take new subtle forms and can hide even under the cloak of militant African nationalism, the cry for dead authentic symbolism and other native racist self assertive banners.

NGUGI WA THIONG'O[1]

*I feel the need to scream
the hard-scissoring nightmares of men
hiding behind ancestral masks
masks of illusions,
carved out of the wish to escape
if only for a day
the saw-blade kiss of reality*

ODIA OFEIMUN[2]

In this chapter I try to locate the meeting point of the bulk of conflicting but mutually inclusive positions in the discourse of modern African literature and culture in what may be termed *traditionalist aesthetics*. This is a complex of theoretical standpoints and critical statements which seek to define the authenticity, standards of creative performance and critical evaluation of African literature in terms of values and models freely selected and adapted from the so-called "traditional," pre-colonial African cultural matrix. This ever-growing and now almost hegemonic intellectual tradition finds its most recent and most trenchant expression in what I call the *decolonization rhetoric* of the sort exemplified by the necessary but problematic book, *Toward the Decolonization of African Literature* by Chinweizu et al.[3] Paradoxically, this theoretical viewpoint finds legitimation in Soyinka's powerful but equally troublesome *Myth, Literature and the African World*.[4]

My basic contention is that for all its attractiveness and desirability as an intellectual "fashion," traditionalist aesthetics is fundamentally flawed by its inherent ahistorical, undialectical and ultimately idealist conception of the relationship between literature as an aspect of culture and the socio-economic processes which overdetermine other aspects of contemporary African experience in particular. Therefore, to use traditionalist aesthetics as the exclusive and decisive point of departure for a rhetorical decolonization of African literature, or for the definition of immutable aesthetic value system for that literature, is not only reactionary and diversionary but also, in itself, a colonial attitude. Additionally, it is a negation of the primordial social involvement of pre-colonial African art as well as the putative historical predication of modern African literature and art.

To this extent, the current hegemony and popularity of traditionalist aesthetics (especially among Nigerian students and their teachers) constitutes a formidable cognitive road-block to the emergence of a tradition of rigorous theorizing on African literature, thus condemning the literature in question and its critical discourse to a state of perpetual underdevelopment.

The intellectual climate

The perennial yearning for the lost ideals of racial infancy; the nostalgic groping for the nipples of the pristine African maternal breast; the selective resuscitation of ancestral myths, values and institutions; the indiscriminate appropriation and application of the tools of Western bourgeois rationalism to contemporary African culture; the endless quest for "traditional" criteria for the evaluation of a literature that has since lost its cultural innocence: these and their variants are the manifestations of the present crisis of consciousness and confidence in bourgeois intellection of modern African society and culture in general and literature in particular.

This conjunction of theoretical contradictions which has unfortunately been consecrated into the dominant intellectual tradition of Africa (in the field of culture at least) betokens an ambiguous sense of nostalgia which looks in two principal directions for inspiration: African cultural scholarship has looked insistently either back at traditional pre-colonial Africa or to the dominant (bourgeois) cultural tradition of the West for theoretical moorings. In either direction, a certain preoccupation with tradition in its idealist (static) sense seems cultural to contemporary discourse on African literature and culture. Whether our point of reference is literature or the figurative arts, dance or fashion, architecture or cuisine, the pendulum of discourse and controversy swings either to pre-colonial "Africa" or "the West."

While granting that the dilemma in question is historically inevitable, one is perturbed by a certain insidious ambiguity in the conception of the two opposing geo-cultural regions, namely Africa and Europe. The Africa that is usually projected is the pristine, unspoilt world of migrant herdsmen, naked tribesmen and dancing damsels; the highest indices of its achievement in terms of material culture are the ever-present Ife and Benin bronze heads, the Dogon masks, the Terracotta relics, Nok culture, the great walls of Zimbabwe and so on. Accordingly, these achievements and relics are artfully insulated from history in its dynamic meaning. On the other hand, European models are carefully selected from the highest points in Western civilization usually dating from the Renaissance to the present era of guided missiles and computer chips. In an attempt to erect a comparative paradigm between "the two worlds," the Western and pro-Western media and intellectual establishment have consciously or unconsciously come to adopt an unbalanced North–South framework. Thus, for instance, a comparison of Western and African architectural models in Western scholarship and media would tend to compare say Igbo thatch huts with New York skyscrapers. In short, there is a basic reluctance on the part of the Western intellectual establishment and their African protégés to concede a certain measure of motion or dynamism to the African world.

The sense of intellectual anguish which lies at the root of these observations does not arise from what the West (or certain sections of it) have chosen to believe about Africa but from the more debilitating realization that prominent African intellectuals have tacitly acquiesced to this unbalanced comparative paradigm. Thus, we are assailed from all directions by indiscriminate bandyings of such clichés as "the African world," "African culture," "African values," etc. by African bourgeois scholars. Implicit in all this is a basic reluctance on the part of these scholars to see Africa not only as part of a changing world but also as a highly heterogeneous and multivalent geo-political entity whose problems need to be confronted at the level of theories with practical value for both the present and the future.

There is a kind of defensive intellection which seeks to rationalize the African contribution to world culture exclusively in terms of the past glories of illustrious ancestors conceived in broad continental terms. It needs to be underlined that this kind of rationalization belongs in a general tradition of affirmative consciousness which is a continuation of the reflex response to the cultural denigration and psychological emasculation which were implicit in colonialist ideology. It is the appropriateness of this response in the heydays of nationalist politics and black collective race retrieval that confers historical importance on men like Caseley Hayford, Wilmot Blyden, Leopold Senghor and others. Negritude and allied philosophies with their inherent class limitation were the appropriate vehicles for the expression of that sense of racial injury. It also needs to be underlined that such affirmative philosophies had inherent *revolutionary* significance in the days when they were current.

The contemporary problematization of the question of an aesthetic reference point for African literature is a by-product of this tradition of black affirmative consciousness. But, the African literary intelligentsia came to the realization that they had a cultural task to perform rather belatedly and through a curious backyard route.

The emergence of African literature in the European languages was greeted by the European literary establishment with a spontaneous spate of reviews and critical essays characterized by a patronizing condescension couched in glamorous eulogy. Underlying these critical celebrations was a certain nebulous universalism which saw African literature as part of the "human" literary heritage which did not necessitate the adoption of fresh evaluative criteria. Since ... the logical index and reference point of universal humanism was the Western world, standards of performance and critical values from the Western tradition could freely be adopted for exegetizing and evaluating African literature. The excesses of colonialist criticism have more recently mellowed into a liberal absolute relativism which claims that there could be as many evaluations of an African literary work as there are critics provided we are sufficiently intelligent to distinguish between "good" and "bad" critics. Characteristically, Bernth Lindfors articulates the essence of this growing fashion: "A reasonable alternative ... would be an approach which recognised the validity of various interpretations of the same work of art, a relative approach in matters of aesthetic discrimination."[5] Predictably, the response of African writers and critics to the underlying assumptions of this critical attitude has consisted of a series of defences of the authenticity, peculiarity and historical predication of African literature. Accordingly, the necessity for the adoption of African aesthetic criteria has come to be forcefully articulated while attention has duly been drawn to the existence, albeit latent, of a body of aesthetic values and artistic practices in pre-colonial African cultures which only need to be exhumed, refurbished and systemized to provide an alternative aesthetic of African literature and thus call the bluff of the Western literary establishment.

This position, once articulated, provided the basis for a new diversionary theology. In conference after conference on African literature and in the now familiar avalanche of amputated reviews and subjective exegeses that inundate journals in the field, it would appear that the bulk of intellectual energy in African literary discourse has been dissipated on the quest for an "African" aesthetic value system for our literature. The road to authentic African aesthetic values and artistic practices has led inexorably to pre-colonial and often destroyed or forgotten socio-cultural formations. Understandably, therefore, Africanist literary scholarship has had to fall back on those disciplines traditionally equipped to handle the past of societies. In this regard, history, anthropology and religious studies would ordinarily provide ready services. But here again, we come face to face with the ubiquitous West. Colonialist history of Africa of the sort associated with early Rowland Oliver and Eurocentric (primitivist) anthropology of the brand linked with Placide Tempels, Levi-Bruhl and Jack Goody has had only stock European prejudices to offer.[6] Most scandalous perhaps, is the work of African professional religionists like Idowu and Mbiti whose sense of divinity and the sacred is so steeped in Judeo-Christian mythology that it cannot but see a hierarchy of Christian angels in African pantheons![7] We shall return to this point later.

Given the discordant tone and suspicious nature of information form these auxiliary disciplines, traditionalist aesthetics of African literature has tended to content itself with vague generalizations about the "African oral narrator," "the African world view," "the traditional poet" and so on. In some cases, the quest for an African aesthetic of African literature has been hijacked from African scholars by the Euro-American counterparts. I am referring specifically to the flurry of centers and institutes of African studies in North America in the last decade. These are programs established with American blood-money and whose staple diet has been all manner of tape recordings, films, relics and allied exotica collected from some carefully chosen remote African village. The unrelenting collector (often in ragged denim outfit) soon returns from the African Tartarus to a well deserved professional chair in the American Olympus as an Africanist or "specialist" on African culture. The readiest victims and consumers of the products of these programs have understandably been Afro-Americans whose endless quest for roots has led them to invent all manner of interesting mythologies about Africa. Some of them have become so obsessed with the "golden past" that their sense of identity would be fatally damaged if they woke up one morning to find that the whole of Africa was swarming like jet planes, computerized assembly lines and bullet trains! Like the sympathizer who mourns more than the bereaved, American scholars of African literature have recently over-reached themselves in this quest for an African aesthetic of African literature. In a recent publication *Toward Defining the African Aesthetic*,[8] the American-based African Literature Association displayed the most scandalous ignorance about the subject, for none of the series of unrelated essays in the collection defines or shows the faintest awareness of the ingredients or implications of the so-called African aesthetic. Such examples could be multiplied indefinitely in the works of the ever-increasing specialists on African in the West.

As a hegemonic intellectual preoccupation, the quest for an African aesthetic must be viewed as a prominent product of an intellectual climate in which African scholarship about Africa has been unconsciously performing a task assigned to it by the West. In the discharge of this task, there has emerged a body of pronouncements that fit out earlier definition of traditionalist aesthetics. The shortcomings of this intellectual formation will emerge more concretely if we examine the broad philosophical assumptions that underlie the pronouncements of some of its most glorified advocates.

An African world view: Illusion or reality?

To the extent that aesthetic theories are almost always predicated on a philosophical premise, traditionalist aestheticians of African literature have relentlessly invoked a certain amorphously defined "African world view" as the informing metaphysical bedrock of their postulations. As it is popularized and bandied around by anthropologists, religionists and professional philosophers, *the* African world view refers to an absolute fairly homogeneous, immutable and eternal mode of perceiving reality and explaining phenomena by which African can be distinguished from the West in particular. As we had indicated earlier, the erection of this concept must be seen as a deliberate attempt to provide a rational mooring for the identity crisis which the Western imperialist assault has inflicted on Africans and peoples of African descent. As a result, in the pronouncements of this group of intellectuals, the African world view always has a past pre-scientific, pre-colonial time reference. Kwasi Wiredu reinforces this explanation when he asserts that:

> African nationalists in search of an African identity, Afro-Americans in search of their African roots, and foreigners in search of exotic diversion—all demand an African philosophy fundamentally different from Western philosophy, even if it means the familiar witches' brew.[9]

In a bid to project to so-called African world view as a coherent philosophical proposition, every attempt is made to submerge the ethnic heterogeneity of the continent and put forward a set of beliefs, customs, taboos and practices as typically and uniformly African. One area in which this generalizing tendency is most evident is in the area of religious belief. The dominant tendency has been to posit animistic religion as the definitive mode of African religious practice. Consequently, the African sense of the real is presented as a conflation of the mundane world of working, waking and sleeping and a supra-mundane world of spirits, gods, and other numinous influences intricately matrixed in a complex cosmogonic design. As in Senghorian negritude, African man in the context of this world view intuitively grasps the essence of things and can change his material circumstances through an act of will mediated by supernatural collaboration. Says Kofi Awoonor in his book, *The Breast of the Earth*:

> The African established, from time immemorial, a spiritual hierarchy which reveals a cunning understanding of natural phenomena and a clever talent for manipulating them toward good for himself and evil for his enemies.[10]

Accordingly, advocates of this distinctive African metaphysics posit an interesting conception of deity. In establishing a certain hierarchical relationship among gods in whatever ethnic pantheon they choose to discuss, they have not quite played safe of stock Judaeo-Christian models. Kofi Awoonor, in the book in question, proffers a hierarchical ordering of gods in which there is a creator God somewhere spatially and metaphysically distanced from a chain of lesser gods:

> Beneath the Creator God is a host of minor deities. By the light of his own logic, the African assigns to the creator God a certain degree of distance and unapproachability, not because he considers Him unconcerned, but rather because he thinks of Him in his primal ancestral role as the supreme paterfamilias who must not be bothered with the petty details of the universe. He, Himself, appoints lieutenants and assistants who become overseers and guardians of various natural phenomena and faculties.[11]

Other features of this world view include a certain cyclic conception of time, a belief in reincarnation and allied superstitions.

It is crucial to interject at this point that this conception of deity is Christian-based and largely a falsification of the reality of religious practice in most, if not all, African cultures. Pre-colonial Africa was essentially humanistic and, to that extent, the existence of human society was the precondition for the existence of religion and gods. As it were, people said: let there be gods and proceeded to create them! In turn, they were imbued with humanistic attributes (a point to which I shall return in my discussion of Achebe's *Arrow of God in* Chapter Six) and accordingly assigned them duties within the emergent concept of the social division of labor. The provinces (or "ministries") allocated to various gods corresponded to what, in the particular tie and place, were conceived of as areas not totally within human control and competence—control of thunder, hail, earthquake, rainfall and so on. Thus, pre-scientific (or *traditional*) African gods were and have remained terrestrial, rather than celestial; they can be felt (through their molded or sculpted symbolizations), touched, carved, cursed, reproached and dismantled or starved to death in response to material exigencies of social existence which formed the basis for the existence of gods in the first place. In most cases, the gods were essentially intensifications of existing personages who attaining deification through a process of apotheosis by virtue of socially recognized acts of heroism and distinction. In conceptual terms, therefore, the abode of gods was a terrestrial but spatially intangible realm of spirituality which nevertheless mortal man could penetrate through acts of augury, invocation, and other magical feats. In objective terms, it was an imaginative extension of the real world furnished by human material necessity. That world did not exist as an objective reality. All in all, the relationship between people and their gods was essentially an instrumental one; they made the gods, who existed in human image to serve them. Belief in the gods in turn influenced social action in a dialectical process.

It is, in addition, illogical to use the metaphysics of a particular phase in the development of a society to generalize on and posit an immutable philosophical paradigm for the world view of members of that culture— dead, living and unborn. The religious practices and beliefs which have been used to characterize the African world view belong to an advanced neolithic phase in the development of human societies in general, a phase characterized by primitive communal social relations arising from a dependence on pastoral, subsistence, agricultural production. This stage of social evolution is the natural breeding ground of animism, totemism and their attendant profusion of ritualistic observances. Says Arnold Hauser:

> With the awareness of man's dependence on good and bad weather, on rain and sunshine, lightning and hail, plague and famine, on the fertility or infertility of the earth and abundance or meagerness of litters, arises the conception of all kinds of demons and spirits—the beneficent and malignant—distributing blessings and curses . . . The world is divided into two halves; man himself seems divided into two halves. This is the phase of animism, of spirit-worship, of belief in the survival of the soul and the cult of the dead.[12]

The similarities which Soyinka has noted between the rituals of Ogun worship and those of Dionysos are best grasped in such socio-economic terms. By positing these practices in a specific evolutionary context, however, one is not suggesting the animistic religion and the modes of perception attendant on it are things of the past in Africa. On the contrary, the reality of contemporary African experience is the active co-existence of a pre-scientific mode of perceiving reality with a modernizing tendency. This corresponds to the co-existence of pre-literate communal agricultural village societies with modern industrial urban centers; the former with its herbalists, shrines, hoes, etc. and the latter complete with its computers, Mercedes cars and skyscrapers. And this is largely the case in most societies of the world, for at no point in time does a given national or transnational society attain a perfect uniformity in mode of production and world view. If this happens, such a society or culture is ready for a change into its antithesis. One must of course concede the preponderance of pre-scientific (traditional) modes of existence and experience with modern modes in contemporary Africa. According to Wiredu,

> Contemporary African societies are still largely traditional in the anthropological sense. Nevertheless, it is important for the future that the significance of the current processes of modernisation in Africa should be realised not only in terms of material changes, but also in terms of intellectual developments.[13]

From this perspective, it is undialectical to insist on an African world view as a static irreducible.

Against the foregoing background, therefore, it is my contention that the entire concept of an African world view—immutable, undifferentiated in time and space—is a mythical and illusory concept propagated and popularized to satisfy the hunger of African bourgeois intellectuals for an ideological sanctuary in the face of incessant harassments from a Western intelligentsia socialized by the exploits of their forefathers into thinking of other peoples, especially Africans, as inherently inferior.

The reality of the African situation must be rigorously confronted in its dynamic multivalence by a dialectical intelligence equipped with an acute sense of history. To drown oneself in a so-called African world view that thrives on romanticizations and complex rationalizations of bygone days is the height of a nihilistic narcissism which has nothing to do with defending one's African identity and dignity. It is, in addition, to lag behind the African masses themselves who, in their rural poverty and urban squalor and dispossession, are progressively losing confidence in gods, shrines and amulates that have no answers to rising costs of imported food, drugs, electricity and even the schnapps used in pouring libation to the gods. Fanon realized the limitation of an unrelenting obsession with a retrogressive conception of tradition and put the matter quite pointedly and analogically in the following quotes:

> All the proofs of a wonderful Songhai civilization will not change the fact that today Songhais are underfed and illiterate, thrown between sky and water with empty heads and empty eyes.[14]

> It is not enough to try to get the people back to that past out of which they have already emerged, rather we must join them in that fluctuating movement which they are just giving shape to.[15]

In spite of its myriad flaws, however, the notion of an African world view has informed an impressive body of aesthetic pronouncements on African literature which also embody the basic contradictions inherent in that philosophical proposition.

Pitfalls of traditionalist aesthetics

The indeterminacy and ambiguity inherent in the very concept of an African world view also bedevil attempts to distil an aesthetic from that world view. The resultant traditionalist aesthetics is from the outset, therefore, prodigal proposition. The concept *tradition* which informs our subsequent characterization of the aesthetics in question needs initial clarification. Traditionalist thought in Africa and elsewhere describes a pre-scientific mode of perceiving reality, explaining events and seeking to effect changes in the objective world through subjective (often magical) impulses uncorrected by rational enquiry. Thus the term traditional in this context is not a temporal category but a modal one; it is a way of saying that traditionalist thought and perception, although a dominant mode in pre-colonial African societies, still features in post-colonial Africa and can be identified in specific formations even within advanced industrialized societies.

Against this background, the contradiction inherent in traditionalist aesthetics of African literature can be identified in three dominant tendencies:

1. a pseudo-universalist idealism which takes a pan-Africanist view of African literature and seeks to see that literature in terms of a universal world culture;

2. a narrow ethnocentric particularism which distils the aesthetic values of a particular ethnic culture and uses knowledge derived therefrom to pontificate on African literature and art;

3. a crusading neo-negritudist polemic that correctly identifies the need for the decolonization of African literature but conceives of

that process in romantic idealist terms to the exclusion of the vital determinants of culture.

The first tendency is the product of an adulteration of the recognition of the specificity and peculiarity of African culture with a liberal universalist conception of literature and art. Stanley Macebuh, in his otherwise brilliant essay, "African Aesthetics in Traditional African Art,"[16] typifies the main liabilities of this tendency. Probably because of a certain intellectual socialization into the best traditions of Western liberal idealist aesthetics, Macebuh attempts to define and situate the aesthetic referent of traditional African figurative and verbal arts in the realm of what amounts to Platonic ideals:

> What the artist seeks to represent in the sculpted figure is his direct apprehension of the ideal, mediated by an oppressive sense of the real, for the "real" is not merely phenomenological, but embraces . . . the mind of God.[17]

Which God (Stanley)? It is perhaps permissible to impose a rationalist-idealist order on the African world. But to proceed therefrom and impose the Christian God to preside over "order" in the African world, is, to say the least a veritable abomination. There is no single God in whose image the African was sculpted (or molded) nor is there a static monolithic conception of "the Ideal" or the real to which the African creative imagination aspires. What existed, and still exists, is the individual artist's active perception of reality defined in terms of the dialectics of social experience in his or her particular community. This perception was livened and given concrete artistic form as an expression of the artist's perennial commitment to the process of change and to the advancement of the consciousness of his or her society.

Macebuh's essay contains several other interesting off-hand generalizations about traditional literary art in particular which deserve quoting at some length:

> Traditional African narrative tends to be fluid, repetitious, incantatory, even "structureless," but far from being formless, it seeks indeed to recapture through . . . direct mimesis, the oceanic infinitude and the interpenetration of things in the universe.[18]

> In traditional African literature, content, theme and subject matter had often to conform to the facts of immediate experience, structure, organization, and meaning derived ultimately from a metaphysical consciousness.[19]

A much more disarming feature of this aspect of traditionalist aesthetics is its innocence of the inevitable socio-political implication of all artistic undertakings. In his essay, "An African Literary Aesthetic: A Prolegomena" (sic), Charles Nnolim contributes to the ongoing debate by arguing for an African literary renaissance sanitized of politics and political commitment, features which he sees as the source of the "trouble" with contemporary African literature. Hear Nnolim:

> African literature as it is written today is maggot-ridden to the core: it is flawed by the very nature of its concerns, for it is, in the main, *littérature engagée*, and committed literature has a way of dying a natural death— certain to be dulled and dimmed by the fog of time when the issues it fought over are no longer current.[20]

> African nationalism should be a-political and should only be a nationalism that celebrates and revitalizes African oral tradition and its folkways. Such nationalism, therefore, should shun all the "isms" of modern political, economic, social and ideological struggles.[21]

Much as Nnolim's pronouncements speak for themselves, it would be necessary to ask whether in fact the age-long marriage between literature and politics has ever been dissolved. From the Homeric epics to the medieval morality play; from Elizabethan theatre to romantic poetry; from the literature of the Chinese cultural revolution to Russian socialist realism; from the literature of negritude to that of the Harlem renaissance; from African cultural nationalist literature to the most contemporary, anti-imperialist writings, has literature ever parted company with politics? Nationalism itself is a term that belongs squarely in the realm of politics. For an African professor of literature to speak of "artistic nationalism" without political content is anachronistic and tragic to say the least.

In this universalist idealist formation of the African aesthetic movement, a note of relief emerges in the writings Isidore Okpewho. In his highly informative essay, "The Aesthetics of Old African Art,"[22] Okpewho recognizes the compulsive social predication of traditional African art as well as the dynamic relationship between the artist and his society:

> In view of . . . the traditional society's pressing sense of the real, the desire to have "the inapprehensible world grasped", it seems logical to suggest that it has human experience as its fundamental frame of reference . . . the traditional African artist is then first and foremost a realist artist.[23]

> I have chosen to see the traditional African artist as an active mind operating in a dynamic context.[24]

Perhaps Okpewho's most crucial contribution to the debate on traditional aesthetics consists of his recognition of the dialectical essence of tradition itself as "a pattern of growth rather than a rigid invariable."

The second traditionalist aesthetics—that of elevating a particular ethnic mythology into a continental imperative—finds expression in Wole Soyinka's *Myth, Literature and the African World*. Soyinka's theoretical intervention in the question of Africa's position in world culture and civilization is partly a direct response to the romanticist and retrospective fixations of writers like Cheik Anta Diop who had relied almost solely on ethnological evidence to support their equally rigorous re-mythificiation of the African world and essence. Unlike Anta Diop, however, Soyinka insists on a process of racial apprehension rooted in myth. As Okpewho remarks, "[from] Soykinka's point of view this is the inward eye of mythic essence, which probes more deeply into the springs of a people's cultural life than anything we can derive from feeble archival resources."[25]

More specifically, Soyinka writes in response to promptings from two "hostile" and, in his view, equally insidious ideological camps: firstly, there are the "radicals" and "sophisticates" (African and non-African)—who maintain that traditionalist cultural reaffirmation is a reactionary diversion. Secondly and more immediately, he writes to address and confront that kind of racist arrogance which has continued to blind the English academic (especially at Oxford and Cambridge) to the specificity of the African world.

> This volume . . . is engaged in what should be the simultaneous act of eliciting from history, mythology and literature, for the benefit of both genuine aliens and alienated Africans, a continuing process of self-apprehension whose temporary dislocation appears to have persuaded many of its non-existence or its irrelevance . . . in contemporary world reality.[26]

The underlying assumption of the book, therefore, is the existence of an African world view, a homogeneous, immutable and eternal metaphysics by which Africa can be distinguished from the West in particular. This idealist construct is here elevated into a cultural mini-catechism which is adumbrated with relentless fervor and articulated in a characteristically turgid idiom.

Predictably, the notion of an African world view on which Soyinka predicates his aesthetic pronouncements in this book is a familiar landscape to those who are conversant with his obsession with the mythic realm. In *Myth, Literature and the African World*, a metasocial, transhistorical and mythic "reality" is juxtaposed with the phenomenological universe of everyday prosaic reality. A combination of both levels of "reality" is posited as the African sense of the real and the essence of the African world view. In the resultant world, man, nature and supernatural agencies are united in a complex cosmogonic design in which the laws of logic and causality peter out into irrelevance. Man is primarily a spiritual being and his social experience is submerged in ritual. Accordingly, conventional notions of space and time are dissolved in an oceanic continuum that denies periodicity and specificity to human experience and action. The lineal progression of events is replaced by a cyclic determinism: "Traditional thought operates, not a linear conception of time, but a cyclic reality."[27]

At the level of what remains of social reality, human existence is perpetually haunted by a plethora of ominous forebodings from the ever-present world of ancestors. Explanations for human action or for mishaps are to be sought from the great beyond through oracles. Most interestingly, human action is portrayed as in blind obedience to subliminal impulses radiating from the cosmic *will* of some god. Like in the world of the ancient Greeks as recreated by Nietzsche, human character is to be understood in terms of fixed *types* deducible from the peculiar attributes of different gods in the ethnic pantheon. For Soyinka, the metaphysical models for human action are furnished by numerous deities in the Yoruba pantheon. This quality, the immanence of divine purpose in human essence, constitutes for him an invariable attribute of the African world which has been lost modern Western man:

> In Asian and European antiquity . . . man did, like the African, exist within a cosmic totality, did possess a consciousness in which his own earth being, his gravity-bound apprehension of self, was inseparable from the entire cosmic phenomenon.[28]

In addition to the essentially Yoruba-centeredness of Soyinka's "African World" and its resultant dramatic theory, there is a disturbingly paradoxical Eurocentrism about Soyinka's conceptualization of the metaphysical identity of Yoruba deities. This is in the sense that he delights in finding equivalents between key Yoruba gods and ancient Greek gods. It is this obsession with cross-cultural equivalents that informs his adaptation of Euripides' *The Bacchae*, an obsession which is theoretically illuminated and concretized in his essay. "The Fourth Stage": "Ogun . . . is best understood in Hellenic values as a totality of the Dionysian, Appollonian and Promethean virtues."[29] What is here being questioned is no Soyinka's right to perceive equivalents among cultures but the idea of legitimizing African deities by matching them with the gods of the ancestors of Europeans.

The crucial challenge for Soyinka, however, seems to be one of distinguishing a peculiarly African mode perceiving and apprehending reality which will necessarily differ from what we have come to associate with the West (and here there are echoes of the ugly controversy: Is there anything like African philosophy?). In an attempt to see this quality in a certain "irrational" cast of mind, Soyinka falls into the familiar Senghorian trap of dismissing rational, philosophical and logical thinking as part of the reification and dehumanization of Western man. This rather unfortunate argument comes out when he tries to distinguish between Western and African dramatic traditions:

> The serious divergences between a traditional African approach to drama and the European . . . will be found more accurately in what is a recognisable Western cast of mind, a compartmentalising habit of thought which periodically selects aspects of human emotion, phenomenal observations, metaphysical intuitions and even scientific deductions and turns them into separatist myths (or "truths") sustained by a proliferating super-structure of presentation idioms, analogies and analytical modes.[30]

Implicit in this assertion is a certain romanticization of the African mind as non-rational but capable of "cohesive understanding of irreducible truths." And here the wheel has come full cycle, for the neo-negritudist, neo-nationalist has begun to speak the language of Levi-Bruhl!

If one is sufficiently courageous to penetrate Soyinka's linguistic barrier, and resist the rhetorical seductiveness of his prose and the sheer eclectic expanse of his erudition, we come face to face with the pitfall of his brand of traditionalist myth-making. We can safely itemize these shortcomings as contained in *Myth, Literature* as follows.

a) The excessive fixation on myth blurs the historical predication of myth itself.

b) History is almost totally excluded in the attempt to polarize mythic reality and prosaic reality.

c) There is a certain dissonance between the Yoruba-centeredness of the ethnographic evidence and the Pan-Africanist reference of the book itself.

d) In the attempt to project an undifferentiated African cultural continuum, Soyinka dissolves the obvious contradictions in consciousness that we find in African literature in a general sea of apprehension. Consequently, obvious ideological and class divergences between writers are omitted or conveniently ignored in this fixation with continental/race retrieval.

Our quest for a definitive, coherent and systematic articulation of the aims and methods of traditionalist aesthetics leads to the doorstep of the third formation of the intellectual fashion itself—that represented by the troika of Chinweizu, Jemie and Madubuike. The now familiar book, *Toward the Decolonization of African Literature*, is the manifesto of this formation. The absence of history in the earlier formations is remedied here by situating the quest for an authentic African literary aesthetic in the context of decolonization, which is now posited as a cultural challenge in a purely superstructural sense:

> The cultural task in hand is to end all foreign domination of African culture, to systematically destroy all encrustations of colonial and slave mentality, to clear the bushes and stake out new foundations for a liberated African modernity.[31]

The warning shots of this thesis had earlier been fired in Chinweizu's deservedly controversial book, *The West and the Rest of Us*:

> A modern African culture, whatever else it might be, must be a continuation of old African culture. Whatever else it includes, it must include seminal and controlling elements from the African tradition, elements which determine its tone, hold it together, and give it a stamp of distinctness.[32]

This thesis is later adumbrated into the catechism of the troika in the later book.

It is important to preface our observations on the limitations of this "important" book with certain qualifications about its significance in African cultural scholarship. Firstly, it is the first systematic fairly incisive identification of the ills of modern African literary creativity and its criticism. In this regard, it punctures the naked under-belly of bourgeois criticism of African literature. More crucially, because of its intrinsic recognition of the fact that artistic values are often geo-politically and racially determined, it distinguishes between Afrocentric and Eurocentric values in matters of literary taste and thereby deflates the bogey of liberal humanist universalism. For an African audience, the crucial import of the book belongs in the psycho-affective domain of cultural perception and consumption in the sense that the authors earnestly, even if idealistically, ginger their African audience to shake of their Eurocentricity.

Beyond the foregoing admissions, however, the ideological and theoretical shortcomings of the book (which are legion) need to be highlighted if only for the purpose of advancing its ostensibly noble cause. The following critique of the positions in the book in question must be seen as an attempt to promote meta-criticism and the history of ideas in African scholarship. In short, *certain ideas come into being, enjoy prominence and fade out of fashion because of certain determinate socio-historical conditions. It is the responsibility of committed scholarship to identify these moments and conditions so that intellectual fashions and schools occupy their rightful historical positions. Reality can then be confronted with the tools of new ideas.*

Again, for purposes of clarity, we can itemize the pitfalls of the Chinweizu et al. contribution to traditionalist aesthetics as contained in *Toward the Decolonization of African Literature* in particular:

a) The pursuit of cultural (literary) decolonization rests on the false assumption that economic and political decolonization have been completed. It is common knowledge that the cultural domination of Africa by the West is only a symptom of a more fundamental domination. The interconnection between economic and cultural domination on one hand and liberation on the other is only hinted at but not articulated in clear structural terms. Cultural imperialism is only an outward superstructural manifestation of economic imperialism. The crucial task before Africa is economic liberation which will in turn encourage a liberated literary culture. Existence (economics) precedes essence (literature). This dialectic is apparently alien to the authors of this book.

b) The posting of Afrocentric values vis-à-vis Eurocentric values is undialectical. It negates the internal differences and putative heterogeneity of the two opposing geo-cultural zones. What is actually being juxtaposed and opposed are traditional (pre-colonial African animistic values versus bourgeois Western values). Values in Africa and the West are group and class values and are in turn dynamic and historical.

c) There is a certain hypersensitivity to the Western hegemony that leads to a romanticization of the traditional African literary heritage. Negritude is smuggled back in through the back door under the guise of irreverent rhetoric.

d) In turn, tradition itself is conceived of in rather static terms. Again, it is obvious that the forces that are responsible for the shaping of a given tradition often lie outside the tradition itself. Similarly, whether modern African literature should be *traditionalist* in a pre-colonial sense is the function of a complex of factors primarily predicated on the nature of social experiences that constitute the motivation and content of literature. The kind of mechanical experimentation with tradition which the troika advocate will result in simulated, synthetic art.

e) The conception of the political commitment of the writer which emerges from this book is extremely indeterminate and diffuse and smacks of familiar liberal equivocation:

> None can decide for the writer, as none can decide for the cook, the teacher, the soldier, doctor, merchant, lawyer ... or politician. Each would have to decide which cause to serve by donation of

his or her skill . . . [The writer] can defend or attack the state, if that is where his impulse leads him.[33]

Political commitment is one thing; artistic profundity is another. Political commitment is socio-historically determined. In certain social situations, some writers end up being irrelevant or plain traitors of their people.

f) In its pan-Africanist aspiration, the book does not give sufficient attention to the reality of individual national literatures which constitutes the most advanced stage in the evolution of African literature to date. Fanon had seen the danger signal implicit in this particular deficiency when he said that:

> [The] historical necessity in which the men of African culture find themselves to racialize their claims and to speak more of African culture than of national culture will tend to lead them up a blind alley.[34]

Nor do the troika give sufficient attention to the regional and ethno-national contradictions and variations in African literary consciousness.

g) There is also the erroneous impression that cultural/literary renaissance is a self-generating phenomenon which can be pursued in its own terms and by itself. Whatever literary culture in the Western Renaissance itself bred was the logical outcome of decisive alterations in the economic, social and political orientations of Europe. Elizabethan drama, for instance, was merely the cultural expression of the economic proposition symbolized by the Medicis or the increased secularization of political life represented by Queen Elizabeth I. Elsewhere in the world, where there has been a literary renaissance of the scope advocated by the troika, such a renaissance has always formed part of far-reaching changes at the political and economic levels. The literary harvest and the democratization of literary consumption that accompanied the Chinese revolution were organic outgrowths of the Chinese revolution. Similarly, movements like Russian formalism and socialist realisms, respectively, were products of developments in Russian revolution of 1917.

What are the ideological, socio-economic and political predicators of the traditionalist aesthetic renaissance being advocated by Chinweizu et al.? Is the task in hand strictly that of cultural decolonization? Can a dependent neo-colonial economy sustain a decolonized literary culture?

From the foregoing observations we can hazard certain tentative conclusions about the present hegemonic status of the kind of ideas expressed in *Toward the Decolonization of African Literature*. It would appear that the situation of complete cultural decolonization which it envisages would ordinarily flow from a situation of economic and political freedom, for it is not possible to achieve a decolonized literary culture in an atmosphere of imperialist tutelage.

It therefore needs to be said, and quite pointedly too, that for all its pseudo-radical posturing, its affected irreverence and its revisionist fervor, *Toward the Decolonization of African Literature* remains a fatally flawed book. Its cardinal premise is suspended on a precarious idealist proposition—that culture can be sequestered from its economic and political moorings. Its emotional appeal is founded on a dying anti-racist racism; its idea of tradition is static while its notion of society is undialectical. It is the kind of fundamentalist cultural nationalism which is capable of diverting the minds of the young and the young-at-heart from perceiving the integral nature of cultural struggles in the larger struggles for economic freedom and social justice which currently stare Africa in the face.

Most dangerously, there is a certain intellectual and theoretical superficiality and philistinism about this book which is deliberately submerged in pugilistic phraseology and an unnecessarily quarrelsome tone. Ultimately, the book is in fact a very *colonial* book in the sense that it defines the African world in decadent animistic terms, thus advocating for African an image based on backward integration, which is the staple diet of European racist mythology. It is no wonder then that Chinweizu et al. have had only a nuisance value in African cultural scholarship. Nor could they be said to have influenced any writers or critics of note. Their book is ultimately mythic and its brand of myth-making is good only for the Black-Power-mongering, fist-clenching adolescent and for the lazy intellectual unwilling to apply himself rigorously to the real challenge of an intellectual calling.

All the foregoing formations of traditionalist aesthetics are united by a common fundamental historical ideational dislocation. They fail to recognize that in all traditional societies, theorizing about aesthetics was not a distinct social undertaking divorced from the consumption and creation of art. Says Terry Eagleton of the rise of aesthetics as a discipline:

> Previously, men and women had written poems, staged plays or painted pictures for a variety of purposes, while others had read, watched or viewed them in a variety of ways. Now these concrete, historically variable practices were being subsumed into some special mysterious faculty known as the "aesthetic."

> Art was extricated from the material practices, social relations and ideological meanings in which it is always caught up, and raised to the status of a solitary fetish.[35]

The rise of traditionalist aesthetics in African literary discourse must also be seen as part of a general process of reification which has little to do with faithfulness to traditional artistic practice in its original manifestation.

The abiding significance of traditionalist aesthetics however resides in its contribution to the necessary task of imparting more knowledge about African artistic traditions, ethno-philosophies and extant aesthetic value systems to an indifferent world while imbuing the ignorant and miseducated African with greater confidence to understand both himself and the position of his mortally injured race in the world. But the crucial task of compelling the world, especially the West, to recognize Africa through its practical achievements demands more than self-definition and rhetorical reaffirmation. Accordingly, in the area of culture, it calls for a theoretical framework in which the absolutist separation between idea and praxis is finally banished. We need a theoretical framework which would seek to integrate cultural liberation into the larger struggle for economic and political liberation. In this regard, a dialectical theory of African literature, corrected by an anti-imperialist ideological stance, seems most suited for consolidating the gains of traditionalist aesthetics and transcending its particular limitations to a greater understanding of the African reality.

Notes

1 Ngugi wa Thiong'o, *Writers in Politics* (London: Heinemann, 1982), 25.
2 Odia Ofeimun, *The Poet Lied* (London: Longman, 1982), 35.
3 Chinweizu, Onwuchekwa Jemie, and Ihechukwu Madubuike, *Toward the Decolonization of African Literature* (Enugu: Fourth Dimension, 1980).
4 Wole Soyinka, *Myth, Literature and the African World* (Cambridge: Cambridge University Press, 1976).
5 Bernth Lindfors, "The Blind Men and the Elephant," *African Literature Today* 7 (1974): 63.
6 See, for instance Levi-Bruhl's *The Primitive Mentality* and also, with some modifications, Robin Horton's essay, "African Traditional Thought and Western Science," in *Rationality*, ed. B. R. Wilson (Oxford: Basil Blackwell, 1970).
7 John Mbiti, *African Religions and Philosophy* (London: Heinemann, 1969).
8 Lemuel A. Johnson, Bernadette Cailler, Russell Hamilton, and Mildred Hill-Lubin, ed, *Toward Defining the African Aesthetic* (Washington, DC: Three Continents Press, 1982).
9 Kwasi Wiredu, *Philosophy and African Culture* (Cambridge: Cambridge University Press, 1976).
10 Kofi Awoonor, *The Breast of the Earth* (New York/Enugu: NOK, 1975), 51.
11 Ibid.
12 Arnold Hauser, *The Social History of Art*, vol. I, trans. Stanley Godman (London: Routledge & Kegan Paul, 1977) 11.

13 Wiredu, *Philosophy and African Culture*, 38.
14 Frantz Fanon, *The Wretched of the Earth* (Harmondsworth: Penguin, 1967), 168.
15 Ibid., 183.
16 Stanley Macebuh, "African Aesthetics in Traditional African Art," *Okike* 5 (1974): 13–25.
17 Ibid., 15.
18 Ibid., 20.
19 Ibid.
20 Charles E. Nnolim, "An African Literary Aesthetic: A Prolegema," *Ba Shiru* 17 (1976): 71.
21 Ibid., 61–2.
22 Isidore Okpewho, "The Aesthetics of Old African Art," *Okike* 8 (1975): 38–55.
23 Isidore Okpewho, "The Principles of Traditional African Art," *The Journal of Aesthetics & Art Criticism* 35:3 (1977): 305.
24 Ibid., 311.
25 Isidore Okpewho, *Myth in Africa* (Cambridge: Cambridge University Press, 1985), 242.
26 Soyinka, *Myth, Literature and the African World*, xi.
27 Ibid., 10.
28 Ibid., 3.
29 Ibid., 41.
30 Ibid., 37.
31 Chinweizu et al., *Toward the Decolonization of African Literature*, 1.
32 Chinweizu, *The West and the Rest of Us* (Lagos: NOK, 1978), 298.
33 Chinweizu et al., *Toward the Decolonization of African Literature*, 254.
34 Fanon, *The Wretched of the Earth*, 172.
35 Terry Eagleton, *Literary Theory: An Introduction* (Oxford: Blackwell, 1983), 21.

CHAPTER TWENTY TWO

Marxist Literary Theory, Then and Now

Imre Szeman

From Mediations *24 (2) (Spring 2009): 37–47.*

Neither is philosophy turning to advantage the approach of that professor who, in the pre-Fascist era, experienced an urge to rectify the ills of the times, and examined Marlene Dietrich's film, The Blue Angel, *in order to obtain, at first hand, an idea of how bad things really were. Excursions of that kind into tangible realities turn philosophy into the refuse of history, with the subject-matter of which it is confused, in the manner of a fethisistic belief in culture per se.*

THEODOR ADORNO "WHY PHILOSOPHY?"[1]

"Traditional" Marxism, if "untrue" during this period of a proliferation of new subjects of history, must necessarily become true again when the dreary realities of exploitation, extraction of surplus value, proletarianization, and the resistance to it in the form of class struggle, all slowly reassert themselves on a new and expanded world scale, as they seem currently in the process of doing.

FREDRIC JAMESON "PERIODIZING THE 60s"[2]

What has Marxism contributed to literary criticism? And what does its encounter with literature in the twentieth century mean for the directions that Marxist criticism might take in the twenty-first? These are huge questions—too large for a short paper; to answer them properly would require, to begin with, some assessment of the state of various Marxisms today (whatever existence they eke out here and there) as well as the situation in which the profession of literary criticism finds itself. Nevertheless, I thought it might be useful to take the subject head-on, however briefly—a sketch with inevitable gaps, but one that could offer a starting point to the project of filling in the bigger picture.

There is no such thing as *a* Marxist literary criticism: no established approaches, no clear methodology, no agreed-upon ideas about how to approach a text or what count as appropriate texts to read, or, indeed, no clearly established sense of why one might expend energy on literary analysis to begin with. It is difficult even to establish a core set of interests and commitments that mark it off from other forms of literary criticism. Marxist literary criticism need not make reference back to Marx (who liked Shakespeare but didn't discuss literature in relation to historical materialism); it certainly doesn't deal with a stock set of questions or topics—say, class or labor, in the way sometimes imagined in introductory texts on literary criticism. There are numerous modes of Marxist criticism related to one another through a theoretical family resemblance and perhaps a shared, general political outlook. The taxonomies of Marxist approaches offered by Raymond Williams, Terry Eagleton, and others not only differ from one another, but show enough internal variation as to leave things confused in the extreme. For the form of Marxist criticism which Eagleton, for instance, calls "economic"—a category including such things as the sociology of literature and book history—words in books don't really matter, or at least aren't the primary source of literature's social and political function and importance. But for the other forms of criticism he discusses, from social realism to *Ideologiekritik*, the marks on the page that are the typical focus of literary criticism are the main things to be assessed and analyzed.

There are, it seems to me, three primary forms or modes of intervention that Marxist literary criticism has taken, especially since the 1920s, beginning with the early work of Adorno, Benjamin, Bloch, Lukács, and others. These modes of Marxist criticism have changed in content, but less so in form—though the conditions under which they are practiced and carried out have changed, a fact not always reflected within newer practices of Marxist criticism, which make use of (say) the old insistence on the relation of literary form to social form even while the former has declined in importance and the latter has been reshaped in response to new forces and historical circumstances. Hopefully, spelling out these three modes can help to show us where Marxist literary criticism stands today and what might be on the horizon.

In perhaps its most simple and basic form, Marxist criticism has taken the form of a series of methodological criticisms and challenges to existing forms of criticism. These are reminders of what to do or not to do—to "Always historicize," for example, or to remember the centrality of class struggle and the determining role of the forces and relations of production to social life and to literary and cultural production. Such critical imperatives are meant to shape literary criticism as such, pulling it away from idealist forms of historicism and formalism and toward a commitment to the social character of literary writing. In *Marxism and Literature*, Williams remarks that "'Marxist criticism' and 'Marxist literary studies' have been most successful . . . when they have worked with the received category of 'literature', which they may have extended or even revalued, but never radically questioned or opposed."[3] Adorno on Mann, Lukács on Scott, Jameson on Gissing, Schwarz on Brás Cubas: each of these analyses might introduce new insights into the objects and authors being studied, but they still largely take the form of learned commentaries of objects known in advance for being ones filled with significance and in need of study with the tools of literary analysis. Here, Marxism piggybacks on received definitions of literature and literary study in a manner that defines it as a theoretical approach to texts—one of a handful which can be substituted for one another depending on context or even an individual critic's analytic sensibilities.

The second mode of Marxist criticism builds on the impulse of this first, but extends it significantly. Here, the received category of literature around which institutional practices such as professional organizations and university departments are organized is scrutinized and placed into question. Marxism has at the core of its theory and practice the analysis of history and of the shifts that take place within it; it assumes that the economic is ("in the last instance") of prime importance in how human social life is organized. With respect to literature and literary criticism, it thus tries to understand the existing social and political function of these practices by mapping out the manner in which they have developed and changed over time—that is, both how these practices themselves have changes *and* shifts in their social and political function. This is a form of metatheory: a view of the status and practice of the literary in general which focuses more on social form than on aesthetic content; it is something akin to a history of ideas traced out within materialist philosophy. Williams and others remind us that literature developed into "an apparently objective category of printed works of a certain quality" out of something more inchoate, something once linked to reading ability and not limited to creative or imaginative works defined by taste or sensibility.[4] But beyond this acknowledgment of definitional shifts with the category of literature is an insistence on the politics of literature in relation to larger social developments: "*Literature and criticism* are, in the perspective of historical social development, forms of a class specialization and control of a general social practice, and of a class limitation on the questions which it might raise."[5]

If the first mode of Marxist criticism introduces more complex forms of literary analysis into existing forms of criticism, the second aims to shatter the self-certainties of literary analysis by insisting on the ways in which culture and power are necessarily bound together, perhaps especially so in the constitution of literary criticism as a practice. Terry Eagleton has written that "Nobody is much bothered by materialist readings of *Titus Andronicus* . . . but a materialist theory of culture—a theory of culture as production before it is expression—sounds, in the spontaneously idealist milieu of middle-class society, something of a category mistake or a contradiction in terms."[6] The most important intervention made by cultural criticism in the twentieth century—and not just in Marxism, but in the work of scholars from Thorstein Veblen to Pierre Bourdieu—was to desacralize and demythologize ideas of literature and culture, highlighting the social and political violence which shaped the consecration of these categories into practices immediately associated with transcendent value; the insistence on culture as always already a form of production is only the beginning of this effort. While political reflections on the category of literature and culture itself have contributed to the practice of literary criticism, they have just as frequently pushed critical analysis in other directions—toward sociological approaches to literature and culture (the latest of which is exemplified by the work of Franco Moretti) or to the study of numerous other modes of cultural expression and practice. Challenges to the institutions of literary analysis make it—or at least should make it—hard to continue with criticism as usual.

"Culture for Marxism is at once absolutely vital and distinctly secondary: the place where power is crystallized and submission bred, but also somehow 'superstructural', something which in its more narrow sense of specialized artistic institutions can only be fashioned out of a certain economic surplus and division of labor, and which even in its more generous anthropological sense of a 'form of life' risks papering over certain important conflicts and distinctions."[7] This tension lies at the heart of most forms of Marxist criticism that deal with culture as opposed to economics, politics, or the social. Culture is an object of suspicion as a result of its structural function and, indeed, its very existence, but is also a field which requires critical study—and not just because of its ideological function (to which Eagleton points here), but because it is also imagined as a space in which the crystallization of power can be interrupted or halted, and submission turned into autonomy and genuine self-expression. If literature and culture were simply the space of ideological expression, if ideology was simply false consciousness or a blunt substitute for religion, they wouldn't create such headaches and problems for Marxist criticism. Rather, culture is also imagined within Marxism as a space of political possibilities and alternative imaginings—not "politics by other means" in any simple and direct way, but also not ultimately separable from politics.

Marxism may be "deeply suspicious of the cultural, which it views as in the end the offspring of labor, as well as, often enough, a disownment of it," but it also can't give up on culture or literature.[8] The longstanding anxieties within Marxism about what Herbert Marcuse called "affirmative culture" or what others name as "instrumental culture" aren't meant to close down the horizon of possibility offered by culture, but to show the enormous difficulties for criticism in addressing culture without participating in its reification and instrumentalization. Adorno's worries in "Cultural Criticism and Society" and elsewhere echo those of Marcuse: both worry about the tendency of criticism to be interested in culture because of its links with the spiritual and the transcendent.[9] "Man does not live by bread alone; this truth is thoroughly falsified by the interpretation that spiritual nourishment is an adequate substitute for too little bread"; and Marcuse again: "The culture of souls absorbed in a false form those forces and wants which could find no place in everyday life."[10] The challenge for Marxist criticism has been to name or identify alternative or antagonistic forms of life expressed in culture, while keeping the lie also named by culture firmly in mind. A difficult task: playing with and against the false autonomy of culture established by bourgeois social life since the late eighteenth century. The criticism of the past several decades, whether looked at individually or as a whole, has taken this challenge up with more or less rigor, but without any coherent plan of attack. With respect to literature, some forms of criticism have sought to separate out reified forms of culture from other, more revolutionary forms; in many cases this has reflected existing taxonomies, with (say) mass culture being seen as the most ideological, and forms of experimental or explicitly political literature being seen as having escaped instrumentalization and so having special significance (Jameson speaks of modernism in this fashion, even if at other points he insists on the opposite point). Marxist criticism which places wagers on the utopian dimension of this or that novel or genre—"serious" science fiction, for instance—seems to forget the second mode to which I've pointed concerning the political and economic conditions of possibility of literary writing *and* criticism, with the effect being a curious, uncritical acceptance of (for instance) writerly aims and intentions, and of the category of the literary more generally.

More interestingly, other forms of Marxist criticism have imagined that it is "possible to find the material history which produces a work of art somehow inscribed in its very texture and structure, in the shape of its sentences or its play of narrative viewpoints, in its choice of a metrical scheme or its rhetorical device."[11] This is to use symbolic responses to an objective historical situation as a way to read back through to those circumstances, whether in a direct, unmediated form, or perhaps with the added bonus that inscribed in symbolic forms is some hint of the Real or the social unconscious of a given historical period. The most powerful of these approaches is found in the work of Fredric Jameson, who famously views literature as a symbolic practice that provides imaginary and ideological solutions to unresolved sociopolitical contradictions. In Jameson's "Reification and Utopia in Mass Culture," the divide between mass and high culture is collapsed; each is now seen as a different way of managing the same set of social contradictions, thus providing materials valuable for critics who want to better understand the ways in which culture is reified.[12] It is the "utopian" content of mass culture that most readers of Jameson's essay seize on, the idea that a latent element of any form of cultural expression casts doubt on the fixity of the political present and its self-certainties. Here, the hope that culture yields political tools and insights (if not transcendence of an older, spiritual kind) is tied together with a more sociological, institutional approach: one gets the rewards of literary criticism while approaching things from a Marxist perspective. What's still left out of the picture is how and why certain forms of culture might be seen to escape the instrumentalization that worried the Frankfurt School. If everything has a utopian content (even if perhaps only in the minimal sense outlined by Williams: "*No mode of production and therefore no dominant social order and therefore no dominant culture ever in reality excludes or exhausts all human practice, human energy, and human intention*"), then there's no need to make distinctions about what to study as especially significant forms of culture.[13] Literature is displaced from the center of Marxist critical concern, but in the process culture becomes a space of study primarily for what it reveals about conditions and developments at other, more socially significant levels.

If one way of addressing the crisis that affirmative culture introduces into Marxist criticism was to divide culture into serious work and junk, avant-garde modernism and mass culture, Jameson manages this problem (in part) by considering different zones of capitalism in which "culture" takes different forms. The utopia which is supposed to go hand-in-hand with reification is divided spatially, with utopia being displaced from the West to the rest. Already in the "Reification" essay we find him introducing the idea that revolutionary cultural expressions can be found only in those places whose conditions of possibility—formal, but not yet real, subsumption into global capital—allow for forms of cultural production that don't obey the inexorable logic of affirmative culture. This spatial move is also a temporal one—it suggests (questionably) that literature and other cultural forms once lived out the political promise of their semi-autonomy from social life, before collapsing into the undifferentiated murk of instrumentality. For Jameson, the phenomenon called "globalization" seems to have eliminated this possible political opening in the gap between formal and real, so that now what we read in his work and that of other Marxist critics is an insistence on the fact that everything is now cultural—an assertion whose implications have been difficult to ascertain or to properly make sense of, perhaps especially so when it comes to the question of what it is one imagines one is doing in engaging with this or that literary text from a Marxist perspective. Everything is cultural: should we take this as a further intensification (or even dialectical transfiguration) of the drama of the spectacle to which Guy Debord alerted us, or as announcing a welcome social immanence whose outcome can be nothing other than the multitude and the commons described by Michael Hardt and Antonio Negri?

Where are we then left? The first mode is inadequate; the second, reductive; and the third, confused by the movement between the repudiation of culture as an ideological category and a belief in its potential redemptive and/or political possibilities—a politics grounded in older critical ontologies and epistemologies, even if these are troubled by Marxist categories. How, then, do we relate these approaches to literature and its potential end(s)? Literature always has a truth value of some kind. Even if its slow marginalization as a social practice has made it tempting to insist more strongly on its class basis and social untruth, it would be a mistake for Marxism to think that it is done with it once and for all. Literature still provides cognitive, utopian, or aesthetic insights, and writing itself remains a political practice—"one of the most transgressive and most easily exchanged cultural forms through which dissidence can be articulated, not least because the material prerequisites of pen and paper"—or the keyboard and the wireless connection—"are relatively easy to acquire."[14] But this persistence of literature (a persistence which finds analogs in the figures of excess animating poststructuralist philosophy or Deleuzian politics) doesn't find an easy counterpoint in Marxist literary criticism, much of which seems to me to continue to work within one of the three modes I've just outlined, if (to be ungenerous) with an increasing lack of purpose and direction. What other path could it follow? To a large degree, literary criticism has absorbed Marxism's methodological pointers and grasps the implications of its larger critique of literary institutions, even if it hasn't acted on them (here, the institutional instinct for self-preservation kicks in). As for its own attempts to grasp the strands of culture that slip out from under affirmative culture, this seems to have brought Marxist criticism back to a sense of culture as pure ideology *or* as pure political possibility, without a clear sense of which situation holds where or when, convinced of neither outcome, but energized by these breaks, gaps, and incompletions.

To get a sense of why this might be the case—and what might come next—we need to think about the historical conditions of Marxist criticism itself. More than thirty years ago, Perry Anderson diagnosed a paradigm shift in Marxism—a shift away from political practices intimately connected to the activities of parties and unions to a phenomenon he named "Western Marxism," which roughly comes into being with the work of the Frankfurt School. For Anderson, the "first and most fundamental of its characteristics has been the structural divorce of this Marxism from political practice."[15] In Western Marxism, the divide of theory and practice isn't something to be actively engaged, but has become affirmed as a given, with energies thus devoted entirely to theory at the expense of practice. Marxism shifts toward philosophy, and becomes an "ever increasing academic emplacement"; its central focus is on culture and aesthetics, particularly of the bourgeois kind; and it becomes "Western," which is to say, "utterly provincial and uninformed about the theoretical cultures of neighbouring countries."[16] For Anderson, this strain of Marxism is also characterized by a consistent pessimism as it develops "new themes absent from classical Marxism—mostly in a speculative manner."[17] "Where the founder of historical materialism moved progressively from philosophy to politics and then economics," Anderson writes, "the successors of the tradition that emerged after 1920 turned back from economics and politics to philosophy."[18]

Anderson's characterization of Western Marxism is meant to sound alarm bells about the draining of energies from what he would have understood (in 1976 at least) as a "proper" form of politics. He writes that "the hidden hallmark of Western Marxism as a whole is that it is a product of *defeat*."[19] This criticism comes at a moment in which actually-existing socialisms— even given their very real flaws and their distance from Marxist theory— presented a viable alternative to forms of liberal democratic capitalism and unionism remained a strong movement across the world. In the context of our circumstances, it is easy enough to see the depth of this defeat as something we are still in the process of coming to understand. Many of the points that Anderson makes with respect to Western Marxism seem characteristic of Marxist criticism today: it is largely divorced from political parties or even from social movements (though perhaps not at its anarchist edges); its practitioners are primarily university-based and generally accepted there as one variant of a multiplicity of critical approaches; and they are interested in philosophy more than in (say) the nitty-gritty of re-establishing an international party operating above and beyond parochial nationalisms. These points are, of course, directed at Marxist criticism in general and not just at Marxist *literary* critics, who were in relatively short supply before Lukács (despite Plekhanov and Lenin and Trotsky's writings on art and literature).

The intervening thirty years and the end of state socialism have brought about new geopolitical configurations within which Marxisms circulate, and, as such, new criteria with which to assess their political possibilities. Western Marxism looks like a defeat if one imagines politics to have to take a certain form—that which characterized Marxist and socialist movements of the late nineteenth and early twentieth centuries. The political and historical terrain has altered so much in the global era that it would be a mistake to measure success or failure on these grounds (a point made repeatedly since at least Ernesto Laclau and Chantal Mouffe's *Hegemony and Socialist Strategy*).[20] Anderson laments the break of Western Marxism with an international party and criticizes its parochialism. While there remains nothing like a new international socialist party, the palpable sense of having to frame one's political imaginings and activities in a global context ensures that the "Westernness" of Western Marxism has now dissipate—though, in part, this is because of the global circulation and re-purposing of Western Marxism in places around the globe (university-based Marxists even in Russia, Eastern Europe, and China are Western Marxists in terms of the archives they draw upon and their broad interest in culture over politics and economics). Nor does culture hold the attention of Marxist criticism as it once did, and, where it does capture critical attention, the focus is certainly not bourgeois culture alone. If anything, the shift from economics to philosophy that Anderson describes seems to have been reversed in recent years. The very absence of the socialist world (at least on its former scale) has brought the structuring force of economics to the surface in a way that has rendered its foundational role apparent to everyone: political economy is back in style. One of the real limits of Western Marxism was that despite its best intentions to do otherwise, it, too, tended to treat culture as in the end semi-autonomous from politics, and so as a space necessitating a careful mapping by those whose political commitments demanded a search for alternative social forms and imaginings. Anderson writes that while Gramsci dealt extensively with Italian literature in the *Prison Notebooks*, he "took the autonomy and efficacy of cultural superstructures as a *political* problem, to be explicitly theorized as such—in its relationship to the maintenance or subversion of the social order."[21] In this sense, we are all Gramsci now, with the difference being that the political problem with respect to culture today is, in fact, its *lack* of autonomy and efficacy, its equivalence with the political in a manner that leaves conceptions of its function as ideological or anti-ideological unhelpful and beside the point.

Western Marxism's focus on culture generated contributions to literary criticism that have been productive even for those who don't understand themselves to be Marxists. However we might assess the status of its activities—a distraction from real politics or a contribution to understanding the complexity of social signification and meaning-making without which there can be no politics—we are in new historical circumstances that have pushed Marxist criticism toward new objects of study and modes of intervention. This is an ongoing process; the three approaches to literature or culture that I described above continue to describe much of what is done under the name of Marxism. But the changed political circumstances of the present moment—one which finds capitalism under question, widespread expressions of anxiety about ecological futures, and so on—have pushed critical energies in other directions, and will continue to do so. One of the only positive things that Anderson says about Western Marxism is that it proved to be unexpectedly immune to reformism. Marxism is a theory of social and political transformation—of revolution, not evolution, since it understands that no amount of amelioration of existing political and economic frameworks will address the broad social injustices that capitalism produces. At the moment, studies of literature within universities may not be the main site for such transformations to be better understood, or actualized—which isn't the same as saying that such studies don't have any value at all.

Notes

1   Theodor Adorno, "Why Philosophy?" in *The Adorno Reader*, ed. Brian O'Connor (Oxford: Blackwell, 2000), 53.
2   Fredric Jameson, "Periodizing the 60s," in *The Ideologies of Theory, Essays 1971–1986*, Vol. 2 (Minneapolis, MN: University Minnesota Press, 1988), 208.
3   Raymond Williams, *Marxism and Literature* (Oxford: Oxford University Press, 1977), 53.
4   Williams, *Marxism and Literature* 48.
5   Williams, *Marxism and Literature* 49.
6   Terry Eagleton, "Introduction Part I" in *Marxist Literary Theory: A Reader*, ed. Terry Eagleton and Drew Milne (New York: Blackwell, 1996), 14.
7   Eagleton, "Introduction" 7.
8   Eagleton, "Introduction" 6.
9   See Theodor Adorno, "Cultural Criticism and Society," in *Prisms*, translated by Samuel Weber and Shierry Weber Nicholsen (Cambridge: MIT Press, 1997), 17–34.
10 Herbert Marcuse, *Negations: Essays in Critical Theory*, translated by Jeremy J. Shapiro (London: Free Association Books, 1988), 109–110.
11 Eagleton, "Introduction" 11.
12 See Fredric Jameson, "Reification and Utopia in Mass Culture," *Social Text* 1 (1979): 130–48.
13 Williams, *Marxism and Literature* 125.
14 Drew Milne, "Introduction Part II: Reading Marxist Literary Theory," in *Marxist Literary Theory: A Reader*, ed. Terry Eagleton and Drew Milne (New York: Blackwell, 1996), 27.
15 Perry Anderson, *Considerations on Western Marxism* (London: New Left Books, 1976), 29.
16 Anderson, *Western Marxism* 49 and 69.
17 Anderson, *Western Marxism* 93.
18 Anderson, *Western Marxism* 52.
19 Anderson, *Western Marxism* 42.
20 See Ernesto Laclau and Chantal Mouffe, *Hegemony and Socialist Strategy* (New York: Verso, 1985).
21 Anderson, *Western Marxism* 78.

CHAPTER TWENTY THREE

The Antinomies of Postmodernity

Fredric Jameson

From The Seeds of Time. *New York: Columbia University Press, 1994: 50–72.*

Even after the "end of history," there has seemed to persist some historical curiosity of a generally systemic—rather than merely anecdotal—kind: not merely to know what will happen next, but as a more general anxiety about the larger fate or destiny of our system or mode of production. On this, individual experience (of a postmodern kind) tells us that it must be eternal, while our intelligence suggests this feeling to be most improbable indeed, without coming up with plausible scenarios as to its disintegration or replacement. It seems to be easier for us today to imagine the thoroughgoing deterioration of the earth and of nature than the breakdown of late capitalism; perhaps that is due to some weakness in our imaginations.

I have come to think that the word *postmodern* ought to be reserved for thoughts of this kind. The term and its various substantives seem instead to have evolved into various partisan expressions of value, mostly turning on affirmation or repudiation of this or that vision of pluralism. But these are arguments better conducted in concrete social terms (those of the various feminisms, or the new social movements, for example). Postmodernism as an ideology, however, is better grasped as a symptom of the deeper structural changes in our society and its culture as a whole, or in other words, in the mode of production.

Inasmuch as those changes still remain tendencies, however, and out analyses of actuality are governed by the selection of what we think will persist or develop, any attempt to say what postmodernism is can scarcely be separated from the even more problematic attempt to say where it is going—in short, to disengage its contradictions, to imagine its consequences (and the consequences of those consequences), and to conjecture the shape of its agents and institutions in some more fully developed maturity of what can now at best only be trends and currents. All postmodernism theory is thus a telling of the future, with an imperfect deck.

It is conventional to distinguish an antimony from a contradiction, no least because folk wisdom implies that the latter is susceptible of a solution or a resolution, whereas the former is not. In that sense, the antimony is a cleaner form of language than the contradiction. With it, you know where you stand; it states two propositions that are radically, indeed absolutely, incompatible, take it or leave it. Whereas the contradiction is a matter of partialities and aspects—only some of it is incompatible with the accompanying proposition—indeed, it may have more to do with forces, or the state of things, than with words or logical implications. Contradictions are supposed, in the long run, to be productive; whereas antimonies—take Kant's classic one: the world has a beginning, the world has no beginning—offer nothing in the way of a handle, no matter how diligently you turn them around and around.

Our antinomies will concern Kant's "a priori representations"; namely time and space, which we have generally come to think of in historical terms as implicit formal frames that nonetheless vary according to the mode of production. We may presumably, then, learn something about our own mode of production from the ways in which we tend to think of change and permanence, or variety and homogeneity—ways that prove to have as much to do with space as with time.

I

Time is today a function of speed, and evidently perceptible only in terms of its rate or velocity as such: as though the old Bergsonian opposition between measurement and life, clock time and lived time, had dropped out, along with that virtual eternity or slow permanence without which Valéry thought the very idea of a work of art as such was likely to die out (something he seems to have been confirmed in thinking). What emerges then is some conception of change without its opposite; and to say so is then helplessly to witness the two terms of this antinomy folding back into each other, since from the vantage point of change it becomes impossible to distinguish space from time, or object from subject. The eclipse of inner time (and its organ, the "intimate" time sense) means that we read our subjectivity off the things outside: Proust's old hotel rooms, like old retainers, respectfully reminded him every morning how old he was, and whether he was on vacation or "at home," and where—that is to say, they told him his name and issued him an identity, like a visiting card on a silver salver. As for habit, memory, recognition, material things do that for us (the way the servants were supposed to do our living, according to Villiers de l'Isle Adam). Subjectivity is an objective matter, and it is enough to change the scenery and the setting, refurnish the rooms, or destroy them in an aerial bombardment for a new subject, a new identity, miraculously to appear on the ruins of the old.

The end of the subject–object dualism, however—for which so many ideologues have yearned for so long—carries with it hidden retroparadoxes, like concealed explosives: Paul Virilio's, for example, in *War and Cinema*, which shows how the seeming speed of the outside world is itself a function of the demands of representation. Not, perhaps, the result of some new subjective idea of velocity that projects itself on to an inert exterior, as in stereotypes of classical idealism, but rather technology versus nature. The apparatus—and very specifically the photographic and filmic one—makes its own demands on reality, which, as in the Gulf War, reality then scrambles to fulfil (like a time-lapse photo in which the photographer himself can be seen breathlessly sliding into place at the end of the row of already posing faces):

> [T]he disappearance of the proximity effect in the prosthesis of accelerated travel made it necessary to create a wholly simulated appearance that would restore three-dimensionality to the message in full. Now a holographic prosthesis of the military commander's inertia was to be communicated to the viewer, extending his look in time and space by means of constant dashes, here and there, today and yesterday . . . Already evident in the flashback and then in the feedback, this miniaturisation of chronological meaning was the direct result of a military technology in which events always unfolded in theoretical time.[1]

Such a "return of the repressed" (an old-fashioned, now relatively metaphorical name for it to be sure) means that eliminating the subject does not leave us with the object *wie es eigentlich gewesen*, but rather with a multiplicity of simulacra. Virilio's point, like that of so many others today, is that it is the cinema that is the truly centered subject, perhaps indeed the only one: the Deleuzian schizo being only a confused and contradictory idea alongside this apparatus that absorbs the former's subject–object pole triumphantly into itself. But it raises the embarrassing secondary question of whether, in that case, there ever was a (centered) subject to begin with: did we ever have to wait? Is boredom a figment of the imagination along with its cousin eternity? Was there a time when things did not seem to change? What did we do before machines? All flesh is grass: and life in the ancient *polis* strikes us at the being more fragile and ephemeral than anything in the modern city, even though we ought to be able to remember how many changes this last has undergone. It is as though an illusion of slower permanence accompanies the lived present like an optical projection, masking a change that only becomes visible when it falls outside the temporal frame.

But to put it this way is to measure a gap and to assure ourselves of everything that is radically different from the modernist form-projects and the modernist "time-sense" in the postmodern dispensation, where the formerly classical has itself been unmasked as sheer fashion, albeit the fashion of a slower, vaster world that took ages to cross by caravan or caravel, and through whose thickened time, as through a viscous element, items descended so slowly as to acquire a patina that seemed to transform their contingencies into the necessities of a meaningful tradition. For a world population, the languages of Periclean Athens can no longer be any more normative than that of other tribal styles (although it is very easy to imagine a cultural United Nations Security Council operation in which the "great civilizations" pooled their various classical traditions with a view toward imposing some more generally "human" classical canon): time thereby also becomes multicultural, and the hitherto airtight realms of demography and of industrial momentum begin to seep into each other, as though there were some analogies between great crowds of people and dizzying rates of speed. Both then spell the end of the modern in some renewed and paradoxical conjunction, as when the new styles seem exhausted by virtue of their very proliferation, while their bearers, the individual creators, prophets, geniuses and seers, suddenly find themselves unwanted owing to sheer population density (if not the realization of the democratic ethos as such).

That the new absolute temporality has everything to do with the urban my references have suggested, without underscoring the requirement in that case of revising traditional notions of the urban as such, in order to accommodate its postnaturality to technologies of communication as well as of production and to mark the decentered, well-nigh global, scale on which what used to be the city is deployed. The modern still had something to do with the arrogance of city people over the provincials, whether this was a provinciality of peasants, other and colonized cultures, or simply the precapitalist past itself: that deeper satisfaction of being *absolument moderne* is dissipated when modern technologies are everywhere, there are no longer any provinces, and even the past comes to seem like an alternative world, rather than an imperfect, primitive stage of this one. Meanwhile, those "modern" city dwellers or metropolitans of earlier decades themselves came from the country or at least could still register the coexistence of uneven worlds; they could measure change in ways that become impossible once modernization is even relatively completed (and no longer some isolated, unnatural and unnerving process that stands out to the naked eye). It is an unevenness and a coexistence that can also be registered in a sense of loss, as with the slow partial changes and demolitions of Baudelaire's Paris, which almost literally serve as the objective correlative of his experience of passing time: in Proust all this, although apparently more intensely elegiac (and in any case surcharging the text of Baudelaire itself) has already been subjectivized, as though it were the self and its past that were regretted and not its houses (but Proust's language knows better: *"la muraille de l'escalier où je vis monter le reflet de sa bougie, n'existe plus depuis longtemps"*;[2] as does his spatial plot construction). Today the very meaning of demolition has been modified, along with that of building: it has become a generalized postnatural process that calls into question the very concept of change itself and the inherited notion of time that accompanied it.

These paradoxes are perhaps easier to dramatize in the philosophical and critical realm, than in the aesthetic one, let alone in urbanism as such. For demolition has surely defined the modern intellectual's vocation ever since the *ancien régime* tended to identify its mission with critique and opposition to established institutions and ideas: what better figure to characterize the strong form of the cultural intellectual from the Enlightenment *philosophies* all the way to Sartre (who has been called the last of the classical intellectuals), if not beyond? It is a figure that has seemed to presuppose an omnipresence of Error, variously defined as superstition, mystification, ignorance, class ideology and philosophical realism (or "metaphysics"), in such a way that to remove it by way of the operations of demystification leaves a space in which therapeutic anxiety goes hand in hand with heightened self-consciousness and reflexivity in a variety of senses, if not, indeed, with Truth as such. By attempting to restore, alongside this negative tradition, the intellectual's other mission of the restoration of meaning, Ricoeur sharply dramatized everything the various strands of what he called "the hermeneutics of suspicion" had in common, from the Enlightenment and its relationship to religion all the way to the destructive relationship to "Western metaphysics," emphasizing above all the three great formative moments of Marx, Nietzsche and Freud, to which even postmodern intellectuals still owe join allegiance in some form or another.

What has changed is then perhaps the character of the terrain in which these operations are carried out: just as the transitional period between aristocratic and clerical, *ancien régime* societies and mass-democratic industrial capitalist ones has been much longer and slower than we tend to believe (Arno Mayer suggests that significant remnants of the former survived in Europe until the end of World War Two), so also the objective role of intellectuals to implement modernization's cultural revolution long remained a progressive one. But the process itself often tended to impress observers and participants alike by its self-perpetuating and indeed self-devouring energies. It is not only the Revolution that eats its own children; any number of visions of pure negativity as such do so as well, from Hegel's account of freedom and the Terror to the Frankfurt School's grim theory of the "dialectic of enlightenment" as an infernal machine, bent on extirpating all traces of transcendence (including critique and negativity itself).

Such visions seem even more relevant for one-dimensional societies like our own, from which the residual, in the forms of habits and practices of other modes of production, has been tendentially eliminated, so that it might be possible to hypothesize a modification or displacement in the very function of ideology-critique itself. This is at least the position of Manfredo Tafuri, who offers a kind of functionalist analysis of the avant-garde intellectual, whose "anti-institutional phase" essentially involved "the criticism of outworn values."[3] The very success of such a mission, however, coterminous with the modernizing struggles of capital itself, "serves to prepare a clean-swept platform from which to depart in discovery of the new "historic tasks" of intellectual work."[4] Not surprisingly, Tafuri identifies these new "modernizing" tasks with rationalization as such: "what the ideologies of the avant-garde introduced as a proposal for social behavior was the transformation of traditional ideology into Utopia, as a prefiguration of an abstract final moment of development coincident with a global rationalisation, with a positive realisation of the dialectic."[5] Tafuri's formulations become less cryptic when one understands that for him Keynesianism is to be understood as a planification, a rationalization of the future.

Thus seen, demystification in the contemporary period has its own secret "ruse of history," its own inner function and concealed world-historical missions; namely, by destroying traditional societies (not merely the Church and the old aristocracies but above all the peasants and their modes of agricultural production, their common land and their villages), to sweep the globe clean for the manipulations for the great corporations: to prepare a purely *fungible* present in which space and psyches alike can be processed and remade at will with a "flexibility" with which the creativity of the ideologues busy coining glowing new adjectives to describe the potentialities of "post-Fordism" can scarcely keep up. Demolition, under these circumstances, begins to take on new and ominously urbanistic overtones, and to connote the speculations of the developers far more than the older heroic struggles of opposition intellectuals; while just such objections to and critiques of demolition itself are relegated to a tiresome moralizing and undermine themselves by virtue of their vivid dramatization of outmoded mentalities that are better off being demolished anyhow (*"denn alles, was entsteht/Ist wert, dass es zugrunde geht"*).

These are now media paradoxes, which result from the speed and tempo of the critical process, as well as the way in which all ideological and philosophical positions as such have in the media universe been transformed into their own "representations" (as Kant might put it)—in other words into images of themselves and caricatures in which identifiable slogans substitute for traditional beliefs (the beliefs having indeed been forced to transform themselves into just such recognizable ideological positions in order to operate in the media marketplace). This is the situation in which it is easier to grasp the progressive value of conservative or residual modes of resistance to the new thing than to evaluate the range of ostensibly left-liberal positions (which, as in Tafuri's model, often functionally prove to indistinguishable from the structural requirements of the system itself). The diagnosis also projects the mirage of some possible sound barrier, like a telltale line blurring away against the sky; and indeed the obvious question of how much speed the human organism can bear may play its part in naturalist revivals; while the new fact itself does seem to offer a fleeting but vivid dramatization of Engels's old law about the transformation of quantity into quality (or at least of that "law"'s afterimage).

In this form, the paradox from which we must set forth is the equivalence between an unparalleled rate of change on all the levels of social life and an unparalleled standardization of everything—feelings along with consumer goods, language along with built space—that would seem incompatible with such mutability. It is a paradox that can still be conceptualized, but in inverse rations: of that modularity, for example, where intensified change is enabled by standardization itself, where prefabricated modules, everywhere from the media to a henceforth standardized private life, from commodified nature to uniformity of equipment, allow miraculous rebuildings to succeed each other at will, as in fractal video. The module would then constitute the new form of the object (the new result of reification) in an informational universe: that Kantian point in which raw material is suddenly organized by categories into an appropriate unit.

But the paradox can also incite us to rethink our conception of change itself. If absolute change in our society is best represented by the rapid turnover in storefronts, prompting the philosophical question as to what has really changed when video stores are replaced by T-shirt shops, then Barthes's structural formulation comes to have much to recommend it, namely that it is crucial to distinguish between rhythms of change inherent in the system and programmed by it, and a change that replaces one entire system by another one altogether. But that is a point of view that revives paradoxes of Zeno's sort, which derive from the Parmenidean conception of Being itself, which, as it *is* by definition, cannot be thought of as even momentarily becoming, let along failing to be for the slightest instant.

The "solution" to this particular paradox lies of course in the realization (strongly insisted on by Althusser and his disciples) that each system— better still, every "mode of production"—produces a temporality that is specific to it: it is only if we adopt a Kantian and a historical view of time as some absolute and empty category that the peculiarly repetitive temporality of our own system can become an object of puzzlement and lead to the reformulation of these old logical and ontological paradoxes.

Yet it may not be without its therapeutic effects to continue for one long moment to be mesmerized by the vision attributed to Parmenides, which however little it holds for nature might well be thought to capture a certain truth of our social and historical moment: a gleaming science-fictional stasis in which appearances (simulacra) arise and decay ceaselessly, without the momentous spellbound totality of everything that is ever flickering for the briefest of instants or even momentarily wavering in its ontological prestige.

Here, it is as if the logic of fashion had, accompanying the multifarious penetration of its omnipresent images, begun to bind and identify itself with the social and psychic fabric which tends to make it over into the very logic of our system as a whole. The experience and the value of perpetual change thereby comes to govern language and feelings, fully as much as the buildings and the garments of this particular society, to the point at which even the relative meaning allowed by uneven development (or "nonsynchronous synchronicity") is no longer comprehensible, and the supreme value of the New and of innovation, as both modernism and modernization grasped it, fades away against a steady steam of momentum and variation that at some outer limit seems stable and motionless.

What then dawns is the realization that no society has even been so standardized as this one, and that the steam of the human, social and historical temporality has never flowed quite so homogeneously. Even the great boredom or ennui of classical modernism required some vantage point or fantasy subject position outside the system; yet our seasons are of the post-natural and post-astronomical television or media variety, triumphantly artificial by way of the power of their National Geographic or Weather Channel images: so that their great rotations—in sports, new model cars, fashion, television, the school year or *rentée*, etc.—simulate formerly natural rhythms for commercial convenience and reinvent such archaic categories as the week, the month, the year imperceptibly, without any of the freshness and violence of, say, the innovations of the French revolutionary calendar.

What we now begin to feel, therefore—and what begins to emerge as some deep and more fundamental constitution of postmodernity itself, at least in its temporal dimension—is henceforth, where everything now submits to the perpetual change of fashion and media image, that nothing can change any longer. This is the sense of the revival of that "end of history" Alexandre Kojève thought he could find in Hegel and Marx, and which he took to mean some ultimate achievement of democratic equality (and the value of equivalence of individual economic and juridical subjects) in both American capitalism and Soviet communism, only later identifying a significant variant of it in what he called Japanese "*snobisme*," but that we can today identify as postmodernity itself (the free play of masks and roles without content or substance). In another sense, of course, this is simply the old "end of ideology" with a vengeance, and cynically plays on the waning of collective hope in a particularly conservative market climate. But the end of history is also the final form of the temporal paradoxes we have tried to dramatize here: namely that a rhetoric of absolute change (or "permanent revolution" in some trendy and meretricious new sense) is, for the postmodern, no more satisfactory (but not less so) than the language of absolute identity and unchanging standardization cooked up by the great corporations, whose concept of innovation is best illustrated by the neologism and the logo and their equivalents in the realm of built space, "life-style" corporate culture, and psychic programming. The persistence of the Same through absolute Difference—the same street with different buildings, the same culture through momentous new sheddings of skin— discredits change, since henceforth the only conceivable radical change would consist in putting an end to change itself. But here the antinomy really does result in the blocking or paralysis of thought, since the impossibility of thinking another system except by way of cancellation of this one ends up discrediting the utopian imagination itself, which is fantasized as the loss of everything we know experientially, from our libidinal investments to our psychic habits and in particular the artificial excitements of consumption and fashion.

Parmenidean stasis or Being, to be sure, knows at least one irrevocable event, namely death and the passage of the generations: insofar as the system of Parmenidean simulacrum or illusion is a very recent one, constituted in what we call postmodernity, the temporality of the generations in all their mortal discontinuity is not yet visible in results, except retroactively and as a materialist historiographic imperative. But death itself, as the very violence of absolute change, in the form of the nonimage—not even bodies rotting off stage but rather something persistent like an odor that circulates through the luminous immobility of this world without time—is inescapable and meaningless, since any historical framework that would serve to interpret and position individual deaths (at least for their survivors) has been destroyed. A kind of absolute violence, then, the abstraction of violent death, is something like the dialectical correlative to this world without time or history.

But it is more appropriate to conclude this section with a remark about the relationship of this temporal paradox—absolute change equals stasis— to the dynamics of the new global system itself, for here too we can observe an effacement of the temporalities that seemed to govern an older period of modernity, of modernism and modernization alike. For in that older period, most Third World societies were torn by a penetration of Western modernization that generated over against itself—in all the variety of cultural forms characteristic of those very different societies—a counterposition that could generally be described as traditionalism: the affirmation of a cultural (and sometimes religious) originality that had the power to resist assimilation by Western modernity and was indeed preferable to it. Such traditionalism was of course a construction in its own right, brought into being as it were, by the very activities of the modernizers themselves (in some more limited and specific sense than the one now widely accepted, that all traditions and historical pasts are themselves necessarily invented and constructed). At any rate, what one wants to affirm today is that this second reactive or antimodern term of tradition and traditionalism has everywhere vanished from the reality of the former Third World or colonized societies, where a neotraditionalism (as in certain Chinese revivals of Confucianism, or in religious fundamentalism) is now rather perceived as deliberate political and collective choice, in a situation in which little remains of a past that must be completely reinvented.

This is to say that, on the one hand, nothing but the modern henceforth exists in the Third World societies; but it is also to correct this statement, on the other, with the qualification that under such circumstances, where only the modern exists, "modern" must now be rebaptized "postmodern" (since what we call modern is the consequence of incomplete modernization and must necessarily define itself against a nonmodern residuality that no longer obtains in postmodernity as such—or rather, whose absence defines this last). Here too then, but on a social and historical level, the temporality that modernization promised (in its various capitalist and communist productivist forms) has been eclipsed to the benefit of a new condition in which that older temporality no longer exists, leaving an appearance of random changes that are mere stasis, a disorder after the end of history. Meanwhile, it is as though what used to be characterized as the Third World has entered the interstices of the First one, as the latter also demodernizes and deindustrializes, lending the former colonial otherness something of the centered identity of the former metropolis.

With this extension of the temporal paradox on a global scale something else becomes clear as well, a kind of second paradox or antimony that begins to make its presence felt behind and perhaps even with the first. Indeed the repeated spatial characterizations of temporality here—from Proust to storefronts, from urban change to global "development"—now begin to remind us that if it is so that postmodernity is characterized by some essential spatialization, then everything we have been trying to work out in terms of temporality will necessarily have passed through a spatial matrix to come to expression in the first place. If time has in effect been reduced to the most punctual violence and minimal irrevocable change of an abstract death, then we can perhaps affirm that in the postmodern time has become space anyhow. The foundational antinomy of postmodern description lies then in the fact that this former binary opposition, along with identity and difference themselves, no longer is an opposition as such, and ceaselessly reveals itself to have been at one with its other pole in a rather different way than the old dialectical projection back and forth, the classical dialectical metamorphosis. In order to see what this involves, we now necessarily turn to the other spatial antinomy, which apparently we have been rehearsing all along its temporal version, with a view toward determining whether spatiality has any genuine thematic priority.

II

It is at least certain that the form by which one dimension of the antithesis necessarily expresses itself by way of figurality of the other, time being required to express itself in spatial terms, is not repeated here; nor is the time–space antithesis symmetrical or reversible in this sense. Space does not seem to require a temporal expression; if it is not what absolutely does without such temporal figurality, then at the very least it might be said that space is what represses temporality and temporal figurality absolutely, to the benefit of other figures and codes. If Difference and Identity are at stake in both the temporal and the spatial antinomy, then the difference pre-eminent in considerations of space is not so much that of change in any temporal understanding of the form, as rather variety and infinity, metonymy and—to reach some more influential and seemingly definitive and all-encompassing version—heterogeneity.

Historically, the adventures of homogeneous and heterogeneous space have most often been told in terms of quotient of sacred and of the folds in which it is unevenly invested: as for its alleged opposite number, the profane, however, one supposes that it is a projection backward in time of post-sacred and commercial peoples to imagine that it was itself any single thing or quality (a nonquality, rather); a projection indeed to think that anything like simple dualism of the profane and the sacred ever existed as such in the first place. For the sacred can be supposed to have meant heterogeneity and multiplicity in the first place: a nonvalue, an excess, something irreducible to system or to thought, to identity, to the degree to which it not merely explodes itself, but its opposite number, positing the spaces for normal village living alongside the chthonic garbage heaps of the *im-monde* (Henri Lefebvre's account, in *The Production of Space*⁶) but also the empty spaces of waste and desert, the sterile voids that punctuate so many naturally expressive landscapes. For by definition there must also have been as many types or kinds of the sacred as there were powers, and one must drain these words of their feeble archaic overtones before we realize that abstractions such as *sacred* or *power* have, in the face of the realities they were meant to designate, about the same expressive force as the abstraction *color* for the variety of intensities that absorb our gaze.

This also bears on the meaning of landscape, whose secular and painted modern version is a very recent development, as interpreters such as Deleuze or Karatani have so often reminded us. I hesitate to lapse into the fantasies of Romantics like Runge, with his languages of the plants; but they are certainly attractive fantasies, at least until they become socially stabilized in the form of kitsch (with its "language of flowers"). Such notions of a space that is somehow meaningfully organized and on the very point of speech, a kind of articulated thinking that fails to reach its ultimate translation in propositions or concepts, in messages, ultimately find their justification and theoretical defence in Lévi-Strauss's description, in *La Pensée sauvage*,[7] of prephilosophical "perceptual science"; while their aesthetic reaches at least one kind of climax in the same anthropologist's classic reading of the Pacific Northwest Coast Indian, *La Geste d'Asdiwal*, where the various landscapes, from frozen inland wastes to the river and the coast itself speak multiple languages (including those of the economic mode of production itself and of the kinship structure) and emit a remarkable range of articulate messages.

This kind of analysis effectively neutralizes the old opposition between the rational and the irrational (and all the satellite oppositions—primitive versus civilized, male versus female, West versus East—that are grounded on it) by locating the dynamics of meaning in texts that precede conceptual abstraction: a multiplicity of levels is thereby at once opened up that can no longer be assimilated to Weberian rationalism, instrumental thought, the reifications and repressions of the narrowly rational or conceptual. It is thereby to be characterized as heterogeneity; and we can go on to describe the sensory articulations of its object, in the mobile landscapes of *Asdiwal*, as heterogeneous space. As Derrida has famously shown, in one of the inaugural documents of what later comes to be called poststructuralism ("Structure, Sign, and Play"[8]), Lévi-Strauss's analysis remains somehow centered around homologous meanings: it fails to reach the ultimately aleatory and undecidable; it persists in clinging for dear life to the very concept of meaning proper; and in a situation that ought to put an end to that concept, it does not even attain the openness of Bakhtinian polyphony or heteroglossia, since there is still a collective agency—the tribe—that speaks through its multiplicities.

But that then becomes the failure of Lévi-Strauss to reach true heterogeneity rather than the historical insufficiency of this latter concept as such, about which Bataille's whole life's work demonstrates that it exists in situation and is, like the surrealism from which it derived and that it repudiates, a strategic reaction against a modern state of things. This leads one to wonder whether heterogeneity has historically emerged, to confer upon it the value and the force of a specific oppositional tactic. What has to be described, therefore, is not so much the prestige of such forms of multiplicity and excess that overspill the rational modern mind and rebuke it, as their values as reactions against it whose projection into the past is at best a doubtful and suspicious matter. The prior object of description is rather the gradual colonization of the world by precisely that homogeneity whose tendential conquests it was Bataille's historical mission (as of so many others) to challenge, along with the setting in place of forms of identity that only after the fact allow the anachronistic illusion of heterogeneity and difference to come to seem the logic of what they organized and flattened out.

That process, as far as space is concerned, can surely be identified with some precision: it is the moment in which a Western system of private property in real estate displaces the various systems of land tenure it confronts in the course of its successive enlargements (or, in the European situation itself, from which it gradually emerges for the first time in its own right). Nor does a language of violence—otherwise perfectly appropriate for these supersessions and still observable in settler colonies such as Israel and also in the various "transitions to capitalism" in Eastern Europe—convey the way in which the substitution of one legal system for another, more customary one is a matter of calculation and elaborate political strategy.[9] The violence was no doubt always implicit in the very conception of ownership as such when applied to the land; it is a peculiarly ambivalent mystery that mortal beings, generations of dying organisms, should have imagined they could somehow "own" parts of the earth in the first place. The older forms of land tenure (as well as the more recent socialist forms, similarly varied from country to country) at least posited the collectivity as the immortal governor into whose stewardship portions of the soil are given over; nor has it ever been a simple or easy matter to undo these social relationships and replace them with the apparently more obvious and manageable ones based on individualized ownership and a juridical system of equivalent subjects—East Germany in this respect today rather resembling what the North American had to do with the conquered South after the Civil War; while the Israeli settlements often remind one of the brutal displacements of Native American societies in the West of the United States.

The point is, however, that where the thematic opposition of heterogeneity and homogeneity is invoked, it can only be this brutal process that is the ultimate referent: the effects that result from the power of commerce and then capitalism proper—which is to say, sheer number as such, number now shorn and divested of its own magical heterogeneities and reduced to equivalencies—to seize upon a landscape and flatten it out, reorganize it into a grid of identical parcels, and expose it to the dynamic of a market that now reorganizes space in terms of an identical value. The development of capitalism then distributes that value most unevenly indeed, until at length, in its postmodern moment, sheer speculation, as something like the triumph of spirit over matter the liberation of the form of value from any of its former concrete or earthly content, now reigns supreme and devastates the very cities and countrysides it created in the process of its own earlier development. But all such later forms of abstract violence and homogeneity derive from the initial parcellization, which translates the money form and the logic commodity production for a market back on to space itself.

Our own period also teaches us that the fundamental contradiction in this reorganization of space, which seeks to stamp out older and customary forms of collective land tenure (that then swim back into the modern historical imagination in the form of religious anthropological conceptions of "the sacred" or of the archaic heterogeneity), is to be identified as what we equally used to call agriculture itself when that was associated with a peasantry or even yeoman farmers. In a postmodern global system, in which the tendency of a hitherto overwhelming peasant population to drop to some 7 or 8 per cent of the nation can be observed everywhere in the modernizing fully as much as in the "advanced" countries, the relationship between peasant agriculture and traditional culture has become only too clear: the latter follows the former into extinction, and all the great precapitalist cultures prove to have been peasant ones, except where they were based on slavery. (Meanwhile, as for what has until today passed for a capitalist culture—a specifically capitalist "high culture," that is—it can also be identified as the way in which a bourgeoisie imitated and aped the traditions of its aristocratic feudal predecessors, tending to be eclipsed along with their memory and to give way, along with the older classical bourgeois class-consciousness itself, to mass culture—indeed to a specifically American mass culture at that.)

But the very possibility of a new globalization (the expansion of capital beyond its earlier limits in its second, or "imperialist," stage) depended on an agricultural reorganization (sometimes called the Green Revolution owing to its technological and specifically chemical and biological innovations) that effectively made peasants over into farm workers and great estates or latifundia (as well as village enclaves) over into agribusiness. Pierre-Philippe Rey has indeed suggested that we understand the relationship of modes of production to one another as one of the imbrications or articulations, rather than as one of the simple supersessions: in this respect, he suggests the second or "modern" moment of capital—the stage of imperialism— retained an older precapitalist mode of production in agriculture and kept it intact, exploiting it in tributary fashion, deriving capital by extensive labor, inhuman hours and conditions, from essentially precapitalist relations.[10] The new multinational stage of capital is then characterized by the sweeping away of such enclaves and their utter assimilation into capitalism itself, with its wage-labor and working conditions: at this point, agriculture— culturally distinctive and identified in the superstructure as the Other of Nature—now becomes an industry like any other, and the peasants simple workers whose labor is classically commodified in terms of value equivalencies. This is not to say that commodification is evenly distributed over the entire globe or that all areas have been equally modernized or postmodernized; rather, that the tendency toward global commodification is far more visible and imaginable than it was in the modern period, in which tenacious premodern life realities still existed to impede the process. Capital, as Marx showed in the *Grundrisse*, necessarily tends toward the outer limit of a global market that is also its ultimate crisis situation (since no further expansion is then possible); this doctrine is for us today much less abstract than it was in the modern period; it designates conceptual reality that neither theory nor culture can any longer postpone to some future agenda.

But to say so is to evoke the obliteration of difference on a world scale, and to convey a vision of the irrevocable triumph of spatial homogeneity over whatever heterogeneities might still have been fantasized in terms of global space. I want to stress this as an ideological development, which includes all the ecological fears awakened in our own period (pollution and its accompaniments also standing as a mark of universal commodification and commercialization): for in this situation ideology is not false consciousness but itself a possibility of knowledge, and our constitutive difficulties in imagining a world beyond global standardization are very precisely indices and themselves features of just that standardized reality or being itself.

Such ideological limits invested with certain affective terror as a kind of dystopia are then compensated by other ideological possibilities that come into view when we no longer take the countryside as our vantage point but rather the city and the urban itself. This is of course already an opposition that has left significant traces in the science-fictional or utopian tradition: the antithesis between a pastoral utopia and an urban one, and in particular the apparent supersession in recent years of images of a village of tribal utopia (Ursula Le Guin's *Always Coming Home* of 1985[11] was virtually the last of those) by visions of an unimaginably dense urban reality (therein nonetheless somehow imagined) that is either explicitly placed on the utopian agenda, as in Samual Delany's 1976 *Trouble on Triton*[12] or Raymond Williams's prescient forecast that socialism, if possible, will not be simpler than all this but far more complicated, or by masquerades under a dystopian appearance whose deeper libidinal excitement, however, is surely profoundly utopian in spirit (as in most current cyberpunk).

Once again, however, we have to deal with the conceptual difficulties in which we are plunged by the disappearance of one of the terms of a formerly functioning binary opposition. The disappearance of Nature—the commodification of the countryside and the capitalization of agriculture itself all over the world—now begins to sap its other term, the formerly urban. Where the world system today tends toward one enormous urban system—as a tendentially ever more complete modernization always promised, a promise which has however been ratified and delivered in an unexpected way by the communications revolution and its new technologies: a development of which the immediately physical visions, nightmares of the "sprawl from Boston to Richmond, or the Japanese urban agglomeration," are the merest allegories—the very conception of the city itself and the classically urban loses its significance and no longer seems to offer any precisely delimited objects of study, any specifically differentiated realities. Rather, the urban becomes the social in general, and both of them constitute and lose themselves in a global that is not really their opposite either (as it was in the older dispensation) but something like their outer reach, their prolongation into a new kind of infinity.

Ideologically, what this dissolution of the boundaries of the traditional city and the classically urban enables is slippage, a displacement, a reinvestment of older urban ideological and libidinal connotations under new conditions. The city always seemed to promise freedom, as in the medieval conception of the urban as the space of escape from the land and from feudal labor and serfdom, from the arbitrary power of the lord: "city air" from this perspective now becomes the very opposite of what Marx famously characterized as "rural idiocy," the narrowness of village manners and customs, the provinciality of the rural, with its fixed ideas and superstitions and its hatred of difference. Here, in contrast to the dreary sameness of the countryside (which is also, however, inaccurately, fantasized as a place of sexual repression), the urban classically promised variety and adventure, often linked crime just as the accompanying visions of pleasure and sexual gratification are inseparable from transgression and illegality. What happens, then, when even that countryside, even that essentially provincial reality, disappears, becomes standardized, hears the same English, sees the same program, consumes the same consumer goods, as the former metropolis to which, in the old days, these same provincials and country people longed to go as to a fundamental liberation? I think that the missing second term—provincial boredom, rural idiocy—was preserved, but simply transferred to a different kind of city and a different kind of social reality, namely the Second World city and the social realities of a nonmarket or planned economy. Everyone remembers the overwhelming power of such Cold War iconography, which has perhaps proved even more effective today, after the end of the Cold War and in the thick of the current offensive of market propaganda and rhetoric, than it was in a situation of struggle where visions of terror were more quintessentially operative. Today, however, it is the memory of the imagined drabness of the classic Second World city—with its meager shelves of consumer goods in empty central from which the points of light of advertising are absent, streets from which small stores and shops are missing, standardization of clothing fashions (as most emblematically in Maoist China)—that remains ideologically operative in the campaigns for privatization. Jane Jacob's fundamental identification of a genuine urban fabric and street life with small business is ceaselessly rehearsed ideologically, without any reminder that she thought the diagnosis applied fully as much to the North American or capitalist city in which corporations have equally, but in a different fashion, driven small business out of existence, and created canyons of institutional high-rises without any urban personality at all.

This urban degradation, which characterizes the First World, has, however, been transferred to a separate ideological compartment called postmodernism, where it duly takes place in the arsenal of attacks on modern architecture and its ideals. As for the Second World city, its vision is rather enlisted in the service of a rather different operation, namely to serve as the visual and experiential *analogon* of a world utterly programmed and directed by human intention, a world therefore from which the contingencies of change—and thereby the promise of adventure and real life, of libidinal gratification—are also excluded. Conscious intention, the plan, collective control, are then fantasized as being at one with repression and renunciation, with instinctual impoverishment: and as in the related postmodern polemic, the absence of ornament from the Second World city—as it were the involuntary enactment of Adolf Loos's program—serves as a grim caricature of the puritanical utopian values of a revolutionary society (just as it had served as that of the equally puritanical utopian values of high modernism in the other campaign that in certain recent theory in the Eastern countries[13] is explicitly linked to this one in an instructive and revealing way).

Only the spatial features of this particular ideological tactic are new: Edmund Burke was of course the first to develop the great anti-revolutionary figure, according to which what people consciously and collectively do can only be destructive and a sign of fatal hubris: that only the slow "natural" growth of traditions and institutions can be trusted to form a genuinely human world (a deep suspicion of the will and of unconscious intention that then passes over into a certain Romantic tradition in aesthetics). But Burke's pathbreaking attack on the Jacobins was aimed at the middle-class construction and formation of market society itself, about whose commercialism it essentially expressed the fears and anxieties of an older social formation in the process of being superseded. The market theorists today, however, marshal the same fantasies in defence of a market society now supposed itself to be somehow "natural" and deeply rooted in human nature; they do so against the Promethean efforts of human beings to take collective production into their own hands and, by planning, to control or at least to influence and inflect their own future (something that no longer seems particularly meaningful in a postmodernity in which the very experience of the future as such has come to seem enfeebled, if not deficient).

But this is precisely the ideological and imaginary background against which it is possible to market and to sell the contemporary capitalist city as well-nigh Bakhtinian carnival of heterogeneities, of differences, libidinal excitement and a hyperindividuality that effectively decenters the old individual subject by way of individual hyperconsumption. Now the associations or connotations of provincial misery and renunciation, of petty bourgeois impoverishment, of cultural and libidinal immiseration, systematically reinvested in our images of the urban space of the Second World, are pressed into service as argument against socialism and planning, against collective ownership and what is fantasized as centralization, at the same time that they serve as powerful stimuli to the peoples of Eastern Europe to plunge into the freedoms of Western consumption. This is no small ideological achievement in view of difficulties, a priori, in staging the collective control over their destinies by social groups in a negative way and investing those forms of autonomy with all the fears and anxieties, the loathing and libidinal dread, which Freud called counterinvestment or anticathexis and that must constitute the central effect of any successful anti-utopianism.

This is then also the point at which everything most paradoxical about the spatial form of the antinomy under discussion here becomes vivid and inescapable; our conceptual exhibit comes more sharply into view when begin to ask ourselves how it is possible for the most standardized and uniform social reality in history, but the merest ideological flick of the thumbnail, the most imperceptible of displacements, to emerge as the rich oil-smear sheen of absolute diversity and of the most unimaginable and unclassifiable forms of human freedom. Here homogeneity has become heterogeneity, in a movement complementary to that in which absolute change turned into absolute stasis, and without the slightest modification of a real history that there was thought to be at an end, while here it has seemed finally to realize itself.

Notes

1 Paul Virilio, *War and Cinema*, trans. Patrick Camiller (London: Verso, 1989), 56–60.
2 Marcel Proust, *A la recherche du temps perdu*, vol. I (Paris, 1987), 36.
3 Manfredo Tafuri, *Architecture and Utopia*, trans. Barbara Luigia La Penta (Cambridge: MIT Press, 1976), 70.
4 Ibid.
5 Ibid., 62.
6 Henri Lefebvre, *The Production of Space*, trans. Donald Nicholson-Smith (Oxford: Blackwell, 1991).
7 Claude Lévi-Strauss, translated as *The Savage Mind* (Chicago: University of Chicago Press, 1966).
8 See Jacques Derrida, *Writing and Difference*, trans. Alan Bass (London: Routledge, 1990).
9 See Ranajit Guha, *A Rule of Property for Bengal* (Durham: Duke University Press, 1963).
10 See Pierre Philippe Rey, *Les Alliances de classes* (Paris: Maspero, 1978).
11 Ursula Le Guin, *Always Coming Home* (London: Harper & Row, 1985).
12 Samuel R. Delany, *Trouble on Triton: An Ambiguous Heterotopia* (Middleton: Middleton Press, 1996).
13 For the identification of aesthetic modernism with Stalinism, see, in particular, Boris Groys, *Gesamtkunstwerk Stalin* (Munich: Hanser, 1998); translated by Charles Rougle as *The Total Art of Stalinism: Avant Garde, Aesthetic Dictatorship and Beyond* (Princeton NJ: Princeton University Press, 1992).

CHAPTER TWENTY FOUR

Reading Dialectically

Carolyn Lesjak

From Literary Materialisms, *ed. Mathias Nilges and Emilio Sauri, New York: Palgrave Macmillan, 2013: 17–48.*

This, then, is the limit of common sense. What lies beyond involves a Leap of Faith, faith in lost Causes, Causes that, from within the space of skeptical wisdom, cannot but appear as crazy. And the present book speaks from within this Leap of Faith—but why? The problem, of course, is that, in a time of crisis and ruptures, skeptical empirical wisdom itself, constrained to the horizon of the dominant form of common sense, cannot provide the answers, so one must risk a Leap of Faith.

SLAVOJ ŽIŽEK, *In Defense of Lost Causes*

Fredric Jameson ends his recent book on the dialectic, *Valences of the Dialectic*, with a careful reading of Paul Ricoeur's *Narrative and Time*. On the face of it, a book about the dialectic in 2009 might seem destined for the remainder shelves. Especially one that concludes with a long, final section closely reading a work of narrative theory with which few scholars today would be familiar, in order to argue that the task of criticism is to "make time and history appear"—at a moment when, as Jameson himself diagnosed in *Postmodernism, or, the Cultural Logic of Late Capitalism*, our ability to think historically has all but disappeared. Against the specter of the dialectic's obsolescence, I want to suggest however that *Valences of the Dialectic* in fact constitutes a timely polemic against the new disciplinary conservatism, and a spirited defense of theory, which is also a defense of reading.

Theory and reading: in the contemporary climate, these two endeavors, more often than not, tend to be pitted against one another. Simply put, theory is on its way out; reading is (back) in. Beleaguered by post-structuralism and Foucault, social constructionism, interdisciplinarity, cultural studies, and the like—all of which get collapsed under the umbrella bogeyman "theory"—a group of literary critics are once again arguing for an emphasis on the literary in literary criticism, and claiming, in essence, that reading literature is what we literary scholars do best and hence what we ought to return to doing, after having lost our way in the heady theory days of the 1960s–1990s.[1] As the former president of the MLA, Marjorie Perloff, wrote in her 2006 presidential address, "a specter is haunting the academy, the specter of literature."[2] And the means of exorcism: "It is time to trust the literary instinct that brought us to this field in the first place and to recognize that, instead of lusting after those other disciplines that seem so exotic primarily because we don't really practice them, what we need is more theoretical, historical and critical training in our own discipline. Rhapsodes [discussed in the context of her preceding argument regarding the absence of poetics in interdisciplinary literary studies, which she renames 'other-disciplinary' to capture its total disregard for the literary], it turns out, can and should serve a real function in our oral, print and digital culture" (655, 662).

This claim echoes those made by New Formalists of various stripes, as well as a slew of other new "isms" committed to "returns" of one sort or another, which are also presented as reclamations—the need to reclaim the aesthetic, or reading, human nature or pleasure, and so on. In her review essay on New Formalism, Marjorie Levinson identifies two strains within the movement, normative and activist new formalism. She characterizes the former as a "backlash new formalism," for its rejection of new historicist claims and because it "assigns to the aesthetic norm-setting work that is cognitive and affective and therefore also cultural-political"; activist formalism, on the other hand, aims to restore the importance of form within historical reading, thereby positioning itself along the continuum of new historicism rather than as a break with it.[3] For our purposes here, normative new formalism most directly dramatizes the conservatism of these movements in its advocacy of a return to the pleasures of a kind of reading theory has supposedly made impossible. (I will return to the status of new historicism and its relationship to theory.) As Levinson notes, "normative new formalism makes a strong claim for bringing back pleasure as what hooks us on and rewards us for reading." Following a list of such claims by critics such as Susan Wolfson, Denis Donoghue, Charles Altieri, and George Levine, Levinson concludes: "Normative new formalism holds that to contextualize aesthetic experience is to expose its hedonic dimension as an illusion, distraction, or trap. It is hard not to hear in this worry a variant of the classic freshman complaint that analyzing literature destroys the experience of it" (562).

Also arguing against the abuses theory has propagated against contemporary readers, New Darwinism advocates for a return to the concept of human nature, a concept out of favor in a climate dominated by theories of social constructionism with their championing of the virtually infinite malleability of human individuals, and the power, therefore, of social contexts, institutions, and cultural factors to change and mold individuals. One of New Darwinism's main proponents, Steven Pinker, for example, argues against what he sees as an historical triad of ideas that have been used, sometimes erroneously, to discount the role of human nature in modern life: the "blank slate" (Locke), the "Noble Savage" (Rousseau), and the "Ghost in the Machine" (Descartes).[4] Given new developments in evolutionary psychology, cognitive science, and neuroscience, Pinker argues, there is ample evidence to prove that, within contemporary theory, social factors are unduly privileged over the biological imperatives of human nature. His motive for writing *The Blank Slate: The Modern Denial of Human Nature*, he states, stemmed from his utter frustration with social constructivist models of human development:

> I first had the idea of writing this book when I started a collection of astonishing claims from pundits and social critics about the malleability of the human psyche: that little boys quarrel and fight because they are encouraged to do so; that children enjoy sweets because their parents use them as a reward for eating vegetables; that teenagers get the idea to compete in looks and fashion from spelling bees and academic prizes; that men think the goal of sex is an orgasm because of the way they were socialized.[5]

In the realm of the arts, specifically, Pinker suggests that an attentiveness to human nature would illuminate the false claims of both modernism and postmodernism and their shared allegiance to the constructedness of perception, formal innovation (the desire to "make it new"; the embracing of nonnarrative form), and relativism, all of which go against human nature's privileging of beauty, pleasure, middlebrow realistic fiction, narrative, and representational art. But Pinker also perceives progressive seeds of change in the humanities:

> A revolt has begun. Museum-goers have become bored with the umpteenth exhibit on the female body featuring dismembered torsos or hundreds of

pounds of lard chewed up and spat out by the artist. Graduate students in the humanities are grumbling in emails and conference hallways about being locked out of the job market unless they write in gibberish while randomly dropping the names of authorities like Foucault and Butler. Maverick scholars are doffing the blinders that prevented them from looking at exciting developments in the sciences of human nature. And younger artists are wondering how the art world got itself into the bizarre place in which beauty is a dirty word. (416)

Pinker provides a long list of other movements sympathetic to "these currents of discontent" that are "coming together in a new philosophy of the arts, one that is consilient with the sciences and respectful of the minds and senses of human being," and which include New Formalism, along with the artistic movement Derrière Guard ("which celebrates beauty, technique, and narrative"), the New Narrativism, Stuckism, and the Return of Beauty, as well as literary critics such as Joseph Carroll, Elaine Scarry, Wendy Steiner, and Frederick Turner, characterized as a "growing number of mavericks . . . looking to evolutionary psychology and cognitive science in an effort to reestablish human nature at the center of any understanding of the arts."[6]

While these movements sound somewhat like the Tea Party contingent of a new literary criticism—"Give us back our literature and our socially unencumbered aesthetic!" the rallying call in this case—less bombastic, more solidly centrist voices, to continue the analogy, also call for the renewal of formalist analyses, as well as other kinds of scientific approaches to literature, more moderate and nuanced than Pinker's and from within the humanities. In her call for a "strategic formalism," for example, the Victorian scholar Caroline Levine proposes a model of "social close reading" (Herbert Tucker's term) that would allow critics to move more deftly and flexibly between the micro- and macro-levels of a text.[7] "Formalism," Levine writes,

emerges as an ideal set of methods for thinking about competing modes of order, and it is particularly well suited to the apprehension of subtle interactions among different ordering tactics. The point is not that societies are just like poems, but that literary critics, long practiced at articulating the subtle shaping patterns that both reinforce and destabilize one another in a given textual object, are ideally suited to extend those reading practices to the analysis of cultural life more broadly, understanding cultural entities as sites where many conflicting ways of imposing order jostle one another, overlap, and collide.[8]

Despite the complexity of a formalism that is reservedly "strategic," and thereby mirrors the knowingness of Gayatri Spivak's notion of a "strategic essentialism" rather than the knee-jerk return of normative new formalism, Levine's less extreme, and on the face of it utterly reasonable, model of reading best captures, I want to suggest paradoxically, the increasingly conservative mood within literary criticism and its key theoretical gestures. The overarching message seems to be: scale back, pare down, small aims met are better than grand ones unrealized. Reclaim our disciplinary territory and hold on to it. Perloff even makes an instrumental case for such an approach: as she notes, the demand outside the academy, as witnessed by the enthusiasm surrounding Beckett's centennial, is for reading literature, not theory, so by returning to our roots, we will not only satisfy ourselves but the market as well. And in the process, this line of reasoning implies, perhaps save our jobs as humanities' professors by (cynically) complying with the instrumentalization of knowledge and thought driving the very educational and university policies that see the humanities as obsolete. (Again, this is an extreme version of what I will argue defines the status quo.) And all in the name of getting back to basics, while seemingly forgetting that we have been there before and it is no longer the same place it used to be, if it ever was that place.[9]

It goes without saying that the sometimes catholic, at other times simple and purportedly neutral imperatives (accounting for the multiplicity of discourses in any text, or "the many conflicting ways of imposing order," getting back to basics, respecting human nature) driving the spectrum of readings from normative new formalism to strategic formalism, to narratology, and to cognitive science studies are premised on a rejection of Marxist literary criticism, a point Levine makes explicit when she notes that her vision of "contests and encounters among different forms of order" only holds true if there is no single determining force among the colliding, overlapping forms: "When we are faced with the competing imperatives not only of race, class, and gender, but of imperial expansion, nationality, sexuality, and disability, the result—unless one is seen as the root cause of all the others—is not an orderly political culture but a highly contestatory one."[10] Except in isolated instances, I think it's fair to say that Marxism is not even part of the conversation, despite the continued popularity of Slavoj Žižek (many of whose fans and readers seem perfectly capable of enjoying his work without adhering in any way to its Marxism).[11]

By opening with a reference to the timeliness of Jameson's *Valences of the Dialectic*, I mean to frame the argument to follow in the context of the ongoing necessity of a Marxist literary criticism and of a dialectical Marxist criticism, in particular. Indeed, I hope to show why a Marxist critique is more necessary than ever, given the current crisis in the humanities and the turn against theory—two events that Vincent Leitch argues are deeply interconnected. Leitch identifies the close connection between theory and the university when he suggests that claims of theory's demise are also signs of anxiety about what is to come: the so-called passing of theory equally reflects wider fears about the role or place of critical thinking within an increasingly corporatized university. In short, for Leitch, the status of theory in such debates is inseparable from the status or future of the university. But whereas Leitch ends up embracing the proliferation of theories and new fields—from affect and animal studies to whiteness, fashion, and disability studies—as a sign of the continuing vitality of critical thinking, I want to make a case for narrowing the field: I want to suggest that the task the humanities need to set themselves now is akin to what Max Horkheimer claimed for critical theory in 1937: "the task of the critical theoretician is to reduce the tension between his [sic] own insight and oppressed humanity in whose service he [sic] thinks."[12] What is counterintuitive here, obviously, is that an anti-humanist, revitalized Marxism—itself supposedly dead, along with theory—offers the way forward for humanist study, given how irreducibly bound to the economy the humanities are today.

Equally against the grain of mainstream dismissals of theory, Jameson in *Valences of the Dialectic* (as well as elsewhere) distinguishes between philosophy and theory and aligns reading with the latter, drawing on Ricoeur to characterize reading as "the momentary and ephemeral act of unification in which we hold multiple dimensions of time together for a glimpse that cannot prolong itself into the philosophical concept."[13] If philosophy tries to solve aporias, literature, in contrast, produces them. While Jameson will enlarge his frame of reading to historiographic texts such as Fernand Braudel's, he nonetheless maintains an emphasis on the value of narrative (via Ricoeur's notion of "narrative intelligence" and Hayden White's idea of "emplotment") and its unique capacity to hold multiple temporalities together, in short, as noted above, to make time and History appear. Framed by Jameson's plea that theory still matters, I want to examine more closely the role new historicism has played in the production of two very specific articulations of what today constitutes reading, in order to suggest both what is missing from this conversation and to speculate on how we might better pose properly dialectical questions in response to the current, inseparably intertwined crises of literary criticism, the humanities and the university.

Against theory redux

The backlash against theory has been gradual and fairly quiet. Refusing to be theory, or have a methodology or belong to a school of thought, the anti-theory camp disavows itself as an event and positions itself as the Other to theory. Catherine Gallagher and Stephen Greenblatt's introduction to *Practicing New Historicism* (2000) muses on this otherness; as they conclude their non-mission, mission statement: "Writing the book has convinced us that new historicism is not a repeatable methodology or a literary critical program. Each time we approached that moment in the writing when it might have been appropriate to draw the 'theoretical' lesson, to scold another school of criticism, or to point the way toward the paths of virtue, we stopped, not because we're shy of controversy, but because we cannot bear to see the long chains of close analysis go up in a puff of abstraction. So we sincerely hope you will not be able to say what it all adds up to; if you could, we would have failed."[14] I want to spend a little time with Greenblatt's and Gallagher's explicit articulation of their anti-programmatic principles in order to review their vision of reading, which, paradoxically, given their stated aims, has become something of a new critical orthodoxy. Their essay plots a series of theoretical moves in which earlier, primarily Marxist terminology is supplanted by language meant to open up the "textual archive": ideology critique is rejected in favor of discourse analysis; determinism is replaced by "an aesthetic appreciation of the individual instance"; and Herder's notion of diversification becomes the means to highlight "the singular, the specific, and the individual" (16, 6). Throughout, Herder provides the framework for properly encountering what they refer to, giddily, as the "vastness of the textual archive" (16). The coupling of the archive (a stand-in for the real) and the aesthetic (culture) alleviates Gallagher and Greenblatt's discomfort with key Marxist concepts—base and superstructure, class consciousness, totality—and with any form of systematization whatsoever. Relieved of what they perceive as the pre-rehearsed protocols of Marxist literary criticism, they imagine themselves free to see cultural texts "independently"—in terms of "the single voice, the isolated scandal, the idiosyncratic vision, the transient sketch" (16). Only in this way, they claim, can the aesthetic qualities of culture as text be appreciated.

Despite espousing a new historicism, this reading of the archive is of a piece with what Alexander Kluge calls the "assault of the present on the rest of time": the key is to grasp that these ostensible representations of the past emerge from within what Kluge has called a "universalized present," a present that simultaneously forecloses horizons of the past and of the future, and that also colonizes our very understanding of the past so that representations of the past—like new historicist readings—appear to us as little more than reflections or reaffirmations of the status quo and the given moment.[15] (Kluge's perspective is deeply Benjaminian; this sort of historicism must be distinguished from the liberatory historicism of which Benjamin spoke.) In its invocation of the "vastness of the archive" new historicism fantasizes about a plenitude of the present cloaked in the artifacts of the past (there are so many more objects available to be read and interpreted!). It gives new life to tired critics who have "never given up or turned [their] backs on the deep gratification that draws [them] in the first place to the study of literature and art"—but in the benign form of a comfortable skepticism allied with appreciation, in which there are seemingly no limits to what culture can do.[16] It is a materialism, that is to say, in which materiality conveniently never gets in the way. The sheer increase in reading material equates to a material reading that is, by dint of its expansiveness, "democratizing" (11). Hierarchies and contradictions— between texts, between horizons of the social, between texts and contexts— are dissolved, replaced by a kind of ecumenical lateralness, in which the operative movement is outward or across surfaces rather than downward, as in surface/depth hermeneutical models.[17]

From critique to analysis, from revolutionary to democratizing: this pallid middle ground tends to define "reading" these days. Indeed, the "smallness" of new historical claims essentially puts literary scholarship on par with "middle-level research," an identification so unremarkable in the present climate that its coiner, David Bordwell, actively advocates for such a diminished critical project with no sense of chagrin or irony.[18] But he is certainly not alone. As Žižek characterizes our age of cynical reason, "skeptical wisdom" both carries the day and "cannot provide the answers" given the fact that it is "constrained to the horizon of the dominant form of common sense."[19] The middle reader, like Žižek's enlightened conservative liberal, accommodates herself to the given, to common sense, against the now discredited excesses of the theory years, with a kind of Blairite Third-Way of reading, which is neither new criticism nor Marxism but a nice compromise midway between them, a blend of cultural liberalism with a "minimally 'authoritarian' spirit of community (the emphasis on social stability, 'values' and so forth)" (2). Small, pious claims are claims nonetheless, though, as the historian Carolyn Steedman's alternate analysis of the archive as itself a counter to this blending and its fantasy of inclusiveness makes clear: pace Derrida, the archive, she reminds us, has everything to do with state power and state authority: "The Archive is not potentially made up of everything, as is human memory . . . In the Archive, you cannot be shocked at its exclusions, its emptinesses, at what is not catalogued . . . Its condition of being deflects outrage: in its quiet folders and bundles is the neatest demonstration of how state power has operated, through ledgers and lists and indictments, and through what is missing from them."[20]

Middling and mousy, the archival researcher adapts beautifully to the dictates of the neoliberal university, enjoying "management's designer culture" (Marc Bousquet's term) and learning to live with and benefit from its empty slogans about "the culture of quality" and the "pursuit of excellence."[21] (Infusing academic culture with a competitive business ethos, this language offers equally good justification for market differentials— the awarding of higher salaries to faculty who could otherwise work in the private sector, thus instituting marked income disparities among the faculty—and for a pervasive and willful blindness to the conditions of other university workers.)[22] Against middle reading, I will propose a form of what I'll call extreme reading, which, as my title suggests, is also a form of dialectical reading. Again following Žižek, I'll also argue for a fidelity to the failure of Marxist literary criticism, and for the need to "go on and fail better" (7)—or, in this context, read better (to borrow a phrase from Zadie Smith).

The middle way

Initially delivered as part of the Tanner Lectures on Human Values in 1998, and subsequently published as a book, Elaine Scarry's *On Beauty and Being Just* performs a paean to beauty's capaciousness in the face of its banishment from the humanities over the course of the last 20 years. Against arguments that characterize beauty as meretricious or see it leading only to an empty materialism and possessiveness and/or dangerous forms of reification via the gaze, Scarry avers that beautiful things are not only generative, "[inciting] the desire to bring new things into the world" from infants to sonnets to laws and philosophical dialogues, but also "prepare us for justice."[23] Scarry grants to beauty a pliancy or elasticity (46): it both moves us forward in its "impulse toward begetting" (10), and backward, when it compels us to rethink our assessment of whether something is beautiful or not. In other words, it teaches us about "being wrong," making it a model for the very process of "consciousness in education" (46). Unlike the constraints of the material world, which compel us "to see each person and thing in its time and place, its historical context" (48), the mental processes we undergo in the presence of beauty have a porousness, or limitlessness, which "ignites the desire for truth by giving us, with an electric blindness shared by almost no other uninvited, freely arriving perceptual event, the experience of conviction and the experience, as well, of error" (52).

In the second part of the essay, Scarry then directly links beauty to justice, suggesting that the very symmetry at the heart of beauty inspires a consonant desire for symmetry or fairness in social arrangements. Etymologically, she notes, "fairness" refers both to something being aesthetically pleasing to the eye and "fitting" or "joining," as in making two things fair. In short, fair skies call out for fair legal arrangements (101) and those skies also have the advantage of being available to the senses, unlike legal arrangements. They, along with beautiful flowers, underground caves, music, and Matisse paintings, give sensory concreteness to otherwise abstract notions of justice or equality and thus serve as moral prompts in times of inequality. In its call for distributive justice, buttressed by the unself-interestedness it inspires in its beholder (117) beauty brings out the best in us: we wish for the existence of the beautiful whether we will be its beneficiary or not. These claims about beauty are anything but speculative for Scarry: "the vote on blossoms has been taken (people over many centuries have nurtured and carried the flowers from place to place, supplementing what was there)"; likewise, "the vote on the sky has been taken (the recent environmental movement)" and so on. "We are not guessing," the last sentence of the essay definitively concludes, "the evidence is in" (124).

Like this final evidentiary claim, Scarry's rhetoric throughout appeals to what is before us, to what is immediately apprehensible via the senses. Performing the aesthetic as much as arguing for it—beauty, after all, begets beauty in the essay's line of reasoning—Scarry lavishly appreciates individual objects, like Matisse's palm fronds and Gallé vases, in order to enact a seemingly natural progression from particular individual experiences of beauty to beauty's universal claims. If in Adorno, beauty holds out the promise of the nonidentical at the same time that it, as a consciously experienced phenomenon, denies it, in Scarry, beauty holds out the promise of more of the same—beauty has a bar code just like the Gallé vase; and one must suspect that the abstract equality that denies authentic equality lies at the heart of her notion of democracy. Marcuse would call this kind of culture Affirmative, written with a capital A. Individual, class-based standards—what is a Gallé vase anyhow; this reader had to google it. And how, *the Sopranos'* psychiatrist Jennifer Malfi might ask, does it compare to Murano glass?—are universalized in the surety of the concrete: "the evidence is in." The essay therefore restores beauty's humanizing effects by way of a categorical imperative, leaving the individual perceiver of beauty subject to and yet also not determined in any way by a beauty that "comes to us, with no work of our own; then leaves us prepared to undergo a giant labor" (53). But laboring toward what ends? The very terms requiring thought, debate, struggle, are contentless, reduced to the tautology, "fair social arrangements," in which fair means fair. Plenitude, capaciousness, the aspiration for truth: divorced from any social content whatsoever beauty's qualities have no meaning and they've already been realized anyhow: "the evidence is in." "Uninvited" and determined in advance, there's really not much left for individual subjects to do but wait to be taken.

A kind of humanism with guarantees, Scarry's enactment of beauty celebrates the transcendental nature of the beautiful soul. On its own, this is nothing new. But coming as it does in the wake of the theory years, and couched in the language of common sense, its willful disregard for the institutions and practices within which beauty exists and circulates signals something new. There's a determination here to find plenitude in the present at all costs but with nothing really at stake. And, of course, this is exactly where its appeal lies: free of negative, ugly considerations, which all would only entail "imperfect [instances] of an otherwise positive" (7) process, the institutional and social contexts and consequences of the aesthetic dissolve in the spirit, no less, of a professed inclusiveness. We can see beauty with our own eyes, there is nothing hidden, there are no Leonard Basts here: this is, in a word, cynical.

But also par for the course. In its championing of a naïve empiricism, Scarry's essay shares theoretical allegiances with the larger critical shift away from symptomatic readings or ideological critique, in which models of depth, unveiling, and decoding are eschewed in favor of a variety of "surface" readings. In both cases, a hermeneutics of suspicion is replaced by a suspicion of hermeneutics, a disavowing of interpretation itself, which is part and parcel of the so-called death of theory. One starting point for this movement can be located in Eve Sedgwick's 1995 essay "Shame in the Cybernetic Fold: Reading Silvan Tomkins," in which she catalogues the routinized moves considered de rigueur within applied theory at the time. In addition to identifying a series of theoretical assumptions, which had become, in her view, dogmatic, Sedgwick also registered and fueled a sense of theoretical exhaustion within literary critical studies. Revelations that earlier had prompted surprise now seemed stale and predictable, raising larger questions about the aims of literary criticism and the status and role of knowledge, which she continued to develop in her later essay on paranoid reading and in her work on Tomkins and theories of affect. As she comments in "Paranoid Reading, Reparative Reading," "in a world where no one need be delusional to find evidence of systemic oppression, to theorize out of anything but a paranoid critical stance has come to seem naïve, pious, or complaisant."[24]

Fast-forward 15 years and compare this to Sharon Marcus and Stephen Best's introduction to "Surface Reading," where they write:

> The assumption that domination can only do its work when veiled, which may once have sounded almost paranoid, now has a nostalgic, even utopian ring to it. Those of us who cut our intellectual teeth on deconstruction, ideology critique, and the hermeneutics of suspicion have often found these demystifying protocols superfluous in an era when images of torture at Abu Ghraib and elsewhere were immediately circulated on the internet; the real-time coverage of Hurricane Katrina showed in ways that required little explication the state's abandonment of its African American citizens; and many people instantly recognized as lies political statements such as "mission accomplished." Eight years of the Bush regime may have hammered home the point that not all situations require the subtle ingenuity associated with symptomatic reading, and they may also have inspired us to imagine that alongside nascent fascism there might be better ways of thinking and being simply there for the taking, in both the past and the present.[25]

Now there are significant differences to be noted between Sedgwick's subsequent work on reparative reading and the varied approaches taken by the contributors to "The Way We Read Now." In the interests of space, though, I want simply to note that both share the assumption that ideological critique is primarily a practice of unveiling, in which surface appearances are shown to be illusory, and the hidden or latent meaning beneath the surface the truth. And, crucially, the reader who practices such readings is assumed to be in a position of mastery over the text. (This point is specifically taken up by Jameson in "Making Time Appear" when he notes that the act of interpretation, contrary to populist bias, in no way asserts the superiority of the interpreter or reader over an assumed "plebeian readership," in an aside noting that "in that sense, we are all plebeians when we read." Rather "it simply offers an interpretive hypotheses, which the reader or re-reader is free to explore or to abandon (as sterile, as far-fetched, or as mistaken)." But "what the reader is not free to abandon is the interpretive process itself") (492–93). To counter the model of false consciousness, which warns that you cannot believe what you see, surface reading upends the binary, and claims that the truth is, in fact, readily available on the surface. Because we all watched the twin towers collapse, or saw the Abu Ghraib photos, their meaning is "there for the taking." To recognize that a regime peddles in lies is to know already what we need to know about that regime.[26]

To state the obvious: ideological critique, at its best, was never simply about unmasking, a recognition this collection of writers might have recalled, given the fact that the conference where these papers were delivered commemorated the twenty-fifth anniversary of *The Political Unconscious*, the most systematic articulation of Jameson's two-fold hermeneutic model in which the unmasking of determinant social relations is only half the story, the other half of course being the positive Utopian impulses that lie along negative critique.[27] But perhaps the more telling occlusion in dismissals of ideological critique is the dialectic. Surface reading hopes to freeze time, to stay in the present in its appeal to the commonsensical, to a thing's face value. Sharon Marcus, for example, in her work on women's friendships, *Between Women*, introduces the idea of "just reading": "Just reading attends to what Jameson, in his pursuit of hidden master codes, dismisses as 'the inert given and materials of a given text' . . . Just reading strives to be adequate to a text conceived as complex and ample rather than as diminished by, or reduced to, what it has had to repress. Just reading accounts for what is in the text without construing presence as absence or affirmation as negation."[28] Marcus does qualify her "just," adding that her approach "recognizes that interpretation is inevitable: even when attending to the givens of a text, we are always only—or just—constructing a meaning." Nor is it "to make an inevitably disingenuous claim to transparently reproduce a text's unitary meaning," nor to "dismiss symptomatic reading," since surface reading itself inevitably relies on the absences of other theories of the novel, such as Jameson's (75–76). But what "just reading" does not account for is the impact these qualifications have on the very project of analyzing "what is in the text," or what "texts present on their surface" (75).

The push and pull Marcus attempts to be theoretically savvy about evokes, significantly, the language of dialectics, a language conspicuously absent from characterizations of ideological critique. The impulse to be affirmative, to talk about what texts do rather than what they don't do, occludes the negation upon which such affirmation is based—in this example, the ontological assumptions structuring what appears "in the text"—but unlike a dialectical reading, offers no way of actually registering or thinking the occlusion that structures the surfaces being privileged. In short, surface readings have no real capacity to understand themselves as symptoms, despite the fact that they are, as Marcus confirms, at the very least symptoms of once dominant hermeneutic models of interpretation. Given this, it is not clear why they might not also be symptoms of larger structures; why stop at the horizon of a genre, when surely genres too constitute particular modes of historical thinking, simply at a different level of the social? Seen in this light, surface reading entails a form of fetishistic disavowal in its insistence on the real surface of texts; as Žižek's describes the function of the fetish, "what [it] gives body to is precisely my disavowal of knowledge, my refusal to subjectively assume what I know" (300). Surface reading's advocacy of neutrality, of "minimal critical agency," of "objectivity, validity, [and] truth" involves a fantasy of stepping outside the subject altogether; addressing the recent turn to computers and what their intelligence might provide in terms of new models of reading, Best and Marcus suggest: "Where the heroic critic corrects the text, a nonheroic critic might aim instead to correct for her critical subjectivity, by using machines to bypass it, in the hopes that doing so will produce more accurate knowledge about texts."[29] The ultimate aim, then, is toward more accurate descriptions, in which subjectivity can seemingly come and go, as needed: "Sometimes," the essay concludes, "our subjectivity will help us see a text more clearly, and sometimes it will not."[30] Neutral, objective, self-effacing, humbled before the text: this reader is, above all, benign.

Going to extremes

It is not enough to simply dismiss the new critical orthodoxies as reactive, culturally conservative, or anti-Marxist, since, as the dialectic itself demonstrates, there is no value in taking the moral high ground, and nothing to be gained by simply repeating old methods. Indeed, one of the reasons I have spent so much time on Scarry and surface reading is because, regardless of the paucity of their so-called solutions, their challenges to ideological critique nonetheless identify something of an impasse within Marxist literary and cultural criticism, namely the fact that the unearthing of the so-called real processes behind surface phenomenon has come to prove insufficient to the material life to be interpreted and changed. In his reading of commodity histories, Bruce Robbins identifies something similar when he asks: "Looking through a commodity to the human relations behind it, what exactly should one see? Capitalism? Class? Culture? The state? After all, what is the right way to describe a commodity?"[31] The same might be asked of Marxist approaches to a text: what are we hoping to see behind it? What are we demystifying and why? What, after all, is the right way to describe or read a text?

Borrowing one of Gayatri Spivak's formulations, I want to consider how, in the current debate around why and how we read, the extremes of surface reading and Marxist literary and cultural criticism bring each other into crisis. In Spivak's version, "practice persistently brings the notion of theory into crisis. And theory—just as persistently, and depending upon the situation—asymmetrically brings the vanguardism of practice into crisis as well." In the more limited confines of reading, I want to think more about how notions of surface and depth can be seen in productive tension or unease with one another, such that "neither one of the two can really take 'first' place."[32]

Many of the ways in which ideological critique brings surface reading into crisis have already been either alluded to or enumerated. The most obvious, and as yet only indirectly stated, is that Marxist criticism, as a theory and a practice, makes clear that reading alone is never enough. As Žižek articulates the consequences of a properly dialectical relationship between theory and practice, "at its most radical, theory is the theory of a failed practice" (3), a description that nicely captures, as well, Steven Helmling's description of Jameson's thinking as driven by a self-imposed "failure imperative."[33] Žižek also underscores that to theorize out of failure "confronts us with the problem of fidelity: avoiding the twin trap of nostalgic attachment to the past and of all-too-slick accommodation to 'new circumstances'" (3). In their attempts to be affirmative, to counter the negativity of critique with analysis, surface readers not only belie their humility before texts (success has already been realized; "the evidence is in"), but also fall prey to nostalgia and accommodation. The very substitution of reading for theory both harkens back to a more innocent time of ordinary, commonsensical reading ("just reading") and, as we have seen, easily allows for a complaisant accommodation to the given. In this way, surface readers give up on reading as much as they give up on theory, its role reduced to stating the obvious, even as they continue to fetishize the text in their celebration of its surface. They embody in their particular practice what Žižek has said about the age of cynical reason more generally: just as "cynical reason, with all its ironic detachment, leaves untouched the fundamental level of ideological fantasy, the level on which ideology structures the social reality itself" (27), so, too, do surface readers leave untouched the level on which ideology structures the apparent contiguity and coherence of the surface of the text itself. In short, they proceed as if the age of cynical reason is synonymous with a post-ideological world.

Žižek's distinction helps to illuminate the central point of contention between surface and symptomatic readers, namely the very status of the object of reading. Surface readers claim, in essence, that Marxist reading practices "de-materialize" the text—recall Marcus's claim that Jameson "dismisses the inert given and materials of a given text"—whereas Marxists argue that surface readers falsely materialize texts, thereby enhancing their inertness, and forgetting about the real things and real people behind them. In the former reading, surfaces seem to promise solidity, or an affirmative inertness that would render them unsusceptible to the vagaries of self-reflective thought; in the latter, surfaces are what we have to be wary about. Clearly, no simple averaging of the two extremes will do. But again, neither will simply choosing one or the other. Instead, it is the gap between them that creates what Spivak refers to as a productive unease that cannot settle on either side, a tension rather than a balance in which each side, she ventriloquizes, call outs: "Look here, you know you are dependent upon me and you're ignoring it."[34]

But for a moment let us reify the sides again and return briefly to the issue of how surface reading brings ideological critique to crisis by asking what the good of sheer negativity is when ideology critique has no leverage, and when we already know what will be revealed. At heart, this claim captures the way in which Marxist critique can fall prey to reified protocols of reading. The very fact that Eve Sedgwick can catalogue these protocols as she does (and I recognize that not all of them pertain directly or only to Marxist criticism) registers their failure to be properly dialectical as well as their attachment to old lessons already learned. They succumb in this way to a success regarding method, whose failure surface reading aims to correct. There is a deeper pressure here, though, regarding the force of negativity, which resonates with recent comments by both Žižek and Jameson. Commenting on Adorno's "implacable negative dialectic," Jameson writes, "[his] desperate attempt to avoid positivities, which he instinctively felt always to be ideological, by embracing a resolutely negative equipollence, is a prophetic but unsatisfying response to our historical situation," which might better be characterized by varying Žižek's famous title to "they know what they are doing (but they do it anyway)" (60). Likewise, Žižek suggests the need to distinguish between the symptomal mode of ideology under attack in surface reading and the fetishistic mode, which, he argues, predominates today. If the symptom marks the return of the repressed, that which disrupts the ideological lie, the fetish is the symptom turned inside out, as it were, "the embodiment of the lie which enables us to sustain the unbearable truth" (296). The fetish, that is to say, does its work in plain sight.[35] "Fetishists," Žižek notes, "are not dreamers lost in their private worlds, they are thoroughly 'realist,' able to accept the way things effectively are—since they have their fetish to which they can cling in order to cancel the full impact of reality" (296). It is hard not to see this characterization as tailor-made for surface readers. With the text as their fetish, surface readers are unencumbered by the "full impact of reality"—hence, perhaps the sense that you can easily hear their claims about texts coming out of the mouths of university deans. But this recognition, needless to say, does not negate their critique of negativity per se, a critique that finds a foothold within Marxism itself.

Nor does it dissipate, to my mind, the demand they make to give an account of the surface. But what is needed is a better way of reading surfaces *in relation to each other*, which requires a more rather than less expansive reading practice. Surface readers, as I have already noted, upend the surface/depth binary and thereby essentially remain within the same structure they want to criticize; they also tend to treat surfaces as if they are one with themselves. Given these limitations, it is important, as I noted earlier, to distinguish between surface readers and the work of Eve Sedgwick, for even as they share a suspicion of hermeneutics, Sedgwick's work on reparative reading and touch offers a substantive and affectively powerful demonstration of the spatial relations missing from surface reading—the challenges of which Marxist literary criticism would do well to heed. In particular, Sedgwick's attentiveness to the sensory aspects of experience can, I believe, help us rethink the relationship between lived experience and structure, itself a recoding of the relationship between immanence and transcendence, or event and system, all attempts to conceptualize, as Jameson notes in the preface to *Marxism and Form*, the new spatial relations within what he then termed industrial capitalism, and then more fully developed in his work on postmodernism as the cultural logic of late capitalism.[36] Ultimately I aim to show how the spatial dialectic Jameson gestures toward in *Valences of the Dialectic* and Sedgwick's emphasis on touch as opposed to sight share a desire to reimagine the lividness of contemporary social relations by way of their spatiality. (Whereas Jameson, in the face of the radical transformation of space within postmodernity, invoked the need to grow new organs, Sedgwick turns to different, already available but neglected sensory modes such as touch to capture this same space.) These distinct perspectives—a Hegelian Marxism, on the one hand, and a nondualistic queer/affect theory, on the other—together define the challenge of conceptualizing lived experience and structure in dialectical relation to one another, which, in turn, constitutes the challenge of how to think space dialectically.

Extreme or perverse reading

In her Introduction to *Touching Feeling*, a book whose central project is "to explore promising tools and techniques for nondualistic thought and pedagogy" (1), Sedgwick invokes a set of spatial concepts as one avenue through which to understand and feel (to literally come up next to) the deeply textured, often nonlinguistic nature of knowledge and social relations. Specifically, she places the spatial concept of "beside" in relation to "beneath" and "beyond," and suggests that "invoking a Deleuzian interest in planar relations, the irreducibly spatial positionality of beside also seems to offer some useful resistance to the ease with which beneath and beyond turn from spatial descriptors into implicit narratives of, respectively, origin and telos" (8). Trying to stop the emptying out of space (the "air of neutrality or indifference with regard to its contents"[37]) that temporal narratives enact, Sedgwick hopes to allow for the possibility of the reverse: halting linear, causal narratives, which flatten out lived material experience, and instead feeling the difference space makes. (In a different context, Zadie Smith characterizes the emphasis on the former as the "filling of space with time," which she links to "realism's obsession" with "convincing us that time has passed" and the latter as "filling time up with space."[38]) Moreover, as Sedgwick imagines the meaning of beside, "a number of elements may lie alongside one another, though not an infinity of them. Beside permits a spacious agnosticism about several of the linear logics that enforce dualistic thinking: noncontradiction or the law of the excluded middle, cause versus effect, subject versus object." Sedgwick is quick to note that at the same time, "its interest does not, however, depend on a fantasy of metonymically egalitarian or even pacific relations, as any child knows who's shared a bed with siblings" (8). These side by side, lateral relations, for her, are "tensile" and "proximate"; they feel or register the recalcitrance of the material and acknowledge what Jonathan Goldberg, referencing a 1999 talk of Sedgwick's, "Reality and Realization," where she describes the difference between thinking your cancer is in remission and learning that it is incurable, calls the "mental shuttle-pass between knowing and realizing," another way perhaps for articulating the need to redeem the failure of ideological critique by reading better.[39] Is this not in some sense a project that begins to read lateral relations as at once material and figural, of time and space, but neither that of surface reading nor ideological critique alone? Whereas the latter two protocols might be characterized as "ways of knowing what we see," the kind of reading Sedgwick practices here entails "ways of seeing what we know." As with Žižek's description of the fetishistic mode of ideology, no accumulation of documents, however large, can do this kind of interpretive work.[40] Against the archive piety of historicists, the recognition or realization involved in "seeing what we know" is one of qualitative difference rather than quantitative sameness, of perverse relations rather than commonsensical surfaces in which the status of the real is an interpretive problem rather than a given.[41]

A perverse reader, Sedgwick suggests in an earlier essay, "Queer and Now," is an ardent reader. Looking back on the development of her own reading practices, she situates them in the context of a broader field of passional investments in and deep attachments to cultural objects more generally, which became for her (and, she imagines, for many queer writers and teachers), "a prime resource for survival," a way of reading that is at one and the same time a way of being in the world—so much so, she adds, that "it's almost hard for me to imagine another way of coming to care enough about literature to give a lifetime to it."[42] Reading is by necessity overreading: intense rather than cool (as in "just reading"); political rather than historicist; highly interpretive rather than descriptive. Rather than the less is more logic of surface reading, perverse or ardent reading requires more reading, at once close given our attachments, and distant, given the reach of perverse relations. "The demands on both the text and the reader from so intent an attachment," Sedgwick writes, "can be multiple, even paradoxical"—and be engaged, no less, by a formalist investment in texts, which Sedgwick characterizes, in her own case, as a "visceral near-identification with the writing [she] cared for, at the level of sentence structure, metrical pattern, rhyme," all a "way of trying to appropriate what seemed the numinous and resistant power of the chosen objects" (3).

Formalism need not, however, be dispassionate nor eschew the political and the world outside the text:

> For me, this strong formalist investment didn't imply (as formalism is generally taken to imply) an evacuation of interest from the passional, the imagistic, the ethical dimensions of the texts, but quite the contrary: the need I brought to books and poems was hardly to be circumscribed, and felt I knew I would have to struggle to wrest from them sustaining news of the world, ideas, myself, and (in various senses) my kind. The reading practices founded on such basic demands and intuitions had necessarily to run against the grain of the most patent available formulae for young people's reading and life . . . At any rate, becoming a perverse reader was never a matter of my condescension to texts, rather of the surplus charge of my trust in them to remain powerful, refractory, and exemplary. (4)

In this articulation of reading, texts are both fully here in their "resistant power" (and akin to the recalcitrance of the material she will later evoke in lateral relations), and wholly elsewhere, in their "numinous power." They produce a "near-identification" that is neither a loss of the self nor or an affirmation of an autonomous self, nor, significantly, some kind of compromise between the two. Instead such reading relations embody the perversity of the nonidentical.

In earlier works of Sedgwick's, the catalogue or list illustrates and enacts the potential richness of relations of nonidentity. As she asks in "Queer and Now" in the context of a list of all the different meanings of "the

family," which, within the constraints of dominant ideology, are "meant
to line up perfectly with each other": "What if . . . there were a practice
of valuing the ways in which meanings and institutions can be at loose
ends with each other? What if the richest junctures weren't the ones where
everything means the same thing?" (6). Sedgwick's later attention to
touch specifically highlights the spatial nature of (non) identity, the way,
as Judith Butler frames it, that we live "beside ourselves" (24), that being
"beside oneself" (with grief or rage) and hence profoundly vulnerable to
and "implicated in lives that are not our own" (28) illuminates identity
itself as a state of dispossession.[43] In a similar vein, Jameson, in his analysis
of the "Three Names of the Dialectic," suggests that older equations of
identity, such as Hegel's I = I to denote self-consciousness, are by nature
spatial (69). For Sedgwick, tarrying with the space of "besideness" is not
only a way "around the topos of depth or hiddenness, typically followed
by a drama of exposure" (8), which she identifies with a hermeneutics
of suspicion, but a way of thinking nondualistically and ecologically. It
also prompts, importantly, new forms of recognition or realization and
alternate conceptions of pedagogy, inspired, in particular, by Buddhist
practices. Here the "near-identification" Sedgwick describes with texts
finds something like its corollary in the "near-miss pedagogy" of what in
Buddhist writing is called "pointing at the moon": an example of which
is the mundane and oft-repeated exchange familiar to cat owners in
which, wanting a cat to look at something, we point and the cat, rather
than looking where we want it to, sniffs our finger instead. Spatial and
pedagogical relations: both offer new forms of relationality that help to
refigure the relationship between lived experience and structure, which,
in a somewhat different language, Sedgwick refers to when she states:
"Spatializing disciplines such as geography and anthropology . . . have the
advantage of permitting ecological or systems approaches to such issues
as identity and performance" (8). As Sedgwick's sustained meditations on
space and pedagogy also demonstrate, the two are inextricably linked,
much like the finger pointing at the moon and the moon itself turns out to
be inseparable within Buddhism.

The anthropologist Esther Newton's work on drag clubs makes visible,
in a most concrete way, the gains for Sedgwick of an "ecological attention
to space" (*Touching*, 9). In her analysis of drag, Newton focuses not just
on the drag performance and performers, but also on the floor plans of two
drag clubs, thereby including in drag a set of spatial relations comprising
"a heterogeneous system, an ecological field whose intensive and defining
relationality is internal as much as it is directed toward the norms it may
challenge" (9). (As I suggest below, Jameson's comments on the absence
within narratives of globalization of analyses of the changed space of
national cultures can be seen to parallel, I think, the kind of distinction
Sedgwick makes here between internal and outward-directed forms of

relationality.) Judith Butler's reading of drag, which draws on Newton's work, dramatizes this difference for Sedgwick. By leaving out Newton's incorporation of space, Butler's account stresses instead the temporal aspects of drag: "With its loss of spatiality, the internally complex field of drag performance suffers a seemingly unavoidable simplification and reification." In fact, Sedgwick surmises, "I think this loss of dimension may explain why many early readers, wrongly, interpreted Butler's discussion as prescribing a simplistic voluntarity" (9). With the shift from space to time, not only are the transindividual relations within drag lost, thereby making it into a solo or "single act," but also lost are the ways in which space is productive; the fact that it produces us as much as we produce it.[44]

But, importantly, the converse shift from single act to heterogeneous system is not a disavowal of lived experience in the interests of structure—a loss of the livedness of the diachronic or of narrative, which Ricoeur feared in synchronic or structuralist models of the social—but rather a recognition of identity as *in proximity*, a different articulation of which Sedgwick traces in the pedagogy of Buddhism. In the opening of Sogyal Rinpoche's *The Tibetan Book of Living and Dying*, she sees Rinpoche's mode of teaching as at once intensely personal and emotional and a "mysteriously powerful solvent of individual identity" (160). Beginning with his own disorienting initiation as an infant into the monastery, a result of being chosen as a reincarnation of one of the great masters, Rinpoche initiates the reader into the text through a series of pedagogical scenes, in which his identity as student (grateful to "[his] master") and teacher (he is now a master himself, indeed has been "'recognized' as an incarnation of his master's own teacher"; 159) become indistinguishable—or more accurately, the idea of choosing between student and master is rendered moot: "Rather than into 'Buddhism,' a reader who begins this book is, by means of her disorientation, interpellated into a rich yet dissolvent relationality of pedagogy itself. In this world it is as though relation *could only be* pedagogical—and for *that* reason, radically transindividual" (160).

To learn within such a pedagogical relation radically alters not only how one learns but also what exactly is to be learned. A process of recognition, learning is unabashedly tautological: we learn what we already know. That which constitutes a problem within Western modes of knowing becomes in Buddhism "a deliberate defining practice" (166); in place of the "paradox/ impasse/scandal" of the tautological nature of learning, "of being able to learn only versions of what you already know or find only what you have already learned to look for" (166), Buddhism embraces the complexity of recognizing what we know. Recognition in this sense is processural, makes no distinction between means and ends, and can take a lifetime. And like dialectics, Buddhism includes within it a scrutiny of the very mental categories with which we "know." It is also perhaps another way of "thinking" the perversity of Žižek's formulation of ideology as "they know it, but they are doing it anyway," which is in turn, for Žižek, a matter of "saving appearances" or recognizing the paradox of "objective appearance" (which I will return to below). And again, as with the mobility of teacher/student relations, the idea of choosing between the terms in such formulations loses all meaning.

The pedagogical nature of relation and of spatiality, more particularly, that Sedgwick recognizes in Buddhism lies at the center of Jameson's speculations on a spatial dialectic as well. Despite occupying a completely different affective register, Jameson, like Sedgwick, finds in the reading of space an articulation of identity and the social that unsettles the "lightning-flash simultaneity of self and world" privileged by temporal models of identity and their concomitant "ideologies of self-consciousness or reflection" (68). He, too, that is, finds in spatial relations embodiments of the nonidentical; he wagers that "space . . . is the source of difference and time . . . that of identity" (69).

To be sure, they accent their respective accounts differently. While Sedgwick, for example, characterizes relations of "besideness" as tensile and proximate, her emphasis ultimately on a reparative reading (to counter what she sees as the deficiencies of ideological critique) leads her to stress the creative richness of nonidentical relations. Hers is a pedagogy of cerebral "feltness"; of touch and textiles that, like Rinpoche's initiatory "opening," initiates her readers into alternate relations without herself being at the center in any way.[45] Jameson, on the other hand, working explicitly within the tradition of Hegelian dialectics, emphasizes the dissonance, violence, or negativity among the multiple horizons of the social, which alone allow us to perceive time and change (key features of any dialectic)—and without which a Marxist politics is impossible. In his account, then, the pedagogical need for a spatial dialectic arises in response to the twin narratives of the "end of history" and globalization, which, together, express the coordinates of late capitalism in terms, respectively, of time and space. The gesture toward a spatial dialectic not only speaks to the lost sense of historicity within the present, the sense that it has become increasingly difficult to imagine an other to capitalism in temporal terms (either as a memory of a not yet fully commodified *before* or past, or the possibility of an uncommodified *after* or future), but more pointedly aims to recognize space as newly "dominant" within globalization and to register this dominance in theory and practice. This shift, Jameson clarifies, "is not meant to suggest that one dimension [within the 'spatio-temporal continuum'] replaces the other but rather to convey the fact that their ratios have been modified, or in other words that there has been a shift in the structure of their 'form of appearance'" (68).[46] "Saving appearances" within this changed structure will therefore entail learning to read space in dialectical relation to time, which in turn, presupposes new constructions of consciousness or "seeing." In this light, the proposal for a spatial dialectic can be seen as an extension or enlargement of Jameson's notion of cognitive mapping in which cognition itself undergoes a further dialectical twist.

Perhaps the most dramatic example of the difference an attentiveness to space can make comes in Jameson's analysis of Fernand Braudel's history of the Mediterranean. This analysis develops by way of Jameson's close reading of Ricoeur's *Narrative and Time* in which, as Jameson demonstrates, Ricoeur makes existential time in modernist novels such as *Mrs. Dalloway* and *The Magic Mountain* appear "in the intersection of multiple kinds of temporality" (500). The fact of multiple temporalities is not in and of itself, however, to be celebrated. Indeed, Jameson's polemic against contemporary humanist invocations of difference and multiplicity rests on his distinction between the mere existence of multiple temporalities and the intersection of these temporalities, in which the gaps or aporia between temporalities are made evident. Ricoeur, in this context, figures for Jameson as an exemplar of humanism and its limits, then and now. "The appearance of Time or History as such," Jameson underscores, "depends not on the multiplicity and variety of these trajectories, but rather on their interference with each other, with their intersection now understood as dissonance and as incommensurability rather than as a conjuncture which augments them all, in the fashion of a synthesis, by the central space of some harmonious meeting and combination" (543). The intersection of these varied and multiple intersections is indeed often violent—and necessary "in order for this dissonant conjunction to count as an Event, and in particular as that Event which is the ephemeral rising up and coming to appearance of Time and History as such" (543).[47] Like Badiou's notion of the Event, in other words, this process entails something like a cut into the social, which Žižek describes as a "subtraction *from* the hegemonic field which, simultaneously, forcefully intervenes *into* this field, reducing it to its occluded minimal difference" (411).

One way of seeing these intersecting gaps or incommensurabilities is by extending the very frame of time, as Braudel does when he attends to three temporalities in his study of the Mediterranean: the long *durée* of geological time, the middle time of institutional practices, and the short *durée* of historical events. Humanists err in looking only at the short *durée*, equivalent to existential time. In their reading, history remains the history of the individual; the only "real event," for Ricoeur, is the "existential one" (542). But geological time fundamentally challenges Ricoeur's humanism in its Darwinian rebuke to human consciousness and understanding; it is, Jameson writes, "a temporality so deep the human senses and even human storytelling, historical memory, the records and the archives, cannot register it" (539). Which is not to say, however, that it does not nevertheless have "its own temporality and its own narrative possibilities, just as the solar system does, or the galaxies" (539). The incommensurability between different temporalities, between objective and subjective time, the cosmological and the existential, marks the site, or rather, lack of a site, where time itself, which is also now seen to be inseparably connected to space, is expressed. (Jameson hazards the term "synchronicity" to reflect this connectedness.) These discordances also point to one of the dialectic's basic forms: namely "the way that success brings failure, winner loses, and good fortune brings all kinds of new problems which in the end may well prove fatal" (537). In Braudel's historiography, this dialectical reversal occurs when the success of the Mediterranean meets its limit in its own geography—in its inability to bring in enough people to ply its trade—and world trade moves on and forms a new center in the Atlantic and Northern Europe (541). This story differs from the story told when Philip II is at the center of the narrative; in that version of history, the story of the Mediterranean ends with Phillip's death in 1598 rather than decades later, as it does in geographical time. It is precisely the gap between the two stories—the way the two deaths, as it were, do not meet up—that needs to be retained, because it is only in the disparity between them, in "their interference with each other" (543), that Time or History can be apprehended. A holding open of negativity, a refusal to close the gap or synthesize the differences constitutes reading here— what Ricoeur, describing the structure of narrative, refers to as "discordant concordance," and which Jameson likes for its ability to remind us of the processural nature of mimesis, of emplotment as an act and a process (506), but which Jameson also crucially modifies to allow for a theorization of "agency on the level of the collective" (501).

Jameson's reading of Braudel's historiography also implies a kind of "knowing" that no longer relies on self-reflexivity as the means toward the apprehension of history. In place of self-consciousness, which Jameson argues we must see as integrally linked to a "temporal thematics," a spatial dialectic refigures the coming to consciousness non-associated with self-consciousness as a "mode of quasi-spatial enlargement: to the old non-reflexive I or ordinary consciousness there is added something else, which allows us to grasp that former non-reflexive self as itself an object within a larger field" (69). "Seeing what we know" entails seeing not only larger socio-temporal relations spatially, but our very identity as well. "It is an operation structurally analogous," Jameson suggests, "to the way in which two distinct spatial objects are set in relationship to each other by perception as such (what I have called 'difference relates')" (69–70). The ability to think the world and ourselves spatially is thus in a sense a response to the need to "grow new organs" referenced above. Numerous examples in the last section of *Valences of the Dialectic* attest to the representational potency of an attentiveness to space, from the Greimasian boxes that illustrate the presence of hitherto unseen but present historical actors, such as the "formerly employed," to the spatial enlargements that are part of the process of *anagnorisis* (one of the three Aristotelian narrative categories Jameson adapts from Ricoeur to "open up new perspectives on the narrative structure history shares with fiction" 565).[48] In his discussion of *anagnorisis*, commonly understood as "recognition," for example, Jameson notes that an alternate translation renders *anagnorisis* as "discovery." In this light, the recognition, historically, of a new class, for instance, becomes something more like an "enlargement of historical knowledge which is then at one with practical political consequences" (571) than the kind of recognition advocated within liberal political thought and assimilable within bourgeois society. In Subaltern Studies, for example, this "discovery" involves the radical reconstitution of the peasantry by way of the notion of "the subaltern" into a "genuine 'subject of history,' whose acts and interventions are not simply blind and spontaneous reflexes of *jacquerie* and irrational mob behavior, but rather know an intentionality of a kind not hitherto recognized or acknowledged," thereby effecting a "kind of agnagnorisis . . . in which History can itself be glimpsed in a new and more energizing way" (572).

Like the space of "besideness," to which Sedgwick is drawn for its potency to read relations *as pedagogical*, the enlarged scope of a spatial dialectic and the processes of reversal and recognition it allows on a historical scale represent the possibility of a Marxist pedagogy attuned to the geography of globalization: the contradictions between the positive and negative aspects of capitalist development play out spatially, be it in the disparity between developed and underdeveloped economies, between capitalist and failed states, or between those in the thick of history and those who have "fallen out of history" (576). But, how, exactly is this different from older recognitions of capitalism's drive to colonize more and more of the globe, dramatized by Marx in the *Communist Manifesto* as giving "a cosmopolitan character to production and consumption in every country"?[49] Classical Marxist models produce two contending classes, the bourgeoisie and the proletariat, both of which are positively determined in the sense that they are produced by the movement of capitalism, and its dynamic of exploitation and development. But, as Žižek highlights, the problem today is "how are we to think the singular universality of the emancipatory subject as not purely formal, that is, as objectively-materially determined, but without the working class as its substantial base?" (420). His answer is to say that "the solution is a negative one: it is capitalism itself which offers a negative substantial determination, for the global capitalist system is the substantial 'base' which mediates and generates the excesses (slums, ecological threats, and so on) that open up sites of resistance" (421). In other words, the excesses or exclusions of the global capitalist system become the object of inquiry, along with those individuals and groups who are negatively rather than positively determined by capitalism, namely the slum dwellers, the excluded, those who, as Jameson phrases it, have literally "fallen out of history," who are, along with the spaces they inhabit, the detritus or waste left in capitalism's wake.

Closest to the lumpenproletariat whom Marx deemed inconsequential to the class struggle, these negatively determined subjects differ in being *formerly* rather than chronically unemployed. The significance of this distinction, the discovery, to use Jameson's language, that it prompts arises directly from a reading of capitalist development in spatial rather than temporal terms. For as Jameson underlines, the "closure of the world market" when seen from the vantage point of these excluded spaces and workers, can no longer be understood as the "filling up of an empty container," or the complete colonization and homogenization of space. Instead, capitalism needs to be understood as "the progress of an epidemic" (582)—in which the excluded or slum-dweller, whom Žižek refers to as "a *homo sacer*, the systemically generated 'living dead' of global capitalism," becomes newly visible. This distinction, in essence, gives the lie to the possibility ever of the real subsumption of all social relations and labor processes under capital. "Abandoned by capital in its *fuite en avant*," Jameson writes, these spaces are "now fully commodified at the same time that they are blighted and devastated" (582).

Of course, this view of global spatial relations is not an endpoint, but only a beginning, defining a contemporary Marxist politics explicitly in terms of globalization: "The 'destructured' masses, poor and deprived of everything, situated in a non-proletarianized urban environment, constitute one of the principal horizons of the politics to come" (426), according to Žižek; "they occupy a *proletarian* position, the position of the 'part of no-part'" (428). In his view, then, a "genuine form of globalization, today, would be found in the organization of these masses—on a worldwide scale, if possible—whose conditions of existence are essentially the same" (426). Jameson, likewise, speculates on the necessity of such a transformation, from a subject negatively determined by the global capitalist system to a positively determined subject or social agent capable of opposing capitalism. But his interest here also rests in understanding the narrative processes themselves that are employed to conceptualize or theorize such transformations, namely "the inseparability of the figurative process from any more properly cognitive mapping as such" (582). At the same time that we must recognize the descriptions used to distinguish between the filling of a container and an epidemic as figures, with "specific disadvantages and constitutive distortions," the very repositionings that take place as a result are theoretically—and potentially politically—productive. Phrased as a thought experiment, Jameson writes:

> The unlikely possibility of the industrialization of the abandoned populations of the postmodern world nonetheless allows us to reconceptualize, and cognitively remap, their structural positions within the world system, and to recreate actants, agents, narrative characters, in a far more inclusive narrative about late capitalism or globalization,

than the ones in which this whole range of debates has hitherto moved. Here, in other words, we grasp anagnorisis as an act of theoretical production, in which new characters are produced for our collective and political discovery and recognition. (582)

Whether in the vision of a primary antagonism between the Included and the Excluded, or the enlargement of space that permits us to see that "there is no difference between consciousness and self-consciousness," both Žižek and Jameson illustrate the persistence of the dialectic within a fully global capitalism given its unique capacity to read space relationally, which, to return to where we began, can never be only read "on the surface," given the paradoxical nature of "objective appearance." To remain at the level of appearance, as surface readers advocate, is the most ideological of positions in its refusal to distinguish between that which is "constituted" and that which is "constitutive"; in the different context of the claims of democracy, Žižek asserts that "while democracy can more or less eliminate constituted violence, it still has to rely continuously on constitutive violence" (413). Likewise, without a means of reading ourselves into the equation, as it were, and thereby responding to the challenge to read lived experience and structure dialectically, in proximate relationship to one another, we are left with variants of empirical thinking, whose limitations Heidegger bluntly captures when he warns: "Science doesn't think." Ill-equipped to capture the livedness of space as an individual and transindividual process and structure, social scientific accounts miss the pedagogical aspect of cognitive mapping or a spatial dialectic, which, like Sedgwick's reading of pedagogy, relies on a notion of recognition rather than an abstract conceptual mastery of the real.[50] How to see the real's "aching gaps," to borrow one of Sedgwick's phrases, if we only fetishize its surfaces? Or, as the epigraph that begins this essay puts this declaratively, "in a time of crisis and ruptures, skeptical empirical wisdom itself, constrained to the horizon of the dominant form of common sense, cannot provide the answers, so one must risk a Leap of Faith."

Remaining on the surface, in other words, is simply not an option, at least if reading is about something other than the performance of reading. "The very concept of objective appearance," Jameson cautions, "warns us that any such resolution of the contradiction in favor of either essence or appearance, truth or falsehood, is tantamount to doing away with the ambiguous reality itself. The dialectic stands as an imperative to hold the opposites together" (65). The particular challenge of a spatial dialectic is to hold together the visceral, affective, and local textures of experience and the global, virtual, derivative-driven flows of capital. For, as Adorno reminds us, "dialectical mediation is not a recourse to the more abstract, but a process of resolution of the concrete in itself."[51] A fidelity to the lost cause of reading dialectically, in other words, is the only way to keep faith with history.

If, in an earlier moment, we could perhaps still envision enclaves (especially intellectual ones) seemingly protected from a not yet fully global capitalism, local crises today, such as those of theory, the humanities, and the university dispel such myths, and set in motion the kind of mental shuttle-pass Sedgwick identifies between knowing and realizing. The neoliberalization of the university has made talk of the "death" of the humanities a reality—and one more and more directly felt on the ground, as it were.[52] Once the idea of the humanities (or the university or theory) as an enclave becomes impossible to sustain, saving the university has no meaning if divorced from a larger, systemic politics. What then becomes indistinguishable is reading and a fidelity to revolution.

Notes

1 Turning the tables on this particular narrative, Vincent Leitch writes: "I prefer to think not that literary studies (or university education) was tragically politicized in recent decades, say since the 1960s, but that it was peculiarly depoliticized in the 1940s and 1950s as part of the 'end of ideology' campaign waged during the early years of the Cold War . . . In this scenario, cultural studies represents something like a return to normal after an aberrant period of reaction that tended to fetishize disembodied great works along with pure science and unending progress." *Theory Matters* (New York: Routledge, 2003), 7–8; see also Leitch, "Theory Ends," *Profession* 2005 (New York: Modern Language Association, 2005), 122–28.

2 Marjorie Perloff, "Presidential Address 2006: It Must Change," *PMLA* 122, no. 3 (May 2007): 652.

3 Marjorie Levinson, "What Is New Formalism?" *PMLA* 122, no. 2 (March 2007): 559.

4 In his review of *The Blank Slate*, the philosopher Simon Blackburn rightly notes that the doctrines comprising Pinker's "unholy Trinity" are inconsistent with one another, surely complicating Pinker's diagnosis of their domination of modern life. As he also notes, though:

"Still, it is not for its cultural history that people are buying this book in alarming numbers, but for the promise of a new synthesis, a science of the mind that finally tells us who we are, what is possible for us, how our politics should be organized, how people should be brought up, what to expect of ethics—in short, how to live." And this turn to a science of the mind indicates one more way in which the classic role of the humanities is being displaced: "In the old days," Blackburn rues, "philosophers, dramatists, historians, anthropologists, writers and poets monopolized these subjects. Now behavioral economists, biologists, cognitive scientists, evolutionary theorists and neurophysiologists occupy the territory. A brave new dawn is upon us."

"Meet the Flintstones," review of *The Blank Slate: The Modern Denial of Human Nature*, by Steven Pinker, *The New Republic*, November 25, 2002, http://www.tnr.com/article/meet-the-flintstones.

5 Steven Pinker, *The Blank Slate: The Modern Denial of Human Nature* (New York: Viking, 2002), x.

6 Ibid., 417. In a glowing review of *The Blank Slate* (part of a two-part article on "The New Darwinism in the Humanities"), Harold Fromm lauds Pinker as among these mavericks. Interestingly though, even as he celebrates Pinker's (and E. O. Wilson's) virtuosity in crossing the science–humanities divide, he does find it necessary to qualify his praise when it comes to their aesthetic judgments:

> "They [Pinker and Wilson] practice the consilience they recommend to others. While valuing their insights, we don't have to accept their aesthetic judgments as the last word, since the matter of 'beauty' in the arts is complex. We know that the late Beethoven, late Wagner, Mahler, Stravinsky, Picasso, some of James Joyce and T.S. Eliot, etc., were at first regarded as 'ugly' and now are so naturalized as to present few problems. What hasn't been assimilated—*Finnegan's Wake, Moses und Aron*—may be the sort of artifacts that affirm Pinker's judgment."

"The New Darwinism in the Humanities, Part I: From Plato to Pinker," *The Hudson Review* vol. LVI, no. 1 (Spring 2003): 99. The very fact that beauty is complex in this way, however, fundamentally undercuts Pinker's argument. See also "The New Darwinism in the Humanities, Part II: Back to Nature, Again," *The Hudson Review* LVI, no. 2 (Summer 2003): 315–327.

7 Caroline Levine, "Strategic Formalism: Toward a New Method in Cultural Studies," *Victorian Studies* 48, no. 4 (Summer 2006): 633–34; and Herbert Tucker, "Tactical Formalism: A Response to Caroline Levine," *Victorian Studies* 49, no. 1 (Autumn 2006): 85–93.

8 Levine, "Strategic Formalism," 633–34. Despite Levine's clarification regarding the role of the poem within a "strategic formalist" analysis, it seems telling that not only does she choose to illustrate the benefits of her method by way of a reading of a poem, but that the two responses to her essay in the *Victorian Studies* critical response forum also use poems to illustrate their shared interest in reinvigorating questions of form within literary studies. As with New Criticism, the poem seems to offer an especially manageable site for the kind of close, local reading certain variants of formalism inspire. See Carolyn Dever, "Strategic Aestheticism: A Response to Caroline Levine," *Victorian Studies* 49, no. 1 (Autumn 2006): 94–99; and Tucker, "Tactical Formalism."

9 In the case of narratological, cognitive, and other data-based systems of literary criticism, the hope seems to be that literature can be analyzed within the same kinds of supposedly objective paradigms as science, its findings verifiable and valid rather than subject to interpretation and hence relative. A recent article in the *New York Times* frames this work in the crudest of instrumental ways, asking in a sidebar, "Can combining neuroscience and Jane Austen get a literature Ph.D. a job?" Patricia Cohen, "Next Big Thing in English: Knowing They Know That You Know," *The New York Times*, March 31, 2010. More nuanced responses in the "Room for Debate" forum also however embody many of the key concerns and aims enumerated above regarding the capitulation of these various movements to the status quo or the given. Blakey Vermeule, for example, notes that younger scholars "bring a suite of skills that are fully compatible with science. They are highly tech-savvy and open to using digital techniques to mount broad, ambitious research

programs." The value of such research is that "Energies are distributed and results are empirical and (one hopes) testable and falsifiable . . . Striking about all of this work is how practical, positive, cooperative and empirical it is. So to say that the humanities are floundering in theory's wake is misleading. The theory wars are long gone and nobody regrets their passing. What has replaced them is just what was there all along: research and scholarship, but with a new openness to scientific ideas and methods." "Practical and Positive Research," *The New York Times*, April 5, 2010.

10 Levine, "Strategic Formalism," 630, 629.

11 See for example Jean-Jacques Lecercle's "Return to the Political," *PMLA* 125, no. 4 (2010): 916–19, devoted to the topic of "Literary Criticism for the Twenty-First Century," as well as an interview, in the same issue, with Gayatri Chakravorty Spivak.

12 Max Horkheimer, "Traditional and Critical Theory," trans. Matthew J. O'Connell, in *Critical Theory: Selected Essays* (New York: Herder & Herder, 1972), 221.

13 Fredric Jameson, *Valences of the Dialectic* (New York: Verso, 2009), 532.

14 Catherine Gallagher and Stephen Greenblatt, *Practicing New Historicism* (Chicago: University of Chicago Press, 2000), 19.

15 Alexander Kluge, "The Assault of the Present on the Rest of Time," trans. Tamara Evans and Stuart Liebman,*New German Critique* 49 (Winter 1990): 11–22.

16 Gallagher and Greenblatt, *Practicing*, 9.

17 Jameson describes this lateralness in terms of "a return to immanence and to a prolongation of the procedures of 'homology' which eschews homology's theory and abandons the concept of 'structure.'" He goes on to characterize New Historicism's discourse "as a 'montage of historical attractions,' to adapt Eisenstein's famous phrase, in which extreme theoretical energy is captured and deployed, but repressed by a valorization of immanence and nominalism that can either look like a return to the 'thing itself' or a 'resistance to theory.'" *Postmodernism, or, The Cultural Logic of Late Capitalism* (Durham, NC: Duke University Press, 1991), 188 and 190–91.

18 David Bordwell, "Contemporary Film Studies and the Vicissitudes of Grand Theory," in *Post-Theory: Reconstructing Film Studies*, ed. David Bordwell and Noël Carroll (Madison, WI: University of Wisconsin Press, 1996), 3–36.

19 Slavoj Žižek, *In Defense of Lost Causes* (New York: Verso, 2008), 2.

20 Carolyn Steedman, *Dust* (Manchester: Manchester University Press, 2001), 68.

21 Marc Bousquet, *How the University Works: Higher Education and the Low-Wage Nation* (New York: New York University Press, 2008), 107.

22 Bousquet is particularly interested in analyzing the commercialization of the university and changes in the university's organizational structure in tandem with one another. In the subtitle of his article "Worlds to Win," part of a collection of essays honoring Cary Nelson's contributions to these debates, Bousquet names his approach "Toward a Cultural Studies of the University Itself." See "Worlds to Win: Toward a Cultural Studies of the University Itself," in *Cary Nelson and the Struggle for the University: Poetry, Politics and the Profession*, ed. Michael Rothberg and Peter K. Garrett (Albany, NY: SUNY Press, 2009), 95–111.

23 Elaine Scarry, *On Beauty and Being Just* (Princeton, NJ: Princeton University Press, 1999), 46, 78.

24 Eve Kosofsky Sedgwick, *Touching Feeling: Affect, Pedagogy, Performativity* (Durham, NC: Duke University Press, 2003), 125–26.

25 Stephen Best and Sharon Marcus, "Surface Reading: An Introduction," in *The Way We Read Now*, ed. Sharon Marcus and Stephen Best, special issue, *Representations* 108 (Fall 2009): 2.

26 If Errol Morris's film *Standard Operating Procedure* shows anything, it is that the meaning of these Abu Ghraib images—even as evidence of a malign power that seems unquestionable—are far from obvious, transparent, and "there for the taking." In an editorial he wrote after the release of a videotape showing an Iraqi insurgent being killed by a US marine in Fallujah, Morris positions "pictures" as "a point around which other pieces of evidence collect. They are part of, but not a substitute for, an investigation . . . Believing is seeing and not the other way around." "Not Every Picture Tells a Story," *The New York Times*, November 20, 2004, A19; and *Standard Operating Procedure* (New York: Sony Pictures Classics, 2008).

27 See Fredric Jameson, *The Political Unconscious: Narrative as a Socially Symbolic Act* (Ithaca, NY: Cornell University Press, 1981). Jameson was also present throughout the conference and gave the keynote address, making it all the more plausible that his claims regarding the status of theory and reading in *Valences* are attuned to these recent articulations of surface reading.

28 Sharon Marcus, "Just Reading: Female Friendship and the Marriage Plot," in *Between Women: Friendship, Desire, and Marriage in Victorian England* (Princeton, NJ: Princeton University Press, 2007), 75.

29 Best and Marcus, "Surface Reading," 17. If surface reading makes a renewed claim for "truth, validity and objectivity," New Formalism codes this renewal in terms of value. In her 1999 article "In Defense of Poetry," for example, Marjorie Perloff comments that in cultural studies' approaches to texts,

> A poem or a novel or film is discussed, not for its intrinsic merits or as the expression of individual genius, but for its political role, the "cultural work" it performs, or what it reveals about the state of the society. In this scheme of things, questions of value simply vanish, there being no reason why Henry James's novels are a better index to or symptom of the cultural aporias of turn-of-the century America than the best-sellers of the period—or, for that matter, early twentieth century domestic architecture, popular periodicals, or medical treatises. Read the list of topics currently being studied by the fellows at a university humanities center and you will find that "literature" functions almost exclusively in this way: the project titles would suggest to anyone outside the academy that all the fellows come from a single department—history.

"In Defense of Poetry: Put the Literature Back into Literary Studies," *Boston Review*, February/March 2000, http://bostonreviewnet/BR24.6/perloff.html. While these calls may appear to be at odds with one another, given their divergent positions with respect to historical reading, they both nonetheless reduce reading to the level of the text, thereby not only disavowing the symptom but also arguing for an impossible textual immanence, in which, like Scarry's formulation "fair equals fair," what is "valid" or a work of "genius" requires no recourse to the larger structures within which the concepts of validity and genius are delineated and given meaning in the first place.

30 Best and Marcus, "Surface Reading," 18.

31 Bruce Robbins, "Commodity Histories," *PMLA* 120, no. 2 (March 2005): 455.

32 Gayatri Chakravorty Spivak, "Rhetoric and Cultural Explanation: A Discussion with Gayatri Charkravorty Spivak," *JAC* 10, no. 2 (Winter 1990): n.p.

33 Steven Helmling, *The Success and Failure of Fredric Jameson: Writing, the Sublime, and the Dialectic of Critique* (Albany, NJ: SUNY Press, 2001). As his title indicates, Helmling develops this notion throughout *The Success and Failure of Fredric Jameson*, one formulation of which is the following: "[a 'dialectical project'] can succeed only by failing, and by failing only in especially and appropriately demanding ways. It must evoke the difficulties it aspires to solve, but to the extent that any solution it proposes seems to succeed, the statement of the problem will seem to have failed, by underestimating the problem" (8).

34 Spivak, "Rhetoric."

35 Our relationship to money exemplifies how this kind of fetishism works: "When individuals use money, they know very well that there is nothing magical about it—that money, in its materiality, is simply an expression of social relations . . . So, on an everyday level, the individuals know very well that there are relations between people behind the relations between things. The problem is that in their social activity itself, in what they are *doing*, they are *acting* as if money, in its material reality, is the immediate embodiment of wealth as such. They are fetishists in practice, not in theory." Slavoj Žižek, *The Sublime Object of Ideology* (New York: Verso, 2008), 28.

36 As this language suggests, this is also why Jameson holds that the issues of Hegelian philosophy are "once again the order of the day": namely "the relationship of part to whole, the opposition between concrete and abstract, the concept of totality, the dialectic of appearance and essence, the interaction between subject and object." *Marxism and Form: Twentieth-Century Dialectical Theories of Literature* (Princeton, NJ: Princeton University Press, 1971), xix. In his later essay on cognitive mapping, then, Jameson employs one variation of these themes, the distinction between lived experience and structure, to describe the changes that take place during the period of monopoly capitalism and the imperial expansion that accompanies it. See Fredric Jameson, "Cognitive Mapping," in *Marxism and the Interpretation of Culture*, ed. Nelson, Cary and Lawrence Grossberg (Urbana, IL: University of Illinois Press, 1988), 347–60.

37 This description is Lefebvre's and is quoted by Edward W. Soja in "The Socio-Spatial Dialectic," *Annals of the Association of American Geographers* 70, no. 2 (1980): 210. The full quote is as follows:

    "Space is not a scientific object removed from ideology and politics; it has always been political and strategic. If space has an air of neutrality and indifference with regard to its contents and thus seems to be 'purely' formal, the epitome of rational abstraction, it is precisely because it has been occupied and used, and has already been the focus of past processes whose traces are not always evident on the landscape. Space has been shaped and molded from historical and natural elements, but this has been a political process. Space is political and ideological. It is a product literally filled with ideologies." Lefebvre, "Reflections on the Politics of Space," *Antipode* 8, no. 2 (May 1976): 31.

38 Zadie Smith, *Changing My Mind: Occasional Essays* (New York: Penguin Press, 2009), 96.

39 Jonathan Goldberg, "On the Eve of the Future," *PMLA* 125, no. 2 (March 2010): 375.

40 Although not referencing surface reading directly and its appeal to the objectivity of the computer as a means of collecting and collating without the interference of subjective interpretation, Jameson in *Valences of the Dialectic* cautions: "Global capitalism today is clearly not to be thought of in terms of a sum of positivities; and any number of disastrous political strategies and calculations testify to the folly of approaching it in terms of common sense and of empirical facts, even when it is acknowledged that the multiplicity of such facts demands something more complicated than individual reasoning (generally it is the computer which is appealed to in such cases)." (67)

41 Describing the inexplicable impulse that led her to distribute to a graduate class sections from a 1981 *Semiotext(e)* containing (questionably) historical documents detailing nineteenth-century medical cases involving masturbation, Sedgwick, in "Jane Austen and the Masturbating Girl," writes: "I hadn't even the new historicist's alibi for perpetuating and disseminating the shock of the violent narratives in which they trade: 'Deal,' don't they seem tacitly but moralistically to enjoin, 'deal with your own terror, your own arousal, your disavowals, in your own way, on your own time, in your own [thereby reconstituted as invisible] privacy; it's not our responsibility, because *these awful things are real*'." "Jane Austen and the Masturbating Girl," *Critical Inquiry* 17, no. 4 (Summer 1991): 835. In my account, new historicist's fetishize via the archive what Sedgwick refers to as the "pretext of the real."

42 Eve Kosofsky Sedgwick, "Queer and Now," in *Tendencies* (Durham, NC: Duke University Press, 1993), 3.

43 Judith Butler, *Precarious Life: The Powers of Mourning and Violence* (London: Verso, 2004), 24, 28.

44 As Henri Lefebvre defines space, "it is not a thing among things, nor a product among products: rather, it subsumes things produced, and encompasses their interrelationships in their coexistence and simultaneity—their (relative) order and/or (relative) disorder." *The Production of Space* (1974; Cambridge, MA: Blackwell, 1991), 73.

45 Writing about her experience in the classroom, in the midst of the AIDS crisis, and at the time of her cancer diagnosis, Sedgwick reflects that "finding myself as teacher, as exemplar, as persuader, as reader to be less and less at the center of my own classroom, I was also finding that the voice of a certain abyssal displacement—and mine was certainly not the only such displacement going on in these classrooms—could provide effects that might sometimes wrench the boundaries of discourse around in productive if not always obvious ways" (*Touching*, 34). The notion of "abyssal displacement" functions not unlike negativity within Hegelian dialectics and Jameson's account of a spatial dialectic in its "putting out of place." Sedgwick also uses the language of displacement to describe her unsettled place and its politics at an AIDS demonstration about black queer invisibility: "Displacements: the white skin of someone to whom black queer invisibility had come to feel—partly through representational work like *Tongues Untied*, partly in the brutalities of every day's paper, partly through transferentially charged interactions with students—like an aching gap in the real" (33).

46 Sedgwick makes a similar clarification when she acknowledges: "Although temporal and spatial thinking are never really alternative to each other, I've consistently tried in *Touching Feeling* to push back against an occupational tendency to underattend to the rich dimension of space" (9).

47 The violence within the concept of intersection is also to be distinguished from Althusser's model of overdetermination and structural causality, which, although useful in its time, lacks the negative force of the dialectic, namely contradiction. Instead "overdetermination now seems to imply that a singular event, in all its uniqueness, has many causes whose conjuncture is aleatory (and which could conceivably omit the economic); while structural causality formulates the differential relationship of the various levels with one another in terms of a specific distance which is itself an effect of 'structure'" (545).

48 Key in the representation of these categories is the fact that they are known but not seen: "This empty slot [which constitutes one of the oppositions between work and unemployment] is already implicitly identified in *Capital*, which presciently includes a withering attack on pious notions of retraining in its epic account of whole industries driven out of business: but it remained for globalization to dramatize this category far more visibly by projecting it out into visible geographical space" (580).

49 Karl Marx and Frederick Engels, *The Communist Manifesto* (New York: Verso, 1998), 39.

50 Jameson defined cognitive mapping as "a pedagogical political culture which seeks to endow the individual subject with some heightened sense of its place in the global system." *Postmodernism*, 54. Introducing the concept of cognitive mapping at the "Marxism and the Interpretation of Culture" conference in the summer of 1983, he specifically identifies it as an "aesthetic task" to be distinguished from the social sciences, a distinction corresponding to the Althusserian distinction between science and ideology: "Now I think you can teach people how this or that view of the world is to be thought or conceptualized, but the real problem is that it is increasingly hard for people to put that together with their own experience as individual psychological subjects, in daily life. The social sciences can rarely do that, and when they try (as in ethnomethodology), they do it only by a mutation in the discourse of social science, or they do it at the moment that a social science becomes an ideology; but then we are back into the aesthetic. Aesthetics is something that addresses individual experience rather than something that conceptualizes the real in a more abstract way." "Cognitive Mapping," 358.

51 Theodor Adorno, *Minima Moralia: Reflections on a Damaged Life*, trans. E. F. N. Jephcott (New York: Verso, 2005), 74.

52 In response to SUNY Albany President George M. Philip's announcement cutting the Italian, French, Russian, classics, and theater programs, Stanley Fish notes in "The Crisis of the Humanities Officially Arrives" that it is no longer a question of when the humanities will collapse as a result of public defunding; it has already happened. Stanley Fish, "The Crisis of the Humanities Officially Arrives," *The New York Times*, October 11, 2010.

CHAPTER TWENTY FIVE

Creative Labor

Sarah Brouillette

From Mediations *24 (2) (2009): 140–149.*

This essay compares two influential conceptions of contemporary labor, which emerge from and contribute to radically divergent interpretive traditions, but share common ground. First is the largely celebratory idea of a "creative class" branded by Richard Florida, management professor and globe-trotting consultant to government and industry. Second is the account of "immaterial labor" assembled by a group of thinkers tied to autonomia, a radical Marxist formation with origins in the Italian workerist movement. This group, now in a "post-workerist" mode, includes Michael Hardt, Antonio Negri, Maurizio Lazzarato, and Paolo Virno. I will refer to them as autonomists, a poor but convenient shorthand. Florida's research has influenced recent government policy and management literature in which individuals appear as born innovators, the origins of enterprise, naturally predisposed to be against what exists and to try to perfect it through invention; and in which the economy discovers this pre-existing tendency and then nurtures it into an engine for ceaseless renewal. The autonomists' theories, which imagine a resistant subjectivity that is at once subsumed within, outside of, and the source of liberation from capitalism, are hardly equivalent to Florida's. Nevertheless, I suggest they are likewise more symptoms than diagnoses of the pervasive vocabulary that fathoms creative expression as an essence of experimentation emanating from an internal and natural source, and that finds one of its models in idealized apprehension of artists' ostensible resistance to routine, to management, to standardization, and to commodification. For Florida, the fact that this vocabulary is one that contemporary capitalism clearly requires and reinforces is not a problem: his creative subject is the fruit of the progress of modernization, of the spread of self-reflexivity and freedom. The autonomists' case is more difficult. They themselves tend to lament that the expressive self-realization at the core of their theory is the same one nurtured and expropriated by capital, yet they do not offer any alternative to this conception of human motivation and behavior. Instead, their immaterial producer, her character assumed rather than interpreted, appears largely destitute of any significant history.[1]

To begin, Florida and the autonomists broadly agree that over the past few decades more work has become comparable to artists' work. For Florida this is a positive development. For the autonomists it is ambivalent, but they state with little equivocation that the kind of aesthetic expression subsumed within capitalist production is not real creativity, but rather its codified and corrupted appearance in commodity form. Still, both camps imagine creativity as located within individuals' uncontainable experimental energies and self-expressive capacities. In Florida's work, these capacities are often facilitated and liberated by development of one's career within an expanding marketplace for creative work. For the autonomists, they are instead threatened by such incorporation. In fact, they are quashed by the sheer process of individuation, since that, too, has by now been subsumed into capitalist relations, until only a "monad" of pure "potential," existing somehow before socialization, can be the source of real creativity. Nevertheless, this "potential," imagined as an inherent germ available for development, is for the autonomists also crucial to capitalism's demise. New currents in production trigger the rise of "the multitude," and with it, in time, the fruition of something resembling Marx's postcapitalist "social individual": the worker who does tasks that a thing cannot do, whose work is so satisfying it will be done for its own sake, under no distant compulsion or direct domination.[2]

For Florida, under capitalism's benevolent watch, the ideal of nonalienated labor, performed by the "whole person" en route to self-development, has passed out of the realm of utopian fantasy and into the workplace. A once-tenable distinction between bourgeois and bohemian values has collapsed into the "shared work and lifestyle ethic" that Florida calls "the creative ethos."[3] Like bohemians before them, the creative class values diversity, openness, and nonconformity, eschewing "organizational or institutional directives" and embracing city living as freedom from the tradition.[4] However, like the bourgeoisie, they are also quite willing to connect self-worth to career success, and they feel little "distaste for material things"— not because they wish to grow rich per se, but because they are living in an era of "post-scarcity."[5] Whereas the bohemian artist suffered for her work, members of the creative class tap into creativity precisely to the extent that they are free from worry about poverty.[6] Indeed, a successful creative career is important because it means being granted the freedom to pursue creative inclinations without too much concern for market necessities. Thus materialistic motivations exist in tandem, rather than tension, with the desire for self-expression and personal development; the wish to do creative work and identify with a community of creative people is perfectly reconcilable with the desire to live in prosperity. The creative process need only be organized in such a way that its essential indivisibility is respected, its autonomy assumed and structured into the workplace.

For the autonomists, meanwhile, via immaterial labor—the post-factory work which "produces the informational and cultural content of the commodity"—capital is busily orchestrating the incorporation of creativity into itself.[7] It is doing this by treating all social experience as a factory, in which the universal inclination toward creative play becomes the laboratory from which new products emerge. The personality of the worker, including her desire for variety and self-expression, are made "susceptible to organization and command."[8] Thus, when we are all enjoined to explore our subjectivity that by no means does away with the "antagonism" between "autonomy and command," instead, it simply "re-poses the antagonism at a higher level, because it both mobilizes and clashes with the very personality of the individual worker."[9] The shifting world of available ideas, which the autonomists call "the mass intellect," is something capital is always trying to access and capture, so it creates spaces where novel agglomerations will emerge and be accessible. In this, the "struggle against work" is simply useful. Immaterial production "nurtures, exploits, and exhausts" its labor force by ongoing affective social production of self-sacrificing and self-motivated workers, people who freely offer their labor because it is experienced as non-laborious pleasure or as moral compulsion.[10] Key here is capital's desire for a worker-subject in whom command can simply "reside": workers may disobey command, but disobedience is a prerequisite for productivity.[11] For the autonomists, then, Florida's mistake is seeing the commingling of capitalism and creative expression as a benign or even ideal realization of the end of soul-destroying labor. It is, rather, an intensification of exploitation, though it is often experienced as the opposite.

In tandem, as the distinction between work and leisure is eroded, what one experiences and consumes "outside" of labor time becomes part of the production of commodities.[12] As immaterial labor is a matter of social relations *in toto*, and its economic value stems from this fact, for the autonomists the consumer, too, "is inscribed in the manufacturing of the product from its conception."[13] Consumption doesn't just "realize" the product. It is itself the product, as at once the tracked assumption behind the product's creation and as its desired outcome. Thus, the material reworked by immaterial labor is the general world of subjectivity and the environment in which it is produced; the content of immaterial labor's commodities is the general social milieu. Immaterial workers satisfy a demand and produce it at the same time. The social world, as the factory, is the space in which the worker is reproduced; all the culture that is consumed works to infect and influence and re-create the consumer's situation. In other words, the consumer is thoroughly incorporated into the cycle of production, and the cultural producer is herself conceived as a consumer, as the member of a class defined by the accoutrements of lifestyle and leisure, as one whose habits of consumption do so much to define her, and whose experiences as a consumer are what generate the ideas that are later codified in rights to intellectual property. The process of immaterial production is thus cyclical and all-pervasive, incorporating everyone.

Having painted this portrait, the autonomists are nevertheless careful to theorize the mass intellect as something that cannot be fully incorporated. In trying to explain this resistance, several look to Marx's mention of a general intellect, especially as articulated in the "Fragment on Machines," where, in Virno's terms, Marx argues that abstract knowledge "begins to become, precisely by virtue of its autonomy from production, nothing less than the principle productive force, relegating parcelized and repetitive labor to a peripheral and residual position."[14] In brief, Virno interprets Marx's short text as support for his own claim that it is perverse to hold that knowledge and the worker exist independently of one another: the general intellect is the mutual interrelation of living labor and machinery, which is the fixed capital in which abstracted knowledge about working processes is embedded; and the knowledge held by the general intellect "cannot be reduced to fixed capital" because it is "inseparable from the interaction of a plurality of living subjects."[15]

"Mass intellectuality is the composite group of post-Fordist living labor," Virno writes, and it "cannot be objectified in machinery."[16] Indeed, as the general intellect is constantly recombined and reconstituted within the expanse of living labor, whenever it is translated into fixed capital, a conflict emerges. Capital's constant struggle to fix knowledge is met by living labor's lack of willingness to have its knowledge abstracted. For Virno, the general intellect is, exactly, "the intellect in general": it is the basic human ability to think and process information; it is the inherent creativity possessed by everyone, "rather than the works produced by thought." Post-industrial accumulation taps this unending resource; indeed, it requires the inexhaustible resource potential of the creative impulse, grounded fundamentally in the "potential of labour to execute contingent and unrepeatable statements."[17] This is a social knowledge that is the opposite of that possessed by the new "labour aristocracy." It is the "immeasurable" site of "heterogeneous effective possibilities." It arises from the faculties for thinking, perception, language, memory, feeling, all part of the "fundamental biological configuration" that distinguishes the human animal.[18] It is a neverending potentiality—in the autonomists' vocabulary, a "virtuality."[19] It is this that capital attempts to transform into productive labor, and that Hardt and Negri have located at the utopian center of the political promise of "the multitude."

It is in understanding the relationship between this potentiality and its transformation through immaterial labor that the autonomists tend to invoke aesthetic models. Virno prefers to figure innovation as the "virtuosity" of the live performer, whose activity "finds its own fulfillment (that is, its own purpose) in itself, without objectifying itself into an end product . . . or into an object which would survive the performance."[20] It would seem, then, that real creativity cannot survive transformation into "product" or "object"; its rightful aura cannot be preserved or accessed by others outside a singular moment of its own expression, interpreted as "its own purpose." For his part, Lazzarato applies the literary circuit of "the author, reproduction, and reception."[21] He positions the author as a consumer who puts together a unique amalgam of materials available within mass intellectuality and then offers up that assemblage of her labor to capital. That offering up is the crucial thing; in its absence one remains and continues to perform as living labor or "virtuoso," capital's ceaseless countermeasure, the thing that it will never fully "subordinate it to its own values."[22] In other words, to engage in immaterial production is to author something, which inevitably means to work in a way that "distorts or deflects the social imaginary that is produced in the forms of life." At the same time, though, those forms of life are the ultimate and final source of innovation—in the simple process of being alive, ideas occur—and so the actual production of immaterial commodities is dependent and secondary. Everything is, of course, socially authored, since it is "the whole of the social relation," embodied in the author–work–audience relationship, that bring any kind of meaning "into play."[23] But through the author of immaterial products, who possesses what Lazzarato calls autonomous "synergies," capital will "attempt to control" and "subordinate" these irreducible energies to itself.[24]

Thus, in the case of immaterial labor's theorists, as for the creative class's enthusiasts, ideas about the status and work of the artist-author shape how they present what contemporary labor entails. For the latter, it seems that the old ideal of the artist's aversion to market success no longer holds. The artist has been subsumed into the creative class, bohemian values persist only as lifestyle choices, and creativity and market circulation are synonymous and unfold in tandem. The authenticity and subjectivity of the creative act are in no way threatened by market circulation. Instead, they are protected by it. For the former, in turn, the artist is the model for the absorption of subjectivity into the market. She is the figure for any worker who "originates" the authored and authorized discourse that is inseparable from capitalism but separate from something else it cannot contain: inherent human creativity, understood as the variability of the human personality's infinite potential for recombination.

The Floridean and autonomist viewpoints are thus similar in their assumption that creativity and capital are merged now in some novel ways, as the production of various kinds of symbolic content—information, entertainment, art—have ostensibly become economically dominant, and as artists' vaunted resistance to routine work has been thus generalized throughout the workforce. But the autonomists try to preserve a space between the "mass intellect" and entrepreneurial appropriation of its products for personal gain. Their theories of virtuosity and virtuality constantly return to what authorized speech cannot capture through immaterial production of intellectual property, and so the sense remains that there is some pressing contradiction between creative expression and work. Their writings evince a clear wish to maintain a sublime mass which is at once outside of property relations and the source of everything available for transposition into them. This wish is perhaps most evident in their continual return to oppositions that are resonantly ethical: quantities are pitted against the unquantifiable; actual products are pitted against future potential for the creation of anything; the model of the solo author is pitted against the collective intelligence that is actually held by everyone and merely appropriated for the author's use; writing and codification are pitted against the universal possession of language that can be constantly recombined and redeployed; intellectual property rights are pitted against the "the commons" and the multitude; and measure and all it implies about quantification and exchange are pitted against immeasure, figured as the endless fecundity of social knowledge and its irreducibility to exchange relations (or, its unavailability for abstraction in machinery).

Thus, where Florida and the autonomists confer, we find an image of an economy in which individual human creativity has become the vanguard driving force and key productive engine. Where they diverge, we glimpse continued conflict over what it means that so much labor is now being called creative, or that respect for the productive powers of creative impulses is now so general. For Florida and his students and allies, artists are models of successful and fulfilling work within the marketplace, while non-creatives are simply a problem. It isn't that they have nothing to offer—like the autonomists, Florida states that everyone is creative—but that, because they are trapped in deadening work, their potential isn't being accessed, which means "wasting that great reservoir of our creative capital."[25] This represents a problem both for them and for the businesses that might trade in their creativity.

In marked contrast, for the theorists of immaterial labor, these noncreatives are actually where true creativity resides, because their ceaseless ability to recombine is the source of all knowledge. These theorists thus transmogrify those who don't author—or those who "refuse"—into the only source of resistance to capital, a resistance that capital always does and does not incorporate. So whereas the Floridean approach positions creativity as the market meeting minds, for the autonomists it can only be minds as they meet outside of market logic, as the author becomes any figure whose thinking being is exploited by capital, and also, quite simply, capital itself. Both the figure and the system require that whole social world that remains outside of authorship or authored experience, the source of potential which can't be reduced to capital. In other words, once your labor has become available for this reduction to product, by expropriating potentiality, you've become an author. It is only the non-author, in possession of a non-market mass intellect, who holds on to non-market integrity.

Literary scholars have shown how indispensable imagining the subject as "origin of expression" has been to the history of capitalist cultural markets and of private rights to intellectual property.[26] In future writing, I hope to show the relevance of their findings to theories of creative labor, while taking my cue from Michael Ryan's argument that Negri's valorization of "expressive subjectivity" depends upon omission of the "instrumental and contextual factors" that are its actual conditions of possibility.[27] Ryan laments this as an "absolutism of the subject," and claims that the individual Negri imagines as embodiment of irreducible difference and source of ceaseless experimentation is continuous with the liberal subject as site of personal choice and self-referencing desire.[28] Since Ryan's appraisal, theories of creative production have tended to extend and generalize the approach to subjectivity he faulted, activating particular figures of artist-authors in the process. The continued life of these figures involves a confluence of social and economic forces that are of precious little interest to Florida or to the autonomists, whose theories tend instead to remove the subject they assume from historical comprehension. Lost in both sets of analyses is, thus, any sense of the contradictory, material, and constitutive histories of artists' labor and of images of artists at work that subtend the conception of subjectivity they maintain. Labor theories of aesthetic production, as part of a broader political economy of culture, should provide an alternative, by considering, for example, the development of the contradictory relationship between artists and the markets for their work, or the concomitant mainstreaming of the figure of the artist as valorized mental laborer. Accounting for the historicity and the particular emergence and spread of the vocabulary that makes contemporary labor an act of self-exploration, self-expression, and self-realization is an essential task in denaturalizing the character of contemporary capitalism.

Notes

1 For pressing critique of the theory of immaterial labor, see Timothy Brennan, "The Empire's New Clothes," *Critical Inquiry* 29 (2003): 337–67. For broad treatment of creative labor, see Mark Banks, *The Politics of Cultural Work*

(London: Palgrave, 2007), and Andrew Ross, *Nice Work If You Can Get It* (New York: New York University Press, 2009).

2 On the "social individual," see Moishe Postone, *Time, Labor, and Social Domination: A Reinterpretation of Marx's Critical Theory* (Cambridge: Cambridge University Press, 1993) 33; compare Karl Marx, *The Grundrisse* [1857–61] (London: Penguin, 1973), 325, 705–706.

3 Richard Florida, *The Rise of the Creative Class* (New York: Basic Books, 2002), 193.

4 Florida, *Rise of the Creative Class*, 77.

5 Florida, *Rise of the Creative Class*, 194.

6 Florida, *Rise of the Creative Class*, 81.

7 Maurizio Lazzarato, "Immaterial Labor," in Paolo Virno and Michael Hardt (eds), *Radical Thought in Italy* (Minneapolis, MN: University of Minnesota Press, 1996), 133.

8 Lazzarato, "Immaterial Labor," 134.

9 Lazzarato, "Immaterial Labor," 135.

10 Tiziana Terranova, "Free Labor: Producing Culture for the Digital Economy," *Social Text* 63 (2000): 51.

11 Lazzarato, "Immaterial Labor," 136.

12 Paolo Virno, "General Intellect," translated by Arianna Bove. <http://www.generation-online.org/p/fpvirno10.htm>, para 5.

13 Lazzarato, "Immaterial Labor," 141.

14 Paolo Virno, "The Ambivalence of Disenchantment," in Paolo Virno and Michael Hardt (eds) *Radical Thought in Italy* (Minneapolis, MN: University of Minnesota Press, 1996), 21. Compare Marx, *Grundrisse* 692–93.

15 Virno, "General Intellect," para 6.

16 Virno, "General Intellect," para 7.

17 Virno, "General Intellect," para 7.

18 Paolo Virno, *A Grammar of the Multitude*, trans. Isabella Bertoletti, James Cascaito, and Andrea Casson (Los Angeles: Semiotext[e], 2004), 98.

19 Virno, "General Intellect," para 8.

20 Virno, *Grammar*, 52.

21 Lazzarato, "Immaterial Labor," 144.

22 Lazzarato, "Immaterial Labor," 145.

23 Lazzarato, "Immaterial Labor," 146.

24 Lazzarato, "Immaterial Labor," 145.

25 Richard Florida, *The Flight of the Creative Class* (New York: HarperCollins, 2005), 188.

26 Two representative studies are Mark Rose, *Authors and Owners: The Invention of Copyright* (Cambridge: Harvard University Press, 1993), and Martha Woodmansee, *The Author, Art, and the Market: Rereading the History of Aesthetics* (New York: Columbia University Press, 1994).

27 Michael Ryan, *Politics and Culture: Working Hypotheses for a Post-Revolutionary Society* (Baltimore, MD: Johns Hopkins University Press, 1989), 46.

28 Ryan, *Politics and Culture*, 57.

CHAPTER TWENTY SIX

The Work of Art in the Age of its Real Subsumption Under Capital

Nicholas Brown

From nonsite.org *(March 13, 2012): http://nonsite.org/editorial/ the-work-of-art-in-the-age-of-its-real-subsumption-under-capital*

Whatever previous ages might have fancied, we are wise enough to know that the work of art is a commodity like any other. Chances are that we don't have any very clear idea what we mean by that. Marx, however, does.

> What chiefly distinguishes the commodity-owner from the commodity is the circumstance that the latter treats every other commodity as nothing more than the form of appearance of its own value. Born leveler and cynic, it is therefore always on the jump to exchange not only soul but body with any other commodity, be it plagued by more deformities than Maritornes herself. With his five and more senses, the owner of the commodity makes up for the latter's lack of a feel for the concrete in other commodities. His commodity has for him no unmediated use value. Otherwise he would not bring it to market. It has use value for others. For him its only unmediated use value is to be the bearer of exchange value, and so to be a medium of exchange. That is why he wants to dispose of it in exchange for commodities whose use values appeal to him. All commodities are non-use-values for their owners, use values for

their non-owners. Consequently, they must all change hands. But this change of hands constitutes their exchange, and their exchange relates them to one another as values and realizes them as values. Commodities must be realized as values before they can be realized as use values. (*K* 100/*C* 179)[1]

This is a knotty passage (and one whose gender politics are thankfully not entirely legible in English). Its difficulty and indeed "literariness" seem all out of proportion to the matter in hand. Should it not be among the easiest things in the world to distinguish commodity-owner from commodity? Is it not rather an odd flourish to stack the deck by personifying the commodity, and then to feign perplexity in distinguishing the personification from the person? But the operation is the opposite of this: we have been told in the previous paragraph that "the characters who appear on the economic stage are merely personifications of economic relations" (*K* 100/*C* 179). So it is not only that the commodity is personified, but rather, it proving easier to talk of the commodity as a "she" than the owner as an "it," that the owner is. The distinction is therefore between two logical standpoints—something which the fact that one of them is occupied by a consciousness tends to obscure—and the distinction is simply this: from the standpoint of the commodity, all commodities are qualitatively indifferent. If you imagine a market without buyers and sellers, you are left with a mass of commodities that are exchangeable in various ratios, but none of which is not exchangeable, which is to say none of which possesses any qualities that cannot be expressed as quantity. (The basis of this qualitative indifference, established in Marx's previous chapter, does not concern us at the moment.) But from the standpoint of the commodity owner—who, because he owns a commodity and not some other kind of thing, is both buyer and seller—his commodity is qualitatively different from all the others in that his alone has no qualities. To be more precise, his has only one quality that matters, which is its lack of qualities: that is, its qualitative equality with other commodities: its exchangeability.[2]

All other commodities—that is, the commodities he encounters as a buyer rather than a seller—are, for his "five and more senses" full of qualities. Quality, use value, counts for him as a buyer: otherwise he would not want to buy. Quality, use value, counts nothing for him as a seller: otherwise he would not be willing to sell. Of course, as a seller, he knows that the commodities he brings to market must "stand the test as use-values before they can be realized as values" (*K* 100/*C* 179). "But"—and this is a Hegelian "but," the conjunction which changes everything—"only the act of exchange can prove whether or not [the human labor expended in them] is useful for others, whether the product of such labor can therefore satisfy alien needs" (*K* 100–101/*C* 180). We thus find ourselves in a chicken-and-egg loop—exchange value precedes use value precedes exchange value precedes use value—that Marx's imaginary commodity owner wants no part of: "he wants to realize his commodity as value . . . whether or not his own commodity has any use value for the owner of the other commodity" (*K* 101/*C* 180). The problem can only be resolved—for the time being, for it will reemerge in several forms, including what our contemporary Keynesians will call a liquidity trap—by giving the contradiction "room to move" (*K* 118/*C* 198). Marx is preparing the ground for the appearance of money, which turns the relationship to a single buyer into a relationship with the market, and provides a practical basis for the radical exchangeability of the commodity.

For our present purposes, however, what is important is that even in the case of the individual buyer, and therefore also in the case of the market, it is only the exchangeability that matters to the commodity owner, as frustrated as he might be by the fact that its use value is from one angle prior. If he sells you a salad bowl and you use it as a chamber pot, that is strictly your business. As far as the seller is concerned, the use value of "his" commodity only makes its appearance as exchange value: "only the act of exchange can prove whether that labor is useful to others." The commodity owner wants to realize the exchange value of his commodity by producing something that is a use-value for others. But he isn't in the business of legislating or even knowing what that use-value should be; he doesn't even know it has a use value until it sells. Indeed, the more potential uses it has—it slices, it dices, it's a typewriter and a shoe store and a status symbol and a peepshow—the less he legislates what its actual use-value should be, and the happier he is.

If this were the only possible state of affairs, there would be no reason to demonstrate its peculiarity. So what is the other of "a society of commodity producers" (*K* 93/*C* 172)? We are given several options in the previous chapter: Robinson Crusoe, the medieval corvée, the peasant family, hints of various historical non-capitalist societies, and finally the famous "association of free people, working with the means of production held in common, and, in full self-awareness, expending their many individual labor powers as one social labor power" (*K* 92/*C* 171). These are all others of commodity production, but its determinate other, the other that the capitalist market produces as its own internal frame, is Hegel's image of collective labor, which Marx here and there explicitly recalls. This image appears most explicitly in Hegel's idealized evocation of Greek ethical life, an evocation which refers not to the Greek polis as it actually was or as Hegel imagined it actually was, but rather to its own immanent horizon, an ideal Greek customary life must presuppose but can only realize in an unsatisfactory, contradictory and unstable way:

> The individual's labor to satisfy his own needs is as much a satisfaction of the needs of others as his own, and the satisfaction of his own needs

is achieved only through the labor of others. As the individual in his individual labor already unconsciously accomplishes a common labor, so again he also produces the common as his conscious object; the whole becomes, as whole, his work, for which he sacrifices himself, and precisely thus is himself restored by it. (265/§351)[3]

The problem—the satisfaction of "universal" or social needs through individual labor, irreducibly particular talents and drives—is the same in Marx and Hegel, though for Marx "full self-awareness" will mark a crucial difference. Marx, however, considers this problem by means of a different social formation, namely capitalism, one in which there is nothing customary about what is produced or who produces it; one in which, as we have seen, exchange precedes use. In Marx's version—"only the act of exchange can prove whether or not [such labor] is useful for others, whether the product of such labor can therefore satisfy alien needs"—the two subordinate clauses appear to say the same thing. The function of the second clause is to emphasize the shift from the neutral "other" to "alien" (*fremde*); that is, to point out the peculiarity of commodity exchange in which "the needs of others," taken for granted in the Hegelian version of customary life, are reduced to a cipher whose index is exchangeability. As Fredric Jameson has recently reminded us, the logic of alienation (*Entfremdung*) in Marx is intimately related to that of Hegelian externalization (*Entäusserung*, though neither Hegel nor Marx adheres rigorously to the linguistic distinction).[4] The other or negative horizon of commodity exchange is what Hegel calls *die Kraft der Entäusserung*, "the power of externalization, the power to make oneself into a thing" (483/§658).

Let us then take a moment to establish the precise contours of this negative, Hegelian horizon of commodity exchange. Plenty has been said about the lordship and bondage theme in *Phenomenology of Spirit*, and we have no interest in revisiting it here, even if the relation of buyer to seller—logically encompassing the two moments of indifference and petulance—does, in its utter failure to produce anything like subjectivity (it produces instead a market where the parties can safely face one another in the aggregate rather than as antagonists) ironically recall it. What is important here is how we get out of this dialectic. As is well known, this is through the labor of the bondsman who, in forming and shaping the thing, in externalizing himself in the production of the lifeworld of both himself and his master, comes to find in that world not the master's power but his own:

Thus the form [of the product of labor], set outside himself, is not an other to him, for this form is precisely his own pure being-for-self, which to him becomes the truth. What he rediscovers, precisely through labor which appears to harbor only an alien purpose, is nothing other than his own purpose, arrived at through his own means. (154/§196)

This is Hegel's materialism—the exact opposite, it might be said in passing, of causal or vulgar materialism—and indeed it represents a kind of ideological core to *Phenomenology of Spirit*. But the point to be made here is that the object the bondsman shapes is not just made—Marx's commodity will also be the product of labor—but intended: a purpose arrived at by his own means. The thing is not a cipher whose use is indexed by its exchange, but rather a use whose purpose is legible, which is to say normative. The master can and presumably does find another purpose in it; but that will now be an occasion for conflict. The owner of commodities, on the other hand, doesn't care what purpose a buyer finds in his commodity, as long as someone will buy it.

What we have arrived at is the distinction between the exchange-formula C-M-C (Commodity-Money-Commodity or Hegelian *Sittlichkeit*, the satisfaction of individual needs as the universal satisfaction of needs through the social metabolism, as use-values are exchanged through the medium of money) and M-C-M, the same relation but now understood as the kernel of capitalism itself, where use-value is only a vanishing moment in the valorization of capital. What we have arrived at is the distinction between an object whose use (or purpose or meaning) is normatively inscribed in the object itself—a meaning that is in Hegel's terms universal, which is simply "*allgemein*," available for everyone and not therefore a private matter— and an object whose use is a matter of indifference from one position, and a matter of possibly intense but necessarily private concern from another. What we have arrived at is the distinction between an object that embodies, and must seek to compel, conviction, and one that seeks to provoke interest in its beholder—or perhaps all kinds of different interest from different beholders. What we have arrived at, no doubt through an unusual route, is the distinction between art and objecthood.[5]

The distinction is of course Michael Fried's, but it has become central to the debate over the dominant strand in contemporary cultural production, or, more likely, the dominant strand in the cultural production of the very recent past, a period for which the term "postmodernism" will do as well as any other. Everything Fried finds objectionable in the "object" is on the other hand perfectly legitimate for a certain class of objects we are already familiar with, namely commodities. Or, to put this another way, Fried's "formalist" account of the distinction between art and non-art is also an historicist one, fully derivable from the Marxian problematic of the "real subsumption of labor under capital," or the closure of the world market.

To return, then, to *Capital*. As we just saw, one way of understanding Marx's analysis is to say that in commodity exchange, the site of purpose or intention shifts. If I make a bowl for myself, it is a bowl because I wanted to make a bowl, and I will be concerned about all kinds of concrete attributes the bowl might have. If it is shallow rather than deep, wood rather than metal, these attributes are as they are because I intend them to be that way, and we are in the world of Hegelian externalization. If I make a bowl for the market, I am primarily concerned only with one attribute, its exchangeability: that is, the demand for bowls. And that demand, and therefore all of the concrete attributes that factor into that demand, are decided elsewhere, namely on the market. So while I might still make decisions about my bowls, those decisions no longer matter as intentions even for me, because they are entirely subordinated to more or less informed guesses about other people's desires. This has obvious repercussions for cultural interpretation. If a work of art is not a commodity—or if it is not only a commodity, which is to say that a moment of externality to the commodity form is analytically isolable, which is to say that there is something in the work that is not a commodity—then it makes entirely good sense to approach it with interpretive tools, since it can plausibly be intended to mean something. (In the passage from Hegel cited above—"his own purpose, arrived at through his own means"—"*Sinn*," a multivalent word translated here as "purpose," could also be translated as "meaning," and indeed the conflict immanent in the normativity of the formed object will, in *Phenomenology of Spirit*, devolve in skepticism and stoicism to a mere conflict of interpretation. But that is another story.) If a work of art is only a commodity, interpretive tools suddenly make no sense at all, since the form the object takes is determined elsewhere than where it is made, namely on the market. So it is not really that interpretation as such no longer makes any sense, so much as that interpreting the artwork no longer makes any sense. It is rather the desires represented by the market that are subject to analysis and elucidation.

It might seem absurd to say the art commodity is uninterpretable, but think for a moment of an industrial spectacle like James Cameron's *Avatar*. The sight of critics producing a welter of completely incompatible (but also generally plausible) interpretations was an amusing one that did not go unnoticed by the critics themselves. This empirical profusion is insignificant in itself: all of these interpretations could be wrong. But it is also possible that since the film is only concerned with producing a set of marketable effects, it cannot at the same time be concerned with producing the minimal internal consistency required to produce a meaning. And in fact, James Cameron himself is pretty clear that this is the case. When asked why female Na'vi have breasts, Cameron replies: "Right from the beginning I said, 'She's got to have tits,' even though that makes no sense because her race, the Na'vi, aren't placental mammals."[6] Cameron is more precise than he probably means to be when he says that "makes no sense." Pressed in a different interview, Cameron responds that the female Na'vi have breasts "because this is a movie for human people."[7] In other words, people—enough of them anyway—will pay to see breasts, so the breasts go in. But this "makes no sense": there is no point in interpreting it, because the salient fact is not that Cameron wanted them there but that he thought a lot of other people would want them there, and the wildly inconsistent ideology of the film is likewise composed of saleable ideologemes that together make no sense. This is not to say that all art commodities are similarly inconsistent: some audiences will pay for ideological or narrative or aesthetic consistency, so we have Michael Moore, middlebrow cinema, and independent film. But this consistency doesn't add up to a meaning, since what looks like meaning is only an appeal to a market niche.

But this is nothing new but rather a very old line, essentially Adorno's critique of the culture industry.[8] The lineaments of that critique are well known; it will be enough for the present to remind ourselves that in that essay Adorno has no interest in explicating works because in commercial culture there are no works to critique and no meanings to be found. The culture industry as it appears in Adorno is simpler than ours, seemingly only differentiated vertically rather than splintered into potentially infinite socio-aesthetico-cultural niches, but the essential situation is the one we are attempting to understand. "The varying production values in the culture industry have nothing to do with content, nothing to do with the meaning of the product" (*DA* 132/*DE* 124) because the varying production values are aimed at different markets rather than different purposes, and this principle is "the meaningful content of all film, whatever plot the production team may have selected" (*DA* 132/*DE* 124). So while one can ask sociological questions about art commodities—Why do people like violent movies?—interpretive questions—Why is there a love scene in the middle of *Three Days of the Condor?*—do not have interesting answers.

It will not have escaped notice that, under conditions of Hegelian externalization, meaning is equated with intention, while under market conditions, "meaning" is simply what can be said about the appropriation of commodities. Sociological questions have answers without necessarily involving intentions; interpretive questions, if they have answers, require intentions. It may be worth taking a moment to emphasize the fact that this equation is deeply Hegelian, and that there is nothing in it that is threatening to Marxist interpretation as such. The strong claim for the identity of intention and meaning (very briefly, the claim that meaning includes neither causes nor effects of the meaning in question) already implies the social.[9] The medium of meaning is (always in the Hegelian sense) a universal, which is to say a social machine, be it language as such or a particular signifying network like literature or the royal court. (Meaning is necessarily a socially symbolic act.) While meanings exist *sub specie aeternitatis*, the media or social machines in which they mean are, it seems almost too obvious to point out, historical: if one insists on understanding meaning proper as externalization, one must begin with an account of the social machine. (Always historicize.) Further, nothing in the reduction of meaning to intention prevents us from chasing down what a meaning might entail as a logically necessary consequence (as opposed to an effect) or condition of possibility (as opposed to a cause), even if these are not intended. Indeed, this is Marx's procedure in the chapter we have been discussing. The future capitalist, for now simply an owner of commodities, wants to sell his goods. That is all. "In their confusion, the commodity owners think like Faust: In the beginning was the deed. They have already acted before thinking" (*K* 101/*C* 180). The logical contortions embodied in the act of exchange (the confusion or embarrassment, *Verlegenheit*, of the commodity-owners—indeed, their ideology) are nowhere in the mind of the capitalist, but are rather the logical preconditions of the act of exchange itself. In this Hegelian-Marxian sense, the unconscious is simply everything entailed or presupposed by an action that is not present to consciousness in that action: in *Phenomenology of Spirit*, the ignorance of the provincial *type* at court, which necessarily turns every attempt at sincerity into its opposite, or the politics of the "beautiful soul," who imagines himself to be beyond politics but whose very aloofness from politics is itself a politics. An intention includes such necessary presuppositions or entailments. (The identity of intention and meaning insists upon a political unconscious.)[10]

Finally, the identity of meaning and intention does not entail any position on the desirability of something like cultural studies, if the latter is taken to mean the sociological study of cultural production, distribution, and consumption. What it does entail is the distinction between such study—which will be crucial in what follows, in the form of a sociological understanding of the universal in which contemporary artworks make their way—and interpretation. And indeed, this last position can also be derived from Hegel. In the section in the *Phenomenology* on "the matter in hand," the relation between sociological motivation (ambition) and scientific purpose (*die Sache selbst*, the matter in hand) is, as it is in Bourdieu, undecidable: it is always possible that a given intervention is attempted for money or fame or position. But this very undecidability means that nothing concrete can be said about the relation of ambition to work, which is to say that, as regards what is in the work (as opposed to what caused it or what effect it may have) nothing useful can be divined from sociological research.

To return, then, to the art-commodity and its other. For Adorno the art-commodity had a plausible other or negative horizon, namely modernism (even if this is usually referred to collectively in the essay as "bourgeois artworks," and usually in the past tense), where Hegelian externalization—compensatory, tragic, but an externalization nonetheless—holds. Adorno accounts for this possibility by the residual phenomenon of tributary backwaters within capitalism, spaces left behind by the expansion of capital. The persistence of such spaces "strengthened art in this late phase against the verdict of supply and demand, and increased its resistance far beyond the actual degree of protection" (*DA* 141/*DE* 133). What differentiates Adorno's culture industry from the self-representation of our contemporary moment is that the art-commodity now has no other. Fredric Jameson, bringing the problem up to the day before yesterday, simply says, matter-of-factly, that "What has happened is that aesthetic production today has become integrated into commodity production generally."[11] From this, everything follows.

The logic of this transition is already available in Marx, in a draft chapter for *Capital I* that was not available in the West until the 1960s. What we have is often fragmentary, but the basic distinction in the "Results of the Immediate Process of Production" between the "formal subsumption" and the "real subsumption of labor under capital" is clear.[12] Under conditions of formal subsumption, an industry or production process is drawn into a capitalist economy, but "there is no change as yet in the mode of production itself" (*R* 106/*C* 1026). Under conditions of "real subsumption," on the other hand, the production process itself is altered, such that the producers are no longer selling their surplus product to the capitalist, but are instead selling their labor to the capitalist, who will eventually be compelled to reorganize the production process altogether. (Production, as well as exchange, has both a C-M-C or "customary" in the Hegelian sense and an M-C-M or capitalist form. The latter haunts the former until the phase change to capitalism proper, when the former haunts the latter.) Logically speaking, the distance between formal and real subsumption is vanishingly small (just as C-M-C and M-C-M are the same process, examined from different standpoints); but the status of the product of labor, and eventually the work process itself, is fundamentally different under each. Indeed, as will no doubt already be apparent, "formal subsumption" allows for Hegelian externalization to continue under capitalism, since it is, for example, only accidental surplus that is sold: "Milton produced *Paradise Lost* as a silkworm produces silk, as the manifestation of his own nature. He later sold the product for £5 and thus became a dealer in commodities" (*R* 128/*C* 1044). Under "real subsumption," on the other hand, we are already in the world of Marxian separation, where the whole production process is oriented toward exchange. But what this logical proximity means is that directly "capitalist production has a tendency to take over all branches of industry . . . where only formal subsumption obtains" (*R* 118/*C* 1036). In order for formal subsumption in a given corner of industry to obtain with any permanence, it must be afforded some degree of protection: professional guilds, research-based tenure, Adorno's well-funded state cultural institutions, or, as we shall consider shortly, something like Bourdieu's concept of a field of restricted production.

For once underestimating capitalism, Marx seems to think in these fragments that the arts are, by their very nature, unsuitable candidates for real subsumption (see *R* 133/*C* 1048). Little did he imagine that once the means of distribution were fully subsumed, whatever is genuinely inassimilable in artistic labor would cease to make any difference; that the artist, when not genuinely a cultural worker, would be forced to conceive of herself, in true neoliberal fashion, as an entrepreneur of herself; that any remaining pockets of autonomy would effectively cease to exist by lacking access to distribution and, once granted access, would cease to function as meaningfully autonomous. Adorno has no trouble imagining a still-incomplete real subsumption, which is the culture industry, with modernism as the last holdout of merely formal subsumption.[13] For Jameson, finally, the real subsumption of cultural labor under capital is an established fact. The result is a "dissolution of an autonomous sphere of culture" that is at the same time "a prodigious expansion of culture throughout the social realm" (48).

This end of autonomy directly implies the end of modernism. If canonical modernism conceived of itself as autonomous—as producing the "critical distance" (48) that Jameson sees as having been "abolished," along with any "autonomous sphere of culture . . . in the new space of postmodernism" (48)—then today we tend to understand this critical distance as nothing more than modernism's aesthetic ideology; modernist artworks are and were commodities after all.[14] So far we have done no more than reconstruct the logic that lends the contemporary common sense we began with its plausibility.

Nobody could be more skeptical of modernism's self-representation than Pierre Bourdieu. And yet Bourdieu produced, in his two-field theory of aesthetic production, an account of the real referent of modernism's self-representation in the development of a "field of restricted production," which lies behind the ability of artists to "affirm, both in their practice and their representation of it, the irreducibility of the work of art to the status of a simple commodity."[15] This dual affirmation is key, for the ideological representation of autonomy has its basis in the real autonomization of aesthetic practice in the struggle by artists to institute a "field of restricted production," which forcibly substitutes for the "unpredictable verdicts of an anonymous public" (54)—the problem of the seller of commodities—a "public of equals who are also competitors" (58). In other words, the establishment of a field of restricted production forcibly carves a zone of formal subsumption out of the field of large-scale production which is really and entirely subsumed under capital. (It is worth pointing out that such a restricted field is not a market in any meaningful sense: judgments by peers, struggles over the significance of particular interventions, are precisely the opposite of purchases on a market, which cannot provoke disagreement because, as we have seen, no agreement is presupposed.) Adorno's more ad hoc version of the two-field hypothesis conceives of its restricted zone as a residual rather than an emergent space; but he and Bourdieu share an understanding of the essentiality of such a zone to meaning as such, as well as a sense of its precariousness.

In Bourdieu's account, the establishment of such a zone directly implies the tendency of art produced in a restricted field to gravitate toward formal concerns, toward the progressive working-out of problems specific to individual media. What a restricted public of (for example) painters, critics of painting, and connoisseurs of painting share is nothing other than expertise in painting. "Painting was thus set on the road toward a conscious and explicit implementation or setting-into-work of the most specifically pictorial principles of painting, which already equals a questioning of these principles, and hence a questioning, within painting itself, of painting itself" (66). In other words, modernism: "Especially since the middle of the nineteenth century, art finds the principle of change within itself, as though history were internal to the system and as though the development of forms of representation and expression were nothing more than the product of the logical development of systems of axioms specific to the various arts" (126). But for the characteristic "as though," which marks this as an imaginary relation whose real referent is the logic of the restricted field, the words could have been written by Clement Greenberg.[16] Indeed, the Bourdieusian restricted field is the condition of possibility of modernism as such, the condition of possibility of a Hegelian concern for "the matter in hand" under full-blown capitalism.

With the collapse of an autonomous field, with the real subsumption of aesthetic labor under capital, the possibility of something bearing a family resemblance to modernism abruptly disappears. What had been central was a problem to be addressed—a problem in which the general market, because it is a market, has no interest—and all the old solutions had been ruled out of bounds not because they were not nice to hang on a wall or to read, but because they had been absorbed into the game of producing new ones. For this reason, what appears as loss from the perspective of autonomy is at the same time a tremendous liberation of formal energies. The leapfrogging, dialectical modernist game—in which every attempt to solve the central problem represented by a medium becomes, for every other producer, a new version of the problem—becomes more hermetic and difficult to play over time. One can immediately see that the isolation of an autonomous field is not only the necessary condition of possibility (within market society) for the production of any meaning whatsoever, it is also a condition that leads to the increasing difficulty of producing meaning or, more accurately, the increasing formalization of meaning itself. Meanings are made possible by autonomization, but these meanings themselves are increasingly only formally meanings—that is, they are legible as intentions, but the only meanings they convey are specifically painterly, musical, writerly, etc. The very dynamic that makes modernism possible tends at the same time to restrict its movement to an increasingly narrow ambit.

With the real subsumption of art under capital and the end of the modernist game, then, all of the old "solutions," each one of which had been invalidated by subsequent solutions, suddenly become available for use. A certain historicism—Jamesonian postmodern pastiche—becomes possible.

Such a historicism is null as historicism, since what it doesn't produce is precisely anything like history; but on the other hand it is practically bursting with the excitement at being allowed to apply its galvanic fluid to the great gallery of dead forms, which are suddenly candidates for resuscitation. Friedian "objecthood" is also liberated at this same moment: the reaction of the spectator, or customer, assumes importance in precise correlation to the recession of the formal problem confronted by the artist.

But, as is probably obvious by now, liberation from the strictures of the old modernist games is at the same time subjection to something else, namely the "anonymous market" from which the autonomous field had wrested a degree of autonomy. If artworks can now make use of all the old styles (or become objects), it is not clear why one would call them artworks at all, since the honest old art-commodity, precisely because it was more interested in the appeal to a market (the effect on an audience) than on formal problems, was able to make use of the old styles (or be an object) all along. In other words, there is nothing new in unabashedly borrowing indiscriminately from the great gallery of dead forms, or in appealing theatrically to consumer desires. These procedures are in fact the norm. The innovation of postmodern pastiche is—by definition—not formal, but in the collapse of art into what was already the status quo of the culture at large. Postmodernism's innovation is precisely in evacuating the distinction between industrial spectacle—Cameron's ideological mishmash—and the Jamesonian postmodern art-object, assembled from its "grab bag or lumber room of disjointed subsystems and raw materials and impulses of all kinds" (31).

Of course, this is the point. And indeed there is nothing implausible about a scenario in which artworks as such disappear, to be entirely replaced by art-commodities, and in which the study of artworks would have to be replaced with the study of reception, of desires legible in the market, and so on. There is a deeply egalitarian promise in such a scenario, precisely because the formal concerns addressed by artworks are in general the province of a few—in the absence of a strong public education system, are necessarily the province of a few. The problem is that a world where the work of art is a commodity like any other is the world neoliberalism claims we already live in and have always lived in, a world where everything is (and if it isn't, should be) a market. The old vanguardist horizon of equivalence between art and life—which only made sense as a progressive impulse when "life" was understood as something other than the status quo—reverses meaning and becomes deeply conformist. Against this market conformism the assertion of autonomy—even as its very plausibility now seems in doubt—becomes vital once again.

A host of consequences follows from this reversal. The assertion of autonomy means that an artwork must contain its own interpretation; that is, the artwork must be a theory of itself. The assertion of autonomy, in other words, demands a return to immanent critique, to the notion of self-legislating form; in other words, to the conception of literature formulated by the German Romantics at the turn of the 19th century: "Poetry should represent itself in every representation, and be at every point at once poetry and the poetry of poetry" (Friedrich Schlegel, Athenaeum Fragment 238 [1798]).[17] In fact, the Romantic reinvention of literature and the other arts undergirds more contemporary critical practice than we like to imagine, and indeed alone justifies a practice like close reading. The assertion of aesthetic autonomy returns the discipline of literary studies, which, absent such an assertion, can only flounder in search of a relevance it lacks by definition, to theoretical coherence.

A more substantial consequence is that the charge of "elitism," or the class stratification of aesthetic response, accrues to the claim to universal heteronomy rather than to autonomous art. For if nothing essential distinguishes between art and non-art, the only distinction left—and some distinction is necessary in order for the word "art" to have any referent, not to mention in order to populate the institutions that still exist to preserve, transmit, and consecrate it—is between expensive art and cheap art, or art whose means of appropriation are expensive or cheap to acquire. Indeed, rather than affirm emphatically the status of the work of art as nothing more than the luxury good that it undoubtedly also is, it would be prettier to claim heteronomy as a critique of autonomy. But this would mean affirming a meaning, and as we have seen this would necessarily entail a claim to autonomy from the market even as that claim is disavowed.

Under contemporary conditions, the assertion of aesthetic autonomy is, in itself, a political assertion. (A minimal one, to be sure.) This was not always the case. In the modernist period, for example, the convincing assertion of autonomy produced, as it does now, a peculiar non-market space within the capitalist social field. But there is no natural political valence to modernism's distance from the market, since modernism does not make its way under anything like the dominance of market ideology that we experience today.[18] (It was also easier to confuse personal with aesthetic autonomy. Today their opposition is clear. Personal autonomy—choice—takes place in the market. Aesthetic autonomy—meaning—can take place only in a non-market. Outside of the work, the assertion of autonomy is advertising copy.) Modernism tends to be hostile to the culture market, but all kinds of politics (Heidegger as much as Adorno) are hostile to the market. Indeed, Lisa Siraganian has suggested that underlying the panoply of modernist radicalisms is nothing other than a deeper commitment to classical political liberalism, to a zone of deliberative autonomy.[19] Modernist hostility to the market only acquires a definite political valence after modernism: when the claim of the universality of the market is, as it is today, the primary ideological weapon wielded in the class violence that is the redistribution of wealth upwards. The upwards redistribution of wealth in the current conjuncture would be unthinkable without this weapon: the entire ideology of neoliberalism hinges on the assertion that this redistribution is what a competitive market both produces and requires as a precondition. If the claim to autonomy is today a minimal political claim, it is not for all that a trivial one. A plausible claim to autonomy is in fact the precondition for any politics at all other than the politics of acquiescence to the dictates of the market.

In the new dispensation, in other words, the assertion of autonomy is no longer a commitment to liberalism. The horizon of the liberal commitment to disagreement is agreement. Aesthetic autonomy today is, on the other hand, locked in a life or death struggle with the market. Our social machine is not the market itself but rather capitalism, which requires (among other things, like exploitation) both markets and institutions autonomous of them. There is then nothing archaic about the institution of art, nothing rearguard about the assertion of autonomy. As with the enlightenment in Hegel (who referred rather to "the struggle of Enlightenment with Supersition"), capitalism is not one thing but rather the struggle between two things. (To be more precise, it is many such struggles, or one such struggle with many forms of appearance.) Autonomous institutions, "matters in hand," are, in other words, not mere spaces of critique, somehow removed from the social machine; they are rather integral to it. The assertion of autonomy is the assertion that, rather than in the heat-death of the closure of the market, or in the static symbiosis of markets and regulation, history lies in the struggle between autonomy and the market.

But how to make the claim to autonomy plausible? Haven't we, in outlining the collapse of modernism, done no more than confirm the wisdom that the work of art is a commodity like any other? In fact, it is the claim to universal heteronomy that is implausible. Markets—and this was recognized in some of the precursors to neoliberal discourse—depend on a host of non-market actors and institutions, even as these are always at the same time under threat from the market itself.[20] And a major consequence of Bourdieu's discovery of the restricted field was the demonstration that the field of large-scale cultural production, the culture industry as such, is utterly dependent on the persistence of the restricted field.[21] If the old modernist autonomy has been revealed to be an aesthetic ideology, there is no reason to believe that the new heteronomy therefore represents the truth. Like modernist autonomy, it is a productive ideology: it frees artists to do something other than the old modernist games, and it allows them to work in the culture industry without facing the accusation of selling out, which now seems like an anachronistic accusation indeed. But that doesn't mean that aesthetic heteronomy corresponds to the actual state of affairs, though it must refer to something real in order to be effective. And at any rate, it takes half a second to realize that both heteronomy and autonomy are, taken separately, deeply contradictory positions that could not be occupied by any actual cultural production worth talking about. Pure autonomy would have no relation to the world; pure heteronomy would be indistinguishable from it. Rather, the question is: how and where is autonomy asserted, what are the mechanisms that make it possible? How, in short, does heteronomy produce or presume the autonomous?

Two answers suggest themselves, though both Fried and Jameson have their own solutions with which readers will already be familiar. The first is what one might call, in search of a better term, positive historicism, as a necessary logical advance from null historicism or pastiche. As long as an artwork is making a claim to be an artwork, the very heteronomy proclaimed by historicism can only be the appearance of heteronomy. The "grab bag or lumber room" is only an apparent grab-bag or lumber-room; it is in fact governed by a principle of selection. If it is an actual grab bag or lumber room, it is the Internet or an archive or a mall or simply everyday experience itself, and we don't need artists for those. As a disavowed principle of selection it may be weak or inconsistent; but from disavowed principle to conscious principle is but a tiny Hegelian step, and weak or null historicism turns into strong or positive historicism. So in this case the legible element of form, its meaning—the moment of intention—is not so much in the formal reduction of an art into the problem of its medium as it is in the process of framing: in the selection a particular formal or thematic problem as central, and the rewriting of the history of the medium or genre or even socio-cultural aesthetic field as the history of that problem. Possibly because of the one-time dominance of the album form, this solution is most abundantly audible in popular music. (Meanwhile, in large-format photography, precisely because it does open up an entirely new arena to be formally reduced to the problem of medium, and because this arena can be explored on the basis of an already existing restricted field, this solution is less urgent.)[22]

One of the best examples in music is the Brazilian Tropicália movement, one of the first pastiche postmodernisms. But it becomes obvious almost immediately that Tropicália's "lumber room" is a national lumber room, and that the materials it cobbles together are only those materials that register what had been the thematic center of Brazilian modernism. Brazilian modernism had been concerned with the perverse coexistence of the archaic and the hypermodern typical of Brazil's insertion into the world economy as a relatively wealthy peripheral economy. Tropicália, rather than search for a form adequate to express this content, will scour the cultural landscape for forms that already embody it: for example, slave culture electrified in *trio eléctrico* or submitted to modernist compositional technique in *bossa nova*.[23] The two musical forms—a street music invented for Carnaval in Salvador and a chamber music invented for bourgeois living rooms in Rio—would seem to have nothing to do with each other until Tropicália asserts their identity, at which point they can only be understood as forms of appearance of the same essential contradiction. And indeed now purely commercial forms like *iê-iê-iê* (from "yeah, yeah, yeah": derivative pop) can be seen, properly framed, to take part of this same contradiction from the other direction, since the attempt to keep up with the metropolitan culture industry is already the failure to keep up with it. A more formalized version of the historicist solution can be seen in the U.S. in, for example, the White Stripes project, which was essentially a theory of rock in musical form, and Cee-Lo Green's most recent album *The Lady Killer*, which produces a history of that sliver of black music that for a time assumed a dominant presence in the mass market, from the girl groups of the early 1960s to Prince and Michael Jackson even Lionel Richie in the early 1980s.[24]

A second possibility, which bears a family resemblance to the first but is closer in structure to Fried's version of the problem than to Jameson's, is the aestheticization of genre. In a recent discussion, David Simon, the creator of the television show *The Wire*, points to genre fiction as the one place where stories other than the now-standard, character-driven family narratives of contemporary high populism can be reliably found.[25] But why should genre fiction be a zone of autonomy? Isn't genre fiction the quintessential art commodity? In an interview, this time with Nick Hornby, Simon repeatedly says, in various ways, "Fuck the average reader."[26] This is a completely modernist statement, an assertion of autonomy from the culture market.[27] But how can someone who writes for TV possibly imagine his work as autonomous from the culture market? Because a genre, already marketable or it wouldn't be a genre, is also governed by rules. The very thing that invalidates genre fiction in relation to modernist autonomy—"formulas," Adorno called them—opens up a zone of autonomy within the heteronomous space of cultural commodities. The requirements are rigid enough to pose a problem, which can now be thought of as a formal problem like the problem of the flatness of the canvas or the pull of harmonic resolution. "Subverting the genre" means doing the genre better, just as every modernist painting had to assume the posture of sublating all the previous modernisms. Simon's only concession to the market is to the genre itself: Simon has to "solve the problem" of the police procedural—in other words, to produce a new way of satisfying the requirements of the genre—and he is free within that genre to use what narrative materials he likes. Ultimately, he is free to orient the entire work toward a plausible left project, namely a classically realist mapping of social space.

The assertion of autonomy implied in positive historicism, above, can lead to an attractive politics, as it does (not without ambivalence) in Tropicália, but it can also produce no legible politics at all beyond the minimal one entailed in the claim to autonomy (The White Stripes, Cee-Lo). Similarly, even when the aestheticization of genre doesn't lead to an obviously attractive politics, it does lead to better art, or rather to the possibility of art as such—a possibility which, I have tried to show, today itself entails a minimal politics. A time-travel narrative can only have one of two endings: either history can be changed, or it can't: *Back to the Future* or *La jetée*. So the problem of the time-travel flick is how to keep these two incompatible possibilities in play until the end, and if possible even beyond the end, so you can have a sequel. And James Cameron can, within this genre, make all kinds of intentional choices that can only be read as intentional choices, because they can only be understood as manipulations of a formal problem. And *Terminator II* can be a work of art, while *Avatar* is only an art commodity.

Notes

1 Karl Marx, *Das Kapital: Kritik der politischen Ökonomie, Erster Band*, in Karl Marx and Friedrich Engels, *Werke*, vol. 23 (Berlin: Dietz, 2008) is cited in the text as *K*. Karl Marx, *Capital: A Critique of Political Economy, Volume One*, trans. Ben Fowkes (London: New Left Review, 1976) is cited in the text as *C*. My translations will often differ substantially from the English text.

2 The logic here is enough to differentiate the Hegelian-Marxian concept of standpoint from the contemporary notion of viewpoint. The denotations of the words in English are more or less indistinguishable, but standpoint in the Hegelian-Marxian tradition means virtually the opposite of what we usually mean by viewpoint. "Standpoint" refers to a logical position within a system of logical positions, where the system is not posited as unknowable a priori. Since standpoints are logical positions, they can be adopted at will, even if they are empirically native to this or that social position. In the master–slave dialectic, one can adopt either position at will, and presumably the relation between the two only becomes clear in the shuttling back and forth between the two positions. But one can also adopt the standpoint of non-persons: the State in Hegel, the proletariat in Lukács. Viewpoint, however, can only apply to persons. Marx's distinction between M-C-M and C-M-C, which will have a role to play in what follows, is also one of standpoint, since both are merely segments in the unsegmented process of continuous exchange. The "small master" may experience exchange as C-M-C, and the capitalist proper may experience exchange as M-C-M, but the distinction is not reducible to their subject positions or viewpoints. The point here is that the commodity has a standpoint as much as the capitalist. The capitalist can of course also have a viewpoint. But Marx's point in "personifying" the capitalist is that the viewpoint, to the extent that it diverges from the standpoint, is irrelevant.

3 Page references are to G.W.F. Hegel, *Phänomenologie des Geistes* (Frankfurt: Suhrkamp, 1970); paragraph numbers follow Miller's English translation (*Phenomenology of Spirit* [Oxford: Oxford University Press, 1977]). Translations are my own.

4 Fredric Jameson, *Representing Capital* (London: Verso, 2011). See, e.g. 81: "What the figure of externalization and the return or taking back into self is for Hegel, the trope of separation and its various cognates and synonyms is for Marx."

5 The reference is to Michael Fried, "Art and Objecthood," in *Art and Objecthood* (Chicago and London: University of Chicago Press, 1998), 148–172.

6 http://gawker.com/5403302/james-cameron-reveals-his-quest-to-build-more-perfect-cgi-boobs.

7 http://uinterview.com/news/james-cameron-why-the-navi-have-breasts-985.

8 Max Horkheimer and Theodor W. Adorno, "The Culture Industry: Enlightenment as Mass Deception," in Horkheimer and Adorno, *Dialectic of Enlightenment*, trans. John Cumming (New York: Continuum, 1996), is cited in the text as *DE*. As elsewhere, my translations will diverge substantially from the cited text. *Dialektik der Aufklärung: Philosophische Fragmente* (Frankfurt: Fischer, 1969) is cited in the text as *DA*.

9 For an efficient statement of the intentionalist position, see Jennifer Ashton's rewriting of the Wimsatt and Beardsley prohibitions as the "Causal" and "Effective" fallacies in her "Two Problems with a Neuroaesthetic Theory of Interpretation," *nonsite.org* 2.

10 The distinction between the Hegelian and the Freudian unconscious can be seen most starkly in Hegel's few words in *Phenomenology of Spirit* on *Oedipus Rex* (§468), where *das Unbewußte* (unusually nominalized, as opposed to the more common, adjectival *bewußtlos*) is simply the unknown that is nonetheless part of the deed. I am inclined to think that in Fredric Jameson's work the Freudian positivity of the unconscious is relatively inconsequential and can be re-written in terms of the negative, Hegelian-Marxian unconscious, but I have not done the work of attempting such a translation. Certainly when Jameson writes, for example, of class-consciousness in Wyndham Lewis, the point is that petty-bourgeois class consciousness logically presupposes working-class consciousness, is unnecessary and unthinkable without it, and that Lewis is not aware of that entailment and presumably would have disavowed it. It doesn't mean that some secret part of Lewis's brain is aware of that entailment. Any Freudian "return of the repressed" would then have to be understood instead as the Hegelian "ruse of reason," that is, the proof that logical entailments are real entailments. At any rate, the claim here is not that Jameson doesn't rely on a positive unconscious but that work which follows his lead would be better off working with a negative one.

11 Fredric Jameson, *Postmodernism: Or, the Cultural Logic of Late Capitalism* (Durham, NC: Duke University Press, 1991), 4.

12 English text in *C*, 948–1084. Karl Marx, *Das Kapital 1.1: Resultate des unmittelbaren Produktionsprozesses* (Berlin: Karl Dietz, 2009) is cited in the text as *R*. The distinction occurs elsewhere in *Capital*, notably *K* 533/*C* 645.

13 Marx's notes on formal and real subsumption were not available to Adorno when he and Horkheimer were writing *Dialectic of Enlightenment*, but the logic, operative here and there in the published text of *Capital* (see particularly the section on "Absolute and Relative Surplus Value" [*K* 531–542/*C* 644–654], two terms that map roughly onto "formal and real subsumption," which also make a brief appearance there), is clearly operative in Adorno's work.

14 It is by no means self-evident that the formal subsumption of aesthetic labor under capitalism is an effect of capitalism's triumphant march, rather than a consequence of its ever more desperate search for profits once the rate of profit native to industrial capital has begun a secular decline. See Part One, "The

Trajectory of the Profit Rate," in Robert Brenner, *The Economics of Global Turbulence* (London: Verso, 2006), 11–40.

15 Pierre Bourdieu, "Le marché des biens symboliques," *L'Année sociologique* 22 (1971): 49–126, 52–53.

16 "The essence of Modernism lies, as I see it, in the use of characteristic methods of a discipline in order to criticize the discipline itself. . . . [What quickly emerges is] that the unique and proper area of competence of each art coincide[s] with all that [is] unique in the nature of its medium. The task of self-criticism [becomes] to eliminate from the specific effects of each art any and every effect that might conceivably be borrowed from or by the medium of any other art." Clement Greenberg, "Modernist Painting," in *The Collected Essays and Criticism*, Volume 4: *Modernism with a Vengeance, 1957–1969* (Chicago: University of Chicago Press, 1993), 85–86.

17 Friedrich Schlegel, *Kritische Fragmente, Kritische Friedrich Schlegel Ausgabe*, ed. E. Behler and U. Eichner, 2 (Paderborn: Ferdinand Schöningh, 1958–), 204.

18 Though we know from his letters that Joyce was hostile to the publishing market, he imagines himself from the beginning as superior to it, which is what makes his hostility so entertaining: graver threats to autonomy are church and nation, though it is really the latter that threatens aesthetic, as opposed to personal autonomy. Astonishingly, the same logic holds with South African writer Es'kia Mphahlele. Mphahlele is disgusted with the South African publishing industry and his position within it, and, in a country where until 1953 all education for black students had been run through mission schools, is frustrated with everpresent "South African 'churchianity'" (Ezekiel Mphahlele, *Down Second Avenue* [1959; New York: Anchor, 1971], 210). Apartheid South Africa is nothing like a neoliberal state, requiring a massive bureaucracy to administer Apartheid and to keep white unemployment low; under Apartheid, the market is far from the most obvious threat. The astonishing thing is that despite the almost unimaginable humiliation of living under Apartheid, Mphahlele exiles himself from South Africa not only because of Apartheid ("I can't teach [having been banned], and I want to teach"), but because of the threat to aesthetic autonomy represented by a resistance with which he is in full sympathy: "I can't write here and I want to write," and he can't write not because he has been banned, but because the situation itself, a political urgency which is as much internal as external to Mphahlele himself, represents "a paralyzing spur" (199). This is not to endorse Mphahlele's decision over other possible ones, but to point out that the Adornian option between engagement and autonomy—the strong version of the heteronomy/autonomy problem, a version in which both sides have a plausible attraction for the Left, but which presupposes, as this example underscores, something plausibly Left to be heteronomous to—is far from a parochial concern and cannot be overcome at will.

19 Lisa Siraganian, *Modernism's Other Work: The Art Object's Political Life* (Oxford and New York: Oxford University Press, 2012).

20 Even the most laissez-faire theories of the market require at least one non-market institution, namely money. Foucault's lectures on neoliberalism have become the locus classicus for the understanding of neoliberalism as the recognition that non-intervention in the mechanisms of the market requires strong intervention on the conditions of the market. Foucault's lecture of

14 February 1979 (138) paraphrases Walter Euken, quoted in the footnotes: "Die Wirtschaftpolitische Tätigkeit des Staates sollte auf die Gestaltung der Ordnungsformen der Wirtschaft gerichtet sein, nicht auf die Lenkung des Wirtschaftprozesses." Michel Foucault, *The Birth of Biopolitics: Lectures at the College de France, 1978–1979*, trans. Graham Burchell (New York: Palgrave, 2008), 154 fn. 37. The neoliberal utopia is in fact an upgrade of Hegel's much more naïve one in *Philosophy of Right*, which essentially lets capitalists accumulate as much as they like—for Hegel understands that, under capitalism, the wealth of capital is the wealth of nations—as long as they are not, heaven forefend, allowed to usurp the job of intellectuals, which is to make decisions about the whole. What neither Hegel nor the neoliberal utopians allow for is that once you understand that wealth is itself a power that can be arrayed against the regulatory apparatus, you understand that some degree of what the economists call "regulatory capture" is implied by the concept regulation itself.

21 See "Les relations entre champ de production restreinte et champ de grande production," "Le marché des biens symboliques" 81–100, especially 90.

22 This is not to say that such a solution is unthinkable in photography; the Bechers' industrial "albums" bear a family resemblance to the musical solution, though the representational and political project is completely different. The discovery of large-scale photography as precisely a new medium in the Greenbergian sense is of course Michael Fried's. Michael Fried, *Why Photography Matters as Art as Never Before* (New Haven: Yale, 2008).

23 See Nicholas Brown, "Postmodernism as Semiperipheral Symptom," in *Utopian Generations: The Political Horizon of Twentieth-Century Literature* (Princeton, NJ: Princeton University Press, 2005), 173–199.

24 The White Stripes example shows the family resemblance of these two solutions. Producing a narrative account of rock involves, in this case, producing a set of formal prohibitions; that is, (paraphrasing Greenberg on painting) eliminating from the specific effects of rock any and every effect that might conceivably be borrowed from or by the medium of any other music. "70 to 80 percent of what we do is constriction, and the other 20 to 30 percent is us breaking that constriction to see what happens." http://www.avclub.com/articles/jack-white,14117/.

25 http://www.nypl.org/audiovideo/death-boom-culture-walter-benn-michaels-david-simon-susan-straight-dale-peck.

26 http://www.believermag.com/issues/200708/?read=interview_simon.

27 Compare Simon's "Fuck the reader" with a statement plausibly attributed to Steve Jobs, that "Consumers aren't in the business of knowing what they want." There's a certain similarity of attitude, but what they mean is completely different. Steve Jobs's claim is that consumers aren't in the business of knowing what they want, but that he is precisely in the business of knowing what consumers want or will want. "Fuck the reader" does not say "Readers don't know what they want, but I do": it says rather, "what the reader wants is irrelevant to what I do."

PART FIVE

Machinations of the Political

Introduction

Marx famously had less to say about anything we could call an explicitly political theory than he did about the specific consequences and contradictions of the science most enthusiastic about capitalism's industrial phase. With the exception of a few key texts written not in the mode of *Capital* but along the lines of "The Civil War in France," the Marxism of the 19th century (despite its historical genesis in the furnace of labor unrest) developed most precisely its critique of the then new science of political economic study. So while there is no shortage of political implication to the positions developed by Marx, Marxism is, strictly speaking, not itself a *politics*.

One thus can't get too far into a Marxist theory of politics before the methodology developed by Marx must give way, at least in appearance, to a mode capable of speculation, prescription, and perlocution, which is to say a mode oriented more enthusiastically at communism (which is not currently of this world) instead of capitalism (which is). The double bind of the object on which Marx spent most his energy, though, is that the latter (communism) is neither autonomous from nor even imaginable in its fullest form without a historical and methodological working through of the former (capitalism). Add to this the inexact alignment between two mirror poles of materialist criticism—political/economic and domination/exploitation—and the precise location, let alone operations of a Marxist *political theory* are cloudy at best, though nonetheless fundamental to its dual commitment to immanent critique (of capitalism) and imminent forecast (of communism).

One way then to interpret the ostensible deficit in Marxist *political* decibels in the post-1989 moment is to say what one healthy strand of "post-Marxism" has insisted, which is that today's postindustrial economy is much closer to the communism we have been thinking about for a long time now, and that our habits, references, and praxis must too change in tune with the "accidental revolution." Another way to think about the shape of Marxist political theory after 1989, however, is as a maturation period during which a more robust and accomplished (and thus abhorrent) capitalist postmodernity pushes back on actual and imagined realities housed in Marxism's core principles, not least that of the identity and difference of politics and economics. On the other side of what was the political downturn of the nineties are some unexpected ideas, this part suggests, about the specifically *political* content of economic life (and thus the obverse, too) and some possible directions moving forward.

Our aim in this part is to bring into chorus new (and perhaps forgotten) directions in Marxist political theory. In order to do so without abandoning either adjective ("Marxist" or "political") or their noun ("theory")—which more often than not results in a bid for something like a Marxist political practice, an oxymoron to which we will return in a moment—we have committed to endorsing projects that update the way we isolate the political content of today's uneven accumulation, and that then say a thing or two about how we might continue that older principle of *politicization*. This part includes new theories regarding the state and law; the new subjects of history; the specific character of contemporary politics and the challenges confronting ideas about emancipation and liberation today; and the unexpected scale at which an internationalist standpoint must today struggle.

* * *

In a series of exchanges in 1897 with Georges Sorel published later as *Correspondence on Philosophy and Socialism*, the influential Italian Marxist Antonio Labriola credits the slow growth and relative paucity of historical materialism amongst Europe's workers and parties to a political imaginary reluctant to dispense with self-preservation: "this vast *system of economic contradictions*," he concludes the second of three letters, "appears in its entirety as a *sum of social injustices* to all sentimental socialists, *rational* socialists, and all shades of declaiming radicals."[1] That Labriola and Sorel will shortly thereafter come to emblematize variants of communism and fascism, respectively, is unsurprising given the alignment on display: a struggle (and thus theory) against political domination remains "sentimental"—or worse, fundamentalist—without the simultaneous struggle against economic exploitation. How, this part addresses, has Marxist political theory after 1989 attempted to do both at the same time?

With no shortage in the number of political positions interested in a post-capitalist future—whether out of concern for ecological catastrophe; factory conditions where things are made cheap and human energy even cheaper; pensions and social security in rich and poor economies alike; or struggles to keep urban- and cyber-space common—what seems often lacking is a transition from what Labriola, Lenin and later Mao criticized as a political practice devoid of materialist theory to a labor *force* (broadly understood) politically at odds with, rather than defensive of, its own economic identity. Fundamental to any historical or dialectical materialist theory is that the transition from the former (idealism) to the latter (materialism) can occur only once the economic content of social and objective contradiction is grasped, and struggled against. Marxist political theory takes place, thus, at the level of knowledge and practice at the same time.

Our first selection comes from the architect of and running mate to Evo Morales' successful campaign in 2005. Álvaro García Linera's "State Crisis and Popular Power" from the following year charts the specifically economic and ideological contents of Bolivia's indigenous-revolutionary force and its *epochal* influence on what he calls the new "reconfiguration."[2] Unique, in Línera's account of Boliva, is the hypothesis that a gradualist electoral trajectory to revolutionary change and an immediate insurrection on the part of its indigenous majority "are not necessarily antagonistic" strategies so long as the country's recent history is understood at the scale of Marx's "revolutionary epoch."[3] Línera's Marxist theory of the political thus hinges on an image not of a static state but instead on a form of the state capable of shielding and embodying revolutionary duration.[4]

On "the political" as an abstraction more generally, Antonio Negri offers an interrogation of what legal theorists call "constituent power" in order to arrive at a revolutionary moment of *un-constitutional* political contradiction (where constitutional power is that most counter-revolutionary period in the dialectic between system and subject). Building on Hannah Arendt's mid-century distinction between social and political power—the former leading without much obstacle to a form of fascist thinking, and the latter somewhere fundamentally incompatible with totalitarianism as such—Negri aims to "identify . . . a strength adequate to structure, and a subject adequate to absolute procedure" in the context of today's political economy. The answer is no longer the proletariat, for Negri, but a sociopolitical *capacity* contemporaneous to the latest stages of economic organization on a global scale, which is the labor of cooperation, or more precisely: "Cooperative living labor [which] produces a social ontology that is constitutive and innovative, a weaving of forms that touch the economic and the political; living labor produces an indistinct mixture of the political and economic that has a creative figure." Revolutionary politics, in Negri's account, is about the very ground upon which creativity occurs, and not the *laborers* or *producers* more familiar to leftist thinking. Contrary to how Negri and his American counterpart, Michael Hardt, are routinely characterized, we offer here a theoretical position far more compatible with older and new forms of Marxism, before their project turned in 2000 to delimiting that subject in *Empire*.

Chantal Mouffe's more recent chapter on "Radical Politics Today" from her 2013 *Agonistics* takes issue, however, with what she sees as the dual tendencies toward "immanentism" and "radical negativity" in the political thought of Negri on the one hand and Bruno Latour on the other. Mouffe's rejoinder is one much more familiar to social democrats—namely, that true political transformation occurs not through a mutually exclusive "antagonism" but through the democratic principle of "agonism"—but nonetheless insists that socialists and communists alike plan their staying power not against but through power and its institutions.[5] Hers is a political theory of socialist emancipation that has challenged many of the habits in leftist thought since the collapse of the Soviet Union, especially on the political function of mediation versus the apparently more attractive commitment to immediacy and transparency.

Peter Hallward's 2005 "The Politics of Prescription" was one of the strongest positions on political will and structural change we've seen in decades, providing much welcome relief to a more commonly melancholy and fatalistic Marxism. In this more recent development of that theoretical project, "On Political Will," Hallward manages to align his political theory with an often impossible anthropological materialism, where "the people" and the possibility of its collective and willed force is taken back from those populists and idealists to whom such terms usually belong. Any revolution worth speaking of, on Hallward's account, will be (and has been) neither accidental nor entirely unexpected (they are *willed*) and so we have every reason to speak of principles as a material force in the world. To this he adds the important caveat that "[T]o will an end or outcome is not to will a fully formed solution in advance of engaging with the problem; it is rather the readiness to follow through on a decision and the principles that orient it, the willingness to do what is required to overcome the obstacles, both predictable and unforeseen, that may emerge over the course of its imposition."[6]

Never before in human history has it been possible to instantly communicate with as many people across the globe as we can today. And yet, as Jodi Dean insists in "Communicative Capitalism," we seem further than ever from developing a truly counterhegemonic political force.[7] Even as millions of activists coordinate demonstrations reminiscent of the 1960s via social networking technologies at a scale unimaginable even a decade ago, the capitalist mode of production appears as defiant and durable as ever. Politicization, on Dean's account, is prevented somehow by the very technologies on which we've recently come to rely for mass mobilization: "communicative exchanges, rather than being fundamental to democratic politics," she claims, "are the basic elements of capitalist production."[8]

Our final three selections conclude our anthology on perhaps the most pressing question facing Marxism today, which is how to characterize and politicize what Jacques Rancière calls "the outside," Claus Peter Ortlieb understands as the ecological precondition to capitalist accumulation, and Aaron Benanav and John Clegg of *Endnotes* characterize as labor superfluous to political and economic life after globalization. Rancière's intervention into the widespread celebration of "the end of politics," which is in no uncertain terms an indictment of the bad social fetishizing committed by lazy liberals and Marxists alike, is to insist that "Democracy is . . . precisely not a political regime in the sense of a particular constitution that determines different ways of assembling people under a common authority"—which later he will call the *policing* of consensus—but is instead "*the* institution of politics—the institution of both its subject and its mode of relating."[9] Rancière thus reinvigorates, against much of the celebrated agonism of Ernesto Laclau and Chantal Mouffe (see above) and others in recent decades, a theory of antagonism that operates both on a supra- and infra-social level.

Taken from a collection on German *Wertkritik* (value critique), *Marxism and the Critique of Value*, Ortlieb's contribution to both Marxist political theory and the political economy of ecology is to insist that social and environmental collapse are both simultaneously certain, and internal guarantees to the logic of capitalist value. Neither are deviations from a properly operating economic system, on Ortlieb's account; instead, the production of a crisis in labor (less and less of it is needed and so more and more of it "vegetate[s] aimlessly as commodity subjects without commodities"[10]) and an ecological crisis (more and more natural wealth is logically required to realize the same amount of value) has already amounted to what others associated with *wertkritik* call the "final crisis." Neither eco-socialism nor deep ecology will do much of anything to slow or reverse it. Without a revolutionary "overcoming of capitalism—and therefore of wealth in the value form, and of the subject form that it constitutes,"[11] Ortlieb's economic and ecological forecast is of a certain and permanent apocalypse.

From the perspective of labor as a socio-economic category in crisis today, "Misery and Debt" from *Endnotes 2* provides Marx's general law of accumulation with concrete and political urgency on global scale. What this means today is that the most general law internal to capitalist development—that more and more value will be congealed in the constant part of capital, or products of previous labor, while more and more living labor will be shed from the production process—has exploded into a volatile and critical condition for populations ostensibly superfluous to capitalism's needs, as well as for the impoverished majority internal to it. *Endnotes'* more general participation in the debates surrounding communization, to which this anthology has given space in earlier parts, is in this essay brought closest to Marxist value theory by way of the immiseration thesis. If politicization is the historical project to which Marxism is designed to give shape, and internationalization gives that project its historicity, then "Misery and Debt" offers a complex, but eminently legible map for a Marxism after globalization.

Notes

1   Antonio Labriola to George Sorel, April 24, 1897 https://www.marxists.org/archive/labriola/works/al03.htm.
2   Álvaro Garcia Línera, "State Crisis and Popular Power," *New Left Review* 37 (January–February 2006): 75.
3   Línera, 85 and 81.
4   For an extended consideration of Línera's political theory in relation to the power of the plebs, see Bruno Bosteels's final chapter in *The Actuality of Communism*.
5   Chantal Mouffe, *Agonistics* (London: Verso, 2013), 84.
6   Peter Hallward, "On Political Will," forthcoming in *Culture and Politics*.
7   Jodi Dean, "Communicative Capitalism: Circulation and the Foreclosure of Politics," *Cultural Politics* 1, no. 1 (March 2005): 53.
8   Ibid., 56.
9   Jacques Rancière, "Ten Theses on Politics," *Theory and Event* 5, no. 3 (2001): 5.
10 Claus Peter Ortlieb, "A Contradiction between Matter and Form: On the Significance of the Production of Relative Surplus Value for the Dynamics of the Final Crisis," trans. Neil Larsen, Mathias Nilges, Josh Robinson, and Nicholas Brown, in *Marxism and the Critique of Value*, ed. Neil Larsen, Mathias Nilges, Josh Robinson, and Nicholas Brown (Chicago and Alberta: MCM', 2014), 109.
11 Ibid.

CHAPTER TWENTY SEVEN

State Crisis and Popular Power

Álvaro García Linera

From New Left Review *37 (January–February 2006): 73–85.*

Three factors define the functioning, stability and representative capacity of a state. The first is the overall framework of social forces: the correlation between the different coalitions, both dominant and subordinate, contesting the reconfiguration of what Bourdieu called "state capital"—the ability to influence decisions on matters of common import. Secondly, there is the system of political institutions and rules that mediate the coexistence of hierarchical social forces. In effect, this institutional framework is a materialization of the founding correlation of forces that give rise to a particular state regime, and the means by which it legally reproduces itself. Thirdly, every state depends upon a structure of common categories of perception, a series of mobilizing beliefs that generates a degree of social and moral conformity among both ruling and ruled, and which takes material form through the state's cultural repertoire and rituals.

When these three components of a country's political life are visibly healthy and functioning, we can speak of an optimal correspondence between state regime and society. When one or all of these factors is suspended or ruptured, we are presented with a crisis of the state, manifested in the antagonism between the political world and its institutions on the one hand, and the opposing actions by large-scale social coalitions on the other. This is precisely what has been happening in Bolivia in recent years. The successive uprisings and popular upheavals that have rocked the country since 2000 may best be understood as symptoms of a profound state crisis.

This crisis has a double character. In the short term, it is a crisis of the neoliberal model, and the social and ideological basis on which it has been constructed in Bolivia. But it is also, to paraphrase Braudel, a crisis of the *longue durée*: an institutional and ideological crisis of the republican state, premised since its foundation on a colonial relationship to the indigenous majority of the Bolivian people. Let us examine how these aspects are manifested at the social, institutional and ideological levels in Bolivia today.

Framework of social forces

The starting point for analysis of the balance of social forces in Bolivia since the mid-1980s is the political and cultural defeat of the labor movement organized around the COB.[1] For decades after the popular revolution of 1953, this had articulated the needs of a wide front of urban and rural working classes, representing popular demands regarding the administration of the social surplus through structures such as union membership and workers' joint management. After the dispersal of this labor movement, a social bloc consisting of business fractions connected to the world market, elite political parties, foreign investors and international regulatory bodies was consolidated, which then took center stage in the definition of public policy. For the next fifteen years, these forces became the sole subjects of decision-making and initiative in public administration, reconfiguring the economic and social organization of the country under promises of modernization and globalization—first and second-generation structural reforms, privatizations, decentralization, tariff-cutting and so forth.

Since the turn of the millennium, this relationship of forces has been challenged from below, and the guaranteed elitism of the "neoliberal-patrimonial state" thrown into question, as new forms of organization and politicization have reversed the footing of the subaltern classes. The protests and road blockades of April and September 2000, July 2001 and June 2002 signalled a regional reconstitution of social movements capable of imposing public policies, legal regimes and even modifications to the distribution of the social surplus through the strength of their mobilizations.[2] Laws such as No. 2029, which sought to redefine ownership of water, and laws enabling the sale of state enterprises into private hands, tax increases, etc., were annulled or modified under pressure from social movements and popular uprisings. Presidential decrees such as that closing the coca market or mandating interdiction in the Yungas had to be withdrawn for the same reason. Financial legislation was amended in line with the national demands of organized popular groups (indigenous communities, retirees, coca-growing peasants, cooperative miners, policemen), demonstrating the emergence of social blocs which, at the margins of parliament, and—following the mass successes in 2002—with support from within it, have the strength to stop the implementation of government policies, and impose the redistribution of public resources by non-parliamentary means.

The important thing to note about these popular groupings, hitherto excluded from decision-making, is that the demands they raise immediately seek to modify economic relations. Thus their recognition as a collective political force necessarily implies a radical transformation of the dominant state form, built on the marginalization and atomization of the urban and rural working classes. Moreover—and this is a crucial aspect of the current reconfiguration—the leaderships of these new forces are predominantly indigenous, and uphold a specific cultural and political project. In contrast to the period that opened with the 1930s, when the social movements were articulated around a labor unionism that held to an ideal of *mestizaje*, and was the result of an economic modernization carried out by business elites, today the social movements with the greatest power to interrogate the political order have an indigenous social base, and spring from the agrarian zones excluded from or marginalized by the processes of economic modernization. The Aymaras of the *altiplano*, the *cocaleros* of the Yungas and Chapare, the *ayllus* of Potosí and Sucre and the Indian people of the east have replaced trade unions and popular urban organizations as social protagonists. And despite the regional or local character of their actions, they share a matrix of indigenous identity that calls into question what has been the unvarying nucleus of the Bolivian state for 178 years: its monoethnicity.

In addition, the elite coalition is itself showing signs of fatigue and internal conflict. The economic program of the past twenty years—privatization of public enterprises, externalization of profit, coca eradication—has resulted in a narrowing of opportunities for some sections of the national bourgeoisie, exacerbated by the shrinking of tax revenues owing to the growth of the informal sector. As their long-term outlook has darkened, the different elite fractions have begun to pull apart, squabbling over the reduction of profits transferred to the state, the refusal by foreign refiners to adjust the purchase price of petrol, the renegotiation of gas prices with Brazil,[3] land taxes, etc. Their shared project of the last decade is over.

The backdrop to the current crisis of the business bloc and to the insurgency of social movements is the Bolivian economy's primary-export, enclave character.[4] The fact that industrial modernity is present only as small islands in a surrounding sea of informality and a semi-mercantile peasant economy limits the formation of an internal market capable of supporting value-added business activity, even if it reduces wage costs. Vulnerability to the fluctuations of world commodity prices is an endemic feature. In that sense we can say that the *longue durée* crisis of the state is the political correlate of an equally long-term economic crisis of the primary-export model, which is incapable of productively retaining surpluses, and hence unable to deploy the capital necessary for national development. Thus the Santa Cruz Civic Committees' proposals for departmental autonomy, renewed every time there is a discussion about how income from hydrocarbons is to be allocated, or the demands for self-government by the indigenous communities, not only question the configuration of state power, but also reveal the underlying crisis of the established economic order.

Political institutions

Since 1985, Bolivia's elite political parties have sought, with the authoritarian support of the state, to substitute themselves for the old regime of political mediation carried out by the trade unions, which had linked the communal heritage of traditional societies with the collective actions of workers in large-scale enterprises. The party system, under Bolivia's particularly skewed constitution, was prescriptively defined as the mechanism through which the exercise of citizenship should function. However, it is clear that the old party groupings have not proved able to turn themselves into genuine vehicles for political mediation, capable of channelling social demands toward the state. They remain, above all, familial and business networks through which members of the elite can compete for access to the state administration as if it were a patrimonial possession; connections to the voting masses are largely organized around clientelist links and ties of privilege.[5]

With the syndical basis of Bolivian citizenship destroyed, and a new form of electoral participation barely perceptible, other popular forms of political mediation began to emerge with the turn of the century. Social movements, new and old, have asserted their own modes of deliberation, mass meetings and collective action. There are thus two types of institutional system in Bolivia today. In the Chapare, Yungas and Norte de Potosí regions, community forms are superimposed not only on party organization, but also on state institutions themselves, to the extent that mayors, *corregidores* and subprefects are de facto subordinated to peasant confederations. In the case of the northern *altiplano*, several subprefectures and police posts have disappeared over the last three years and "community police" have been created in provincial capitals to preserve public order in the name of the peasant federations. During the blockades that accompanied the anti-privatization protests of 2003–05, hundreds of communities on the *altiplano* constituted what they call the "great indigenous barracks" of Q'alachaca, an ad hoc confederation of militant *ayllus* and villages.

The Bolivian theorist René Zavaleta's notion of the "apparent state" is of clear relevance here. Due to the social and civilizational diversity of the country, large stretches of territory and sections of the population remain outside, or have not interiorized, the disciplines of the capitalist labor process; they recognize other temporalities, other systems of authority, and affirm collective aims and values different from those offered by the Bolivian state.[6] Through the political and economic struggles of the last five years, these layers have undergone a process of increasing institutional consolidation, in some cases permanent (politicized agrarian indigenous territories) and in others sporadic (urban areas of Cochabamba, La Paz and El Alto). As a result, the neoliberal state has been confronted with a fragmenting institutional order and robbed of governing authority. The alternative system, anchored in the world of indigenous experience marginalized by Bolivia's uneven modernization process, is challenging the state's centuries-long pretence at a modernity based on texts and institutions that are not even respected by the elites who propound them; and who themselves have never abandoned the methods of seigneurial and patrimonial politics. The generalized corruption in the state apparatus is nothing other than the modernized representation of these habits through which elites in power take on and reproduce state functions.

The liberal-capitalist political culture and institutions that are both being overtaken by the social movements, and traduced by the actual behavior of the elites in power, presuppose the individuation of society: the dissolution of traditional loyalties, seigneurial relations and non-industrial productive systems. These processes, in Bolivia, have affected at most one third of the population. The Bolivian state, however, including its current "neoliberal" variant, has, as a sort of political schizophrenia, constructed normative regimes and institutions that bear no correspondence to the "patchwork" reality of our society which, in its structural majority, is neither industrial nor individuated. The effect of the indigenous and plebeian social movements, which in Habermasian terms stress "normative" over "communicative" action, is thus to call into question the validity of republican state institutions that present a mere simulacrum of modernity, in a society which still lacks the structural and material bases upon which such modernity might be based.

Mobilizing beliefs

Since 1985, the ideological blueprints offered to the Bolivian population have been the free market, privatization, governability and representative democracy. All these proposals were illusions, but well-founded ones, since although they never materialized in any substantial sense, they did bring about a realignment of actions and beliefs in a society which imagined that, through them and the sacrifices they demanded, it would be possible to attain wellbeing, modernity and social recognition. The upper, middle and subaltern urban classes—the latter having abandoned all expectations of protection from the state and workplace unions—saw in this offer a new path to stability and social betterment.

By 2000, the gulf between expectations and realities was driving a disappointed population into conflict with state authority. The promise of modernity had resulted only in intensified exploitation and an increase in informal labor (from 55 to 68 per cent in 20 years); that of social betterment, in a greater concentration of wealth and a refinement in forms of ethnic discrimination. Privatization, especially of hydrocarbons, far from expanding the internal market, has seen an accelerated flight of earnings into foreign hands. This breakdown between official schemas and lived reality has left large sections of the population highly receptive to new loyalties and mobilizing beliefs. Among these are the national-ethnic claims of the indigenous masses, which have produced a sort of indigenous nationalism in the Aymara section of the *altiplano*; state recovery of privatized public resources—water, hydrocarbons—and the broadening of social participation and democracy through recognition of non-liberal political practices of a collective and traditional bent (indigenous community, union, etc.). These convictions are actively displacing loyalties to the liberal, privatizing ideology of the state.

We could say that the Bolivian state has lost its monopoly over the capital of recognition, and that we are passing through a period of transition in the structures of allegiance. A striking feature of the new movements is that they dispute both the discourses of neoliberal modernity and the founding certainties of the republican state—that there is an inherent inequality between indigenous and *mestizos*, and that Indians are not capable of governing the country. The fact that the Indians, accustomed to giving their votes to the "mist'is" (*mestizos*), have over the past few years voted extensively for the emerging indigenous leaders, denotes a watershed in the symbolic structures of a profoundly colonial and racialized society. For indigenous social forces, the construction of urban hegemony is posed as a central strategic task, for it is here that their identity confronts its own hybridity or dissolution in face of the composition—not without ambiguities—of *mestizo* identities, both elite and popular.

In Bolivia, then, the pillars of both the "neoliberal" model and the republican state have deteriorated rapidly. It is this conjunction of crises that helps to explain not just the radical nature of the political conflict over the past five years, but also its complexity and irresolution. Such crises cannot endure for long, because no society can withstand long periods of political vacuum or uncertainty. Sooner or later there will be a lasting recomposition of forces, beliefs and institutions that will inaugurate a new period of state stability. The question for Bolivia is what kind of state this mutation will create. There could be increased repression, leading to the introduction of a "neoliberal-authoritarian" state as the new political form, which might perhaps solve the crisis of the *courte durée*, but not that of the *longue durée*, whose problems would soon manifest themselves again. Or there could be instead an opening of new spaces for the exercise of democratic rights (multicultural political forms, combined communitarian-indigenous and liberal institutions) and economic redistribution (a productive role for the state, self-management, etc.), capable of addressing both dimensions of the crisis. In the latter scenario, a democratic resolution of the neoliberal state crisis will have to involve a simultaneous multicultural resolution of the crisis of the colonial republican state.

Hegemonies, Zavaleta argues, can grow tired: there are moments when the state ceases to be irresistible, when the population abandons the ideological frameworks that allowed it to accept the elite's ordering of society as desirable. The uprising of October 2003 was the maximal expression of the masses' dissent from the "neoliberal-patrimonial" state, and hence of the exhaustion of its form of hegemony.[7] If each state crisis generally goes through four phases—manifestation of the crisis; transition or systemic chaos; conflictive emergence of a new principle of state order; consolidation of the new state—October, with its hundreds of thousands of Indians and urban masses in revolt in the cities of La Paz and El Alto, and its culmination in the flight of President Sánchez de Lozada, inescapably marked the Bolivian state's entry into the transitional phase. The initial acceptance of the constitutional succession of Vice-President Carlos Mesa was due not so much to deference toward parliamentarism as to a popular attachment to the old prejudice of the personalization of power, the belief that a change of personnel is in itself a change of regime. But there was also a certain historical lucidity with regard to the further consequences implicit, given the present correlation of forces, in the abandonment of liberal democratic institutions.

But if there can be no state domination without the consent of the dominated—progressively eroded in Bolivia since the blockades of 2000—there can be no successful opposition without the capacity to postulate an alternative order. This is precisely what the insurgents discovered: they were able to paralyze the state with their blockades but were unable to put forward an alternative and legitimate power project. Hence the ambiguous and confused truce of the Mesa period (2003–05), during which the distinguished broadcaster attempted to channel the insurgents' minimum program (resignation of Sánchez de Lozada, constituent assembly, new hydrocarbons law), while leaving in place the entire governmental machinery of neoliberal reforms.

Revolutionary epochs

It was Marx who proposed the concept of the "revolutionary epoch" in order to understand extraordinary historical periods of dizzying political change—abrupt shifts in the position and power of social forces, repeated state crises, recomposition of collective identities, repeated waves of social rebellion—separated by periods of relative stability during which the modification, partial or total, of the general structures of political domination nevertheless remains in question.

A revolutionary epoch is a relatively long period, of several months or years, of intense political activity in which: (a) social sectors, blocs or classes previously apathetic or tolerant of those in power openly challenge authority and claim rights or make collective petitions through direct mobilizations (gas and water *coordinadoras*, indigenous, neighborhood organizations, *cocaleros*, small-scale farmers); (b) some or all of these mobilized sectors actively posit the necessity of taking state power (MAS, CSUTCB, COB);[8] (c) there is a surge of adherence to these proposals from large sections of the population (hundreds of thousands mobilized in the Water War, against the tax hike, in the Gas War, in the elections to support Indian candidates); the distinction between governors and governed begins to dissolve, due to the growing participation of the masses in political affairs; and (d) the ruling classes are unable to neutralize these political aspirations, resulting in a polarization of the country into several "multiple sovereignties"[9] that fragment the social order (the loss of the "authority principle" from April 2000 till today).

In revolutionary epochs societies fragment into social coalitions, each with proposals, discourses, leaderships and programs for political power that are antagonistic to and incompatible with one another. This gives rise to "cycles of protest,"[10] waves of mobilization followed by withdrawals and retreat, which serve to demonstrate the weakness of those in power (Banzer in April and October 2000 and June 2001; Quiroga in January 2002; Sánchez de Lozada in February and October 2003). Such protests also serve to incite or "infect"[11] other sectors into using mass mobilization as a mechanism to press their demands (teachers, the retired, the landless, students). At the same time, these mobilizations fracture and destabilize the social coalition of the ruling bloc, giving rise to counter-reactions (the so-called business–civic–political "crescent" in the east of the country), which in turn produce another wave of mobilizations, generating a process of political instability and turbulence that fuels itself. Not every revolutionary epoch ends in a revolution, understood as a change of the social forces in power, which would have to be preceded by an insurrectionary situation. There are revolutionary epochs that lead to a restoration of the old regime (coup d'état), or to a negotiated and peaceful modification of the political system through the partial or substantial incorporation of the insurgents and their proposals for change into the power bloc.

The present political period in Bolivia can best be characterized as a revolutionary epoch. Since 2000, there has been a growing incorporation of broader social sectors into political decision-making (water, land, gas, Constituent Assembly) through their union, communal, neighborhood or guild organizations; there has been a continual weakening of governmental authority and fragmentation of state sovereignty; and there has been an increasing polarization of the country into two social blocs bearing radically distinct and opposed projects for economy and state.

At one pole, the fundamental nucleus is the indigenous movement, both rural (peasant) and urban (worker) in composition; this clearly represents a different political and cultural project for the country to any that has previously existed. The economic program of this pole is centered on the internal market, taking as its axis the peasant community, urban-artisanal and micro-business activity, a revitalized role for the state as producer and industrializing force, and a central role for the indigenous majority in driving the new state. At the other pole is the ascendant agro-export, financial and petroleum business bloc, which has played the most dynamic role in the liberalizing sectors of the economy. This bloc has a clear image of how Bolivia should relate to external markets and of the role of foreign investment, and it favors the subordination of the state to private enterprise and the preservation, or restoration, of the old political system. Anchored in the eastern and southeastern zones of the country, beyond the current organizational reach of the social movements, it deploys an openly racialized discourse.

This political polarity is thus further structured by three underlying cleavages: ethno-cultural (indigenous/*qaras-gringos*), class (workers/ businessmen) and regional (Andean west/Amazonian crescent). In the case of the "left" pole, the mobilizing identity is predominantly ethnocultural, around which worker identity is either dissolved (in a novel type of indigenous proletarianism) or complements indigenous leadership at a secondary level. For the "right" pole, mobilizing identity is primarily regional in nature; hence the importance of the Civic Committees, agitating for regional autonomy, for these conservative forces.

This polarization has led to a dissociation between economic dominance and political dominance, creating a period of instability since the components of power are divided between two different zones, neither of which has any immediate possibility of displacing the other. Economic power has moved from west to east (reinforced by foreign investment in hydrocarbons, services, agro-industry), while the sociopolitical power of mobilization has been reinforced in the west, giving rise to a new geographical uncertainty at the level of the state. The interesting thing about the "paradox of October," the period opened up by the insurrection that overthrew Sánchez de Lozada, is that this regional separation simultaneously expresses a confrontation of sharply differentiated ethnicities and classes: businessmen in the east (Santa Cruz, Beni, Tarija), and the indigenous and mass sectors in the west (La Paz, Cochabamba, Potosí, Oruro), both waiting to pounce on a state administration which, in territorial, social and cultural terms, can no longer express the new economic and political configuration of Bolivian society. It is true that there are businessmen, indigenous, *mestizos*, workers and peasants in every part of Bolivia; but the ascendant discourses and identities articulated within each region are differentiated by these class, ethnic and territorial roots.

Overall, the map of sociopolitical forces in Bolivia shows a highly political field, with tendencies on both sides pushing for solutions through force, either by coup d'état (MNR)[12] or insurrection (CSUTCB/COB), or through electoral resolution, either via a restoration of the old regime (ADN)[13] or its progressive transformation (MAS). None of these tendencies has yet managed to construct a bloc with a majority over the other components, still less over the other sections of the population that would be indispensable for a social leadership capable of a long-term hold on state power.

From the point of view of the social movements and their prospects for an indigenous-popular transformation of the state, there are two alternatives: a path of gradual, institutional change by electoral means led by Evo Morales, and an insurrectional path for the revolutionary transformation of the state. The first would require the construction of an electoral bloc around Morales, negotiated with other leaders and social movements, that would be strong enough to generate a unified popular and indigenous pole with the ability to rule. The broad social backing needed would require proposals for change robust enough to attract those urban sectors— middle-class, upwardly mobile popular, and even business layers linked to the internal market—who are at present reluctant to accept an indigenous governmental solution, and without whose support an indigenous electoral triumph would be rendered unviable.

The two paths, electoral and insurrectionary, are not necessarily antagonistic; they could turn out to be complementary. On both, however, the indigenous-popular pole should consolidate its hegemony, providing intellectual and moral leadership of the country's social majorities. There will be neither electoral triumph nor victorious insurrection without wide-ranging, patient work on the unification of the social movements, and a practical education process to realize the political, moral, cultural and organizational leadership of these forces over Bolivia's popular and middle strata.

Notes

1   Central Obrera Boliviana: organization of workers from large enterprises in different branches of production. In the wake of labor flexibilization, closures of businesses and privatizations implemented since 1985, its social base has been reduced to teachers, public hospital employees, university students and some urban guilds.

2   [In 2000, a rate hike imposed on the department of Cochabamba's newly privatized water supply led to massive protests, with strikes and blockades shutting down the city. On April 4, some 100,000 strikers and protesters broke through the military cordon surrounding the city's central square and held a mass open-air assembly. On April 8, Aguas del Tunari's contract on the water supply was revoked by the Banzer government. The same months saw the mobilization of *cocaleros* and peasant colonizers against the threat of coca eradication, with indigenous people's organizations playing a leading role in mounting road blockades that threatened to cut food supplies to La Paz. In June 2001 *cocaleros* in the Yungas valleys succeeded in driving out the joint us—Bolivian eradication force. Two months later, Banzer ceded the presidency to his deputy, Quiroga—NLR.]

3   [The state-owned Brazilian company Petrobras is a major purchaser of Bolivian natural gas, along with the Spanish Repsol—NLR.]

4   José Valenzuela, *¿Qué es un patrón de acumulación?* (Mexico City: Universidad Nacional Autónoma de México, 1990).

5   Patricia Chávez, *Los límites estructurales de los partidos de poder como estructuras de mediación democrática: Acción Democrática Nacionalista*, degree thesis in sociology (Universidad Mayor de San Andrés: La Paz, 2000).

6   Luis Tapia, *La condición multisocietal: multiculturalidad, pluralismo, modernidad* (Muela del Diablo Editores: La Paz, 2002).

7   [Protests at the Sánchez de Lozada government's scheme to export gas reserves through Chile (a national enemy since it had robbed Bolivia of access to the sea in the 1879–83 War of the Pacific), rather than process them domestically, escalated into a full-scale insurrection in La Paz and El Alto in October 2003, ending in the ouster of the president—NLR.]

8   Movimiento al Socialismo: political organization led by the indigenous peasant leader Evo Morales. Rather than a party, it is an electoral coalition of several urban and rural social movements. csutcb: organization of indigenous and peasant communities founded in 1979, led by Felipe Quispe.

9   Charles Tilly, *European Revolutions, 1492–1992* (Oxford: Blackwell, 1993).

10 Sidney Tarrow, *Power in Movement: Social Movements, Collective Action and Politics* (Cambridge: Cambridge University Press, 1994).

11 Anthony Oberschall, *Social Movements: Ideologies, Interests and Identities* (New Brunswick: Transaction, 1993).

12 Movimiento Nacionalista Revolucionario: nationalist party that led the
    popular revolution of 1952 and in the 1980s pushed through the liberal
    reforms of the Washington Consensus.
13 Acción Democrática Nacionalista: party founded in 1979 by the dictator Hugo
    Banzer, which he led in subsequent elections, gaining the presidency from 1997
    to 2001.

CHAPTER TWENTY EIGHT

Constituent Power: The Concept of a Crisis

Antonio Negri

From Insurgencies: Constituent Power and the Modern State. *Translated by Maurizia Boscagli. Minneapolis: University of Minnesota Press, 1990: 1–35.*

. . . From structure to the subject

Up to this point we have accumulated a series of problems. We have before us a productive source of rights and juridical arrangement that refuses to close and stubbornly repeats its claims in the face of juridical theory's and political philosophy's attempts to fix it in a final form. It seems that the issues on the table cannot be addressed except through the intervention of a force capable of mediating the radicalness of constituent power. This force must be able to interpret the structure when this structure is presented as absolute procedure, as continually reactualized strength, but nonetheless positively grounded in reality. An adequate answer to the question that motivates my investigation will be found by identifying a strength adequate to structure, and a subject adequate to absolute procedure. The problem of constituent power thus becomes a question about the construction of a constitutional model capable of keeping the formative capacity of constituent power itself in motion: it is a question of identifying a subjective strength adequate to this task.

If this subject is the subject of an absolute procedure, then it is not enough to pose the question of the subject raised by constituent power. In juridical theory this question arises whenever the voluntary nature of law is affirmed and the subject of this will must be discovered.[1] Posed in these terms the search is too generic because it does not insist on the logically adequate relationship between subject and structure. The history of juridical thought, however, does provide a series of examples that come close to this objective. We should examine them more closely.

The first hypothesis: the subject in question is the nation.[2] This concept seems to be, at first sight, particularly appropriate to that of absolute procedure, except that, on the one hand, it is a generic concept, real only in the imaginary (and therefore indefinitely manipulable); on the other, it is a concept that is historically determined at different times, often with the function of breaking and limiting the constituent process. The generic conception of the nation (resulting from an intricate play of ethnic determinism, historical judgments, political necessities, juridical demands, but above all a strong naturalistic overdetermination) produces a polysemy that allows for sophistic interpretations of the concept and instrumental uses of it in practice.[3] The latter conception, which refers to historical determinations, sets in motion a constitutional dynamic that, far from procedurally reopening the relationship between the subject and the constitutional structure, hypostatizes and blocks it.[4]

A second hypothesis aimed at posing an adequate relationship between subject and structure (in the dynamic sense) sees the subject as the people.[5] The concept of "people," however, is no less generic than that of "nation." This definition also soon falls prey to the juridical mechanism of qualification. The generic essence of the concept is reread in a constitutional key: if the "people" is the subject of constituent power, it can be so only insofar as it first undergoes an organizational process capable of expressing its essence. Indeed, to imagine and above all to assume as scientific subject "an ordering force that can be ordered by a multitude without order" would represent a contradiction in terms.[6] This conception does go beyond the limitations and the naturalistic and organicist mystifications of the idea of constituent power as an attribute of the nation. The theoretical desire to clear away the ambiguity of the nation is clear. Equally clear, however, is the will to break the expansive force of the concept of constituent power.[7] The fact that any definition of the constituent subject in terms of the people boils down to a normativist conception and a celebration of the constituted law is not an accident but a necessity.[8] This normative conception confuses constituent power with one of the internal sources of law and with the dynamics of its revision, its constitutional self-renovation. Briefly stated, constituent power is the people only in the context of representation.

A third hypothesis: constituent power as subject is already materially defined by juridical mechanisms inherent in its composition, and constituent power is itself a multiplicity of juridical powers set in a singular relationship—such that elements of juridical mediation are always necessarily presupposed.[9] From this point of view, which is eclectic but still effective, the possibility that constituent power is represented as absolute procedure is taken away or transfigured from the beginning. The point here is not to insist on the singularity of the historical definition of every emergence of constituent power, but to pose this determination as an unsurpassable limit, as materially determined self-limitation. Juridical theory has become clever. It does not deny constituent strength but affirms its singularity. It does not, however, consider constituent power a process and a precarious ontological insistence but, rather, a limit. Limitation is posed à la Hegel as determination.[10] Mediation and compromise are assumed within constituent power as the subject that founds the material constitution—not outside but within it: this is the effectiveness of mystification. This is in fact a matter of mystification because the problem of constituent power cannot be solved by making singularity the limit of its absolute character—a temporal, spatial, and procedural limit. The fact that the absolute character of constituent power lies in its singularity is perfectly evident, but this, and not something else, is the problem.

At this point we could examine other theories that try to connect constituent power to absolute procedure in order to domesticate the former, but they would really tell us nothing new. It is more interesting to notice that the negation in absolute terms of the adequate relationship between subject and procedure is the figure of a metaphysical negation—that is, a negation of the fact that multiplicity can be represented as a collective singularity, that the multitude can become a unitary and ordering force, that this relationship (open and impossible to bring to a conclusion) between subject and procedure can be real and effectively constitute a real temporality. On the contrary, any formation of power must be constituted outside this human context—by the divinity or some other ideal overdetermination, in transcendence or transcendentality. The negation of an adequate relationship between subject and structure is thus always embedded in an external and hypostatic figure for the justification of power. The radicalness of constituent power cannot be negated in reality, but here it is simply denied in principle.

It is not enough, however, to expose and denounce the metaphysical partiality of the positions that relativize constituent power in a transcendental manner in order to resolve our problem, the problem of its absolute character. Denunciation cannot take the place of a constructive argument. Thus we must pose once again the problem of the adequate relationship between subject and absolute procedure.

Michel Foucault is undoubtedly the one who has made the most substantial progress in defining a concept of power that, in its relationship to the subject, allows for constructive dimensions and absolute openings.

In Foucault, humanity appears as a set of resistances that release (outside any finalism that is not an expression of life itself and its reproduction) an absolute capacity for liberation. Life is liberated in humanity and opposes anything that encloses it and imprisons it.[11] What we need to stress here is that the relationship between subject and procedure is free. In other words, after demonstrating how power can subjugate humanity to the point of making it function as a cog of a totalitarian machine (we could accept this specific use of the term *totalitarianism*), Foucault shows instead how the constitutive process running through life, biopolitics and biopower, has an absolute (and not totalitarian) movement. This movement is absolute because it is absolutely free from determinations not internal to the action of liberation, to the vital assemblage [agencement].[12]

Starting from this viewpoint, which permits us to ground the question of the constituent subject, Foucault allows us to go still further. Indeed, he shows us that the subject is, first, strength, production. Certainly, the subject can be reduced to a pure phantom, a residue of the totality of the system of repression. But how productive it remains, even in this reductive horizon and imprisoned within these mechanisms! It is productive because on this limit the subject goes back into itself and rediscovers there the vital principle. Second, besides being strength, the subject is also action, a time of action and freedom, an assemblage—open because no teleology conditions or prefigures it. Foucault critically performs a process of disarticulation of the real and then, constructively, reopens a process that assumes the disarticulation as a positive condition. What was a path through necessity opens the way for a process of freedom.[13] This is essentially the same process we find in Spinoza.[14] Third, Foucault develops the paradigm of subjectivity as the place of the recomposition of resistance and public space.[15] Here we are confronted by a figure of the subject that formally and methodologically has characteristics adequate to absolute procedure. In effect this subject is strength, time, and constitution: it is the strength of producing constitutive trajectories; it is time that is in no way predetermined; and it is thus a singular constitution. When this critique has destroyed the prisons of constituted power, it identifies itself as ontological strength, constituent power capable of producing absolute events. The political is here production, production *par excellence*, collective and non-teleological. Innovation constitutes the political; constitution cannot but be constant innovation. What Arendt tried to articulate in terms of the inessentiality of liberal politics as alternative to a Heideggerian void of being Foucault constructs in the fullness of being, as an apparatus of positive freedom. The social, negated by Arendt as the suffocation of the political, reveals itself as the space of biopolitics—of that human radicalness of the political that constituent power reveals in its absoluteness.[16]

Absoluteness is under no circumstance totalitarianism. The latter is not a necessary corollary of the former, but this accusation springs up whenever the sacred principles of liberalism are not glorified and thus demands our attention.[17] If our "adequate subject" is in no way tied to liberal principles, or, rather, if in some ways it contradicts them, it need not for this reason be totalitarian. The equation "refusal of liberal principles equals totalitarianism" is reductive and mystifying. It is founded on a tradition of modern thought that presumes to found human rights on contractualism. Contractualism, however, cannot be the ground for human rights, cannot give them that material and immanent basis, that worldly absoluteness that is the only guarantee of the rights themselves. The perspective of constituent power puts the contractualist position under attack and recognizes in it the inevitable deferral to transcendence, to constituted power and its apology. This is indeed the outcome of contractualism, the logical demand that it claims it cannot resist, whether expressed by Hobbes as a God that transforms the association of individuals into sovereignty and the *contractum unionis* into *contractum subjectionis*, or by Rousseau as the "will of all" that is sublimated in a "general will," or by idealist transcendentalism as the process of the economic and the ethical that leads the contingent and the singular to the totality of the spirit and its State configurations.[18]

On the other hand, another tradition of modern metaphysics, from Machiavelli and Spinoza to Marx, sees the development of the dynamic of constituent power as absolute, but here that absoluteness never becomes totalitarian. In Machiavelli and Spinoza strength is expressed and nourished by discord and struggle; in both authors the process extends between singularity and multitude, and the construction of the political is the product of permanent innovation. What in Machiavelli is involved in the analysis of popular movements and the conflictuality of republics, in Spinoza develops in a high metaphysics. And it is precisely when we compare it to Spinoza's metaphysical absolute that the claim of pushing constituent power, its procedure, and its subject toward totalitarianism (even as a hypothesis) becomes ridiculous. There does indeed exist a totalitarianism in which the enigma of constituent power is not revealed, where its powerful effectiveness is denied or mystified in constituted power, and where the radicalness of its metaphysical strength and collective desire [*cupiditas*] is refused. In the lack of desire, the political becomes disciplinary totality, totalitarianism. Neither in Machiavelli nor in Spinoza, however, does the revolutionary process that embodies and establishes the constitution present itself as closure; rather, it is always open, both temporally and spatially. It flows as potently as freedom. It is at the same time resistance to oppression and construction of community; it is political discussion and tolerance; it is popular armament and the affirmation of principles through democratic invention. The constituent absolute and the democratic absolute have nothing to do with the totalitarian conception of life and politics. This absolute that builds the social and the political together has nothing to do with totalitarianism. Once again, then, political philosophy finds its dignity and its primary distinctions in metaphysics—on the one hand, the idealist metaphysics that, from Hobbes to Hegel, produces a transcendental concept of sovereignty; on the other, the historical materialism that develops a radical concept of democracy from Machiavelli to Spinoza to Marx. In this framework it is evident that the opposite of democracy is not totalitarianism but the concept of sovereignty itself, and it is now clear that the concept of democracy is not a subspecies of liberalism or subcategory of constitutionalism but a "form of governability"[19] that tends to destroy constituted power, a process of transition that frees constituent power, a process of rationalization that provides "the solution to the *riddle* of every constitution."[20]

We thus reach a turning point where we can verify what we have been arguing until now—that is, where we can verify our claim of having identified, at least formally, an image of the subject that allows us to sustain adequately the concept of constitution as absolute procedure. It seems to me that this formal figure must now be confronted with reality, with the history of subjects and constitutions, with life and politics. This is an open subject, projected into a totality without closure. To begin, let's again consider a characteristic, between the formal and the material, already attributed to our subject: that of temporality. Our subject is, and cannot but be, a temporal subject, a temporal constitutive strength. That said, once again two paths open in front of us. On the one hand, temporality is brought back to and confused in being, emptied of the elements that constitute it and therefore reduced to mysticism—in short, necessarily rooted in a firm principle that is the relation of being with itself.[21] On the other hand, temporality can be grounded in human productive capacity, in the ontology of its becoming—an open, absolutely constitutive temporality that does not disclose Being but instead produces beings.

A rereading of Marx's thought in this context can allow us to make progress in the definition of a materially adequate relationship between the constituent subject and absolute procedure. Marx's metaphysics of time is much more radical than Heidegger's.[22] Time is for both a matter of beings. Social time is the apparatus through which the world is quantified and qualified. But here we are once again, always at the same point: Marx frees what Heidegger imprisons. Marx illuminates with praxis what Heidegger reduces to mysticism. Heideggerian time is the form of being, the indistinctness of an absolute foundation. Marxian time is the production of being and thus the form of an absolute procedure. Marxian temporality represents the means by which a subject formally predisposed to being adequate to an absolute procedure becomes a subject materially capable of becoming part of this process, of being defined as constituent power.[23] Clearly, it is not only by comparison with the Heideggerian conception of time that this characteristic of Marxian temporality becomes clear, and from now on we will go along Marx's independent path. It is useful, however, to keep in mind this clash of perspectives because some crucial showdowns over it take place in contemporary philosophy: between Benjamin and Arendt, between Sartre and Foucault and Deleuze. Through the same clash, one might say, the whole political-constitutional debate of our times takes place as well.

Let's thus focus on Marx, on the crucial point where the critique of power and the critique of labor intersect, because this is what we are talking about, and it is on this crux that the contradictions of the history of constituent power develop. The definition of constituent power, when we move from the concept to the real, is decided on this problem. Naturally, Marx's path is a long one. From the critique of ideology to the critique of power to the critique of labor, an extraordinary accumulation of theoretical initiatives unravels.

We begin with *The Holy Family* and "On the Jewish Question" of 1844. Marx's demystification of the concept of equality here leads to a critique of labor, or, better, the proclamation of human rights leads to the discovery of the universality of exploitation and private appropriation, to the denunciation of individualism and the exaltation of the community of workers.[24] Political emancipation is nothing but the attempt to displace the meaning of the impulse to revolt, the juridical hypostasis of the social status quo. Human rights and all the constituent propositions of the bourgeoisie represent neither productive forces nor Utopia. They are nothing but mystifications and celebrations of the status quo. So-called political emancipation celebrates the force of the constituted while pretending to exalt the constituent.[25]

In *The German Ideology* of 1845–46 constituent power is defined twice. In its bourgeois formulation it is immediately class consciousness, a universal that through its affirmation adjusts the State constitution to the demands of bourgeois rule and the productive necessities of the division of labor. Constituent power is also expressed as communism: "Communism is for us not a *state of affairs* that is to be established, an *ideal* to which reality [will] have to adjust itself. We call communism the *real* movement that abolishes the present state of things. The conditions of this movement result from the premises now in existence."[26] This defining process results in a further development: "Thus things have now come to such a pass that the individuals must appropriate the existing totality of productive forces, not only to achieve self-activity, but, also, merely to safeguard their very existence. This appropriation is first determined by the object to be appropriated, the productive forces, which have been developed to a totality and which only exist within a universal intercourse"; and "the appropriation of these forces is itself nothing more than the development of the individual capacities corresponding to the material instruments of production. The appropriation of a totality of instruments of production is, for this very reason, the development of a totality of capacities in the individuals." Further: "Only the proletarians of the present day, who are completely shut off from all self-activity, are in a position to achieve a complete and no longer restricted self-activity, which consists in the appropriation of a totality of productive forces and in the thus postulated development of a totality of capacities." Finally, "All earlier revolutionary appropriations were restricted. In all expropriations up to now, a mass of individuals remained subservient to a single instrument of production; in the appropriation by the proletarians, a mass of instruments of production must be made subject to each individual, and property to all. Modern universal intercourse can be controlled by individuals, therefore, only when controlled by all."[27]

The idealist residues that so heavily resound in these pages have to be dispelled, and they are defused in Marx's later historical writings. In his writings of 1851–52 on revolution and counterrevolution in Germany the opposition between "universal class" and "real movement" is brought back to the model of constituent power—an open constituent power that takes the form of a permanent revolution, in other words, a process in which the subject's independence is affirmed at the moment when it continually rolls back the enemy's oppression and simultaneously expresses, accumulates, and organizes its own power.[28] Here, therefore, constitutive temporality is foregrounded and defined as the continuity of the process and a dimension of ontological accumulation.

In Marx's writings on the Paris Commune of 1871, constituent power emerges finally as a perfect synthesis of a historical subject, the Parisian proletariat in arms, and an absolute process. The proletarian Commune itself is "essentially a working class government, the product of the struggle of the producing against the appropriating class, the political form at last discovered under which to work out the economical emancipation of labor." Further: "The working class did not expect miracles from the Commune. They have no ready-made Utopias to introduce *par decret du peuple*. . . . They have no ideals to realize, but to set free the elements of the new society with which old collapsing bourgeois society itself is pregnant." Finally: "The great social measure of the Commune was its own working existence. Its special measures could but betoken the tendency of a government of the people by the people."[29] This is where the concept of constituent power reaches its highest poignancy in Marx, when the project of the abolition of the State is not subordinated to anarchist spontaneity but focused on the nexus (dynamic and expansive, and yet precise) between political movement and political power.[30] If there were in English the terminological distinction that many languages mark between two kinds of power—*potestas* and *potentia* in Latin, *pouvoir* and *puissance* in French, *potere* and *potenza* in Italian, *Macht* and *Vermögen* in German (which we have been marking as *power* and *strength* in this translation)—it would reside in this distinction between political movement and political power. Indeed, Marx translates strength [*potenza*] as "political movement," that constituent force of a radical democracy in which the critique of power is combined with the emancipation of labor, the "real movement."

But this is not enough. As long as we follow the political Marx, political revolution and social emancipation are two historical matrices that intersect on the same terrain—the constitutional terrain—but still in an external manner, without a metaphysical logic of this intersection being given. There must be something deeper and more urgent that demonstrates that this encounter is in no way accidental and makes necessary the materialist rule according to which political liberation and economic emancipation are one and the same thing. This necessity resides at the core of Marx's theory of capital, where living labor appears as the foundation and the motor of all production, development, and innovation. This essential source also animates the center of our investigation. Living labor against dead labor, constituent power against constituted power: this single polarity runs through the whole schema of Marxist analysis and resolves it in an entirely original theoretical-practical totality.[31] The basis of Marxian discourse in the passage from the critique of power to the critique of labor and vice versa therefore consists in the deployment of the concept of living labor as an instrument that, while destroying the equivocal quality of the bourgeois theory of labor (consolidated, accumulated, dead labor set against the creativity of living labor), shows the bourgeois theory of power itself to be an overdetermination of living labor by dead labor.

Living labor, instead, embodies constituent power and offers it general social conditions through which it can be expressed: constituent power is established politically on that social cooperation that is congenital in living labor, thus interpreting its productivity or, better, its creativity. In the immediacy, the creative spontaneity of living labor, constituent power finds its own capacity for innovation; in the cooperative immediacy of living labor, constituent power finds its creative massification.[32] One must look carefully at this nucleus of living labor, this creative tension that is at the same time political and economic, productive of civil, social, and political structures—in a word, constituent. Cooperative living labor produces a social ontology that is constitutive and innovative, a weaving of forms that touch the economic and the political; living labor produces an indistinct mixture of the political and economic that has a creative figure.[33]

More than a century has passed since Marx elaborated this theory of constituent power, identifying the proletariat as its historical carrier. Doubtless, this theory has had wide effect, even though, like other theories, it has by now reached its historical limit.[34] What remains of it is not so much the effort to identify the proletariat as the agent of a permanent revolution and thus the adequate subject of an absolute constitutional procedure, as much as the terrific metaphysical effort to propose constituent power as the general genealogical apparatus of the sociopolitical determinations that form the horizon of human history. This problematic is more contemporary than ever; and in the conclusion of this book we will certainly have to take into account the answer to the Marxian question about what the nexus between constituent power and that word *communism* might be—the nexus on which Marx synthesized the entire historical process. In any case, here we must keep in mind for the next stage of our inquiry some relations that Marx, above all, in concluding the materialist tradition of the definition of democracy as expression of strength, has helped to identify. In particular I am thinking of the relation that attaches the constitutive temporality of constituent power to an adequate subject and the one that poses the absoluteness of the nexus of subject and structure at the center of the creative process of the political.

One last reflection. Our argument will trace the conceptual formation of constituent power from a historical point of view, but it will not follow a continuous process: rather, it will move among various hypotheses. In each of the next five chapters we will analyze a particular figure of the formulation of the concept of constituent power and its singular destiny. In Machiavelli constituent power opens toward a strong dialectic between virtue and fortune—a dialectic that sets in play the revolutionary adventure of the Renaissance. In the English Revolution we will focus on Harrington's thought and his reading of the concept of constitution, but also the blockage of the constitution or, better, that "reversed" revolution that after 1688 fixed the constitutional conditions of the affirmation of the gentry and capitalist accumulation. The American Revolution and the clash of constituent positions among Adams, Jefferson, and the authors of *The Federalist* will illustrate how the ideology of freedom was made the constituent principle of a dynamic constitution of space, where democracy and imperialism confront each other.

The French Revolution poses for the first time the constituent principle as the principle of an absolute procedure, which is recognized in the movement of the popular classes against the bourgeois demand to restore the principle of sovereignty. In the Russian Revolution, finally, constituent power concretely measures itself with a Utopian conception of time and tries to embody an absolute procedure. The tragedy of the Russian Revolution, in its greatness and misery, relates directly to the core of our investigation. Therefore, we are not proposing a genealogy of the concept: concepts have no history except in the materiality of the history of humans and societies. Rather, we will try to define through the alternatives of constituent power the differentiated set of its possibilities: not a set of different expressions united by the custom of linguistic usage, but an expressive potential (of desires, wills, constructive experiences) accumulated inside our fundamental being from past experiences.

We are not interested in the archaeology of constituent power; we are interested in a hermeneutics that, beyond words and through them, can grasp the life, the alternatives, the crisis and the recomposition, the construction and the creation of a faculty of humankind: a faculty to construct a political arrangement. Therefore, what does the virtue [virtus] of Machiavelli's people in arms and the discovery of the material determinations of the relations of power in Harrington have in common? And how does the American renovation of classical constitutionalism overlap with the French ideology of social emancipation? How does the egalitarian impulse of communism dramatically coexist with the enterprising spirit of the Bolsheviks? It is clear that each of these enterprises will discover its meaning within the set of events that shapes them individually. But it is also true that the meaning of these events is inscribed in the consciousness of us all and etched in our being because it has somehow determined it. These events have for us a meaning worth investigating because they have constructed new horizons of reason and have proposed new dimensions of historical being. The journey we propose will be neither concluded by ideological syntheses nor contented with tracing the evolution of the concept; instead, it will try to lead us to the analysis of the strength of contemporary humanity. To understand our desire through the thousand stratifications that underlie it is the only path if we want to understand the concept.[35]

The concept of constituent power is the core of political ontology. Thus, it is evident that the conclusion of the journey that we are now beginning will involve confronting the contemporary crisis of constitutionalism and asking ourselves what subject today is adequate to sustain an absolute constitutional procedure capable of opposing the concept of sovereignty. At the same time we will attempt to determine where the living labor of strength resides, how it is represented, how it operates today.

Notes

1 Herbert Sauerwein, "Die Omnipotenz des 'pouvoir constituant,'" in Ein Beitrag zur Staats- und Verfassungstheorie (Frankfurt, 1960), chapter 5. The limitations of this author's discourse lie in his referring the thematic of subjectivity to the currents of neonatural law in the 1950s.

2 On the continuity of the "national" tradition as foundation of constituent power, see also Erich Tosch, *Die Bindung des verfassungsändernden Gesetzgebers an den Willen des historischen Verfassungsgebers* (Berlin: Duncker & Humblot, 1979). In general, on Sieyès and the tradition connected to him, see chapter 5 of *Insurgencies*.

3 Etienne Balibar and Immanuel Wallerstein, *Race, Nation, Class: Ambiguous Identities*, trans. Chris Turner (London and New York: Verso, 1991).

4 Hans Kohn, *The Idea of Nationalism: A Study in Its Origins and Background* (New York: Macmillan, 1967); Hannah Arendt, *The Origins of Totalitarianism* (New York: Harcourt Brace, 1951).

5 It is Carl Schmitt in *Verfassungslehre* who, outside of the ambiguous Anglo-Saxon constitutionalist tradition, offers the most accomplished conceptual

construction of "the people" as constitutional foundation. But see also Dietrich Schindler, *Verfassungsrecht und soziale Struktur* (Zurich: Schulthess, 1950).

6   Luigi Taparelli d'Azeglio, *Saggio teoretico di dritto naturale appoggiato sulfatto* (Rome: 1949), 2: 28.

7   See Santi Romano, "Mitologia giuridica," in *Frammenti di un dizionario giuridico* (Milan: Giuffrè, 1953), 131ff., 126ff.; Giovanni Sartori, (New York: Praeger, 1965).

8   See the first section of this chapter.

9   Romano, *Frammenti*, 223 ff.; Costantino Mortati, *La costituzione in senso materiale*. Ernst Forsthorf, "Zur heutigen Situation einer Verfassungslehre," in *Festgabe fur Carl Schmitt* (Berlin: Duncker & Humblot, 1968), 1:185 ff.

10 Michael Theunissen, *Hegels Lehre vom absoluten Geist als theologisch-politischer Traktat* (Berlin: de Gruyter, 1970); *Sein und Schein: Die kritische Funktion der Hegelschen Logik* (Frankfurt: Suhrkamp, 1980).

11 The reference is obviously to the "second" Foucault, the author of *History of Sexuality*, vol. I, of *The Uses of Pleasure*, of *The Care of the Self*, trans. Robert Hurley (New York: Random House, 1978–1986). On the "first" Foucault, see my "Sul metodo della critica della politica," in *Macchina Tempo*, 70–84.

12 Gilles Deleuze, *Foucault*, trans. and ed. Sean Hand (Minneapolis: University of Minnesota Press, 1988).

13 Foucault developed these positions in the lectures he gave in the 1970s.

14 Gilles Deleuze, *Expressionism in Philosophy: Spinoza*, trans. Martin Joughin (New York: Zone, 1990).

15 From this perspective Foucault's position is opposed, on metaphysical and sociological terrain, to Habermas's theory of the "public sphere." In my view, however, Foucault interprets the lessons of the Frankfurt School more faithfully than do its direct descendants.

16 On the impossibility of considering the social in purely political terms, and thus of redirecting it toward "totalitarianism" (as Arendt does), as well as on the abstract emptiness and purely polemical use (in the worst ideological sense) of the concept of "totalitarianism," see Karl Polyani, *The Great Transformation: The Political and Economic Origins of Our Time* (Boston: Beacon Press, 1957). See also Richard Bernstein, *The Restructuring of Social and Political Theory* (Oxford: Oxford University Press, 1976).

17 Arendt's *The Origins of Totalitarianism* (New York: Harcourt Brace, 1966), in which she explores the theme of totalitarianism in its full range, is certainly her worst book. The categories of the so-called Cold War are deeply imbricated in her argument at all turns. The great social movements that brought about the destruction of the system of "real socialism" have demonstrated how false and heuristically dangerous these categories were.

18 On the tradition of contractualism as the ground for the definition of the transcendence of power, see my book *The Savage Anomaly*.

19 Foucault introduced the analysis of the concept of democracy onto the terrain of the "forms of governability" or "government."

20 Karl Marx, *Critique of Hegel's Doctrine of the State*, in Marx, *Early Writings*, trans. Rodney Livingstone (Harmondsworth: Penguin, 1975), 87.

21 Heidegger maintains this position in the 1927 Marburg seminar and also in section 3 of Part I of *Being and Time*, which he never saw published and which has appeared in print only recently.

22 On Marx's theorization of time, we should keep in mind in addition to the famous passages from the *Grundrisse*, about which see my book *Marx beyond Marx: Lessons on the Grundrisse*, trans. Harry Cleaver, Michael Ryan, and Maurizio Viano, ed. Ian Fleming (South Hadley: Burgin & Savey, 1984); *The Poverty of Philosophy* (New York: International Publishers, n.d.); and *Letter to Annenkov*, English translation in Karl Marx and Friedrich Engels, *Selected Correspondence* (Moscow: Progress Publishers, 1975), 29–39. We will return to this topic later in the course of this book. On the prehistory of the category of time in Marx, see Eric Alliez, *Capital Times: Tales from the Conquest of Time*, trans. Georges Van Den Abbeele (Minneapolis: University of Minnesota Press, 1996).

23 See Jean-Marie Vincent, *Abstract Labor: A Critique*, trans. Jim Cohen (New York: St. Martin's Press, 1991).

24 Karl Marx, *The Holy Family*, trans. R. Dixon (Moscow: Foreign Languages Publishing House, 1956), chapter 4.

25 Karl Marx, "On The Jewish Question," in *Early Writings* (New York: Penguin, 1975), 211–41. As we will see later, in the polemic that divides them concerning the problem of the "two revolutions," Jürgen Habermas rightly reproaches Arendt for treating the Marxian theme of the emancipation of the political in purely formal terms, or, better, for having exalted as positive what Marx criticized from the point of view of social liberation. If she maintained this style of argumentation but changed its sense and referents, Arendt would produce, according to Habermas, a classical sophism.

26 Karl Marx, *The German Ideology*, pt I, ed. C. J. Arthur (New York: International Publishers, 1991), A4: 56–57.

27 Ibid., D2: 92–93.

28 Karl Marx, *Revolution and Counter-Revolution*, ed. Eleanor Aveling Marx (London: Unwin, 1971), chap, 18.

29 Karl Alarx, *The Civil War in France, in The First International and After*, ed. David Sternbach (New York: Penguin, 1974), 213, 217.

30 Karl Marx, *Letter to Bolte*, in Marx and Engels, *Selected Correspondence*, 253–55.

31 Once again allow me to refer the reader to my *Marx beyond Marx*. For the passages from Marx quoted up to this point, see chapters 5 and 6 of *Insurgencies*, where they are discussed in detail.

32 E. P. Thompson, *The Making of English Working Class* (London: Gollancz, 1968).

33 On this question, permit me to refer the reader once again to my *Fabbriche del soggetto* (Livorno: XXI Secolo, 1987).

34 Antonio Negri, *The Politics of Subversion* (Cambridge: Polity Press, 1989), part 1.

35 Gilles Deleuze and Felix Guattari, *A Thousand Plateaus: Capitalism and Schizophrenia*, trans. Brian Alassumi (Minneapolis: University of Minnesota Press, 1987).

CHAPTER TWENTY NINE

Radical Politics Today

Chantal Mouffe

From Agonistics. London: Verso, 2013: 65–85.

The years in which the hegemony of neo-liberalism was unchallenged have fortunately come to a close. With the multiplication of protest movements, we are witnessing a renewed interest in a type of radical politics that might be able to bring about an alternative to the current neo-liberal globalization. There is, however, no agreement on the modalities and the objectives of such a politics. What kind of strategy should be implemented? How should such a movement deal with existing institutions?

   In this chapter I will discuss two different proposals: the first, which is very influential among social movements, promotes a strategy of "withdrawal from institutions"; the second, which is the one that I advocate, calls for an "engagement with institutions." To start, I will examine the main divergences between these two proposals regarding political strategy, and then I will scrutinize their respective philosophical frameworks. This will allow me to show how the political disagreements between those two conceptions stem from their different ontologies.

Critique as withdrawal from

The model of radical politics put forward by Michael Hardt and Antonio Negri in *Empire*, *Multitude* and *Commonwealth* calls for a break with modernity and the elaboration of a different approach that they first termed "post-modern," but which they now prefer to designate as "altermodern."[1] In their view, such a break is required because of the crucial transformations undergone by our societies since the last decades of the twentieth century. These transformations, which they present as the consequences of globalization and of the transition from fordism to post-fordism—a change in the work process brought about by workers' struggles—can be briefly summarized in the following points:

1   Sovereignty has taken a new form, composed of a series of national and supranational organisms united under a single logic of rule. This new global form of sovereignty, which they call "Empire," has replaced the Imperial Age that was based on the attempt by nation-states to extend their sovereignty beyond their borders. In contrast to what happened in the stage of imperialism, the current Empire has no territorial center of power and no fixed boundaries; it is a decentered and deterritorialized apparatus of rule that progressively incorporates the entire global realm with open, expanding frontiers.

2   These transformations are linked to the transformation of the capitalist mode of production in which the role of industrial factory labor has been reduced and replaced by communicative, cooperative and affective labor. In the post-modernization of the global economy, the creation of wealth tends toward biopolitical production. The object of the rule of Empire, therefore, is social life in its entirety, the paradigmatic form of biopower.

3   We are witnessing the passage from a "disciplinary society" to a "society of control" characterized by a new paradigm of power. In the disciplinary society, which corresponds to the first phase of capitalist accumulation, command is constructed through a diffuse network of dispositifs or apparatuses that produce and regulate customs, habits and productive practices with the help of disciplinary institutions like prisons, factories, asylums, hospitals, schools and others.

    The society of control, in contrast, is one in which mechanisms of command become immanent within the social field. The modes of social integration and exclusion are increasingly interiorized through mechanisms that directly organize the brains and bodies of the citizens. This new paradigm of power is "biopolitical" in nature. What is directly at stake in power is the production and reproduction of life itself.

4   Hardt and Negri assert that the notions of "mass intellectuality," "immaterial labor" and "general intellect" help us to grasp the relation between social production and biopower. The central role previously occupied by the labor-power of mass factory workers

in the production of surplus-value is today increasingly filled by intellectual, immaterial and communicative labor-power. The figure of immaterial labor involved in communication, cooperation and the reproduction of affects occupies an increasingly central position in the schema of capitalist production.

5   In the passage to post-modernity and biopolitical production, labor-power has become increasingly collective and social. A new term is needed to refer to this collective worker. It is the "Multitude." The construction of Empire is seen as a response to the various machines of power and the struggles of the Multitude. Multitude, they say, called Empire into being, and globalization, in so far as it operates a real deterritorialization of the previous structures of exploitation and control, is a condition of the liberation of the Multitude.

Incorporating, although not always in a faithful way, the analyses of Foucault and Deleuze, Hardt and Negri claim that the end of the disciplinary regime that was exercised over bodies in enclosed spaces, like schools, factories and asylums, and its replacement by the procedures of control linked to the growth of networks is leading to a new type of governance. This style of rule permits more autonomous and independent forms of subjectivity. With the expansion of new forms of cooperative communication and the invention of new communicative forms of life, those subjectivities can express themselves freely. They will contribute to the formation of a new set of social relations that will finally replace the capitalist system.

Indeed, Hardt and Negri are adamant that the passage to Empire opens new possibilities for the liberation of the Multitude. The creative forces of the Multitude that sustain Empire are capable of constructing a counter-empire, an alternative political organization of the global flows of exchange and globalization, so as to reorganize them and direct them toward new ends.

As outlined in his book *Grammar of the Multitude*, the analyses of Paolo Virno, another post-operaist thinker, dovetail in many respects with those of Hardt and Negri.[2] But there are also some significant differences. For instance, Virno is much less sanguine about the future. While Hardt and Negri have a messianic vision of the role of the Multitude, which will necessarily bring down Empire and establish an "Absolute Democracy," Virno sees current developments as an ambivalent phenomenon, acknowledging the new forms of subjection and precarization that are typical of the post-fordist stage.

It is true that people are not as passive as before, but it is because they have now become active actors of their own precarization. So instead of seeing the generalization of immaterial labor as a type of "spontaneous communism" like Hardt and Negri, Virno tends to see post-fordism as a manifestation of the "communism of capital." He notes that, today, capitalistic initiatives orchestrate for their own benefits precisely those material and cultural conditions that could, in other conditions, have opened the way for a potential communist future.

When it comes to envisaging how the Multitude could liberate itself, Virno declares that the post-fordist era requires the creation of a "Republic of the Multitude," by which he understands a sphere of common affairs that is no longer state-run. He proposes two key terms to grasp the type of political action characteristic of the Multitude: "exodus" and "civil disobedience." "Exodus" is a fully-fledged model of political action capable of confronting the challenges of modern politics. It consists in a mass defection from the state aiming at developing the "publicness of Intellect" outside of work and in opposition to it. This requires the development of a non-state public sphere and a radically new type of democracy framed in terms of the construction and experimentation of forms of non-representative and extra-parliamentary democracy organized around leagues, councils and soviets.

The democracy of the Multitude expresses itself in an ensemble of acting minorities that never aspire to transform themselves into a majority and develop a power that refuses to become government. It is "acting in concert," and while tending to dismantle the supreme power, it is not inclined to become state in its turn. This is why civil disobedience needs to be emancipated from the liberal tradition within which it is generally located. In the case of the Multitude, "civil disobedience" does not mean ignoring a specific law because it does not conform to the principles of the constitution. This would still be a way of expressing loyalty to the State. What should be at stake is a radical disobedience that puts into question the State's very faculty of command.

Regarding the type of political action better suited to the liberation of the Multitude, there is no fundamental difference between Virno and Hardt and Negri, who also advocate desertion and exodus. Whereas in the disciplinary era sabotage was the fundamental form of resistance, in the era of imperial control they claim that it is desertion. It is indeed through desertion, through the evacuation of the places of power, that they think that battles against Empire might be won. Desertion and exodus are for them a powerful form of class struggle against imperial post-modernity.

Another important point of agreement among Hardt, Negri and Virno concerns their conception of the democracy of the Multitude. To be sure, Virno never uses the term "absolute democracy," but in both cases we find a rejection of the model of representative democracy and the drawing of a stark opposition between the Multitude and the People. The problem with the notion of the People, they claim, is that it is represented as a unity, with one will, and that it is linked to the existence of the State. The Multitude, on the contrary, shuns political unity. It is not representable because it is a singular multiplicity. It is an active self-organizing agent that can never achieve the status of a juridical personage and can never converge in a general will. It is anti-state and anti-popular. Virno, like Hardt and Negri, claims that the democracy of the Multitude cannot be conceived anymore in terms of a sovereign authority that is representative of the People, and that new forms of democracy which are non-representative are needed.

Radical politics is envisaged, according to this approach, in terms of a "withdrawal" from existing institutions so as to foster the self-organization of the Multitude. Such a strategy is justified by the claim that, under the new post-fordist forms of production characterized by the centrality of immaterial labor, capitalists are no longer necessary for the organization of production. They have become parasites who simply appropriate the value produced by the general intellect, without playing any positive role. In a theme reminiscent of Marx's assertion that capitalism is its own grave-digger, they see the development of "cognitive capitalism" as creating the conditions for the dismissal of those parasitic capitalists. The Multitude should accelerate this process by disengaging itself from all the institutions through which capitalists desperately try to keep it enslaved.

Critique as hegemonic engagement with

In contrast to this strategy of "withdrawal," I want to offer a different conception of radical politics envisaged in terms of "engagement" with institutions, with the aim of bringing about a different hegemony. I agree with the previous writers on the need to take account of the crucial transformations in the mode of the regulation of capitalism brought about by the transition from fordism to post-fordism. In addition, it is necessary not to judge those transformations as the mere consequence of technological progress. In my view, however, this transition is better apprehended within the framework of the theory of hegemony. Many factors have contributed to this transition, and it is necessary to recognize their complex articulation.

The problem with the operaist and post-operaist viewpoints is that they tend to see the transition from fordism to post-fordism as driven by one single logic: workers' resistance to the process of exploitation, which forces the capitalists to reorganize the process of production and to move to post-fordism, where immaterial labor is central. For them, capitalism can only be reactive; they refuse to accept the creative role played by both capital and labor. What they deny is in fact the role played in this transition by the hegemonic struggle.

To envisage the transition from fordism to post-fordism in terms of an hegemonic struggle means abandoning the view that one single logic—workers' struggles—is at work in the evolution of the work process. It means acknowledging the pro-active role played by capital in this transition. In order to grasp this role, we can find interesting insights in the work of Luc Boltanski and Eve Chiapello. In their book *The New Spirit of Capitalism*, they bring to light the way in which capitalists managed to use the demands for autonomy made by the new movements that developed in the '60s, harnessing them in the development of the post-fordist networked economy and transforming them into new forms of control.[3] What they call "artistic critique" to refer to the aesthetic strategies of the counter-culture—the search for authenticity, the ideal of self-management, the anti-hierarchical exigency—was used to promote the conditions required by the new mode of capitalist regulation, replacing the disciplinary framework characteristic of the fordist period.

From my point of view, what is important in this approach is that it shows how a crucial aspect of the transition from fordism to post-fordism consisted in a process of discursive re-articulation of existing discourses and practices. This is why it allows us to visualize this transition in terms of an hegemonic intervention. To be sure, Boltanski and Chiapello never use this vocabulary, but their analysis is a clear example of what Gramsci called "hegemony through neutralization" or "passive revolution," a situation where demands which challenge the hegemonic order are appropriated by the existing system so as to satisfy them in a way that neutralizes their subversive potential.

When the transition from fordism to post-fordism is apprehended within such a framework, we can understand it as an hegemonic move by capital to re-establish its leading role and restore its legitimacy, which had been seriously challenged in the late '60s and early '70s. This will in turn permit us to envisage how to challenge the new capitalist order by launching a counter-hegemonic offensive in a variety of fields where the nodal points securing the new post-fordist mode of regulation of capitalism have been established. This is a complex process that cannot merely consist in separating the different elements whose discursive articulation constitutes the structure of the current hegemony. The second moment, the moment of re-articulation, is crucial. Otherwise, we will be faced with a chaotic situation of pure dissemination, leaving the door open for attempts at re-articulation by non-progressive forces. Indeed, we have many historic examples of situations in which the crisis of the dominant order led to right-wing solutions. The critique and disarticulation of the existing hegemony cannot be conceived in terms of desertion because it should go hand in hand with a process of re-articulation.

This double moment, of dis-articulation and re-articulation, is not only missed by the exodus theorists. It is also missed by all the approaches that rely on the idea of reification or false consciousness, which believe that it is enough to lift the weight of ideology in order to bring about a new order free from oppression and power.

Another point of divergence between the two strategies comes from the importance that hegemonic politics attributes to the establishment of a "chain of equivalences" between the various democratic demands. It is clear that those demands do not necessarily converge and they can even be in conflict with each other. To transform them into claims that will challenge the existing structure of power relations, they need to be articulated politically.

What is at stake is the creation of a common will, a "we," and this requires the determination of a "they." This need for a "they" to secure the unity of the common will is neglected by the various advocates of the Multitude, who believe that the Multitude is endowed with a natural unity and that it does not need political articulation. According to Virno, for instance, the singularities that constitute the Multitude already have something in common: the general intellect. His critique of the notion of the People (shared by Hardt and Negri) as being homogeneous and expressed in a unitary general will which does not leave room for multiplicity is totally misplaced when directed at the construction of the People through a chain of equivalence. Indeed, in this case we are dealing with a form of unity that respects diversity and does not erase differences. A relation of equivalence does not eliminate difference—that would simply be identity. It is only to the extent that democratic differences are opposed to forces or discourses that negate all of them that these differences can be substituted for each other. This is why the construction of a collective will requires designating an adversary.

Such an adversary cannot be defined in broad general terms like "Empire," or for that matter "Capitalism," but in terms of nodal points of power that need to be targeted and transformed in order to create the conditions for a new hegemony. It is a "war of position" (Gramsci) that has to be launched in a multiplicity of sites, and this requires establishing a synergy between a plurality of actors: social movements, parties and trade unions. What is at stake is not any "withering away" of the state or of the variety of institutions through which pluralism is organized. Rather, through a combination of parliamentary and extra-parliamentary struggles we must bring about a profound transformation of those institutions, so as to make them a vehicle for the expression of the manifold of democratic demands which would extend the principle of equality to as many social relations as possible. This is how radical politics is envisaged by the hegemonic approach, and such a project requires an agonistic engagement with the institutions.

The important democratic advances made in recent years by progressive governments in South America testify to the possibility of making profound institutional transformations through representative forms of politics. In Venezuela, Bolivia, Ecuador, Argentina and Brazil, left-wing governments have been able to challenge neo-liberal forces and to implement a set of reforms which have significantly improved the condition of the popular sectors. This was made possible by the state's collaboration with a variety of social movements. These experiences prove that, contrary to what is claimed by the exodus theorists, the state and representative institutions, instead of being an obstacle to social change, can contribute to it in a crucial way.

The case of Argentina is particularly interesting for my argument. In the exodus literature, it is common to find a celebration of the *piqueteros*, the movement of impoverished, mainly unemployed workers who in the end of the 1990s began to organize road-blocking pickets to protest against the neo-liberal policies of President Carlos Menem. During the economic crisis of 2001–2002, they organized themselves in cooperatives and were very active in the popular protests that brought down the de la Rúa government in 2001.

With their motto "Que se vayan todos" (Away with them all) they proclaimed their rejection of all politicians and called for a self-organization of the popular sectors. Post-operaist theorists see in the *piqueteros* a paradigmatic example of the political expression of the Multitude and present their refusal to collaborate with political parties as a model for the strategy of desertion. But they do not seem to realize that what the movement of the *piqueteros* shows is precisely the limits of such a strategy. To be sure, they played a role in bringing down a president, but when the time came to offer an alternative, their refusal to participate in the elections rendered them unable to influence the further course of events. If it had not been for the fact that Nestor Kirchner won the elections and began to implement progressive measures to restore the Argentinian economy and improve the conditions of the poor, the outcome of the popular protests could have been completely different.

The democratic progress made in Argentina under Nestor Kirchner and Cristina Fernandez de Kirchner has been possible thanks to the synergy that was established between the government and a series of social movements (among them some *piquetero* groups that accepted Kirchner's offer to collaborate with him), with the aim of tackling the social and socio-economic challenges confronting the country. Far from providing a successful example of the strategy of desertion, what the Argentinian case reveals are the shortcomings of such a strategy. It brings to light the importance of combining parliamentary with extra-parliamentary struggles in a common fight to transform the configuration of power within the institutional framework.

It is for that reason that, despite having sympathy for recent forms of protest like the *Indignados* in Spain or the various forms of "Occupy," there is reason to be concerned about the type of anti-institutional strategy that they have adopted and that is inspired by the exodus model. To be sure, these movements are very diverse and not all of them are influenced by the exodus theorists, but many of them share these theorists' total rejection of representative democracy. Moreover, they also believe in the possibility for social movements, on their own, to bring about a new type of society where a "real" democracy could exist without the need for the state or other forms of political institutions. Without any institutional relays, they will not be able to bring about any significant changes in the structures of power. Their protests against the neo-liberal order risk being soon forgotten.

Immantism versus radical negativity

Having contrasted the political strategies of the "withdrawal from" and "engagement with" approaches, I would now like to scrutinize their respective philosophical postulates. My claim is that the kind of radical politics advocated by the exodus approach proceeds from a flawed understanding of politics, one that does not acknowledge "the political" with its ineradicable dimension of antagonism. The strategy of exodus advocated by Hardt and Negri is based on an ontology of immanence whose primary ontological terrain is one of multiplicity.

The problem with this immanentist ontology is its inability to give an account of radical negativity, i.e. antagonism. True, negation is present in the work of these theorists, and they even use the term "antagonism," but this negation is not envisaged as radical negativity. It is either conceived on the mode of dialectical contradiction or simply as a real opposition. In fact, the strategy of exodus is the reformulation in a different vocabulary of the idea of communism as it was found in Marx, and there are clearly analogies between the views of the post-operaists and traditional Marxist conceptions. Of course, in the case of the post-operaists, it is no longer the proletariat but the Multitude which is the privileged political subject. But in both cases, the State is seen as a monolithic apparatus of domination that cannot be transformed. It has to "wither away" in order to leave room for a reconciled society beyond law, power and sovereignty. Indeed, absolute democracy presupposes the possibility of a redemptive leap into a society beyond politics and sovereignty where the Multitude can immediately rule itself and act in concert without the need of law or the State—a society where antagonism has disappeared.

If our approach has been called "post-Marxist," it is precisely because we have challenged the type of ontology subjacent to such a conception. As I and Ernesto Laclau have shown in *Hegemony and Socialist Strategy*, to envisage negation on the mode of antagonism demands a different ontological approach.[4] It is not possible to make room for radical negativity without abandoning the immanentist idea of a homogeneous, saturated social space and acknowledging the role of heterogeneity. Indeed, as pointed out by Laclau, the two poles of antagonism do not belong to the same space of representation and they are essentially heterogeneous with respect to each other. It is out of this irreducible heterogeneity that they emerge.[5]

This is why politics always takes place in a field crisscrossed by antagonisms. To envisage it as "acting in concert" leads to erasing the ontological dimension of antagonism that I call "the political," which provides its quasi-transcendental condition of possibility. There will always be a struggle between conflicting hegemonic projects aiming at presenting their views of the common good as the "true" incarnation of the universal. No rational resolution of that conflict will ever be available. As far as political critique is concerned, it can never be merely oppositional or conceived as desertion because it always engages with a certain aspect of the existing hegemony in order to disarticulate/re-articulate its constitutive elements.

I would like to emphasize that the aim of a counter-hegemonic intervention is not to unveil "true reality" or "real interests," but to re-articulate a given situation in a new configuration. Envisaging the critical process in these terms shows that, contrary to what Bruno Latour has affirmed, critique has not run out of steam. Although conceding that critique might have done a good job in debunking prejudices and illusions, Latour claims that critique has finally revealed its limits because of its reliance on a sharp distinction between nature and culture and its assumption that there is a "true" world behind the veil of appearances. Nowadays, belief in the existence of such a world has been discredited, and it is time, he says, to find an alternative. He describes his project in the form of a question: "Is it really possible to transform the critical urge in the ethos of someone who *adds* reality to matters of fact and not *substracts* reality?"[6] It is such an alternative that Latour puts forward under the name of "compositionism." To overcome the bifurcation between nature, objectivity and reality on one side, and culture, subjectivity and appearances on the other, the solution he proposes is to "compose" the common world. Contrasting it with critique and its belief in a world beyond this world, he declares that "for compositionism, there is no world of beyond. It is all about *immanence*."[7] This means that, according to the compositionists, one should discard the opposition between what is constructed and what is not constructed. Instead, the question to ask is whether something is well constructed or badly constructed.

I agree with Latour that it is important to challenge the traditional modernist epistemology that postulates a radical divide between human subjects and non-human objects. Our discursive approach dovetails with his constructivism on several points. There are, of course, many differences stemming from the fact that our fields of enquiry are not of the same nature, but we could say that we broadly belong to the same epistemological camp that rejects the separation between culture and nature and the thesis of the existence of a world of facts independent of what he calls "matter of concerns."

However, when it comes to envisaging the question of the political, there are significant divergences. The best way to apprehend their nature is probably by pointing out that, instead of saying, like Latour, that the common world has to be "composed," Laclau and I assert that it has to be "articulated." This terminological difference is meant to highlight the fact that the process of composition always takes place in a terrain informed by power relations—or to put it in our vocabulary, that the common world is always the result of an "hegemonic" construction. As a consequence, it is not enough for us to ask if this world is badly or well constructed. It is also necessary to examine the power relations that are at play in composition. Latour writes that "what is to be composed, may, at any point, be *de*composed."[8] Indeed, this is what we refer to as the process of disarticulation/re-articulation that is constitutive of the counter-hegemonic struggle. But this process is eminently political and it does not take place in a neutral terrain in which the observers could impartially decide if things have been composed in a "good" or a "bad" way. Conflicting interests are at stake in the hegemonic articulation of the common, and this is why an element of critique is always involved in any attempt at disarticulation (*de*composition). Latour's move to eliminate the critical dimension because it is grounded in a deficient epistemology and his attempt to redirect the critical urge toward compositionism have, in my view, disempowering political effects because they preclude the possibility of revealing and challenging power relations.

I would like to suggest that when it comes to politics, the divergence between our discursive hegemonic approach and Latour's compositionism has its origin in our different ontologies. This has to do with the inability of the immanentist approach to acknowledge radical negativity and the ineradicability of antagonism. As with the exodus theorists, although in the context of very different political strategies, the problem with Latour's compositionism is that it relies on an ontology that is unable to give account of the division of the social. In the case of Hardt and Negri, this leads them to believe in the availability of an "absolute democracy" to be reached once the Multitude has overcome Empire. Latour is very far from this kind of messianism and his politics does not pretend to be radical, but his compositionism is similarly unable to acknowledge the hegemonic nature of every kind of social order.

In both cases, what also is foreclosed is the possibility of visualizing a "war of position" aiming at a profound transformation of existing power relations. Hardt and Negri's failure to grasp the hegemonic nature of socio-economic orders precludes their envisaging the possibility of transforming them through an internal process of re-articulation. For his part, Latour rightly wants to convert matters of fact into matters of concern, and he praises debate and contestation. But his political posture is close to the "agonism without antagonism" whose shortcomings I discussed in the first chapter; what is lacking here again is the antagonistic dimension of the political.

Communism or radical democracy

Given my insistence on the importance of acknowledging radical negativity and of relinquishing the idea of a society beyond division and power, it will not come as a surprise that I disagree with the attempt by a group of left intellectuals to revive the "Idea of communism."[9] They claim that the "communist hypothesis" is absolutely necessary for envisaging a politics of emancipation. They argue that the egalitarian ideal is so intrinsically linked to the horizon of communism that its future depends on bringing back such a model.

They are no doubt right in refusing the widely accepted view that the disastrous failure of the Soviet model forces us to reject the entirety of the emancipatory project. But I do believe that there are important lessons to be learned from the tragic experience of "really existing socialism," and this calls for a serious rethinking of some central tenets of the communist project.

It would indeed be too easy to simply declare that the Soviet model represents a flawed realization of an ideal that remains to be truly implemented. To be sure, many of the reasons for which the communist ideal went astray could be avoided and the current conditions might provide a more favorable terrain. But some of the problems that it encountered cannot be reduced to a simple question of application. They have to do with the way this ideal was conceptualized. To remain faithful to the ideals that inspired the different communist movements, it is necessary to scrutinize how they conceived their goal so as to understand why those ideals could have become so disastrously misled.

It is the very notion of "communism" that needs to be problematized because it strongly connotes the anti-political vision of a society where antagonisms have been eradicated and where law, the state and other regulatory institutions have become irrelevant. The main shortcoming of the Marxist approach lies in its inability to acknowledge the crucial role of what I call "the political." While traditional Marxism asserted that communism and the withering away of the state logically entailed each other, Laclau and I assert that the emancipatory project can no longer be conceived of as the elimination of power and the management of common affairs by social agents identified with the viewpoint of the social totality. There will always be antagonism, struggles and division of the social, and the need for institutions to deal with them will never disappear.

By locating socialism in the wider field of the democratic revolution, we indicated in *Hegemony and Socialist Strategy* that the political transformations that will eventually enable us to transcend capitalist society are founded on the plurality of social agents and their struggles. Thus the field of social conflict is extended rather than being concentrated in a "privileged agent" such as the working class.

It is for this reason that we reformulated the emancipatory project in terms of a radicalization of democracy. We emphasized that the extension and radicalization of democratic struggles will never have a final point of arrival in the achievement of a fully liberated society. This is why the myth of communism as a transparent and reconciled society—which clearly implies the end of politics—must be abandoned.

Notes

1 Michael Hardt and Antonio Negri, *Empire*, Cambridge, MA: Harvard University Press, 2000; Michael Hardt and Antonio Negri, *Multitude: War and Democracy in the Age of Empire*, New York: Penguin Press, 2004; Michael Hardt and Antonio Negri, *Commonwealth*, Cambridge, MA: Harvard University Press, 2009.
2 Paolo Virno, *A Grammar of the Multitude*, Los Angeles: Semiotext(e), 2004.
3 Luc Boltanski and Eve Chiapello, *The New Spirit of Capitalism*, London and New York: Verso, 2005.
4 Ernesto Laclau and Chantal Mouffe, *Hegemony and Socialist Strategy: Towards a Radical Democratic Politics*, Second Edition, London and New York: Verso, 2001.
5 See Ernesto Laclau, *On Populist Reason*, London and New York: Verso, 2005, chapter 5.
6 Bruno Latour, "Why Has Critique Run out of Steam? From Matters of Fact to Matters of Concern," *Critical Enquiry* 30, no. 2 (2004): 232.
7 Bruno Latour, "An attempt at a 'Compositionist Manifesto,'" *New Literary History* 41, no. 3 (2010): 475.
8 Ibid., 474.
9 Costas Douzinas and Slavoj Žižek, *The Idea of Communism*, London and New York: Verso, 2010.

CHAPTER THIRTY

On Political Will

Peter Hallward

From Politics and Culture, *forthcoming (2014).*

The best way to address questions about emancipatory political practice, I think, is to pose them in terms of political will. Right away, this foregrounds the basic difference between the involuntary and the voluntary dimensions of social life, and thus helps reduce or transform the one in favor of the other. In every situation where it applies, it helps clarify a version of what I take to be the most important question of political practice: how can a dominated and coerced group or class of people free themselves from this coercion and acquire the power they need to determine their own course of action, consciously, deliberately or "willingly," in the face of the specific obstacles and resistance this course will confront?

I

The guiding intuition of this project is that the homely and clichéd phrase, "the will of the people," remains the best way of approaching the question of democratic politics, and of making distinctions between genuine and deceptive forms of democracy. In direct opposition to oligarchy, genuine democracy means the rule of the people—the people as distinct from a privileged few or ruling elite, the people understood as the many, or as the great majority of the population. Democracy applies in situations where the will of the people (however this is formulated or expressed) can overpower the will or wills of those few who might seek to exploit, oppress, or deceive them.

These two vague terms, people and will, are both notoriously difficult to pin down. Despite their revolutionary history and implications, both have been yoked to reactionary and in some cases ultra-reactionary political projects. Taken on their own, both terms are now widely considered to be almost indefensible as political categories; the notion of will, in particular, has been the object of varied but relentless philosophical assault for much of the past century, going back at least to Heidegger's critique of Nietzsche, and recurring in the work of thinkers as varied as Althusser, Derrida, Agamben, Deleuze, and many others. I'd like to suggest, however, that the combination of these two terms, in the formulation of a will of the people, serves to frame if not answer most of the general questions that a theory of emancipatory politics needs to address.

Compared to other, more conventional ways of formulating the question of democracy (for instance in terms of state institutions, electoral mechanisms, market structures, "civil society," "liberal values," etc.), our cliché has a couple of advantages.

First of all, nobody quite knows what it means. Of all the basic concepts at issue in modern political theory and philosophy, the notion of a will of the people is perhaps the most indeterminate. Everyone is familiar with the words, and their combination, but as things stand today their meaning is quite literally up for grabs, and in the last couple of years in particular, it has been invoked in all kinds of ways, and in all kinds of situations.

On the one hand, diplomatic reference to "the will of the people" has long been one of the most formulaic turns of phrase in the modern political lexicon. In mainstream discussion of current affairs this usually amounts to nothing more than a token nod to "formal democratic" mechanisms for ensuring some sort of minimal choice in the selection of political representatives. So long as such selection is controlled in ways that restrict any challenge to the established order of things, apparent respect for the will of the people is an integral aspect of the status quo, and has been so for a long time. Even so conservative a constitution as the one described by the French writer Benjamin Constant in 1815 "recognizes the principle of the sovereignty of the people, that is, the supremacy of the general will over every particular will,"[1] and today there is perhaps no modern political principle more widely shared than the one that condemns as illegitimate any attempt to govern people against their will. It's in this sense that even so aristocratic an oligarch as Winston Churchill might defer to a representation of the people's will,[2] and it's in this sense that presidents of the United States like to remind the world they dominate that they "support the democratic aspirations of all people," including a few places "where the will of the people [has] proved more powerful than the writ of a dictator."[3] Even the president whom Cornel West memorably derided as "a black mascot of Wall Street oligarchs and a black puppet of corporate plutocrats"[4] does not hesitate to define "self-determination" as "the chance to make of your life what you will."[5]

On the other hand, the concentration and assertion of the people's will has been central to the whole modern trajectory of revolutionary practice. From the Jacobin constitution of 1793 France through the ANC's Freedom Charter of 1955 to the new Bolivian constitution of 2009 and the Arab revolutions of 2011, a long and versatile emancipatory tradition has affirmed the will of the people as the basis of political action and legitimacy. The ANC's Charter, for instance, before it denounces apartheid, racism and social inequality, opens with the assertion that "no government can justly claim authority unless it is based on the will of all the people," and insists as its first demand: "The People shall govern!" National liberation movements from Algeria to Zimbabwe took shape around a similar "will to independence."[6] The 2011 uprisings in Tunisia and Egypt, likewise, crystallized around a literal assertion of the people's will, expressed in the innumerable variations of the slogan that has already transformed the Middle East: "the people want to topple the regime."[7] Reference to emancipatory political will is also essential to the political theory and practice of a wide range of revolutionary thinkers, from Robespierre and Saint-Just through Lenin and Gramsci to Mao and Fanon. Insofar as what is at stake is the empowerment of people to determine their own destiny and their own political program, Tony Benn is right to insist that democracy remains the most revolutionary program of all, "the most revolutionary thing in the world."[8]

This uncertainty in the status of our phrase gives it a unique strategic purchase. Unlike concepts that are more directly associated with orthodox Marxist or Communist traditions, reference to the will of the people evokes a revolutionary practice that also retains a thoroughly "mainstream" significance.

A second and more important advantage stems from the peculiar and problematic conjunction of the two terms in question, "people" and "will." If we leave the partial exception of ancient Athens to one side, the connection of these two notions was scarcely thinkable before the world was "turned upside down" by the Levellers, Diggers and other egalitarian mobilizations during the English revolution of the 1640s, and among the privileged classes it has remained the primary source of political anxiety ever since. Although important initial contributions were made by early modern thinkers like Machiavelli and Hobbes, I think that it's only with Rousseau that the notion of a collective or "general" will began to receive adequate theoretical definition. It is only with Rousseau's Jacobin admirers, furthermore, during the French and Haitian revolutions, that such a notion came to orient political practice, and it is only after Marx that such practice gained the sort of historical determination required to give it far-reaching strategic purchase on a situation. If we can clarify what is meant by these elusive terms "people" and "will," and what their combination requires and implies, then we may also clarify what is required to move from merely formal to actual democracy.

My hypothesis is that their conjunction is enough all by itself to provide a normative basis for democratic practice, and thus for the political project of changing a world ruled by and for the few into a world ruled by and for the many. Precisely on account of their generic and transhistorical quality, these terms offer a useful basis for getting a grip on a wide range of situations. Compared with emancipatory perspectives that filter the category of the people through pre-existing categories of identity, occupation or history, or with conceptions of volition filtered through (or displaced by) notions of instinct, intellect, appetite, affect, or communication, the terms will and people are as wide-ranging and versatile as the notions of empowerment and liberation themselves.

It's equally important to stress, however, that they also prescribe a certain specificity. The category of "the people," as is well known, is always bound up with the tension between abstract inclusion (the people simply as everyone, or as the whole population, the "realm" or nation as a more or less harmonious totality) and concrete exclusion (whereby the category of the people excludes those "enemies" who exploit, oppress or dominate them); it is only through its articulation with concrete political practice that its orientation is decided, in one direction or the other. The practice of political will likewise mediates the norm of free self-determination and the necessity to engage with the constraints that inhibit popular participation in such determination, the obstacles or tendencies that might divide, isolate or deceive those who seek to formulate and impose their will.

Will and people: rejecting the merely formal i.e. oligarchic conceptions of democracy that disguise the established balance of class power, a genuinely or literally democratic politics can be described as the effort to think and practice one term through the other. A will of the *people* must of course involve association and collective action, and shall depend on a capacity to invent and preserve forms of inclusive assembly (e.g. through demonstrations, meetings, unions, parties, networks, websites, . . .). If an action is prescribed by popular *will*, on the other hand, then what's at stake is a free or voluntary course of action, decided on the basis of informed and reasoned deliberation. Since there's no agreement on the meaning of the term will (or even on its very existence), its usage calls for some further clarification.

By "will" I mean, first of all, the actual exercise of willing a particular purpose or end. For precisely this reason I will prefer the generic term *actor* over the term "subject," since it avoids or recasts some of the well-known ambiguities of latter (as both agent and substrate, active and passive, free and "subjected," etc.) in favor of a direct derivation from the verb *to act*, a verb whose own ambiguity is productive and illuminating. To will is a practical rather than theoretical matter, and as a matter of practice it involves direct participation, action and effort on the part of its subject or actor, undertaken as deliberate and purposeful (rather than conceived as an "authentic" expression of an essence or identity). There is an essential difference between active involvement in an act of willing, and its representation, measurement or interpretation by external observers.

There is likewise an essential difference between voluntary and involuntary kinds of action. Unlike an involuntary action or movement, for instance a movement determined by a reflex or instinct, or one that has become routine by force of repetition or habit, and unlike action that is coerced or compelled, a voluntary or willed action is more or less freely chosen, intended and sustained, on the basis of more or less well-informed rational deliberation. (As opposed to a metaphysical understanding of the will as endowed with a kind of absolute or quasi-divine freedom, the freedom at issue is indeed always a matter of "more of less," since freedom is also to be understood here as a practice, as a process of *freeing* or emancipating—a practice through which actors liberate themselves, more or less, from the various constraints they confront, and thereby acquire a degree of autonomy).

The kinds of purpose at issue in an act of will are also more or less distinct from those involved with mere impulses of whim or wish. Whereas much of the scholarly work done on the problem of free will might better be described as reflection on "free whim," the notion of political will that interests me, and that has its roots in Rousseau and in Machiavelli, instead associates will and "virtue" with power and the capacity to act. Unlike mere whim or wish, or the simple expression of an opinion or preference, to will a purpose is itself to embark on the course of action that may realize it, in spite of the obstacles and vagaries of fortune it must confront. No doubt the difference here is more a matter of dialectical transition than of categorical distinction: a certain quantity of wish, so to speak, may well cross the qualitative threshold that separates it from will. But once this threshold is crossed, in ways that will vary with the situation and the obstacles involved, then the old truisms remain true: where there's a will there's a way, so long as those who will the end will the means.

Examples of the sort of egalitarian political will I have in mind are easy to list: along with the Bolivarian projects of Latin America and the recent mobilizations in north Africa (along with, on what remains for the time being a more modest scale, the anti-neoliberal demonstrations across Europe and much of the world), they could include the political determination of South Africa's United Democratic Front, Haiti's Lavalas and Palestine's Intifada to confront forms of inequality and injustice based on race, culture, privilege and class. For me the most instructive examples remain the great revolutions that took place in France and Haiti, and then in Russia, China and Cuba, along with the anti-colonial liberation movements that drew much of their inspiration from these revolutions.

In each case, a threshold is crossed when the actors in these sequences apply a version of Danton's principle, later cited by Engels, Lenin and many others: *"de l'audace, de l'audace, encore de l'audace!"*[9] In each case, a decisive element in the struggle is the respective actors' capacity and willingness to act—the capacity of those who control the economic levers of power and the repressive machinery of the state, on the one hand, versus the people's collective capacity to act deliberately and forcefully in pursuit of common goals. When a struggle reaches a decisive point, those waging it must decide between fright or fight. Anyone involved in a popular struggle knows that if we are to continue to fight, and to fight to win, then we need to maintain solidarity and unity, to resist fragmentation and dispersal, to invent forms of discipline and organization, and to encourage means of leadership that are both responsive and decisive. A popular mobilization prevails when its sense of purpose is strong and its principles are clear, and when it is prepared to take the steps needed to apply them. As Frederick Douglas realized early in a long cycle of anti-imperialist struggle, "power concedes nothing without a demand"[10]—but by the same token, as the Vietnamese general Vo Nguyen Giáp argued later in that same cycle, when a popular demand is clear, conscious and well-organized, when it is made with "unshakeable conviction," then it commands "invincible strength" and can "overcome all difficulties and hardships to defeat an enemy who at first was several times stronger."[11] Along the way, uncounted numbers of people struggling against all sorts of powerful enemies have repeated the slogan that prevails whenever it is put into practice with the determination it requires: "the people, united, will never be defeated!" Popular determination, in the past, has put an end to slavery, colonialism, child labor and apartheid; only similar determination can, in the future, put an end to capitalist exploitation, imperialist oppression, nuclear proliferation and environmental catastrophe.

II

I'm currently trying to tackle this cluster of ideas and historical sequences from two angles, one broadly synthetic, the other more genealogical. The synthetic project is intended to be a somewhat systematic study of the notion and practice of the will of the people as such, with sections devoted to accounts of the people on the one hand and of the will on the other, along with the most fruitful attempts to think them together, for instance via the effort made by Marx and Blanqui, followed by Luxemburg, Lenin and their contemporaries, to think the notion of a resolute, determined and autonomous proletariat, as the "leading edge" of a mobilization in pursuit of the political and economic emancipation of the people as a whole. This project also includes some discussion of several of the essential practices that figure as conditions for the organized exercise of such a political will: practices of association, combination and assembly (for instance in the Jacobin clubs, or municipal sections of the French Revolution, in trade unions, workers' councils and political parties, in the *ti legliz* and base ecclesial communities of liberation theology, etc.); practices of education, information, deliberation and debate, that allow for the formulation and assertion of collective priorities, goals and decisions; practices that enable these decisions to be imposed and these goals to be realized, in the face of whatever opposition they might encounter from more privileged members of the situation; practices that encourage the cultivation of a collective spirit, discipline and courage (practices that Rousseau, followed by e.g. Mao and Che, described in terms of political "virtue"), to counter the inevitable tendencies that encourage the pursuit of private, factional or divisive interests; practices that enable a popular political will to persevere as united (but not uniform), determined (but not dogmatic), self-critical (but not cynical), steadfast (but not rigid), and so on.

Several broad suppositions underlie this approach to emancipatory politics. One is that the conscious and deliberate intentions of the actors are an important (though certainly not the exclusive) factor in the determination of political struggle. This factor has been systematically downplayed if not dismissed by many of the most innovative figures in continental philosophy, ever since the turn against Sartre and existentialism in the early 1960s—and in many ways, ever since the turn away from the voluntarist conceptions of moral and political philosophy defended, in various ways, by Rousseau, Kant and Hegel, but then rejected by figures as diverse as Schopenhauer, Nietzsche, Wittgenstein, Stalin and his epigones, the later Heidegger, Deleuze, Derrida, and so on. Any analysis of imperial and neo-colonial policies, for instance, or of neo-liberal policies, or of the policies that in recent years have targeted the labor movement, immigrant workers, anti-imperialist "insurgents," etc., that doesn't/don't pay attention to the perfectly explicit, perfectly deliberate intentions of the actors involved, has no chance of grasping the class and power dynamics involved—and the same goes, of course, for the emancipatory movements resisting these policies.

In the absence of any "neutral" means of deciding the issue, the sort of voluntarism I'm defending here implies a readiness to treat both oppressive and emancipatory processes less as reflections of "objective tendencies" or "systemic laws" than as more or less deliberate strategies conceived by conscious and specific actors, albeit in circumstances that are forced upon rather than chosen by them. Against the theoretical reflexes that have long dominated the human sciences in general and contemporary European philosophy in particular, this approach involves recognition that no adequate account of political action can proceed without considering its "psychological" or psycho-political dimension, and without addressing the hopes and motivations of the actors themselves. It involves a willingness to listen to the reasons actors give for acting the way they do, before jumping to the conclusion that these reasons simply mask "deeper" (unconscious, involuntary, ideological, . . .) forms of determination. It accepts that some kinds of situation are only intelligible from the perspective of those who are engaged in the process of its transformation, and that people should be treated as the "authors and actors of their own drama," rather than as puppets subjected to the play of forces they cannot understand.[12]

A second and equally self-evident supposition is that the actors who seek to exploit and dominate target groups or populations usually go to a good deal of trouble to disguise their intentions, and to control the way they are represented in what passes for the public means of information and education. The ideal form of domination, of course, is one that can be represented, and perhaps even lived, as "voluntarily" accepted by those it targets, and thus not as a form of domination at all. The genius of capitalism, as the coercive "command of unpaid labour,"[13] is that despite its violent origins and premises its coercion eventually comes to take on an apparently free or voluntary form, as mediated by the labor market, in which buyers and sellers appear to meet on an "equal" footing. The genius of "humanitarian" forms of imperial intervention—for instance as recently perfected by the "donor" countries who have long controlled Haiti's economy and government—likewise focuses on the apparent dependence and presumed gratitude of its beneficiaries, their need to be "protected" from home-grown political projects that might threaten the status quo.

A third supposition turns on the relation between a will and its consequences, and qualifies the primacy of willed intention. Even so austere a political voluntarist as Saint-Just understood, of course, that "the force of circumstance [*la force des choses*] may lead us to results that we never thought of" (February 26, 1793). To insist on the importance of deliberate intention and conscious purpose is not to pretend that intentions alone might determine what happens over a course of action. An intention is not the virtual blueprint for a series of deeds that simply brings it to fruition in actuality. To will an end or outcome is not to will a fully formed solution in advance of engaging with the problem; it is rather the readiness to follow through on a decision and the principles that orient it, the willingness to do what is required to overcome the obstacles, both predictable and unforeseen, that may emerge over the course of its imposition. If to will the end is also to will the means, then participation in a political will is participation in the effort, which is invariably specific to a particular situation of struggle, to align means and ends in the way that appears to promise maximum conformity of the former to the latter. A will cannot dictate its consequences in advance, but the people who affirm it can be more or less capable of following the partially contingent sequence of its consequences, and of doing what is necessary to see them through, without falling prey to dogmatic rigidity on the one hand or opportunistic compromises on the other.

A further presumption concerns the nature of the actor or subject of political will. I take the capacity to will to be a universal and thoroughly ordinary human ability, like the capacity to speak or think, an ability whose most fundamental conditions of possibility stem from the way that we evolved as a species. Among other things, this evolution dictates that the actor who speaks, thinks or wills is an individual (rather than a group) while at the same time ensuring that willing individuals are always more or less "grouped," in keeping with the commonplace idea that human individuals are always constitutively and irreducibly social. There is then a kind of continuum, one that crosses multiple thresholds of scale and capacity, between individual and collective acts of will. "The individual is the element of humanity," as Blanqui argues, "like the stitch in a piece of knitting"—without willing and politically educated individuals nothing is possible, but if the political fabric they form is too lose or shapeless then when it comes to social or economic struggles such isolated individuals are reduced to impotence.[14] Only individuals can will, but as a matter of course only organized groups of individual have the capacity to engage in a political will, and thus challenge the terms of their employment, confront the class of people who exploit them, or struggle with those who dominate them.

Running through all these assumptions is the correlation of will and capacity, the capacities to deliberate with others, to formulate an end, follow its consequences, and so on. The second of the two projects I'm currently engaged in aims to unpack these assumptions and to explore the link between will and capacity. There are lots of ways you could try to do this, but for the time being I've decided that the most economical way is to focus on what I take to be the three most important figures to have contributed to the modern practice of emancipatory politics—Rousseau, Blanqui and Marx.

III

By framing the theoretical roots of political will in terms of this trio, I mean to emphasize the fact that no single philosopher or political thinker provides an adequate account of its practice, or deserves to be taken as a sufficient guide on their own. Rousseau, Blanqui and Marx differ in many ways, of course, and sometimes spectacularly so. Nevertheless, I hope to show that they can be productively read as contributions to a common project, and that taken together they provide the most concise way of laying the foundations for a general account of political will in this activist and emancipatory sense. Of course many other thinkers should be added to create a more complete list (for instance Machiavelli, Kant, Robespierre, Marat, Fichte, Babeuf, . . .), but I've chosen these particular three, beyond their canonical status and their direct influence on other figures, because together they seem to offer, with a minimum of direct overlap, the most forceful and suggestive way of framing the issue.

On both historical and conceptual grounds, Rousseau clearly figures as the first, most fundamental figure of this modern tradition, insofar as he posits as a primary and irreducible point of departure that "the principle of every action is in the will of a free being," such that "it is not the word freedom which means nothing; it is the word necessity."[15] A person's freedom, Rousseau concludes, "doesn't consist in doing merely what he wills or wants, but rather in never doing what he does not want to do."[16] It is the constitutive alignment of willing and doing, which has to be worked out through practice and experiment, that establishes the ground for a collective and egalitarian notion of freedom. Rousseau then sketches a normative account of political community and social justice on the basis of this principle, a sketch that Robespierre and Marat, along with a host of other Jacobins and *sans-culottes*, would soon strive to put into revolutionary practice.[17] Against the many variations of the argument that downplays the significance of the French revolution, and that tries either to limit its implications or confine them to an outdated historical moment, I side with those who affirm it as the inauguration of a revolutionary period that remains open to this day, and in particular as the initiation of what might be called a "Jacobin-Bolshevik" project whose significance, however battered and maligned over recent decades, is far from exhausted.

If Robespierre emerged as the dominant political figure of the Jacobin phase of the French Revolution it's because he understood most clearly why, to accomplish its goals, "we need a single will, ONE will [*une volonté UNE*]," the will of the people in general—and since the main resistance to such a general will "comes from the bourgeois" so then Robespierre recognized that "*to defeat the bourgeois* we must *rally the people*."[18] After Robespierre, Saint-Just summarized the whole Jacobin political project when he rejected "purely speculative" or "intellectual" conceptions of justice, as if "laws were the expression of taste rather than of the general will." The only legitimate basis for autonomous self-determination, from this perspective, is instead "the material will of the people, its simultaneous will; its goal is to consecrate the active and not the passive interest of the greatest number of people."[19] In the wake of Thermidorian reaction, Babeuf quickly realized that the "first and crucial step" toward a more equal distribution of resources and opportunities was "the achievement of a truly effective democracy through which the people's will could be expressed."[20]

After Babeuf and Buonarrati, Blanqui again adopts the ends and means of this neo-Jacobin project, and his lifelong effort "to continue the revolution" is first and foremost a confrontation with the specific obstacles that now prevent conversion of *la volonté du peuple* into a sovereign political reality. Considered as a revolutionary activist, Marx shares rather more with Blanqui than most recent critics acknowledge. Though Marx is more concerned with the socio-economic dimensions of this conversion, of course, if we read him as a political theorist then Lucio Colletti isn't far off the mark when he suggests that Marx adds little or "nothing to Rousseau, except for the analysis (which is of course rather important) of the 'economic basis' for the withering away of the state."[21]

We might say that Rousseau imagines an autonomous community governed by a general will, Blanqui considers the steps that need to be taken in order to actualize it, and Marx the historical and economic tendencies that may enable or discourage the taking of these steps. In terms of what they contribute to a general theory of revolutionary emancipation, then, these three contributions are best understood in a way that inverts their chronological order: it is Marx who reconstructs the roots and causes of a popular revolution, Blanqui who considers what is needed to trigger and sustain one, and Rousseau who ponders its consequences and continuation.

Or else, to risk a still more abstract formulation: Rousseau considers aspects of our capacity to act, the constitution of a collective actor and the determination of a common purpose (the who and the why of action), Marx considers the conditions and tendencies that enable or discourage emancipatory political action (its where and when), and Blanqui the taking of action itself (what it involves and how it might prevail).

Although much recent work on Rousseau remains preoccupied by his allegedly authoritarian inclinations (and the consequent problems this poses for trying to read him as compatible with approaches he heartily detests: parliamentary democracy and free-market liberalism), I hope that few readers will dispute his foundational place in this wider project. Blanqui too, although marginalized for more than a century, as much by a certain Marxist tradition as by more "moderate" forms of republicanism, is a relatively obvious choice. Although certainly not as thorough, original or influential a thinker as Rousseau or Marx, and despite the clear limits and ambiguity of some of his positions, Blanqui deserves to be rescued from neglect because he poses with unrivalled force the essential question of revolutionary politics—the question of taking and retaining the political power that alone can change a society structured in dominance and oppression. Although they may not have known it (or been willing to admit it), the next generation of revolutionary activists, the generation of Luxemburg, Lenin, Trotsky, and Gramsci (to say nothing of Mao, Che or Giáp), followed Blanqui almost as much as they did Marx.[22]

The association of Marx with any kind of voluntarism may be more controversial. As his every reader knows, Marx is certainly critical of the sort of "merely" political will he associates, in different places, with Robespierre, Hegel, or Bauer, and with some of Blanqui's own supporters in exile. There are also aspects of Marx's own work that in my opinion go too far in the opposite, anti-voluntarist, direction, and that help to justify some of the recurring attempts to dismiss him as guilty of a reductive socio-historical determinism. One-sided emphasis on the ways that "social being determines consciousness," if not corrected by consideration of political practice and organization, sometimes encourages Marx to downplay questions of proletarian agency and purpose in favor of an analysis of *"what the proletariat is*, and what, in accordance with this *being*, it will historically be compelled to do."[23] Marx rarely worries that proletarian actors might think and act in ways that could conflict with the underlying tendencies shaping their proletarian being and "forcing" them into revolutionary conflict with those who exploit them.[24] A similar confidence will enable him to assume, with remarkable brevity and nonchalance, that "capitalist production begets its own negation with the inexorability of a natural process."[25] There is no denying the problematic consequences of this side of his legacy.

Nevertheless, along with others who have argued that Marx is more concerned with political possibility than with historical necessity, I hope to show that his most fundamental concerns can be traced back to precisely that central relation of freedom and necessity which Hegel and Kant inherited from Rousseau. The young Marx insists on the distinctive way that, unlike other animals, "man makes his life activity itself an object of his will and consciousness,"[26] and in a crucial chapter of *Capital* the older Marx insists in comparable terms on man's "sovereign power" and capacity to "change his own nature," his ability consciously and deliberately to determine his own ends, and to sustain the disciplined, "purposeful will" required to realize them.[27] The young Marx likewise insists on "the self-determination of the people,"[28] and emphasizes the unique virtues of democracy as the political form of a fully "human existence," in which "the law exists for the sake of man" rather than vice versa,[29] and is formulated as "the conscious expression of the will of the people, and therefore originates with it and is created by it";[30] the older Marx will embrace the Paris Commune of 1871 (inspired and organized in large part by Blanqui's supporters) as an exemplary instance of precisely this sort of democracy in action. Understood from this perspective, political decisions are in no sense limited to passively registering changes that occur at the level of the material "base" of social life. Among other things, the Commune illustrates our capacity to invent a political lever that can wedge its way "underneath" this very base, "a lever for uprooting the economical foundation upon which rests the existence of classes, and therefore of class rule."[31] The base itself, moreover, is both shaped by the irreducibly political inflection of class relations, and sustained by the irreducibly "human" and thus purposeful and inventive character of the forces of production. At least during periods of revolutionary opportunity, as in 1871, or 1848–1850, what is primary is not some sort of inexorable historical determinism so much as the taking of vigorous and lucid action, carried out by an independent, resolute and fully conscious political actor, on the model of another (temporarily) fruitful collaboration between supporters of both Marx and Blanqui: the Communist League.[32]

Early and late, Marx understands communism as "the true appropriation of the human essence through and for man," and "the true resolution of the conflict . . . between freedom and necessity."[33] What is at stake in the revolutionary transition from capitalism to communism is the "development of all human powers as such,"[34] together with "the control and conscious mastery of these powers, which, born of the action of men on one another, have till now overawed and governed men as powers completely alien to them."[35] Once we understand the way we shape our social relations, Engels will add, "it depends only upon ourselves to subject them more and more to our own will, and, by means of them, to reach our own ends. . . . Man's own social organization, hitherto confronting him as a necessity imposed by Nature and history, now becomes the result of his own free action," and confirms "the ascent of man from the kingdom of necessity to the kingdom of freedom."[36]

With far more depth and precision than Rousseau or Blanqui, Marx also exposes how capitalist forms of coercion take on an apparently "voluntary" form, and shows, once it has completed the brutal work of its "originary accumulation," how capital's "command of unpaid labour" binds it not with the flagrant chains of slavery but with the "invisible threads" and "silent compulsion" of dependence and precarity.[37] Marx helps us to understand how modern forms of coercion move beyond mere strategies of overt exclusion and direct domination, to encompass more subtle manipulations of our will itself. In doing so he frames what remains the central problem for a contemporary account of political will: how might we challenge forms of servitude and oppression that are represented, in the prevailing neoliberal order of things, as the very form of freedom? If the most salient historical developments of the last thirty or so years have involved, in almost every part of the world, the massive transfer of power and resources from the relatively poor to the relatively rich, perhaps the most far-reaching aspect of these developments is the way their advocates have managed to induce large numbers of people to accept and even to embrace them as necessary and unavoidable. Until we renew our capacity for political will, we will have no convincing answer to the dreary refrain: "there is no alternative."

IV

Considered in terms of the contribution they make to an understanding of the practice of political will, if read in isolation each of these three thinkers appears one-sided and incomplete. Rousseau affirms the freedom and power of a popular or general will, but (anticipating Kant) relies too much on the abstract determination of "pure" will as such, and downplays the historical and economic context in which it takes shape and operates. Marx emphasizes "developmental" factors (following Hegel), to the occasional detriment of political action and intention. Rousseau tends to presume too much of pure volition and intention, and Marx can rely too much on the course of historical development. Blanqui stakes everything on the immediate pursuit of justice and equality, but without doing enough to consider either its relations to the people and popular organization on the one hand or its historico-material determinants on the other. What is needed today is less the renewal of Marxism per se, and still less of Blanquism or Rousseauism (or of Leninism, Maoism, or any other proper-name-ism), so much as the construction of a more robust and assertive political *voluntarism* in general, i.e. an account of the emancipation from necessity that is fully prepared to foreground its partial but decisive dependence on a whole series of political-psychological factors, including purpose, intention, consciousness, deliberation and volition. If it is to prevail and endure, the movement from necessity to freedom must itself be freely undertaken.

Taken in isolation, Rousseau, Blanqui and Marx all have clear limitations, but taken together, I think it's not much of an exaggeration to say that they anticipate most of the concepts and concerns of a whole series of subsequent voluntarist political thinkers, including for instance Lenin, Trotsky, Serge, Gramsci, Mao, Sartre, Che, Fanon, Giáp, Dussel, Bensaïd, Badiou, . . . For all the obvious differences in context and priority, there is a striking degree of internal consistency along this voluntarist line of political thought (so long as we don't try to trace it back to a single foundational thinker). There are few significant political concepts developed by Lenin or Mao, for instance, that weren't anticipated by either Marx, Rousseau or Blanqui, and both of them are better understood through the lens of this triple and thoroughly integrated influence than simply as orthodox Marxists. Although it would be a sterile and reductive exercise to try to read them as mere variations in a paradigm, of course, I think it would be easy to show how Fanon and Che renew certain motifs in Rousseau, or Bensaïd and Badiou some motifs in Blanqui, and so on, in each case conditioned by particularities of context and priority. Overall, the underlying continuity is more significant, with these and other comparable figures, than their (otherwise noteworthy) innovations and peculiarities.

Gramsci is perhaps the most suggestive and fertile instance of this triple legacy, if we can call it that. Gramsci seeks, in terms that seem to draw as much on Rousseau and Blanqui as on Marx or Lenin, "to put the 'will,' which in the last analysis equals practical or political activity, at the base of philosophy."[38] Reality itself is best understood as "a product of the application of human will to the society of things," so "if one excludes all voluntarist elements . . . one mutilates reality itself. Only the man who wills something strongly can identify the elements which are necessary to the realization of his will."[39] In a more specifically Marxist sense, Gramsci explains, "will means consciousness of ends, which in turn implies having an exact notion of one's own power, and the means to express it in action." Participation in such a will implies a capacity to determine and pursue our "specific ends, without deviations or hesitations. It means cutting a straight and direct path through to the ultimate end, without detours into the green meadows of happy brotherhood"[40] and the false community of the "realm."

No less than Rousseau, Gramsci knows that "before it can be physical, movement must always be intellectual" and that "every action is the result of various wills, with a varying degree of intensity and awareness and of homogeneity with the entire complex of the collective will."[41] As they combine through forms of assembly and association to "forge a social, collective will," Gramsci anticipates that people will eventually gain the ability to "control economic facts with their will, until this collective will becomes the driving force of the economy, the force which shapes reality itself, so that objective reality becomes a living, breathing force, like a current of molten lava, which can be channelled wherever and however the will directs."[42]

No less than Blanqui, Gramsci puts his "faith [in] man, and man's will and his capacity for action,"[43] and defines man as "concrete will, that is, the effective application of the abstract will or vital impulse to the concrete means which realise such a will."[44] Gramsci understands partisan political struggle as "a conscious struggle for a precise, determinate end: it is a lucid act of the will, a discipline already forged within the mind and the will," one that allows "workers in the Party [to] become an industrial vanguard within the workers' State, just as they are a revolutionary vanguard in the period of struggle for the introduction of proletarian power."[45]

No less than Marx, finally, Gramsci knows that if "society does not pose itself problems for whose solution the material preconditions do not already exist," acceptance of this proposition "immediately raises the problem of the formation of a collective will":

> In order to analyse critically what this proposition means, it is necessary to study precisely how permanent collective wills are formed, and how such wills set themselves concrete short-term and long-term ends—i.e. a line of collective action. It is a question of more or less long processes of development, and rarely of sudden, "synthetic" explosions. It requires an extremely minute, molecular process of exhaustive analysis in every

detail, the documentation for which is made up of an endless quantity of books, pamphlets, review and newspaper articles, conversations and oral debates repeated countless times, and which in their gigantic aggregation represent this long labour which gives birth to a collective will with a certain degree of homogeneity—with the degree necessary and sufficient to achieve an action which is coordinated and simultaneous in the time and the geographical space in which the historical event takes place.[46]

There is no better way to begin the renewal of such study and analysis, I think, than by recalling its point of departure in the political philosophy of Jean-Jacques Rousseau. That will be my priority for the coming months, to be followed in quick succession by brief studies of Blanqui and Marx. And after this, I hope, I should be in a better position to work out a more synthetic account of political will in general, and to head off some of the objections that might be leveled at a politics of prescription.

Notes

1   Benjamin Constant, *Principes de politique*, in his *Écrits politiques* (Paris: Gallimard [Folio], 1997), 310.
2   Martin Gilbert, *The Will of the People: Churchill and Parliamentary Democracy* (2006).
3   Barak Obama, "State of the Union Address," January 25, 2011, http://www.whitehouse.gov/the-press-office/2011/01/25/remarks-president-state-union-address, accessed February 2, 2014.
4   Chris Hedges, "The Obama Deception: Why Cornel West Went Ballistic," *Truthdig* May 16, 2011, http://www.truthdig.com/report/print/the_obama_deception_why_cornel_west_went_ballistic_20110516, accessed February 2, 2014.
5   Obama, speech of May 19, 2011, http://www.guardian.co.uk/world/2011/may/19/barack-obama-speech-middle-east, accessed February 2, 2014.
6   Cf. Peter Hallward, "Fanon and Political Will," *Cosmos and History: The Journal of Natural and Social Philosophy* 7(1) (2011): 104–127, http://www.cosmosandhistory.org/index.php/journal/article/view/244/329.
7   Cf. John Rees and Joseph Daher, *The People Demand: A Short History of the Arab Revolutions* (London: Counterfire, 2011); Elliott Colla, "The People Want" (May 2012), http://www.merip.org/mer/mer263/people-want; Gilbert Achcar, *The People Want: A Radical Exploration of the Arab Uprising* (London: Saqi Books, 2013).
8   Tony Benn, interviewed in Michael Moore, *Sicko* (2007).
9   Antoine Saint-Just offered a more distilled variant: "We must dare! [Osez!]—this motto compresses the whole political logic of our revolution" (Antoine Saint-Just, speech to the National Convention, February 26, 1794). And again: "Those who undertake revolutions resemble those who are the first to navigate in unknown waters, guided by their audacity" (Report to the National Convention, March 13, 1794).

10 "If there is no struggle, there is no progress. Those who profess to favor freedom, and yet deprecate agitation, are men who want crops without plowing up the ground. . . . Power concedes nothing without a demand. It never did and it never will. Find out just what any people will submit to, and you have found out the exact amount of injustice and wrong which will be imposed upon them; and these will continue till they are resisted with either words or blows, or with both. The limits of tyrants are prescribed by the endurance of those whom they oppress" (Frederick Douglass, "The Significance of Emancipation in the West Indies" [August 3, 1857], *The Frederick Douglass Papers*, ed. John W. Blassingame [New Haven: Yale University Press], vol. 3, 204).

11 Vo Nguyen Giáp, "The South Vietnamese People Will Win" (January 1966), in *The Military Art of People's War* (New York: Monthly Review Press, 1970), 204.

12 Karl Marx, *The Poverty of Philosophy* [1847], *Collected Works* (London: Lawrence & Wishart, 1975–2000), vol. 6, 170.

13 Marx, *Capital*, vol. 1, trans. Ben Fowkes (London: Penguin, 1976), 672.

14 Louis-Auguste Blanqui, Manuscripts, Bibliothèque Nationale Collection NAF9591(2), f. 520 (October 19, 1866).

15 Rousseau, *Emile*, in his *Oeuvres complètes*, vol. 4 (Paris: Gallimard [Pléiade], 1969), 576.

16 Rousseau, *Reveries of the Solitary Walker*, in his *Oeuvres complètes*, vol. 1, 1059.

17 "We have turned into imposing realities," Robespierre proudly declared in 1794, "the laws of eternal justice that used to be contemptuously called the dreams of well-meaning people. Morality was once limited to the books of philosophers; we have put it into the government of nations" (Maximilien Robespierre, *Oeuvres complètes* [Paris: PUF, 1910–1967], vol. 10, 229).

18 Robespierre, notes written in early June 1793, in J. Marx Thompson, *Robespierre*, Blackwell, Oxford, 1935, II, 33–34.

19 Saint-Just, *Oeuvres complètes* (Paris: Gallimard [Folio], 2004) 547.

20 R.B. Rose, *Gracchus Babeuf: The First Revolutionary Communist* (Stanford: Stanford University Press, 1978), 104; cf. Ian Birchall, *The Spectre of Babeuf* (Houndmills: Palgrave, 1997).

21 Lucio Colletti, "Rousseau as Critic of 'Civil Society,'" *From Rousseau to Lenin* (London: NLB, 1972), 185; cf. Eugene Kamenka, *Ethical Foundations of Marxism* (London: Routledge & Kegan Paul, 1962), 37–47.

22 It's for precisely this reason that critics keen to drive a wedge between a "democratic" Marx and the "authoritarian" Lenin regularly ground their interpretation in a critique of Blanqui. See for instance Hal Draper, *The Dictatorship of the Proletariat from Marx to Lenin* (New York: Monthly Review Press, 1987), 13, 25–6; Richard Hunt, *The Political Ideas of Marx and Engels* (University of Pittsburgh Press, Pittsburgh, 1974), 1, 13–16, 191, 289.

23 Marx and Friedrich Engels, *The Holy Family*, in *Collected Works* vol. 4, 37.

24 Marx and Engels, *The German Ideology*, in *Collected Works* vol. 5, 52. There are echoes of this emphasis on compulsion and forcing even in so allegedly "voluntarist" a reading of Marx as Lukács's *History and Class Consciousness* (Cambridge, MA: MIT Press, 1972); see for instance, pages 41–42.

25 Marx, *Capital*, vol. 1, 929.

26 Marx, "Economic and Philosophical Manuscripts" [1844], *Early Writings*, 329.

27 Marx, *Capital*, vol. 1, 283–4.
28 Marx, *Critique of Hegel's Doctrine of the State* [1843], *Early Writings*, 89.
29 Marx, *Critique of Hegel's Doctrine of the State* [1843], *Early Writings*, 88.
30 Marx, "The Divorce Bill" [1842], *Collected Works*, vol. 1, 309.
31 Marx, *Class Struggles in France* [1871], *Collected Works*, vol. 22, 334.
32 See in particular Karl Marx and Friedrich Engels, "Address of the Central Committee to the Communist League" [March 1850], *Collected Works* vol. 10, 277–87.
33 Marx, *Economic and Philosophical Manuscripts* [1844], *Early Writings*, 348; cf. Marx, *Capital* vol. 3, 959.
34 Marx, *Grundrisse*, 488.
35 Marx and Engels, *The German Ideology* [1846], *Collected Works* vol. 5, 51–2.
36 Engels, *Anti-Dühring* [1877], *Collected Works* vol. 25, 266, 270.
37 Marx, *Capital*, vol. 1, 719, 899.
38 Antonio Gramsci, "Study of Philosophy," *Selections from the Prison Notebooks*, ed. and trans. Quintin Hoare and Geoffrey Nowell Smith (London: Lawrence & Wishart, 1971), 345; cf. Gramsci, "The Modern Prince," *Selections*, 125–133, 171–172.
39 Gramsci, "The Modern Prince," *Selections*, 171. Compared with the apparent solidity of actually-existing reality, "what 'ought to be' is therefore concrete; indeed it is the only realistic and historicist interpretation of reality, it alone is history in the making and philosophy in the making, it alone is politics" (ibid., 172).
40 Gramsci, "*Our* Marx," *Pre-Prison Writings* (Cambridge: Cambridge University Press, 1994), 57.
41 Gramsci, "Class Intransigence and Italian History," *Pre-Prison Writings*, 69; Gramsci, *Selections*, 364.
42 Gramsci, "The Revolution Against Capital," *Pre-Prison Writings*, 40.
43 Gramsci, "Socialism and Co-operation," *Pre-Prison Writings*, 14.
44 "Men create their own personality, 1. by giving a specific and concrete ("rational") direction to their own vital impulse or will; 2. by identifying the means which will make this will concrete and specific and not arbitrary; 3. by contributing to modify the ensemble of the concrete conditions for realizing this will to the extent of one's own limits and capacities and in the most fruitful form" (Gramsci, *Selections*, 360).
45 Gramsci, "The Communist Groups," *Pre-Prison Writings*, 176.
46 Gramsci, *Selections*, 194, referring to Marx: "mankind thus inevitably sets itself only such tasks as it is able to solve" (Marx, *A Contribution to the Critique of Political Economy* [1859], *Collected Works* vol. 29, 263).

CHAPTER THIRTY ONE

Communicative Capitalism: Circulation and the Foreclosure of Politics

Jodi Dean

From Cultural Politics *1 (1) (March 2005): 51–74.*

No response

Although mainstream US media outlets provided the Bush administration with supportive, non-critical and even encouraging platforms for making his case for invading Iraq, critical perspectives were nonetheless well represented in the communications flow of mediated global capitalist technoculture. Alternative media, independent media and non-US media provided thoughtful reports, insightful commentary and critical evaluations of the "evidence" of "weapons of mass destruction" in Iraq. Amy Goodman's syndicated radio program, "Democracy Now," regularly broadcasts shows intensely opposed to the militarism and unilateralism of the Bush administration's national security policy. The *Nation* magazine offered detailed and nuanced critiques of various reasons introduced for attacking Iraq. Circulating on the Internet were lists with congressional phone and fax numbers, petitions and announcements for marches, protests and direct-action training sessions. As the march to war proceeded, thousands of bloggers commented on each step, referencing other media supporting their positions. When mainstream US news outlets failed to cover demonstrations such as the September protest of 400,000 people in London or the October march on Washington when 250,000 people surrounded the White House, myriad progressive, alternative and critical left news outlets supplied frequent and reliable information about the action on the ground. All in all, a strong anti-war message was out there.

But, the message was not received. It circulated, reduced to the medium. Even when the White House acknowledged the massive worldwide demonstrations of February 15, 2003, Bush simply reiterated the fact that a message was out there, circulating—the protestors had the right to express their opinions. He didn't actually respond to their message. He didn't treat the words and actions of the protestors as sending a message to him to which he was in some sense obligated to respond. Rather, he acknowledged that there existed views different from his own. There were his views and there were other views; all had the right to exist, to be expressed—but that in no way meant, or so Bush made it seem, that these views were involved with each other. So, despite the terabytes of commentary and information, there wasn't exactly a debate over the war. On the contrary, in the days and weeks prior to the US invasion of Iraq, the anti-war messages morphed into so much circulating content, just like all the other cultural effluvia wafting through cyberia.

We might express this disconnect between engaged criticism and national strategy in terms of a distinction between politics as the circulation of content and politics as official policy. On the one hand there is media chatter of various kinds—from television talking heads, radio shock jocks, and the gamut of print media to websites with RSS (Real Simple Syndication) feeds, blogs, e-mail lists and the proliferating versions of instant text messaging. In this dimension, politicians, governments and activists struggle for visibility, currency and, in the now quaint term from the dot.com years, mindshare. On the other hand are institutional politics, the day-to-day activities of bureaucracies, lawmakers, judges and the apparatuses of the police and national security states. These components of the political system seem to run independently of the politics that circulates as content.

At first glance, this distinction between politics as the circulation of content and politics as the activity of officials makes no sense. After all, the very premise of liberal democracy is the sovereignty of the people. And, governance by the people has generally been thought in terms of communicative freedoms of speech, assembly and the press, norms of publicity that emphasize transparency and accountability, and the deliberative practices of the public sphere. Ideally, the communicative interactions of the public sphere, what I've been referring to as the circulation of content and media chatter, are supposed to impact official politics.

In the United States today, however, they don't, or, less bluntly put, there is a significant disconnect between politics circulating as content and official politics. Today, the circulation of content in the dense, intensive networks of global communications relieves top-level actors (corporate, institutional and governmental) from the obligation to respond. Rather than responding to messages sent by activists and critics, they counter with their own contributions to the circulating flow of communications, hoping that sufficient volume (whether in terms of number of contributions or the spectacular nature of a contribution) will give their contributions dominance or stickiness. Instead of engaged debates, instead of contestations employing common terms, points of reference or demarcated frontiers, we confront a multiplication of resistances and assertions so extensive that it hinders the formation of strong counterhegemonies. The proliferation, distribution, acceleration and intensification of communicative access and opportunity, far from enhancing democratic governance or resistance, results in precisely the opposite—the post-political formation of communicative capitalism.

Needless to say, I am not claiming that networked communications never facilitate political resistance. One of the most visible of the numerous examples to the contrary is perhaps the experience of B92 in Serbia. Radio B92 used the Internet to circumvent governmental censorship and disseminate news of massive demonstrations against the Milošević regime (Matic and Pantic 1999). My point is that the political efficacy of networked media depends on its context. Under conditions of the intensive and extensive proliferation of media, messages are more likely to get lost as mere contributions to the circulation of content. What enhances democracy in one context becomes a new form of hegemony in another. Or, the intense circulation of content in communicative capitalism forecloses the antagonism necessary for politics. In relatively closed societies, that antagonism is not only already there but also apparent at and as the very frontier between open and closed.

My argument proceeds as follows. For the sake of clarity, I begin by situating the notion of communicative capitalism in the context of other theories of the present that emphasize changes in communication and communicability. I then move to emphasize specific features of communicative capitalism in light of the fantasies animating them. First, I take up the fantasy of abundance and discuss the ways this fantasy results in a shift in the basic unit of communication from the message to the contribution. Second, I address the fantasy of activity or participation. I argue that this fantasy is materialized through technology fetishism. Finally, I consider the fantasy of wholeness that relies on and produces a global both imaginary and Real. I argue that this fantasy prevents the emergence of a clear division between friend and enemy, resulting instead in the more dangerous and profound figuring of the other as a threat to be destroyed. My goal in providing this account of communicative capitalism is to explain why in an age celebrated for its communications there is no response.

. . .

Communicative capitalism

The notion of communicative capitalism conceptualizes the commonplace idea that the market, today, is the site of democratic aspirations, indeed, the mechanism by which the will of the demos manifests itself. We might think here of the circularity of claims regarding popularity. McDonald's, Walmart and reality television are depicted as popular because they seem to offer what people want. How do we know they offer what people want? People choose them. So, they must be popular.

The obvious problem with this equation is the way it treats commercial choices, the paradigmatic form of choice per se. But the market is not a system for delivering political outcomes—despite the fact that political campaigns are indistinguishable from advertising or marketing campaigns. Political decisions—to go to war, say, or to establish the perimeters of legitimate relationships—involve more than the mindless reiteration of faith, conviction and unsupported claims (I'm thinking here of the Bush administration's faith-based foreign policy and the way it pushed a link between Iraq and Al Qaeda). The concept of communicative capitalism tries to capture this strange merging of democracy and capitalism. It does so by highlighting the way networked communications bring the two together.

Communicative capitalism designates that form of late capitalism in which values heralded as central to democracy take material form in networked communications technologies (cf. Dean 2002). Ideals of access, inclusion, discussion and participation come to be realized in and through expansions, intensifications and interconnections of global telecommunications. But instead of leading to more equitable distributions of wealth and influence, instead of enabling the emergence of a richer variety in modes of living and practices of freedom, the deluge of screens and spectacles undermines political opportunity and efficacy for most of the world's peoples.

Research on the impact of economic globalization makes clear how the speed, simultaneity and interconnectivity of electronic communications produce massive concentrations of wealth (Sassen 1996). Not only does the possibility of superprofits in the finance and services complex lead to hypermobility of capital and the devalorization of manufacturing but financial markets themselves acquire the capacity to discipline national governments. In the US, moreover, the proliferation of media has been accompanied by a shift in political participation. Rather than actively organized in parties and unions, politics has become a domain of financially mediated and professionalized practices centered on advertising, public relations and the means of mass communication. Indeed, with the commodification of communication, more and more domains of life seem to have been reformatted in terms of market and spectacle. Bluntly put, the standards of a finance- and consumption-driven entertainment culture set the very terms of democratic governance today. Changing the system— organizing against and challenging communicative capitalism—seems to require strengthening the system: how else can one organize and get the message across? Doesn't it require raising the money, buying the television time, registering the domain name, building the website and making the links?

My account of communicative capitalism is affiliated with Georgio Agamben's discussion of the alienation of language in the society of the spectacle and with Slavoj Žižek's emphasis on post-politics. And, even as it shares the description of communication as capitalist production with Michael Hardt and Antonio Negri, it differs from their assessment of the possibilities for political change.

More specifically, Agamben notes that "in the old regime . . . the estrangement of the communicative essence of human beings was substantiated as a presupposition that had the function of a common ground (nation, language, religion, etc.)" (Agamben 2000: 115). Under current conditions, however, "it is precisely this same communicativity, this same generic essence (language), that is constituted as an autonomous sphere to the extent to which it becomes the essential factor of the production cycle. What hinders communication, therefore, is communicability itself: human beings are being separated by what unites them." Agamben is pointing out how the commonality of the nation state was thought in terms of linguistic and religious groups. We can extend his point by recognizing that the ideal of constitutional states, in theories such as Jürgen Habermas's, say, has also been conceptualized in terms of the essential communicativity of human beings: those who can discuss, who can come to an agreement with one another at least in principle, can be in political relation to one another. As Agamben makes clear, however, communication has detached itself from political ideals of belonging and connection to function today as a primarily economic form. Differently put, communicative exchanges, rather than being fundamental to democratic politics, are the basic elements of capitalist production.

Žižek approaches this same problem of the contemporary foreclosure of the political via the concept of "post-politics." Žižek explains that post-politics "emphasizes the need to leave old ideological divisions behind and confront new issues, armed with the necessary expert knowledge and free deliberation that takes people's concrete needs and demands into account" (1999: 198). Post-politics thus begins from the premise of consensus and cooperation. Real antagonism or dissent is foreclosed. Matters previously thought to require debate and struggle are now addressed as personal issues or technical concerns. We might think of the ways that the expert discourses of psychology and sociology provide explanations for anger and resentment, in effect treating them as syndromes to be managed rather than as issues to be politicized. Or we might think of the probabilities, measures and assessments characteristic of contemporary risk management. The problem is that all this tolerance and attunement to difference and emphasis on hearing another's pain prevents politicization. Matters aren't represented— they don't stand for something beyond themselves. They are simply treated in all their particularity, as specific issues to be addressed therapeutically, juridically, spectacularly or disciplinarily rather than being treated as elements of larger signifying chains or political formations. Indeed, this is how third-way societies support global capital: they prevent politicization. They focus on administration, again, foreclosing the very possibility that things might be otherwise.

The post-political world, then, is marked by emphases on multiple sources of value, on the plurality of beliefs and the importance of tolerating these beliefs through the cultivation of an attunement to the contingencies already pervading one's own values. Divisions between friends and enemies are replaced by emphases on all of us. Likewise, politics is understood as not confined to specific institutional fields but as a characteristic of all of life. There is an attunement, in other words, to a micropolitics of the everyday. But this very attunement forecloses the conflict and opposition necessary for politics.

Finally, Hardt and Negri's description of the current techno-global capitalist formation coincides with Agamben's account of communication without communicability and with Žižek's portrayal of a global formation characterized by contingency, multiplicity and singularity. For example, they agree that "communication is the form of capitalist production in which capital has succeeded in submitting society entirely and globally to its regime, suppressing all alternative paths" (Hardt and Negri 2000: 347; cf. Dean 2002b: 272–275). Emphasizing that there is no outside to the new order of empire, Hardt and Negri see the whole of empire as an "open site of conflict" wherein the incommunicability of struggles, rather than a problem, is an asset insofar as it releases opposition from the pressure of organization and prevents co-optation. As I argue elsewhere, this position, while inspiring, not only embraces the elision between the political and the economic but also in so doing cedes primacy to the economic, taking hope from the intensity and immediacy of the crises within empire. The view I advocate is less optimistic insofar as it rejects the notion that anything is immediately political, and instead prioritizes politicization as the difficult challenge of representing specific claims or acts as universal (cf. Laclau 1996: 56–64). Specific or singular acts of resistance, statements of opinion or instances of transgression are not political in and of themselves; rather, they have to be politicized, that is articulated together with other struggles, resistances and ideals in the course or context of opposition to a shared enemy or opponent (cf. Laclau and Mouffe 1986: 188). Crucial to this task, then, is understanding how communicative capitalism, especially insofar as it relies on networked communications, prevents politicization. To this end, I turn now to the fantasies animating communicative capitalism.

The fantasy of abundance: From message to contribution

The delirium of the dot.com years was driven by a tremendous faith in speed, volume and connectivity. The speed and volume of transactions, say, was itself to generate new "synergies" and hence wealth. A similar belief underlies the conviction that enhanced communications access facilitates democracy. More people than ever before can make their opinions known. The convenience of the Web, for example, enables millions not simply to access information but also to register their points of view, to agree or disagree, to vote and to send messages. The sheer abundance of messages, then, is offered as an indication of democratic potential.

In fact, optimists and pessimists alike share this same fantasy of abundance. Those optimistic about the impact of networked communications on democratic practices emphasize the wealth of information available on the Internet and the inclusion of millions upon millions of voices or points of view into "the conversation" or "public sphere." Pessimists worry about the lack of filters, the data smog and the fact that "all kinds of people" can be part of the conversation (Dyson 1998; cf. Dean 2002a: 72–3). Despite their differing assessments of the value of abundance, then, both optimists and pessimists are committed to the view that networked communications are characterized by exponential expansions in opportunities to transmit and receive messages.

The fantasy of abundance covers over the way facts and opinions, images and reactions circulate in a massive stream of content, losing their specificity and merging with and into the data flow. Any given message is thus a contribution to this ever-circulating content. My argument is that a constitutive feature of communicative capitalism is precisely this morphing of message into contribution. Let me explain.

One of the most basic formulations of the idea of communication is in terms of a message and the response to the message. Under communicative capitalism, this changes. Messages are contributions to circulating content—not actions to elicit responses.[1] Differently put, the exchange value of messages overtakes their use value. So, a message is no longer primarily a message from a sender to a receiver. Uncoupled from contexts of action and application—as on the Web or in print and broadcast media—the message is simply part of a circulating data stream. Its particular content is irrelevant. Who sent it is irrelevant. Who receives it is irrelevant. That it need be responded to is irrelevant. The only thing that is relevant is circulation, the addition to the pool. Any particular contribution remains secondary to the fact of circulation. The value of any particular contribution is likewise inversely proportional to the openness, inclusivity or extent of a circulating data stream—the more opinions or comments that are out there, the less of an impact any one given one might make (and the more shock, spectacle or newness is necessary for a contribution to register or have an impact). In sum, communication functions symptomatically to produce its own negation. Or, to return to Agamben's terms, communicativity hinders communication.

Communication in communicative capitalism, then, is not, as Habermas would suggest, action oriented toward reaching understanding (Habermas 1984). In Habermas's model of communicative action, the use value of a message depends on its orientation. In sending a message, a sender intends for it to be received and understood. Any acceptance or rejection of the message depends on this understanding. Understanding is thus a necessary part of the communicative exchange. In communicative capitalism, however, the use value of a message is less important than its exchange value, its contribution to a larger pool, flow or circulation of content. A contribution need not be understood; it need only be repeated, reproduced, forwarded. Circulation is the context, the condition for the acceptance or rejection of a contribution. Put somewhat differently, how a contribution circulates determines whether it has been accepted or rejected. And, just as the producer, labor, drops out of the picture in commodity exchange, so does the sender (or author) become immaterial to the contribution. The circulation of logos, branded media identities, rumors, catchphrases, even positions and arguments exemplifies this point. The popularity, the penetration and duration, of a contribution marks its acceptance or success.

Thinking about messages in terms of use value and contributions in terms of exchange value sheds light on what would otherwise appear to be an asymmetry in communicative capitalism: the fact that some messages are received, that some discussions extend beyond the context of their circulation. Of course, it is also the case that many commodities are not useless, that people need them. But, what makes them commodities is not the need people have for them or, obviously, their use. Rather, it is their economic function, their role in capitalist exchange. Similarly, the fact that messages can retain a relation to understanding in no way negates the centrality of their circulation. Indeed, this link is crucial to the ideological reproduction of communicative capitalism. Some messages, issues, debates are effective. Some contributions make a difference. But more significant is the system, the communicative network. Even when we know that our specific contributions (our messages, postings, books, articles, films, letters to the editor) simply circulate in a rapidly moving and changing flow of content, in contributing, in participating, we act as if we do not know this. This action manifests ideology as the belief underlying action, the belief that reproduces communicative capitalism (ŽRižek 1989).

The fantasy of abundance both expresses and conceals the shift from message to contribution. It expresses the shift through its emphases on expansions in communication—faster, better, cheaper; more inclusive, more accessible; high speed, broadband, etc. Yet even as it emphasizes these multiple expansions and intensifications, this abundance, the fantasy occludes the resulting devaluation of any particular contribution. Social network analysis demonstrates clearly the way that blogs, like other citation networks, follow a power law distribution. They don't scale; instead, the top few are much more popular than the middle few, and the middle few are vastly more popular than the bottom few. Some call this the emergence of an "A list" or the 80/20 rule. As Clay Shirkey summarily puts it, "Diversity plus freedom of choice creates inequality, and the greater the diversity, the more extreme the inequality" (Shirkey 2003).[2] Emphasis on the fact that one can contribute to a discussion and make one's opinion known misdirects attention from the larger system of communication in which the contribution is embedded.

To put it differently, networked communications are celebrated for enabling everyone to contribute, participate and be heard. The form this communication takes, then, isn't concealed. People are fully aware of the media, the networks, even the surfeit of information. But, they act as if they don't have this knowledge, believing in the importance of their contributions, presuming that there are readers for their blogs. Why? As I explain in the next section, I think it involves the way networked communications induce a kind of registration effect that supports a fantasy of participation.

The fantasy of participation: Technology fetishism

In their online communications, people are apt to express intense emotions, intimate feelings, some of the more secret or significant aspects of their sense of who they are. Years ago, while surfing through Yahoo's home pages, I found the page of a guy who featured pictures of his dog, his parents, and himself fully erect in an SM-style harness. At the bottom of his site was the typical, "Thanks for stopping by! Don't forget to write and tell me what you think!" I mention this quaint image to point to how easy many find it to reveal themselves on the Internet. Not only are people accustomed to putting their thoughts online but also in so doing they believe their thoughts and ideas are registering—write and tell me what you think! Contributing to the infostream, we might say, has a subjective registration effect. One believes that it matters, that it contributes, that it means something.

Precisely because of this registration effect, people believe that their contribution to circulating content is a kind of communicative action. They believe that they are active, maybe even that they are making a difference simply by clicking on a button, adding their name to a petition or commenting on a blog. Žižek describes this kind of false activity with the term "interpassivity." When we are interpassive, something else, a fetish object, is active in our stead. Žižek explains, "you think you are active, while your true position, as embodied in the fetish, is passive . . ." (1997: 21). The frantic activity of the fetish works to prevent actual action, to prevent something from really happening. This suggests to me the way activity on the Net, frantic contributing and content circulation, may well involve a profound passivity, one that is interconnected, linked, but passive nonetheless. Put back in terms of the circulation of contributions that fail to coalesce into actual debates, that fail as messages in need of response, we might think of this odd interpassivity as content that is linked to other content, but never fully connected.

Weirdly, then, the circulation of communication is depoliticizing, not because people don't care or don't want to be involved, but because we do! Or, put more precisely, it is depoliticizing because the form of our involvement ultimately empowers those it is supposed to resist. Struggles on the Net reiterate struggles in real life, but insofar as they reiterate these struggles, they displace them. And this displacement, in turn, secures and protects the space of "official" politics. This suggests another reason communication functions fetishistically today: as a disavowal of a more fundamental political disempowerment or castration. Approaching this fetishistic disavowal from a different direction, we can ask, if Freud is correct in saying that a fetish not only covers over a trauma but that in so doing it also helps one through a trauma, what might serve as an analogous socio-political trauma today? In my view, in the US a likely answer can be found in the loss of opportunities for political impact and efficacy. In the face of the constraining of states to the demands and conditions of global markets, the dramatic decrease in union membership and increase in corporate salaries and benefits at the highest levels, and the shift in political parties from person-intensive to finance-intensive organization strategies, the political opportunities open to most Americans are either voting, which increasing numbers choose not to do, or giving money. Thus, it is not surprising that many might want to be more active and might feel that action online is a way of getting their voice heard, a way of making a contribution.

Indeed, interactive communications technology corporations rose to popularity in part on the message that they were tools for political empowerment. One might think of Ted Nelson, Stewart Brand, the People's Computer Company and their emancipatory images of computing technology. In the context of the San Francisco Bay Area's anti-war activism of the early seventies, they held up computers as the means to the renewal of participatory democracy. One might also think of the image projected by Apple Computers. Apple presented itself as changing the world, as saving democracy by bringing technology to the people. In 1984, Apple ran an ad for the Macintosh that placed an image of the computer next to one of Karl Marx. The slogan was, "It was about time a capitalist started a revolution." Finally, one might also recall the guarantees of citizens' access and the lure of town meetings for millions, the promises of democratization and education that drove Al Gore and Newt Gingrich's political rhetoric in the nineties as Congress worked through the Information and Infrastructure Technology Act, the National Information Infrastructure Act (both passing in 1993) and the 1996 Telecommunications Act. These bills made explicit a convergence of democracy and capitalism, a rhetorical convergence that the bills brought into material form. As the 1996 bill affirmed, "the market will drive both the Internet and the information highway" (Dyer-Witheford 1999: 34–5). In all these cases, what is driving the Net is the promise of political efficacy, of the enhancement of democracy through citizens' access and use of new communications technologies. But, the promise of participation is not simply propaganda. No, it is a deeper, underlying fantasy wherein technology functions as a fetish covering over our impotence and helping us understand ourselves as active. The working of such a fantasy is clear in discussions of the political impact of a new device, system, code or platform. A particular technological innovation becomes a screen upon which all sorts of fantasies of political action are projected.

We might think here of peer-to-peer file sharing, especially in light of the early rather hypnotic, mantra-like appeals to Napster. Napster—despite that fact that it was a commercial venture—was heralded as a sea change; it would transform private property, bring down capitalism. More than piracy, Napster was a popular attack on private property itself. Nick Dyer-Witheford, for example, argues that Napster, and other peer-to-peer networks, present "real possibilities of market disruption as a result of large-scale copyright violation." He contends:

> While some of these peer-to-peer networks—like Napster—were created as commercial applications, others—such as Free Net—were designed as political projects with the explicit intention of destroying both state censorship and commercial copyright. . . . The adoption of these celebratory systems as a central component of North American youth culture presents a grassroots expansion of the digital commons and, at

the very least, seriously problematizes current plans for their enclosure. (Dyer-Witheford 2004: 142)

Lost in the celebratory rhetoric is the fact that capitalism has never depended on one industry. Industries rise and fall. Corporations like Sony and Bertelsmann can face declines in one sector and still make astronomical profits in others. Joshua Gamson's point about the legacy of Internet-philia is appropriate here: wildly displaced enthusiasm over the political impact of a specific technological practice results in a tendency "to bracket institutions and ownership, to research and theorize uses and users of new media outside of those brackets, and to let 'newness' overshadow historical continuity" (Gamson 2003: 259). Worries about the loss of the beloved paperback book to unwieldy e-books weren't presented as dooming the publishing industry or assaulting the very regime of private property. Why should sharing music files be any different?

It shouldn't—and that is my point; Napster is a technological fetish onto which all sorts of fantasies of political action are projected. Here of course the fantasy is one deeply held by music fans: music can change the world. And, armed with networked personal computers, the weapons of choice for American college students in a not-so-radical oh-so-consumerist entertainment culture, the wired revolutionaries could think they were changing the world comforted all the while that nothing would really change (or, at best, they could get record companies to lower the prices on compact disks).

The technological fetish covers over and sustains a lack on the part of the subject. That is to say, it protects the fantasy of an active, engaged subject by acting in the subject's stead. The technological fetish "is political" for us, enabling us to go about the rest of our lives relieved of the guilt that we might not be doing our part and secure in the belief that we are after all informed, engaged citizens. The paradox of the technological fetish is that the technology acting in our stead actually enables us to remain politically passive. We don't have to assume political responsibility because, again, the technology is doing it for us.

The technological fetish also covers over a fundamental lack or absence in the social order. It protects a fantasy of unity, wholeness or order, compensating in advance for this impossibility. Differently put, technologies are invested with hopes and dreams, with aspirations to something better. A technological fetish is at work when one disavows the lack or fundamental antagonism forever rupturing (yet producing) the social by advocating a particular technological fix. The "fix" lets us think that all we need is to universalize a particular technology, and then we will have a democratic or reconciled social order.

Gamson's account of gay websites provides a compelling illustration of this fetish function. Gamson argues that in the US, the Internet has been a major force in transforming "gay and lesbian media from organizations answering at least partly to geographical and political communities into businesses answering primarily to advertisers and investors" (2003: 260). He focuses on gay portals and their promises to offer safe and friendly spaces for the gay community. What he notes, however, is the way that these safe gay spaces now function primarily "to deliver a market share to corporations." As he explains, "community needs are conflated with consumption desires, and community equated with market" (Ibid.: 270–1). Qua fetish, the portal is a screen upon which fantasies of connection can be projected. These fantasies displace attention from their commercial context.

Specifying more clearly the operation of the technological fetish will bring home the way new communications technologies reinforce communicative capitalism. I emphasize three operations: condensation, displacement and foreclosure.

The technological fetish operates through condensation. The complexities of politics—of organization, struggle, duration, decisiveness, division, representation, etc.—are condensed into one thing, one problem to be solved and one technological solution. So, the problem of democracy is that people aren't informed; they don't have the information they need to participate effectively. Bingo! Information technologies provide people with information. This sort of strategy, however, occludes the problems of organizing and political will. For example, in the United States—as Mary Graham explains in her study of the politics of disclosure in chemical emissions, food labeling and medical error policy—transparency started to function as a regulatory mechanism precisely at a time when legislative action seemed impossible. Agreeing that people had a right to know, politicians could argue for warning labels and more data while avoiding hard or unpopular decisions. Corporations could comply—and find ways to use their reports to improve their market position. "Companies often lobbied for national disclosure requirements," Graham writes. "They did so," she continues,

> because they believed that disclosure could reduce the chances of tougher regulation, eliminate the threat of multiple state requirements, or improve competitive advantage . . . Likewise, large food processing companies and most trade associations supported national nutritional labeling as an alternative to multiple state requirements and new regulations, or to a crackdown on health claims. Some also expected competitive gain from labeling as consumers, armed with accurate information, increased demand for authentically healthful productions. (Graham 2002: 140)

Additional examples of condensation appear when cybertheorists and activists emphasize singular websites, blogs and events. The MediaWhoresOnline blog might be celebrated as a location of critical commentary on mainstream and conservative journalism—but it is also so small that it doesn't show up on blog ranking sites like daypop or Technorati.

The second mode of operation of the technological fetish is through displacement. I've addressed this idea already in my description of Napster and the way that the technological fetish is political for us. But I want to expand this sense of displacement to account for tendencies in some theory writing to displace political energies elsewhere. Politics is displaced upon the activities of everyday or ordinary people—as if the writer and readers and academics and activists and, yes, even the politicians were somehow extraordinary. What the everyday people do in their everyday lives is supposed to overflow with political activity: conflicts, negotiations, interpretations, resistances, collusions, cabals, transgressions and resignifications. The Net—as well as cell phones, beepers and other communications devices (though, weirdly, not the regular old telephone)—is thus teeming with politics. To put up a website, to deface a website, to redirect hits to other sites, to deny access to a website, to link to a website—this is construed as real political action. In my view, this sort of emphasis displaces political energy from the hard work of organizing and struggle. It also remains oddly one-sided, conveniently forgetting both the larger media context of these activities, as if there were not and have not been left and progressive print publications and organizations for years, and the political context of networked communications—the Republican Party as well as all sorts of other conservative organizations and lobbyists use the Internet just as much, if not more, than progressive groups.

Writing on Many-2-Many, a group web log on social software, Clay Shirkey invokes a similar argument to explain Howard Dean's poor showing in the Iowa caucuses following what appeared to be his remarkable successes on the Internet. Shirkey writes:

> We know well from past attempts to use social software to organize groups for political change that it is hard, very hard, because participation in online communities often provides a sense of satisfaction that actually dampens a willingness to interact with the real world. When you're communing with like-minded souls, you feel [original emphasis] like you're accomplishing something by arguing out the smallest details of your perfect future world, while the imperfect and actual world takes no notice, as is its custom.

> There are many reasons for this, but the main one seems to be that the pleasures of life online are precisely the way they provide a respite from the vagaries of the real world. Both the way the online environment flattens interaction and the way everything gets arranged for the convenience of the user makes the threshold between talking about changing the world and changing the world even steeper than usual.[3] (Shirkey 2004)

This does not mean that web-based activities are trivial or that social software is useless. The Web provides an important medium for connecting and communicating and the Dean campaign was innovative in its use of social software to build a vital, supportive movement around Dean's candidacy. But, the pleasures of the medium should not displace our attention from the way that political change demands much, much more than networked communication and the way that the medium itself can and does provide a barrier against action on the ground. As the Dean campaign also demonstrates, without organized, mobilized action on the ground, without responses to and from caucus attendees in Iowa, for example, Internet politics remains precisely that—a politics of and through new media, and that's all.

The last operation of the technological fetish follows from the previous ones: foreclosure. As I have suggested, the political purchase of the technological fetish is given in advance; it is immediate, presumed, understood. File sharing is political. A website is political. Blogging is political. But this very immediacy rests on something else, on a prior exclusion. And, what is excluded is the possibility of politicization proper. Consider this breathless proclamation from Geert Lovink and Florian Schneider:

> The revolution of our age should come as no surprise. It has been announced for a long time. It is anticipated in the advantage of the open source idea over archaic terms of property. It is based on the steady decline of the traditional client–server architecture and the phenomenal rise of peer-to-peer technologies. It is practiced already on a daily basis: the overwhelming success of open standards, free software and file-sharing tools shows a glimpse of the triumph of a code that will transform knowledge-production into a world-writable mode. Today revolution means the wikification of the world; it means creating many different versions of worlds, which everyone can read, write, edit and execute. (Lovink and Schneider 2003; cf. King 2004)

Saying that "revolution means the wikification" of the world employs an illegitimate short circuit. More specifically, it relies on an ontologization such that the political nature of the world is produced by particular technological practices. Struggle, conflict and context vanish, immediately and magically. Or, they are foreclosed, eliminated in advance so as to create a space for the utopian celebration of open source.

To ontologize the political is to collapse the very symbolic space necessary for politicization, a space between an object and its representation, its ability to stand for something beyond itself. The power of the technological fetish stems from this foreclosure of the political. Bluntly put, a condition of possibility for asserting the immediately political character of something, web radio or open-source code, say, is not simply the disavowal of other political struggles; rather, it relies on the prior exclusion of the antagonistic conditions of emergence of web radio and open source, of their embeddedness within the brutalities of global capital, of their dependence for existence on racialized violence and division. Technologies can and should be politicized. They should be made to represent something beyond themselves in the service of a struggle against something beyond themselves. Only such a treatment will avoid fetishization.

The fantasy of wholeness: A global zero institution

Thus far I've discussed the foreclosure of the political in communicative capitalism in terms of the fantasy of abundance accompanying the reformatting of messages as contributions and the fantasy of participation accompanying the technology fetishism. These fantasies give people the sense that our actions online are politically significant, that they make a difference. I turn now to the fantasy of wholeness further animating networked communications. This fantasy furthers our sense that our contributions to circulating content matter by locating them in the most significant of possible spaces—the global. To be sure, I am not arguing that the world serves as a space for communicative capitalism analogous to the one the nation provided for industrial capitalism. On the contrary, my argument is that the space of communicative capitalism is the Internet and that networked communications materialize specific fantasies of unity and wholeness as the global. The fantasies in turn secure networked transactions as the Real of global capitalism.

To explain why, I draw from Žižek's elucidation of a concept introduced by Claude Lévi-Strauss, the zero institution (Žižek 2001: 221–3). A zero institution is an empty signifier. It has no determinate meaning but instead signifies the presence of meaning. It is an institution with no positive function—all it does is signify institutionality as such (as opposed to chaos, for example). As originally developed by Lévi-Strauss, the concept of the zero institution helps explain how people with radically different descriptions of their collectivity nevertheless understand themselves as members of the same tribe. To the Lévi-Straussian idea Žižek adds insight into how both the nation and sexual difference function as zero institutions. The nation designates the unity of society in the face of radical antagonism, the irreconcilable divisions and struggles between classes; sexual difference, in contrast, suggests difference as such, a zero level of absolute difference that will always be filled in and overdetermined by contextually given differences.

In light of the nation's failing capacity to stand symbolically for institutionality, the Internet has emerged as the zero institution of communicative capitalism. It enables myriad constituencies to understand themselves as part of the same global structure even as they radically disagree, fail to co-link, and inhabit fragmented and disconnected network spaces. The Internet is not a wide-open space, with nodes and links to nodes distributed in random fashion such that any one site is equally likely to get hits as any other site. This open, smooth, virtual world of endless and equal opportunity is a fantasy. In fact, as Albert-Laszlo Barabasi's research on directedness in scale-free networks makes clear, the World Wide Web is broken into four major "continents" with their own navigational requirements (Barabasi 2003: 161–78). Following links on one continent may never link a user to another continent; likewise, following links in one direction does not mean that a user can retrace links back to her starting point. So despite the fact that its very architecture (like all directed networks) entails fragmentation into separate spaces, the Internet presents itself as the unity and fullness of the global. Here the global is imagined and realized. More than a means through which communicative capitalism intensifies its hold and produces its world, the Internet functions as a particularly powerful zero institution insofar as it is animated by the fantasy of global unity.

The Internet provides an imaginary site of action and belonging. Celebrated for its freedoms and lack of boundaries, this imagined totality serves as a kind of presencing of the global. On the one hand the Internet imagines, stages and enacts the "global" of global capital. But on the other this global is nothing like the "world"—as if such an entity was possible, as if one could designate an objective reality undisturbed by the external perspective observing it or a fully consistent essential totality unruptured by antagonism (Žižek 2002: 181).

The oscillations in the 1990s debate over the character of the Internet can clarify this point. In the debate, Internet users appeared either as engaged citizens eager to participate in electronic town halls and regularly communicate with their elected representatives, or they appeared as web-surfing waste-of-lives in dark, dirty rooms downloading porn, betting on obscure Internet stocks or collecting evidence of the US government's work with extraterrestrials at Area 51 (Dean 1997). In other versions of this same matrix, users were either innocent children or dreadful war-game playing teenage boys. Good interactions were on Amazon. Bad interactions were underground and involved drugs, kiddie porn, LSD and plutonium. These familiar oscillations remind us that the Net has always been particular and that struggles over regulating the Internet have been struggles over what kind of particularity would and should be installed. Rather than multiply far-reaching, engaging and accessible, the Internet has been constituted in and through conflict over specific practices and subjectivities. Not everything goes.

We might even say that those who want to clean up the Internet, who want to get rid of or zone the porn and the gambling, who want to centralize, rationalize and organize commercial transactions in ways more beneficial to established corporations than to small, local businesses, express as a difference on the Internet what is actually the starker difference between societies traversed and mediated through electronic communications and financial networks and those more reliant on social, interpersonal and extra-legal networks. As Ernesto Laclau argues, the division between the social and the non-social, or between society and what is other to it, external and threatening, can only be expressed as a difference internal to society (Laclau 1996: 38). If capital today traverses the globe, how can the difference between us and them be expressed? The oscillations in the Internet debate suggest that the difference is between those who are sexualized, undisciplined, violent, irrational, lazy, excessive and extreme on the one hand, and those who are civilized, mainstream, hard-working, balanced and normal on the other. Put in psychoanalytic terms, the other on the Internet is the Real other—not the other I imagine as like me and not the symbolic other to be recognized and respected through abstract norms and rights. That the other is Real brings home the fact that the effort to clean up the Internet was more than a battle of images and involved more than gambling and porn. The image of the Internet works as a fantasy of a global unity. Whatever disrupts this unity cannot be part of the global.

The particularity of the fantasies of the global animating the Internet is striking. For example, Richard Rogers's research on linking practices on the World Wide Web brings out the Web's localism and provincialism. In his account of the Dutch food safety debate, Rogers notes "little in the way of 'web dialogue' or linkage outside of small Dutch 'food movement'" (Rogers 2002). Critics of personalized news as well as of the sheltered world of AOL click on a similar problem—the way the world on the Web is shrunken into a very specific image of the global (Patelis 2000). How would fringe culture fans of blogs on incunabula.org or ollapodrida.org come into contact with sites providing Koranic instruction to modern Muslims—even if there were no language problems? And, why would they bother? Why should they? Indeed, as a number of commentators have worried for a while now, opportunities to customize the news and announcements one reads—not to mention the already undigestible amount of information available on topics in which one is deeply interested—contribute to the segmentation and isolation of users within bubbles of opinions with which they already agree.

The particularity of these fantasies of the global is important because this is the global that networked communications produce. Our networked interactions produce our specific worlds as the global of global capital. They create the expectations and effects of communicative capitalism, expectations and effects that necessarily vary according to one's context.

And, precisely because the global is whatever specific communities or exchanges imagine it to be, anything outside the experience or comprehension of these communities either does not exist or is an inhuman, otherworldly alien threat that must be annihilated. So, if everything is out there on the Internet, anything I fail to encounter—or can't imagine encountering—isn't simply excluded (everything is already there), it is foreclosed. Admitting or accessing what is foreclosed destroys the very order produced through foreclosure. Thus, the imagined unity of the global, a fantasy filled in by the particularities of specific contexts, is one where there is no politics; there is already agreement. Circulating content can't effect change in this sort of world—it is already complete. The only alternative is the Real that ruptures my world, that is to say the evil other I cannot imagine sharing a world with. The very fantasy of a global that makes my networked interactions vital and important results in a world closed to politics on the one hand, and threatened by evil on the other.

Conclusion

A Lacanian commonplace is that a letter always arrives at its destination. What does this mean with respect to networked communications? It means that a letter, a message, in communicative capitalism is not really sent. There is no response because there is no arrival. There is just the contribution to circulating content.

Many readers will likely disagree. Some may say that the line I draw between politics as circulating content and politics as governance makes no sense. Dot.orgs, dot.coms, and dot.govs are all clearly interconnected and intertwined in their personnel, policies and positions. But, to the extent that they are interconnected, identifying any impact on these networks by critical opponents becomes all the more difficult.

Other readers might bring up the successes of MoveOn (www.moveon. org). From its early push to have Congress censure Bill Clinton and "move on," to its presence as a critical force against the Iraq war, to recent efforts to prevent George W. Bush from acquiring a second term, MoveOn has become a presence in mainstream American politics and boasts over two million members worldwide. In addition to circulating petitions and arranging e-mails and faxes to members of Congress, one of MoveOn's best actions was a virtual sit-in: over 200,000 of us called into Washington, DC at scheduled times on the same day, shutting down phone lines into the capital for hours. In early 2004, MoveOn sponsored an ad contest: the winning ad would be shown on a major television network during the Super Bowl football game. The ad was great—but CBS refused to broadcast it.

As I see it, far from being evidence against my argument, MoveOn exemplifies technology fetishism and confirms my account of the foreclosure of the political. MoveOn's campaigns director, Eli Pariser, says that the organization is "opt-in, it's decentralized, you do it from your home" (Boyd 2003: 14). No one has to remain committed or be bothered with boring meetings. Andrew Boyd, in a positive appraisal of the group, writes that "MoveOn's strength lies . . . in providing a home for busy people who may not want to be a part of a chapter-based organization with regular meetings . . . By combining a nimble entrepreneurial style with a strong ethic of listening to its members—via online postings and straw polls—MoveOn has built a responsive, populist and relatively democratic virtual community" (Ibid.: 16). Busy people can think they are active—the technology will act for them, alleviating their guilt while assuring them that nothing will change too much. The responsive, relatively democratic virtual community won't place too many (actually any) demands on them, fully aware that its democracy is the democracy of communicative capitalism—opinions will circulate, views will be expressed, information will be accessed. By sending an e-mail, signing a petition, responding to an article on a blog, people can feel political. And that feeling feeds communicative capitalism insofar as it leaves behind the time-consuming, incremental and risky efforts of politics. MoveOn likes to emphasize that it abstains from ideology, from division. While I find this disingenuous on the surface—MoveOn's politics are progressive, anti-war, left-democratic—this sort of non-position strikes me as precisely that disavowal of the political I've been describing: it is a refusal to take a stand, to venture into the dangerous terrain of politicization.

Perhaps one can find better reasons to disagree with me when one looks at alternative politics, that is when one focuses on the role of the Internet in mass mobilizations, in connecting activists from all over the world and in providing an independent media source. The February 15, 2003 mobilization of ten million people worldwide to protest the Bush administration's push against Iraq is perhaps the most striking example, but one might also mention MoveOn's March 16, 2003 candlelight vigil, an action involving over a million people in 130 countries. Such uses of the Internet are vitally important for political activists—especially given the increasingly all-pervasive reach of corporate-controlled media. Through them, activists establish social connections to one another—even if not to those outside their circles. But this does not answer the question of whether such instances of intense social meaning will drive larger organizational efforts and contribute to the formation of political solidarities with more duration. Thus, I remain convinced that the strongest argument for the political impact of new technologies proceeds in precisely the opposite direction, that is to say in the direction of post-politics. Even as globally networked communications provide tools and terrains of struggle, they make political change more difficult—and more necessary—than ever before. To this extent, politics in the sense of working to change current conditions may well require breaking with and through the fantasies attaching us to communicative capitalism.

Notes

1   A thorough historical analysis of the contribution would spell out the steps involved in the uncoupling of messages from responses. Such an analysis would draw out the ways that responses to the broadly cast messages of television programs were configured as attention and measured in terms of ratings. Nielsen families, in other words, responded for the rest of us. Yet, as work in cultural studies, media and communications has repeatedly emphasized, ratings are not responses and provide little insight into the actual responses of viewers. These actual responses, we can say, are uncoupled from the broadcast message and incorporated into other circuits of communication.
2   I am grateful to Drazen Pantic for sending me a link to this site.
3   Special thanks to Auke Towslager for this URL and many others on blogspace.

Works cited

Agamben, Giorgio. (2000), *Means Without End: Notes on Politics*, trans. by Vincenzo Binetti and Cesare Casarino, Minneapolis, MN: University of Minnesota Press.

Barabasi, Albert-László. (2003), *Linked: How Everything is Connected to Everything Else and What It Means*, New York: Plume.

Boyd, Andrew. (2003), "The Web Rewires the Movement," *The Nation* (August 4/11): 14.

Dean, Jodi. (1997), "Virtually Citizens," *Constellations* 4 (2) (October): 264–82.

—. (2002), *Publicity's Secret: How Technoculture Capitalizes on Democracy*, Ithaca, NY: Cornell University Press.

—. (2004), "The Networked Empire: Communicative Capitalism and the Hope for Politics," in Paul A. Passavant and Jodi Dean (eds), *Empire's New Clothes: Reading Hardt and Negri*, New York: Routledge, pp. 265–88.

Dyer-Witheford, Nick. (1999), *Cyber-Marx: Cycles and Circuits of Struggle in High Technology Capitalism*, Urbana, IL: University of Illinois Press.

—. (2004), "E-Capital and the Many-Headed Hydra," in Greg Elmer (ed.), *Critical Perspectives on the Internet*, Lanham, MD: Rowman & Littlefield.

Dyson, Esther. (1998), "The End of the Official Story," *Brill's Content* (July/August): 50–1.

Gamson, Joshua. (2003), "Gay Media, Inc.: Media Structures, the New Gay Conglomerates, and Collective Sexual Identities," in Martha McCaughey and Michael D. Ayers (eds), *Cyberactivism: Online Activism in Theory and Practice*, New York: Routledge.

Graham, Mary. (2002), *Democracy by Disclosure: The Rise of Technopopulism*, Washington, DC: The Brookings Institution.

Habermas, Jürgen. (1984), *The Theory of Communicative Action, Volume I: Reason and the Rationalization of Society*, trans. by Thomas McCarthy, Boston, MA: Beacon Press.

Hardt, Mihael and Negri, Antonio. (2000), *Empire*, Cambridge, MA: Harvard University Press.

King, Jamie. (2004), "The Packet Gang," *Mute* 27 (Winter/Spring), available at www.metamute.com.

Laclau, Ernesto. (1996), *Emancipations*, London: Verso.

Laclau, Ernesto and Mouffe, Chantel. (1986), *Hegemony and Socialist Strategy*, London: Verso.

Lovink, Geert and Schneider, Florian. (2003), "Reverse Engineering Freedom," available at http://www.makeworlds.org/?q=node/view/20

Matic, Veran and Pantic, Drazen. (1999), "War of Words," *The Nation* (November 29), available at http://www.thenation.com/doc.mhtml?i=19991129&s=matic

Patelis, Korianna. (2000), "E-Mediation by America Online," in Richard Rogers (ed.) *Preferred Placement: Knowledge Politics on the Web*, Maastricht: Jan van Eyck Academie, pp. 49–64.

Rogers, Richard. (2002), "The Issue has Left the Building," paper presented at the *Annual Meeting of the International Association of Internet Researchers*, Maastricht, the Netherlands, October 13–16.

Sassen, Saskia. (1996), *Losing Control?* New York: Columbia University Press.

Shirkey, Clay. (2003), "Power Laws, Weblogs, and Inequality," available at http://shirky.com/writings/powerlaw_weblog.html. First published February 8, 2003 on the "Networks, Economics, and Culture" mailing list.

—. (2004), "Is Social Software Bad for the Dean Campaign?" Many-2-Many, posted on January 26, available at http://www.corante.com/many/archives/2004/01/26/is_social_software_bad_for_the_dean_campaign.php.

Žižek, Slavoj. (1989), *The Sublime Object of Ideology*, London: Verso.

—. (1997), *The Plague of Fantasies*, London: Verso.

—. (1999), *The Ticklish Subject*, London: Verso.

—. (2001), *Enjoy Your Symptom* (second edition), New York: Routledge.

—. (2002), "Afterward: Lenin's Choice," in *Revolution at the Gates: Selected Writings of Lenin from 1917*, London: Verso.

CHAPTER THIRTY TWO

Ten Theses on Politics

Jacques Rancière

From Theory and Event *5 (3) (2001): 1–16.*

Thesis 1:[1]

Politics is not the exercise of power. Politics ought to be defined on its own terms, as a mode of acting put into practice by a specific kind of subject and deriving from a particular form of reason. It is the political relationship that allows one to think the possibility of a political subject(ivity) [*le sujet politique*],[2] not the other way around.

1   To identify politics with the exercise of, and struggle to possess, power is to do away with politics. But we also reduce the scope of politics as a mode of thinking if we conceive of it merely as a theory of power or as an investigation into the grounds of its legitimacy. If there is something specific about politics that makes it something other than a more capacious mode of grouping or a form of power characterized by its mode of legitimation, it is that it involves a distinctive kind of subject considered, and it involves this subject in the form of a mode of relation that is its own. This is what Aristotle means when, in Book I of the *Politics*, he distinguishes between political rule (as the ruling of equals) from all other kinds of rule; or when, in Book III, he defines the citizen as "he who partakes in the fact of ruling and the fact of being ruled." Everything about politics is contained in this specific relationship, this "*part-taking*" [*avoir-*

part],[3] which should be interrogated as to its meaning and as to its conditions of possibility.

2   An interrogation into what is "proper" to politics must be carefully distinguished from current and widespread propositions regarding "the return of the political." In the past several years, and in the context of a state consensus, we have seen the blossoming of affirmations proclaiming the end of the illusion of the social and a return to a "pure" form of politics. Read through either an Arendtian or Straussian lens, these affirmations focus on the same Aristotelian texts gestured to above. These readings generally identify the "proper" political order with that of the *eu zen* (i.e., a conception of the good) as opposed to a *zen* (conceived as an order of mere living). On this basis, the frontier between the domestic and the political becomes the frontier between the social and the political; and to the idea of a city-state defined by its common good is opposed the sad reality of modern democracy as the rule of the masses and of necessity. In practice, this celebration of pure politics entrusts the virtue of the "political good" to governmental oligarchies enlightened by "experts;" which is to say that the supposed purification of the political, freed from domestic and social necessity, comes down to nothing more (or less) than the reduction of the political to the state [*l'étatique*].

3   Behind the current buffooneries of the "returns of the political" (that include "the return of political philosophy"), it is important to recognize the vicious circle that characterizes political philosophy; a vicious circle located in the link between the political relationship and the political subject. This vicious circle posits a way of life that is "proper" to politics. The political relationship is subsequently deduced from the properties of this specific order of being and is explained in terms of the existence of a character which possesses a good or a specific universality, as opposed to the private or domestic world of needs or interests. In short, politics is explained as the accomplishment of a way of life that is proper to those who are destined for it. This partition—which is actually the object of politics—is posited as its basis.

4   What is proper to politics is thus lost at the outset if politics is thought of as a specific way of living. Politics cannot be defined on the basis of any preexisting subject. The political "difference" that makes it possible to think its subject must be sought in the form of its relation. If we return to the Aristotelian definition, there is a name given to the subject (*politès*) that is defined by a *part-taking* (*metexis*) in a form of action (*archein*—ruling) and in the undergoing that corresponds to this doing (*archesthai*—being

ruled). If there is something "proper" to politics, it consists entirely in this relationship which is not a relationship between subjects, but one between two contradictory terms through which a subject is defined. Politics disappears the moment you undo this knot of a subject and a relation. This is what happens in all fictions, be they speculative or empiricist, that seek the origin of the political relationship in the properties of its subjects and in the conditions of their coming together. The traditional question "For what reasons do human beings gather into political communities?" is always already a response, and one that causes the disappearance of the object it claims to explain or to ground—i.e., the form of a political part-taking that then disappears in the play of elements or atoms of sociability.

Thesis 2:

That is proper to politics is the existence of a subject defined by its participation in contrarieties. Politics is a paradoxical form of action.

5   The formulations according to which politics is the ruling of equals, and the citizen is the one who *part-takes* in ruling and being ruled, articulate a paradox that must be thought through rigorously. It is important to set aside banal representations of the *doxa* of parliamentary systems that invoke the reciprocity of rights and duties in order to understand what is extraordinary in the Aristotelian articulation. This formulation speaks to us of a being who is at once the agent of an action and the one upon whom the action is exercised.[4] It contradicts the conventional "cause-and-effect" model of action that has it that an agent endowed with a specific capacity produces an effect upon an object that is, in turn, characterized by its aptitude for receiving that effect.

6   This problem is in no way resolved by reverting to the classic opposition between two modes of action: *poiesis*, on the one hand, governed by the model of fabrication that gives form to matter; and *praxis*, on the other, which excludes from this relation the "inter-being" [*l'inter*-être][5] of people devoted to politics. As we know, this opposition—replacing that of *zen* and *eu* zen—sustains a conception of political purity. In Hannah Arendt's work, for instance, the order of *praxis* is that of equals with the power of *archein*, conceived of as the power to begin anew: "To act, in its most general sense," she explains in *The Human Condition*, "means to take an initiative, to begin (as the Greek word *archein*, 'to begin,' 'to lead,' and eventually 'to rule' indicates);" she concludes this thought by subsequently linking *archein* to "the

principle of freedom."[6] Once Arendt defines both a proper mode and sphere of action, a vertiginous shortcut is formed that allows one to posit a series of equations between "beginning," "ruling," "being free," and living in a city-state ("To be free and to live in a *polis* is the same thing" as the same text puts it).

7   This series of equations finds its equivalent in the movement that engenders civic equality from the community of Homeric heroes; equals, that is, in their participation in the power of *arche*. The first witness against this Homeric idyllic, however, is Homer himself. Against the garrulous Thersites—the man who is an able public speaker despite the fact that he is not qualified to speak— Odysseus recalls the fact that the Greek army has one and only one chief: Agamemnon. He reminds us of what *archein* means: to walk at the head. And, if there is one who walks at the head, the others must necessarily walk behind. The line between the power of *archein* (i.e., the power to rule), freedom, and the *polis*, is not straight but severed. In order to convince oneself of this, it is enough to see the manner in which Aristotle characterizes the three possible classes of rule within a *polis*, each one possessing a particular title: "virtue" for the *aristoi*, "wealth" for the *oligoi*, and "freedom" for the *demos*. In this division, "freedom" appears as the paradoxical part of the *demos* about whom the Homeric hero tells us (in no uncertain terms) that it had only one thing to do: to keep quiet and bow down.

8   In short, the opposition between *praxis* and *poiesis* in no way resolves the paradoxical definition of the *politès*. As far as *arche* is concerned, as with everything else, the conventional logic has it that there is a particular disposition to act that is exercised upon a particular disposition to "be acted upon." Thus the logic of *arche* presupposes a determinate superiority exercised upon an equally determinate inferiority. In order for there to be a political subject(ivity), and thus for there to be politics, there must be a rupture in this logic.

Thesis 3:

Politics is a specific rupture in the logic of *arche*. It does not simply presuppose the rupture of the "normal" distribution of positions between the one who exercises power and the one subject to it. It also requires a rupture in the idea that there are dispositions "proper" to such classifications.

9   In Book III of the *Laws*, Plato devotes himself to a systematic inventory of the qualifications (*axiomata*) for ruling, along with

certain correlative qualifications for being ruled. Out of the seven he retains, four are traditional qualifications of authority based on a natural difference; that is, the difference in birth. Those qualified to rule are those "born before" or "born otherwise." This grounds the power of parents over children, old over young, masters over slaves, and nobles over serfs. The fifth qualification is introduced as the principal principle that summarizes all natural differences: It is the power of those with a superior nature, of the stronger over the weak—a power that has the unfortunate quality, discussed at length in the *Gorgias*, of being indeterminate. The sixth qualification, then, gives the only difference that counts for Plato; namely, the power of those who know [*savoir*] over those who do not. There are thus four couplings of traditional qualifications to be had, along with two theoretical couplings that claim priority over them: namely, "natural" superiority and the rule of "science" *qua* knowledge.

10　The list ought to stop there. But there is a seventh qualification: "the choice of god," otherwise referring to a drawing of lots [*le tirage au sort*] that designates the one who exercises *arche*. Plato does not expand upon this. But clearly, this kind of "choice" points ironically to the designation by god of a regime previously referred to as one only god could save: namely, democracy. What thus characterizes a democracy is pure chance or the complete absence of qualifications for governing. Democracy is that state of exception where no oppositions can function, where there is no pre-determined principle of role allocation. "To partake in ruling and being ruled" is quite a different matter from reciprocity. It is, in short, an absence of reciprocity that constitutes the exceptional essence of this relationship; and this absence of reciprocity rests on the paradox of a qualification that is absence of qualification. Democracy is the specific situation in which there is an absence of qualifications that, in turn, becomes the qualification for the exercise of a democratic *arche*. What is destroyed in this logic is the particular quality of *arche*, its redoubling, which means that it always precedes itself within a circle of its own disposition and its own exercise. But this exceptional state is identical with the very condition for the specificity of politics more generally.

Thesis 4:

Democracy is not a political regime. Insofar as it is a rupture in the logic of *arche*—that is, in the anticipation of rule in the disposition for it—democracy is *the* regime of politics in the form of a relationship defining a specific subject.

11   What makes possible the *metexis* proper to politics is the rupture
     of all those logics of allocation exercised in the partaking of *arche*.
     The "freedom" of a people that constitutes the *axiom* of democracy
     has as its real content the rupture of the axioms of domination: a
     rupture, that is, in the correlation between a capacity for rule and
     a capacity for being ruled. The citizen who partakes "in ruling and
     being ruled" is only thinkable on the basis of the *demos* as a figure
     that ruptures the correspondence between a series of correlated
     capacities. Democracy is thus precisely not a political regime in the
     sense of a particular constitution that determines different ways of
     assembling people under a common authority. Democracy is *the*
     institution of politics—the institution of both its subject and its
     mode of relating.

12   As we know, democracy is a term invented by its opponents, by
     all those who were "qualified" to govern because of seniority,
     birth, wealth, virtue, and knowledge [*savoir*]. Using it as a term of
     derision, they articulated an unprecedented reversal of the order
     of things: the "power of the *demos*" means that those who rule
     are those who have no specificity in common, apart from their
     having no qualification for governing. Before being the name of
     a community, *demos* is the name of a part of the community:
     namely, the poor. The "poor," however, does not designate an
     economically disadvantaged part of the population; it simply
     designates the category of peoples who do not count, those who
     have no qualifications to part-take in *arche*, no qualification for
     being taken into account.

13   This is exactly what Homer describes in the Thersites episode
     evoked above. Those who want to speak, though they belong to
     the *demos*, though they belong to the undifferentiated collection of
     the "unaccounted for" [*l'hors-compte*] (*anarithmoi*), get stabbed
     in the back by Odysseus's scepter. This is not a deduction but a
     definition: The one who is "unaccounted for," the one who has no
     speech to be heard, is the one of the *demos*. A remarkable passage
     from Book XII of the Odyssey illustrates this point: Polydamas
     complains because his opinion has been disregarded by Hector.
     With you, he says, "one never has the right to speak if one belongs
     to the *demos*." Now Polydamas is not a villain like Thersites; he is
     Hector's brother. *Demos* thus does not designate a socially inferior
     category: The one who speaks when s/he is not to speak, the one
     who part-takes in what s/he has no part in—that person belongs
     to the *demos*.

Thesis 5:

The "people" that is the subject of democracy—and thus the principal subject of politics—is not the collection of members in a community, or the laboring classes of the population. It is the supplementary part, in relation to any counting of parts of the population that makes it possible to identify "the part of those who have no-part" [*le compte des incomptés*][7] with the whole of the community.

14   The people (*demos*) exists only as a rupture of the logic of *arche*, a rupture of the logic of beginning/ruling [*commencement/ commandement*]. It should not be identified either with the race of those who recognize each other as having the same origin, the same birth, or with a part of a population or even the sum of its parts. "People" [*peuple*] refers to the supplement that disconnects the population from itself, by suspending the various logics of legitimate domination. This disjunction is illustrated particularly well in the crucial reforms that give Athenian democracy its proper status; namely, those reforms enacted by Cleisthenes when he rearranged the distribution of the demes[8] over the territory of the city. In constituting each tribe by the addition of three separate boundaries—one from the city, one from the coast, and one from the countryside—Cleisthenes broke with the ancient principle that kept the tribes under the rule of local aristocratic chieftainships whose power, legitimated through legendary birth, had as its real content the economic power of the landowners. In short, the "people" is an artifice set at an angle from the logic that gives the principle of wealth as heir to the principle of birth. It is an abstract supplement in relation to any actual (ac)count of the parts of the population, of their qualifications for part-taking in the community, and of the common shares due to them according to these qualifications. The "people" is the supplement that inscribes "the count of the unaccounted for" or "the part of those who have no-part."

15   These expressions should not be understood in their more populist sense but rather in a structural sense. It is not the laboring and suffering populace that comes to occupy the terrain of political action and to identify its name with that of the community. What is identified by democracy with the role of the community is an empty, supplementary, part that separates the community from the sum of the parts of the social body. This separation, in turn, grounds politics in the action of supplementary subjects that are a surplus in relation to any (ac)count of the parts of society. The whole question of politics thus lies in the interpretation of this void. The criticisms that sought to discredit democracy brought

the "nothing" which constitutes the political people back to the overflow of the ignorant masses and the greedy populace. The interpretation of democracy posed by Claude Lefort gave the democratic void its structural meaning.[9] But the theory of the structural void can be interpreted in two distinct ways: First, the structural void refers to *an-archy*, to the absence of an entitlement to rule that constitutes the very nature of the political space; Secondly, the void is caused by the "disincorporation" of the king's two bodies—the human and divine body.[10] Democracy, according to this latter view, begins with the murder of the king; in other words, with a collapse of the symbolic thereby producing a disincorporated social presence. And this originary link is posed as the equivalent of an original temptation to imaginatively reconstruct the "glorious body of the people" that is heir to the immortal body of the king and the basis of every totalitarianism.

16   Against these interpretations, let us say that the two-fold body of the people is not a modern consequence of the sacrifice of the sovereign body but rather a given constitutive of politics. It is initially the people, and not the king, that has a double body and this duality is nothing other than the supplement through which politics exists: a supplement to all social (ac)counts and an exception to all logics of domination.

17   The seventh qualification, Plato says, is "god's part." We will maintain that this part belonging to god—this qualification of those who have no qualification—contains within it all that is theological in politics. The contemporary emphasis on the theme of the "theologico-political" dissolves the question of politics into that of power and of the grounding event that is its fundamental. It redoubles the liberal fiction of the contract with the representation of an original sacrifice. But the division of *arche* that conjoins politics and democracy is not a founding sacrifice: It is, rather, a neutralization of any founding sacrifice. This neutralization could find its exact fable at the end of *Oedipus at Colonus*: it is at the price of the disappearance of the sacrificial body, at the price of not seeking Oedipus's body, that Athenian democracy receives the benefit of its burial. To want to disinter the body is not only to associate the democratic form with a scenario of sin or of original malediction. More radically, it is to return the logic of politics to the question of an originary scene of power; in other words, to return politics to the state. By interpreting the empty part in terms of psychosis, the dramaturgy of original symbolic catastrophe transforms the political exception into a sacrificial symptom of democracy: It subsumes the litigiousness proper to politics under any of the innumerable versions of an originary "crime" or "murder."

Thesis 6:

If politics is the outline of a vanishing difference, with the distribution of social parts and shares, then it follows that its existence is in no way necessary, but that it occurs as a provisional accident in the history of the forms of domination. It also follows from this that political litigiousness has as its essential object the very existence of politics.

18 Politics cannot be deduced from the necessity of gathering people into communities. It is an exception to the principles according to which this gathering operates. The "normal" order of things is that human communities gather together under the rule of those qualified to rule—whose qualifications are legitimated by the very fact that they are ruling. These governmental qualifications may be summed up according to two central principles: The first refers society to the order of filiation, both human and divine. This is the power of birth. The second refers society to the vital principle of its activities. This is the power of wealth. Thus, the "normal" evolution of society comes to us in the progression from a government of birth to a government of wealth. Politics exists as a deviation from this normal order of things. It is this anomaly that is expressed in the nature of political subjects who are not social groups but rather forms of inscription of "the (ac)count of the unaccounted for."

19 There is politics as long as "the people" is not identified with the race or a population, inasmuch as the poor are not equated with a particular disadvantaged sector, and as long as the proletariat is not a group of industrial workers, etc. Rather, there is politics inasmuch as "the people" refers to subjects inscribed as a supplement to the count of the parts of society, a specific figure of "the part of those who have no-part." Whether this part exists is *the* political issue and it is the object of political litigation. Political struggle is not a conflict between well defined interest groups; it is an opposition of logics that count the parties and parts of the community in different ways. The clash between the "rich" and the "poor," for instance, is the struggle over the very possibility of these words being coupled, of their being able to institute categories for another (ac)counting of the community. There are two ways of counting the parts of the community: The first only counts empirical parts—actual groups defined by differences in birth, by different functions, locations, and interests that constitute the social body. The second counts "in addition" a part of the no-part. We will call the first *police* and the second *politics*.

Thesis 7:

> Politics is specifically opposed to the police. The police is a "partition of the sensible" [*le partage du sensible*] whose principle is the absence of a void and of a supplement.

20   The police is not a social function but a symbolic constitution of the social. The essence of the police is neither repression nor even control over the living. Its essence is a certain manner of partitioning the sensible. We will call "partition of the sensible" a general law that defines the forms of part-taking by first defining the modes of perception in which they are inscribed. The partition of the sensible is the cutting up of the world and of "world;" it is the *nemeïn* upon which the *nomoi* of the community are founded. This partition should be understood in the double sense of the word: on the one hand, that which separates and excludes; on the other, that which allows participation (see note 2). A partition of the sensible refers to the manner in which a relation between a shared "common" [*un commun partagé*] and the distribution of exclusive parts is determined through the sensible. This latter form of distribution, in turn, itself presupposes a partition between what is visible and what is not, of what can be heard from the inaudible.

21   The essence of the police is to be a partition of the sensible characterized by the absence of a void or a supplement: society consists of groups dedicated to specific modes of action, in places where these occupations are exercised, in modes of being corresponding to these occupations and these places. In this fittingness of functions, places, and ways of being, there is no place for a void. It is this exclusion of what "there is not" that is the police principle at the heart of statist practices. The essence of politics, then, is to disturb this arrangement by supplementing it with a part of the no-part identified with the community as a whole. Political litigiousness/struggle is that which brings politics into being by separating it from the police that is, in turn, always attempting its disappearance either by crudely denying it, or by subsuming that logic to its own. Politics is first and foremost an intervention upon the visible and the sayable.

Thesis 8:

> The principal function of politics is the configuration of its proper space. It is to disclose the world of its subjects and its operations. The essence of politics is the manifestation of dissensus, as the presence of two worlds in one.[11]

22 Let us begin from an empirical given: police intervention in public spaces does not consist primarily in the interpellation of demonstrators, but in the breaking up of demonstrations. The police is not that law interpellating individuals (as in Althusser's "Hey, you there!") unless one confuses it with religious subjectification.[12] It is, first of all, a reminder of the obviousness of what there is, or rather, of what there isn't: "Move along! There is nothing to see here!" The police says that there is nothing to see on a road, that there is nothing to do but move along. It asserts that the space of circulating is nothing other than the space of circulation. Politics, in contrast, consists in transforming this space of "moving along" into a space for the appearance of a subject: i.e., the people, the workers, the citizens: It consists in refiguring the space, of what there is to do there, what is to be seen or named therein. It is the established litigation of the perceptible, on the *nemeïn* that founds any communal *nomos*.

23 This partition constituting politics is never given in the form of a lot, of a kind of property that obliges or compels politics. These properties are litigious as much in their understanding as in their extension. Exemplary in this regard are those properties that, for Aristotle, define a political ability or are intended for "the good life." Apparently nothing could be clearer than the distinction made by Aristotle in Book I of the *Politics*: the sign of the political nature of humans is constituted by their possession of the *logos*, the articulate language appropriate for manifesting a community in the aisthesis of the just and the unjust, as opposed to the animal *phone*, appropriate only for expressing the feelings of pleasure and displeasure. If you are in the presence of an animal possessing the ability of the articulate language and its power of manifestation, you know you are dealing with a human and therefore with a political animal. The only practical difficulty is in knowing which sign is required to recognize the sign; that is, how one can be sure that the human animal mouthing a noise in front of you is actually voicing an utterance rather than merely expressing a state of being? If there is someone you do not wish to recognize as a political being, you begin by not seeing them as the bearers of politicalness, by not understanding what they say, by not hearing that it is an utterance coming out of their mouths. And the same goes for the opposition so readily invoked between the obscurity of domestic and private life, and the radiant luminosity of the public life of equals. In order to refuse the title of political subjects to a category—workers, women, etc.—it has traditionally been sufficient to assert that they belong to a "domestic" space, to a space separated from public life; one from which only groans or

cries expressing suffering, hunger, or anger could emerge, but not actual speeches demonstrating a shared *aisthesis*. And the politics of these categories has always consisted in requalifying these places, in getting them to be seen as the spaces of a community, of getting themselves to be seen or heard as speaking subjects (if only in the form of litigation); in short, participants in a common *aisthesis*. It has consisted in making what was unseen visible; in getting what was only audible as noise to be heard as speech; in demonstrating to be a feeling of shared "good" or "evil" what had appeared merely as an expression of pleasure or pain.

24   The essence of politics is *dissensus*. Dissensus is not the confrontation between interests and opinions. It is the manifestation of a distance of the sensible from itself. Politics makes visible that which had no reason to be seen, it lodges one world into another (for instance, the world where the factory is a public space within the one where it is considered a private one, the world where workers speak out vis-à-vis the one where their voices are merely cries expressing pain). This is precisely why politics cannot be identified with the model of communicative action since this model presupposes the partners in communicative exchange to be preconstituted, and that the discursive forms of exchange imply a speech community whose constraint is always explicable. In contrast, the particular feature of political dissensus is that the partners are no more constituted than is the object or the very scene of discussion. The ones making visible the fact that they belong to a shared world the other does not see—cannot take advantage of—the logic implicit to a pragmatics of communication. The worker who argues for the public nature of a "domestic" matter (such as a salary dispute) must indicate the world in which his argument counts as an argument and must demonstrate it as such for those who do not possess a frame of reference to conceive of it as argument. Political argument is at one and the same time the *demonstration* of a possible world where the argument could count as argument, addressed by a subject qualified to argue, upon an identified object, to an addressee who is required to see the object and to hear the argument that he or she "normally" has no reason to either see or hear. It is the construction of a paradoxical world that relates two separate worlds.

25   Politics thus has no "proper" place nor does it possess any "natural" subjects. A demonstration is political not because it takes place in a specific locale and bears upon a particular object but rather because its form is that of a clash between two partitions of the sensible. A political subject is not a group of interests or ideas: It is

the operator of a particular mode of subjectification and litigation through which politics has its existence. Political demonstrations are thus always of the moment and their subjects are always provisional. Political difference is always on the shore of its own disappearance: the people are close to sinking into the sea of the population or of race, the proletariat borders on being confused with workers defending their interests, the space of a people's public demonstration is always at risk of being confused with the merchant's *agora*, etc.

26 The deduction of politics from a specific world of equals or free people, as opposed to another world lived out of necessity, takes as its ground precisely the object of its litigation. It thus renders compulsory a blindness to those who "do not see" and have no place from which to be seen. Exemplary, in this regard, is a passage from Arendt's *On Revolution* discussing the manner in which John Adams identifies the unhappiness of the poor with the fact of "not being seen."[13] Such an identification, she comments, could itself only emanate from a man belonging to a privileged community of equals. And, by the same token, it could "hardly be understood" by the people comprising the relevant categories. We could express amazement at the extraordinary deafness of this affirmation in the face of the multiplicity of discourses and demonstrations of the "poor" concerning precisely their mode of visibility. But this deafness has nothing accidental about it. It forms a circle with the acceptance of an original partition, a founding politics, with what was in fact the permanent object of litigation constituting politics. It forms a circle with the definition of *homo laborans* as a partition of the "ways of life." This circle is not that of any particular theoretician; it is *the* circle of "political philosophy."

Thesis 9:

Inasmuch as what is proper to "political philosophy" is to ground political action in a specific mode of being, so is it the case that "political philosophy" effaces the litigiousness constitutive of politics. It is in its very description of the world of politics that philosophy effects this effacement. Moreover, its effectiveness is perpetuated through to the nonphilosophical or antiphilosophical description of the world.

27 That the distinguishing feature of politics is the existence of a subject who "rules" by the very fact of having no qualifications to rule; that the principle of beginnings/ruling is irremediably

divided as a result of this, and that the political community is specifically a litigious community—this is the "political secret" that philosophy first encounters. If we can speak of the privileged stature of the "Ancients" over the "Moderns," it is a consequence of their having first perceived this "secret" and not of having been the first to oppose the community of the "good" to that of the "useful." At the head of the anodyne expression "political philosophy" one finds the violent encounter between philosophy and the exception to the law of *arche* proper to politics, along with philosophy's effort to resituate politics under the auspices of this law. The *Gorgias*, the *Republic*, the *Politics*, the *Laws*, all these texts reveal the same effort to efface the paradox or scandal of a "seventh qualification"—to make of democracy a simple case of the indeterminable principle of "the government of the strongest," against which one can only oppose a government of those who know [*les savants*]. These texts all reveal a similar strategy of placing the community under a unique law of partition and expelling the empty part of the *demos* from the communal body.

28   But this expulsion does not simply take place in the form of the opposition between the "good" regime of the community that is both one and hierarchised according to its principle of unity, and the "bad" regimes of division and disorder. It takes place within the very presupposition that identifies a political form with a way of life; and this presupposition is already operating in the procedures for describing "bad" regimes, and democracy in particular. All of politics, as we have said, is played out in the interpretation of democratic "anarchy." In identifying it with the dispersal of the desires of democratic man, Plato transforms the form of politics into a mode of existence and, further, transforms the void into an overflow. Before being the theorist of the "ideal" or "enclosed" city-state, Plato is the founder of the anthropological conception of the political, the conception that identifies politics with the deployment of the properties of a type of man or a mode of life. This kind of "man," this "way of being," this form of the city-state: it is there, before any discourse on the laws or the educational methods of the ideal state, before even the partition of the classes of the community, the partition of the perceptible that cancels out political singularity.

29   The initial gesture of political philosophy thus has a two-fold consequence: On the one hand, Plato found a community that is the effectuation of a principle of unity, of an undivided principle—a community strictly defined as a common body with its places and functions and with its forms of interiorisation of

the common. He found an archipolitics[14] based on a law of unity between the "occupations" of the city-state and its "ethos," (in other words its way of inhabiting an abode), as law but also as the specific "tone" according to which this ethos reveals itself. This ethology of the community once again makes politics and police indistinguishable. And political philosophy, inasmuch as it wants to give to the community a single foundation, is condemned to have to reidentify politics and police, to cancel out politics through the gesture that founds it.

30   But Plato also invents a "concrete" mode for describing the production of political forms. In a word, he invents the very forms of the refusal of the "ideal state," the settled forms of opposition between philosophical "*a-prior-ism*" and concrete sociological or political-scientific analyses of the forms of politics as expressions of ways of life. This second legacy is more profound and more long lasting than the first. The sociology of the political is the second resource—the *deuteron plous*—of political philosophy that accomplishes (sometimes against itself) its fundamental project: to found the community on the basis of a univocal partition of the sensible. In particular, de Tocqueville's analysis of democracy, whose innumerable variants and ersatz versions feed the discourses on modern democracy, the age of the masses, the mass individual, etc., fits into the continuity of the theoretical gesture that cancels out the structural singularity of "the qualification without qualifications" and the "part of the no-part," by redescribing democracy as a social phenomenon, of the collective effectuation of the properties of a type of man.

31   Inversely, the claims for the purity of the *bios politikos* (of the republican constitution and of the community versus the individual or democratic mass, and the opposition between the political and the social) share in the effectiveness of the same knot between the *a-prior-ism* of the "republican" refounding, and the sociological description of democracy. No matter which side one rests on, the opposition between the "political" and the "social" is a matter defined entirely within the frame of "political philosophy;" in other words, it is a matter that lies at the heart of the philosophical repression of politics. The current proclamations of a "return to politics" and "political philosophy" are an imitation of the originary gesture of "political philosophy," without actually grasping the principles or issues involved in it. In this sense, it is the radical forgetting of politics and of the tense relationship between politics and philosophy. The sociological theme of the "end of politics" in postmodern society and the "politico" theme

of the "return of politics" both derive from the initial double
gesture of "political philosophy" and both move towards the same
forgetting of politics.

Thesis 10:

The "end of politics" and the "return of politics" are two complementary
ways of canceling out politics in the simple relationship between a state
of the social and a state of statist apparatuses. "Consensus" is the vulgar
name given to this cancellation.

32   The essence of politics resides in the modes of dissensual
     subjectification that reveal the difference of a society to itself. The
     essence of consensus is not peaceful discussion and reasonable
     agreement as opposed to conflict or violence. Its essence is the
     annulment of dissensus as the separation of the sensible from itself,
     the annulment of surplus subjects, the reduction of the people
     to the sum of the parts of the social body, and of the political
     community to the relationship of interests and aspirations of
     these different parts. Consensus is the reduction of politics to
     the police. In other words, it is the "end of politics" and not the
     accomplishment of its ends but, simply, the return of the "normal"
     state of things which is that of politics' nonexistence. The "end of
     politics" is the ever-present shore of politics [*le bord de la politique*]
     that, in turn, is an activity of the moment and always provisional.
     "Return of politics" and "end of politics" are two symmetrical
     interpretations producing the same effect: to efface the very concept
     of politics, and the precariousness that is one of its essential
     elements. In proclaiming the end of usurpations of the social and
     the return to "pure" politics, the "return of politics" thesis simply
     occludes the fact that the "social" is in no way a particular sphere
     of existence but, rather, a disputed object of politics. Therefore, the
     subsequently proclaimed end of the social is, simply put, the end of
     political litigation regarding the partition of worlds. The "return
     of politics" is thus the affirmation that there is a specific place for
     politics. Isolated in this manner, this specific space can be nothing
     other than the place of the state and, in fact, the theorists of the
     "return of politics" ultimately affirm that politics is outdated. They
     identify it with the practices of state control which have, as their
     principal principle, the suppression of politics.

33   The sociological thesis of the "end of politics" symmetrically
     posits the existence of a state of the social such that politics
     no longer has a necessary *raison-d'être*; whether or not it has
     accomplished its ends by bringing into being precisely this state

(i.e., the exoteric American Hegelian-Fukayama-ist version) or whether its forms are no longer adapted to the fluidity and artificiality of present-day economic and social relations (i.e., the esoteric European Heideggerian-Situationist version). The thesis thus amounts to asserting that the logical telos of capitalism makes it so that politics becomes, once again, out dated. And then it concludes with either the mourning of politics before the triumph of an immaterial Leviathan, or its transformation into forms that are broken up, segmented, cybernetic, ludic, etc.—adapted to those forms of the social that correspond to the highest stage of capitalism. It thus fails to recognize that in actual fact, politics has no reason for being in any state of the social and that the contradiction of the two logics is an unchanging given that defines the contingency and precariousness proper to politics. Via a Marxist detour, the "end of politics" thesis—along with the consensualist thesis—grounds politics in a particular mode of life that identifies the political community with the social body, subsequently identifying political practice with state practice. The debate between the philosophers of the "return of politics" and the sociologists of the "end of politics" is thus a straightforward debate regarding the order in which it is appropriate to take the presuppositions of "political philosophy" so as to interpret the consensualist practice of annihilating politics.

Notes

1 The original translation of the "Ten Theses" was done by Rachel Bowlby. However, some phrases were modified by Davide Panagia in consultation with Jacques Rancière. Terms in square brackets are Rancière's original French expressions.
2 Our English "political subject(ivity)" does not give an adequate sense of Rancière's "le sujet politique," a term that refers both to the idea of a political subjectivity and to the "proper" subject of politics.
3 Rancière plays on the double meaning of the *avoir-part* as both a "partaking" and a "partition."
4 The reference is to Arendt's claim that "the human capacity for freedom, which, by producing the web of human relationships, seems to entangle its producer to such an extent that he appears much more the victim and the sufferer than the author and the doer of what he has done" (*The Human Condition*, pp. 233–234; Chicago: The University of Chicago Press, 1989).
5 The word-play, here, is on the idea of an "*inter-est*" referring both to a principle of inter-relating and to the idea of societal "interest." Rancière is invoking an Arendtian distinction found in her *The Human Condition* (see pages 50–58).

6   Hannah Arendt, *The Human Condition*, p. 177.

7   Though the literal translation of the French is "the count of the unaccounted-for" the formulation found in the English translation of *Dis-agreement: Politics and Philosophy*, (Julie Rose trans., Minneapolis: University of Minnesota Press, 1999) is retained for the sake of consistency.

8   Demes were townships or divisions of ancient Attica. In modern Greece the term refers to communes.

9   See *Democracy and Political Theory* (Minneapolis: University of Minnesota Press, 1988) especially Part IV: "On the Irreducible Element."

10 Rancière is invoking Ernst Kantorowicz's work on medieval political theology, also present in Lefort's study.

11 Rancière's conception of dissensus counts as an instance of the paradox of the "one and the many" characteristic of democratic politics.

12 Rancière here refers to Althusser's "Ideology and Ideological State Apparatuses" (see *Lenin and Philosophy*, New York: Monthly Review Press, 1971).

13 See Arendt's chapter entitled "The Social Question" from *On Revolution*; especially pages 68–71 (New York: Penguin Books, 1990).

14 See Rancière's *Dis-agreement* (Chapter 4) for an extended discussion of this concept.

CHAPTER THIRTY THREE

A Contradiction between Matter and Form

Claus Peter Ortlieb

From "A Contradiction between Matter and Form: On the Significance of the Production of Relative Surplus Value for the Dynamics of the Final Crisis," in Marxism and the Critique of Value, *ed. Neil Larsen, Mathias Nilges, Josh Robinson, and Nicholas Brown Chicago and Alberta: MCM', 2014: 71–113.*

. . .

The inner compulsion toward growth, the historical expansion of capital, and the material limits thereof

In a society oriented solely toward material wealth—a society that merely by virtue of that fact would not be capitalist—growth in productivity would only cause a few problems, which could easily be solved technically and could unburden human life, leading to a reduction of labor but nonetheless to an increase in the number of useful goods. This is also precisely the way that the blessings of growing productivity become public knowledge, as the potential for the technical solutions to virtually all human problems. But of course such ideals, constrained within the unquestioned framework of a capitalist mode of production, would imply the belief in a capitalism that could somehow coexist with a constantly shrinking mass of surplus value.[1] This, of course, capitalism cannot do.

"When value is the form of wealth, the goal of production is necessarily surplus value. That is, the goal of capitalist production is not simply value but the constant expansion of surplus value."[2] The reason for this is the fact that in the capitalist process of production, self-valorizing capital must reproduce itself "on a progressively increasing scale,"[3] and therefore also "produce" a surplus value that is constantly growing, by incorporating and exploiting a correspondingly growing number of labor powers.

As productivity increases, this compulsion to growth increases exponentially once again on the material level: if the production of more and more material wealth becomes necessary for the realization of the same surplus value, capital's material output must accordingly grow even more rapidly than the mass of surplus value. As we have seen, this holds for the phase of the fall of the production of surplus value, a phase that was reached some time ago. Now, if this movement of expansion comes up against limits, because the perpetually growing material wealth must not simply be produced, but also find a buyer, an irreversible crisis dynamic gets underway: a material output that remains constant, or even that increases, but less quickly than productivity, results in permanently shrinking production of surplus value, through which in turn the opportunities for the sale of the material output become fewer, which then has a greater effect on the fall in the mass of surplus value, and so on. It is by no means the case that such a downward movement afflicts all individual capitals uniformly: those affected are in the first instance the less productive, which must disappear from the market, culminating in the collapse of entire national economies such as, for example, in the eastern European countries at the start of the 1990s. The remaining capital can burst into the resulting empty spaces, and for the time being can expand again, which at the surface gives the impression that everything is fine for capital. This may indeed be the case for the survivors in each case—and for the moment—but it changes nothing of the character of the movement as a whole.

The growth of the mass of surplus value and—as long as productivity is increasing—the related and even stronger growth of the material output is the unconscious *raison d'etre* of capital and the condition *sine qua non* of the continued existence of the capitalist mode of production. In the past, capital has followed its compulsion to growth—that is, the necessity of its unlimited accumulation—in a process of expansion that is without historical parallel. Kurz names as its essential moments: first, the step-by-step conquering of all branches of production already existing before and independently of capital, and the concomitant condemnation of its working population to wage dependency, which also involves the conquering of geographical space (admired, though with a shudder, in the *Communist Manifesto* as the compulsion for a "constantly expanding market for its products") that "chases the bourgeoisie across the entire surface of the globe," and second, the creation of new branches of production for new needs (which themselves have first to be created), bound up, by means of mass consumption, with the additional conquering of the "dissociated," feminine realm of the reproduction of labor power, and recently the gradual suspension of the division between labor time and leisure time.[4]

The spaces into which capital has expanded are of material nature, and therefore necessarily finite and at some point, by equal necessity, bound to be full. As concerns the spatial expansionism that is capitalism's first essential moment (see above), this exhaustion of the planet itself as one, global mass of material for the valorization of capital has without doubt become a fait accompli today: there is now no spot on the earth and no branch of production that has not been delivered up to into the grip of capital. This is in no way altered even by the subsistence production that exists in some places, for this is not the remains of premodernity, but a makeshift means by which those who have fallen out of capitalist production can attempt, after a fashion, to secure their survival.

The question, in contrast, of whether the second moment of the capitalist process of expansion—the generation of new branches of production—has finally reached its end, is unresolved. This moment essentially relied on an expansion of mass consumption—which, however, is only possible if there is a sufficient real-terms rise in wages, which in turn affects the production of relative surplus value. In the high phase of Fordism after World War II—times of full employment—it was for a time even possible to implement trade-union demands for wage increases of the magnitude of the growth in productivity. . . . Kurz summarizes the situation as it appeared in the mid-1980s as follows:

> But both essential forms or moments of the process of capitalist expansion are today starting to come up against absolute material limits. The saturation point of capitalization was reached in the 1960s; this source of the absorption of living labor has come to a final standstill. At the same time, the confluence in microelectronics of natural-scientific technology and the science of labor implies a fundamentally new stage in the revolution of the material labor process. The microelectronic revolution does not eliminate living labor in immediate production only in this or that specific productive technology, but sets out on a wider front, throughout all branches of production, seizing even the unproductive areas. This process has only just started, and will not fully gain traction until the second half of the 1980s; it seems likely that it will continue until the end of the century and beyond. To the extent that new branches of production are created by means of this process, such as in the production of microelectronics itself or in gene technology, they

are by their nature from the outset not very labor intensive in respect to immediate production. This brings about the collapse of the historical compensation that has existed up until this point for the absolute immanent limit, embedded within relative surplus value, to the capitalist mode of production. The elimination on a massive scale of living productive labor as a source of the creation of value can no longer be recuperated by newly mass-produced cheap products, since this process of mass production is no longer mediated by a process of reintegrating a labor population that has been made superfluous elsewhere. This brings about a historically irreversible overturning of the relationship between the elimination of living productive labor through scientification on the one hand, and the absorption of living productive labor through processes of capitalization or through the creation of new branches of production on the other: from now on, it is inexorable that more labor is eliminated than can be absorbed. All technological innovations that are to be expected will also tend only in the direction of the further elimination of living labor, all new branches of production will from the outset come to life with less and less direct human productive labor.[5]

Heinrich describes, somewhat derisively, the direct reference of "Kurz's theory of collapse" to the "microelectronic revolution" as "technological determinism," which he claims is wonderfully appropriate "to the 'workers-movement Marxism' that is otherwise criticized so very fiercely by Kurz."[6] However, what is at stake here, as Heinrich is certainly aware, is not a particular individual technology, but the fact that technology is making labor to a great extent superfluous—an argument against which Heinrich marshals no argument even in his "more extensive critique."[7] But this ought really to give a theorist of value pause for thought, for a crisis of capital could in that case only fail to result if value and surplus value were not measured in labor time, but natural-scientific technology had instead replaced the application of immediate labor as a source of value, as someone like Habermas believes. But Heinrich does not go this far.

It is correct, on the other hand—and if this had been what Heinrich had said, he would have been right—that a prognosis, based on the here and now, according to which "it is inexorable that more labor is eliminated than can be absorbed," cannot be derived solely from the category, established on a more abstract level, of relative surplus value. Empirical observations are also required. These exist in great numbers, and Kurz also alludes to them. But empirical semblance can of course deceive, and capital can pull itself together once more—the question is only what the consequences would be for capital and for humanity.

This uncertainty as to the future development of the crisis dynamic changes nothing of the fact that capital must perish as a result of its own dynamic, if it is not overcome by conscious human actions before then. This results simply from the limitless compulsion to growth on one hand,

and on the other hand the finitude of the human and material resources on which it depends.

Knut Hüller has already drawn attention to the fact that the total social rate of profit (rate of accumulation) must fall for no other reason than the fact that the labor power available to capital on this earth is simply finite, whereas a constant rate of profit would presuppose an exponentially growing working population.[8] And this conclusion was reached without once taking the production of relative surplus value into consideration. If one does so, it becomes clear that constant or even exponentially growing material production leads, if the rate of "real growth" is too low (under the rate of growth of productivity), to an exponential fall in the mass of surplus value (and accordingly to falls in the productively working population).

The observation that "it is inexorable that more labor is eliminated than can be absorbed" is essentially based on the presupposition that capital will no longer be able to compensate for the losses, induced by process innovations, in the production of value and surplus value, by means of product innovations. There is much in favor of this claim, but even today, twenty-two years later, no innovations of this kind are anywhere to be found. As stated, here it is a matter not of new products and their associated needs as such, but of those whose production requires labor on such a mass scale that it would be possible at least to compensate for the streamlining potential of microelectronics. However, if this prognosis was to reveal itself to be false, the contradiction revealed here between matter and form would in no way be resolved, but would in that case result in a violent discharge in another direction.

The Inner Compulsion Toward Growth and Environmental Destruction Moreover, all progress in capitalist agriculture is a progress in the art, not only of robbing the worker, but of robbing the soil; all progress in increasing the fertility of the soil for a given time is a progress toward ruining the more long-lasting sources of that fertility. The more a country proceeds from large-scale industry as the background of its development, . . . the more rapid is this process of destruction. . . . Capitalist production, therefore, only develops the techniques and the degree of combination of the social process of production by simultaneously undermining the original sources of all wealth—the soil and the worker.[9]

Capital requires material wealth as the bearer of value; as such the latter is indispensable, and in quantitative terms (see above) it will become even more so. But capital is not concerned with the material wealth that is freely available and that therefore does not become part of the mass of value and surplus value that is produced. In comparison with the necessity of capital accumulation, the preservation of this wealth is at best of lesser importance—or in other words, if the destruction of material wealth serves the valorization of value, then material wealth will be destroyed. It's that simple. Into this category fall all of its forms which have come into view or been mentioned over the last fifty years in the context of environmental destruction: the long-term fertility of the soil, to which Marx had already referred; air and water of a quality that they can be breathed and drunk without danger to life or limb; biodiversity and undamaged ecosystems, even merely with respect to their function as renewable sources of food; or a climate that is hospitable to human life.

The question is not, therefore, whether the environment is destroyed for the sake of the valorization of value, but at best of the extent of this destruction. And in this matter the growth of productivity, to the extent that it, as the production of relative surplus value, remains bound to value as the predominant form of wealth, plays a thoroughly sinister role because the realization of the same mass of surplus value requires an ever-greater material output and even greater consumption of resources: for the transition from old to new technologies with the purpose of reducing the labor time required is usually achieved by replacing or accelerating human labor with machines. We may assume, for example, in an ideal-typical case . . . it is possible to make 10,000 shirts in 1,000 working days by the old technology, and this production only requires cloth and labor. The new technology could consist in the reduction of the labor time necessary for the production of the same number of shirts to 500 working days, but to introduce and employ machines and additional energy which for their part could be produced in 300 working days. In the situation . . . this would mean that in the case of the new, more profitable technique for the realization of the same surplus value as in the old, it would be necessary to produce not only more than 10,000 shirts in a capitalist manner, but also the additional machinery and energy which are used in the process of production. This means that ever-greater consumption of resources becomes necessary for the same surplus value, a consumption that is greater than, and grows even more quickly than, the required material output.

That is, if Kurz was wrong, and the accumulation of capital could continue without restriction, it would sooner or later have as its inevitable consequence the destruction not only of the material foundations of the valorization of capital, but also of human life as such.

Postone draws the following conclusion from his analysis of the contradiction between material wealth and wealth in the value form as it is brought forth by the production of relative surplus value:

> Leaving aside considerations of possible limits or barriers to capital accumulation, one consequence implied by this particular dynamic— which yields increases in material wealth far greater than those in surplus value—is the accelerating destruction of the natural environment. According to Marx, as a result of the relationship among productivity, material wealth, and surplus value, the ongoing expansion of the latter increasingly has deleterious consequences for nature as well as for humans.[10]

In explicit opposition to Horkheimer and Adorno, for whom the domination of nature is itself already the "Fall," Postone emphasises that "the growing destruction of nature should not simply be seen . . . as a consequence of increasing human control and domination of nature."[11] Such a critique is inadequate because it does not distinguish between value and material wealth, although it is the case that in capitalism nature is exploited and destroyed not because of material wealth, but because of surplus value. The increasing imbalance between the two forms of wealth leads him to come to this conclusion:

> The pattern I have outlined suggests that, in the society in which the commodity is totalized, there is an underlying tension between ecological considerations and the imperatives of value as the form of wealth and social mediation. It implies further that any attempt to respond fundamentally, within the framework of capitalist society, to growing environmental destruction by restraining this society's mode of expansion would probably be ineffective on a long-term basis—not only because of the interests of the capitalists or state managers, but because failure to expand surplus value would indeed result in severe economic difficulties with great social costs. In Marx's analysis, the necessary accumulation of capital and the creation of capitalist society's wealth are intrinsically related. Moreover . . . because labor is determined as a necessary means of individual reproduction in capitalist society, wage laborers remain dependent on capital's "growth," even when the consequences of their labor, ecological and otherwise, are detrimental to themselves and to others. The tension between the exigencies of the commodity form and ecological requirements becomes more severe as productivity increases and, particularly during economic crises and periods of high unemployment, poses a severe dilemma. This dilemma and the tension in which it is rooted are immanent to capitalism: their ultimate resolution will be hindered so long as value remains the determining form of social wealth.[12]

The dilemma described here manifests itself in a many-faceted form. To give an example: while there is a consensus in environmental contexts that the global spread of the "American way of life" or even only of the western European lifestyle would bring with it environmental catastrophes to a degree that has not yet been seen, development organizations must nonetheless pursue precisely this goal, even if it has now become unrealistic. Or, in the terminology of this essay, the employment of labor power that would be necessary for the continued accumulation of capital, even of only half the globally available labor power, at the level of productivity that has been attained, with the corresponding material output and consumption of resources, would result in the immediate collapse of the earth's ecosystem.

This dilemma also manifests itself in the weekly walk on eggshells as to what is "ecologically necessary" and what is "economically feasible"—the two are now irreconcilable—in the political treatment of the expected climate catastrophe, which is indeed only one of many environmental problems. Politics cannot emancipate itself from capital, since it depends on successful production of surplus value even for its tax revenue and therefore its own ability to act. It already has to go against its own nature in order to pass even resolutions that remain well below the objective requirements of the problem that is to be solved, and that even then nonetheless are softened within a week under pressure from some or other lobby on behalf of what is "economically feasible." What remains is pure self-dramatization on the part of "doers" who claim still to have the objectively insoluble problems under control.

Conclusion

This chapter presents a relatively meager analysis of a particular perspective that is nonetheless determinant of the capitalist dynamic—the production of relative surplus value and its consequences for the valorization of capital. The reduction of complexity necessary to carry out this analysis—and with it the occasional obscuring of all other aspects of a commodity-producing patriarchy that has entered a period of crisis—is the price to pay for a (hopefully successful) comprehensible presentation. For example, the ideological distortions that accompany the development of the crisis thus remain obscured, as does the increasing inequality with which different groups of the population bear the brunt of the crisis: women more strongly than men, and the middle class (for the moment) to a lesser extent than the majority that has already been precarized.[13]

The role of finance capital has also remained hidden—about which a few words should be said at this point, because some consider it to be the true cause of the crisis, while others believe that it could save capitalism from the ultimate collapse. Both views are false. What is true is that in late capitalism, the valorization of value would not be possible without finance capital, because the huge capitalist aggregates that are necessary at the level of productivity that has been attained today could not by a long way any longer be financed by private capital. But this makes finance capital an indispensable "lubricant," but not the "fuel" of the production of surplus value, which remains bound to the expenditure of labor. The valorization of value has not come to a standstill because capital has fled, maliciously, into the financial sector—rather, it is the other way round. Because it has already been the case for decades that the valorization of capital has come to a standstill, capital flees into the financial sector with its higher (if fictitious, seen from the perspective of the economy as a whole) yields. The effect of this flight is—in the fashion of global Keynesian deficit spending, against all neoliberal ideology—in the first instance to delay the crisis. But the longer this succeeds, the harder the impact with which the crisis must ultimately assert itself. In any case, the idea, that has its origins in the postmodern fantasy of virtuality, of a capitalism that could be "regulated" on a long-term basis by an escalating financial sector which is no longer counterbalanced by any real production of surplus value, is at least as adventurous as that of the production of surplus value without labor by means of science as productivity alone.

If, however, the production of surplus value presupposes the application of immediate labor and the production of material wealth that is bound up with it, the production of surplus value that according to Marx is appropriate to developed capitalism—that is, the production of relative surplus value—leads to the requirement of an ever-greater material output and a still greater consumption of resources for the realization of the same mass of surplus value. The capitalist process of accumulation and expansion thus comes up against absolute material limits, the observance of which must lead to the burning-out of the capitalist logic of valorization, and the disregard for which to the destruction of its material foundations and the possibility of human life as such.

The choice that this presents, between the devil of the gradual disappearance of labor and the social consequences that are, in capitalism, bound up with it, and the deep blue sea of ecological collapse, is not even an either–or choice. It seems rather that both are approaching together: falling production of surplus value at the same time as growing consumption of resources, overladen by the prospect of wars over increasingly scarce material resources, squandered in the valorization of capital, and for the chance to valorize the last remains.

Prognoses made on the basis of the investigations carried out here as to the course of such demise would therefore be pure speculation; but we ought, one way or another, to speak of the end of capitalism as a social formation— just not in the same sense as Heinrich does when he writes in relation to "Kurz's theory of collapse": "Historically, the theory of collapse always had an exonerating function for the left: however bad the contemporary defeats, the demise of its antagonist was ultimately certain."[14]

Here, too, he is wrong. It is a matter not of the end of an "antagonist," but of our own end. Whether as a slow, lingering sickness or in a great explosion, the foreseeable demise of a social form the members of which, bound to it by means of a value form they regard as natural and thus lack any idea of what is happening to them, could at best leave its survivors to vegetate aimlessly as commodity subjects without commodities. It would merely be one more—albeit the last—defeat. And conversely, the only chance for some sort of liberated postcapitalist society presents itself to us as the overcoming of capitalism—and therefore of wealth in the value form, and of the subject form that it constitutes—brought about by conscious human action. This must come, however, before the compulsion to growth in the valorization of capital, in combination with the production of relative surplus value, leaves behind nothing other than scorched earth. Time is running out.

Notes

1   In addition, unburdening human life on a global scale would require conscious planning oriented toward material wealth, that is to say more or less the opposite of an orientation toward the market. Besides, in a noncapitalist society with today's level of production it would not be a matter merely of less labor, but rather of the abolition of labor as a category.

2   Moishe Postone, *Time, Labor, and Social Domination: A Reinterpretation of Marx's Critical Theory* (Cambridge: Cambridge University Press, 1993): 308.

3   Karl Marx, *Capital: A Critique of Political Economy*, Volume I, trans. Ben Fowkes (London: Harmondsworth, 1976): 725 and following.

4   Karl Marx and Friedrich Engels, "Manifesto of the Communist Party," trans. Samuel Moore, *The Marx-Engels Reader*, 2nd ed., ed. Robert C. Tucker (New York: W. W. Norton, 1978): 476, and Kurz, "Crisis" (23). What is at issue here is exclusively the quantitative aspect of the objective dynamics of the valorization of capital. Under the aspect of the dissociation of value as the dark flipside of the process of disciplining the (masculine) subject so as to be fit for the valorization of value (and its necessary prerequisite, socialization in the shape of the value form), it would be worthwhile carrying out our own investigation as to whether and to what extent capital undermines its own foundations by capitalizing the "feminine," value-dissociated sphere within the social division of labor, destroying, in the process, the long-term prospects for the vital reproductive function of this sphere for the valorization of capital. The increase in mental illness and in the premature inability to work for reasons of mental health weigh in favor of this hypothesis, as do the disastrous conditions, which to a great extent have already become intolerable, in state-funded care for children, the sick, and the elderly, once these services too have been subjected to the microeconomic time regime of capital.

5   "The Crisis of Exchange Value," trans. Neil Larsen, Mathias Nilges, Josh Robinson, and Nicholas Brown, in *Marxism and the Critique of Value*, ed. Neil Larsen, Mathias Nilges, Josh Robinson, and Nicholas Brown (Chicago and Alberta: MCM', 2014): 71–113, 48–9.

6   *Kritik der politischen Ökonomie. Eine Einführung* (Stuttgart: Auflage, 2005): 178.

7   Michael Heinrich, "Untergang des Kapitalismus? Die Krisis und die Krise." *Streifzüge* 1 (1999).

8   Knut Hüller, *Eine Aufwertung des Werts gegenüber dem Preis*, 2006. The so-
    called Okishio Theorem, which has its origin in the neo-Ricardian
    critique of Marx, in contrast, supposedly refutes the "law of the tendency
    of the rate of profit to fall": even Heinrich, *Die Wissenschaft vom Wert*
    (Münster: Westfälisches Dampfboot, 1991): 327 and following; *Kritik*,
    148) accepts this theorem as is, and likes to assert it against capital's
    "tendency to collapse." The Okishio Theorem says nothing more than that
    a particular mathematical model (a comparatively static, linear model of
    production, that is ridiculously laid at Marx's door), cannot demonstrate the
    fall of the rate of profit, but rather implies its rise. This shows nothing more
    than that one should not simply abstract from absolute figures and their
    limits, as linear models always do.

9   Marx, *Capital* I, 638.

10 Postone, 311.

11 Max Horkheimer and Theodor W. Adorno, *Dialectic of Enlightenment*,
    trans. Edmund Jephcott (Stanford, CA: Stanford University Press, 2002);
    Postone, 312.

12 Postone, 313.

13 Compare Frank Rentschler, "Die kategoriale Abwesenheit des Geschlechts,"
    EXIT! 3 (2006) 176–209; Roswitha Scholz, "Überflüssig sein und
    'Mittelschichtsangst,'" *EXIT!* 5 (2008): 58–104.

14 Heinrich, "Untergang," 178.

CHAPTER THIRTY FOUR

Misery and Debt: On the Logic and History of Surplus Populations and Surplus Capital

Aaron Benanav and John Clegg (Endnotes)

From Endnotes 2 (April 2010): 20–51.

We tend to interpret the present crisis through the cyclical theories of an older generation. While mainstream economists root around for the "green shoots" of recovery, critical critics ask only if it might take a little longer to "restore" growth. It's true that if we begin from theories of business cycles, or even long waves, it's easy to assume that booms follow busts like clockwork, that downturns always "prepare the way" for resurgent upswings. But how likely is it that, if and when this mess clears, we will see a new golden age of capitalism?

We might begin by remembering that the miracle years of the previous golden age (roughly 1950–1973) depended not only on a world war and an enormous uptick in state spending, but also on an historically unprecedented transfer of population from agriculture to industry. Agricultural populations proved to be a potent weapon in the quest for "modernization," since they provided a source of cheap labor for a new wave of industrialization. In 1950, 23 percent of the German workforce was employed in agriculture, in France 31, in Italy 44 and in Japan 49 percent—by 2000, all had agricultural populations of under 5 percent.[1] In the 19th and early 20th centuries, capital dealt with mass unemployment, when it occurred, by expelling urban proletarians back to the land, as well as by exporting them to colonies. By eliminating the peasantry in the traditional core at the same time as it came up against the limits of colonial expansion, capital eliminated its own traditional mechanisms of recovery.

Meanwhile, the wave of industrialization that absorbed those who had been pushed out of agriculture came up against its own limits in the 1970s. Since then, the major capitalist countries have seen an unprecedented decline in their levels of industrial employment. Over the past three decades, manufacturing employment fell 50 percent as a percentage of total employment in these countries. Even newly "industrializing" countries like South Korea and Taiwan saw their relative levels of industrial employment decline in the past two decades.[2] At the same time the numbers of both low-paid service-workers and slum-dwellers working in the informal sector have expanded as the only remaining options for those who have become superfluous to the needs of shrinking industries.

For Marx, the fundamental crisis tendency of the capitalist mode of production was not limited in its scope to periodic downturns in economic activity. It revealed itself most forcefully in a permanent crisis of working life. The *differentia specifica* of capitalist "economic" crises—that people starve in spite of good harvests, and means of production lie idle in spite of a need for their products—is merely one moment of this larger crisis—the constant reproduction of a scarcity of jobs in the midst of an abundance of goods. It is the dynamic of *this* crisis—the crisis of the reproduction of the capital–labor relation—which this chapter explores.[3]

Simple and expanded reproduction

Despite the complexity of its results, capital has only one essential precondition: people must lack direct access to the goods they deem necessary for life, finding that access instead only through the mediation of the market. Hence the very term "proletariat," referring originally to landless citizens living in Roman cities. Lacking work, they were pacified first by state provision of bread and circuses, and ultimately by employment as mercenaries. However, the proletarian condition is historically uncommon: the global peasantry have, throughout history, mostly had direct access to land as self-sufficient farmers or herders, even if they were almost always coerced into giving a portion of their product to ruling elites. Thus the need for "primitive accumulation": separating people from land, their most basic means of reproduction, and generating an all-round dependence on commodity exchange.[4]

The initial separation of people from the land, once achieved, is never enough. It has to be perpetually repeated in order for capital and "free" labor to meet in the market time after time. On the one hand, capital requires, already present in the labor market, a mass of people lacking direct access to means of production, looking to exchange work for wages. On the other hand, it requires, already present in the commodity market, a mass of people who have already acquired wages, looking to exchange their money for goods. Absent those two conditions, capital is limited in its ability to accumulate: it can neither produce nor sell on a mass scale. Outside of the US and UK before 1950, the scope for mass production was limited precisely because of the limitation of the size of the market, that is, because of the existence of a large, somewhat self-sufficient peasantry not living primarily by the wage. The story of the post-war period is that of the tendential abolition of the remaining global peasantry, first as self-sufficient, and second as peasants at all, owning the land on which they work.

Marx explains this structural feature of capitalism in his chapter on "simple reproduction" in volume one. We will interpret this concept as the reproduction, in and through cycles of production–consumption, of the relationship between capital and workers.[5] Simple reproduction is maintained not out of "habit," nor by the false or inadequate consciousness of workers, but by a material compulsion. This is the exploitation of wage-workers, the fact that all together, they can purchase only a portion of the goods they produce:

> [Capital prevents its] self-conscious instruments from leaving it in the lurch, for it removes their product, as fast as it is made, from their pole to the opposite pole of capital. Individual consumption provides, on the one hand, the means for their maintenance and reproduction: on the other hand, it secures by the annihilation of the necessaries of life, the continued re-appearance of the workman in the labor-market.[6]

The accumulation of capital is not a matter, then, of the organization of either the sphere of production or the sphere of consumption. Over-emphasis on either production or consumption tends to generate partial theories of capitalist crises: "over-production" or "under-consumption." Wage-labor structures the reproduction process as a whole: the wage allocates workers to production and, at the same time, allocates the product to workers. This is an invariant of capital, independent of geographic or historical specificities. The breakdown of reproduction creates a crisis of both over-production *and* under-consumption, since under capital they are the same.

However, we cannot move so directly from an unfolding of the structure of simple reproduction to a theory of crisis. For simple reproduction is, of its very nature, also expanded reproduction. Just as labor must return to the labor market to replenish its fund of wages, so too capital must return to the capital market to reinvest its profits in an expansion of production. All capital must accumulate, or it will fall behind in its competition with other capitals. Competitive price formation and variable cost structures within sectors lead to divergent intra-sectoral profit rates, which in turn drives efficiency-increasing innovations, for by reducing their costs beneath the sectoral average firms can either reap super profits, or lower prices to gain market share. But falling costs will in any case lead to falling prices, for the mobility of capital between sectors results in an equalization of inter-sectoral profit rates, as the movement of capital in search of higher profits drives supply (and thus prices) up and down, causing returns on new investment to fluctuate around an inter-sectoral average. This perpetual movement of capital also spreads cost-reducing innovations across sectors—establishing a law of profitability which forces all capitals to maximise profits, irrespective of the political and social configuration in which they find themselves. Conversely, when profitability falls, there is nothing that can be done to re-establish accumulation short of the "slaughtering of capital values" and the "setting free of labor" which re-establish the conditions of profitability.

Yet this formalistic conception of the valorization process fails to capture the historical dynamic to which Marx's analysis is attuned. The law of profitability alone cannot ensure expanded reproduction, for this also requires the emergence of new industries and new markets. Rises and falls in profitability act as signals to the capitalist class that innovations have occurred in specific industries, but what is important is that over time the composition of output—and therefore employment—changes: industries that once accounted for a large portion of output and employment now grow more slowly, while new industries take a rising share of both. Here, we have to look at the determinants of demand, as independent from the determinants of supply.[7]

Demand varies with the price of a given product. When the price is high, the product is purchased only by the wealthy. As labor-saving process innovations accumulate, prices fall, transforming the product into a mass-consumption good. At the cusp of this transformation, innovations cause the market for a given product to expand enormously. This expansion stretches beyond the capacity of existing firms, and prices fall more slowly than costs, leading to a period of high profitability. Capital then rushes into the line, pulling labor with it. At a certain point, however, the limits of the market are reached; that is, the market is saturated.[8] Now innovations cause total capacity to rise beyond the size of the market: prices fall more quickly than costs, leading to a period of falling profitability. Capital will leave the line, expelling labor.[9]

This process, which economists have called the "maturation" of industries, has occurred many times. The agricultural revolution, which first broke out in early modern England, eventually hit the limits of the domestic market for its products. Labor-process innovations such as the consolidation of fragmented land holdings, the abolition of the fallow, and the differentiation of land use according to natural advantages meant—*under capitalist conditions of reproduction*—that both labor and capital were systematically pushed out of the countryside. England rapidly urbanised as a result, and London became the largest city in Europe.

It is here that the key dynamic of expanded reproduction comes into play. For the workers thrown out of agriculture were not left to languish indefinitely in the cities. They were eventually taken up in the manufacturing sector of an industrializing Britain, and especially in the growing textile industry, which was transitioning from wool to cotton cloth. But once again, labor-process innovations such as the spinning jenny, spinning mule, and the power loom meant that eventually this industry, too, began to throw off labor and capital. And the decline in the industries of the first Industrial Revolution, as a percentage of total labor employed and capital accumulated, made way for those of the second Industrial Revolution (chemicals, telecommunications, electric and engine-powered commodities). It is this movement of labor and capital into and out of lines, based on differential rates of profit, that ensures the continued possibility of expanded reproduction:

> [E]xpansion . . . is impossible without disposable human material, without an increase in the number of workers, which must occur independently of the absolute growth of the population. This increase is effected by the simple process that constantly "sets free" a part of the working class; by methods which lessen the number of workers employed in proportion to the increase in production. Modern industry's whole form of motion therefore depends on the constant transformation of a part of the working population into unemployed or semi-employed hands.[10]

Expanded reproduction is, in this way, the continual reproduction of the conditions of simple reproduction. Capitals that can no longer reinvest in a given line due to falling profitability will tend to find, available to them on the labor market, workers who have been thrown out of other lines. These "free" quantities of capital and labor will then find employment in expanding markets, where rates of profit are higher, or come together in entirely new product lines, manufacturing products for markets that do not yet exist. An increasing number of activities are thus subsumed as capitalist valorization processes, and commodities spread from luxury into mass markets.

The bourgeois economist Joseph Schumpeter described this process in his theory of the business cycle.[11] He noted that the contraction of older lines rarely happens smoothly or peacefully, that it is usually associated with factory closures and bankruptcies as capitals attempt to deflect losses onto one another in competitive price wars. When several lines contract simultaneously (and they usually do, since they are based on linked sets of technological innovations), a recession ensues. Schumpeter calls this shedding of capital and labor "creative destruction"—"creative" not only in the sense that it is stimulated by innovation, but also because destruction creates the conditions for new investment and innovation: in a crisis, capitals find means of production and labor-power available to them on the market at discount prices. Thus, like a forest fire, the recession clears the way for a new bout of growth.

Many Marxists have espoused something similar to Schumpeter's conception of cyclical growth, to which they merely add the resistance of workers (or perhaps the limits of ecology) as an external constraint. Hence the Marxist notion of crisis as a self-regulating mechanism is complemented by a conviction that crises provide opportunities to assert the power of labor (or correct the ecologically destructive tendencies of capitalism). In these moments, "another world is possible." Yet Marx's theory of capitalism contains no such distinction between "internal" dynamics and "external" limits. For Marx it is in and through this process of expanded reproduction that the dynamic of capital manifests itself *as its own limit*, not through *cycles* of boom and bust but in a *secular* deterioration of its own conditions of accumulation.

The crisis of reproduction

People usually look for a theory of secular decline in Marx's notes on the tendential fall in the rate of profit, which Engels edited and compiled as chapters 13 to 15 of volume three of *Capital*. There, the tendency of the profit rate to equalise across lines—combined with the tendency of productivity to rise in all lines—is held to result in an economy-wide, tendential decline in profitability. Decades of debate have centered on the "rising organic composition of capital," to which this tendency is attributed, as well as on the complex interplay of the various tendencies and counter-tendencies involved. Yet those engaged in this debate often neglect that the same account of the composition of capital underlies *another law*, expressing itself in both cyclical and secular crisis tendencies, one that may be read as Marx's more considered re-formulation of this account—chapter 25 of *Capital* volume one: "The General Law of Capitalist Accumulation."[12]

This chapter, which follows immediately after the three chapters on simple and expanded reproduction, is typically read as having more limited ends. Readers focus on the first part of Marx's argument only, where he provides an account of the endogenous determination of the wage rate. There Marx shows how, through the structural maintenance of a certain level of unemployment, wages are kept in line with the needs of accumulation. The "industrial reserve army" of the unemployed contracts as the demand for labor rises, causing wages to rise in turn. Rising wages then eat into profitability, causing accumulation to slow down. As the demand for labor falls, the reserve army grows once again, and the previous wage gains evaporate. If this was the sole argument of the chapter, then the "general law" would consist of nothing more than a footnote to the theories of simple and expanded reproduction. But Marx is just beginning to unfold his argument. If the unemployed tend to be reabsorbed into the circuits of capitalism as an industrial reserve army—still unemployed, but essential to the regulation of the labor market—they then equally tend to outgrow this function, reasserting themselves as *absolutely redundant*:

> The greater the social wealth, the functioning capital, the extent and energy of its growth, and therefore also the greater the absolute mass of the proletariat and the productivity of its labor, the greater is the industrial reserve army. The same causes which develop the expansive power of capital, also develop the labor-power at its disposal. The relative mass of the industrial reserve army thus increases with the potential energy of wealth. But the greater this reserve army, the greater is the mass of a consolidated surplus population, whose misery is in inverse ratio to the amount of torture it has to undergo in the form of labor. The more extensive, finally, the lazarus-layers of the working class, and the industrial reserve army, the greater is official pauperism. *This is the absolute general law of capitalist accumulation.*[13]

In other words, the general law of capital accumulation is that—concomitant with its growth—capital produces a relatively redundant population out of the mass of workers, which then tends to become a consolidated surplus population, absolutely redundant to the needs of capital.[14]

It is not immediately obvious how Marx reaches this conclusion, even if the tendency Marx describes seems increasingly evident in an era of jobless recoveries, slum-cities and generalised precarity. Marx makes his argument clearer in the French edition of volume one. There he notes that the higher the organic composition of capital, the more rapidly must accumulation proceed to maintain employment, "but this more rapid progress itself becomes the source of new technical changes which further reduce the relative demand for labor." This is more than just a feature of specific highly concentrated industries. As accumulation proceeds, a growing "superabundance" of goods lowers the rate of profit and heightens competition across lines, compelling all capitalists to "economise on labor." Productivity gains are thus "concentrated under this great pressure; they are incorporated in technical changes which revolutionise the composition of capital in all branches surrounding the great spheres of production."[15]

What, then, about new industries; won't they pick up the slack in employment? Marx identifies, in and through the movements of the business cycle, a shift from labor-intensive to capital-intensive industries, with a resulting fall in the demand for labor in new lines as well as old: "On the one hand . . . the additional capital formed in the course of further accumulation attracts fewer and fewer workers in proportion to its magnitude. On the other hand, old capital periodically reproduced with a new composition repels more and more of the workers formerly employed by it."[16] This is the secret of the "general law": *labor-saving technologies tend to generalise, both within and across lines*, leading to a relative decline in the demand for labor. Moreover, these innovations are irreversible: they do not disappear if and when profitability is restored (indeed, as we shall see, the restoration of profitability is often conditioned on further innovations in new or expanding lines). Thus left unchecked this relative decline in labor demand threatens to outstrip capital accumulation, becoming absolute.[17]

Marx did not simply deduce this conclusion from his abstract analysis of the law of value. In chapter 15 of *Capital* he attempts to provide an empirical demonstration of this tendency. There he presents statistics from the British census of 1861 which show that the new industries coming on line as a result of technological innovations were, in employment terms, "far from important." He gives the examples of "gas-works, telegraphy, photography, steam navigation, and railways," all highly mechanised and relatively automated processes, and shows that the total employment in these lines amounted to less than 100,000 workers, compared to over a million in the textile and metal industries whose workforce was then shrinking as a result of the introduction of machinery.[18] From these statistics alone it is clear that the industries of the second industrial revolution had not absorbed anything like as much labor as those of the first in the moment of their initial appearance. In chapter 25 Marx provides additional statistical evidence that, from 1851 to 1871, employment continued to grow substantially only in those older industries in which machinery had not yet been successfully introduced. Thus Marx's expectation of a secular trajectory of a first relative then absolute decline in the demand for labor was born out by the available evidence in his time.

What Marx is here describing is not a "crisis" in the sense usually indicated by Marxist theory, i.e. a periodic crisis of production, consumption or even accumulation. In and through these cyclical crises, a secular crisis emerges, *a crisis of the reproduction of the capital–labor relation itself.* If expanded reproduction indicates that workers and capital pushed out of contracting industries will try to find places in new or expanding lines, the general law of capital accumulation suggests that, over time, more and more workers and capital will find that they are unable to reinsert themselves into the reproduction process. In this way the proletariat tendentially becomes an externality to the process of its own reproduction, a class of workers who are "free" not only of means of reproduction, but also of work itself.

For Marx this crisis expresses the fundamental contradiction of the capitalist mode B of production. On the one hand, people in capitalist social relations are reduced to workers. On the other hand, they *cannot be workers* since, by working, they undermine the conditions of possibility of their own existence. Wage-labor is inseparable from the accumulation of capital, from the accretion of labor-saving innovations, which, over time, reduce the demand for labor: "The working population . . . produces both the accumulation of capital and the means by which it is itself made relatively superfluous; and it does this to an extent which is always increasing."[19] It might seem that the abundance of goods, which results from labor-saving innovations, must lead to an abundance of jobs. But in a society based on wage-labor, the reduction of socially-necessary labor-time—which makes goods so abundant—can only express itself in a scarcity of jobs, in a multiplication of forms of precarious employment.[20]

Marx's statement of the general law is itself a restatement, a dramatic unfolding of what he lays out as his thesis at the beginning of chapter 25. There, Marx writes, somewhat simply: "Accumulation of capital is therefore multiplication of the proletariat." Marxists of an earlier period took this thesis to mean that the expansion of capital necessitates an expansion of the industrial working class. But the proletariat is not identical to the industrial working class. According to what Marx sets out in the conclusion to this chapter, the proletariat is rather a working class in transition, a working class tending to become a class excluded from work. This interpretation is supported by the only definition of the proletariat Marx provides in *Capital*, located in a footnote to the above thesis:

"Proletarian" must be understood to mean, economically speaking, nothing other than "wage-laborer," the man who produces and valorises "capital," *and is thrown onto the street as soon as he becomes superfluous to the need for valorisation.*[21]

From re-industrialization to deindustrialization

The "general law of capitalist accumulation," with its clear implications for the interpretation of *Capital*, has been overlooked in our own time because under the name of the "immiseration thesis" it was taken up and abandoned many times over in the course of the 20th century. It was held that Marx's prediction of rising unemployment, and thus the increasing immiseration of the working population, has been contradicted by the history of capitalism: after Marx's death, the industrial working class both grew in size and saw its living standards rise. Yet quite apart from the fact that these tendencies are often over-generalised, more recently their apparent reversal has made the immiseration thesis seem more plausible. The last 30 years have witnessed a global stagnation in the relative number of industrial workers. A low-wage service sector has made up the difference in the high GDP countries alongside an unparalleled explosion of slum-dwellers and informal workers in the low GDP countries.[22] So is the immiseration thesis correct after all? That is the wrong question. The question is: under what conditions does it apply?

Marx wrote about the growth of consolidated surplus populations in 1867. Yet the tendency he described—by which newer industries, because of their higher degree of automation, absorb proportionally less of the capital and labor thrown off by the mechanization of older industries— did not play out as he had envisaged. As we can see from Figure 34.1, Marx's view was correct, in his own time, for the UK: the rising industries of the early second Industrial Revolution—such as chemicals, railways, telegraph, etc.—were not able to compensate for declining employment in the industries of the first Industrial Revolution. The result was a steady fall in the rate of growth of manufacturing employment, which looked set to become an absolute decline sometime in the early 20th century. What Marx did not foresee, and what actually occurred in the 1890s, was the emergence of new industries that were simultaneously labor and capital absorbent, and which were able to put off the decline for more than half a century. The growth of these new industries, principally cars and consumer durables, depended on two 20th-century developments: the increasing role of the state in economic management, and the transformation of consumer services into consumer goods (Figure 34.1).[23]

FIGURE 34.1 *Employment in UK Manufacturing: 1841–1991.*
Source: Brian Mitchell, International Historical Statistics: Europe, 1750–2005 *(Basingstoke: Palgrave Macmillan, 2007).*

The emergent industries of which Marx wrote in the 1860s—gas-works, telegraphy, and railways (we would add only electrification)—were already in his time beginning to be made available to consumers. Yet the consumer services generated from these technologies—initially reserved for the enjoyment of a wealthy elite—were secondary to the services they provided within the internal, planned economy of industrial firms. Railways emerged as a labor-saving innovation within mining, which was subsequently extended to other industries. It became a service offered to consumers only after extensive national-rail infrastructures had been developed by state-supported cartels. Even as costs fell and mechanised transportation via rail became available to more and more people, as a consumer service it preserved many of the features of its initial employment as a "process innovation" within industry. National railways, carrying passengers in addition to freight, absorbed large amounts of capital and labor in their construction but were subsequently relatively automated processes requiring less capital and labor for their upkeep.[24]

The advent of the automobile industry, subsidised by state funding of roads, eventually transformed the consumer service of mechanised transport into a good that could be purchased for individual consumption. This segmentation and replication of the product—the transformation of a labor-saving process innovation into a capital-and-labor absorbing "product innovation"—meant that this industry was able to absorb more capital and labor as its market expanded. A similar story can be told of the shift from telegraphy to telephones, and from electronic manufacture to consumer electronics. In each case, a collectively consumed service—often emerging from an intermediary service within industry—was transformed into a series of individually purchasable commodities, opening up new markets, which in turn became mass markets as costs fell and production increased. This provided the basis for the "mass consumerism" of the 20th century, for these new industries were able to simultaneously absorb large amounts of capital and labor, even as productivity increases reduced relative costs of production, such that more and more peasants became workers, and more and more workers were given stable employment.

Yet, as the unprecedented state deficit-spending which supported this process indicates, there is no inherent tendency to capital that allows for the continual generation of product innovations to balance out its labor-saving process innovations. On the contrary, product innovations themselves often serve as process innovations, such that the solution only worsens the initial problem.[25] When the car and consumer durables industries began to throw off capital and labor in the 1960s and 70s, new lines like microelectronics were not able to absorb the excess, even decades later. These innovations, like those of the 2nd industrial revolution described above, emerged from specific process innovations within industry and the military, and have only recently been transformed into a diversity of consumer products. The difficulty in this shift, from the perspective of generating new employment, is not merely the difficulty of policing a market in software—it is that new goods generated by microelectronics industries have absorbed tendentially diminished quantities of capital and labor. Indeed computers not only have rapidly decreasing labor requirements themselves (the microchips industry, restricted to only a few factories world-wide, is incredibly mechanised), they also tend to reduce labor requirements across all lines by rapidly increasing the level of automation.[26] Thus rather than reviving a stagnant industrial sector and restoring expanded reproduction—in line with Schumpeter's predictions—the rise of the computer industry has contributed to deindustrialization and a diminished scale of accumulation—in line with Marx's.

Surplus populations under deindustrialization: Service work and slums

Deindustrialization began in the US, where the share of manufacturing employment started falling in the 1960s before dropping absolutely in the 80s, but this trend was soon generalized to most other high-GDP countries, and even to countries and regions that are seen as "industrializing."[27] The explosive growth of a low-wage service-sector partially offset the decline in manufacturing employment. However, services have proven incapable of replacing manufacturing as the basis of a new round of expanded reproduction. Over the last 40 years average GDP has grown more and more slowly on a cycle-by-cycle basis in the US and Europe, with only one exception in the US in the late 90s, while real wages have stagnated, and workers have increasingly relied on credit to maintain their living standards.

If, as we have argued, expanded reproduction generates dynamic growth when rising productivity frees capital and labor from some lines, which then recombine in new or expanding industries, then this has an important consequence for an understanding of service industry growth. Services are, almost by definition, those activities for which productivity increases are difficult to achieve otherwise than on the margin.[28] The only known way to drastically improve the efficiency of services is to turn them into goods and then to produce those goods with industrial processes that become more efficient over time. Many manufactured goods are in fact former services—dishes were formerly washed by servants in the homes of the affluent; today, dishwashers perform that service more efficiently and are themselves produced with less and less labor. Those activities that remain services tend to be precisely the ones for which *it has so far proven impossible to find a replacement in the world of goods.*[29]

Of course the bourgeois concept of "services" is notoriously imprecise, including everything from so-called "financial services" to clerical workers and hotel cleaning staff, and even some outsourced manufacturing jobs. Many Marxists have tried to assimilate the category of services to that of unproductive labor, but if we reflect on the above characterization it becomes clear that it is closer to Marx's conception of "formal subsumption." Marx had criticised Smith for having a metaphysical understanding of productive and unproductive labor—the former producing goods and the latter not—and he replaced it with a technical distinction between labor performed as part of a valorization process of capital and the labor performed outside of that process for the immediate consumer. In the *Results of the Direct Production Process* Marx argues that theoretically all unproductive labor can be made productive, for this means only that it has been formally subsumed by the capitalist valorization process.[30] However, formally subsumed activities are productive only of absolute surplus value. In order to be productive of relative surplus value it is necessary to transform the material process of production so that it is amenable to rapid increases in productivity (co-operation, manufacture, large-scale industry and machinery)—i.e. real subsumption. When bourgeois economists like Rowthorn speak of "technologically stagnant services" they recall without knowing it Marx's concept of a labor process which has been only formally but not really subsumed.

Thus as the economy grows, real output in "services" tends to grow, but it does so only by adding more employees or by intensifying the work of existing employees, that is, by means of absolute rather than relative surplus value production. In most of these sectors wages form almost the entirety of costs, so wages have to be kept down in order for services to remain affordable and profitable, especially when the people purchasing them are themselves poor: thus McDonald's and Walmart in the US—or the vast informal proletariat in India and China.[31]

It is a peculiar failure of analysis that today, in some circles, the deindustrialization of the high-GDP countries is blamed on the industrialization of the low-GDP countries, while in other circles, the deindustrialization of low-GDP countries is blamed on IMF and World Bank policies serving the interests of high-GDP countries. In fact, almost all the countries of the world have participated in the *same global transformation*, but to different degrees. In the early post-war period, many countries turned to "Fordism"—that is to say, the import of methods of mass production, made possible by government-sponsored "technology transfers" from high-GDP countries. Fordism is often taken to be a national economic-development policy, based on an "agreement" between capital and workers to share the gains of productivity increases. But Fordism was, almost from the beginning, predicated on an internationalization of trade in manufactures. Europe and Japan benefited the most from the resurgence of international trade in the 1950s and 60s: capitals in these countries were able to achieve massive economies of scale by producing for international trade, thereby overcoming the limits of their own domestic markets. By the mid-60s, capitals in low-GDP countries like Brazil and South Korea were doing the same thing: even if they could capture only a small portion of the rapidly expanding international export market, they would still grow far beyond what was possible in their home markets. Thus, in the period before 1973, *the internationalization of trade was associated with high rates of growth in all industrializing countries.*

After 1973, the situation changed. Markets for manufactures were becoming saturated, and it was increasingly the case that a few countries could provide the manufactures for all of the world (one Chinese firm currently supplies over half the world's microwaves). Thus the resulting crisis of the capital–labor relation, which is to say, a combined crisis of over-production and under-consumption, signalled by a global fall in the rate of profit and issuing in a multiplication of forms of unemployment and precarious employment. As the capital–labor accord snapped, having always been based on healthy rates of growth worldwide, wages stagnated. Capital in all countries became even more dependent on international trade, but from now on, *capitals in some countries would expand only at the expense of those in others.* Though they had not yet caught up to the high-GDP countries, the low-GDP countries took part in the same international crisis. Structural Adjustment Programs only accelerated their transition to a new, unstable international framework. Deindustrialization, or at least the stagnation of industrial employment, set in almost universally among industrializing countries in the 1980s and 90s.[32]

For countries that remained agricultural, or relied on traditional or resource exports, the crisis was even more devastating, as prices of "traditional" commodities collapsed in the face of falling demand. Here, too, we must look back at longer-term trends. In the early post-war period, developments in agriculture radically increased the availability of cheap food. First, synthetic fertiliser was manufactured in demobilised munitions-factories after World War II, making it possible to raise the productivity of land with new high-yield varieties of crops. Second, motor-mechanization raised the productivity of agricultural labor. Both technologies were adapted to production in tropical climates. Thus, almost immediately after the global peasantry was drawn into the market by high agricultural-prices stemming from the Korean War boom, those same prices began to fall continuously. Exit from agriculture in the low-GDP countries was therefore already underway in the 1950s. It was the result, not only of the differentiation and expulsion of the peasantry according to market viability, but also of the massive boost to population itself (sustained by cheap food and modern medicine). Rising household sizes meant that traditional forms of inheritance now pulverised land holdings, while rising population density strained ecological limits, as resources were used unsustainably.[33] Again, the Structural Adjustment Programs of the 1980s and 90s, which forced indebted countries to lift agriculture subsidies, merely dealt the knockout blow to peasants who were already on their last legs.

It should thus be clear that de-industrialization is not caused by the industrialization of the "third world." Most of the world's industrial working-class now lives outside the "first world," but so does most of the world's population. The low-GDP countries have absolutely more workers in industry, but not relative to their populations. Relative industrial employment is falling even as agricultural employment collapses. Just as deindustrialization in the high-GDP countries entails both the exit from manufacturing and the failure of services to take its place, so also the explosive growth of slums in the low-GDP countries entails both the exit from the countryside and the failure of industry to absorb the rural surplus. Whereas the World Bank used to suggest that the growing surplus populations throughout the world were a mere transitional element, they are now forced to admit the permanence of this condition. More than a billion people today eke out a terrible existence via an endless migration between urban and rural slums, searching for temporary and casual work wherever they can find it.[34]

Surplus capital alongside surplus populations

We have described how accumulation of capital over long periods leads old lines to throw off labor and capital, which are then recombined in new and expanding lines. This is the dynamic of capital, which becomes at the same time its limit. Since capital is thrown off whether or not it can find productive avenues of investment, a point is reached at which "surplus" capital begins to build up in the system, beside the surplus labor it no longer employs. Marx discusses these phenomena in a section of *Capital* vol. 3, entitled "surplus capital alongside surplus population."[35] For most of this chapter we have focused on the latter phenomenon, due in large part to the neglect of this tendency among readers of Marx. In this final section we look at some recent manifestations of the former, as the story of surplus capital both mediates and distorts the story of surplus populations. Unfortunately we will be able to do little more than touch on this subject matter here, leaving a more extended treatment to *Endnotes* no. 3.

The US emerged unscathed from World War II as the most advanced capitalist country, with the largest domestic market, the smallest agricultural population (as a percentage of employment), and the most advanced industrial technologies. By some estimates it was responsible for more than half of the world's output.[36] It also emerged from the war as the global creditor *par excellence*, owning two thirds of global gold reserves and with most allied powers owing it tremendous sums of money. Under these conditions, the US was able to reconstruct the international monetary order, in a shamble since the Great Depression, on its own terms. At Bretton Woods, the dollar was established as the international reserve currency, the only one to be directly backed by gold, and all other currencies were pegged to the dollar (creating a fixed exchange rate system, which nevertheless allowed for periodic adjustments). On the one hand, by fixing their own currencies to the dollar, European powers were given temporary relief from balancing their budgets during reconstruction. On the other hand, the US, by facilitating reconstruction, was assured of markets for its capital exports, which in turn facilitated the European purchase of American goods. In this way European budget deficits were funded by US capital exports, and a persistent trans-Atlantic trade imbalance was effectively written into the Bretton Woods agreements. It was an imbalance, however, which soon evaporated.

On the back of an influx of dollars, via direct foreign investment (often military), loans and credit, European countries, as well as American firms operating in Europe, had been importing US capital goods to expand European productive capacity. The same process occurred in Japan, with the Korean War playing the role of the Marshall Plan (though in Japan, US subsidiaries were notable by their absence). All this was encouraged by the US, which facilitated the transfer of its technologies of mass production and distribution all over the world. Yet by the 1960s, many countries had developed their productive capacity to the extent that they no longer relied on US imports. Furthermore, some of those countries were beginning to compete with the very US producers on whom they had previously relied. This competition played out first in third markets and then in the US domestic market itself. The resulting reversal of the US balance of trade in the mid sixties signified that the build out of global manufacturing capacity was approaching a limit. Henceforth competition for export share would become a zero-sum game.

While during the post-war boom the export of dollars via foreign direct investment had enabled rapid growth in deficit countries, this phase change meant that US capital exports became increasingly inflationary.[37] The spiralling US budget deficits of the Vietnam War only intensified this problem of inflation, as the seemingly inevitable devaluation of the dollar threatened to undermine the reserves, and hence the balance of payments, of all nations, straining the fixed exchange rate system to its limits. The result was that on the one hand many central banks began to cash in their dollars for gold (forcing the US to effectively end convertibility in 1968), while on the other hand surplus dollars accumulated in Eurodollar markets began to put speculative pressure on the currencies of export-based economies who were most at risk from the effects of dollar devaluation. These included both those developing countries which had pegged their currencies to the dollar, and thus risked seeing their primary commodity exports fall in value relative to the manufactured imports on which their development depended, as well as developed nations whose export markets risked being undermined by the revaluation of their currencies relative to the dollar. In its subsequent abandonment of Bretton Woods and its policy of "benign neglect" of the deficit, the US used this threat of dollar devaluation to impose a new flexible dollar reserve currency standard on the rest of the world, effectively delegating the job of stabilizing the dollar to foreign central banks who would be compelled to spend their surplus dollars on US securities in order to maintain the dollar value of their own currencies. This, to all intents and purposes, removed budgetary constraints from the US, allowing it to run up deficits and issue dollars at will, knowing that foreign nations would have no choice but to recycle them back to US financial markets, particularly into US government debt which quickly replaced gold as the global reserve currency.[38]

Recycled surplus dollars provided an enormous boost to global financial markets, where they became the key factor in the suddenly highly volatile currency markets—as both the reason for this volatility and the only available resource for hedging against it. Yet surplus dollars also transformed the landscape and shaped the growth of the global economy for the next 30 years. Because it was far in excess of global investment demand, this "giant pool of money" became the source of expanded state and consumer debt, as well as speculative financial bubbles. In the latter sense surplus dollars have become something of a specter stalking the planet, running up unprecedented asset bubbles in whichever national economy has the misfortune to absorb their attention.[39]

This chain of bubbles and busts began in Latin America in the late 70s. An influx of recycled petro-dollars (stimulated by sub-zero real interest rates on the dollar) generated a whole series of risky financial innovations (including the infamous "adjustable rate loan"), which all collapsed when the Volcker shock brought interest rates back up. It was recycled surplus dollars from Japan that saved the US economy from the subsequent deflation and enabled Reagan's redoubled Keynesian spending programs. Yet the US thanked Japan for its kindness by devaluing the dollar relative to the Yen in the Plaza Accords of 1985, sending the Japanese economy into an asset-price bubble of even greater proportions, which finally collapsed in 1991. This in its turn set off a series of bubbles in the East Asian economies, to which Japan had exported its manufacturing capacity (in order to get around an appreciating Yen). These economies, as well as other Latin American economies that had pegged their currencies to the dollar, then imploded as a delayed result of the dollar revaluation in the reverse Plaza Accords of 1995. Yet this merely shifted the bubble back to the US, as the US stock market bonanza created by the appreciating dollar gave way to the dot-com bubble. In 2001 the latter turned over into a housing bubble, when US corporate demand for debt proved to be an insufficient sink for global surplus dollars. If the last two bubbles were largely restricted to the United States (although the housing bubble also extended its reach to Europe), it is because due to its size and senior age privileges it is now the only economy able to withstand the influx of these surplus dollars for any sustained time period.

If we place this phenomenon in the context of the story of deindustrialization and stagnation described above, it becomes plausible to envisage it as a game of musical chairs in which the spread of productive capacity across the world, compounded by rising productivity, continually aggravates global overcapacity. Excess capacity is then only kept in motion by a continual process that shifts the burden of this excess on to one inflated economy after another. These latter are only able to absorb the surplus by running up debt on the basis of excessively low short term interest rates and the fictitious wealth this generates, and as soon as interest rates begin to rise and the speculative fever abates the bubbles must all inevitably collapse—one after another.

Many have called this phenomena "financialization," an ambiguous term suggesting the increasing dominance of financial capital over industrial or commercial capital. But the "rise of finance" stories, in all their forms, obscure both the sources of financial capital, and the reasons for its continued growth as a sector even as finance finds it increasingly difficult to maintain its rate of return. For the former, we must look not only at the pool of surplus dollars, which we have already described, but also the fact that stagnation in non-financial sectors has increasingly shifted investment demand into *IPO*'s, mergers and buy-outs, which generate fees and dividends for financial companies. As for the latter, the dearth of productive investment opportunities, combined with an expansive monetary policy, kept both short and long-term interest rates abnormally low, which compelled finance to take on greater and greater risk in order to make the same returns on investment. This rising level of risk (finance's measure of falling profitability) is in turn masked by more and more complex financial "innovations," requiring periodic bailouts by state governments when they break down.

Unprecedented weakness of growth in the high-GDP countries over the 1997–2009 period, zero-growth in household income and employment over the whole cycle, the almost complete reliance on construction and household debt to maintain GDP—all are testament to the inability of surplus capital in its financial form to recombine with surplus labor and give rise to dynamic patterns of expanded reproduction.[40] The bubbles of mid-19th century Europe generated national rail systems. Even the Japanese bubble of the 1980s left behind new productive capacity that has never been fully utilized. By contrast the two US-centered bubbles of the past decades generated only a glut of telecommunication wires in an increasingly wireless world and vast tracts of economically and ecologically unsustainable housing. The "Greenspan put"—the stimulation of "a boom within the bubble"—was a failure. It merely demonstrated the diminishing returns of injecting more debt into an already over-indebted system.

. . . and China?

A common objection to the account we have so far provided would be to point to China as an obvious exception to this picture of global stagnation, particularly in so far as it relates to otherwise global trends of deindustrialization and under-employment. Of course, over these years China became a global industrial powerhouse, but it did so not through opening new markets or innovating new productive techniques, but rather by massively building out its manufacturing capacity at the expense of other countries.[41] Everyone assumes that this expansion must have brought about a historic increase in the size of the Chinese industrial working class, but that is flatly false. The latest statistics show that, on balance, *China did not create any new jobs in manufacturing between 1993 and 2006*, with the total number of such workers hovering around 110 million people.[42] This is not as surprising as it must seem at first glance, for two reasons.

First, over the last thirty years, the industrialization of the new southern industries—based initially on the processing of exports from Hong Kong and Taiwan—has kept pace with the gutting of the old, Maoist industrial northeast. That may provide part of the explanation of why China, unlike Germany, Japan, or Korea (earlier in the postwar period), saw almost no rise in real wages over decades of miracle growth rates.

Second, China has not only grown on the basis of labor-intensive manufacturing. Its low wages have helped it to compete across a spectrum of industries, from textiles and toys to cars and computers. The incorporation of existing labor-saving innovations into the firms of developing countries, including China, has meant that, even with growing geographic expansion, each set of industrializing countries has achieved lower heights of industrial employment (relative to total labor force). That is to say, not only has China lost manufacturing jobs in its older industries; the new industries have absorbed tendentially less labor relative to the growth of output.

In the 19th century when England was the workshop of the world, 95 percent of that world were peasants. Today, when the vast majority of the world's population depends on global markets for their survival, the ability of one country to produce for all the others spells ruin, both for those who must be kept impoverished in order to maintain export prices, and for the vast multitudes whose labor is no longer necessary, but who, equally, can no longer rely on their own resources to survive. In this context the remainder of the world's peasantry can no longer act as a weapon of modernization, i.e. as a pool of both labor and consumer demand that can be drawn on in order to accelerate the pace of industrialization. It becomes a pure surplus. This is true in India and sub-Saharan Africa—*and in China.*

Conclusion

Today many speak of a "jobless recovery," but if the "general law of capital accumulation" applies then all capitalist recoveries are tendentially jobless. The tendency of "mature" industries to throw off labor, whilst facilitating expanded reproduction, also tends to consolidate a surplus population not fully absorbed by the subsequent expansion. This is due to the adaptability of labor-saving technology across lines, which mean that the manufacture of new products tends to make use of the most innovative production processes. Yet process innovations last forever, and they generalize across new and old capitals, while product innovations are inherently limited in their ability to generate a net expansion of output and employment. Here the problem is not merely that product innovations have to emerge at an accelerated rate to absorb the surplus thrown off by process innovations, it is that an acceleration of product innovation itself gives rise to an acceleration of process innovation.[43]

Yet if the "general law" was suspended for much of the 20th century for the reasons we have outlined above, the current growing global masses of under-employed cannot be attributed to its reassertion, at least in any simple sense. For the trajectory of surplus capital distorts the trajectory of surplus labor described by Marx, and not only in the ways that we have already described. Most importantly, surplus capital built up in international money markets over the last 30 years has masked some of the tendencies to absolute immiseration, through the growing debt of working class households. This tendency, which has kept the bottom from falling out of global aggregate demand, has equally prevented any possibility of recovery, which would be achieved only through the "slaughtering of capital values" and "setting free of labor." For while asset-price deflation may raise the possibility of a new investment boom, the devalorization of labor-power will, in this context, only lead to increasing levels of consumer default and further financial breakdowns.[44] Thus it is not only its capacity to generate employment, but the sustainability of the recovery itself which remains in question today.

The coming decades may see a series of blowouts, if states fail to manage global deflationary pressures, or they may see a long and slow decline. While we are not catastrophists by inclination, we would warn against those who might forget that history sometimes rushes forward unpredictably. Regardless, the catastrophe for which we wait is not something of the future, but is merely the continuation of the present along its execrable trend. We have already seen decades of rising poverty and unemployment. Those who say of the still-industrialized countries that it is not so bad, that people will soldier on—in a phrase, that the proletariat has become indifferent to its misery—will have their hypothesis tested in the years to come, as levels of debt subside and household incomes continue their downward trend.[45] In any case, for a huge chunk of the world's population it has become impossible to deny the abundant evidence of the catastrophe. Any question of the absorption of this surplus humanity has been put to rest. It exists now only to be managed: segregated into prisons, marginalised in ghettos and camps, disciplined by the police, and annihilated by war.

Notes

1 *FAOSTAT* Statistical Database, Food and Agriculture Organization of the United Nations, http://www.fao.org/FAOSTAT (2009).
2 Robert Rowthorn and Ken Coutts, "Deindustrialisation and the Balance of Payments in Advanced Economies," United Nation Conference on Trade and Development Discussion Paper 170 (May 2004): 2.
3 By noting the tendency of capital to generate a scarcity of jobs amidst an abundance of goods (which are thereby made artificially scarce in relation to effective demand) we are not, of course, lending sustenance to demands for "more jobs." Such demands will always be futile as long as selling one's labor remains the primary way of acquiring the means of life.
4 This need not always occur through the violent means described by Marx. In the 20th century many peasants lost direct access to land not by expropriation but rather through an excessive subdivision of their holdings as land was passed from generation to generation. Becoming thus increasingly market dependent, small farmers found themselves at a disadvantage to large farmers and eventually lost their land. In Europe, this process was completed in the 1950s and 1960s. On a global scale it is only now—with the exceptions of sub-Saharan Africa, parts of South Asia, and China—beginning to approach completion.
5 Marx sometimes refers to simple reproduction as an abstract thought experiment—capitalism without growth—but to leave it at that is to miss what the concept tells us about the inner mechanism of the process of accumulation. The chapter on simple reproduction concludes: "Capitalist production, therefore, under its aspect of a continuous connected process, of a process of reproduction, produces not only commodities, not only surplus-value, but it also produces and reproduces the capitalist relation; on the one side the capitalist, on the other the wage-laborer." Marx, *Capital*, vol. 1 (*MECW* 35), p. 573.
6 Marx, *Capital*, vol. 1 (*MECW* 35), p. 573.
7 Marxists have tended to avoid issues of demand because of a supposed neoclassical monopoly on the discourse, but Marx had no such reticence. The compulsion to expand markets and fight over market share is fundamental to the workings of the law of value, e.g. Marx, *Capital*, vol. 1 (*MECW* 35), p. 434.

8 Saturation is a matter, not of the absolute amount of a product bought and sold, but of a changed relationship between the rates of growth of capacity and of demand.

9 This process applies only to consumer-goods industries. Capital-goods industries tend to expand and contract in accordance with the needs of the particular consumer-goods which "lead" each cycle. But the relationship between the two "departments" is never so simple. As we will show, labor-saving "process-innovations" in dept 1 may lead to "product innovations" in dept 2, expanding the market as a whole.

10 Marx, *Capital*, vol.1 (*MECW* 35), p. 627 (Fowkes's translation).

11 Joseph Schumpeter, *Business Cycles: A Theoretical, Historical and Statistical Analysis of the Capitalist Process* (Mansfield Centre, CT: Martino Pub, 2005).

12 Though earlier in the series, the published version of volume one—written in 1866–67—actually postdates volume three, most of the material for which was written in 1863–5. It thus seems plausible to account for the striking parallels between chapter 25 of volume one and chapter 15 of volume three on the supposition that Marx introduced key elements of the volume three material into the published version of volume one in anticipation of the difficulty of finishing volume three in a reasonable time.

13 Marx, *Capital*, vol. 1 (*MECW* 35), p. 638.

14 This surplus population need not find itself completely "outside" capitalist social relations. Capital may not need these workers, but they still need to work. They are thus forced to offer themselves up for the most abject forms of wage slavery in the form of petty-production and services.

15 Translations of the French edition of *Capital*, vol. 1 from Simon Clarke, *Marx's Theory of Crisis* (New York: St Martin's Press, 1994), pp. 172–5.

16 Marx, *Capital*, vol. 1 (*MECW* 35), pp. 622–3.

17 Marx sometimes envisages this as a revolutionary crisis: "A development of productive forces which would diminish the absolute number of laborers, i.e., enable the entire nation to accomplish its total production in a shorter time span, would cause a revolution, because it would put the bulk of the population out of the running" (Marx, *Capital*, vol. 3 (*MECW* 37), p. 262).

18 Marx, *Capital*, vol. 1 (*MECW* 35), p. 449.

19 Ibid., p. 625.

20 It is possible to imagine a world in which labor-saving innovations would lead to a reduction, not of the number of workers in a given line, but the amount of time each of them works. Yet because capitalists derive their profit from the value added by the worker beyond that required to pay his wages, it is never in the interest of capitalists to reduce the number of hours each individual works (unless, of course, they are forced to do so by action of the state or agitation of workers). Such reductions would cut directly into profits unless wages were also reduced concomitantly. Because of the peculiarities of a social form based on wage-labor, therefore, capitalists must shed the individuals themselves rather than the hours each individual works, decreasing the costs of labor relative to value added, and pushing great masses of people into the streets.

21 Ibid., p. 609 (emphasis added).

22 In this chapter we have opted to use the epithets "high-GDP"/"low-GDP" (meaning GDP per capita) to describe the division of the world between a wealthy minority of capitalist states and a more impoverished majority.

We adopt these not entirely satisfactory terms because of the absence of associations with dubious political and theoretical analyses that are carried by other divisions (e.g., first world/third world, core/periphery, developed/underdeveloped, imperialist/oppressed).

23 In the following we deal only with the latter phenomenon. For an account of the former see the article "Notes on the New Housing Question", *Endnotes* 2 (April 2010), 52–66.

24 The difference between the economy of time that rail transport offered to the consumer and the economy of time and labor it offered to the capitalist was itself a vanishing difference as the capitalist notion of time as a scarce resource to be allocated with maximum efficiency increasingly came to dominate society at large.

25 "It is not merely that an accelerated accumulation of total capital, accelerated in a constantly growing progression, is needed to absorb an additional number of laborers, or even, on account of the constant metamorphosis of old capital, to keep employed those already functioning. In its turn, this increasing accumulation and centralization becomes a source of new changes in the composition of capital, of a more accelerated diminution of its variable, as compared with its constant constituent." Marx, *Capital*, vol. 1 (*MECW* 35), pp. 623–4.

26 See Beverly Silver, *Forces of Labor* (Cambridge and New York: Cambridge University Press, 2003).

27 In no country (with the exception of the UK) did deindustrialization involve a decline in real industrial output. In 1999, manufacturing still accounted for 46 percent of total US profits, but only 14 percent of the labor force.

28 Robert Rowthorn and Ramana Ramaswamy, "Deindustrialization: Causes and Implications" (*IMF* Working Paper 97/42, April 1997).

29 Jonathan Gershuny, *After Industrial Society?: The Emerging Self-Service Economy* (Atlantic Highlands, NJ: Humanities Press, 1978).

30 Marx, "Results of the Direct Production Process" (*MECW* 34), pp. 121–46.

31 Many service jobs only exist because of wage differentials—that is, massive social inequality. Marx noted that domestic servants outnumbered industrial workers in Victorian Britain (Marx, *Capital*, vol. 1 [*MECW* 35], p. 449). With rising real wages it became increasingly untenable for middle class households (such as Marx's) to employ servants. For much of the 20th century this destitute labor force was reduced to a memory, only to reappear as "service" workers in every corner of the modern world.

32 Sukti Dasgupta and Ajit Singh, "Will Services be the New Engine of Indian Economic Growth?" *Development and Change* 36, no. 6 (2005).

33 This does not mean that the world is overpopulated relative to food production. As we have shown, exit from the countryside was related to a massive increase in the productivity of agriculture. Food production per person has constantly risen even as population growth slows with the coming completion of the world demographic transition. It would be even higher if the overproduction of grains had not led to subsidizing the corn-feeding of animals for meat production. There is nothing Malthusian about the Marxian concept of surplus populations, which are surplus with regard to capital accumulation and nothing else.

34 See Mike Davis, *Planet of Slums* (London: Verso, 2006).

35 "It is no contradiction that this over-production of capital is accompanied by more or less considerable relative over-population. The circumstances which increased the productiveness of labor, augmented the mass of produced commodities, expanded markets, accelerated accumulation of capital both in terms of its mass and its value, and lowered the rate of profit—these same circumstances have also created, and continuously create, a relative overpopulation, an over-population of laborers not employed by the surplus-capital owing to the low degree of exploitation at which alone they could be employed, or at least owing to the low rate of profit which they would yield at the given degree of exploitation." Marx, *Capital*, vol. 3 (*MECW 37*), pp. 254–5.

36 Daniel Brill, "The Changing Role of the United States in the World Economy" in John Richard Sargent, Matthijs van den Adel (eds), *Europe and The Dollar in the World-Wide Disequilibrium* (Leiden: Brill, 1981), p. 19.

37 Most Marxists attribute inflation in this period either to the exploding US budget deficit (due in large part to the Vietnam War) or to the rising strength of labor. Yet Anwar Shaikh convincingly argues that the restricted supply in relation to which inflation is the index of excess demand is not full employment or labor recalcitrance, but rather the maximum level of accumulation, or the maximum capacity profit rate—whose decline during this period is the leading factor behind stagflation. Anwar Shaikh, "Explaining Inflation and Unemployment" in Andriana Vachlou, ed., *Contemporary Economic Theory* (London: Macmillan, 1999).

38 See Michael Hudson, *Super Imperialism: The Origin and Fundamentals of U.S. World Dominance* (London: Pluto Press, 2003).

39 The following account owes much to Robert Brenner's analysis. See in particular the prologue to the Spanish translation of *Economics of Global Turbulence*: "What is Good For Goldman Sachs is Good For America: the Origins of the Current Crisis" (2009).

40 Josh Bivens and John Irons, "A Feeble Recovery: The Fundamental Economic Weaknesses Of the 2001–07 Expansion," *EPI Briefing Paper* 214, Economic Policy Institute (2008).

41 In the 1990s Japan devolved its more labor-intensive industries onto developing countries in Asia—first to the East Asian Tigers, then to the *ASEAN* countries and then to China. But the absorption of industries by China has undermined the hierarchy of production within the region.

42 Erin Lett and Judith Banister, "Chinese Manufacturing Employment and Compensation Costs: 2002–2006," *Monthly Labor Review* 132 (April 2009): 30.

43 See note 27 above.

44 See Paulo Dos Santos, "At the Heart of the Matter: Household Debt in Contemporary Banking and the International Crisis," *Research On Money And Finance*, Discussion Paper no. 11 (2009). On the capital side, Phelps and Tilman outline a series of limitations to the potential of innovators to exploit the crisis: Edmund Phelps and Leo Tilman, "Wanted: A First National Bank of Innovation," *Harvard Business Review* (January–February 2010).

SOURCES

The authors and publisher gratefully acknowledge the permissions granted to reproduce the copyright materials in this book:

Félix Guattari and Eric Alliez, "Capitalist Systems, Structures, and Processes," *Molecular Revolution*. New York: Penguin, 1984: 273–287. Reprinted by permission of Penguin.

Moishe Postone, "Rethinking Marx's Critical Theory," *History and Heteronomy*. Tokyo: University of Tokyo Center for Philosophy, 2009: 31–48. Reprinted by permission of University of Tokyo Center for Philosophy.

Alain Lipietz, "The Impasses of Liberal Productivism," *Towards a New Economic Order: Postfordism, Ecology and Democracy*. New York and Oxford: Oxford University Press, 1992: 30–47. Reprinted by permission of Oxford University Press and Polity.

Paulin Hountondji, "Recapturing," *The Surreptitious Speech: Présence Africaine and the Politics of Otherness 1947–1987*, ed. V. Y. Mudimbe. Chicago: University of Chicago Press, 1992: 238–248. Reprinted by permission of University of Chicago Press.

Maurizio Lazzarato, "Immaterial Labor," *Radical Thought in Italy: A Potential Politics*, ed. Paolo Virno and Michael Hardt. Minneapolis: University of Minnesota Press, 1996: 133–150. Reprinted by permission of University of Minnesota Press.

Silvia Federici, "Women, Land-Struggles, and Globalization," *Journal of Asian and African Studies* 39, no. 1–2 (April 2004): 47–62. Reprinted by permission of the author.

Arif Dirlik, "The Idea of a 'Chinese Model,'" *International Critical Thought* 1, no. 2 (August 2011): 129–137. Reprinted by permission of Copyright Clearance Center.

Étienne Balibar, "Is There a Neo-Racism?" *Race, Nation, Class: Ambiguous Identities*. London: Verso, 1991: 17–28. Reprinted by permission of Verso.

Dipesh Chakrabarty, "Marx After Marxism: A Subaltern Historian's Perspective," *Economic and Political Weekly*, 28, no. 22 (May 29, 1993): 1094–1096. Reprinted by permission of the author.

Maya Gonzalez and Jeanne Neton, "The Logic of Gender: On the Separation of Spheres and the Process of Abjection," *Endnotes 3* (September 2013): 56–91. Reprinted by permission of Autonomedia.

Slavoj Žižek, "Postmodernism or Class? Yes Please," Judith Butler, Ernesto Laclau and Slavoj Žižek, *Contingency, Hegemony, Universality*. London: Verso, 2000: 90–135. Reprinted by permission of Verso.

Théorie Communiste, "Communization in the Present Tense," *Communization and its Discontents*, ed. Benjamin Noys. New York: Minor Compositions, 2011: 41–60. Reprinted by permission of Autonomedia.

Roswitha Scholz, "Patriarchy and Commodity Society: Gender without the Body," in *Marxism and the Critique of Value*, ed. and trans. Neil Larsen, Mathias Nilges, Josh Robinson, and Nicholas Brown (Chicago and Alberta: MCM′, 2014) 115–132. Reprinted by permission of MCM′.

Gayatri Spivak, "Scattered Speculations on the Question of Value," *Diacritics* 15, no. 4 (Winter, 1985): 73–93. Reprinted by permission of the Johns Hopkins University Press.

Pierre Macherey, "Philosophy as Operation," *In a Materialist Way*, ed. Warren Montag. London: Verso, 1998: 28–41. Reprinted by permission of Verso.

Kojin Karatani, "What is Transcritique?" *Transcritique*. London: MIT Press, 2003: 1–26. Reprinted by permission of MIT Press.

Alain Badiou, "The Idea of Communism," *The Idea of Communism*, ed. Costas Douzinas and Slavoj Žižek. London: Verso, 2010: 1–14. Reprinted by permission of Verso.

Boris Groys, "The Kingdom of Philosophy: The Administration of Metanoia," *The Communist Postscript*. London: Verso, 2009: 103–127. Reprinted by permission of Verso.

Imre Szeman and Nicholas Brown, "Twenty-five Theses on Philosophy in the Age of Finance Capital," *A Leftist Ontology*, ed. Carsten Strathausen. Minneapolis: University of Minnesota Press, 2009: 33–55. Reprinted by permission of University of Minnesota Press.

Roberto Schwarz, "Misplaced Ideas: Literature and Society in Late-Nineteenth-Century Brazil," *Misplaced Ideas: Essays on Brazilian Culture*, ed. John Gledson. London: Verso, 1992: 19–32. Reprinted by permission of Verso.

Chidi Amuta, "Traditionalism and the Quest for an African Literary Aesthetic," *The Theory of African Literature*. London: Zed Books and Institute for African Alternatives, 1989: 33–50. Reprinted by permission of Zed Books.

Imre Szeman, "Marxist Literary Theory, Then and Now," *Mediations* 24, no. 2 (Spring 2009) 37–47. Reprinted by permission of *Mediations*.

Fredric Jameson, "The Antinomies of Postmodernity," *The Seeds of Time*, New York: Columbia University Press, 1994: 50–72. Reprinted by permission of Columbia University Press.

Carolyn Lesjack, "Reading Dialectically," *Literary Materialisms*, ed. Mathias Nilges and Emilio Sauri. New York: Palgrave Macmillan, 2013: 17–48. Reprinted by permission of *Criticism*.

Sarah Brouillette, "Creative Labor," from *Mediations* 24, no. 2 (Spring 2009): 140–149. Reprinted by permission of *Mediations*.

Nicholas Brown, "The Work of Art in the Age of its Real Subsumption Under Capital," *nonsite.org* (March 13, 2012): http://nonsite.org/editorial/the-work-of-art-in-the-age-of-its-real-subsumption-under-capital. Reprinted by permission of nonsite.org.

Álvaro García Linera, "State Crisis and Popular Power," *New Left Review* 37 (January–February 2006): 73–85. Reprinted by permission of New Left Review.

Antonio Negri, "Constituent Power: The Concept of a Crisis," *Insurgencies: Constituent Power and the Modern State*, trans. Maurizia Boscagli. Minneapolis: University of Minnesota Press, 1990: 1–35. Reprinted by permission of University of Minnesota Press.

Chantal Mouffe, *Agonistics*, London: Verso, 2013: 65–85. Reprinted with permission by Verso.

Peter Hallward, "On Political Will," *Politics and Culture* (forthcoming 2014). Reprinted by permission of *Politics and Culture*.

Jodi Dean, "Communicative Capitalism: Circulation and the Foreclosure of Politics," *Cultural Politics* 1, no. 1 (March 2005): 51–74. Reprinted by permission of Duke University Press.

Jacques Rancière, "Ten Theses on Politics," *Theory and Event* 5, no. 3 (2001): 1–16. Reprinted by permission of The Johns Hopkins University Press.

Claus Peter Ortlieb, "A Contradiction between Matter and Form: On the Significance of the Production of Relative Surplus Value for the Dynamics of the Final Crisis," in *Marxism and the Critique of Value*, ed. and trans. Neil Larsen, Mathias Nilges, Josh Robinson, and Nicholas Brown (Chicago and Alberta: MCM', 2014) 71–113. Reprinted by permission of MCM'.

Aaron Benanav and John Clegg (Endnotes), "Misery and Debt," *Endnotes* 2 (April 2010): 20–51. Reprinted by Permission of Autonomedia.

INDEX

1960s 204, 506, 575
1970s 56, 78, 168–9, 204, 506, 586
1980s 1, 205, 217, 220, 314
1990s 2–6, 9, 217–18, 549, 574,
 608n. 41

abject, the 169, 171, 174n. 35
abolition 49, 203, 212
 of slavery 350–1
Abu Ghraib 417–18
Adorno, Theodor 218, 224, 324, 326,
 327, 380, 383, 416, 432, 455–6,
 579
aesthetic 87–8, 91n. 2, 415–16, 439n.
 50, 506
 autonomy 459–65
affect 228, 247, 422
affirmative culture 383–4, 416, 418
Africa 67–76, 94–5, 305
 aesthetics 358–76
African National Congress (ANC) 517
Agamben, Giorgio 516, 537, 539–40
Aglietta, Michel 39n. 15
agriculture 23, 94–104, 105, 215, 284,
 364–5, 402, 403, 483, 577, 585,
 588, 598
alienation 219, 277–8, 289, 300, 439n.
 47, 452, 537, 565
Alliez, Eric 19–20
altermodern 502
Althusser, Louis 7, 239, 249, 300, 565
Amin, Samir 71, 253
Amuta, Chidi 338–9
anarchism 287–8, 386, 494
 anarcho-syndicalism 290–1
Anderson, Benedict 285
Anderson, Perry 385–7
animals 137, 264–5, 296, 412, 526,
 565

antagonism 126, 176–7, 183, 190–1,
 193–4, 322, 443, 473, 509, 535,
 537
 and agonism 472, 511–12
antinomy 276, 339, 390
Anti-Oedipus 239–40, 329
anti-semitism 135, 139n. 8, 183–4,
 190–1, 195
Apple Computers 543
Arab Spring 517
arche 558–9
architecture 349, 394–5
archive 412–14
Arendt, Hannah 471, 490, 557–8, 567
Argentina 209, 215, 507–8
Aristotle 261–2, 266, 555–6, 565
art 312, 449–50
 and objecthood 453
asceticism 312–13
Assis, Machado de 338, 343, 348–53
associationism 285, 287
Attali, Jacques 326
austerity 21, 65, 169–70
automation 60–1
autonomism 153, 421–47
 autonomia 441
autonomy 82–4, 205, 283, 458–65
 see also aesthetic
Avatar 454–5

Badiou, Alain 194, 196, 236, 313,
 323, 332, 428
Bailey, Samuel 278–9
Bakhtin, Mikhail 90–1, 400, 405
Bakunin, Mikhail 288
Balibar, Étienne 123–4
Bangladesh 100, 209
banlieues 209
Barabasi, Albert-Laszlo 549

base and superstructure 181, 328, 382, 387–8
Bataille, Georges 400
beauty 415–17
Beck, Ulrich 178, 324
Benanav, Aaron 473
Benjamin, Walter 91n. 3, 253, 325, 413
Bernstein, Eduard 287
biopolitics 490, 502–3
biopower *see* biopolitics
Blair, Tony 414
Blanqui, Louis Auguste 520, 523, 525, 528
Bloomberg, Michael 93
body, the 177, 311
    without organs 239, 312
Bolivia 475–84, 507, 517
Boltanski, Luc 506
Bordwell, David 414
Bosteels, Bruno 12
Bourdieu, Pierre 382, 456, 458–9, 475
bourgeoisie, the 10, 56, 179, 191, 197n. 8, 285, 307, 348, 351, 402, 430, 493
brain drain 73–4
Braudel, Fernand 29, 38n. 3, 39n. 9, 428–9, 476
Brazil 338, 343–53, 477, 507
    Constitution 344
Bretton Woods 601
Brezhnev 314
British Empire 96, 343–4
Brouillette, Sarah 340–1
Brown, Nicholas 237, 341
Brown, Wendy 179, 182
Buddhism 425–7
Burke, Edmund 405
Bush, George H.W. 66
Bush, George W. 533–4, 551
    faith-based policy 536
Butler, Judith 126, 164–5, 176, 185–7, 226, 425–6

Cameroon 96
Capital 49–50, 84, 151, 233, 242, 277, 281, 287, 289, 291

capital 7, 50–1, 124, 145, 160, 204, 219–20, 241–7, 278–9, 289, 324, 457–8, 495, 525–8, 543
    communism of 504
    creative 446–7
    and immaterial labor 80, 86, 88–9, 444–5
    productivity of 51, 574–5
    rate of accumulation 577, 585–99
    reproduction of 84, 205–7, 289–90, 586–90, 605n. 5
    see also valorization
    semiotic system of 19–20
capitalism 25–7, 43–4, 125, 211, 220, 278, 280–4, 402, 431, 462, 505, 507, 522, 573
    with Chinese characteristics 118
    circulation 281–2
    communicative *see* communicative capitalism
    and crisis 211, 575–82, 585–6
    and gender 96–7, 149–50, 161–3, 165–9, 221–2, 252
    naturalization of 180
    pre- 147, 158, 221, 286, 392, 402
    turbo- 227–9
carnivalesque 405
castration 174n. 36, 199n. 24
Cellatex 208
centrism 291
Chakrabarty, Dipesh 124–5
Chiapello, Eve 506
children 162, 163, 165
    child care 153–5, 169
    child labor *see* labor
Chile 38n. 7
China 35, 109–19, 206, 209, 309, 314, 603–4
    Cultural Revolution 110, 236, 295–6
Christianity 310
    in Africa 361
citizenship 159–60
city 392–3
    socialist 404
civil society 57
class 90–1, 173n. 19, 203, 205, 324, 430
    colonialism 346–7

and gender 227 *see also* capitalism
and postmodernism 181
struggle 206, 211, 289–90, 502
Clegg, John 473
Clinton, Bill 192, 551
cognitive mapping 176, 428, 431–2,
439n. 50
Cold War 111, 200n. 29, 314, 404,
498n. 17
Colletti, Lucio 525
colonialism 36, 37, 39n. 18, 68–9,
71–6, 95–7, 105n. 3, 142, 210,
345–54, 346, 357–78, 480–1, 520
commodity 46–7, 82, 85, 125, 145–6,
150–2, 219, 278, 282, 443, 450–3
art 449–50 *see also* cultural
production
fetishism 187 *see also* fetish
commons, the 446
communication 80, 87
communicative capitalism 535–9
communism 203, 212–15, 236, 287–8,
295–305, 309, 470, 493–4, 496,
512, 527
of capital 503–4
communist hypothesis, the 512
soviet 317–18
Communist Party, the 204, 304, 316,
386
Second International 50–1
self-abolition of 314
communization 126, 165, 203, 213–14
concrete universal 179, 182–3, 185,
187, 199n. 23
consensual politics 570–1
see also post-politics
constituent power 487, 494–7
constitutionalism 497
constructivism 221, 409, 510
consumption 85, 88–9, 290–1, 405, 443
contraception 163
contractualism 491
contradiction 50–1, 151, 234–5,
271–2, 390
and antinomy 339–40, 390
see also antinomy
performative 185
see also performative

contrat premiére embauch
(CPE) 209–10
Couto, Mia 327
creativity 79, 81, 88–91, 340–1,
421–47, 494–5
creative class 421–3, 446
credit 281 *see also* debt
crisis 204, 211–12, 305, 590–603
see also capitalism
critical theory 412
cultural production 337, 339–40, 447,
456–9
culturalism 217, 229
culture 133–4, 136–7, 339–40, 382–5,
387
bourgeois 346
high culture 402
mass 402
postmodern 389
cybernetic 36, 77, 328
cynical reason 326, 414, 420–1

Dean, Howard 546–7
Dean, Jodi 11, 472–3
Debord, Guy 325, 327
debt 63, 210, 599–600
decentralization 80
Declaration of the Rights of Man,
The 344
deconstruction 8, 141, 143, 217–18,
234, 240, 312
deindustrialization 593–6
Deleuze, Gilles 189, 239, 312, 329,
331, 503
democracy 178–9, 181–4, 432, 473,
491–2, 509, 510–11, 517, 535,
560–1, 568
absolute 503–4
and communication technology 539
demos 560, 568
dependency 68–9, 71–5, 99–100
depolitization 182
deregulation 56
Derrida, Jacques 8, 25, 146, 178, 244,
246, 247, 253, 254–6, 259n. 14,
400, 414
desertification 103
deterritorialization 20, 189, 502–3

development 93, 398
dialectic 234–6, 243–4, 248, 282,
    298, 313, 322, 407–8, 429, 432,
    482
  Hegelian 233–4, 298, 313, 322,
    437n. 36
  materialist 309, 313
  of theory and practice 420–1
Diduk, Susan 96
difference 143–4, 146–8, 161, 323,
    330
Dirlik, Arif 23–4
dissesnsus 564–6
dissociatoin 221, 223
distinction 90
Dow-Jones, the 256
Durkheim, Émile 44
Dyer-Witheford, Nick 543–4

Eagleton, Terry 375, 380, 382
Eastern Europe 38
  collapse of socialist states 217,
    316–18, 401, 406
ecology *see* environment
Economist, The 6
education 205–6
Einstein, Albert 322
empiricism 295–6
  Kant 277
Endnotes 474
Engels, Friedrich 280, 287
England 286
  Revolution 517
Enlightenment, The 142, 147, 348–9,
    462
entrepreneur, the 63, 82, 84, 90, 446
  artist as 458
environment 66, 93–4, 403, 425, 473
  activism 103
  crisis 8–9
  limits of growth 577–82
épistème 188
equality 161–2
essentialism 178–9, 181, 188–9, 207
  strategic 183, 410–11
ethics 12, 285, 289, 446
eugenics 137

eurocentrism 115, 142, 322, 324, 338,
    346–7, 359–61, 370
Europe 338, 344–8, 574
  and Africa 359
  Eastern *see* Eastern Europe
  economic history 64, 429, 586, 594,
    597–602
  European Union 170
event 299, 313, 428
exchange 452
exchange-value *see* value
extraversion 67

factory 78–9
family 163, 166–7, 221, 227
Fanon, Frantz 130
fantasy 420, 535
fascism 34, 132–3, 144, 177, 190, 286
fashion 90
Federici, Silvia 23, 171, 174n. 34
femininity 164–5, 168, 171, 223, 225
feminism 126–7, 149, 153, 155, 217–18
  marxist 172n. 1, 218
fetish 2, 419, 421–2, 437n. 35, 542
  technological 535, 544–6
feudalism 285
Fiat 66–7
file sharing 543–4, 547
finance 205, 326, 327, 580–1, 602–3
  crisis 211
  financialization 602–3
Florida, Richard 441–2, 446–7
food 94–5
Food and Agriculture Association 95
Ford 85
Fordism 21, 55, 59, 78, 502
  and the family 167–8
  gender 225
  transition to post-fordism 505–6
formalism 340, 408, 424–5
  see also literary criticism
Foucault, Michel 4, 6, 48, 138, 142,
    147, 188, 312, 408, 467n. 20,
    489–90, 503
France 57, 129, 132–6, 208–10
  women wage-labor 173n. 18
Frankfurt School, the 44, 384

French Revolution 285, 296
Freud, Sigmund 262, 542
Fried, Michael 453, 460, 463–4
Friedman, Milton 37n. 7
Fukuyama, Francis 114, 197n. 7, 323, 571
fundamentalism 53, 398

Gaudemar, John Paul de 37
gender 125, 130, 143, 149, 157, 159–61, 164–72, 188, 221, 224
general intellect 78, 213, 444–5, 502n. 4, 505, 507
generation 310
Germany 61, 215, 494
  GDR 186
  women wage-labor 173n. 18
Giddens, Anthony 178, 324
globalization 1, 19, 64–6, 71–5, 99–104, 220, 283, 325, 332, 402, 431–2, 476, 501–2
  cultural 326–7, 328, 330, 384
  and gender 227
  and the internet 549–51
Gonzales, Maya 125
governmentality 147, 503
Gramsci, Antonio 131, 181, 327, 387, 506, 528–30
Greece 210
Greenberg, Clement 459, 467n. 16
growth 61, 577, 578–80, 599
Guattari, Felix 19–20
Guinea Bissau 99–100
Gulf War, First 391
Gutenberg, Johannes 349

Habermas, Jürgen 196, 255, 479, 537, 540, 576
Hallward, Peter 472
Haraway, Donna 327
Hardt, Michael 327, 333, 340, 501–5, 507, 511, 537
Harman, Graham 8
Haug, Fridda 222–3
Hayden, Dolores 171
Hayke, Friedrich 29
health care 192

Hegel, G.W.F. 49, 178, 182–3, 189, 233–5, 237, 264–6, 281, 298, 310, 313, 322, 325, 462, 489
  concrete universal see concrete universal
  externalization 453–4
  labor 451–2
  mental 80, 132
  and neoliberalism 467n. 20
hegemony 176–8, 181, 187–8, 204, 481, 501, 506, 510–11
Heidegger, Martin 183, 188, 432, 490
  and Marx 492–3
hermeneutics of suspicion 393, 417
heteronomy 51
heterotopias 312
Hinduism 144
historicism 146, 188, 408, 460, 463–5
history 50, 147–8, 297–8, 300, 302, 324, 428–30, 527–8
hoarding 280
Hobbes, Thomas 491, 517
Holland 43
Hollywood 325
Holocaust, the 193, 196
Homer 558
Horkheimer, Max 412, 579
Hountondji, Paulin 21–2, 328
Hüller, Knut 577
human rights 184
humanism 135, 184, 250–1, 302, 360
Hume, David 278–9
Hurricane Katrina 418
Husserl, Edmund 310
hybridity 330
hygene 168

identity 171
  identity politics 179–80, 185–6
ideology 89, 131, 184–6, 307n. 8, 326, 341, 420–1, 427, 541
  end of 397
  fetish character 421–3
  Ideologiekritik 380
  spatial 437n. 37 see also space
immanence 8, 332, 509–12
immaterial labor see labor

immigration 132–6
imperialism 402
  British 96
  cultural 373
  French 97
import-substitution 71, 73
In and Out 191
India 102, 142–4, 206, 209
indigenous peoples 93, 477–8, 480,
  482–3
indignados, los 12, 508
individualism 58, 296
individuality 206, 405, 523
industrialization 589, 593–6
  see also modernization
infinity 310–11
  bad 310, 331
information 36, 60, 80
institution 501
instrumental culture 383
intellectuals 327, 393
  African 359–60, 362
International Labor Organization
  (ILO) 95
International Monetary Fund
  (IMF) 55, 98
internationalism 316
internet 325, 534–5, 539–53
interpolation 565
Iraq 533–4
Islam 144
  islamophobia 135
Israel 401
Italy 38, 60–1

Jacobins, the 517, 521, 524
Jacobs, Jane 404
Jamaica 98
Jameson, Fredric 5, 291, 321, 333,
  339, 341, 384, 407–8, 418–32,
  452, 456–7
Japan 61–3
Jobs, Steve 468n. 27

Kant, Immanuel 188–9, 235, 263,
  275–6, 277–9, 282, 322, 346,
  390, 395
Karatani, Kojin 234, 400

Keynes, John Maynard 36
  see also Keynesianism
Keynesianism 84, 229, 394, 500, 581
Khrushchev, Nikita 302
Kierkegaard, Søren 281, 313
Kluge, Alexander 413
Kojève, Alexandre 323, 396
Kurz, Robert 219, 221, 480–1,
  574–5

La Capra, Dominick 255
labor 46–8, 151–2, 155–7, 158, 324,
  451, 494–5
  abstract/real 46–7, 145–6, 219–20,
    495
  child 167
  creative 447, 457
  dead/living 495–6
  domestic labor 150, 153, 565
  immaterial 22–3, 77–91, 502–3,
    505
  mental and manual 78, 80, 91, 132,
    447
  subsumption under capital 204,
    220, 457–8 *see also* subsumption
  see also working class
labor-power 152–4, 160, 204, 219,
  239, 251–2, 289–90
Labriola, Antonio 470–1
Lacan, Jacques 190, 192, 255–6,
  298–9, 551
Laclau, Ernesto 126, 176–9, 181–3,
  188–90, 509, 550
land ownership 346, 402
Landless Women Association 100
landscape 400
Lassalle, Ferdinand 288
Latour, Bruno 472, 510–11
Lazarus, Sylvain 296, 306n. 3
Lazzarato, Maurizio 22–3
LeFebvre, Henri 399
Lefort, Claude 181
Leitch, Vincent 411–12
Lenin, Vladimir 195, 288, 301, 314,
  332, 471, 528–9
Leninism 287
Lesjak, Carolyn 340
Lévi-Strauss, Claude 133, 400

liberalism 178–9, 285–6, 330, 462, 491, 534
  and slavery 344–6
Linera, Álvaro García 471
Lipietz, Alan 21
literary criticism 255
  Marxist 379–88, 411
  new formalism 408–9
  see also literature
literature 200n. 29, 408
  African 358–76
  Brazilian 343–53
  canon formation 240, 360
Local Exchange Trading Systems 292
Lozada, Sánchez de 481–3
Lukács, Georg 44–5, 465n. 2
Lumpenproletariat see proletariat
Lutz, Vera 29
Luxemburg, Rosa 302, 520
Lyotard, Jean-François 255

Macebuh, Stanley 367
Macherey, Pierre 234–5
Machiavelli, Niccolò 491, 496–7, 517, 519
McLuhan, Marshall 310
management 37, 61, 63, 87
Mann, Paul de 259n. 14
Mao Zedong 301, 302, 307n. 11, 314, 528
Maoism 35, 110
Marcuse, Herbert 383, 417–19
market, the 32–4, 154, 326, 332, 461–2, 522
  anarchy of 56, 280, 287
marriage 163
Marx, Karl,
  and Blanqui 525
  dialectic 49–50
  equality 159, 493
  Eurocentrism 142–3
  liberalism 277
  literary criticism 380
  religion 284
  revolution 482
  the state 159
  and young Hegelians 276
masculinity 164, 168, 222–3

mass intellectuality *see* general intellect
materialism 4, 7, 234, 239, 249–51, 328, 452–3
  dialectic 309
May '68 5, 304
Meillassoux, Claude 97
Menem, Carlos 508
mercantilism 279, 282
Merkel, Angela 223
metanoia 310
metaphysics 311
  African 363–4
middle-class 215, 227, 405
  see also bourgeoisie
Mies, Maria 94, 104
Milošević, Slobodan 194, 535
Milton, John 457
mode of production 204, 206
  Asiatic 34
  capitalist 151–2, 207, 212–13, 457–8, 502–3, 506, 526, 574–5
  see also capitalism
modernism 341, 349, 396, 459–61, 464, 467n. 16
modernity 144, 178, 219–20, 329, 397
  alter- 502
  Bolivia 477–9
  reflexive 324
modernization 345, 352, 392, 397–8, 403, 442
modularity 395
money 216n. 4, 220, 241–2, 248, 279–80, 290–1, 437n. 35, 453, 467n. 20
  and language 250–1
monopoly 35
Moore, Michael 455
Mouffe, Chantal 472
MoveOn 551–2
multiculturalism 180, 198n. 18, 329
multitude 332, 385, 422, 446, 489, 503–5, 507
music 326, 463–4
  file sharing 544–5

Nabuco, Joaquim 343
Napster 543–4

nation 286, 488
national liberation 517
nationalism 287 *see also* national
    liberation
    African 362
    art 368
natural history 289
natural resource 94, 482, 578
nature 248, 402, 578–9
    disappearance of 403
    gender 165
nazism 34, 139n. 8, 193, 195
negation 243–4, 489, 509, 526
Negri, Antonio 247, 292, 327, 333,
    471, 501–5, 507, 511, 537–8
negritude 360, 366–7
neocolonialism 71
neoliberalism 29–30, 56–9, 99, 137,
    467n. 20, 476, 479, 481
    authoritarian 481
neo-Taylorism 60–2
Neton, Jeanne 125
network 47, 80, 534–7, 539–53
neuroscience 333
new historicism 412–13
New Philosophers, the 302–3
new right, the 197n. 9
New York Times 8, 331
Nietzsche, Friedrich 132, 249–50,
    311–12
Nigeria 99

occupy 12, 508
Odysseus 558, 562
OECD 64–6
Oedipus 267
oikos 158, 171
Okishio Theorem, the 583n. 9
Ong, Walter J. 251
Ortlieb, Claus Peter 473
Owen, Robert 287

Palestine 519
parallax 235, 275–7, 281
Paris Commune 484, 526
Parmenides 395–7
partition of the sensible 556, 564

patriarchy 150, 222–5
    feralization of 227–8
Peasant Women's Commission 100–1
pedagogy 426–7
people, the 472, 488, 504–5, 507, 518,
    561–3
    will of the 515–20
People's Computer Company 543
perestroika 314
performative 185
    see also contradiction
petroleum 477, 483
philanthropy 343–4
photography 13, 276, 463
physiocrats, the 280
Pinker, Steven 409–10
Pinochet, Augusto 38n. 7
Plato 295, 303, 306n. 1, 310, 327,
    558–9, 562, 568–9
Poland 170
    Solidamość 307n. 13, 314
Polanyi, Karl 292
police, the 563–4
political, the 125–6, 158–9, 179, 297,
    469–70, 555–71
political ontology 285, 497
population 165, 173n. 13, 392, 560–1,
    563, 577, 585, 589
    surplus 591, 593–4, 596–604
populism 53, 197n. 9, 464, 472, 561
porn 550
positivism 4, 247, 252
post-communism 315–16
post-Fordism 78, 163, 220, 324–5,
    444, 502
post-industrial economy 60, 62, 444
post-Marxism 509
postmodernism 175, 179–81, 339,
    341, 389–406, 453, 581
    and the city 392–3
    and gender 225–6
    and history 389–90
    pastiche 459–60
Postone, Moishe 20, 219, 578–9
post-politics 535, 536–8, 552
    see also consensual politics
post-structuralism 141–2

post-Taylorism *see* production
potentiality 444
power 484–9, 502
  disciplinary 491, 502
  see also biopolitics
praxis 261–7, 270–4
precarity 80, 81, 208
  and gender 227
  precariate, the 210
  see also indignados, los
primative accumulation 166–7, 586
privatization 316, 329, 477, 478–80
production 50, 60–1, 152, 204, 210
  post-Taylorist 21, 84, 87–8
proletariat 203, 205–12, 214,
    307n. 10, 431, 520, 586, 593
  Lumpenproletariat 431
  proletarianization 215
  as subject of history 494–5
Proudhon, Pierre-Joseph 292
Proust, Marcel 393
public 156, 158–9
public sphere, the 158, 223, 534
  and world wide web 539
pyschology 135

queer 422, 424–5

race 124, 160, 563
racism 123–4, 129–38, 375
Radio B92 535
Rancière, Jacques 307n. 10, 473
rate of profit *see* capital
Reagan, Ronald 7, 55
  Reaganism 65
Real, the 190–1, 298–9, 550–1
Regulation School 39n. 15
relativity 322
religion 182, 278, 313
reproduction 150, 152–4, 159–61,
    162–3, 165, 205, 209–10, 247
  of capital *see* capital
reverse discrimination 134–5
revolution 6, 9, 197n. 8, 203, 213,
    287, 301, 332, 393
  Chinese Cultural 236, 295–6
  Chinese Revolution 110–11

English 517
French 285, 296
revolutionary epoch 482–3
Russian 42, 496
Ricardo, David 278, 282
Ricoeur, Paul 393, 407–8, 413, 426, 428
Rinpoche, Sogyal 426–7
risk society 178
Robbins, Bruce 420
Robespierre, Maximilien de 302, 524
Romanticism 405
  aesthetics 451
Rorty, Richard 188, 196
Rosanvallon, Pierre 57
Rousseau, Jean-Jacques 491, 517, 519,
    523–6, 528
Ryan, Michael 447

Sartre, Jean-Paul 323
Saussure, Ferdinand de 250
Scarry, Elaine 415–17
Schirrmacher, Frank 228–9
Schlegel, Friedrich 237, 321, 461
Scholz, Roswitha 126, 172, 230, 583,
    610
Schumpeter, Joseph 589
Schwarz, Roberto 337–8
science fiction 327, 383, 403
Scrione, Accarias de 33
second world 404–5
Sedgwick, Eve 417–19, 421–7
self-organization 205, 215
semiotics 19–20, 25, 27, 28
Serbia 194
service economy 86, 596–9
sexuality 192
Shiva, Vandana 102–3
Silicon Valley 62
Simmel, Georg 90–1, 257n. 2
Simon, David 464
simulacrum 391
Siraganian, Lisa 461
situation, (state of)the 299–300, 301,
    303, 323
skepticism 278–9
slavery 160, 343–8, 350–1, 402
Smith, Adam 278, 345

Smith, Zadie 423
soccer 183
social Darwinism 137
social democracy 192, 286–7, 472
social networks 541
society 183, 190, 490, 550
  and population 563–4
Socrates 276
Sopranos, The 416
Sorel, Georges 470
Soviet Union 35, 309, 314, 512
  Constitution of 315
  dissolution of 315–16
  and Western Marxism 387
Soyinka, Wole 369–71
space 340, 384, 398–400, 422, 425–9,
  437n. 37
  spatial expansion of capital 575
  see also growth
Spain 135
Spartacus 302
Speed 191
Spinoza, Baruch 267, 490
Spivak, Gayatri 234, 410, 420
Stalin, Joseph 302, 314, 316–18
Stalinism 316–17
  economy 35, 37
state, the 32–4, 156, 161, 204, 213,
  284–6, 304, 504, 507, 564
  apparent 479
  socialist 298, 301
  Stalinist 316
stratification 58, 214, 484
  see also middle-class
students 210
subaltern, the 125, 144
  and history 147–8 *see also* Subaltern
  Studies
Subaltern Studies 141–3, 148, 429
subject, the 49, 79, 190–3, 199n. 24,
  235, 289, 296–8, 307n. 7, 323–4,
  447, 488–91
  materialist 239, 241, 247–52, 256
  subjectivization 296–7
subjectivity 79, 86–7, 124, 145, 289,
  391, 419, 555
  expressivity of 447
sub-prime mortgage 211–12

subsumption, real/formal 88, 168–9,
  204, 384, 453, 457–8, 466n. 13,
  597
superstructure *see* base and
  superstructure
surface reading 417–25
Symbolic, the 190–1
Szeman, Imre 237, 339–40, 341

Tafuri, Manfredo 394–5
Taussig, Michael 146
Tea Party, the 410
television 464
temporality 48–9, 144, 146, 148, 154,
  427–9, 492–3
  postmodern 390–2
Thatcher, Margaret 1, 55
Théorie Communiste 126
theory 261–70, 420–1
  theoretical practice 268
third way 178, 192, 324, 414, 538
Third World 29, 64, 67–76, 228, 252,
  397–8
Tomlinson, John 328
totalitarianism 490–1
totality 9, 36, 149, 290, 330, 331,
  493–4
trade-unions 57, 210, 477
  see also unionism
  declining membership 542
transcriticism 235, 293
Tripp, Aili Mari 101–2
Tropicália 349, 463–4

UN Population Fund 94
underdevelopment 97
unemployment 59, 208, 214–15, 604–5
Union of Soviet Socialist Repoublics
  (USSR) *see* Soviet Union
unionism 386, 477
  Bolivia 477
United States of America 36, 58, 63,
  74, 134, 139n. 4, 252, 325, 511,
  535, 599–600
  Civil War 401
  dollar 599–602
  Revolution 496
  Telecommunications Act (1996) 543

universalism 136, 144, 146–7
universality 182, 184–8, 346
  liberal 348, 351–2
  of market 461
university, the 235, 411–12, 414, 433
Uno, Kozo 284
unproductive labour 98, 155–7
urban 392–3, 404–5, 479
urbanization 585
Usual Suspects, The 192
utopia 322, 327, 331, 341, 384, 493
utopianism 245, 247, 256, 332–3, 384
  anti-utopianism 406

valorization 28–31, 87, 211, 453, 580,
  582n. 4 *see also* reproduction, of
  capital
value 28, 48, 219, 239–57, 279,
  280–1, 291, 577–8
  gender 164, 218
  labor theory of 43–4, 46–8, 151–2
  and price 254
  surplus value 49–50, 212, 251, 292,
  573–82, 599
Veblen, Thorstein 382
Venezuela 507
  Bolivarianism 12, 519
Virilio, Paul 391
Virno, Paolo 444, 503–5
virtuality 445–6

wage 155–7, 211, 587
Wallraff, Günter 62
war 34, 99, 222, 391

Weber, Samuel 44–5
West, Cornel 516
West, the 143, 329, 352, 359, 387
Western Marxism 16, 385–7
Westerns 183
White, Hayden 412
whiteness 159–60
Wichterich, Christa 100
Williams, Raymond 327, 328, 381–2,
  403
Wire, The 464
Wolf, Christa 186
Wolff, Richard A. 253–4
women's movements 93–104
work 156 *see also* labor
  women's 159–60, 167, 220–1
worker 78–81, 290, 565
  see also proletariat
  collective 213
  cultural 457
worker's councils 204
working class 52, 80, 144, 205, 290,
  323, 593 *see also* proletariat
World Bank 10, 55, 98–9, 101,
  598–9
World Trade Organization (WTO) 99
World War I 287
World War II 113, 585, 598

Zapatistas 12, 94, 307n. 13
Zavaleta, René 479, 481
Žižek, Slavoj 11, 125–6, 297, 304n. 6,
  326, 332, 411, 414, 418–21, 537,
  542, 548

CPSIA information can be obtained
at www.ICGtesting.com
Printed in the USA
LVHW030050040522
717815LV00008B/390

9 781441 106285